INKLINGS FOREVER
VOLUME X

PAPERS FROM THE 10th FRANCES WHITE EWBANK
COLLOQUIUM ON C. S. LEWIS & FRIENDS

JOE RICKE AND RICK HILL, EDITORS

Inklings Forever, Volume X
Proceedings from the Frances White Ewbank Colloquium on C. S. Lewis and Friends

Joe Ricke and Rick Hill, Editors

Copyright © 2017 Taylor University

Winged Lion Press
Hamden, CT

All rights reserved. Except in the case of quotations embodied in critical articles or reviews, no part of this book may be reproduced or transmitted in any form or by any means, electronic or mechanical, including photocopying, recording, or by any information storage or retrieval system, without written permission of the publisher. For information, contact Winged Lion Press: www.WingedLionPress.com

Front Cover Image
Sasha_Kopf's_Celtic_knot_ring.jpg: Sasha Kopf derivative work: Ninjatacoshell (talk) (https:/ /commons.wikimedia.org/wiki/File:Sasha_Kopf's_Celtic_knot_ring.svg), 11Sasha Kopf's Celtic knot ring", shades of green by Hailey Smith, https:Ucreativecommons.org/licenses/bysa/3.0/legalcode

ISBN-13 978-1-935668-14-3

This volume is dedicated to a person who has been a friend to the Center and the Colloquium for many years and who, in fact, has worked behind the scenes and without recognition to make sure that they were always so much more than they would have been without him. It would take another book to tell of his many contributions. Enough for now to say, thanks be to God for one of the finest examples of servant leadership we have ever seen.
With gratitude for the dedication, service, and friendship of:

Dan Bowell,
Director of Taylor University's Zondervan Library,

the home of
the Center for the Study of C. S. Lewis and Friends.

photo: Dan Bowell with Carol Stocksdale (daughter of Dave Neuhouser)

TABLE OF CONTENTS

Foreword by Joe Ricke   1

I. Essays on C.S. Lewis   5

- The Perils, Pitfalls, and Pleasures of Writing a New Biography of Lewis by Devin Brown   6
- An Answer for Orual: C. S. Lewis as Defender of the Faith by Donald T. Williams   14
- C. S. Lewis and the Problem of Prayer by Robert Moore-Jumonville   30
- A Beast's Best Friend: Interspecies Friendship in the Thought of C. S. Lewis by Edwin Woodruff Tait   42
- Patriarchy and P'daitaBird: The Artistic Influence of Albert Lewis by Crystal Hurd   57
- Friends at Home: C. S. Lewis's Social Relations at The Kilns by David Beckmann   65
- Separation from the King: Tinidril and Susan's Temptation in the Desert by Kat D. Coffin   73
- The Influence of Richard Wagner's *Ring* Cycle on C. S. Lewis by John MacInnis   81
- Henry More and C.S. Lewis: Cambridge Platonism and its Influence on Lewis's Life and Thought by Susan Wendling   102
- Stories As Friends in C.S. Lewis's Life and Work by Andrea Marie Catroppa   114
- C. S. Lewis: Mere Christian, Evangelist, Author, and Friend by Mark R. Hall   124
- Battlefield of the Mind: Examining Screwtape's Preferred Method by William O'Flaherty   135
- Through the Lens of *The Four Loves*: Love in *Perelandra* by Paulette Sauders   141
- C.S. Lewis and Christian Postmodernism: Jewish Laughter Reversed by Kyoko Yuasa   150
- Being *Hnau*: The Imago Dei in *Gulliver's Travels* and the C.S. Lewis Space Trilogy by Abby Palmisano   159

Two Strategies for Defending Naturalism Against C. S. Lewis's and Victor Reppert's Argument From Reason by Louis J. Swingrover ... 169

An Ekphrasis by C. S. Lewis: "On a Picture by Chirico" by Joe R. Christopher ... 184

Strange Bedfellows: C.S. Lewis and Fred Hoyle by Kristine Larsen ... 204

When Friendship Sours: A Study of Trumpkin, Trufflehunter, and Nikabrik by Victoria Holtz Wodzak ... 216

II. Essays on Dorothy L. Sayers ... 225

Books, Theology, and Hens: The Correspondence and Friendship of C. S. Lewis and Dorothy L. Sayers by Laura K. Simmons and Gary L. Tandy ... 226

Well Met: Common Sense and Humor in the Friendship of G.K. Chesterton and Dorothy L. Sayers by Barbara M. Prescott ... 234

Take This Job and Love It: Dorothy Sayers On Work by Kimberly Moore-Jumonville ... 250

C. S. Lewis and Dorothy L. Sayers: Correspondence by Marsha Daigle-Williamson ... 259

Dorothy L. Sayers and the Mutual Admiration Society: Friendship and Creative Writing in an Oxford Women's Literary Group by Barbara M. Prescott ... 273

III. Essays on George MacDonald ... 293

Mutuality in Wonderland: Charles Dodgson, Adopted Member of the MacDonald Family by Rachel E. Johnson ... 294

Awaking the Reader to Nature's Aesthetics: A Novel Purpose in *The Seaboard Parish* by Cynthia DeMarcus Manson ... 306

But What is the Moral?": A Dramatized Bibliographic Study of the Relationship of George MacDonald's "The Light Princess" to *Adela Cathcart* by Joe Ricke, Abby Palmisano, Blair Hedges, and Cara Strickland — 314

The Performance Text of "The Light Princess" with *Adela Cathcart* frame — 320

IV. Essays on the Inklings (and Friends) — 345

On the Friendship of Books: F.D. Maurice on the Art of Reading, Writing, and Friendship by Robert Trexler — 346

The Inklings and Race: Whiteness, Mythology, and Jesus by Andrew T. Draper — 352

Sister Penelope Lawson CSMV: Her Life, Writings and Legacy by Richard James — 363

Friendship and Hierarchy in Tolkien and Lewis by Grace Tiffany — 378

Beings of Magic: A Comparison of Saruman the White in Tolkien's *The Lord of the Rings* and Simon the Clerk in Williams' *All Hallows' Eve* by Kathryne Hall — 388

"Sufficiently Different to Help One Another": The Central Place of Books in the Friendships of the Inklings by John Stanifer — 396

The Future of Inklings Studies: Keynote Panel Discussion (4 June 2016) by Diana Glyer, Sorina Higgins, and Colin Duriez (with Joe Ricke, moderator) — 405

V. Essays on Charles Williams — 425

Native Language in a Strange Country: Death and Rebirth in the Friendship of C.S. Lewis and Charles Williams by Jennifer Raimundo — 426

Friendship in *The Place of the Lion* by Dan Hamilton	437
The Image of the Library in the Life and Work of Charles Williams by Michael J. Paulus, Jr.	444
C. S. Lewis, Charles Williams, and Esemplastic Friendship by Paul E. Michelson	454

VI. Essays on Owen Barfield — 479

Owen Barfield and C.S. Lewis: A Critical Friendship by Colin Duriez	480
Joy and Poetic Imagination: An Introduction to C.S. Lewis's "Incessant Disputation" with Owen Barfield by Stephen Thorson	502

VII. Creative Work Inspired by C.S. Lewis and Friends — 515

The Words in the World by Luke A. Wildman	516
Can Love be Blind? by Bethany Russell	524
Canto XXXIII by M. J. Paulus	536
DOG CITY AFTER DARK: After reading *The Great Divorce* by Rick Hill	543
Chesterton in Heaven by Jennifer Woodruff Tait	544
"Don't Believe in Anything That Can't Be Told in Colored Pictures:" Notes on a Dramatic Reading of Poetry by Lewis, Tolkien, Chesterton, and Williams by Jennifer Woodruff Tait	546
"The Temptation of Brother Thomas": A Stop-Motion Animated Short Film by J. Stephan Leeper	549
THE INKLINGS, IN MEMORIAM: A Cycle of Poems by Donald T. Williams	557

Afterword: About the Center for the Study of C. S. Lewis and Friends — 565

David and Ruth Neuhouser with Edwin and Pat Brown

Foreword

by Joe Ricke,

Director of the Center for the Study of C. S. Lewis and Friends

Preparing for the 10th Biennial C. S. Lewis and Friends Colloquium at Taylor University, we couldn't help but think of the year 1997 when, under the leadership of Dr. David L. Neuhouser, and with the help of a generous anonymous donor, the outstanding book collection of Dr. Edwin W. Brown came to be housed at Taylor. Later that summer, Dr. Neuhouser was out beating the bushes, promoting both the collection and the first-ever colloquium to be held in November of that year. A substantial part of that story is told in our new book, *Exploring the Eternal Goodness: Selected Writings of David L. Neuhouser*, especially in the introduction, in the long interview with David, and in the many tributes included in the book.

This book, too, tells an important part of that story. For this volume, containing a good number of the eighty-plus essays and creative pieces presented at the 2016 Frances Ewbank Colloquium, suggests that the vision of Neuhouser and Brown is not only ongoing but, if anything, growing. Here, in the middle of the cornfields of Indiana, a fellowship and a friendship began that continues to make a difference in this university, in the long-time friends of the Lewis Center and the Brown Collection, and, perhaps more than ever, in the community of Inklings scholars and fans around the world. This year's colloquium welcomed back many long-time friends, including several who had participated in every one of the previous nine as well. At the same time, a large number of new friends attended, participated, and experienced the special, even unique blend of scholarship and fellowship that the title Lewis and Friends has always designated.

This year's colloquium honored not only the friendship of Neuhouser and Brown, both of whom had died in 2015, but it remembered the 90th anniversary of the first meeting of those two quite different Oxford dons, C. S. Lewis and J. R. R. Tolkien, whose friendship did much to re-shape the literary landscape of twentieth-century imaginative writing. All four were remembered in a number of ways, including papers, special sessions using the Brown Collection resources, art displays, and a video honoring Neuhouser and Brown at the final banquet. More than these, the keynote speakers for the colloquium were chosen partly because of the focus in their own writings on the friendship, fellowship, and collaboration of the Inklings. Diana Glyer's *Bandersnatch* and Colin Duriez's *The Oxford Inklings*, both new in 2016, are key texts in what might be seen as a new and important emphasis in Inklings Studies (and in studies of creativity more generally). In our planning, we wanted to push that even further, announcing that, by our colloquium theme of "friendship," we hoped to inspire participants to extend the so-called "Lewis circle," tracing connections and shedding new light on friendships and influences which had been under-appreciated heretofore.

As a result, we saw an increase in papers on Dorothy Sayers, Charles Williams, and Owen Barfield, as well as a good many papers on the influence of George MacDonald. And not just papers about Sayers and papers about Williams, but papers about the relationship of Sayers and Williams or Sayers and Lewis or Sayers and Chesterton. We also had new papers about Lewis and astronomer Fred Hoyle, about Lewis and Richard Wagner, about Albert Lewis's influence on his two sons, about Lewis Carroll and MacDonald, about Lewis and Sister Penelope Lawson, about Lewis and Henry More (the 17th Century Cambridge Platonist), and about human/animal friendship. And much more.

As always the Lewis and Friends Colloquium and its proceedings feature a great variety of treasures from a wide range of perspectives. We were pleased to welcome senior scholars, Charles Huttar and Joe Christopher, whose volumes on Lewis and the Inklings have shed light on these authors for over forty years. A number of participants had recently published a book on some aspect of Inklings, so much so that we filled an entire room for one of our more open-ended sessions, listening as authors gave 3-5 minute summaries of their most recent work. That wonderful experience of meeting a member of your bibliography for the first time in person occurred more than once that afternoon. And, as usual, we had the newcomers, the first-timers, and the student presenters involved. Once again, as well, we conscripted participants to be part of our traditional readers theater performance: this year a special version of George MacDonald's *The Light Princess*. Of many wonderful performances, Sorina Higgins' wicked turn as the fairy godmother/witch haunts us long after the laughter has died down. One of our keynote presenters, Colin Duriez, included his paper in this volume, and our entire keynote panel on the future of Inklings studies was transcribed and included as well.

There were also numerous creative works presented, including paintings, an animated film in progress, original poetry, original fiction, readings of Inkling poetry, and the dramatic presentation of *The Light Princess*. Not to mention one late-night singalong that did not make it into the book. Suffice to say, the beautiful unrehearsed harmonizing on "Come Thou Fount of Every Blessing" and "Country Roads" fit the conference theme as well.

Those who have been collecting the *Inklings Forever* volumes since their first publication in 1997 will notice a few changes. First, and most obvious, is the shape. For the first time, the book is a standard octavo book rather than the previous folio double-columned volumes. Thanks to Bob Trexler of Winged Lion Press, we hope to make this yet another quality text under the Center for the Study of C. S. Lewis and Friends sponsorship. Another difference, also obvious, is heft. This year's colloquium had far more presentations than any of the previous nine. Even though many of the works presented at the colloquium were not submitted for the publication, we are still confident that this volume represents both the biggest and the best, a fitting tribute especially to David Neuhouser who originally envisioned both the colloquium and the publication of its proceedings.

Finally, a special word of thanks to two people without whom this volume would never have appeared. First, Lisa Ritchie, the program coordinator for the Lewis Center and, therefore, the primary organizer of the colloquium, somehow kept the entire program from spinning out of control. She received the original proposals for the papers, sorted them, put together the schedule, and made sure of all the important details (like registration, housing, meals, conference rooms, etc.). She, more than anyone, made sure the colloquium exceeded all our expectations. To make this more personal, she got people here and took really really good care of them. I know this is so, because I have personally read the post-colloquium feedback.

The other person to thank is, of course, the co-editor of this volume, Rick Hill, Professor of English at Point Loma Nazarene University. Rick was a long-time faculty member at Taylor University. As such, he worked with David Neuhouser not only to make Lewis and Friends an important part of our university life but, more specifically, to make the Lewis and Friends Colloquium the significant event it has become. Since leaving Taylor, he has continued his relationship with the colloquium, going so far this year as to volunteer to help edit the proceedings. He might have changed his mind if he had known when he volunteered, while we were still in the planning stages of the colloquium, that we would have a record number of participants and presentations. Be that as it may, he received the submissions, put them into a format, worked with authors on necessary revisions, and got an entire draft turned around in a timely manner. His friendship, expressed in collaborative work, is another example of the colloquium theme which really came to life for us in 2016.

I also want to thank two people who helped with some further copy-editing and formatting. They are recent Taylor University English Creative Writing graduate, Alex Moore and senior English Education major, Rebekah Swank.

Just a brief note about the text. The authors have used various style guides for their essays (mostly MLA or Chicago Manual of Style). We have done our best to make sure that each essay's style and documentation are logical and consistent, although we have made no attempt to normalize the entire volume. Thus, for example, some essays have footnotes and others have parenthetic references.

I. Essays on C.S. Lewis

The Perils, Pitfalls, and Pleasures of Writing a New Biography of Lewis

by Devin Brown

Devin Brown is a Professor of English at Asbury University. He has written ten books, including the most recent biographies of Lewis and Tolkien. He has taught in the Summer Seminar program at The Kilns and recently wrote the script for *Discussing Mere Christianity* which was shot on location in Oxford with host Eric Metaxas.

In 2013, I published *A Life Observed: A Spiritual Biography of C. S. Lewis*. The increased interest in Lewis generated in 2013 by the fiftieth anniversary of his death and the unveiling of the Lewis memorial in the Poets' Corner of Westminster Abbey helped make it possible for Brazos, my publisher, to release another book about Lewis. Contrary to what many people think, publishing a book about Lewis is no guarantee of commercial success. As the late Chris Mitchell once noted: "While books by C. S. Lewis continue to sell briskly, books about Lewis (and there are many) sell comparatively sluggishly. The public is far more interested in reading Lewis than in reading books about Lewis" (8).

So I considered myself very fortunate in being offered a contract for a new Lewis biography. Growing up on the south side of Chicago where not many of my neighbors or classmates were particularly literary, I never imagined that one day I would write a book about the author who had come into my blue collar world during my teens when I was in special need of a teacher.

Like most big projects, the challenge of writing a new Lewis biography, which had seemed like such a wonderful idea in the proposal stage, suddenly became filled with many difficulties. In this paper, I will discuss some of the perils, pitfalls, and pleasures faced in trying to write a new biography on Lewis.

As I looked through the Lewis books that take up several shelves in my bookcase—eight previous biographies as well as many books that simply contained some biographical information on Lewis—I perceived the first peril (or pitfall): *A biography cannot be just a collection of facts, however accurate or new: it has to bring the person to life*. A biography cannot (or should not) be just a summary, but an analysis and a synthesis. It cannot be just a list of names and dates, but the story of why they are important.

Don King points to this first difficulty in his review of *C. S. Lewis: A Companion and Guide* by Walter Hooper. Although King mentions many positive aspects, he also notes a lack of analysis. "There is no section devoted specifically to analyzing Lewis's achievements as a writer, artist, or apologist," King observes. "Even in the summaries of Lewis's books we rarely find Hooper going beyond the obvious" (245).

Of course at the same time, a biography must of necessity include many names and dates in addition to *some* summary. Figuring out when to do this and how much readers will want or need is what makes writing a biography, like all writing, an art and not a science. Too little can be a problem as well as too much. What seemed to me to be the most deadly for a biographer was not to provide something new—fresh insights and analysis as well as some different perspectives. Laura Miller, with whom I often disagree, touches on this problem in her overall description of the plethora of Lewis books that came out in advance of the first Narnia film. She refers to them as, by and large, "a shelf-full of mediocrity."

Pitfall number one may be extended with the following caution: *Say things that are insightful and valid, not things that are uninteresting or too farfetched.* In the opening section of *A Life Observed*, I wrote this:

> Lewis took his title, *Surprised by Joy*, from a sonnet by the English poet William Wordsworth which begins with these two lines:
>
> *Surprised by joy—impatient as the wind*
>
> *I turned to share the transport. . . .*
>
> Lewis uses Wordsworth's first line on the title page of *Surprised by Joy* as an epigraph for the book. Like the wind, this Joy would come and go in Lewis's life as it wished, sometimes appearing regularly, other times disappearing for long periods. When it did come, its presence was always fleeting, or as the sonnet says, impatient. (3)

In an early draft, I then went on to discuss Wordsworth's second line "I turned to share the transport" in an effort to connect it to Lewis's intentions as I did the first line. But an early reader rightly recommended that I cut this second part because it was more than was needed.

As I then turned to looking specifically at some of the previous Lewis biographies, I realized a second mistake biographers are likely to make, namely that *a biography should not be just a vehicle for the biographer to advance his or her own personal ideology.* For an illustration of this second pitfall, we need to look at what Lewis had to say about his first experience of boarding school life and then look at how one of Lewis's biographers portrayed it. In *Surprised by Joy*, Lewis tell us:

> But I have not yet mentioned the most important thing that befell me at Oldie's. There first I became an effective believer. As far as I know, the instrument was the church to which we were taken twice every Sunday. . . . What really mattered was that I here heard the doctrines of Christianity (as distinct from general 'uplift') taught by men who obviously believed them. . . . The effect was to bring to life what I would already have said that I believed. In this experience there was a great deal of fear. I do not think there was more than was wholesome or even necessary. . . . The effect, so far as I can judge, was entirely good. I began seriously to pray and to read my Bible and to attempt to obey my conscience. (33-34)

If we now turn to how biographer Michael White interprets this passage, we find a very different story. White tells his readers:

> At Wynyard House Lewis was introduced to the Anglo-Catholicism that had dominated Capron's own distorted psyche. . . . This was Lewis's first experience of . . . hour-long, largely meaningless sermons delivered by the local rector. And they succeeded in their purpose, terrifying the boy into acquiescence. . . . After this initiation, and thanks to the power of ritual and fear, he began to read the Bible and to engage in earnest religious conversation with some of the other boys who had also been swept up in the heady atmosphere of suffering and salvation. (26-7)

Having decided in advance that despite what Lewis says, fear could not have been good for Lewis's spiritual development, White sees acquiescence where Lewis sees conversion. Where Lewis sees a wholesome and necessary amount of fear which had an entirely good effect, White claims that Lewis was merely swept up in a terrifying atmosphere of suffering and salvation.

We find a similar illustration of a biographer using a biography to advance his own ideology in a section of A. N. Wilson's book on Lewis. There Wilson asserts that *The Lion, the Witch and the Wardrobe* grew out of Lewis's experience of "being stung back into childhood by his defeat at the hands of Elizabeth Anscombe at the Socratic Club" (220). Wilson then declares: "It is as though Lewis, in all his tiredness and despondency in the late 1940s, has managed to get through the wardrobe door himself; to leave behind the world of squabbles and grown-ups and to re-enter the world which with the deepest part of himself he never left."

Several pages later, Wilson projects even more of his own personal ideology onto Lewis's supposed motivations, claiming: "He has launched back deep into the recesses of his own emotional history, his own most deeply felt psychological needs and vulnerabilities.... We hardly need to dwell on the psychological significance of the wardrobe.... in this tale of a world which is reached through a dark hole surrounded by fur coats" (228).

In evaluating these assertions, Bruce Edwards claims that Wilson "ultimately reduces Lewis to a bundle of quasi-Freudian complexes" and concludes that in writing this biography Wilson the novelist features more prominently than Wilson the historian.

Kathryn Lindskoog makes a similar criticism and argues: "A. N. Wilson substitutes his own ideological Freudian view of C. S. Lewis. Thus the real C. S. Lewis, he claims, was . . . a terrified Oedipal neurotic and a closet misanthrope. The Narnian wardrobe is a symbol of Flora Lewis's private parts."

A third, somewhat similar peril for would-be biographers can be stated as *in general, don't assume you understand your subject better than the subject does*. This is a general principle and certainly need not apply if there is reason to believe that the subject might be lying or deliberately hiding something.

With this rule in mind about not assuming you know more that your subject, consider the following claim that Alister McGrath puts forth in his biography of Lewis:

> Why did Lewis spend three chapters of *Surprised by Joy* detailing his relatively minor woes at Malvern College and pay so little attention to the vastly more significant violence, trauma, and horror of the Great War? . . . The simplest explanation is also the most plausible: *Lewis could not bear to remember the trauma of his wartime experience.* (50)

If Lewis had never told us why he says relatively little about his war experience, McGrath's explanation might deserve to be taken more seriously. However, in *Surprised by Joy* Lewis directly addresses the question raised by McGrath. There Lewis explains: "The war itself has been so often described by those who saw more of it than I that I shall here say little about it" (195). Then a few pages later, he adds, "The rest of my war experiences have little to do with this story" (197).

In an article titled "Does C. S. Lewis Have Something to Hide? Or Is Alister McGrath's Biography Too Preoccupied with What Lewis Declines to Reveal?" Jerry Root tackles McGrath's error head on, writing:

> In one instance, McGrath begins to question why Lewis spends more time discussing his school days than his war

years. Had McGrath appreciated Lewis's respect for literary form, he might have made more sense of this. Since Lewis was writing the story of his pilgrimage to faith, extended discussion of his school days enabled him to emphasize his loneliness and isolation. . . . Lewis writes less about his war experiences because they occupied a shorter period of time and . . . were less formative in his pilgrimage to faith.

Root goes on to discuss a fourth peril which is illustrated by this same passage from McGrath, a pitfall which can be stated as *the spotlight should be on the subject, not the biographer.* Root argues that there are moments in McGrath's book when one senses that "the real Lewis has dropped out of the narrative, or been replaced by a figment of the biographer's imagination." Root concludes: "Based on speculations about what Lewis *didn't* write, a repressed Lewis emerges, hidden from all until McGrath draws him out of the shadows."

A fifth pitfall when writing a biography can be expressed as *biographers should proceed cautiously when there are few or no facts.* In an article written for *Christianity Today*, Gina Dalfonzo points out that in *A Grief Observed*, Lewis portrays his relatively brief marriage to Joy Davidman as blissful. Dalfonzo notes that the Davidman whom Lewis depicts is a woman whose strength, faith, honesty, humor, and loyalty made her "the best of companions, and brought out the best in him."

"That's why I found Alister McGrath's new biography of C. S. Lewis rather jarring," Dalfonzo goes on to state. "For anyone familiar with Lewis's loving portrait of her—or the other portraits we have from her friends, her son, and her biographers—the Joy Davidman Lewis of McGrath's book is virtually unrecognizable. . . . McGrath paints her as an unlikable, determined seducer and money-grubber."

In his biography, McGrath objects to what he sees as our romanticized reading of Lewis's marriage, and he claims that Douglas Gresham, Davidman's youngest son, has gone on record stating that his mother had gone to England with one specific intention which was "to seduce C. S. Lewis" (323).

But, as Dalfonzo points out, this is not what Gresham said. She quotes the newspaper report that McGrath cites, and she notes that what Gresham actually said was: "She was not above telling nosy friends that she was going to England to seduce C. S. Lewis." The tone of this remark, Dalfonzo rightly points out, suggests a joke—the kind that the blunt Davidman was fond of making. Dalfonzo also explains that McGrath's claim also stands in direct contradiction with what

Davidman herself, in a letter to Chad Walsh, explained her intentions were—to soothe her shattered nerves and give her the strength to go on with her marriage.

A sixth peril I encountered, one that takes a different tack, is that *the writing must do the subject justice*. A book about a great writer who inspired millions of people should be (or should attempt to be) inspiring and great. A biography about someone who had an amazing ability to bring clarity to complex issues and to engage all kinds of readers should itself be clear and engaging. Anyone who has read anything by Lewis will understand the difficulty in producing writing about him that will seem fitting or can in some small way measure up.

One final pitfall I tried to avoid is that a *biography must present new material for those who have read other biographies and at the same time must cover previously covered ground for those who have not*. Certainly I was not entirely successful in balancing this paradoxical demand. In his Goodreads review of *A Life Observed,* HaperOne editor Mickey Maudlin—who has certainly read many other Lewis biographies—complains, "I was expecting more."

Having covered a number of pitfalls in writing a new biography of Lewis, I should make it clear that they were vastly outweighed by the pleasures. Here are a few of them.

One of the greatest pleasures in writing a new Lewis biography was discovering something new. As an example of one new discovery, in my book I point out the following previously undocumented connection with George MacDonald. Lewis opens chapter eleven of *Surprised by Joy* with this line from the medieval poem "Sir Aldingar": *When bale is at highest, boote is at next.* Lewis's epigraph may be paraphrased as *when evil is at its greatest, help is at its closest.*

What was this help Lewis alludes to? If we turn to chapter four of MacDonald's *Phantastes,* we find that before Lewis used this epigraph, MacDonald used it himself, though in a slightly different variation: *When bale is att hyest, boote is nyest*—which may be paraphrased as *When evil is greatest, help is nearest*. By repeating MacDonald's epigraph in *Surprised by Joy,* Lewis leads us to believe that the help he is referring to came from MacDonald's book.

Besides discovering something new, another pleasure I found in writing a new Lewis biography was simply to write something new. For example, in the research I did I turned up very little written about the final line of *A Grief Observed*. Believing that it warranted more attention than it had received, I wrote the following:

After telling us, "She smiled, but not at me," Lewis chooses to end *A Grief Observed* with a sentence taken from one of the final cantos of the *Paradiso*: "Poi si torno all' eternal fontana." Here Dante's beloved Beatrice turns away from him and towards the glory of God. *Then she turned back to the Eternal Fountain.* Jack finally lets go of his Helen Joy. But how is he able to do this? How is this even possible? Jack can let go because he knows, truly knows, that he is letting her go into the hands of God, who is the eternal fountain of living water.

Earlier Lewis commented that his notes had been about himself, about Joy, and about God—in an order and proportion that were exactly the opposite of what they ought to have been. *Then she turned back to the Eternal Fountain.* Jack does not include himself in the final sentence at all. It begins Joy and ends with God. Jack finally has the order right. And now that he has the order right, he can let go. This letting go, this acceptance of Joy's death, will not be an end to the burden of grief. But now the burden is bearable. (*A Life Observed* 215)

Two pleasures remain. The first was the unforeseen opportunity of getting to work with Lewis's stepson Douglas Gresham who, after some emailing back and forth with me from his home in Malta, agreed to write a foreword—one which turned out to be extraordinarily gracious and generous.

The final pleasure of writing a new biography of Lewis was the pleasure that comes with creating anything: the sheer pleasure of holding something in your hands that you made yourself. Yes, there was help from many other sources along with a large measure of good fortune, but it is and always will remain your own creation—your chance to join the conversation.

WORKS CITED

Brown, Devin. *A Life Observed*. Grand Rapids: Brazos Press, 2013. Print.

Dalfonzo, Gina. "C. S. Lewis's Joy in Marriage: What I Think Alister McGrath Got Wrong about Lewis's Wife, Joy Davidman." *Christianitytoday.com*, 8 October 2013. Web. 14 July 2016.

Edwards, Bruce. "A Review of *C. S. Lewis: A Biography* by A. N. Wilson." Web. 14 July 2016.

King, Don. "A Review of *C. S. Lewis: A Companion and Guide*." *Plain to the Inward Eye: Selected Essays on C. S. Lewis*. Abilene: Abilene Christian University Press, 2013. 243-45. Print.

Lewis, C. S. *Surprised by Joy*. New York: Harvest, 1955. Print.

Lindskoog, Kathryn. "A. N. Wilson Errata," *Into the Wardrobe*. cslewis.drzeus.net/papers/wilson-errata. Web. 14 July 2016.

McGrath, Alister. *C. S. Lewis - A Life: Eccentric Genius, Reluctant Prophet*. Carol Stream: Tyndale House, 2013. Print.

Miller, Laura. "Return to Narnia," *The Los Angles Times*, 4 December 2005. Print.

Mitchell, Christopher. "Foreword." *The C. S. Lewis Readers' Encyclopedia*. Grand Rapids: Zondervan, 1998. 7-8. Print.

Root, Jerry. "Does C. S. Lewis Have Something to Hide? Or Is Alister McGrath's Biography Too Preoccupied with What Lewis Declines to Reveal?" *Christianitytoday.com*, 22 November 2013. Web. 14 July 2016.

White, Michael. *C. S. Lewis: A Life*. New York: Carroll & Graf Publishers, 2004. Print.

Wilson, A. N. *C. S. Lewis: A Biography*. London: Flamingo, 1991. Print.

An Answer for Orual:
C. S. Lewis as Defender of the Faith

by Donald T. Williams

Donald T. Williams is Forrest Scholar at Toccoa Falls College and past president of the International Society of Christian Apologetics. He has published ten books, including, most recently (with Jim Prothero), *Gaining a Face: C. S. Lewis's Romanticism* (Cambridge: Cambridge Scholar's Press, 2013). He blogs at www.lanternhollow.wordpress.com and http://thefivepilgrims.com/.

You are yourself the answer. Before your face questions die away.
—C. S. Lewis, Orual in *Till We Have Faces*

Many have taken pen in hand to discuss the validity of C. S. Lewis's apologetic arguments. I have been one of them.[1] But here I would like to address what we can learn practically about apologetics as a part of Christian ministry from Lewis's approach to defending the faith. Lewis was not a pastor, though Providence gave him an informal pastoral role in many lives which is often on display in his letters. He was an evangelist of sorts as well as perhaps the most effective apologist the church has known. A fresh look at his approach to these two areas of ministry and how they fit together could be useful to both evangelists and apologists in the twenty-first century.

EVANGELISM

C. S. Lewis did not talk a lot about evangelism. He just did it. He often did it indirectly, but it got done. There is no direct appeal for conversion in the Broadcast Talks that became *Mere Christianity*, but there is an exposition of the Christian faith designed to elucidate its attractiveness as an answer to the problems of fallen man as well as to underscore its truth. And conversion was often the result, as famously with Charles Colson. But while Lewis's approach to evangelism may have been indirect, it was not unintentional. When Sherwood Eliot Wirt of the Billy Graham Evangelistic Association asked Lewis whether he would say that the aim of his writing was "to bring about an encounter of the reader with Jesus Christ," Lewis replied, "That

---

[1] E.g. in *C. S. Lewis's Apologetics: Pro and Con*, ed. Gregory Bassham (Leiden: Brill/Rodopi, 2015), 171-89, 201-4.

is not my language, yet it is the purpose I have in view."[2] He said elsewhere that "Most of my books are evangelistic, addressed to *tous exo* ["those outside"]."[3]

Lewis did not feel he had the gifts for the "direct evangelical appeal of the 'Come to Jesus' type," but he thought that those who could do that sort of thing should "do it with all their might."[4] Lewis not only practiced evangelism by writing, but also in his speaking on the radio, speaking for the RAF in World War II, and in personal letters and other contacts. Lewis's commitment to evangelism and the price he paid for it at Oxford are covered brilliantly in the book edited by David Mills, *The Pilgrim's Guide: C. S. Lewis and the Art of Witness*, especially in the late Chris Mitchell's essay, "Bearing the Weight of Glory."[5]

Through all of these varied experiences, Lewis came to have a good understanding of some of the problems with doing effective evangelism in the modern world. One thing he noticed was that "The greatest barrier I have met is the almost total absence from the minds of my audience of any sense of sin. . . . We have to convince our hearers of the unwelcome diagnosis before we can expect them to welcome the news of the remedy."[6] This was a new situation without precedent in the history of the church. "When the apostles preached, they could assume even in their Pagan hearers a real consciousness of deserving the Divine anger. . . . Christianity now has to preach the diagnosis— in itself very bad news—before it can win a hearing for the cure."[7] This means, not an adjustment to the message, but more work for the evangelist, who can no longer do his work effectively without help from the apologist. "Christ takes it for granted that men are bad. Until we really feel this assumption of His to be true, though we are part of the world He came to save, we are not part of the audience to whom

---

2   C. S. Lewis, "Cross Examination," in *God in the Dock: Essays on Theology and Ethics*, ed. Walter Hooper (Grand Rapids: Eerdmans, 1970), 262.
3   C. S. Lewis, "Rejoinder to Dr. Pittenger," in *God in the Dock*, ed. Walter Hooper (Grand Rapids: Eerdmans, 1970), 181.
4   C. S. Lewis, "Christian Apologetics," in *God in the Dock*, ed. Walter Hooper (Grand Rapids: Eerdmans, 1970), 99.
5   Christopher W. Mitchell, "Bearing the Weight of Glory: The Cost of C. S. Lewis's Witness," in *The Pilgrim's Guide: C. S. Lewis and the Art of Witness*, ed. David Mills (Grand Rapids: Eerdmans, 1998), 3-14.
6   C. S. Lewis, "God in the Dock," in *God in the Dock: Essays on Theology and Ethics*, ed. Walter Hooper (Grand Rapids: Eerdmans, 1970), 243-4; cf. "Christian Apologetics," op. cit., 95.
7   C. S. Lewis, *The Problem of Pain* (N.Y.: MacMillan, 1967), 43.

His words are addressed."[8] There is no hint of the idea that we have to adjust the message to make it more palatable to this new, tougher audience. Rather, we must gird up our loins and do the work required to gain a hearing for this unwelcome diagnosis and the joyous cure that can only make sense when it follows it.

Apologetics

The evangelist increasingly needs help from the apologist because the diagnosis is no longer self-evident, and it is no longer self-evident partly because the Christian world view is now a foreign country to most modern people. They must be *persuaded* (the apologist's job) to try the experiment of looking at the world and their own hearts very differently from the way they habitually do if they are even to understand the relevance of the Gospel to their lives, much less accept it as Good News that is true. The "liberal" approach to this dilemma is to try to accommodate the Gospel to the modern (or now, post-modern) world view, to make it more palatable to the audience that exists. But this approach begs the question. If the Gospel is not *true*, then it is not Good News for anyone; and if it is true, then the modern world view must at points be false. Lewis does not seem to have been tempted at all by the liberal cop-out. He was fully prepared to accept the challenge that, in order to present the Good News today, we must, to an extent that was never necessary before, convince people that not just their behavior and their beliefs but their *thinking* has been mistaken at crucial points.

Apologetics is how we do this job. It is the defense of the faith, that branch of theology which asks of the Gospel, "*Why* should we think it is *true*?" It is the one branch of theology in which Lewis was recognized as an expert, if not a professional. His broad and deep learning, classical, philosophical, and literary, which kept him in touch with the best products of both the human mind and the human heart; his rigorous training in logic and debate by W. T. Kirkpatrick; and the fact that his own conversion was facilitated by reasoned arguments from Chesterton and Tolkien[9]: All these factors combined to make Lewis one of the greatest apologists we have seen. What can he tell us about apologetics as a form of practical theology?

---

8 Ibid., 45.
9 See. Donald T. Williams, "G. K. Chesterton, *The Everlasting Man*," in *C. S. Lewis's List: The Ten Books that Influenced Him Most*, Ed. David Werther and Susan Werther (N.Y.: Bloomsbury, 2015), 31-48.

The Need for Apologetics

Apologetics is needed for many reasons. In the first place it is a biblical mandate: "Sanctify Christ as Lord in your hearts, always being ready to make a defense to everyone who asks you to give an account for the hope that is in you" (1 Pet. 3:15, NASB). The word translated "defense" is (*apologia*), from which we get the English word *apologetics*. It is a courtroom term which refers to the kind of reasoned case a lawyer would make in defense of his client. Lewis was in tune with a number of the reasons why that mandate exists.

One is the very nature of the faith to which the Gospel calls us. Many modern people, Christians included, treat faith as a kind of strange mystical way of knowing unconnected to reason or evidence. They treat it as a zero-sum game in which, the more reason and evidence you have for any given belief, the less of a role is left for faith to play. The New Testament, however, knows nothing of such ideas. For the New-Testament writers, faith is simply trust, and salvation is granted to people who put their personal trust in Christ as God's messiah. "If you confess with your mouth Jesus as Lord and believe in your heart that God raised him from the dead, you shall be saved" (Rom. 10:9 NASB). In Greek the noun *faith* (*pistis*) and the verb *I believe* (*pisteuo*) are built on the same root. You could conceivably have that trust for good reasons or bad reasons or no reasons. It is better to have good reasons. Luke says that Jesus offered "many convincing proofs" of his resurrection (Acts 1:3 NASB), and early preachers like the Apostle Paul were constantly giving reasons and evidence to back up their message. So we could say that apologetics is based on a biblical precept (Peter's command), biblical precedent (the example of the Apostles), and a biblical principle (that the Gospel is *truth* that should be addressed to the whole person, including the mind).

Lewis accepted this biblical perspective fully. This acceptance is shown by his teachings on the nature of truth,[10] by his practice of apologetics, and by direct statement. "My faith is based on reason. . . . The battle is between faith and reason on one side and emotion and imagination on the other."[11] The idea is not that emotion and imagination are inherently opposed to faith (one factor leading to Lewis's conversion was the "baptism" of his imagination by George

---

[10] See Donald T. Williams, "C. S. Lewis on Truth," in *Reflections from Plato's Cave: Essays in Evangelical Philosophy* (Lynchburg: Lantern Hollow Press, 2012), 103-28.
[11] C. S. Lewis, *Mere Christianity* (N.Y.: MacMillan, 1943), 122.

MacDonald), but that in fallen human beings they often are opposed to it. When reason appears to be opposed to faith, on the other hand, this opposition is illusory, because if the Gospel is true, then true reason must support it. We practice apologetics in our evangelism then because of the nature of the Gospel as truth and the nature of human beings as whole people who have minds as well as hearts that need to be reached.

The nature both of the Gospel and of human beings then makes apologetics a necessary part of theology for every generation. The times in which we live can make the need even more pressing. Lewis lived in such times, and the needs he saw have not diminished since he saw them. A skeptical age will have its effects even on people raised in Christian homes. Lewis describes those effects graphically. He wrote to a Mrs. Lockley on 5 March 1951, that "Skeptical, incredulous, materialistic *ruts* have been deeply engraved in our thought."[12] As a result, even committed Christians like Lewis have moments when Christian truth claims look implausible. What then will be the case for those without his apologetic defenses? In such an age, apologetics is essential equipment for believers wanting to preserve and strengthen their faith just as much as it is when they are proclaiming it to others.

The ruts have not only been dug; they are systematically reinforced. Lewis gives an accurate analysis of the spirit of the age:

> As long as this deliberate refusal to understand things from above, even where such understanding is possible, continues, it is idle to talk of any final victory over materialism. The critique of every experience from below, the voluntary ignoring of meaning and concentration on fact, will always have the same plausibility. There will always be evidence, and every month fresh evidence, to show that religion is only psychological, justice only self protection, politics only economics, love only lust, and thought itself only cerebral biochemisty.[13]

The mindset Lewis is describing here is called *reductionism*: Every aspect of reality is reduced to one other thing that is held to explain it exhaustively. For the Marxist, everything is really economics, for the Freudian everything is really just sex, etc. For the materialist everything is only atoms in motion, so in a materialist age various forms of reductionism will be the default setting for understanding

---

12   C. S. Lewis, *The Collected Letters of C. S. Lewis*, 3 vols., ed. Walter Hooper (San Francisco: HarperSanFrancisco, 2004), 3:393.
13   C. S. Lewis, "Transposition," in *The Weight of Glory and Other Addresses*, ed. Walter Hooper (San Francisco: Harper Collins, 1980), 114-115.

any aspect of human experience. The reason you can always find real evidence that seems to support reductionism is that thought, for example, does involve cerebral biochemisty. If you only look at it "from below," biochemistry is all you will see. But there has to be more to it than that, because if thought is reduced to brain chemistry then there is no reason to believe the thought that thought is only brain chemistry. A scientific age only accepts looking "from below" as valid looking (Looking *from below* here would correspond to looking *at* as opposed to looking *along* in Lewis's essay "Meditation in a Toolshed."[14]). We are pounded by this mentality so consistently that it becomes one of the "ruts" Lewis spoke of. We have to make a special and concerted effort to counteract the prejudices that result from such habits of how we look at things in order to be reminded that it cannot be the whole story. Apologetics is how we make that effort.

Our age remains as skeptical as Lewis's was, and to that challenge we have now added the ruts of pluralism and its offspring multiculturalism. Lewis's ruts have been worn deeper and new ones have been added. Neither evangelism nor Christian nurture can be conducted effectively without help in navigating around, smoothing out, or bridging over those ruts. Therefore, Lewis's advice is even more pertinent today than it was when he gave it:

> To be ignorant and simple now—not to be able to meet the enemies on their own ground—would be to throw down our weapons, and to betray our uneducated brethren who have, under God, no defence but us against the intellectual attacks of the heathen. Good philosophy must exist, if for no other reason, because bad philosophy needs to be answered.[15]

APOLOGETIC METHOD

Modern Christian apologists tend to group roughly into three camps in terms of methodology: Classical, Evidentialist, and Presuppositionalist. Classical apologists argue first for the existence of God, and then turn to the evidence for the resurrection of Christ to identify who that God is and how He can be known. Evidentialists differ as to how valid the classical arguments (cosmological, teleological, moral, etc.) are but agree that they only point to an

---

14   C. S. Lewis, "Meditation in a Toolshed," in *God in the Dock*, ed. Walter Hooper. (Grand Rapids: Eerdmans, 1970: 212-15.
15   C. S. Lewis, "Learning in Wartime," in *The Weight of Glory and Other Addresses*, ed. Walter Hooper (San Francisco: Harper Collins, 1980), 58.

abstract God, not the God of the Bible, and so would prefer to cut to the chase and establish the historicity of the resurrection as pointing to Jesus being God incarnate. Presuppositionalists say we cannot argue *to* God, but only *from* God. In other words, our philosophical assumptions (presuppositions) determine how we are going to evaluate the evidence, and non-Christians' secular world view and rebellious hearts will not let them hear the evidence objectively and conclude that Christ is Lord. So we have to start by showing that all starting points save one (the existence of the God of the Bible) lead to contradiction. Only after we accept God as God do we have a basis for using reason to evaluate the evidence.

Increasingly people are coming to see these approaches as complementary and indeed mutually interdependent, rather than as alternative options. Unless you have reason to believe that a creator God exists, the evidence for the resurrection of Jesus only leads to the conclusion that something really weird might have happened. Unless you see the strength of the evidence for the resurrection, the God of the classical arguments remains only an abstract theory, not a personal savior. Analyzing the world view options and seeing the contradictions of secularism provides a context in which the evidence becomes meaningful. Presenting evidence alone surely does not lead to conversion, but presuppositionalism alone is susceptible to a charge of circularity—and no methodology is successful unless it is blessed and used by the Holy Spirit to bring about conviction and faith. And, despite the purists on all sides, the Spirit has managed to use all three approaches in that way.

C. S. Lewis was not a part of the conversation I've summarized in the last two paragraphs, and he does not discuss the advantages and disadvantages of those approaches. He is best understood as a classical apologist who sometimes argued in ways more typical of evidentialists and presuppositionalists. He was, in other words, an eclectic realist with some common sense. Purists in the three approaches will not find an ally in Lewis, but practical apologists will find much good advice in how to approach their task.

Lewis followed what Groothuis calls the "cumulative case approach."[16] Lewis uses many types of arguments: classical (the moral argument, the ontological argument[17]), evidential (the trilemma),

---

16 Douglas Groothuis, *Christian Apologetics: A Comprehensive Case for Biblical Faith* (Downers Grove, IL: Intervarsity Press, 2011), 59.
17 See Donald T. Williams, "Anselm and Aslan: C. S. Lewis and the Ontological Argument," *Touchstone: A Journal of Mere Christianity* 27:6

presuppositional (the argument from reason), and existential (the argument from desire[18]). His case is not ultimately dependent on any one of them so much as on the fact that they all point to the same conclusion. He explains,

> Authority, reason, experience; on these three, mixed in varying proportions, all our knowledge depends. The authority of many wise men in many different times and places forbids me to regard the spiritual world as an illusion. My reason, showing me the apparently insoluble difficulties of materialism and proving that the hypothesis of a spiritual world covers far more of the facts with far fewer assumptions, forbids me again. My experience even of such feeble attempts as I have made to live the spiritual life does not lead to the results which the pursuit of an illusion ordinarily leads to, and therefore forbids me yet again.[19]

Authority, reason, experience: When they agree, one can proceed with a certain amount of confidence.

Practical Apologetics

There are then a number of arguments pointing to the truth of the Christian faith, some of them quite strong. But Lewis realized that having good arguments is not enough. We also need to influence the general climate of opinion. In a secular age, unexamined attitudes and ideas influence our minds in ways that do not affect the validity of the reasons we have always had for believing in God, but may have a powerful effect on their plausibility. For example, Ransom insists that "What we need for the moment is not so much a body of belief as a body of people familiarized with certain ideas. If we could even effect in one per cent of our readers a change-over from the conception of Space to the conception of Heaven, we should have made a beginning."[20] Space is a vast unpopulated emptiness in which life is an anomaly; heaven is a vibrant matrix of being pulsating with life and light. How we imagine the world has an influence on how we

---

(Nov.-Dec. 2014), 36-39.
18   See Donald T. Williams, "The Argument from Desire Revisited," *The Lamp-Post of the Southern California C. S. Lewis Society* 32:1 (Spring 2010), 32-33.
19   C. S. Lewis, "Religion: Reality or Substitute?" in *Christian Reflections*, ed. Walter Hooper (Grand Rapids: Eerdmans, 1967), 41.
20   C. S. Lewis, *Out of the Silent Planet* (NY: Simon & Schuster Inc., 1996), 154.

think about it, the kinds of arguments we will be drawn to, and the kinds of conclusions we will draw about it.

Lewis's arguments were effective then partly because he knew that more than argument was needed. In Lewis's apologetic they were supplemented by attempts to imagine what the world would look like if Christianity were true as well as arguments that were not directly about apologetic issues. Lewis wanted Christians to pursue intellectual excellence in general in order to create a situation in which people were not so unused to seeing things from the perspective of the Christian world view as they were already becoming in his generation. "What we want," he said, "is not more little books about Christianity, but more little books by Christians on other subjects."[21] When the best available treatments of art, literature, politics, philosophy, ethics, science, etc. all speak as if Christianity were true (without directly mentioning it), then when the time comes to make the case for its truth directly, a receptive audience will have been created. We have much work left to do in this area.

Lewis was also an effective apologist because he was winsome and intelligent. One of my favorite passages is one in which he slyly turns the tables on the skeptics. As an atheist Lewis had had to believe that the great majority of the human race was wrong; "When I became a Christian," he remarks, "I was able to take a more liberal view."[22] Here he steals a favorite buzz word, "liberal," and a favorite stance, that of tolerant open-mindedness, from his opponents, and stands them on their heads to be used against them. Who is really open minded? Lewis makes his point, but he doesn't rub it in; he makes it and moves on. We could learn a lot from him in manner as well as in message.

Lewis had a unique gift for being able to express the most profound Christian ideas that apologetics needs to defend in language that normal human beings can understand. This was a gift, but it is also a skill that can be cultivated. Lewis wrote to John Beddow on 7 Oct. 1945, "It has always seemed to me odd that those who are sent to evangelise the Bantus begin by learning Bantu while the Church turns out annually curates to teach the English who simply don't know the vernacular language of England."[23] He also stressed that you do not really even understand a concept if you cannot translate it into the vernacular. He thought such translation ought to be a compulsory

---

21 "Christian Apologetics," op. cit., 93.
22 *Mere Christianity*, op. cit., 43.
23 *Collected Letters*, op. cit., 2:674.

paper for every ordination examination.[24] It was good advice for the apologist as well as the pastor and the evangelist. Sadly today in Academia there is a prejudice to the effect that writing cannot be intellectual if it is intelligible. Lewis's entire corpus gives the lie to that erroneous notion. It would be good if a host of theologians and apologists following his example could give the lie to it too.

Lewis was also careful not to claim too much. He gives multiple arguments to the best explanation and does not typically claim to have a slam-dunk proof. He wrote to Sheldon Vanauken on 23 Dec. 1950, "I do not think there is a *demonstrative* proof (like Euclid) of Christianity, nor of the existence of matter, nor of the good will & honesty of my best & oldest friends. I think all three are . . . far more probable than the alternatives."[25] Not only does this approach relieve us of the burden of trying to prove more than we can, it is also consistent with the nature of the response we are looking for. As Lewis further explained, God does not give us a demonstrative proof because a response of mere intellectual assent is not what He is after. "Are *we* interested in it in personal matters? . . . The very fairy tales embody the truth. Othello believed in Desdemona's innocence when it was proved; . . . Lear believed in Cordelia's love when it was proved: but that was too late."[26] Faith—personal trust—is not indifferent to evidence. But we do not value faith very highly when it is given only if there is no intellectual alternative, or when it wavers with every fluctuation in the ebb and flow of circumstances.

The Final Apologetic

Lewis would have agreed with Francis Schaeffer that "the final apologetic" is a life lived as if the Christian message were true.[27] Lewis noted, "If Christianity should happen to be true, then it is quite impossible that those who know this truth and those who don't should be equally well equipped for leading a good life."[28] Christians so equipped should indeed be leading a life that not only exhibits

---

24 "Christian Apologetics," op. cit., 98-99.
25 *Collected Letters*, op. cit., 3:75.
26 Ibid.
27 Francis Schaeffer, *The God Who is There: Speaking Historic Christianity into the Twentieth Century* (Downers Grove, Il.: Inter-Varsity Press, 1958, 152; cf. *The Mark of the Christian* (Downers Grove, IL.: Inter-Varsity Press, 1970)..
28 C. S. Lewis, "Man or Rabbit?" in *God in the Dock: Essays on Theology and Ethics*, ed. Walter Hooper (Grand Rapids: Eerdmans, 1970), 109.

human thriving from the application of Christian truths but also a sacrificial commitment to showing the love of Christ to each other and to the world. Without this "final apologetic," no argument will be compelling to people from whom we are asking not just intellectual assent but life commitment. And to some, it will be the only argument that can speak. As Lewis wrote to a Miss Gladding on 7 June 1945, "When a person . . . has lost faith under so very great and bewildering a trial, no intellectual approach is likely to avail. But where people can resist and ignore arguments, they may be unable to resist *lives*."[29]

The final practical point is the realization that apologetics is a form of spiritual warfare, and not one without casualties. The best way to be one of those casualties is to ignore the danger. Lewis did not. He realized that "Nothing is more dangerous to one's own faith than the work of the apologist. No doctrine of that faith seems to me so spectral, so unreal, as the one I have just successfully defended. . . . For a moment, you see, it has seemed to rest on oneself."[30] Therefore it is indispensable that we have a serious reckoning with the fact that intellectual preparation is necessary but not enough. The apologist must be a person who walks with the Lord in such a way that he cannot forget on Whom things truly rest.

Conclusion

Why do we need apologetics? We live in a world filled with people who think like Trumpkin: "I have no use for magic lions which are talking lions and don't talk, and friendly lions though they don't do us any good, and whopping big lions though nobody can see them."[31] The only cure for that attitude was for Trumpkin actually to meet Aslan. Well, we are all of us constitutionally unbelieving Narnian dwarfs. "You see," said Aslan. "They will not let us help them. They have chosen cunning instead of belief. Their prison is only in their own minds, yet they are in that prison; and are so afraid of being taken in that they cannot be taken out."[32]

Only the Holy Spirit can take us out of ourselves, out of those internal prisons, to the point that we can hear the evidence for Christ and respond to it with faith. But the Spirit wants us to be ready and able to present that evidence when He does so. Lewis's friend Austin

---

29 *Collected Letters*, op. cit., 2:659.
30 "Christian Apologetics," op. cit., 103).
31 C. S. Lewis, *Prince Caspian* (NY: HarperCollins, 1979), 156.
32 C. S. Lewis, *The Last Battle* (NY: HarperCollins, 1984), 185-6.

Farrer put it well: "Though argument does not create conviction, the lack of it destroys belief. What seems to be proved may not be embraced; but what no one shows the ability to defend is quickly abandoned. Rational argument does not create belief, but it maintains a climate in which belief can flourish."[33]

Lewis, in other words, well understood that the goal of apologetics is not just to win arguments. It must be what he allowed to Sherwood Eliot Wirt was the goal of all his writing: "to bring about an encounter of the reader with Jesus Christ," the kind of encounter Lewis described so well: "There comes a moment when people who have been dabbling in religion ('Man's search for God') suddenly draw back. Supposing we really found him? We never meant it to come to that! Worse still, supposing he found us?"[34]

The purpose of apologetics then is to help people channel the shock of that encounter into a serious consideration of the claims of Christ. It is to ensure that this encounter is with the Christ of history and not a counterfeit, that it is an encounter of the whole person with that Christ, and that the faith we hope these people will put in Him will be a rational and well-considered and well-grounded faith. It is to help believers whose faith is more fragmented and superficial grow into that rational, well-considered, and well-grounded faith themselves so that they may be preserved in it. It is to remind them in their inevitable moments of doubt that faith is "the art of holding onto things your reason has once accepted, in spite of your changing moods."[35]

The goal is not just to win arguments. It matters little that we persuade people that theism is true in the abstract unless this enables them to meet God. Lewis reminds us, "We trust not because 'a God' exists, but because *this* God exists."[36] We want to get people to the place where "What would, a moment before, have been variations in opinion, now become variations in your personal attitude to a Person. You are no longer faced [simply] with an argument which demands your assent, but with a Person who demands your confidence."[37] For

---

33 Austin Farrer, "The Christian Apologist," in *Light on C. S. Lewis*, ed. Jocelyn Gibb (NY: Harcourt, Brace, & World, 1965), 26.
34 C. S. Lewis, *Miracles: A Preliminary Study* (N.Y.: MacMillan, 1947), 96-7.
35 *Mere Christianity*, op. cit., 123.
36 C. S. Lewis, "On Obstinacy in Belief," in *The World's Last Night and other Essays* (N.Y.: Harcourt, Brace & World, 1960), 25.
37 Ibid., 26.

if indeed they can be brought to see the glory of God in the face of Jesus Christ, they will be ready to say with Orual, "You are yourself the answer. Before your face questions die away."[38]

---

[38] C. S. Lewis, *Till We Have Faces: A Myth Retold* (Harcourt Brace & World, 1956; rpt. Grand Rapids: Eerdmans, 1968), 308.

WORKS CITED

Bassham, Gregory, ed. *C. S. Lewis's Christian Apologetics: Pro and Con*. Leiden: Brill/Rodopi, 2015.

Farrer, Austin. "The Christian Apologist." *Light on C. S. Lewis*, ed. Jocelyn Gibb. NY: Harcourt, Brace, & World, 1965: 23-43.

Groothuis, Douglas. *Christian Apologetics: A Comprehensive Case for Biblical Faith*. Downers Grove, IL: Intervarsity Press, 2011.

Lewis, C. S. "Christian Apologetics." 1945. *God in the Dock*, ed. Walter Hooper. Grand Rapids: Eerdmans, 1970: 89-103.

The Collected Letters of C. S. Lewis, 3 vols., ed. Walter Hooper. San Francisco: HaperSanFrancisco 2004.

"Cross Examination." Orig. printed as "I Was Decided Upon," Decision II (Sept. 1963): 3 and "Heaven, Earth, and Outer Space," Decision II (Oct. 1963): 4; rpt. *God in the Dock: Essays on Theology and Ethics*. Ed. Walter Hooper. Grand Rapids: Eerdmans, 1970: 258-67.

"God in the Dock." As "Difficulties in Presenting the Faith to Modern Unbelievers," Lumen Vitae III (Sept. 1948): 421-6; rpt. *God in the Dock: Essays on Theology and Ethics*. Ed. Walter Hooper. Grand Rapids: Eerdmans, 1970: 240-44.

God in the Dock: Essays on Theology and Ethics. Ed. Walter Hooper. Grand Rapids: Eerdmans, 1970.

The Great Divorce. NY: MacMillan, 1946.

The Last Battle. 1955; NY: HarperCollins, 1984.

"Learning in Wartime." Sermon preached at St. Mary the Virgin, Oxford, 22 Oct. 1939. *The Weight of Glory and Other Addresses*. Ed. Walter Hooper. San Francisco: Harper Collins, 1980: 47-63.

The Lion, the Witch, and the Wardrobe. 1950; NY: HarperCollins, 1978.

"Man or Rabbit?" S.C.M., 1946; rpt. *God in the Dock: Essays on Theology and Ethics*. Ed. Walter Hooper. Grand Rapids: Eerdmans, 1970: 108-113.

"Meditation in a Toolshed." *God in the Dock*, ed. Walter Hooper. Grand Rapids: Eerdmans, 1970: 212-15.

Mere Christianity. NY: MacMillan, 1943.

Miracles: A Preliminary Study. NY: MacMillan, 1947.

"On Obstinacy in Belief." *The Sewanee Review*, Autumn, 1955; rpt. *The World's Last Night and other Essays*. NY: Harcourt, Brace & World, 1960: 13-30.

Out of the Silent Planet. NY: Simon & Schuster Inc., 1996.

Prince Caspian. 1951; NY: HarperCollins, 1979.

The Problem of Pain. NY: MacMillan, 1967.

"Rejoinder to Dr. Pittenger." *The Christian Century* LXXV (26 Nov. 1958): 1359-61; rpt. *God in the Dock*, ed. Walter Hooper. Grand Rapids: Eerdmans, 1970: 177-83.

"Religion: Reality or Substitute?" *World Dominion* XIX (Sept.-Oct. 1941); rpt. *Christian Reflections*, ed. Walter Hooper. Grand Rapids: Eerdmans, 1967: 37-43.

Surprised by Joy: The Shape of my Early Life. NY: Harcourt, Brace, and World, 1955.

Till We Have Faces: A Myth Retold. Harcourt Brace & World, 1956; rpt. Grand Rapids: Eerdmans, 1968.

"Transposition." Sermon preached in the chapel of St. Mansfield College, Oxford, 28 May 1944. *The Weight of Glory and Other Addresses*. Ed. Walter Hooper. San Francisco: Harper Collins, 1980: 91-115.

Mills, David, ed. *The Pilgrim's Guide: C. S. Lewis and the Art of Witness*. Grand Rapids: Eerdmans, 1998.

Mitchell, Christopher W. "Bearing the Weight of Glory: The Cost of C. S. Lewis's Witness." In David Mills, ed., *The Pilgrim's Guide: C. S. Lewis and the Art of Witness*. Grand Rapids: Eerdmans, 1998: 3-14.

Schaeffer, Francis. *The God Who is There: Speaking Historic Christianity into the Twentieth Century*. Downers Grove, IL: InterVarsity Press, 1958.

The Mark of the Christian. Downers Grove, IL: InterVarsity Press, 1970.

Williams, Donald T. "Anselm and Aslan: C. S. Lewis and the Ontological Argument." *Touchstone: A Journal of Mere Christianity* 27:6 (Nov.-Dec. 2014): 36-39.

"The Argument from Desire Revisited." *The Lamp-Post of the Southern California C. S. Lewis Society* 32:1 (Spring 2010): 32-33.

"G. K. Chesterton, The Everlasting Man." *C. S. Lewis's List: The Ten Books that Influenced Him Most.* Ed. David Werther and Susan Werther. NY: Bloomsbury, 2015: 31-48.

"Identity Check: Are C. S. Lewis's Critics Right, or Is His 'Trilemma' Valid?" *Touchstone: a Journal of Mere Christianity* 23:3 (May-June 2010): 25-29.

"Lacking, Ludicrous, or Logical? The Validity of Lewis's 'Trilemma.'" *Midwestern Journal of Theology* 11:1 (Spring 2012): 91-102.

Mere Humanity: G. K. Chesterton, C. S. Lewis, and J. R. R. Tolkien on the Human Condition. Nashville: Broadman, 2006.

"Pro: A Defense of C. S. Lewis's 'Trilemma.'" Bassham, Gregory, ed. *C. S. Lewis's Christian Apologetics: Pro and Con.* Leiden: Brill/Rodopi, 2015: 171-89.

Reflections from Plato's Cave: Essays in Evangelical Philosophy. Lynchburg: Lantern Hollow Press, 2012.

C. S. Lewis and the Problem of Prayer

by Robert Moore-Jumonville

Robert Moore-Jumonville, Ph.D. serves Spring Arbor University as Professor of Christian Spirituality in the Department of Theology. He teaches spiritual formation both at the undergraduate and graduate levels. An elder in the United Methodist Church, he has served for seventeen years as senior pastor for three churches.

Joan Chittister writes: "Prayer life is an awareness and acceptance of the self. . . . The temptation . . . is to pray as if we were more than we are. More pious perhaps. . . . But when all we bring to prayer is our holiness, what is the use of being there?" In other words, prayer is about honesty with God, and with ourselves. Chittister then asks: "What am I not facing in myself that really needs my prayer if I am ever to grow . . . to become fully human?"[1] That short paragraph aptly sums up the heart of C. S. Lewis's spiritual theology regarding prayer. True prayer moves us toward spiritual honesty.

Published posthumously in 1964, *Letters to Malcom*, Lewis's last book on prayer, was construed as a fictitious exchange of letters between two colleagues. On the first page Lewis agrees with his "friend's" proposal that their conversation revolve around the topic of prayer: "Prayer, which you suggest, is a subject that is a good deal in my mind. I mean private prayer."[2]

In fact, prayer stood at the heart of Christian spiritual formation for Lewis and surfaced frequently as an important theme in Lewis's writing. In 1945, the essay *Work and Prayer* appeared in *The Coventry Evening Telegraph*. Then in 1953, *Petitionary Prayer: A Problem Without an Answer* was read to the Oxford Clerical Society; and in 1959 *The Efficacy of Prayer* appeared in *The Atlantic Monthly*.[3] His book, *Reflections on the Psalms*, largely an exploration of prayer, was published

---

1   Joan Chittister, *The Breath of the Soul: Reflections on Prayer*. New London; Twenty-Third Publications, 2009, 5.
2   C. S. Lewis, *Letters to Malcom: Chiefly on Prayer*. San Diego: Harcourt Brace & Company, 1964, 3.
3   C. S. Lewis, *Work and Prayer*, in *God in the Dock*. Grand Rapids: Eerdmans, 1970: 104-107; *Petitionary Prayer: A Problem Without an Answer*, in *C. S. Lewis Essay Collection*. London: HarperCollins, 2000: 197-205; *The Efficacy of Prayer*, in *C. S. Lewis Essay Collection*. London: HarperCollins, 2000: 237-41.

in 1958. But Lewis also wove issues regarding prayer throughout other books as well: notably *The Screwtape Letters*, *Till We Have Faces*, *The Problem of Pain*, and *A Grief Observed*.[4]

In this paper, I hope to identify what Lewis considered as the fundamental problem of prayer. For a clue, we might begin by turning to the full title of Lewis's last book: *Letters to Malcom Chiefly on Prayer: Reflections on the Dialogue Between God and Man*. It's interesting to notice the phrase "dialogue between God and Man" here, because in the last years of his life Lewis painfully experienced God's silence as absence. He feared prayer might only consist of monologue, talking to oneself. Recall *A Grief Observed*, where Lewis laments in the early pages: "Where is God? . . . Go to Him when your need is desperate, when all other help is vain, and what do you find? A door slammed in your face, and a sound of bolting and double bolting on the inside. After that, silence."[5]

Lewis, of course, struggled with abandonment issues. His mother, Flora, had been diagnosed with cancer when he was 10. In his early autobiography, *Surprised by Joy*, Lewis recalls he had been taught that "prayers offered in faith would be granted." So he set out praying earnestly, with force of will; and he thought, yes, my mother will recover. Instead, she died. "The thing hadn't worked," lamented Lewis. Prayer hadn't worked. And when Flora Lewis died, Jack's childhood security and happiness vanished overnight: "No more of the old security. It was sea and islands now; the great continent had sunk like Atlantis." Late in life, his beloved Joy Davidman died, too.[6]

However, let us not fall prey to the sensationalist version of Lewis, as a man holding his faith in tatters at the end of his life, with the tabloid headline blinking above in cheap neon lights: "Cruel God Steals Lewis's Love."[7] Doubt was nothing new in Lewis's life. In fact

---

4   C. S. Lewis, *Reflections on the Psalms*. San Diego: Harcourt Brace and Company, 1958; *The Screwtape Letters*. New York: HarperCollins, 1982; *Till We Have Faces*. San Diego: Harcourt Brace and Company, 1984; *The Problem of Pain*. New York: HarperCollins, 1996; *A Grief Observed* New York: Bantam, 1976.
5   Ibid., 4
6   C. S. Lewis, *Surprised by Joy: The Shape of My Early Life*. New York: Harcourt Brace, 1955: 20-21. On Joy Davidman's death and its impact on Lewis, see Roger Lancelyn Green and Walter Hooper, *C. S. Lewis: A Biography*. San Diego: Harcourt Brace: 257-78; and Alister McGrath, *C. S. Lewis: A Life*. Carol Stream: Tyndale House, 2013: 341-360.
7   I intentionally overstate the case, here, in referring to the efforts of some, like A. N. Wilson, to 'debunk' the myth of Lewis. See A.N. Wilson,

he expressed the same sort of doubt about communication with God when he was 32 years old, and moving from atheism toward Christian faith. In a letter to his closest friend, Arthur Greeves, he wrote: "Often when I pray, I wonder if I am not posting letters to a non-existent address."[8] Lewis points to those times when our prayers seem to bounce off the ceiling. Yet he conveyed similar misgivings thirty years later in *Letters to Malcom*: "Are we only talking to ourselves in an empty universe?" Lewis asked. "The silence is so emphatic. And we have prayed so much already." He was identifying "the haunting fear that there is no-one listening, and that what we call prayer is soliloquy: someone talking to himself."[9]

Lewis's words, here, represent a particularly modern version of the problem of prayer. In some ways, it parallels certain laments we find in the Psalms, or perhaps Job's case against God. Yet in Psalms and Job, the reality of communication with God is never in question; the writers know God hears them, the only question is whether or not God cares. Job's laments foreshadow the cries of the disciples in the boat as Jesus lay asleep in the midst of a raging storm: "Master, don't you care if we perish?"[10]

But the modern anxiety is different. A modern thinker easily complains that talking to God is merely autosuggestion (as the early psychology of religion movement liked to assert), or a projection of something within us (as Feuerbach argued), or mere wish fulfillment (as Freud maintained). Lewis undoubtedly felt this intellectual pressure, which flowed out of the Enlightenment's stress on the autonomy of human reason, and theology understood as anthropology.[11]

Of course, Lewis wanted to be reasonable. Since the time he began addressing Britain through his BBC talks in the early 1940's, he had been put in the position of answering questions for the ordinary Christian—men and women who wanted to believe but felt bewildered by the modern world.

C. S. Lewis: A Biography. New York: Norton, 1990: 282-310.
8   C. S. Lewis to Arthur Greeves, December 24th 1930. *The Collected Letters of C. S. Lewis*, vol. 1, ed. Walter Hooper. San Francisco: HarperCollins, 2004: 945.
9   Ibid., 61, 67.
10 Mark 4:38
11 See Robert Moore-Jumonville and Robert Woods, "A Role-taking Theory of Praying the Psalms: Using the Psalms as a Model for Structuring the Life of Prayer," *McMaster Journal of Theology and Ministry* 6 (2003–2005), 81-112.

Lewis served as spiritual director for many believers through his broadcasts, his books, and through the hundreds of letters he wrote each year in response to questions asked by his audience. Consider, for instance when, in 1944, Lewis agreed to visit a factory in Middlesex to answer questions about the Christian faith. The questions were incredibly diverse, ranging from the church's stance on venereal disease to the modern scientific assertion that life on earth is the product of random stellar collisions; to questions much more pastoral in nature—like this one: "Many people feel resentful or unhappy because they think they are the target of unjust fate. These feelings are stimulated by bereavement, illness, deranged domestic or working conditions, or the observation of suffering in others. What is the Christian view of this problem?" Who among us would like to respond to that question?[12]

My point is this: Lewis wanted to remove intellectual and theological obstacles for the common layperson if possible. It was something he discovered he was gifted at; and it was something he felt compelled to succeed at. And so another set of problems regarding prayer gradually arose in Lewis's mind, having to do with what he considered logical inconsistencies. He hoped he could shed light on these matters for his readers. Let me explain three such questions that Lewis addressed.

The first, and seemingly easiest, intellectual problem Lewis tackled appeared in his short essay titled *Work and Prayer* (1945). Why bother to pray at all? That's the question. Lewis observes: If God is all-wise, he already knows our requests before we ask them; and if he is all-good, then he will grant requests that align with his good and perfect will, and he will reject requests not aligning with that will. So why even ask? God already knows. Lewis concludes that God enjoys taking our prayers seriously. When God gladly listens to us, he grants us dignity as creatures (as co-creators, really) by allowing us agency to participate in the causality of the world he has made. Our prayers, then, can actually effect change in the world.

Nevertheless, in evangelical circles, one hears trite truisms about prayer bandied about—phrases like "prayer works," or "prayer changes things"—statements which, of course, are true; right up to the point when they stop being true; right up to the time when it seems like your prayers aren't working; when nothing is "changing," and your prayers only bounce off the ceiling.

At this point, Lewis confronts a second intellectual difficulty

---

12   C. S. Lewis, "Answers to Questions on Christianity," in *God in the Dock*: 36-53.

concerning prayer. Lewis declared in his 1959 essay *The Efficacy of Prayer* (i.e., the effectiveness of prayer), that to claim prayer "works," to even use that language—to say, prayer is "effective"— invites confusion, since it poses more questions, problems, and doubts than it can possibly answer. Here's how the essay begins:

> Some years ago, I got up one morning intending to have my hair cut in preparation for a visit to London, and the first letter I opened made it clear I need not go to London. So I decided to put the haircut off too. But then there began the most unaccountable little nagging in my mind, almost like a voice saying, "Get it cut all the same. Go and get it cut." In the end I could stand it no longer. I went. Now my barber at that time was a fellow Christian and a man of many troubles whom my brother and I had sometimes been able to help. The moment I opened his shop door he said, "Oh, I was praying you might come today." And in fact if I had come a day or so later I should have been of no use to him. It awed me; it awes me still. But of course one cannot rigorously prove a causal connection between the barber's prayers and my visit. It might be telepathy. It might be accident.... The question then arises, "What sort of evidence would prove the efficacy of prayer?" The thing we pray for may happen, but how can you ever know it was not going to happen anyway?[13]

Thus, the question of causal connection arises for Lewis: did this "prayer" obtain this "result"?

Consider, for instance, a medical miracle as an example of Lewis's question of whether or not prayer "works." We pray for a friend's healing—and she gets better. But was it the prayer that "worked?" Or was it going to happen anyway? Was it just the doctor, and good recovery, and no subsequent infection? Or was it auto-suggestion (a psychosomatic cure)? What should we conclude? Lewis believed there are problems with trying to connect prayers and results. How do we really know if there is a connection? Don't we simply invite confusion and doubt? As Uncle Screwtape counsels his nephew Wormwood: Don't forget to use the "'heads I win, tails you lose' argument. If the thing he prays for doesn't happen, then that is one more proof that

---

13 *The Efficacy of Prayer*: 237. In *Letters to Malcom*, Lewis re-shapes his earlier essays on prayer, while adding new material. One of the book's chief themes revolves around prayer and causality, touching on issues such as human and divine agency, or the relationship between time, experienced as sequence by human beings and the divine timelessness of God where all prayers are answered in His eternal present.

petitionary prayers don't work; if it does happen, he will, of course, be able to see some of the physical causes which led up to it, and 'therefore it would have happened anyway', and thus a granted prayer becomes just as good a proof as a denied one that prayers are ineffective."[14]

Instead of considering prayer as effective or ineffective, then, as working or not working, Lewis points out the obvious fact that prayer is request. As a request, prayer becomes a relational matter. If we ask a friend for a loaf of bread, she may or may not grant our request. Thus, to remove the personal equation of the relationship (of prayer)—where the Person (God) may or may not agree to our request—makes prayer either too mechanical or too much like magic. Sometimes God will say, "Yes," sometimes, "No"—as with all relationships. If you ask someone to marry you—and they agree—is that an event you should try to manipulate, calculate, or scientifically explain?

Like Love, Prayer does not make sense in mechanical language. Real relationship goes well beyond formula, beyond certainty—remaining a mystery. Lewis, in the end, changes the direction of our desiring when he says: "But really, for our spiritual life as a whole, the 'being taken into account,' or [being] 'considered,' matters more than the being granted. Religious people [people of real, deep spirituality] don't talk about the 'results' of prayer; they talk of its being 'answered' or 'heard.'" Isn't that true? We want relationship most. And we most fear rejection. We want mercy more than miracle. Lewis elaborates: "We can bear to be refused but not to be ignored. In other words, our faith can survive many refusals if they really are refusals and not mere disregards. The apparent stone will be bread to us if we believe that a Father's hand put it into ours, in mercy or in justice or even in rebuke."

The third intellectual question Lewis sought to answer has to do with two kinds of petitionary prayer Lewis found in the New Testament—which seemed to him, quite incompatible. Lewis labeled these Two Types of Prayer "Type A" and "Type B."[15] Prayer "Type A" represents the prayer of surrender, illustrated best by Jesus in the Garden of Gethsemane. Jesus asks three times for "this cup" to pass from him; but ends his prayer saying, "Not my will, but your will be done." The example we are given by Jesus, then, is to put our prayers in this conditional form—perhaps all of them saying "Let this prayer

---

14   *The Screwtape Letters*: 148.
15   C. S. Lewis, *Petitionary Prayer*. Let me note the difference between prayer as petition (a request for myself) and prayer as intercession (praying on behalf of someone else). In what follows, Lewis really includes both of these in a single category—perhaps what we could label "asking prayer."

be answered, God, IF you so desire it." We trust that God knows best, that God, who is all-knowing, all-loving, and all-wise, will not grant us a foolish request or one contrary to his will. Notice that we're not praying here with any assurance that we will get what we ask for. We confess—at the outset—we don't know what's best. Lewis also points out that if we're growing closer to God increasingly this sort of surrender will govern the heart of our prayer, our very longing and desire will be to want only what God wants. As Lewis says elsewhere, we will gradually learn to put first things ahead of second things. Lewis confessed he would be happy to stick to this one kind of praying: "If this were the only pattern of prayer, I should be quite content."[16]

But then there's another sort of prayer, the Type B prayer, a kind of prayer that Scripture also instructs us to use. In contrast to the subjunctive prayer of surrender, the Type B prayer instructs believers to ask boldly in the imperative that the request be granted. Although Lewis cites many NT texts to illustrate this kind of prayer, the clearest passage occurs in the synoptic Gospels: "Truly I tell you, if you say to this mountain, 'Be taken up and thrown into the sea,' and if you do not doubt in your heart, but believe that what you say will come to pass, it will be done for you. So I tell you, whatever you ask for in prayer, believe that you have received it, and it will be yours."[17] Or consider the clear call reverberating from John 14:13: "If in my name you ask me anything, I will do it." Lewis concludes that it is impossible to both fully believe with confidence when praying and at the same time utter the conditional, "Thy will be done." One cannot utter an imperative prayer in the subjunctive mood. Lewis admits near the end of his essay: "I have no answer to my problem, though I have taken it to about every Christian I know, learned or simple, lay or clerical, within my own [denomination] or without."[18]

Fortunately, Lewis does not end this discussion of prayer on a completely negative note. Instead, he concludes by suggesting that the prayer of faith—ask anything in my name, and I will do it—perhaps ought to be the standard form of prayer, the norm, for Christians. Perhaps we ought to regard the worker of miracles, however rare, as the true Christian pattern and ourselves as spiritual cripples.[19] Lewis resolves that he himself shall continue to pray the Type A prayer, "Thy will be done," until God grants him the faith to pray the Type B

---

16 Ibid., 144.
17 Mark 11:23-24; and its parallel, Matthew 21:21-22.
18 Ibid., 204.
19 Ibid.

prayer, to "move mountains" by faith.

We have to admire Lewis's honesty regarding his religious doubts, don't we? James Huston, in an article on Lewis's prayer life, emphasizes Lewis's notion of prayer as "earthy" (not merely otherworldly) and as full of practical realism.[20] That amounts to another way of saying Lewis was honest. He was honest about his own struggles spiritually; that is partly why we feel we can easily follow Lewis on the spiritual path—because he walks alongside us, rather than simply barking orders from the director's chair. Lewis had a "sane estimate" of himself.[21] For instance, Lewis never approached the topic of prayer as an expert, but instead, as a common "lay person" (as a fellow pew sitter). In *Reflections on the Psalms*, Lewis confessed on the first page: "I write for the unlearned about things in which I am unlearned myself."[22] He went on to explain that sometimes it is better to ask questions of a fellow student—rather than the teacher—because the expert teacher faced the problem so long ago, he or she has long since forgotten what the problem felt like. "I write," he claimed, "as one amateur to another, talking about difficulties I have met, or [insights] I have gained . . . with the hope that this might . . . help, other inexpert readers. I am 'comparing notes,' not presuming to instruct."[23]

So, Lewis very much wants to come alongside us—as an ordinary man, as a Mere Christian. At one point, Lewis went so far as to confess: "The truth is, I haven't any language weak enough to depict the weakness of my spiritual life. If I weakened it enough it would cease to be language at all. As when you try to turn the gas-ring a little lower still, and it merely goes out."[24]

Clearly, Lewis could admit his own weaknesses as a Christian. He declared: "I dare say I am a much more annoying person than I know." Then he adds a thoughtful spiritual formation meditation: "Shall we, perhaps, in Purgatory, see our own faces and hear our own voices as they really were?"[25] Doesn't this remind us of Orual's unveiling? She's descended to make her complaint to the gods, and she has tried. She has played all her cards, and then: "It was a great assembly, all staring upon me, and I uplifted on my perch above their

---

20 James Huston, *The Prayer-Life of C. S. Lewis, Knowing and Doing* (Summer 2006): 1-8, C. S. Lewis Institute (www.cslewisinstitute.org/).
21 Romans 12:3.
22 Lewis, *Reflections on the Psalms*: 1
23 Ibid., 2
24 *Letters to Malcom*: 113.
25 *Reflections on the Psalms*: 8.

heads.... There were tens of thousands of them, all silent, every face watching me....But on the same level with me, though far away, sat the judge.... It was a face veiled.... Uncover her,' said the judge."[26] And Orual stands exposed, naked, wearing Ungit's face.

Aye, here's the rub: the heart of Lewis's problem with prayer. His problem with prayer is not that we don't know what to pray, or how to pray, but that we fear to pray. It's not a result of lack of knowledge. It's not a result of faulty technique. We fear prayer because we fear being known. Precisely because prayer exposes us, it makes us want to run—like rabbits from a low hawk. We fear because prayer can put us into direct contact with God, with others, and with ourselves, and often we'd rather not know the truth. We don't want to "have faces." Prayer lures the turtle out of its shell, so to speak; and who wouldn't rather manage a controlled situation? Hence, in prayer we stand naked, vulnerable, and culpable. Therein lay the human condition: it's what Existentialists like to yowl about.

We could say that the problem of prayer is summed up succinctly in *Letters to Malcom*, where Lewis insists: "The prayer preceding all prayers is, 'May it be the real I who speaks. May it be the real Thou that I speak to.'"[27] Frequently, Lewis directs us to return to this prayer. I am so adept at deceiving myself. And in prayer, first I deceive myself about myself, and second, I deceive myself about God. Moreover, the devil is willing to give me all the help I need to assist me in my self-deception. Screwtape counsels his fellow fiend: "You must bring him to a condition in which he can practice self-examination for an hour without discovering any of those facts about himself which are perfectly clear to anyone who has ever lived in the same house with him or worked in the same office."[28]

Do we really know ourselves: our motives, our inner workings, and our inner lurkings? Lewis elaborates on our human lack of self-consciousness in his essay *The Trouble With 'X.'* There is someone in your life difficult to live with. A friend who knows asks, "Why don't you tell her?" And your response is, "You don't know X. She will never admit her problem." But the problem, as Lewis describes, is not only with X; it's also with us. "It is no good passing over this with some vague, general admission such as 'Of course, I know I have my faults.' It is important to realize that there is some really fatal flaw in you: something which gives the others just that same feeling of despair

---

26 *Till We Have Faces*: 288-89.
27 Ibid., 82
28 *Screwtape Letters*: 12.

which their flaws give you."²⁹ Yet we hesitate to admit, don't we, that we are just as bad (if not worse) than X?

We see this reluctance to accurately face our true self surfacing again and again throughout Lewis's writing: in Edmund blaming his siblings while believing the White Witch; in Eustace's blaming everyone else on the Dawn Treader; in Orual's concealment of herself behind her veil and in her complaint against everyone else, including the gods; and in all of the characters queued up in *The Great Divorce* who encounter the purgatorial pain of seeing themselves ghostly, as they really are, fearing the exposure and ready to blame someone else:

> "You'd be tired out before we got to the mountains. And it isn't exactly true, you know." ... "What isn't true?" asked the Ghost sulkily. "You weren't a decent man and you didn't do your best. We none of us were and none of us did. Lord bless you, it doesn't matter. There is no need to go into it all now." "You!" gasped the Ghost. "You have the face to tell me I wasn't a decent chap?"³⁰

If Satan leads us to a false assessment of ourselves—especially enticing us to run away from honest self-examination, next, he would tempt us to create a caricature of God when we pray. Think of J. B. Phillips' classic little volume, *Your God is Too Small*—and a god too small is no god at all. Screwtape instructs Wormwood: "I have known cases where what the patient called his 'God' was actually located—up and to the left at the corner of the bedroom ceiling, or inside his own head, or in a crucifix on the wall. But whatever the nature of the composite object, you must keep him praying to it—to the thing that he has made, not to the person who has made him."³¹

Eventually—and ironically—the devil's plan includes turning our eyes back upon ourselves (especially in prayer). The diabolical scheme hopes to move us away from the reality of God, and away from any real choice that can be made by the human will in the present, and to move us, instead, toward subjective feelings or thoughts within ourselves—in other words, away from reality (God) and toward unreality (fabricated imaginings).³²

In the end, Lewis shows that we are afraid to face the true God because of what he might ask of us. Again and again, Lewis uses the example of the Honest Tax Payer, who agrees to pay taxes, but certainly

---

29 C. S. Lewis, "The Trouble with 'X'," in *God in the Dock*: 164
30 C. S. Lewis, *The Great Divorce*. San Francisco: HarperCollins, 1973: 26.
31 *Screwtape Letters*: 18.
32 Ibid., 16.

does not want to give more than his share. There's always a reservation in our hearts about what is given up.³³ Just so, we fear putting ourselves completely into God's hands. In a discussion of prayer as irksome duty Lewis admitted that "we shrink from too naked a contact, because we are afraid of the divine demands upon us which it might make too audible. As some old writer says, many a Christian prays faintly 'lest God might really hear him, which he, poor man, never intended.'"³⁴

We do not want to be known in prayer, in other words, because we do not want to have to change. That is why we leave our churches, marriages, and families—because we become too well known in these places—in all our hidden (Ungit) ugliness. We would rather remain veiled and not have faces. Besides, real, honest, relational prayer implies obedience. My father-in-law used to tell me the spiritual discipline underlying all spiritual disciplines is obedience. Else, why go through the practice, if you're not willing to play in the game?

But is real honest relational prayer even possible? Are we only returning to where we began—with the fear of silence and abandonment, with prayer as monologue and us stuck in a closed circuit of inner ramblings we cannot escape? Can we ever truly be honest to God? In *Letters to Malcom*, I think Lewis provides at least two practical paths of hope. First, he lays out the mechanics of the subject-object split—whether the real "I" can ever address the real "Thou" in earnest. Lewis does not sugar coat our predicament: he admits we often become mired in our subjectivity. Yet he believes a "re-awakened awareness" actually might recognize our subjectivity and the distance that spans between our perception and "rock-bottom realities."³⁵ On the one hand, the "I" and the "world" are only façades—subjective constructions I create, as though the world were a stage and I were an actor playing upon that stage.

Yet, on the other hand—and here's the good news—we might become aware of the very play itself, and step off the stage, as it were. I might honestly admit, my construct: "And in prayer this real I struggles to speak, for once, from his real being, and to address, for once, not the other actors, but—what shall we call Him? The Author, for he invented us all? The Producer, for He controls us all? Or the Audience,

---

33 C. S. Lewis, *Mere Christianity*. New York: Macmillan 1952, 140; "A Slip of the Tongue," in *The Weight of Glory and Other Essays*. New York: Touchstone 1980: 137-143.
34 *Letters to Malcom*: 114.
35 Ibid., 81.

for He watches, and will judge, the performance?"[36] Striving for self-honesty, then, we might step off the field as contemplative witnesses of the game itself. This represents a form of prayer often taught by contemplatives.[37]

Second, let me point us to Lewis's Chestertonian call to wonder and gratitude (as a form of prayer)—again, from *Letters to Malcom*. This sort of prayer also resembles Brother Lawrence's practicing the presence of God, or the Buddhist practice of mindfulness, of appreciating the present moment. "If I could always be what I aim at being, no pleasure would be too ordinary or too usual for such [grateful] reception; from the first taste of the air when I look out of the window—one's whole cheek becomes a sort of palate—down to one's soft slippers at bed time." [38] Through gratitude, any given moment may thus turn into prayer as adoration, as dialogue—as communion.

---

36 Ibid.
37 See, for instance: *The Cloud of Unknowing*, translated by Carment Acevedo Butcher, Boston: Shambhala, 2009; Martin Laird, *Into the Silent Land*. Oxford: Oxford University Press, 2006, and *A Sunlit Absence*. Oxford: Oxford University Press, 2011; James Finley, *Christian Meditation*. San Francisco: HarperCollins, 2004, and *The Contemplative Heart*. Notre Dame: Sorin, 2000.
38 Ibid., 90.

A Beast's Best Friend: Interspecies Friendship in the Thought of C. S. Lewis

by Edwin Woodruff Tait

> Edwin Woodruff Tait is a parent, homesteader, and independent scholar living in Richmond, Kentucky. He received his Ph.D. in religion, specializing in sixteenth-century church history, from Duke University in 2005, and is the author of numerous articles in *Christian History*, where he is a contributing editor.

On May 15, 1942, C. S. Lewis wrote to Sister Penelope, "I am establishing quite a friendship with one of the rabbits wh. we now keep along with the deer in Magdalen grove. It was done by the discovery that he relishes chestnut leaves which grow too high for his teeth. He doesn't yet allow me any familiarities but he comes and eats from my hand. If my jaws were as strong in proportion to my size as his I'd be able to pluck down the pinnacles of the tower with my teeth. But oh! The great lollipop eyes and the twitching velvet nose! How does He come to create both this and the scorpion?"[1]

On July 29, he reported that "the Rabbit and I have quarrelled. . . . [H]e has cut me dead several times lately. . . . [S]o fair and yet so fickle!"[2] On December 10 he wrote to Arthur Greeves describing his relationship with the rabbit as "an acquaintance (almost a friendship)" and still lamenting that the rabbit wouldn't look at him.[3] But Lewis eventually found a new rabbit friend. On July 26, 1944, he wrote to Sarah Neylan that he was "getting to be quite friends with an old Rabbit who lives in the Wood at Magdalen," whom he had tamed by picking leaves off the trees and feeding them to the rabbit (the same method he had used with the first rabbit), and whom he named "Baron Biscuit."[4] In December of 1944 he wrote to Laurence Harwood of the same rabbit, whom he had apparently discovered was actually female and was now calling "Baroness Bisket."[5]

Of course these letters are whimsical, and perhaps I am taking them too seriously. But Lewis took friendship very seriously indeed.

---

1 C. S. Lewis, *Collected Letters* 2:520-21.
2 *Collected Letters* 2:525.
3 *Collected Letters* 2:540.
4 *Collected Letters* 2:618-19.
5 *Collected Letters* 2:634.

Ironically, given his willingness to speak of being friends with a rabbit, he complained to Bede Griffiths that he was worried about the "decay of friendship" due to "the endless presence of women everywhere" as a threat to friendship. Friendship—specifically male friendship—was central to Lewis's life. Furthermore, the theme of human-animal or cross-species friendship in particular shows up throughout Lewis's work, as this paper will show. Lewis appears to have been haunted throughout his life by the possibility of a friendship that unites beings who are fundamentally different.

Lewis's reference to his acquaintance with the rabbit as "almost a friendship" in the letter to Arthur Greeves may reflect his awareness of the fact that friendship between humans and "irrational" animals was declared impossible by the Aristotelian tradition. Thomas Aquinas treats the question in Question 25 of *Summa Theologiae* II/II, on "the object of charity."[6] According to Aquinas, charity is fundamentally the act of loving one's neighbor "so that he may be in God" (article 1). Charity "has the nature of friendship" (article 2), which consists in willing good to another. The specific good that charity wills for another is union with God. Thus, when Aquinas comes to deal with the question of whether irrational creatures may be loved out of charity in article 3, only one of his three reasons for answering in the negative pertain to the specific nature of charity (willing eternal happiness to another, which Aquinas argues is impossible in the case of irrational creatures who are not capable of such happiness). The other two apply to friendship more broadly, and are based on separate passages in Aristotle.

Aquinas' first reason why friendship between humans and "irrational" creatures is impossible is that friendship consists in willing good to another. However, an irrational creature cannot, strictly speaking, "possess good," because it lacks free will. Only a being with intellect and will is capable of choosing a good for itself and thus being benefited or harmed. Aquinas cites Aristotle's discussion of chance in Book 2 of the *Physics*. Aristotle argues there (chapter 6) that "an inanimate thing or a lower animal or a child cannot do anything by

---

6   Lewis suggested in a 1958 letter that most elements in his thought that people took to be Thomistic were really Aristotelian, describing Aquinas as a "top form" boy in the same class as Lewis, where Lewis was a "bottom form boy" and Aristotle was the teacher. (*Collected Letters* 3:995). That being said, Aquinas is important for placing Aristotelian ideas in a Christian context, and is often identified by writers on animal rights as a major (negative) influence on Christian attitudes to animals.

chance, because it is incapable of deliberate intention; nor can 'good fortune' or 'ill fortune' be ascribed to them, except metaphorically." Both in his commentary on this text and in the *Summa*, Aquinas explains that this is the case because a being without free will does not have "dominion over its own action" (*dominium sui actus*).[7]

As Judith Barad points out, this view seems inconsistent with Aquinas' recognition elsewhere that animals have inclinations and appetites and are not simply to be equated with plants or inanimate objects.[8] Given that recognition, is it not more reasonable to conclude, on Aquinas' own principles, that animals can experience "good and ill fortune" to some degree, albeit to a lesser degree than humans? This is one of a number of places where it seems to me that Aquinas' reverence for Aristotle has a baleful effect on his thought.

Aquinas' second reason for denying the possibility of human/animal friendship is based in a different passage from Aristotle, this one from Book 8 of the *Nicomachean Ethics*. There Aristotle defines friendship as "living together," or, in Aquinas' terms, a "sharing of life" (*communicatio vitae*).[9] Humans and animals, according to Aquinas, cannot share life together in the way required for friendship. They do not have common goals (in part, again, because animals are not capable of deliberate intentionality according to Aquinas). Without sharing a rational nature, friendship is impossible.

Lewis's account of his friendship with the rabbit follows exactly the lines sketched out by Barad, ascribing to the rabbit exactly the sort of intentionality that Aquinas would allow (a desire for food), but then extrapolating from that to allow for the use of language that Aquinas would no doubt find unacceptably anthropomorphic. The

---

7   Comm. in Phys. 229, http://dhspriory.org/thomas/Physics2.htm#6, accessed 12 May 2016. Similarly, in ST II/II 25.3, Aquinas says that good and bad pertains to "solum creaturae rationalis, quae est domina utendi bono quod habet per liberum arbitrium" (http://www.corpusthomisticum.org/sth3025.html, accessed 12 May 2016).

8   Judith Barad, "Aquinas' Inconsistency on the Nature and the Treatment of Animals." Barad is unfair to Aquinas, I think, in her treatment of his claim that we should not treat animals cruelly because it will make us cruel to people. While it's true that Aquinas doesn't recognize that animals have any intrinsic rights or that we have moral duties to them directly, his "virtue ethics" leads him to conclude that treating animals cruelly develops a "habitus" of cruelty. This is, I think, more significant ethically than Barad recognizes.

9   *Nicomachaen Ethics*, Book 8, chapter 5, http://classics.mit.edu/Aristotle/nicomachaen.8.viii.html (accessed 12 May 2016).

rabbit initially becomes friends with Lewis because he desires to eat leaves that are too high for him to reach. Lewis speculates that the rabbit later rejects his friendship because Lewis had inadvertently given him something to eat that "disagreed with him."[10] A desire for food is, after all, something humans share with other animals, even in the Aristotelian paradigm. A human may therefore seek to satisfy that desire by giving an animal good food, and thus establish precisely that "sharing of life" which Aquinas disallows. Of course I am probably making far too much of this episode, but the frequency with which Lewis refers to the rabbit(s) during the mid-1940s indicates, I think, that it was of some importance to him.

Another incident, this one narrated by George Sayer, confirms Lewis's interest in the capacity of non-human animals for friendship and affection. Sayer describes walking with Lewis late in the latter's life and seeing a young pig give food to an older pig. According to Sayer, Lewis responded excitedly to this incident, declaring the young pig to be a "pog" and the harbinger of a new stage in porcine evolution, and asking for its blessing.[11] Like the rabbit friendships, this incident is obviously playful and humorous, but it is further evidence of Lewis's interest in the possibility of animal behavior that transcended the limits set by Aristotle.

The most systematic discussion of the capacity of non-human animals for friendship in Lewis's work occurs in *That Hideous Strength*. Ivy Maggs, who functions in the novel as a voice of folk wisdom in contrast to the educated folly of characters such as Jane and MacPhee, refers to Mr. Bultitude the bear and Pinch the cat as "friends." MacPhee insists that they can't really be friends, and suggests various physiological explanations for their behavior, including the possibility of unconscious sexual attraction. Ivy responds defensively as if MacPhee were accusing the animals of moral indecency.[12] Ransom intervenes to say that MacPhee is ascribing to the animals a distinction that simply does not exist for them. What we call "friendship" among humans is for us more articulately distinguished from physical comfort, sexual attraction, etc., than it is for other animals, but that doesn't mean that something analogous to friendship does not exist among animals.[13] Lewis further illustrates this theory of animal psychology by narrating a later section of the book from the point of view of Mr. Bultitude,

---

10   *Collected Letters* 2:540.
11   George Sayer, *Jack: A Life of C. S. Lewis*, 335.
12   C. S. Lewis, *That Hideous Strength*, 261.
13   C. S. Lewis, *That Hideous Strength*, 261-62.

or more precisely from the point of view of the omniscient narrator trying to explain how Mr. Bultitude experienced the events.[14]

The events in question include important parts of the novel's climax, in which Merlin, assisted by Mr. Bultitude and inhabited by the eldila, brings heavenly vengeance to the demonic N.I.C.E. And it is no coincidence that one of the N.I.C.E.'s principal activities is experimenting on animals. Mark Studdock betrays the inadequacy of his modern, sociological education as a form of moral formation by the fact that he has no moral revulsion to the awareness that the N.I.C.E. maintains a vast zoo of animals for purposes of experimentation, and no empathy with the animals.[15] They simply represent, for him, evidence of the scale of the N.I.C.E.'s enterprise. This is an example of the way in which one's reaction to vivisection functions, for Lewis, as a moral test. Not to be disturbed by animal suffering—to have a purely "instrumental" view of animals—is evidence of a lack of participation in what Lewis elsewhere calls the "Tao."[16]

The proper understanding of our relationship with non-human animals is found at the end of *That Hideous Strength* in the *epithalamium* of the beasts, in which all the animals (including the human ones) pair up under the benign influence of Perelandra: "she comes more near the earth than she was wont—to make Earth sane."[17] This sanity not only leads to amorous coupling, but to a restoration of the natural state of humanity: "We are now as we ought to be, between the angels who are our elder brothers and the beasts who are our jesters, servants, and playfellows."[18]

This understanding of the human relationship with animals is found at more length in *Perelandra*, where the unfallen "Lady" commands the creatures of Venus and they obey her willingly. They are, as in Ransom's statement quoted above, her "servants." There is clearly a hierarchical relationship. But it is also characterized by joyful companionship. Both Ransom and the "Un-man" benefit from the willingness of Perelandra's animals to serve human beings. The Un-man, of course, abuses that willingness, commandeering a fish in order to escape Ransom with no thought for the fish's welfare.[19]

---

14 *That Hideous Strength*, 306-08, 350.
15 *That Hideous Strength*, 102.
16 C. S. Lewis, *Abolition of Man*, 70,
17 *That Hideous Strength*, 378.
18 *That Hideous Strength*, 378.
19 C. S. Lewis, *Perelandra*, 158.

He (it?) also casually tortures frogs, and Ransom's final confrontation with the Un-man begins when Ransom attempts to stop the torture of a bird.[20] One of the most disturbing signs of the Lady's slow "corruption" by the Un-man's temptations is her willingness to let him dress her in a cloak of feathers to make her more beautiful, and her casual disinterest in the question of just how the Un-man got the feathers.[21] Animals are servants and in some sense instruments in *Perelandra*, but they are not mere instruments, and the slightest movement toward treating them as such is a matter of grave significance.

One of the Un-man's most telling arguments against Ransom in their extensive debate over the fate of the Lady and her planet is that Ransom's discomfort with the prospect of humans replacing non-human sentient beings as the focus of "Maleldil's" purposes in the universe mark Ransom out as "what we call 'Bad,'" which the Un-man defines as someone who turns away from the coming good out of preference for past good.[22] The "Unman ethic," which led the human Weston to surrender himself to demonic forces and become the "Unman" and is identified by Lewis with Bergson's "creative evolution," is a worship of "becoming" for its own sake.[23]

Weston tells Ransom that this ethic transcends conventional notions of good and evil because what is conventionally called evil is actually the driving force pushing into the future, while "good" is the ideal that beckons from the future. Weston admits to Ransom that his earlier views, evident in *Out of the Silent Planet*, were irrationally anthropocentrism. All that matters is "Life," whatever form Life may take.[24] Reading this text for the first time, I took this to be a sign of conversion and spiritual growth in Weston. Weston's violent, colonialist anthropocentrism is condemned throughout *Out of the Silent Planet*. Surely his willingness to recognize "Life" in non-human forms is an improvement?

But of course it is this "conversion" to Life-force worship that leads to "Weston's" horrific transformation from a misguided, perhaps evil human being to a demon wearing a human body, with the fragmented psyche of the original "Weston" still gibbering away somewhere in the depths and occasionally surfacing when the "Un-

---

20   *Perelandra*, 152.
21   *Perelandra*, 134-138.
22   *Perelandra*, 114.
23   *Perelandra*, 90-96, 121.
24   *Perelandra*, 91.

man" allows it to for pragmatic purposes.[25] The primary characteristic of the demonic form of "creative evolution" represented by the Un-man is its total pragmatism, its instrumentalizing of absolutely everything, even (as Ransom observes at one point) rationality itself. In *Out of the Silent Planet*, Oyarsa had identified Weston's loyalty to his own species as a genuine virtue, although a minor one.[26] Weston's loss of this virtue represents not a step forward on the moral and spiritual scale but his final loss of the "good of intellect" and his descent into demonic madness.

Thus, the Un-man's argument to the Lady about Ransom's "badness" is complex and ironic. He is evoking the orthodox anthropocentrism which the Lady assumes, in order to seduce her to his own worship of pointless destruction in the name of change and evolution. Ransom's sorrow that there will be no more sentient "beasts" but only anthromoporphic beings now that the Incarnation has taken place is, in the context of the Space Trilogy, a response to his experiences in the first book and his choice to identify with the nonhuman Malacandrians over Weston's murderous anthropocentrism.

The unfallen Lady cannot understand this impulse. She knows only a healthy hierarchical relationship with animals who are not *hnau* (rational), the kind of relationship sketched by Ransom at the end of the third book.[27] (Indeed, Ransom's own journey to spiritual maturity in the course of *Perelandra* consists in part of his coming to see the beauty and fittingness of this kind of anthropocentrism.) The Lady is thus ironically in danger of accepting Weston's demonic ideology in contrast to Ransom's flawed but basically virtuous sympathy for the "older" forms of rational creation represented by the Malacandrians. Yet Ransom's point of view is not all wrong, as indicated by the "Great Dance" at the end of *Perelandra*, which affirms that *everything* in the universe is in its own way a "center" and that the Malacandrians are not just disposable precursors to the real show.[28]

Moving backwards within the Trilogy, we come finally to *Out of the Silent Planet*, where we find (for the first time in Lewis's work if we don't count the Boxen material) a fictional depiction of a society of non-human rational beings (*hnau*). As Ransom journeys through the Malacandrian landscape, he journeys spiritually from an initial abject fear of non-human life (filtered through the deeply depraved

---

25 *Perelandra*, 96.
26 *Out of the Silent Planet*, 137-138.
27 *That Hideous Strength*, 378.
28 *Perelandra*, 214-219.

imaginations of Weston and Devine), to a gradual understanding and acceptance of the great diversity under which rationality manifests itself.

Ransom's friendship with the *hross* Hyoi is the catalyst for his coming to a sober understanding of his species' place in the universe—which will, ironically, make him reluctant to accept the revelation of just how important humans are in the cosmic scheme in *Perelandra*). When he first meets Hyoi, he interprets him as an "animal," just as he sees the seroni as monsters.[29] Ironically, Hyoi's animality helps Ransom deal with the shock of dealing with a sentient alien lifeform. When he thinks of Hyoi as a man, he finds him monstrous, but when he thinks of him as an animal, he finds him a kind of "animal 2.0," with everything one might wish in a pet plus the ability to function as an intellectual equal.[30]

Weston and Devine's killing of Hyoi induces in Ransom a deep guilt for being human, an awareness of just how murderous and fallen his species is. The narrative has prepared us for the possibility that Hyoi will be killed by the monstrous *hnakra*, but in fact he successfully kills the *hnakra* only to be killed by the humans, driving home Lewis's point about just who the real monsters are in the story.[31]

The multispecies rationality of Malacandra is not essential to its "unfallenness," but Lewis clearly suggests, through Ransom's complete lack of comprehension of the possibility of the three species living in harmony, that it is only possible on an unfallen world and is thus one of the signs of the planet's innocence. One of the *sorns* remarks at one point that the people of "Thulcandra" (our planet) must be "at the mercy of their blood" because we cannot compare thought with thought that "floats on a different blood." Toward the end of the book Ransom stays in a guesthouse with all three Malacandrian species, and realizes that Malacandrian humor arises largely from the interactions of *hnau* who have different biologies.[32] In a purported letter from Ransom to Lewis appended to the book, he claims that while we can have friendship with other humans and affectionate relationships with animal pets, on Malacandra the two experiences may be combined in a single relationship. Hence, the Malacandrians do not need pets.[33]

---

29 *Out of the Silent Planet*, 55, 45.
30 *Out of the Silent Planet*, 58.
31 *Out of the Silent Planet*, 125.
32 *Out of the Silent Planet*, 117.
33 *Out of the Silent Planet*, 156.

Four years after writing this, Lewis was telling various correspondents about his friendship with the rabbit in the Magdalen garden. It is probably not a coincidence that the years during which he writes about these "rabbit friendships" are also years when he was working on the Space Trilogy, developing his first major fictional universe that explored the possibility of multiple rational species and the disastrous consequences of a purely instrumental approach to life.

Lewis's fullest exploration of a world filled with multiple intelligent species was, of course, his *Chronicles of Narnia*. When Lucy Pevensie steps out of the wardrobe into that snowy wood, she steps into a world where our normal assumptions about the place of humanity appear to be upended. Mr. Tumnus is astonished to meet a human, and his library contains books suggesting that humans are mythical creatures.[34] The White Witch attempts at first to put Edmund in Narnian categories, suggesting that he must be an overgrown dwarf who has cut off his beard.[35] The Beavers tell the Pevensies that "there's never been any of your race here before."[36] While the White Witch looks human, the Beavers assure the children that she isn't really human at all.[37]

Yet it turns out that humans are not as alien to Narnia as first appears. There are those four thrones in Cair Paravel destined to be filled by "sons of Adam and daughters of Eve."[38] While humans in this first Narnia book appear to be a novel introduction into Narnia, they are not unheard-of and a place has been prepared for them by prophecy, as rulers of the land under Aslan. At the same time, a "pseudo-human" ruler oppresses the various creatures of Narnia, favoring some (wolves, dwarfs, and various kinds of monsters) over others and mimicking with her tyranny of dark magic the properly hierarchical rule Aslan intends for Narnia. The White Witch's regime is in fact a reversal of the attitudes of the N.I.C.E., although it is similar in its use of dark magic and its ultimate reduction of rights and dignity to one all-powerful figure.

In the sequel, *Prince Caspian*, Lewis returns to themes familiar from the Space Trilogy. A tyranny of *humans* has now slaughtered the sentient non-humans or driven them into exile, and has put in place a

---

34   C. S. Lewis, *The Lion, the Witch, and the Wardrobe*, 115 (all Narnia citations are to the omnibus edition from HarperCollins).
35   *The Lion, the Witch, and the Wardrobe*, 124.
36   *The Lion, the Witch, and the Wardrobe*, 147.
37   *The Lion, the Witch, and the Wardrobe*, 147.
38   *The Lion, the Witch, and the Wardrobe*, 148.

stodgy, boring, materialistic society that denies magic and mystery and suppresses freedom. At the same time, in this book the importance of human rule is emphasized far more than in *The Lion, the Witch, and the Wardrobe*. Trufflehunter insists that things were never right in Narnia except when a Son of Adam was king. It isn't a country for men, but it's a country for a man to be king of.[39]

Finally, in the penultimate book to be published, *Magician's Nephew*, Lewis provides his most systematic account of the Narnian universe. Aslan creates all kinds of creatures and then chooses to breathe sentient life into certain of them, giving the talking animals authority over the non-sentient creatures while exhorting them to treat them gently.[40] He also (proving the Beavers wrong) makes a human couple rulers of Narnia, exhorting them to treat all their subjects with fairness and equality.[41] Uncle Andrew's stubborn insistence on closing himself off from the voice of Aslan makes him unable to hear and understand the voices of his non-human fellow creatures, and makes him similarly opaque to them. But while he regards them as mere "brutes" to be feared or used or destroyed, they show their virtuous character by attempting to treat him kindly according to his nature, even if their efforts are not very successful. By the end of the book they have come to see him as a pet—an exception to the rule that in Narnia, as in Malacandra, there don't seem to be pets.[42]

Thus, in Narnia Lewis depicts a hierarchical society but one where freedom and equality of dignity are highly valued. Friendship among different kinds of creatures is not only possible but highly valued. It is Lucy's friendship with Tumnus that gives him the courage to defy the Witch, and the children a motive for staying in Narnia in spite of the dangers. In *Prince Caspian*, Dr. Cornelius, stranded in a world of hostile humans, tells Caspian "what friend have I in the wide world save Your Majesty?"[43] In the same book, Trumpkin earns the nickname "the dear little friend" from the children. Reepicheep's friendship with Lucy, in particular, is an important theme in *Voyage of the Dawn Treader*. In *The Silver Chair*, the three Narnians respond to the realization that they've been eating Talking Stag in varied ways that correspond to their immersion in Narnian multispecies society: Jill merely feels sorry for the stag, Eustace is horrified because he has

---

39 C. S. Lewis, *Prince Caspian*, 347.
40 C. S. Lewis, *The Magician's Nephew*, 69-71.
41 *The Magician's Nephew*, 81.
42 *The Magician's Nephew*, 71-79, 97-98.
43 *Prince Caspian*, 343.

actually had a talking animal as a friend, while Puddleglum feels as if he had eaten a baby.[44]

But the Narnian book where interspecies friendship plays the most important role is arguably *The Horse and His Boy*. Lewis may be influenced by medieval romances such as Bevis of Hampton in which horses speak to their riders and indeed play an important role in training their riders in chivalry.[45] Bree becomes a tutor to Shasta not only in riding but in courtesy and "free" behavior. At the same time, it turns out that Bree himself has a lot to learn. Friendship between Shasta and Aravis, divided by social class, turns out to be even more difficult than friendship between Shasta and Bree. In the end, the four fugitives, two human and two equine, are brought together by their shared journey from slavery to freedom, in which the strengths of both species, both sexes, and a diversity of social experiences all contribute to make their quest for freedom successful. The key moment in Aravis' development from an arrogant (though honorable) Calormene lady to the future Queen of Archenland is her decision to go across the desert with a lower-class boy and two horses rather than stay in Calormen with Lasaraleen.[46]

In the Chronicles, Lewis explores playfully the theme first suggested in *Out of the Silent Planet*, that a world with multiple intelligent species would have a capacity for rich and varied friendships that surpasses our own and combines the emotional satisfaction we get from friendship and the kind we get from pets. He explores *Perelandra*'s suggestion that there might be different ways of configuring the "center," asking how God might be manifest in a world of talking animals. And yet Narnia is in a sense more robustly anthropocentric than the world of the Trilogy. There humans are central because Maleldil has become human. Narnia is supposedly an entirely other world, with a parallel "incarnation" of the Logos as a lion.

Yet it is also a world where "Sons of Adam" are supposed to reign. Lewis never explains why. Does the significance of the Incarnation radiate outward even to worlds reachable only by magic? Is Narnia, after all, a kind of shadow world to our own? Or did he just not think it through? Nonetheless, the Narnia books underline Lewis's fascination with the possibility of friendship with the "other" and his hatred of all forms of tyranny of one kind of creature over another, and all forms

---

44 C. S. Lewis, *The Silver Chair*, 608.
45 See Bonnie J. Erwin, "Beyond Mastery: Interspecies Apprenticeship in Middle English Romance."
46 C. S. Lewis, *The Horse and His Boy*, 253.

of cruelty to animals—or to anyone. The hierarchy of Narnia, like the hierarchy of the Trilogy, is fundamentally non-coercive. All beings act according to their natures, and thus a spontaneous order emerges in which difference does not involve dominance or competition.

One interspecies friendship in Narnia, however, towers above the rest—that between Aslan and the human children.[47] Of course, Aslan is a special case, because at the end of *The Last Battle* "he no longer looked to them like a lion," and he is clearly intended to be a "parallel incarnation" of Christ in some sense.[48] (Whether this implies a kind of Docetistic Christology, as one Catholic critic has claimed, is a separate issue).[49]

But by making the children experience the divine as an animal, Lewis provides us with his most daring example of interspecies friendship. Aslan really is "the wholly other," and yet he embodies an archetype that has powerful resonance in our world as well. Lewis had always been fond of human-animal relationships as a symbol of our relationship with God, particularly using dogs in this way. In Narnia, he reverses the imagery—the humans have a relationship with an animal who is also a manifestation of the divine. The characters who see Aslan as merely a "wild beast" are characters who at best (like Trumpkin) need some serious spiritual growth, or at worst (like Uncle Andrew) are stubbornly closed off from the divine, and indeed from recognizing the dignity of their fellow creatures no matter the species.

Lewis's imaginative explorations of human interactions with non-human species, as well as his frequent discussions of the subject in letters and nonfictional works, suggest that he was both working within and implicitly challenging the Aristotelian/Thomist framework. He clearly accepted the premise that friendship involves the ability to share goals and a way of life, and he imagined ways in which humans and other animals might do so. He accepted the premise that willing the good of another implies that the other has agency, and again, he repeatedly ascribes agency to "irrational" animals. Furthermore, he developed fictional universes in which non-human "rational" beings existed.

These universes are still (in a qualified sense) anthropocentric, and (in a less qualified sense) hierarchical. But it is also an imaginative celebration of diversity and multiculturalism that (one would think)

---

47   I am indebted to Padmini Sukumaran for pointing this out in conversation.
48   C. S. Lewis, *The Last Battle*, 767.
49   Eric Seddon, "Letters to Malcom and the Trouble With Narnia."

ought to shatter the preconceptions of people who see Lewis as simply a defender of traditional British mores and the privileges of straight white males. In the words of *Perelandra:* "Thus each is equally at the center and none are there by being equals, but some by giving place and some by receiving it, the small things by their smallness and the great by their greatness, and all the patterns linked and looped together by the unions of a kneeling with a sceptred love. . . . We also have need beyond measure of all that He has made. Love me, my brothers, for I am infinitely necessary to you and for your delight I was made. . . . Love me, my brothers, for I am infinitely superfluous, and your love shall be like His, born neither of your need nor of my deserving, but a plain bounty. Blessed be He!"[50]

---

50   *Perelandra*, 217.

Works Cited

Aquinas, Thomas. *Commentary on Aristotle's* Physics. http://dhspriory.org/thomas/Physics.htm (accessed 12 May 2016).

---. *Summa Theologiae.* Textum Leoninum Romae 1895. xzhttp://www.corpusthomisticum.org/ (accessed 12 May 2016).

Aristotle. *Nichomachaen Ethics.* http://classics.mit.edu/Aristotle/nicomachaen.html (accessed 12 May 2016).

Barad, Judith. "Aquinas' Inconsistency on the Nature and The Treatment of Animals." *Between the Species* vol. 4, no. 2 (1988), 102-111. http://digitalcommons.calpoly.edu/cgi/viewcontent.cgi?article=1692&context=bts (accessed 12 May 2016).

Erwin, Bonnie J. "Beyond Mastery: Interspecies Apprenticeship in Middle English Romance." Unpublished paper presented at the 2016 International Congress on Medieval Studies, May 12-15, 2016.

Lewis, C. S. *The Abolition of Man.* New York: Harper Collins, 2001.

---. *The Chronicles of Narnia, Including "An Essay on Writing."* New York: Harper Collins, 2004.

---. *Out of the Silent Planet.* New York: Collier, 1965.

---. *Perelandra.* New York: Collier, 1965.

---. *That Hideous Strength.* New York: Collier, 1965.

Lewis, C. S., ed. Walter Hooper. *Collected Letters, Vol. 2: Books, Broadcasts, and the War.* New York: Harper Collins, 2004.

---. *Collected Letters, Vol. 3: Narnia, Cambridge, and Joy.* New York: Harper Collins, 2007.

Sayer, George. *Jack: A Life of C. S. Lewis.* Wheaton: Crossway, 2005.

Seddon, Eric. "*Letters to Malcolm* and the Trouble With Narnia: C.S. Lewis, J.R.R. Tolkien, and Their 1949 Crisis." *Mythlore,* vol. 26 no. 1/2, Fall/Winter 2007. http://www.thefreelibrary.com/Letters+to+Malcolm+and+the

+trouble+with+Narnia%3a+C.S.+Lewis%2c+J.R.R. . ..-a0171579958 (accessed 29 June 2016).

Patriarchy and P'daitaBird:
The Artistic Influence of Albert Lewis

by Crystal Hurd

> Crystal Hurd is an educator, writer, and poet from Virginia. She is the author of *Thirty Days with C. S. Lewis: A Women's Devotional*, and a contributor for *Women and C. S. Lewis: What His Life and Literature Reveal for Today's Culture*. She has also published in *All Nine Muses, Legendarium, Mythlore, Sehnsucht* and *VII*. She serves as the book review editor for *Sehnsucht*.

Albert Lewis has long been characterized as a failed parent by Lewis enthusiasts. He was a staple of Irish politics at the turn of the century, serving as a court solicitor in Belfast, yet his two sons noted that he was often absent and when present, nearly intolerable. However, a closer examination offered in the unpublished *Lewis Papers* presents a different portrait of Albert Lewis. Albert was a reigning hero of the Belfast Conservative party, and was poised to become a successful politician. He was a lover of literature, filling Little Lea to the brim with books. His political speeches often alluded to various literary works, and he was a member of distinguished literary societies. Perhaps most notable is the surprising literary influence that Albert had on his two sons, Warren, who would become an authority on 17th century French history, and C.S. "Jack" Lewis, the celebrated literary critic, novelist, children's author, and imaginative apologist.

It is perhaps easy to interpret Albert Lewis as an unflattering character. Most literature, including Lewis's own writings concerning his father, portrays a man with a rigid adherence to routine, an unfailing enthusiasm for argument, and a keen talent of suffocating his listener with verbosity. Albert rarely accompanied his family to the Irish coast, where his sons experienced the beauty of the Irish sea. When he did visit, he seemed restless:

> He would sometimes come down for the week-end, but he never stayed with his wife and children throughout the summer holiday. Urgent business was his excuse . . . . I never met a man more wedded to a dull routine, or less capable of extracting enjoyment from life. A night spent out of his house was a penance to him: a holiday he loathed, having not the faintest conception of how to amuse himself. I can still see him on his occasional visits to the seaside, walking moodily up and down the beach, hands in trouser pockets, eyes on the

ground, every now and then giving a heartrending yawn and pulling out his watch. (22)

Weeks after the devastating loss of his wife Flora to abdominal cancer in 1908, Albert reenrolled Warnie (and now Jack) into boarding school. The young Lewis felt that this was a painful exile from the sanctuary of Little Lea and the backdrop of a cherished childhood to the exhaustively competitive climate of early education. Jack admits that Wynyard, a boarding school operated by severe Reverend Robert "Oldie" Capron, was an oppressive and dark experience. Although many scholars argue that Albert's academic selection demonstrated his stubbornness and frugality, it must be mentioned that Albert did not send the boys away without consulting educational agents Messrs. Gabbitas and Thring as to the best academic options for Warnie and Jack (the letters show that Capron dismissed Albert's letters of inquisition). George Sayer posited that Jack "blamed the English schools for the difficulty he and many of his generation had in understanding their parents" (*Jack* 74). At the time, Albert was assured that the school would properly prepare the boys for university entrance exams. However, many men of Lewis's generation struggled to connect with their fathers. In his new biography of Charles Williams, Grevel Lindop quotes a letter from Williams in which he admits that he was "losing his former closeness to his father": "I could show you, I think, the very point in St. Albans where, just as I was posting a letter, it occurred to me that when my father said X I despised it, and when any one of my friends said X I thought it was extremely intelligent. It is in our blood; we are furious with our parents before we know it" (23).

Indeed, *Surprised by Joy*, although it seems to indict Albert as a problematic parent, illustrated a father struggling to connect with the family that remains. Jack admits that Albert desired the company of his sons, although he became an "oppressive" presence. Lewis recalls that they resembled three brothers other than a father and two sons. He often wished to please his boys, quoting, "Liberty Hall, boys, Liberty Hall" and inquiring what time they would like to eat lunch. However, both boys knew that meals, like many aspects of their day, were subject to their father's strenuous obedience to routine. Lewis writes, "I should be worse than a dog if I blamed my lonely father for thus desiring the friendship of his sons; or even if the miserable return I made him did not to this day lie heavy on my conscience.... I could not 'be myself' while he was at home. God forgive me, I thought Monday morning, when he went back to his work, the brightest jewel in the week" (125-126).

Also noted is Albert's absence before Jack's deployment to France and during his wartime convalescence. Jack desired to see his father before being sent to the French frontlines. However, Albert did not comprehend the telegram and requested clarification. Due to Jack's brief leave, the meeting never occurred. Later, after being wounded in battle, Jack wrote a long, emphatic letter begging for a visit from Albert. However, Albert was preoccupied with work and could not spare time to visit his injured son. Jack interpreted this as a confirmation of Albert's apathy and abandonment, further creating distance between them. Although Albert financed Jack's three firsts at Oxford, his son remained emotionally estranged.

It was during Jack's studies at Oxford that Albert was diagnosed with cancer in August 1929. The younger Lewis returned home to attend the bedside of his ailing father. In a letter to Owen Barfield from *The Collected Letters* dated September 9, 1929, he expressed his deep discontent of nursing a man who, to him, was more a stranger than a beloved father:

> As for my present situation, it frightens me for what it implies. I argue thus: 1. I am attending at the almost painless sickbed of one for whom I have little affection and whose society has for many years given me much discomfort and no pleasure . . . . My father and I are physical counterparts: and during these days more than ever I notice his resemblance to me. (*Letters* 1:819)

Shortly after composing this letter, Jack left to return to Oxford with a doctor's assurance that Albert's condition would take "years" of atrophy before resulting in death. With this news, Jack left to prepare for Michaelmas term, only to receive word that Albert's illness had worsened. He immediately began his return voyage to Belfast, but Albert passed before his youngest son could return to his bedside. With Warnie away in Shanghai, Jack was left to handle the burial arrangements and settling of various financial affairs associated with his father's estate. It was then, sifting through his father's remains mingled with the remnants of his childhood that Jack began to seriously reflect and reconsider Albert's influence.

There is a distinct change of tone in Jack's correspondence just days after Albert's death. Lewis assumed that his grief was a natural progression in the process of mourning, but found that from this ostensible sadness sprung a genuine affection for the father he thought he knew. On October 17, 1929, he wrote Warnie:

What you say in your letter is [very] much what I am finding myself. I always before condemned as sentimentalists and hypocrites the people whose view of the dead was so different from the view they held of the same people living. Now one finds out that it is a natural process. Of course, on the spot, one's feelings were in some ways different. I think the mere pity for the poor old chap and for the life he had led really surmounted everything else. It was also (in the midst of home surroundings) almost impossible to believe. A dozen times while I was making the funeral arrangements I found myself mentally jotting down some episode or other to tell him: and what simply got me between wind and water was going into Robinson and Cleaver's to get a black tie and suddenly realizing 'You can never put anything down to his account again'. . . . As time goes on the thing that emerges is that, whatever else he was, he was a terrific *personality*. . . . How he filled a room! How hard it was to realize that physically he was not a very big man. Our whole world, the whole Pigiebotian* world, is either direct or indirect testimony to the same effect. Take away from our conversation all that is imitation or parody . . . of his, and how little is left. (*Letters* 1:827) [*Editor's Note: "Pigiebotian" is an in-joke word between the Lewis brothers that refers to a pet name (Piggiebottoms) given to them by a housekeeper in their youth.*]

Warnie expressed similar impressions on the death of his father as recorded in *Brothers and Friends*. After returning from Shanghai, Warnie felt that Little Lea was now dark and empty:

> There was a chill about the rank untended garden, but inside at first, the house . . . it's lifelessness: silent it has of course been for many years during most of the day, but this was something new and horrible. It brought home to me as nothing else could have done, the tremendous personality of the Pudaitabird— the whole place is as blank as a frame from which a picture has been stripped. (47)

Perhaps both brothers were realizing that they had been severe on their father. Although both sons admitted to feeling suffocated by his presence and irritated by his idiosyncrasies, what remained in the vacuum of Albert's absence was not relief, but instead a tremendous grief. Others did not interpret Albert as insufferably arrogant but rather as a vibrant, intelligent, and humorous individual. This is especially illustrated through Albert's epitaph published in *St. Mark's Parish Magazine* for the late solicitor:

> The threshold of Little Lea was a kind of parable. Only the few and privileged ventured near and crossed it. But once over, the difficulty was to get away. For the width and wisdom and bubbling fun, and his rage of reading and his human touch, made it one continuous privilege and delight to be in the company of Mr. A.J. Lewis. . . . And with his passing, few of that first generation now remain. Now he crosses the mysterious threshold of the other world. Loneliness ends. Tangles are unraveled. There is fullness of joy in that presence "who to know is to love." (*The Lewis Papers* 2: 63)

Some suggest that Albert's death was the impetus for both Jack and Warnie's religious conversions. George Sayer writes that Albert's death and Jack's resulting grief and remorse were the catalyst for a transformation that would shortly after produce the "most reluctant convert in all England":

> Albert's death affected Jack profoundly. He could no longer be in rebellion against the political churchgoing that was part of his father's way of life. He felt bitterly ashamed of the way he had deceived and denigrated his father in the past, and he determined to do his best to eradicate the weaknesses in his character that had allowed him to do these things. Most importantly, he had a strong feeling that Albert was somehow still alive and helping him. He spoke about this to me and wrote about it to an American correspondent named Vera Matthews. His strong feeling of Albert's presence created or reinforced in him a belief in personal immortality and also influenced his conduct in times of temptation. These extrasensory experiences helped persuade him to join a Christian church. (*Jack* 133-34)

Certainly Jack felt a pang of guilt when considering his adolescent dismissal of Albert. He had overlooked the aspects of his father that he had genuinely loved and admired. In a letter dated February 3, 1940, Jack wrote to Warnie that he was being kind to older gentlemen in hopes that it would be "accepted as a kind of penance for my many sins against the P'daitabird: the blackest chapter in my life" (*Letters* 2: 340).

Albert's death left an indelible mark on his sons, but he especially shaped their literary development. Albert was a voracious reader. In *Surprised by Joy*, the youngest Lewis claims that he is a "product of long corridors, empty sunlit rooms, upstairs indoor silences, attics explored in solitude. . . . Also of endless books" (9). This was due to Albert's insistence that books not only be present, but positively overflowing in the household. It was this fact that Jack recognized and thus dedicated his first work of literary criticism, *An Allegory of Love: A Study in Medieval Tradition* to his father. Later, Jack's work would be imbued with imagination and reason, two seemingly irreconcilable aspects which he would blend seamlessly and beautifully throughout his literary works. Like his father, Jack was exemplary at rhetorical sparring and philosophical musing, as well as inserting humor where it would be most effective.

Few know that Albert was an excellent writer himself, penning short stories and poems in various notebooks around Little Lea. His expansive knowledge of literature is referenced throughout various political speeches written early in his career. However, Albert was disgusted with political corruption and opted instead to become a court solicitor, fighting for the common man. In fact, one of his short stories depicting an impoverished man's misfortune in court, is subtitled "The law's an ass," a phrase borrowed from Charles Dicken's *Oliver Twist*. Like his son Jack, Albert enjoyed writing poetry. One such example is an untitled piece scribbled in his Common Book of 1889 which mourns the death of Emperor Frederick of Germany:

> A few short months of Kingly power
> A few short months of Royal state.
> Glory and woe for one brief house,
> Adored by men, and mocked by fate.
>
> A life too short for patriot plan,
> A life too short for purpose high.
> Yet not too short to teach to man
> How Kings should live and Christians die.
>
> One hero midst the carnage falls
> When shouts proclaim the field is won,
> And one in anguish patient calls,
> 'Thy will, not mine, Oh! God, be done.'
>
> Battles and sieges thou hast past
> To make and keep thy people free,
> Yet wilt thy fame such strife outlast,
> Suffering shalt thy memorial be.
>
> Where hearts shall ache for peace and rest
> And death more joy that treasure give,
> Thy name shall comfort and be blessed,
> And God be praised that thou didst live.
>
> (*The Lewis Papers*, 2: 147)

Writing was most certainly "in the blood." Jack admits in *Surprised by Joy* that this propensity to write was due to a "physical defect which my brother and I both inherit from our father; we have only one joint in the thumb" (12). Both boys quickly developed into writers.

Boxen, the brothers' childhood stories of anthropomorphic heroes and villains, has a considerable amount of political tangle in it, no doubt gleaned from Albert's lively discussions of Belfast politics. From an early age, the boys were creating narratives from their father's professional and political life. Warnie began writing after his retirement from the army, but first took it upon himself to type up the voluminous *Lewis Papers* in order to preserve the family correspondence. This was a way to secure the family legacy, but also to acquaint himself with the father and mother of which he admittedly knew so little. His interest in 17th century French history could have easily been influenced by Albert's political enthusiasm.

Additionally, both Jack and Warnie captured Albert's anecdotes, affectionately called "wheezes," in a manuscript titled *Pudaita Pie: An Anthology*. This draft was recently transcribed and appears in the next issue of VII. It includes an introduction by Jack (penned between 1922 and 1924) and includes 100 numerated "wheezes" which reveal the comedic side of their father. Several of these anecdotes appear in *Surprised by Joy*. It is important to note that the manuscript was written *before* Albert's death, illustrating an affection that both boys shared for their father despite their many objections to his overwhelming personality.

Another gesture of devotion resides at St. Mark's Dundela Belfast Diocese, where Flora's father was a rector for many years. Shortly after Albert's death, Warnie and Jack eventually erected a memorial window for their parents. Like the preservation of *The Lewis Papers*, these windows were tokens of appreciation, and also perhaps of reconciliation, for Albert and Flora.

The portrait of Albert Lewis, as fashioned through reading his speeches as well as his artistic prose and poetry, truly demonstrates a lively character who lived transparently, whose logic and emotions could persuade effectively, and ultimately whose passion and good intentions were unmistakable. In general, biographers have not been kind to Albert, but a deeper investigation reveals a warm and witty man who left an unrelenting influence on his sons.

Works Cited

Kilby, Clyde S., and Marjorie Lamp Mead. *Brothers and Friends: The Diaries of Major Warren Hamilton Lewis.* New York: Ballantine, 1988.

Lewis, C. S. *Surprised by Joy.* San Diego: Harvest, 1955. Print.

The Collected Letters of C.S. Lewis. Vol. 1. San Francisco: HarperSanFrancisco, 2005. Print.

The Collected Letters of C.S. Lewis. Vol. 2. San Francisco: HarperSanFrancisco, 2005. Print.

Lewis, C. S., and W. H. Lewis. *Letters of C.S. Lewis.* Ed. Walter Hooper. New York: Harcourt Brace Jovanovich, 1993.

Lindop, Grevel. *Charles Williams: The Third Inkling.* Oxford: Oxford UP, 2015. Print.

Sayer, George. *Jack: C.S. Lewis and His Times.* New York: Harper & Row, 1988. Print.

The Lewis Family Papers or Memoirs of the Lewis Family (1850-1930) in 11 volumes edited by Warren Hamilton Lewis. Unpublished [Leeborough Press], 1933-1935. Copyright The Marion Wade Center and the C.S. Lewis Company, Ltd. Used by permission. All rights reserved.

Friends at Home:
C. S. Lewis's Social Relations at The Kilns
by David Beckmann

The Revd. David Beckmann is the Moderator of the C. S. Lewis Society of Chattanooga and a former Director of the C. S. Lewis Study Centre at The Kilns. He is an Anglican priest and has held faculty positions at Covenant College and the University of Tennessee, Chattanooga.

It would take a much longer essay to survey all of Lewis's social relations during the 33 years he lived at The Kilns. Instead, this essay considers the World War II evacuees and Lewis's relationship with them. Before I go into detail on the evacuees, however, here is a snapshot of the people living at The Kilns during the time span that the evacuees came and went.

The day after England declared war on Germany, Warnie was called back to the colours and sent to France. He was eventually evacuated with the troops at Dunkirk and continued to serve in England until the middle of August, 1940, at which time he returned to live at The Kilns. He was officially retired with the rank of Major from the regular service, but he was obliged to serve with the Home Guard in Oxford, which meant that, during the summer, he got to navigate his boat, *The Bosporus*, up and down the rivers looking for downed Germans. Jack and Warnie, of course, had a very close relationship and it continued through these years and beyond.

The house actually belonged to Mrs. Moore, or "Minto" as they called her, whom Lewis treated as his mother. Being born in 1872, she was by the time the war began on 1 Sept. 1939, 67 years old, and in increasingly poor health. She had begun to suffer from ulcerating varicose veins.

Mrs. Moore's daughter, Maureen, also lived there. She had just turned 33 at the start of the war. Almost exactly a year later (27 Aug 1940), she married Leonard Blake, Music Master at Malvern College. So, one year into the war, she left The Kilns. She and Jack were life-long friends.

When the war began, there was a Mrs. Alice Hamilton Moore (no relation to Minto) staying in one of the two bungalows on the property. She was a friend of Mrs. Moore's family in Ireland who was widowed and had hit upon hard times. The Lewis brothers built the bungalow on the property for her so she could stay with them. She died early in November of that year.

Fred Paxford was 41 by that time, and served as the faithful gardener of The Kilns, living in a bungalow on the property. Later in the war he was assigned to work in the Morris car factory in Cowley, south of Oxford. That cut into his time to help around the house, but he still had time to drive Jack back and forth from town. Jack and Fred got along very well, and enjoyed sharing jokes with each other.

Vera Henry, Mrs. Moore's goddaughter, was in and out, helping with the cooking a couple of times a week.[1] She does not seem to have gotten along well with other folks in the house. Jack himself apparently had to work hard at being civil with her.[2]

There were housekeeping maids now and then. When June Flewett, a young evacuee, first arrived, Miss Muriel Morris was present to help with the gardening in Fred's absence.[3] Muriel was in ill health and only there for about a year. There was also, for a time, a maid named Margaret. According to Lewis, Mrs. Moore, Muriel and Margaret did not get along well with each other at all.

And then there were the animals. There were always a couple of dogs and cats around the place. There were at least a couple dozen hens. By 1 June, 1943, Lewis wrote to Arthur Greeves that they were keeping rabbits. He amusingly described how, walking past the hutch one Sunday evening, he saw the rabbits all in their box, on their hind legs, all facing the same direction, looking very much like they were in a church pew and holding an evening prayer service.[4]

Enough about the folks living at The Kilns during the war. What about the evacuees? Contrary to popular opinion, the evacuees were not young children like the Pevensie children in *The Lion, The Witch, and The Wardrobe*. The children in the Narnia books seemed to be based on the Bastables in the E. Nesbit books.[5] The evacuees at The Kilns were, in fact, all teenage girls.

Our sources for stories about Jack's time with the girls are primarily four. We find information on the students at The Kilns for the fall of 1939 from his letters, mostly to Warnie and Sister Penelope.

---

1   C. S. Lewis, *Collected Letters of C. S. Lewis, Vol. 2*. Walter Hooper, ed. 622.
2   Ibid., 366.
3   Ibid., 587.
4   Ibid., 579.
5   14 September 1957 letter to Lucy Matthews: *Collected Letters of C. S. Lewis, Vol. 2*. Walter Hooper, ed., 882.

A letter from Margaret Leyland, one of the second group (winter of 1940) appears in Volume 1 of *The Lamp-Post*, the newsletter of the Southern California C. S. Lewis Society. Patricia Heidelberger, one of the two who were in the third group (fall of 1940), wrote a letter to Clyde Kilby. This letter is published in Stephen Schofield's *In Search of C. S. Lewis*. And then there are the various reminiscences of Lady Freud which appear in Schofield's book, on the web, and which she has shared with me in personal correspondence.

The first of the girls arrived on 2 September, 1939. This was one day after Warnie had been called back to the colours and the day before England officially declared war. Some authors say there were four girls initially, but there were actually three.[6] By November there were four. This first group included a young girl that Lewis described as being like Rose Macaulay, the author. Lewis thought her the best, and based on a 1940 letter by Lewis, I believe her name was Sheila Morrison.[7] Sadly, in a couple of weeks, her mother took her away and a young girl, Annamarie, was added to the number.[8] Annamarie's school said she might be a problem, and it seems as if she were. By around 5 November, she was replaced, and a new one added, so that they had now a group of four, which made a merry show when they marched to church on Sundays in columns of two, with Jack and Maureen bringing up the rear. By the end of the year, all four were gone, so the fall of 1939 was quite busy.

January of 1940 saw three new girls, Margaret, Mary, and Katherine. All three girls were Roman Catholic and were students at The Convent of the Sacred Heart in Hammersmith. Margaret was the

---

6   E.g., McGrath's *Life*, p. 192: "Within hours of Warnie's departure, The Kilns had four new occupants. . .."
7   In a letter dated 10 September, 1939, Lewis says that the nicest of the three children staying with them was like Rose Macaulay. We learn from a letter dated 18 September that the "nicest" child is taken away. And then, in 1940, Lewis says that they were visited by Sheila Morrison, whom he calls "the nicest of our old lot of evacuees." The nicest child must be Sheila.
8   When the Rose Macaulay-like child was taken away, she was replaced by a sixteen-year-old Jewish girl from Austria. Lewis writes that this girl's school said she might be "difficult" (*Collected Letters*, 18 September, 1939; Vol. II, p. 276). We learn that, as of 5 November, a girl named Annamarie is "being replaced," and, in a letter of 11 November, Lewis forthrightly says that the house was "pleasanter" with her gone (letters of 5 and 11 November; *Collected Letters*, Vol. II, pp. 282 & 289). The conclusion seems to be reasonable that the girl who might be trouble was indeed a bit of a problem; and that her name was Annamarie.

oldest at 17 years. They stayed at The Kilns until July.

The third group entered The Kilns in September of 1940. There were only two at that time: Patricia and Marie, nicknamed "Microbe." Though Lewis tells Sister Penelope a few weeks later that the house is full of delightful children, Patricia, in a letter she wrote years afterward to Clyde Kilby, speaks only of the two of them. Patricia writes to Dr. Kilby, "In all, I look back on those years as two of the happiest of my school life."[9] These two years would have been two school years. According to Lady Freud, the girls left after the school term ended in July 1942. While living at The Kilns, they attended school at Our Lady's Convent in Abingdon, a few miles from the house.[10]

In June of 1942, June Flewett (age 14) was interviewed by Mrs. Moore as a possible resident. At the age of 14, when her school class moved back to London, she had to leave Oxford. The plan was for her to return to the Kilns for a little summer holiday the next year, when her final exams were done.

So, in July of 1943, June Flewett arrived at The Kilns. When she saw how much she was needed there to help, she stayed until the end of the war.

There has been some confusion in the secondary literature about Lady Freud's name. Her name was June Flewett. After she graduated from the Royal Academy of Dramatic Arts, she played a lead in a film at Pinewood Studios, and the Publicity Department claimed that June Flewett was not a suitable name for a rising star, so they changed it to Jill Raymond. After her marriage to Clement Freud, she changed to Jill Freud as her professional name. She became Lady Jill Freud in 1987, when her husband was granted a knighthood.

So, in brief, in the fall of 1939 we have three or four girls at a time with some turnover going on. In 1940, there were two other sets, one of three in the winter and one of two in the fall, the latter staying for two years. After that, it seems there were no more except for June Flewett who was there from July of 1943 until January of 1945.

How did Lewis relate to these girls socially? In his letters, he confesses that he knew little of children, that he seldom talked to them, and just wasn't much good with them. But once the girls show up, he found them "delightful," and, though he was terribly busy, he found lots of ways to spend time with them and to help them.

All of these women testify to the loving kindness that Jack showed to them. Both Margaret and Lady Freud speak of how gently Lewis dealt with them when it came to intellectual issues. For example, Margaret said that Lewis never talked down to the girls. Lady Freud agrees and adds that Lewis even built up her confidence in her intellectual ability. He would often help them with their school work. Patricia writes that he coached her in her

---

9   Stephen Schofield, *In Search of C. S. Lewis*. 54.
10 Personal correspondence with Lady Freud.

Latin and helped her learn a little Greek, since she wanted to attend Oxford. While we sometimes read of Lewis treating his tutorial students somewhat harshly at the college, he did no such thing with these evacuees.

Speaking of the college students, Margaret tell us that Lewis would often bring three or four of his male students from Magdalen over to The Kilns on the weekend to play tennis or go swimming in the lake - and the girls were invited to join in as well. Now that's not the kind of picture we probably carry around with us of Lewis and his students, is it?

Indeed, Margaret's letter is one of the most revealing of the accounts that we have, with lots of surprises, which challenge our stereotypes of Lewis. For example, we know that Mrs. Moore ruled the house with a tight and frugal hand. Margaret says that she and the other two girls with her were only allowed a Marie biscuit, an apple, and a glass of milk for supper; hardly sufficient. Their room was upstairs across the hall from Mrs. Moore's room, but it also was just above what we today call Joy's room, which has bay windows with little roofs on them. Lewis would sometimes climb up on top of the bay window and hand the girls food through their own window. He would also often help them sneak out of their room through the window, and climb down off the roof of the bay window, so they could walk around to the kitchen or listen to records in his study. Every once in a while, he would take them to the local pub and buy them fish and chips, which they would eat out of their boxes on the way home, so Mrs. Moore wouldn't know.

Lewis was compassionate and kind to the children, but he also could be a bit mischievous. I'm sure a lot of the fun of this had to do with his opportunity to sneak around and do things without Mrs. Moore knowing about it.

Sometimes Jack would take the kids into town. You know about the famous singing of the chapel choir at the top of Magdalen College tower on May Day. At least once, Lewis got the girls up early in the morning on May Day, and climbed up with them to the top of Magdalen Tower to listen. He also would take Margaret into town with him on occasion, and would introduce her to his friends. It was on one such occasion she met Tolkien.

Jack would also spend time sitting with the girls in the garden at The Kilns or taking them for walks over Shotover hill and tell them stories. Lewis did enjoy being with the girls, but I think we can confidently imagine that he felt it his duty to care for them and to improve them. He did think they needed improving. He notes in one of his letters that at times the children would be appealing to Maureen for things to do because they were bored. He speaks of how poorly developed their imaginations were, and so he set out to try to do something about it. He spent time with them, trying to enlarge their world and their imaginations with his stories, told amidst the beauties of the Creation around them.

What does the evacuee experience suggest about Lewis and his relationship with Roman Catholicism? You'll recall that Margaret and her friends were students from a convent. She says that she thinks Lewis was disappointed that they were Roman Catholics. So he made a deal with them. When he would preach in church, if they would come and listen to him, he would return the favour and go to Mass with them. It seems they did this, once or twice.

June Flewett had her own good times at The Kilns, but her time there was a bit different because she became so involved with the struggles of the household, both because help was scarcer by that time, and also because of her desire to help. Warnie's 2 January, 1945, entry in his diary is quite revealing. He writes of her "slaving" from seven in the morning to nine at night and he was amazed at how gracious she could be. Of course, there were things about living at The Kilns that Warnie had particular problems with, and so he was amazed that June could go about such chores as cheerfully and with such Christian grace as she did. He knew it would be very difficult for him to do the same. He speaks of her working from 7:00 A.M. to 9:00 P.M., but in the summertime, when the sun is up by 4:00, she had to start the day earlier. I asked her if she liked taking care of the chickens—since I myself like chickens—and she told me that she enjoyed the hens, but she had to let them out of the hut by a half-hour past sunrise—which in the summer was very early indeed.

Jack and Warnie became very attached to June, and they remained good friends for the rest of Jack's and Warnie's lives. They both record their regret of June's leaving in 1945. In a letter to her mother (4 Jan. 1945), Lewis writes:

Dear Mrs. Flewett,

Oh what a sad waking up this morning when we realized that June was gone!—but I try to comfort myself by realising that there was a correspondingly happy waking in your house and thinking how long you and she had waited for it and how you deserve it. . . . I have never really met anything like her in unselfishness and patience and kindness and shall feel deeply in her debt as long as I live. . . . We are the ghost and ruin of a house. . . . Ichabod, Ichabod! God bless her.[11]

It is perhaps no surprise that, according to Douglas Gresham, June was the inspiration for the character of Lucy Pevensie.[12]

There would seem to be plenty of evidence to show that, even though the children were officially the charge of Mrs. Moore, Jack's kind and gracious heart lead him to take on the real guardianship of these young ladies who had had to leave their homes and live with strange people. He made them feel welcome. He thoughtfully took the initiative to care for them. He would sacrificially do things with them that a loving father would have done for his own children. And he took these girls under his wing because he was willing to have his character stretched. He could just have easily said, "I'm no good with children" and ignored them. Instead, he was willing to step out, enlarge the sphere of his interest and experience, and do whatever he had to do to see to it that these children knew the love of Christ through him. His caring for and befriending these girls was one of the great moments of Jack's life.

---

11   Lewis, *Letters, Vol. 2*, 636-637. From the Taylor University Collection.
12   Bond, Paul. "Jill Freud, Inspiration for Lucy in 'Narnia,' Reveals C. S. Lewis Memories." *The Hollywood Reporter.* 8/19/2014 Web 17 June, 2016.

WORKS CITED

Bond, Paul. "Jill Freud, Inspiration for Lucy in 'Narnia,' Reveals C.S. Lewis Memories." The Hollywood Reporter. n.d. Web. 17 June, 2016.

McGrath, Alister. *C. S. Lewis: A Life*. Carol Stream, Illinois: Tyndale House Publishers, 2012. Print.

Lewis, C. S. *The Collected Letters of C. S. Lewis*. Ed. Walter Hooper. Vols. 2 & 3. New York, NY: Harper San Francisco: 2004. Print.

Leyland, Margaret M. "Lewis and the Schoolgirls." *The Lamp-Post of The Southern California C. S. Lewis Society* 1.3. (1977): 1. Print.

Schofield, Stephen, ed. *In Search of C. S. Lewis*. South Pittsburg, NJ: Bridge Publishing, 1983. Print.

Separation from the King:
Tinidril and Susan's Temptation in the Desert

by Kat D. Coffin

Kat D. Coffin is an independent scholar. Her main concentration is in English Literature, with a specialized focus on C.S. Lewis and gender theory. In summer 2016, she attended the Inklings Week in Oxford and pursued specialized research at the Bodleian library. Her research centers on Lewis's female characters and how his correspondence with female writers shaped his writings and his worldview.

> *Ransom perceived that the affair of the robes and the mirror had been only superficially concerned with what is commonly called female vanity. The image of her beautiful body had been offered to her only as a means to awake the far more perilous image of her great soul. The external and, as it were, dramatic conception of the self was the enemy's true aim. He was making her mind a theatre in which that phantom self should hold the stage. He had already written the play.*
> — C.S. Lewis, *Perelandra*

In the fourth chapter of Luke and Matthew, Jesus is led by the Holy Spirit into the wilderness. For forty days He is tempted by the devil to turn from God and worship him. The devil tempts Him in a variety of ways, challenging His authority over the earth, quoting Scripture to test his knowledge. The climax occurs when the devil takes him to a high place and offers Jesus dominion over the earth, telling Him that He will be given the world if He forsakes God and worships him.

Jesus refuses. "Away from me, Satan! For it is written: 'Worship the Lord your God, and serve Him only.'" (Matt. 4:10) The devil disappears, and angels attend to Jesus. This story is remembered during the 40 days of Lent, where Christians across the world sacrifice a "vice" in their lives, in remembrance of Jesus fasting in the wilderness, being tempted by the Enemy.

Christian temptation pervades much of C.S. Lewis's works, especially for his female characters. The temptations are often dismissed by critics as evidence of shallow sexism on the part of Lewis—the White Witch being a sexist caricature of a woman in power, Susan's omission from the final Chronicle due to Lewis's alleged fear of female sexuality. My previous work reexamined Susan's redemption in the context of Orual's, suggesting an alternate interpretation. In this study, I would like to consider Christian temptation—specifically the temptation undergone by the much maligned and misunderstood character, Susan Pevensie. I would like to once again consider Susan in relation to another queen who underwent a similar temptation—Tinidril, the Green Lady, from the second book in Lewis's Cosmic Trilogy, *Perelandra*.

Lewis does not spend much time detailing what happened to Susan. This is part of why there is a 'problem of Susan'—a beloved character disappears without warning from the final book. Jill remarks with disgust that all Susan cared about was "nylons and lipstick and invitations" and that she was "a jolly sight too keen on growing up" (*The Last Battle* 741). Polly elaborates on this, wishing that Susan *would* grow up—expressing the idea "acting grown up" and "being grown up," two concepts Lewis distinguishes sharply (*The Last Battle* 741).

There are two popular critical interpretations of what happened to Susan. The first is that Susan became interested in sex, and that Lewis is "punishing her" for her sexuality. The other is that Lewis hated traditional femininity, and Susan's interest in "lipstick and nylons" represented a type of female vanity he despised. Both interpretations lead to the conclusion that Lewis was a misogynist.

But these interpretations are shallow, and disregard the myriad of other complex female characters who appear throughout Lewis's prolific work: Particularly another queen who faced a similar worldly temptation—the Green Lady Tinidril in *Perelandra*.

Perelandra is a retelling of the Eden story—or a "supposal," as Lewis coined the term. Lewis disliked the idea that the Narnian chronicles were Scriptural allegories; he preferred to think of them as "supposals"—suppose God created a different universe with talking animals that fell into sin, suppose God had to sacrifice Himself for their redemption, suppose God created a new world on Venus with its own Adam and Eve, etc. Lewis's main character, Elwin Ransom, travels to Venus to stop their own version of the Fall from happening. His rival Weston, possessed by Satan, attempts to persuade Tinidril to disobey God. Tinidril may sleep on any of the floating islands of Venus, or Perelandra, but she may not sleep on the "fixed land," a continent with a firm foundation.

Tinidril is the beginning of innocence. She is a remnant of Eve, a reminder to the Christian reader of the purity we lost in the Fall. She is also the Queen of Perelandra, separated from her King, wandering the golden waves of Venus until she comes upon Ransom and Weston. It is in her separation that she is vulnerable to temptation.

Interestingly, when Tinidril acquires new knowledge, she calls it "growing older":

> "I was young yesterday,' she said. "When I laughed at you. Now I know that the people in your world do not like to be laughed at."
>
> "You say you were young?"
>
> "Yes."
>
> "Are you not young today also?"
>
> She appeared to be thinking for a few moments, so intently that the flowers dropped, unregarded, from her hand.
>
> "I see it now," she said presently. "It is very strange to say one is young at the moment one is speaking. But tomorrow I shall be older. And then I shall say I was young today. You are quite right. This is great wisdom you are bringing, O Piebald Man."
> (*Perelandra* 52)

Tinidril continually remarks throughout the text that she has "grown older," especially during various conversations between her and Ransom and her and Weston. Growing older is often synonymous with wisdom in popular culture—we revere those with worldly and mature views and sneer at those who seem childish. There is something to this idea: As most people age, they acquire new knowledge and ideally, become wiser. However, for Lewis, it's not growing older that's the problem, it's the *desire* to grow older.

A loose interpretation of Susan's fate simplifies her desire as sex or to be traditionally feminine. But I would posit that Susan's desire isn't quite as simple as sex or traditional femininity—it's actually a desire that Lewis struggled with himself. The desire to be grown-up, to be more mature and worldly than the next person. Susan's struggle mirrors Lewis's struggle.

Lewis talks about this desire as an intellectual and moral problem in his essay, "Three Ways of Writing for Children":

> Critics who treat 'adult' as a term of approval, instead of as a merely descriptive term, cannot be adult themselves. To be concerned about being grown up, to admire the grown up because it is grown up, to blush at the suspicion of being childish; these things are the marks of childhood and adolescence. And in childhood and adolescence they are, in

> moderation, healthy symptoms. Young things ought to want to grow. But to carry on into middle life or even into early manhood this concern about being adult is a mark of really arrested development. When I was ten, I read fairy tales in secret and would have been ashamed if I had been found doing so. Now that I am fifty I read them openly. When I became a man I put away childish things, including the fear of childishness and the desire to be very grown up. (*Of Other Worlds* 27)

Tinidril exhibits the "healthy symptoms" of the desire to be grown up. As Lewis wrote, young things ought to want to grow. But Susan's "healthy symptoms" evolved into something that led her astray. She fell for a temptation to be worldly and mature, to put these material objects in place of her family. Relegating her entire character arc into "she liked sex" simplifies a complex arc into oblivion.

On the other hand, equating sex with maturity and wisdom is something Lewis explores in *Perelandra*. Weston darkly questions the nature of Ransom's relationship with Tinidril, disbelieving that he could spend time with her without seducing her:

> "Allow me to tell you that I consider the seduction of a native girl as an almost equally unfortunate way of introducing civilization to a new planet.
>
> "Seduction?" said Ransom. "Oh, I see. You thought I was making love to her."
>
> "When I find a naked civilized man embracing a naked savage woman in a solitary place, that is the name I give to it."
>
> "I wasn't embracing her," said Ransom dully, for the whole business of defending himself on this score seemed at that moment a mere weariness of the spirit. "And no one wears clothes here. But what does it matter? Get on with the job that brings you to Perelandra."
>
> "You ask me to believe that you have been living here with that woman under these conditions in a state of sexless innocence?" (*Perelandra* 75)

Weston refers to Tinidril as a savage, someone that Ransom could only be taking advantage of. For Weston, the idea of "remaining in a state of sexless innocence" is ludicrous. Ransom was alone with Tinidril on an alien planet, therefore he could only be trying to seduce her. He makes the same leaps of logic critics do when they claim that Susan's interest in "lipsticks and nylons" represent an interest in sex.

Susan is an adult woman, therefore she must desire sex, therefore her arc must only be about Lewis's disapproval of sexual awakening.

But let us move forward to the second interpretation—Lewis's supposed hatred of traditional femininity and his denouncement of Susan's "female vanity."

In the few lines given that detail Susan's absence from the final chronicle, a few throwaway details are given. Jill claims that all Susan is interested in are "nylons and lipsticks and invitations." All of these objects have a distinctly feminine tone, as most men of the 1940's wore neither lipstick or nylons. Polly opines, "I wish she would grow up. She wasted all her school time wanting to be the age she is now, and she'll waste all the rest of her life trying to stay that age. Her whole idea is to race on to the silliest time of one's life as quick as she can and then stop there as long as she can" (*The Last Battle* 741).

Seemingly, this is an example of female vanity, but it goes much deeper than shallow materialism. Susan becomes more concerned with herself than with others. She laughs at her siblings when they try to talk to her about Narnia. She pretends it was all a game. She has walked out of Aslan's will to pursue her own. Susan's fall mirrors humanity's fall—the terrible history of choosing something other than God to make her happy, to paraphrase Lewis.

This danger is readily apparent in *Perelandra*. Weston—or "the Un-man," as he eventually becomes—attempts to try and convince Tinidril that her own self-interest is more important than following God. But at first, Tinidril does not even understand the concept of disobedience:

> "How can I step out of His will into something that cannot be wished? Shall I start trying not to love Him—or the King—or the beasts? It would be like trying to walk on water or swim through islands. Shall I try not to sleep or to drink or to laugh? I thought your words had a meaning. But now it seems they have none. To walk out of His will is to walk into nowhere." (*Perelandra* 100)

There is no enjoyment, there is no true joy without God. Anything else—to "walk out of His will" as Susan does—leads to nowhere. The more focused she is on herself, the less focused she is on God.

There is a poignant scene in *Perelandra* where the Un-man gives Tinidril a mirror, awakening her self-awareness of her own body. At first, Ransom is relieved: "Thank Heaven,' thought Ransom, 'he is only teaching her vanity'; for he had feared something worse" (*Perelandra*

115). But it becomes clear that shallow vanity is not the final result. This is the awakening of her awareness of self, an encouragement to form personal desires apart from God. Up until this point, her desires were God's desires. But the mirror offered an image to her that was outside of God, that created a false independence.

"A man can love himself, and be together with himself. That is what it means to be a man or a woman—to walk alongside oneself as if one were a second person and to delight in one's own beauty. Mirrors were made to teach this art" (*Perelandra* 117). The Un-man gives a seemingly harmless explanation for the mirror—no mention of sin, no mention of selfishness, an innocuous delight in oneself. As innocent as lipstick and nylons.

But Ransom realizes the trap. It isn't a temptation for physical vanity, it is a temptation to believe one is greater than he or she is. It is a deeper desire to be "grown up," a desire to be plunged into hubris. This is why the Un-man regales Tinidril with tales of great queens and women who came to tragic and awful ends, because the noble tragedy of their circumstances is deeply alluring. Our image of ourselves can become an idol and, as another demon of Lewis's points out elsewhere, "All mortals tend to turn into the thing they pretend to be."

We run the risk of falling into this trap with Susan. Recent criticism has brought forward the idea that perhaps Susan Pevensie is actually a feminist hero for rejecting her fantasy world and King—that her separation from the King is a noble act; that it makes a 'high and lonely destiny,' to quote Jadis in *The Magician's Nephew*. A popular blogpost that went viral in a few years ago reimagines Susan as a feminist radical, fighting against oppression, proudly turning her back on Aslan and her former kingdom. This is a tempting interpretation, especially to readers who were hurt by Susan's absence in the final Chronicle. But it's the very trap the Un-man tempted Tinidril with in *Perelandra*—the desire to separate yourself from God, to inflate yourself with self-importance, and believe your life does not need God. That was Jesus' temptation. That was Susan's temptation. And that was Tinidril's temptation, though through Ransom's sacrifice and God's guidance, she did not fall.

In the final chapter, Tinidril explains to Ransom:

> "It was to reject the wave—to draw my hands out of Maleldil's, to say to Him, 'Not thus, but thus'—to put in our own power what times should roll towards us . . . as if you gathered fruits together today for tomorrow's eating instead of taking what came. That would have been cold love and feeble trust. And out of it how could we ever have climbed back into love and trust again?" (*Perelandra* 179)

The "problem of Susan" is complex and at times unanswerable. It may feel unfair and sexist, but I do not believe Lewis intended it this way. Her temptation is only superficially gendered, in fact, her desire to be "very grown-up" mirrors Lewis's own faults and struggles with this desire. While looking through Tinidril's temptation, we understand Susan's temptation and eventual fall better.

Works Cited

The Holy Bible: Containing the Old and New Testaments with the Apocryphal/Deuterocanonical Books: New Revised Standard Version. New York: Oxford UP, 1989. Print.

Lewis, C.S. *The Chronicles of Narnia.* New York: Barnes & Noble, 2009. Print.

Lewis, C.S. *Of Other Worlds: Essays and Stories.* New York: Harcourt Brace Jovanovich, 1975. Print.

Lewis, C.S. *Perelandra.* New York: Macmillan, 1944. Print.

The Influence of Richard Wagner's Ring Cycle on C. S. Lewis.

by John MacInnis

John MacInnis (Ph.D., Musicology, Florida State University) serves as Assistant Professor of Music and Music Dept. Co-Chair at Dordt College, in Sioux Center, IA. His teaching duties at Dordt College include Music History, Music Theory, and World Music. As an organist and pianist, MacInnis enjoys learning new literature and collaborating with other musicians.

Music listening and discussion factored regularly in C. S. Lewis's relationships, and he drew on his love of music to spur his creative endeavors and to prompt his best thinking. In fact, Lewis credited his imaginative renaissance to the moment when he encountered the titles to music dramas by Richard Wagner, "*Siegfried and the Twilight of the Gods.*"[1] Later, Lewis pointed to his sudden affinity for Wagner and what he called "Northernness" as a grace; that is, he thought God was calling him to faith through these old stories and music.

Though not a musician himself, Lewis often wrote about and mentioned music, its effects, its power, and its proper reception, in some of his most influential works. This essay will examine Lewis's essays, letters, and autobiography, outline his engagement with the composer Richard Wagner throughout his life, and summarize his insights about music.

IMAGINATIVE RENAISSANCE

In his 1955 autobiography *Surprised by Joy*, Lewis described his imaginative renaissance as happening suddenly, when he came across the 1911 Christmas issue of *The Bookman*.[2] Lewis recounted that, as

---

1 C. S. Lewis, *The Inspirational Writings of C. S. Lewis: Surprised by Joy, Reflections on the Psalms, The Four Loves, The Business of Heaven* (New York: Inspirational Press, 1994), 41.

2 *Inspirational Writings of C. S. Lewis: Surprised by Joy*, 40. Lewis described his renaissance as an adolescent as the sort of reawakening that happens when a person seems to experience the beauties and joys of the world with new eyes and ears. Lewis also called this a renaissance because he viewed the intervening years of boyhood, between childhood and adolescence, as a sort of desert. He wrote, "My childhood is at unity with the rest of my life; my boyhood not so."

he read the words "*Siegfried and the Twilight of the Gods*" accompanied by a picture by Arthur Rackham:

> Pure 'Northernness' engulfed me, a vision of huge, clear spaces hanging above the Atlantic in the endless twilight of Northern summer, remoteness, severity. . .and almost at the same moment I knew that I had met this before, long, long ago. . . .[3]

Wagner's *The Ring of the Nibelung* is a cycle of four mammoth music dramas based on Nordic myths that lasts around fifteen hours, in total, and spans three generations of characters; in order, *The Rhinegold, The Valkyrie, Siegfried, The Twilight of the Gods*.[4] Both the librettos and music were written by Wagner himself, and he even built a special theatre to perform his music dramas, at Bayreuth. *The Ring* is a well-loved classic of Western music history, and the plot centers on a golden ring which grants power to rule the world, but requires that its owner forsake all love.[5]

Almost immediately after his personal renaissance, Lewis wrote over 800 lines of an epic tragedy called *Loki Bound* that he considered Norse in subject and Greek in form.[6] The libretto of Wagner's *Ring* cycle was an obvious inspiration for *Loki Bound*, though Lewis had not yet experienced the *Ring* set to music.[7] *Loki Bound* became a collaborative project with Arthur Greeves, Lewis's childhood friend

---

[3] *Inspirational Writings of C. S. Lewis: Surprised by Joy*, 41. Also, in this moment, Lewis remembered Joy: "And with this plunge back into my own past there arose at once, almost like heartbreak, the memory of Joy itself, the knowledge that I had once had what I had now lacked for years, that I was returning at last from exile and desert lands to my own country; and the distance of the Twilight of the Gods and the distance of my own past Joy, both unattainable, flowed together into a single, unendurable sense of desire and loss . . ." Given Lewis's affinity for Neoplatonic thought, his description, here, sounds reminiscent of the Neoplatonic doctrine of recollection. That is, his recollection is not simply of the joys of his childhood; he seems to recall and long for something further back than that.

[4] In German, the titles are *Das Rheingold, Die Walküre, Siegfried*, and *Götterdämmerung*.

[5] The significance of Wagner's music and musical ideas in Western music history are unquestioned, though receptions of his music vary. For example, the composer Gioachino Rossini famously quipped: "Wagner is a composer who has beautiful moments but awful quarter hours."

[6] C. S. Lewis, *The Collected Letters of C. S. Lewis: Family Letters (1905-1931)*, Vol. 1, ed. Walter Hooper (New York: HarperCollins Publishers, 2004), 20.

[7] *Inspirational Writings of C. S. Lewis: Surprised by Joy*, 42.

and longest correspondent; as a musician, Greeves planned to write the music accompanying Lewis's text.

This collaboration of Lewis and Greeves continued into 1914, and Lewis included a plot summary in a letter to Greeves dated 6 October 1914.[8] Lewis intended the part of Loki to be sung by a tenor, Odin by a baritone, and Thor by a bass ("of course"). With his plot summary, Lewis also included some musical ideas for Greeves, which are instructive to gauge his musical sense at this point, in 1914. By now, Lewis had experienced Wagner's music and learned ways in which that music functioned in Wagner's music dramas.[9] In the following, note the variety of musical elements that Lewis considers, e.g., music for atmosphere, music to express an actor's emotions and character, leitmotifs, etc.:

> Of course you would readily see what musical points could be made. Nevertheless I cannot refrain from giving you a few of my ideas. To begin with, Loki's speech would be somber and eerie,—expressive of the fire-god's intrigueing [sic.] soul, and endless hatred. Then (*Parados*) the first song of the chorus would be bright and tuneful, as a relief to the dramatic duet that precedes it. The next great opportunity for 'atmospheric' music comes (Episode I) where the theme of the 'spirit of madness' is introduced. *You* can well imagine what it ought to be like. Then (Episode II) we would have a bluff, swinging ballad for the huge, hearty giant; and of course the 'madness motive' again, where the horse breaks lose. Then some 'Dawn' music as a prelude to (Episode III) and Odin's speech about their position! What an opening for majestic and mournful themes. But the real gem would be some inexpressibly sad, yearning little theme, where (Exodos) Odin expresses his eternal loneliness.[10]

Later, in his autobiography *Surprised by Joy*, Lewis described his work on *Loki Bound* as a reversal of other Nordic stories; here, Loki

---

8   Lewis, *Collected Letters*, Vol. 1, 75.
9   Cf., *Inspirational Writings of C. S. Lewis: Surprised by Joy*, 42. Lewis reported that he first heard Wagner's "Ride of the Valkyries" (from *The Valkyrie*) in a local shop, and that he then began collecting records of Wagner's music. "[T]he *Ride* came like a thunderbolt. From that moment Wagnerian records (principally from the *Ring*, but also from *Lohengrin* and *Parsifal*) became the chief drain on my pocket money and the presents I invariably asked for. My general appreciation of music was not, at first, much altered. 'Music' was one thing, 'Wagnerian Music' quite another, and there was no common measure between them. . ."
10   Lewis, *Collected Letters*, Vol. 1, 78.

is the hero who opposes Odin, because Odin created the world and forced existence upon creatures without their consent. By Lewis's own admission, in this story, Loki is a projection of himself and voices his own questions about God. Lewis wrote: "I was at this time living, like so many Atheists or Antitheists, in a whirl of contradictions. I maintained that God did not exist. I was also very angry with God for not existing. I was equally angry with Him for creating a world."[11] In this account, one may see that, early in Lewis's life, he used his love for Wagner and "Northernness" to express and explore his own religious questions,.

Personal Correspondence

In his many letters to Arthur Greeves, Lewis often mentioned their mutual love for Wagner's music and critiqued concerts he had seen and recordings he enjoyed. Surveying Lewis's correspondence, therefore, especially notes from Lewis to Greeves, is instructive for understanding the importance of Wagner and music generally in Lewis's life and relationships.[12]

For example, on 8 February 1916, in a letter to Greeves, Lewis discussed a new composer as "one of the promising musicians of the day" and lamented not hearing Verdi's *Rigoletto* performed, because he knew the plot. In this letter, Lewis also speculated that listening to gramophone recordings actually spoils one for hearing live music. That is, listening to recordings improves a person's taste through wide exposure, but conditions one to expect a standard of performance that is not often realistic. And, when we return to one of the "best things" in a recording, for repeated hearings, it may not be as powerful to us when we finally hear the music performed live—the original pleasure may elude us.[13]

---

11 *Inspirational Writings of C. S. Lewis: Surprised by Joy*, 64.
12 It is interesting to note that the friendship of Lewis and Greeves remained centered upon common interests, in this case, music. Lewis wrote of friendship in *The Four Loves*: "Friendship arises out of mere Companionship when two or more of the companions discover that they have in common some insight or interest or even taste which the others do not share and which, till that moment, each believed to be his own unique treasure (or burden). The typical expression of opening Friendship would be something like, "What? You too? I thought I was the only one." (*Inspirational Writings of C. S. Lewis: The Four Loves*, 248).
13 Lewis, *Collected Letters*, Vol. 1, 164.

Lewis owned English translations of Wagner's *Ring* cycle, but he also read Wagner in the original German. In a letter to Greeves from 8 July 1917, Lewis mentioned that all morning he had been reading the text of *Siegfried*, in German, and commended the "lovely wild" poetry, which he found to be better in its original language.[14]

On 17 June 1918, Lewis wrote Greeves to describe a performance of Wagner's *The Valkyrie* that he attended at Drury Lane with Thomas Beecham conducting. Lewis wrote: "The dream of years has been realized, and without disillusionment: I have had thrills and delights of the real old sort, I have felt as I felt five years ago [i.e., at his imaginative renaissance]." Lewis described that he had trouble getting seats and could only see part of the stage. He was also frustrated with the people who sat near him because of their enthusiasm:

> One little man in front of me was so moved that at several interesting points he stood up, until at last I became so exasperated that I caught him by his coat tails and pulled him into his seat. Another, who was following the score, kept on giving vent to quite audible criticism such as 'Louder, Louder!' or 'No, no, no' whenever the conductor's design differed from his own.[15]

Despite these frustrations, Lewis enjoyed the performance and went on to describe what he heard:

> The first act as you remember is in Hunding's hut with the tree growing in it: and towards the end you remember how Siegmund draws the sword and how they throw open the great doors at the back. This showed us a most beautiful scene of distant snow covered peaks and a wild valley. The lighting gave a really unusual impression of spring moon light, and that combined with the glorious love-music of the orchestra (you remember the spring song?) simply swept you away—and then all the time creeping in under this the faint horn blown motive of the Niblungs—oh, ami, it was simply heaven! . . . Wotan was magnificent whenever he came on, and all his music is splendid—there are whole hours of music just as wonderful as the little bits we know: the singing was in English, and so clear and un-strained that with my knowledge of the story, I could follow nearly all the dialogue, and so all the poetic and romantic pleasure came to help the musical. As a spectacle the third act was the best, where Brünhilde is hiding from Wotan. The stage is almost dark, lit only from time to time

---

14 Lewis, *Collected Letters*, Vol. 1, 323.
15 Lewis, *Collected Letters*, Vol. 1, 381-82.

> by flashes of lightening [*sic*], as the angry god draws nearer and nearer and at last enters in a glare of red light, glinting on the huge raven-wings of his helmet and the rings of his mail—one gleaming figure in that sinister gloom—and the music, I cannot describe it. . . .
>
> You felt that [the singers] all loved the Ring and took it seriously not merely as an opportunity for noise. Sieglindë particularly, with a sweet voice and clear enunciation, acted very well, quietly & naturally not in the usual operatic style. And oh! The blessed absence of chorus! So you have my verdict that if the Ring is all like this it quite comes up to our old dreams, and that all Italian opera is merely a pastime compared with the great music-drama of Wagner. In spite of all our efforts we could not get a programme and so I cannot send you one.[16]

In this same letter, Lewis also explains to Greeves a solipsistic philosophy that Lewis later came to repudiate—that an individual is essentially trapped in her own head, without true access to the outside world.[17]

> Of course we all start with the idea that our senses put us in direct contact with reality—you think that your eyes are windows by which your brain 'sees' the world. But science teaches you that your eye, or rather the nerve of your eye, is merely a telegraph wire. . . . [W]e still remain dependant [*sic*] on this long chain of communications, traveling by vibration from atom to atom: and we can never have any proof that the sensation which it produces in our brain conveys any true idea of the external Thing. . . . Hence you see we are driven to the conclusion that we have no knowledge of the external world: that it is concievable [*sic*] that there IS no external world at all, and that if it does exist it must be quite different from our usual ideas of it.[18]

His statements are striking here, especially when they are read after such rich and evocative descriptions of what he saw and heard at the opera. Lewis described an experience that was outside himself, powerful and meaningful, and he was confident that his friend would understand him and sympathize. In fact, this is just the sort of disconnect Lewis said he lived with at this time, a disconnect between

---

16   Lewis, *Collected Letters*, Vol. 1, 381-82.
17   Lewis would probably have referred to this philosophical position as Subjective Idealism.
18   Lewis, *Collected Letters*, Vol. 1, 382-83.

his philosophy and the richness of his imaginative life.[19] In another letter to Greeves, earlier that month, Lewis went so far as to assert that beauty is simply a sensation in the mind: "beauty cannot be in the material thing."[20]

Lewis made a point of attending subsequent Wagner performances; for example, on Monday, 23 June 1924, Lewis again saw Wagner's *The Valkyrie* at His Majesty's Theatre in London, with the British National Opera Company performing. Lewis attended with A. Cecil Harwood, who, in 1933, asked Lewis to be godfather to Harwood's son, Laurence. Lewis was visiting Harwood in London at the time, and they sat together in the upper circle of the theatre. Albert Coates was the conductor.[21] The performance was reviewed in *The Times* as poorly attended, but the orchestra was commended, especially the musical details from the woodwinds and horns and a good balance between voices and instruments in the performing space.[22] The reviewer had some criticism for Robert Parker who played Wotan; apparently, he tended to rant and rave excessively.[23] The only letters preserved from Lewis during this time are those to his father, and he does not mention this concert—just politics and his work establishing himself professionally. This silence about the music may have been because his father was helping to support him financially and might not have liked to hear of his son visiting the opera.

On 1 June 1930, in a note to Greeves, Lewis explained that he was sorting through old records and, since he was listening as he sorted, he played the "Magic Fire Music" from the *Valkyrie*:

> Lying on the sofa and hearing these old favourites I had sensations which you can imagine. And at once (here is the advantage of growing older) I knew that the enemy would take

---

19   *Inspirational Writings of C. S. Lewis: Surprised by Joy*, 95. "Such, then, was the state of my imaginative life; over against it stood the life of my intellect. The two hemispheres of my mind were in the sharpest contrast. On the one side a many-islanded sea of poetry and myth; on the other a glib and shallow 'rationalism.' Nearly all that I loved I believed to be imaginary; nearly all that I believed to be real I thought grim and meaningless."
20   Lewis, *Collected Letters*, Vol. 1, 377.
21   To appreciate the sort of performance Lewis may have heard, recordings are available of Albert Coates conducting Wagner's music, e.g., *Albert Coates (Great Conductors of the 20th Century)*, EMI Classics, 0724357548625 (2003).
22   "The Valkyrie [Review]," *The Times*, 24 June 1924, Issue: 43686.
23   This performance was reviewed positively in *The Sunday Times* (29 June 1924, Issue: 5281), but that reviewer was critical of illogical and inconsistent set design choices and the omission of Wotan's monologue to Brünhilde.

advantage of the vague longings and tendernesses to try & make me believe later on that *he* had the fulfillment which I really wanted: so I baulked him by letting the longings go even deeper and turning my mind to the One, the real object of all desire, which (you know my view) is what we are *really* wanting in all wants."[24]

In referring to the "One" here, in 1930, Lewis expressed his current view, Absolute Idealism.[25]

In a letter to Owen Barfield, on 6 May 1932, Lewis asked Barfield to purchase tickets for them to see Wagner's *Siegfried* at Covent Garden Theatre, on 16 May. In a same day reply to what was obviously a negative response from Barfield, Lewis said that he was sorry that Barfield could not manage *Siegfried* but that Lewis could not pass up the opportunity. He asked Barfield to still secure him a ticket as well as one for himself, should he reconsider. In a letter dated 12 May, Lewis thanked Barfield for getting him a ticket and again asked Barfield to join him, though he probably attended the concert alone.[26] In a letter to his brother Warnie dated 14 June, Lewis wrote that this was his first time seeing *Siegfried*, his first visit to Covent Garden, and that he enjoyed the experience enormously. Lewis praised the acting of the performance, but explained that he found some of the singers to be mediocre.[27]

---

24 Lewis, *Collected Letters*, Vol. 1, 898-99.

25 If Lewis's "One" is understandable, in this quotation, Lewis's reference to an "enemy" is puzzling. In *Surprised by Joy*, Lewis explained how he treated Absolute Idealism as a sort of safe religion, in which there was no fear of the Absolute concerning itself with us (*Surprised by Joy*, 115). It was as an Idealist that Lewis reread Euripides' *Hippolytus* and so entered the final stages before his acceptance of Christianity, which Lewis described as the final moves in a losing game of chess (*Surprised by Joy*, 119). It is striking that, in his account of rereading *Hippolytus*, Lewis used the same language as when he first discovered "Northernness," in the titles of Wagner's music dramas, back in 1911. He described the imaginative renaissance of his adolescence as leaving behind the "desert" of boyhood and as a recollection of and reengagement in joyful longing. Here too, after reading *Hippolytus*, Lewis left a desert: "The dry desert lay behind. I was off once more into the land of longing, my heart at once broken and exalted as it had never been since the old days at Bookham."

26 C. S. Lewis, *The Collected Letters of C. S. Lewis: Books, Broadcasts, and the War*, Vol. 2, ed. Walter Hooper (New York, HaperCollins Publishing, 2004), 79n.72.

27 Interestingly, in his letters to Greeves for the remainder of this year, Lewis did not mention attending *Siegfried*. It may be that he was being

The review for *Siegfried* in the *Sunday Times*, on 22 May 1932, lists Robert Heger as the conductor. Heger was a German musician who conducted in England from 1925-35. The *Sunday Times* reviewer apparently agreed with Lewis's assessment of the singers, some of whom are described as "a little tired this year." And, in corroboration of Lewis's praise for the acting, the reviewer wrote:

> Mr. Tessmer's Mime again struck me as the best I have ever seen: this is no mere whimpering weakling, but a thoroughly dangerous little rat who turns, as Mime should do, our sympathies in the direction of Siegfried: we feel that it is by the merest accident that Alberich forestalled him in the matter of the possession of the Rheingold, and that had Mime obtained it first, it might have gone even worse with the gods and the world.

On 2 May 1933, Lewis attended Wagner's *Das Rheingold* at Covent Garden with Owen Barfield. Lewis described the experience, in a letter to Greeves dated 13 June 1933, and said that he enjoyed it less than *Siegfried* and that they had bad seats. A generally positive review of this performance appeared in *The Times* on 3 May 1933; the reviewer's only criticism was of costuming choices which featured "semi-ecclesiastical *négligé*" in place of the "traditional Viking costume."[28] Robert Heger conducted with several other Germans singing leading roles.

In 1934, Lewis had hoped to attend the entire *Ring* cycle with his brother Warnie, Tolkien, Barfield, and Harwood. In preparation, Lewis, Warnie, and Tolkien met periodically to read the operas in German. Harwood was appointed to arrange tickets, and Lewis reminded him of his duty in a mock-serious note in April 1934:

> Pray, pray, Sir, exert yourself. Reflect that no small part of the satisfaction of five persons depends upon your conduct: that the object of their desires is rational and innocent: and that their desires are fervent and of long standing."[29]

Harwood apparently failed to secure tickets, and Lewis wrote him a long sarcastic note on 7 May:

> As soon as you can, pray let me know through some respectable acquaintance what plans you have formed for the

humble and considerate to his friend, or that he regretted not attending with Greeves.
28 "Covent Garden Opera: Opening of Wagner Series [Review]," *The Times*, 3 May 1933, Issue: 46434.
29 Lewis, *Collected Letters*, Vol. 2, 138.

future. In what quarter of the globe do you intend to sustain that irrevocable exile, hopeless penury, and perpetual disgrace to which you have condemned yourself? Do not give in to the sin of Despair: learn from this example the fatal consequences of error and hope, in some humbler station and some distant land, that you may yet become useful to your species.[30]

In a letter to Greeves on 7 December 1935, Lewis commented on a recent performance of Beethoven's 9th Symphony that he heard and that he had "seldom enjoyed anything more."[31] Lewis added that Wagner's *Siegfried Idyll* (a symphonic poem titled for Wagner's own son Siegfried) was included on the program, but that he found it dull.[32] Despite the disappointment of the *Siegfried Idyll*, Lewis went on to state that the only composer, subsequent to Wagner, to affect him as much as Wagner was the Finnish composer Jean Sibelius, a fact that Lewis attributed to his love for Northern things.

Greeves must have pressed Lewis on this point, and, in a note dated 29 December 1935, Lewis explained what he meant. He referenced a previous conversation in which Lewis and Greeves had agreed that Beethoven should be considered Olympian and Wagner Titanic, Beethoven as spiritual and Wagner natural.[33] To Lewis's thinking, Sibelius's music is natural and evocative of Northern landscapes, like Wagner, and not noble, like Beethoven.

Lewis's metaphors, here, are striking in that they reverse the fact that Wagner came after Beethoven—and considered himself to be Beethoven's heir. In Greek mythology, the Titans precede their children, the Olympians, who eventually overthrow them. It may be that Lewis considered Beethoven and Wagner as expressing two independent and contradictory principles, regardless of chronology, and that he identified with the natural over the spiritual. It may also be that Lewis's comments speak to the narrative he presents for his conversion process in *Surprised by Joy*, in which his love for the natural led to love for the spiritual, and his theism led to Christianity. Considered this way, Lewis's comments about Wagner and Beethoven exemplify his account that love for Wagner was a push towards something higher and better, in the first place.[34]

---

30 Lewis, *Collected Letters*, Vol. 2, 139.
31 Lewis, *Collected Letters*, Vol. 2, 171.
32 Lewis, *Collected Letters*, Vol. 2, 171.
33 Lewis, *Collected Letters*, Vol. 2, 175.
34 Lewis, *Collected Letters*, Vol. 2, 175.

To the question of whether Wagner exerted any influence on Lewis's fictional writings, consider a letter dated 29 October 1944 and addressed to Charles Brady, a professor of English at Canisius College. Brady contacted Lewis regarding two articles he had written concerning Lewis's writings. In reply, Lewis emphasized his love for Wagner and noted that Wagner's influence on his creative work can be observed in the "operatic" build and climax in *Perelandra*.[35]

Other mentions of music in Lewis's correspondence are brief and occasional, with the exception of a letter to Mrs. R. E. Halvorson, in March 1956, in which Lewis briefly discussed church music and confirmed his emphatic dislike for hymn singing and organ playing.[36] Lewis's subsequent comments about the direct emotional impact of music and the learned ability to perceive musical structures is instructive, especially given Lewis's previous comments about Wagner's naturalness versus Beethoven's nobility. Lewis confesses his reliance upon direct, emotional content when enjoying music:

> One must first distinguish the effect which music has on people like me who are musically illiterate and get only the emotional effect, and that which it has on real musical scholars who perceive the structure and get an intellectual satisfaction as well.

Wagner's music is emotionally rich, so it is no wonder that Wagner in particular worked powerfully upon Lewis. Whether one is inclined to receive music emotionally, as Lewis did, or equipped to receive it intellectually, Lewis stressed that "each can be a preparation for or even a medium for meeting God but can also be a distraction and impediment. In that respect, music is not different from a good many other things, human relations, landscapes, poetry, philosophy."

Lewis's notion that human experiences and human creativity are capable of orienting an individual toward God, and, in fact, may constitute a medium for meeting God, is actually quite old. For example, Augustine of Hippo taught the same principle, in his treatise *De musica*.[37] For Augustine, and subsequent Medieval writers, God is encountered and known through the created universe.[38] In *De musica*,

---

35 Lewis, *Collected Letters*, Vol. 2, 630.
36 C. S. Lewis, *The Collected Letters of C. S. Lewis*, Vol. 3, ed. Walter Hooper (New York: HarperCollins, 2007), 731.
37 Cf., John MacInnis, "Augustine's *De Musica* in the 21st Century Music Classroom," *Religions* 6 (March 2015): 211-220.
38 To justify this principle, Augustine pointed to Romans 1:20: "For his invisible attributes, namely, his eternal power and divine nature, have been

Augustine extended this principle to the products of human culture, even music; that is, everything presents an opportunity to know God, if you let it. In contrast, any created thing may become an idol, if it becomes an end in itself. Lewis's concluding comments to Halvorson place him squarely in this philosophical tradition and present a reliable test for judging music:

> I think every *natural* thing which is not in itself sinful can become the servant of the spiritual life, but none is automatically so. When it is not, it becomes either just trivial (as music is to millions of people) or a dangerous idol. The emotional effect of music may be not only a distraction (to some people at some times) but a delusion: i.e. feeling certain emotions in church they mistake them for religious emotions when they may be wholly natural. . . . So that the test of music or religion or even visions if one has them is always the same—do they make one more obedient, more God-centered, and neighbour-centered and less *self-centered*? 'Though I speak with the tongues of Bach and Palestrina and have not charity etc.'![39]

"The Funeral of a Great Myth"

In a letter to Christopher Dawson dated 27 September 1948, Lewis developed a train of thought that he had begun earlier, in an essay for *The Socratic Digest*, in 1945, by taking on what he called the "Great Myth" of "Developmentalism" or "The Evolutionary Myth."[40] For Lewis, "Developmentalism" presented a formula for all existence, and he distinguished "Developmentalism" from the biological theory of evolution, which is used to describe changes observed in organic life (i.e., evolution describes change, Developmentalism describes refinement). Lewis's thinking on this topic is fleshed out in his essay "The Funeral of a Great Myth," included in his essay collection *Christian Reflections*.[41] In this essay, Lewis pointed to excellent artistic examples of "Developmentalism" in Keats's *Hyperion* and Wagner's *Ring* cycle and argued that, contrary to what one might assume about

---

clearly perceived, ever since the creation of the world, in the things that have been made."
39   Lewis, *Collected Letters*, Vol. 3, 731.
40   Lewis, *Collected Letters*, Vol. 3, 1584. The earlier essay from *The Socratic Digest* is titled "Is Theology Poetry" (cf., *Christian Reflections*, xiii).
41   C. S. Lewis, *Christian Reflections*, ed., Walter Hooper (Grand Rapids, MI: Eerdmans Publishing, 1967), 82ff.

"Developmentalism" flowing naturally after the writings of Charles Darwin, "Developmentalism" actually predates Darwin's *Origin of the Species*, published in 1859.[42] That is, the science bolstered a theory that actually predated it. Lewis wrote,

> And on the continent we have the *Nibelung's Ring*. Coming, as I do, to bury but also to praise the receding age, I will by no means join in the modern depreciation of Wagner. He may, for all I know, have been a bad man. He may (though I shall never believe it) have been a bad musician. But as a mythopoeic poet he is incomparable. The tragedy of the Evolutionary Myth has never been more nobly expressed than in his Wotan: its heady raptures never more irresistibly than in *Siegfried*. That [Wagner] himself knew quite well what he was writing about can be seen from his letter to August Rockel in 1854. 'The progress of the whole drama shows the necessity of recognizing and submitting to the change, the diversity, the multiplicity, the eternal novelty, of the Real. Wotan rises to the tragic height of willing his own downfall. This is all we have to learn from the history of Man—to will the necessary and ourselves to bring it to pass.'"[43]

Lewis makes consistent reference to the Wagner's *Ring* cycle, in this essay, and one may observe that, for Lewis, the *Ring* story was not just a fantastical tale about dwarfs, giants, and a magical ring. It was not only a moralistic tale about the importance of love. It was not even simply about the lust for power and how such desire can destroy us. Lewis perceived in Wagner's *Ring* a powerful expression of the dominant story told by modernity, one of inexorable progress and development until our eventual undoing, the heat death of the universe—the twilight of the gods:

> All this time Nature, the old enemy who only seemed to be defeated, has been gnawing away, silently, unceasingly, out of the reach of human power. The Sun will cool—all suns will cool—the whole universe will run down. Life (every form of life) will be banished without hope of return from every cubic inch of infinite space. All ends in nothingness, 'Universal

---

42 Lewis is referring to Wagner's libretto to the *Ring* cycle which was completed in 1852 and published in 1853, which is when Wagner began composing music for the cycle.
43 Lewis, *Christian Reflections*, 84. Lewis goes on to say, "Already, before science had spoken, the mythical imagination knew the kind of 'Evolution' it wanted. It wanted the Keatian and Wagnerian kind: the gods superseding the Titans, and the young, joyous, careless, amorous Siegfried superseding the care-worn, anxious treaty-entangled Wotan." (85-86)

darkness covers all.' True to the shape of Elizabethan tragedy, the hero has swiftly fallen from the glory to which he slowly climbed: we are dismissed 'in calm of mind, all passion spent.' It is indeed much better than an Elizabethan tragedy, for it has a more complete finality. It brings us to the end not of a story, but of all possible stories: *enden sah ich die welt*. I grew up believing in this Myth and I have felt—I still feel—its almost perfect grandeur."[44]

With that last bit of German (translated, "I saw the world end"), Lewis quoted an unpublished ending to Wagner's *The Twilight of the Gods* (Act III, Scene 3). Wagner actually struggled with how the *Ring* cycle should conclude, and he wrote several possible endings, one of which is known as the "Schopenhauer Ending," because it evinces the influence of Arthur Schopenhauer's pessimistic philosophy upon Wagner, at that time.[45] In this possible conclusion to the *Ring* cycle, Brünhilde seeks an end to suffering through nonexistence, and she sings,

> Enlightened and redeemed from reincarnation, I shall proceed to the most hallowed chosen land beyond both desire and illusion, the end of the earthly journey. Do you know how I attained the blessed goal of all that is eternal? The deepest pain of grieving love opened my eyes: I saw the world end."[46]

Continuing his critique of "Developmentalism," Lewis went on to explain some reasons why the Great Myth has such power in modern culture. For example, it presents a rationale to disregard one's parents and teachers. We did not descend from them; we emerged from them as something higher and finer. Again, drawing upon Wagner in his explanation, Lewis wrote,

> One then gets a kind of cosmic excuse for regarding one's father as a muddling old Mima [i.e., Mime] and his claims upon our gratitude or respect as an insufferable *stamenlied* [i.e., *stammenlied*]. 'Out of the way, old fool: it is we who know to forge Nothung!'"[47]

---

44   Lewis, *Christian Reflections*, 88.
45   Cf., Warren Darcy, "The Metaphysics of Annihilation: Wagner, Schopenhauer, and the Ending of the *Ring*, *Music Theory Spectrum* 16, no. 1 (Spring 1994): 1-40.
46   Quoted in Roger Hollinrake, *Nietzsche, Wagner, and the Philosophy of Pessimism* (New York, Routledge, 2010), 47-48. By quoting such an obscure portion of the Ring—not the ending usually heard in performances, Lewis assumes a great deal about his reader, in this essay.
47   Lewis, *Christian Reflections*, 92.

Here, Lewis is referencing Act 1 of Wagner's *Siegfried*, and the hero Siegfried's rude dismal of the dwarf Mime, who raised him from an infant. In the story, Siegfried decides to reforge the magical sword Nothung himself, since Mime cannot do it. Nothung is the same sword Siegfried uses when he unknowingly fights with Wotan and breaks Wotan's spear. In this essay, Lewis's condemnation of "Developmentalism" was final, but he emphasized, in his conclusion, that, like all good myths, "Developmentalism" may be certainly enjoyed with good will and pleasure—though, not believed.

Surprised By Joy

Turning to Lewis's autobiography *Surprised by Joy*, one may note that Lewis's concept of joy, the key theme of this book, is tied to Wagner and "Northernness," throughout the narrative. After his imaginative renaissance, in 1911, Lewis immersed himself in Norse mythology, and he recounted how he tried to recapture the initial sensation of joyful longing through subsequent mythological studies. He soon discovered, though, that focusing on the feeling and trying to achieve it through self effort was futile.[48] Lewis concluded that the joy he wanted was only possible while oriented towards an object, even if only its memory, and that to achieve joy, he must forget himself. This insight resonates with Lewis's letter to Greeves, in 1930, in which he applied his Idealist philosophy to the act of listening to Wagner's music "by letting the longings go even deeper and turning my mind to the One, the real object of all desire." Lewis went on to speculate that all pleasures might actually point to the experience of Joy that he so prized, and that Joy itself pointed to something more ultimate: "Inexorably Joy proclaimed, 'You want—I myself am your want of—something other, outside, not you nor any state of you.'"[49]

It is a well-known portion of Lewis's biography, that, though he tried to live out Absolute Idealism consistently, he found that he could not.[50] Through that experience, though, he concluded that there must be a personal God. Lewis did not come to this conclusion willingly; he described it as the sort of instant when a mouse finds the cat. And what was his chosen metaphor to express his state in this moment? "The best image of my predicament is the meeting of Mime and Wotan in the first act of *Siegfried*: *hier brauch' ich nicht Spärer, noch*

---

48   *Inspirational Writings of C. S. Lewis: Surprised by Joy*, 92.
49   *Inspirational Writings of C. S. Lewis: Surprised by Joy*, 121.
50   *Inspirational Writings of C. S. Lewis: Surprised by Joy*, 125.

Späher, Einsam will ich . . . (I've no use for spies and snoopers. I would be private. . . .)."[51] Here, Lewis takes on the persona of treacherous old Mime who, in the first act of *Siegfried* unsuccessfully tries to dismiss the god Wotan.[52]

Lewis's constant reference back to Wagner and Northernness in his theological journey is understandable because those stories worked powerfully upon his imagination. Lewis also thought that God was at work in his life through his engagement with Wagner. He wrote: "Sometimes I can almost think that I was sent back to the false gods there to acquire some capacity for worship against the day when the true God should recall me to Himself."[53] Similarly, while recounting his move to a personal Theism, Lewis explained further how this process was not random, but had a purpose: "Long since, through the gods of Asgard, and later through the notion of the Absolute, He [i.e., God] had taught me how a thing can be revered not for what it can do to us but for what it is in itself."[54]

An Experiment in Criticism

Lewis's most extended engagement with music and the arts is found in his book *An Experiment in Criticism*. In the chapter titled "How the Few and the Many Use Pictures and Music," Lewis, considered illustrations that he had loved in his youth, and saw that he failed to distinguish between their merits. For example, he mentioned Rackham's illustrations to Wagner's *Ring*, noting their admirable composition, but that he later saw that the human figures were often like "dummies." Lewis concluded that his error was in the act of substitution; he substituted the art for what it prompted within him instead of considering what was objectively before him.[55] This understanding, expressed near the end of Lewis's life and well after his conversion to Christianity, is actually of a piece with his previous insight, while an Idealist, about Joy pointing to something more ultimate. In both contexts, Lewis explained that real appreciation, real Joy begins when you lay yourself aside, i.e., your "preconceptions,

---

51 *Inspirational Writings of C. S. Lewis: Surprised by Joy*, 125.
52 It is interesting that Lewis again adopts a character from Wagner's *Ring* in opposition to Wotan, as he did when he used Loki in conflict with Wotan in *Loki Bound* to express his growing doubts about Christianity.
53 *Inspirational Writings of C. S. Lewis: Surprised by Joy*, 43.
54 *Inspirational Writings of C. S. Lewis: Surprised by Joy*, 127.
55 C. S. Lewis, *An Experiment in Criticism* (Cambridge: Cambridge University Press, 1961), 14.

interests, and associations," and take in something on its own terms. It is the difference between using and receiving, and the call is to orient oneself outward and engage the "other."[56]

> The real objection to that way of enjoying pictures is that you never get beyond yourself. The picture, so used, can call out of you only what is already there. You do not cross the frontier into that new region which the pictorial art as such has added to the world. *Zum Eckel find' ich immer nur mich.*[57]

In that last bit of German (translated, "With disgust I find only myself"), Lewis is paraphrasing Wotan in *The Valkyrie* (Act II, Scene 2), and, in this scene, Wotan needs to find a free agent to accomplish a task that he cannot; he calls out for something free of himself, something "other." Here is a larger portion of the text that Lewis paraphrases:

> How can I create a free agent whom I have never protected, who by defying me will be most dear to me? How can I make that other, no longer part of me, who of his own accord will do what I alone desire? What a predicament for a god, a grievous disgrace! With disgust I find only myself, every time, in everything I create. The other man for whom I long, that other I can never find: for the free man has to create himself; I can only create subjects to myself.[58]

With this nuanced example, drawn from Wagner's *Ring*, Lewis explained how one should receive music and other arts, i.e., as an opportunity to have one's perceptions changed, to see the world differently, to become a different person, to get over yourself and, through engagement with the other, find God.

Lewis compared this principle, i.e., an open-hearted, outward orientation, to how different people tend to hear music. Some music listeners seek only a tune to hum or tap their foot to; they disregard the musical structure, the performance, the interpretation, etc. Others listen only as a means of seeking status or so that the music may prompt fanciful imaginings within them:

> In general the parallel between the popular uses of music and of pictures is close enough. Both consist of 'using' rather than 'receiving.' Both rush hastily forward to do things with the work of art instead of waiting for it to do something to them.

---

56 Lewis, *An Experiment in Criticism*, 18.
57 Lewis, *An Experiment in Criticism*, 21-22.
58 "Libretti Die Walküre," accessed 1 July 2016, <http://www.rwagner.net>.

As a result, a very great deal that is really visible on the canvas or audible in the performance is ignored; ignored because it cannot be so 'used.' And if the work contains nothing that can be so used—if there are no catchy tunes in the symphony, if the picture is of things that the majority does not care about—it is completely rejected. Neither reaction need be in itself reprehensible; but both leave a man outside the full experience of the arts in question."[59]

Lewis's aesthetic insights are commanding because of their historical precedent, their intuitiveness, and because they seem true to life. It is also striking to observe the powerful interaction between Lewis's aesthetics and his ethics; that is, he took the lessons he learned from art and about art and allowed them to change his life. To this point, recall Lewis's words from *Surprised by Joy*: "Long since, through the gods of Asgard, and later through the notion of the Absolute, He [i.e., God] had taught me how a thing can be revered not for what it can do to us but for what it is in itself."[60]

Conclusion

In his essay "First and Second Things," in *God in the Dock*, Lewis points out that the Nazis, in their glorification of Nordic mythology, had gotten it all wrong. They made Hagen the hero in place of Siegfried:

> When I read in *Time and Tide* on June 6 [1942] that the Germans have selected Hagen in preference to Siegfried as their national hero, I could have laughed out loud for pleasure. For I am a romantic person who has frankly reveled in my Nibelungs, and specially in Wagner's version of the story, ever since one golden summer in adolescence when I first heard the "Ride of the Valkyries" on the gramophone and saw Arthur Rackham's illustrations to *The Ring*. Even now the very smell of those volumes can come over me with the poignancy of remembered calf love. It was, therefore, a bitter moment when the Nazi's took over my treasure and made it part of their ideology. But now all is well. They have proved unable to digest it. They can retain it only by standing the story on its

---

59 Lewis, *An Experiment in Criticism*, 25-26. Though Lewis does not discuss specific musical repertoires, comparing their relative merits, he leaves the question open as to whether there are songs that are simply bad, which to delight in is to delight in badness.
60 *Inspirational Writings of C. S. Lewis: Surprised by Joy*, 127.

head and making one of the minor villains the hero.[61]

For Lewis, the Nazis had seemed to exchanged all their cultural inheritance for pre-Christian mythology—and then, paradoxically, got the mythology all wrong. Lewis went on to explain that this is an example of a larger principle: "every preference of a small good to a great, or a partial good to a total good, involves the loss of the small or partial good for which the sacrifice was made."[62] Even the love of art, when made an end in itself, may actually constitute a regression and a loss of something more important:

> It was only in the 19th century that we became aware of the full dignity of art. We began to 'take it seriously' as the Nazis take mythology seriously. But the result seems to have been a dislocation of the aesthetic life in which little is left for us but high-minded works which fewer and fewer people want to read or hear or see, and popular works of which both those who make them and those who enjoy them are half ashamed. Just like the Nazis, by valuing too highly a real, but subordinate good, we have come near to losing that good itself.[63]

Lewis's searching statements, here, deserve some reflection. It may be that we are still guilty of such an error, when it comes to music and culture; by making them ends in themselves we lose the real good they offer us. Is Wagner and his Ring taught to students perfunctorily or simplistically, as an example of worthy art that deserves exposure? If so, we may squander the real good that Wagner offers us—the commanding and artful expression of a great narrative that explains so much of the world we observe, grand music that prompts our best thinking and most creative endeavors.[64] It is commonly said that the

---

61 C. S. Lewis, "First and Second Things," in *God in the Dock*, ed. Walter Hooper (Grand Rapids, MI: Eerdmans Publishing, 1970), 278. A similar war-time misappropriation of Wagner by the Germans had occurred a generation earlier. Just before the end of the Great War, Lewis wrote to Greeves (13 October 1918) and mentioned that the Germans had named their trench systems after the heroes of the *Ring*. His own view was that "Anything more vulgar than the application of that grand old cycle to the wearisome ugliness of modern war I can't imagine." (Lewis, *Collected Letters*, Vol. 1, 406)

62 Lewis, "First and Second Things," 280.

63 Lewis, "First and Second Things," 280.

64 This principle concerns me as a music history teacher, and I assume it may find application in other disciplines. Do we teach Shakespeare because he deserves to be known, or to share his timeless insights into the human condition? Do we teach scientific knowledge and methods for their practical

arts are losing their place in our society, in our school curricula, in our shared national life, and there are calls to preserve our cultural inheritance. Lewis's lesson to us, though, is simply this: if our inheritance is not a lived experience—celebrating all the Joy and wonders offered to us in this world—we are no richer.

---

value or because of humanity's call and responsibility to act with justice in our stewardship of this world?

WORKS CITED

Albert Coates (Great Conductors of the 20th Century). EMI Classics. 0724357548625 (2003).

"Covent Garden Opera: Opening of Wagner Series." *The Times*, 3 May 1933. Issue: 46434.

Darcy, Warren. "The Metaphysics of Annihilation: Wagner, Schopenhauer, and the Ending of the *Ring*." *Music Theory Spectrum* 16, no. 1 (Spring 1994): 1-40.

Hollinrake, Roger. *Nietzsche, Wagner, and the Philosophy of Pessimism*. New York, Routledge, 2010.

Lewis, C. S. *An Experiment in Criticism*. Cambridge: Cambridge University Press, 1961.

Lewis, C. S. *Christian Reflections*. Edited by Walter Hooper. Grand Rapids, MI: Eerdmans Publishing, 1967.

Lewis, C. S. "First and Second Things." In *God in the Dock*. Edited by Walter Hooper. Grand Rapids, MI: Eerdmans Publishing, 1970.

Lewis, C. S. *The Collected Letters of C. S. Lewis*, Vol. 1. Edited by Walter Hooper. New York: HarperCollins Publishers, 2004.

Lewis, C. S. *The Collected Letters of C. S. Lewis*, Vol. 2. Edited by Walter Hooper. New York, HaperCollins Publishing, 2004.

Lewis, C. S. *The Collected Letters of C. S. Lewis*, Vol. 3. Edited by Walter Hooper. New York: HarperCollins, 2007.

Lewis, C. S. *The Inspirational Writings of C. S. Lewis: Surprised by Joy, Reflections on the Psalms, The Four Loves, The Business of Heaven*. New York: Inspirational Press, 1994.

"Libretti *Die Walküre*." Accessed 1 July 2016. <http://www.rwagner.net>.

MacInnis, John. "Augustine's *De Musica* in the 21st Century Music Classroom," *Religions* 6 (March 2015): 211-220.

"The Valkyrie." *The Times*, 24 June 1924. Issue: 43686.

"The Week's Music." *The Sunday Times*, 29 June 1924. Issue: 5281.

Henry More and C.S. Lewis: Cambridge Platonism and its Influence on Lewis's Life and Thought

by Susan Wendling

Susan Wendling, a long-term member of the New York C.S. Lewis Society, has presented several papers on Charles Williams and C.S. Lewis at both the Society and at Taylor University's C.S. Lewis & Friends Colloquium. She has also presented papers on J.R.R. Tolkien at Drexel University in Philadelphia.

While scholars commonly acknowledge that C.S. Lewis is a "Neo-Platonist Christian" (Barkman 5), and readers of the *Chronicles of Narnia* are familiar with the quotation "It's all in Plato" (Lewis "The Last Battle" 170), very few scholars have unpacked just how deep this influence runs. The recently published reappraisal of the Inklings entitled *The Fellowship: The Literary Lives of C. S. Lewis, J.R.R. Tolkien, Owen Barfield and Charles Williams* mentions that Lewis read a biography of the life of Henry More as well as More's own writings. However, the authors fail to mention that Jack Lewis began on January 1, 1924, to "read through the philosophical works of Henry More and to make an abstract of them" (Lewis, *All My Road* 280). Even Walter Hooper, the editor of this diary of Lewis from the year 1922 to 1927, merely notes that at this time Jack was hoping to write on him for a D. Phil. degree and was also applying for his first job. Significantly, at this time in Jack's life, he was moving from Atheism to Idealism but was not yet a committed Christian.

Hooper states that Jack "had chosen Henry More because of his own interest in ethics," adding that in March of 1924, Jack read a paper to the Philosophical Society called "The Promethean Fallacy in Ethics" (*All My Road* 280). However, Adam Barkman, a Canadian scholar who published *C.S. Lewis & Philosophy as a Way of Life* in 2009, takes issue with Hooper, saying that the notes that Lewis made when he was reading through More "do not reveal any interest in ethics; rather, they suggest an interest in More's Platonic metaphysics, to which Lewis was increasingly drawn" (Barkman 41). Barkman strengthens this assessment by his footnote documenting that Lewis was also re-reading Plato's *Phaedrus,* and discussing his *Philebus,* at the time (41). This interest in "Platonic metaphysics," combined with the fact that Jack was a trained philosopher whose first job was as a Philosophy Tutor, suggests that scholars should make a more careful investigation into Platonic and Neoplatonic influences. The Glossary in P.H. Brazier's *C. S. Lewis—An Annotated Bibliography and Resource* (2012), encourages such an investigation:

> Platonism is a type of philosophy that he [Lewis] not only subscribed to but which characterized his work throughout his life.... Many Protestant, Reformed, or Evangelical supporters of Lewis's work today object strongly to his Platonism, not realizing that it is fundamental to Lewis's interpretation of the gospel and is at the heart of his understanding of revelation. As a young don Lewis was profoundly influenced by Henry More (1614-87) who was one of the most prominent of seventeenth-century British philosophers. More's parents were both Calvinists; however, the severity of their faith was eschewed as More moved towards Anglicanism.... However, he devoted himself to the study of philosophy. In his youth he espoused skeptical philosophy, until he became absorbed by the study of Plato and Neo-Platonism. More was a leading member of the Cambridge Platonists emphasizing mystical and philosophical theology. (Brazier 156)

With the additional literary knowledge that More was exposed to Spenser's epic poem *The Faerie Queene* at an early age, and that Lewis himself re-read the first book of *The Faerie Queene* in late January of 1924, writing that "I think I never before saw how much real beauty there is in the religious parts" (*All My Road* 286), the question arises: Why is there so little attention given to the fact that Jack Lewis drank deeply and admiringly at the fountain of Henry More's Cambridge Platonism during his formative years of age 24 to 26, the precise time period when he was finishing his formal education and preparing for his first job as a Philosophy Tutor?

A cursory review of the indices in the Hooper/Green biography as well as those in the biographies by George Sayer, A.N. Wilson, Alan Jacobs and most recently, Alister McGrath, fail to turn up any listing of Henry More! The most recent biography, written in honor of the 50th anniversary of C.S. Lewis's death, seems quite at a loss to explain Jack's utter lack of interest in the "Irish Troubles" in 1924— the most violent in 100 years—failing to note that this is precisely when Jack is absorbed in the life and writings of Henry More, who instructs those who would live their lives ethically and morally in the knowledge of God to avoid political entanglements! Since Jack was "mentored" by More (Barkman 133-4) and admired his holiness up to the end of his own life (*Collected Letters* 2: 613), would this not be a reason for Lewis to avoid politics and concentrate on his spiritual philosophical studies?

By 1924 and 1925, Jack Lewis was a trained philosopher whose first job was as a Philosophy Tutor. Further, at least part of what drew Lewis's attention to both *The Faerie Queene* and the writings of Henry More was their Neoplatonic focus on Truth, Goodness and Beauty—the famous Platonic linked triad of spiritual values. Already Lewis was seeing and admiring the beauty of holiness in Spenser, even though he was at this phase of his life an idealist rather than a fully committed Christian. By the time Jack was working as a Philosophy and Literature Tutor at Magdalen College in Oxford, he was well on his way to being a lifelong Spenserian and Neoplatonist in the mold of his mentor from 1924, Henry More. George Sayer, author of the biography *Jack: The Life of C.S. Lewis*, tells how in 1926 or 1927 Jack wrote a character sketch of the senior fellow at Magdalen, Paul Victor Mendelssohn Benecke.

This sketch shows Benecke's "deep love of animals" and "an unusual insight into holiness." Benecke "lived the life of an ascetic, got up early in the morning, and fasted on Fridays. He wore old and ragged clothes and spent his leisure in charitable work." Sayer goes so far as to write that "except for the fact that Benecke drank nothing alcoholic, "a description of his habits resembles Jack's own ten or twenty years later" (Sayer 188). Indeed, looking ahead to 1958, in a letter to Corbin Scott Carnell, Lewis cites the *Theologia Germanica* as a spiritual influence. In an editorial citation, Walter Hooper identifies this work as an "anonymous fourteenth-century German spiritual treatise counselling radical poverty of spirit and renunciation of zeal as a way of union with God" and specifies that the edition used by Lewis was originally published in 1874 but was in a new edition in 1924 — the precise time when Lewis was reading More deeply and widely and learning of this mystical spiritual treatise from him (*Collected Letters* 3: 978). Robert Crocker, More's recent biographer, quotes More's Cambridge tutor, Robert Gell, as saying that More was particularly inspired [in his teenaged years as a student at Christ's College, Cambridge] by the *Theologia Germanica* with its practical emphasis on extinguishing the human will in order to live only by and through the divine (Crocker 1).

All of the foregoing exempla serve as an introductory foundation for the larger thrust of this essay. Moving from the biographical facts of Lewis's personal and professional life at the beginning of his career, this essay will first describe the writings of Henry More which we know Lewis read. Besides their main ideas, some characteristics of More's personal "habits of mind and life" will be noted. To provide some additional theological background, the "mystical Platonic strand" of Anglicanism will be discussed. Finally, I suggest that these Neoplatonic/Christian mystical ideals, seen as an explanatory template, help account for certain anomalies present in Jack Lewis's life but hitherto not adequately accounted for in the biographies and secondary literature available over the past fifty years.

WRITINGS OF HENRY MORE READ BY C.S. LEWIS

The first letter in which Jack Lewis mentions Henry More is dated March 6th, 1924, and is written to his father. After defending his expenses and pleading for his father to continue to help him financially, he states that he has not been idle but has started to work "experimentally on Dr. Henry More—a 17th Century theologian—with the idea of 'doing' him for a D. Phil." He says that he enjoyed this work and learned a great many curious facts in natural history. He continues: "He was a very holy man, this More: his contemporary biographer tells us that his body 'at the putting off of his clothes, exhaled sweet herbaceous smells, and his urine had the natural savour of violets'" (*Collected Letters* 1:623). As this is the first mention of Henry More in *The Collected Letters*, Walter Hooper, the editor, provides readers with a critical footnote:

> Henry More (1614-87), Cambridge Platonist, was educated at Christ's College, Cambridge, became a Fellow of the College in 1639, and remained there for the rest of his life. Those works of his which Lewis was reading included *An Antidote Against Atheism (1653), An Explanation of the Grand Mystery of Godliness (1660)* and *The Immortality of the Soul (1659).* In them More sought to vindicate theism against the materialism represented by Thomas Hobbes. He did this particularly by emphasizing the instinctive reasonableness of divine truth (1: 623 note 7).

The biography read by Lewis is by Richard Ward, entitled *The Life of the Learned and Pious Dr. Henry More, Late Fellow of Christ's College in Cambridge (1710).*

Another letter, written in 1955 to Vera Gebbert, endeavors to help her with translating some Latin phrases she had asked him about. While unpacking *Amor Dei, lux animae* ("The love of God is the light of the soul"), he tells her: "I did a good deal of work on

Henry More once: a beautiful man of whom it was said 'He was often so drunk with happiness that he had much ado to keep himself from falling down & kissing the very stones on the path.' He is also one of the earliest people to mention kindness to animals as a duty" (*Collected Letters* 3: 613 note 176). Walter Hooper again references More's biographer, Richard Ward: "He was transported . . . with Wonder as well as Pleasure, even in the Contemplation of those things that are here below. And he was so enamoured . . . with the Wisdom of God in the Contrivance of things; that he had been heard to say, A good man could be sometimes ready, in his own private Reflections, to kiss the very Stones of the Street" (*Collected Letters* 3: 613).

Returning to the life of Henry More, we note that in addition to his holy living and his general sacramental appreciation for God's good creation, his General Preface outlines his inner conflicts, his studies of the Greek Fathers and his conversion to Christian Platonism. Written at a time of the English Civil War, More's successive publications are often in direct opposition to the "Atheism," "Enthusiasm" and "Superstition" of his age. According to Robert Crocker, More's intellectual system was "part mystical Platonism and part rational Cartesian physics" (Crocker 3). The young More, as well as certain other British intellectuals and "natural philosophers," rejected the dogmatism of contemporary Calvinist theology, and had sought for peace in a millenarian vision of intellectual and spiritual expansion. Crocker summarizes More's writings as being "hierarchic in structure, the argument moving from mystical theology to rational metaphysics, to examples from nature or experience. This can be seen to some extent in all of More's writings, and derives directly from his Neoplatonism" (4).

According to Richard Popkin's essay on More in *Great Thinkers of the Western World*, More's Neoplatonic construction "developed out of the ideas of Plato, Philo, Plotinus, Proclus and the Renaissance Florentine Platonists," offering a "very Latitudinarian (broad-minded) version of Christianity, often stated in Platonic terms" (203). A key point to realize about More, according to Popkin, is that unlike the medieval Scholastics, More did not oppose "the new science" because "he believed that the basic picture of a mathematically explicable material world was entirely compatible with his dynamic spiritualistic metaphysics and with his Platonic reading of Christianity" (203).

Further, he "tried to make people see that not only was modern science compatible with the Bible but that it was actually, when properly understood, part of the ancient wisdom of the Hebrews as revealed by the cabala" (Popkin 203). This confluence of ideas—including opposition to scholastic hair-splitting, a belief in a "mathematically explicable material world," the centrality of the real substance of Scripture seen from the moral and personal life, as well as a belief in ancient wisdom—depends upon "a truly universal conception of the Logos itself" (Cassirer 19).

In his work dealing with theology specifically, *An Explanation of the Grand Mystery of Godliness*, More attacks at some length the most influential figures amongst the sectarian enthusiasts, the purpose being apologetic. More wished to persuade the "godly" to accept a minimum number of essential doctrines, and in this way to remain loyal to the Anglican Church. However, because he had applied the metaphysical ideas he had worked out in his natural theology, More got into some trouble and was attacked as a "heretic" (Crocker 7).

In spite of these political and religious attacks against the "Latitudinarians" in Cambridge, More's most recent biographer Robert Crocker sums up that Henry More was regarded as something of a saint by a number of his younger acquaintances. He states "there can be little doubt regarding More's life-long commitment to the mystical goal of 'deification' or union with God" (10). This lifelong quest for sanctity and illumination undoubtedly influenced Lewis's life.

Mystical Platonism in Anglican Theology

Having briefly outlined the major ideas of More's Christian Platonism, particularly its insistence that man can rationally know God and grow in godliness through embodying the virtues (or deification), and that the Platonic theory of the universe best fits with the findings of modern science), let us at this point try to reconcile this strand of mystical Platonism with More's beforementioned "loyalty to the Anglican Church." Since his 1660 work *An Explanation of the Grand Mystery of Godliness* discusses the dangers of Atheism, Calvinism, Enthusiasm and Roman Catholicism, the reader may wonder "what else is there?" The mystical Platonic stream of Anglicanism has indeed been present down through the centuries but is more hidden. As Brazier's *C.S. Lewis—An Annotated Bibliography and Resource* noted, Lewis's Christian Platonism is often given short shrift, if indeed it is even noticed at all by Protestants who are more Reformed and/or Evangelical. Since Roman Catholics generally follow the heavily authoritarian hierarchy of a Church historically wed to Aquinas's dogmatizing of Aristotelian epistemology, they, too, fail to acknowledge the underground mystical Platonic stream of a more philosophical theology.

This "third element" in Lewis's Anglican Church is described by that classic author on mysticism, William Inge, as follows:

> My contention is that besides the combative Catholic and Protestant elements in the Churches, there has always been a third element, with very honourable traditions, which came to life again at the Renaissance, but really reaches back to the Greek Fathers, to St. Paul and St. John, and further back still. The characteristics of this type of Christianity are—a spiritual religion based on a firm belief in absolute and eternal values as the most real things in the universe—a confidence that these values are knowable by man—a belief that they can nevertheless be known only by whole-hearted consecration of the intellect, will, and affections to the great quest—an entirely open mind towards the discoveries of science—a reverent and receptive attitude to the beauty, sublimity, and wisdom of the creation, as a revelation of the mind and character of the Creator—a complete indifference to the current valuations of the worldling (33).

Since Lewis mentioned in a letter written to his childhood friend Arthur Greeves in June of 1931 that he was reading Inge's *Personal Religion and the Life of Devotion (1924)* and deemed it to be "one of the best books of the kind I have yet struck" (*Collected Letters* 3: 904), it is fair to assume that he had probably also read Inge's 1926 volume on the Platonic tradition in English religious thought, especially since he had been fascinated by Platonic metaphysics since 1924 and had read widely and deeply in the Cambridge Platonists.

HENRY MORE'S CHRISTIAN PLATONISM AS A TEMPLATE FOR C.S. LEWIS

Highlighting how deeply Lewis studied the life and writings of Henry More, and taking note of the key characteristics of this mystical, rational and "latitudinarian" branch of Christianity, this essay can now conclude by noting the similarities in the personal lives and characters of More and Lewis. Such comparisons will demonstrate the "depth of influence" of the life and philosophy of More on the spiritual development of Lewis.

In the Introduction certain characteristics of Henry More's attention to holy living were noted. First of all, he patiently waited two years to receive his Fellowship at Cambridge, where he then remained for the rest of his life. Jack Lewis waited about that long, taking a third "First" in English Literature and a part-time job as a Philosophy Lecturer before gaining his appointment as a Tutor in English Literature at Magdalen College, Oxford. More was noted for his contentment in his life and did not seek worldly preferment, even turning down a promotion. Lewis, too, was content to do what God wanted him to do and always turned aside from worldly praise of his apologetics, saying that he was "not a trained or professional theologian." Second, More advised "the godly" to seek to become more and more divine by imitating Christ and by putting on charity and humility. This action of choosing to embody the virtues and putting to death vices and "the self" is known doctrinally as "divinization" or "theosis." This doctrine is official dogma in the Eastern Church but is less familiar in the churches of the West. Third, and perhaps a corollary to the idea of dying to self and putting on Christ and His virtues is the fact that such a focus on Christ means less attention paid to what we today might call one's "image." Not only did Lewis defend the senior fellow at Magdalen in 1926 when others would mock his shabby clothing, Lewis himself famously paid little attention to his own clothes or his home environment, giving a "general impression of grand decrepitude," as Alister McGrath puts it (McGrath 165).

While Lewis certainly did not live a life of monkish asceticism, he strove to be holy in his inner life. This leads us to a fourth similarity between More and Lewis: their sacramentalism. Like the ancient Platonic philosophers and like the ancient Fathers of the Church, both More and Lewis saw every form in Nature or Creation as participating in the life of God and therefore sacred. All creatures are given life and therefore require humans to treat them with respect and love. In the letter already quoted, we see that Lewis was impressed by More's love of animals and loved animals himself. Besides seeing sacramental significance in animals and trees, Lewis, like Henry More, loved the sacred symbols in Edmund Spenser's *The Faerie Queene* and was a lifelong Spenserian.

Perhaps the most poignant aspect of Henry More's life, according to the *Encyclopedia of Philosophy* article by John Passmore, is that he "quite failed in what he conceived as his main task—to halt the advance of the mechanical world view" (389). Lewis, too, upheld the ancient Platonic cosmology of the Cosmos being arranged hierarchically with "all the angels and archangels" extending from God to humanity in a living universe. According to Lewis's Preface to the Second Edition of *The Screwtape Letters*, he had held that view for his entire life and had no reason from science or his experience to not believe in angels, fallen angels (demons) and a living cosmos. The only author I have come across to connect Lewis's sacramentalism to his almost lifelong crusade against the modernist, mechanistic world view is, not surprisingly, Kallistos Ware, a titular metropolitan bishop of the Greek Orthodox Ecumenical Patriarchate and former Spalding Lecturer of Eastern Orthodox Studies at the University of Oxford. It is not surprising because the Eastern Church tends to embrace a more mystical philosophy and is less given to the dangerous extremes of the Western church which, according to Henry More, are "Calvinism and Roman Catholicism."

Ware says that Lewis was attracted to the teaching of Henry More, "who—in a manner that recalls Maximus the Confessor—looked on reason, *logos*, as a vital and energizing principle active throughout the universe". In this connection Lewis recalls with a certain nostalgia the period in the distant past when trees and plants, springs and rivers, were all regarded as living beings. Underlying this seemingly outdated mythology, so Lewis believes, there is to be discerned an all-important truth: that nature is not dead matter but living energy, vibrant with the immanence of God. As Ware writes:

> The process whereby man has come to know the universe is from one point of view extremely complicated; from another it is alarmingly simple. We observe a single one-way progression. At the outset the universe appears packed with will, intelligence, life and positive qualities; every tree is a nymph and every planet a god. Man himself is akin to the gods. The advance of knowledge gradually empties this rich and genial universe: first of its gods, then of its colours, smells, sounds and tastes, finally of solidity itself. . . . In his imaginative writing Lewis seeks to reverse this 'one-way progression' and to reaffirm the personal, sacramental, 'elf-patterned' character of the world (46-47).

Conclusion

Although this essay has merely scratched the surface of the possible influences of the life and teachings of Henry More, scholars can certainly delve further into these links in order to more fully grasp the life-long growth of Lewis's Christian character. Perhaps More's mystical yet rational Platonic Christianity, hidden through the centuries in the Anglican Church beloved by Jack Lewis, provides "an explanation of the grand mystery of Lewis's own godliness" which was given to rational apologetics, was evangelistic yet not reformed, and which was deeply sacramentalist and personally devout yet not Roman Catholic. Perhaps, even after realizing the depth of Henry More's influence, we could today transcend More's carefully delineated boundary markers and simply identify C.S. Lewis as "Saint Jack," a humble servant of the Lord.

Works Cited

Barkman, Adam. *C.S. Lewis & Philosophy as a Way of Life.* Zossima Press, 2009. Print.

Brazier, P.H. "Platonism." Glossary. *C.S. Lewis—An Annotated Bibliography and Resource.* Eugene, OR: Wipf and Stock Publishers, 2012. Print.

Cassirer, Ernst. *The Platonic Renaissance in England.* Translated by James P. Pettegrove. Austin: University of Texas Press, 1953. Print.

Crocker, Robert. "Henry More: A Biographical Essay." *Henry More (1614-1687) Tercentenary Studies.* Ed. Sarah Hutton. London: Kluwer Academic Publisher. 1990. Print.

Hooper, Walter. "Note." *All My Road Before Me: The Diary of C.S. Lewis 1922-1927.* Ed. Walter Hooper. New York: Harcourt Brace Jovanovich, 1991. Print.

Inge, William. *The Platonic Tradition in English Religious Thought.* London: Longmans Green & Co. 1926. Print.

Lewis, C.S. *All My Road Before Me: The Diary of C.S. Lewis 1922-1927.* Ed. Walter Hooper. New York: Harcourt Brace Jovanovich, 1991. Print.

Collected Letters of C.S. Lewis Volume I. Ed. Walter Hooper. New York: HarperCollins, 2004. Print.

Collected Letters of C.S. Lewis Volume III. Ed. Walter Hooper. New York: HarperCollins, 2007. Print.

The Last Battle. New York: Collier Books. 1st Paperback edition. Second printing. 1971. Print.

McGrath, Alister. *Eccentric Genius, Reluctant Prophet: C.S. Lewis, a Life.* Carol Stream, Illinois: Tyndale House, 2013. Print.

Passmore, John. "Henry More (1614-1687)." *Encyclopedia of Philosophy Volume 5.* New York: Macmillan, 1967. Print.

Popkin, Richard. "Henry More." *Great Thinkers of the Western World.* New York: Harper Collins Publishers. 1992. Print.

Sayer, George. *Jack: The Life of C. S. Lewis.* Wheaton, Illinois: Crossway, 1988. Print.

Ware, Kallistos. "C.S. Lewis, an 'Anonymous Orthodox'?" *C.S. Lewis and the Church.* Ed. Judith Wolfe and Brendan N. Wolfe. London: T & T Clark International, 2011. Print.

Stories As Friends in C.S. Lewis's Life and Work

by Andrea Marie Catroppa

> Andrea Marie Catroppa is a doctoral student in the History Department at the Maxwell School of Citizenship and Public Affairs at Syracuse University. She has a Masters in Library Science from Syracuse University and a B.A. in History from Geneva College.

C.S. Lewis made stories his friends from a very young age, as evidenced in his writing from grade school through adulthood. He wrote repeatedly about the importance of stories and the significance of friendship. According to Lewis, "Scenes and characters from books provide [literary people] with a sort of iconography by which they interpret or sum up their own experience."[1] This paper draws on C.S. Lewis's writing on stories and friendship and argues that having stories as friends powerfully influenced Lewis's life and can also enrich ours.

Stories enable us to see our own lives from a new perspective. They help us see people, events, objects, and experiences differently. Very often, we can be so used to or distracted by various things that we do not see people, situations, or even objects as they really are. Stories can help us to "rediscover" the truth about these different things.[2] They can sharpen our vision so that we can see things as they truly are. According to Lewis:

> The value of the myth is that it takes all the things we know and restores to them the rich significance which has been hidden by 'the veil of familiarity'…By putting bread, gold, horse, apple, or the very roads into a myth, we do not retreat from reality: we rediscover it. As long as the story lingers in our mind, the real things are more themselves…By dipping them in myth we see them more clearly.[3]

Lewis himself used stories to help his readers see things from a new perspective. Most famously, he did this with *The Chronicles of Narnia* with its Christian undertones. In writing about the Narnia

---

1   C.S. Lewis, *An Experiment in Criticism*. (Cambridge: Cambridge University Press, 2015), 3.
2   C.S. Lewis, "Tolkien's *The Lord of the Rings*," in *C.S. Lewis Essay Collection: Literature, Philosophy and Short Stories*, ed. Lesley Walmsley (Hammersmith: HarperCollins, 2002), 117.
3   C.S. Lewis, "Tolkien's *The Lord of the Rings*," 117.

series he said,

> I thought I saw how stories of this kind could steal past a certain inhibition which had paralysed much of my own religion in childhood. Why did one find it so hard to feel as one was told one ought to feel about God or about the sufferings of Christ? I thought the chief reason was that one was told one ought to. An obligation to feel can freeze feelings. And reverence itself did harm. The whole subject was associated with lowered voices; almost as if it were something medical. But supposing that by casting all these things into an imaginary world, stripping them of their stained-glass and Sunday school associations, one could make them for the first time appear in their real potency? Could one not thus steal past those watchful dragons? I thought one could...The inhibitions which I hoped my stories would overcome in a child's mind may exist in a grown-up's mind too, and may perhaps be overcome by the same means.[4]

Stories enrich our lives. When stories are in our lives, our lives expand. They help us have experiences that we would not have had. They allow us to meet people and go places that we would not have otherwise. C.S. Lewis in writing about stories that contain strong elements of the marvelous in them said, "If good novels are comments on life, good stories of this sort (which are very much rarer) are actual additions to life; they give, like certain rare dreams, sensations we never had before, and enlarge our conception of the range of possible experience."[5]

C.S. Lewis knew that stories also allow us to reclaim a sense of delight. Reading stories awakens in us a sense of wonder and "longing."[6] Sometimes we cannot verbalize what we are longing for, but we are glad that we felt it, because of what a positive experience it was.[7] According to Lewis:

---

4   C.S. Lewis, "Sometimes Fairy Stories May Say Best What's To Be Said," in *C.S. Lewis Essay Collection: Literature, Philosophy and Short Stories*, ed. Lesley Walmsley (Hammersmith: HarperCollins Publishers, 2002), 119-120.
5   C.S. Lewis, "On Science Fiction," in *C.S. Lewis Essay Collection: Literature, Philosophy and Short Stories*, ed. Lesley Walmsley (Hammersmith: HarperCollins Publishers, 2002), 51.
6   C.S. Lewis, "On Three Ways of Writing for Children," in *C.S. Lewis Essay Collection: Literature, Philosophy and Short Stories*, ed. Lesley Walmsley (Hammersmith: HarperCollins Publishers, 2002), 103.
7   Ibid.

> It would be much truer to say that fairy land arouses a longing for [a boy] knows not what. It stirs and troubles him (to his life-long enrichment) with the dim sense of something beyond his reach and, far from dulling or emptying the actual world, gives it a new dimension of depth. He does not despise real woods because he has read of enchanted woods: this reading makes all real woods a little enchanted. This is a special kind of longing. . . . [T]he boy reading the fairy tale desires and is happy in the very fact of desiring. For his mind has not been concentrated on himself.[8]

Through stories we can reclaim this sense of delight and can experience greater delight in our day to day lives. This is because stories help us to see ordinary, commonplace things in a new way. Suddenly, a lamppost may seem magical, a picture may be a portal to another world, and opening a door in a wall may lead to adventures, or reunite us with very old friends:

> The child enjoys his cold meat (otherwise dull to him) by pretending it is buffalo, just killed with his own bow and arrow. And the child is wise. The real meat comes back to him more savoury for having been dipped in a story; you might say that only then is it the real meat. If you are tired of the real landscape, look at it in a mirror.[9]

Some people might say that viewing life through stories this way might make us dissatisfied and not ready to deal with life's challenges. However, this is not the case. As noted earlier, stories can help us to enjoy life more. C.S. Lewis in writing about *The Wind in the Willows* said,

> It might be expected that such a book would unfit us for the harshness of reality and send us back to our daily lives unsettled and discontented. I do not find that it does so. The happiness which it presents to us is in fact full of the simplest and most attainable things—food, sleep, exercise, friendship, the face of nature, even (in a sense) religion. That 'simple but sustaining meal' of 'bacon and broad beans and a macaroni pudding' which Rat gave to his friends has, I doubt not, helped down many a real nursery dinner. And in the same way the whole story, paradoxically enough, strengthens our relish for real life. This excursion into the preposterous sends us back with renewed pleasure to the actual.[10]

Lewis understood that some people might think that children's books should be read only by children. C.S. Lewis addressed the issue of adults reading children's books by saying,

---

8   Ibid.
9   C.S. Lewis, "Tolkien's *The Lord of the Rings*," 117.
10 C.S. Lewis "On Stories," in *Essays Presented to Charles Williams*, ed. C.S. Lewis (Grand Rapids: William B. Eerdmans Publishing Company, 1968), 100.

> It is usual to speak in a playfully apologetic tone about one's adult enjoyment of what are called 'children's books.' I think the convention a silly one. No book is really worth reading at the age of ten which is not equally (and often far more) worth reading at the age of fifty—except, of course, books of information. The only imaginative works we ought to grow out of are those which it would have been better not to have read at all. A mature palate will probably not much care for *crème de menthe*: but it ought still to enjoy bread and butter and honey.[11]

Stories can also help us to better face our own fears and challenges. They can give us examples on how to live and what to avoid. They can encourage us with stories of nobility and honor and help us with our fears. C.S. Lewis dealt with this as follows:

> And I think it possible that by confining your child to blameless stories of child life in which nothing at all alarming ever happens, you would fail to banish the terrors, and would succeed in banishing all that can ennoble them or make them endurable. For in the fairy tales, side by side with the terrible figures, we find the immemorial comforters and protectors, the radiant ones; and the terrible figures are not merely terrible, but sublime. It would be nice if no little boy in bed, hearing, or thinking he hears, a sound, were ever at all frightened. But if he is going to be frightened, I think it better that he should think of giants and dragons than merely of burglars. And I think St. George, or any bright champion in armour is a better comfort than the idea of the police.[12]

Also, stories allow us to form friendships. For some of us, this can be a friendship with a particular character. Certain characters can seem as real as people we know. In getting to know these characters, we develop friendships that can enrich our lives. We know more about life through knowing these characters and we share life with them in a powerful way. These characters are our fellow travelers through life, warming our hearts and delighting our hours.[13] They have the inestimable value of giving us joy just by their presence.

Furthermore, we can develop friendships not only with the characters, but also with the authors of certain stories. One of the things that stories help us to do is to pursue truth with authors who

---

11 Ibid.
12 C.S. Lewis, "On Three Ways of Writing for Children," 104.
13 C.S. Lewis, *The Four Loves*. (Boston: Houghton Mifflin Harcourt, 1988), 270.

are concerned about similar issues. We may never actually meet some authors, but we can come to know them in a very deep way through their stories. We may not agree with them as to what the answer to those issues may be, but we can develop a friendship with them because we think certain things are important.[14] C.S. Lewis wrote on friendship and said,

> ...In this kind of love, as Emerson said, *Do you love me?* means *Do you see the same truth?*—Or at least, "Do you *care about* the same truth?" The man who agrees with us that some question, little regarded by others is of great importance can be our Friend. He need not agree with us about the answer.[15]

When we develop these friendships with authors and characters, this pursuit of truth can become an inner "journey" where we are working together, trying to find answers.[16] It becomes a "collaborative" effort where each one is spurring the other on with new insights and ideas.[17] C.S. Lewis describes this "collaborative" effort in his essay on friendship when he wrote, "The Friends will still be...collaborating, but in some work the world does not, or not yet, take account of; still travelling companions, but on a different kind of journey."[18]

In addition, having these kinds of friendships in our lives can be very supportive. The encouragement from these friendships can be as significant as our real life friendships. This is because stories and the authors of stories touch our hearts in ways that other pieces of writing may not be able to. The friends that we make through stories and their authors feed directly into our lives and bring such joy to us. Having their encouragement truly is a wonderful thing.

C.S. Lewis started early having books as friends. Part of this was due to the times and location in which he lived. Lewis himself was born at the end of the nineteenth century where medicine was not what it is now. Also, Lewis lived in Belfast, Northern Ireland which "was an unhealthy place to live and children frequently died of illnesses that, today, children rarely catch at all, and others that most children shrug off with scarcely a second thought."[19] This led to a

---

14   Ibid., 269.
15   Ibid.
16   Ibid., 270.
17   Ibid.
18   Ibid.
19   Douglas Gresham, introduction to *Boxen: Childhood Chronicles Before Narnia*, by C.S. Lewis and W.H. Lewis (Hammersmith: HarperCollinsPublishers, 2008), 7.

great concern on the part of Lewis's parents for preventing any illness in him or his brother. One of the things that they were worried about was their sons getting wet by being out in the rain and becoming sick.[20] This led to C.S. Lewis and his brother Warnie spending a great deal of time indoors.[21] Douglas Gresham, C.S. Lewis's step-son wrote, "They [Albert and Flora Lewis, C.S. Lewis's parents] would keep [Jack (Lewis's nickname) and Warnie] indoors when the weather was wild and wet, or still and gently wet ("soft" as the Irish call it), so the boys would have to find some means of entertaining themselves."[22] This in part led to the two boys writing stories and making up the imaginary land of Boxen with its animals that wore clothes and acted like humans. The stories about Boxen were in fact not written for a wide audience.[23] Instead, the Lewis brothers wrote them for each other.[24] Douglas Gresham in talking about the *Boxen* stories wrote, "The stories that make up *Boxen* were not really written for children. In fact, they were not really written for any of us; these stories were written by two boys, Clive Staples Lewis and Warren Hamilton Lewis, when they were about 8 and 11 years old, each writing for an audience of one—his own brother."[25]

Gresham goes on to share that Lewis and his brother began to write about Boxen in 1906. However, in 1908 their mother, Flora Lewis, passed away. Gresham writes, "The boys were shattered by her sudden death and sought solace in the only safe place left to them, their own imaginations, and much was added to *Boxen* in the winter of that year."[26]

In his later years, C.S. Lewis himself was a prolific author. However, he would rarely read over his books.[27] Walter Hooper in his "History of *Boxen*" wrote, "Jack seldom re-read any of his published works. There is, however, much to suggest that of all he wrote, published and unpublished, it was the Boxen stories that he and Warnie read most often. It was a door into one of the most pleasant parts of their lives."[28]

---

20   George Sayer, *Jack: A Life of C.S. Lewis* (Wheaton: Crossway, 1994), 39-40.
21   Douglas Gresham, 7.
22   Ibid.
23   Ibid.
24   Ibid.
25   Ibid.
26   Ibid., 8.
27   Walter Hooper, "The History of *Boxen*," in *Boxen:* 239.
28   Ibid.

C.S. Lewis himself entered into the world of Boxen. It became for him this other "reality" that seemed real and alive to him.[29] Walter Hooper wrote about this saying, "Finally, when the grown-up C.S. Lewis re-read the stories [of *Boxen*] in preparation for beginning his *Encyclopedia*, he wrote to his brother saying, 'I suppose it is only accident, but it is hard to resist the convictions that one is dealing with a sort of reality.' Perhaps he was. Perhaps we are too."[30] The characters and stories of *Boxen* were truly friends to Lewis.

This practice of having stories as friends continued throughout C.S. Lewis's life. George MacDonald's book *Phantastes* was a significant story in Lewis's spiritual journey. In his autobiography *Surprised by Joy*, Lewis writes that when he read *Phantastes* his "imagination was, in a certain sense, baptized; the rest of me, not unnaturally, took longer."[31] Also, in his book *The Great Divorce*, Lewis made MacDonald and himself characters and had MacDonald be his friend.[32]

> I [Lewis] tried, trembling to tell this man all that his writings had done for me. I tried to tell how a certain frosty afternoon at Leatherhead Station when I first bought a copy of *Phantastes* (being then about sixteen years old) had been to me what the first sight of Beatrice had been to Dante: *Here begins the New Life*. . . . [H]ow hard I had tried not to see that the true name of the quality which first met me in his books is Holiness.[33]

Lewis also enjoyed reading ancient and medieval story poems like *The Aeneid*[34] and *The Faerie Queene*.[35] When C.S. Lewis was staying at the Acland Nursing Home at the end of his life, he told Walter Hooper to bring him among other things, *The Aeneid*.[36] Hooper wrote that *The Aeneid* was Lewis's favourite of all books.[37] In his writing on *The Faerie Queene*, Lewis spoke of how wonderful it was.[38] He said,

---

29 Ibid.
30 Ibid.
31 C.S. Lewis, *Surprised by Joy*. (Boston: Houghton Mifflin Harcourt, 1955), 159.
32 C.S. Lewis, *The Great Divorce*. (New York: HarperOne, 2002), 337.
33 Ibid.
34 Walter Hooper, foreword to *C.S. Lewis's Lost Aeneid: Arms and the Exile*, ed. A.T. Reyes (New Haven: Yale University Press, 2011), xii.
35 C.S. Lewis, *Spenser's Images of Life*, ed. Alastair Fowler (Cambridge: Cambridge University Press, 2013), 140.
36 Walter Hooper, foreword to *C.S. Lewis's Lost Aeneid*, xi.
37 Ibid., xii.
38 C.S. Lewis, *Spenser's Images of Life*, ed. Alastair Fowler (Cambridge:

"Perhaps this is why *The Faerie Queene* never loses a reader it has once gained. . . . Once you have become an inhabitant of its world, being tired of it is like being tired of London, or of life."[39] Stories like these were part of his work as an academic and a literary critic. He wrote numerous books and essays discussing them.

The stories of J.R.R. Tolkien also became Lewis's friends. Lewis greatly encouraged J.R.R. Tolkien's writing of *The Lord of the Rings*.[40] Tolkien writes that "He [Lewis] was for long my only audience. Only from him did I ever get the idea that my 'stuff' could be more than a private hobby. But for his interest and unceasing eagerness for more I should never have brought [*The Lord of the Rings*] to a conclusion."[41]

Having stories as friends was a significant part of C.S. Lewis's life and work. This can be seen in his early life with his friendship with his brother Warnie in creating Boxen.[42] As he grew older, Lewis's friendship with stories continued in the writing his own stories and in his friendships with the Inklings. One of the many authors that C.S. Lewis liked was Anthony Trollope.[43] Trollope wrote, "Book love, my friend, is your pass to the greatest, the purest, and the most perfect pleasure that God has prepared for His creatures. It lasts when all other pleasures fade. It will support you when all other recreations are gone. It will last until your death. It will make your hours pleasant to you as long as you live."[44] Like Lewis, we too can have stories as friends and they can be as significant in our lives as they were in his.

Cambridge University Press, 2013), 140.
39 Ibid.
40 Diana Pavlac Glyer, *The Company They Keep: C.S. Lewis and J.R.R. Tolkien as Writers in Community*. (Kent: The Kent State University Press, 2007), 48.
41 Ibid.
42 Walter Hooper, "The History of *Boxen*," 239.
43 Sayer, 101.
44 Terry W. Glaspey, *A Passion for Books*. (Eugene: Harvest House Publishers, 1998), 12.

Works Cited

Duriez, Colin. *Tolkien and C.S. Lewis: The Gift of Friendship*. Mahwah: HiddenSpring, 2003.

Glaspey, Terry W. *A Passion for Books*. Eugene: Harvest House Publishers, 1998.

Glyer, Diana Pavlac. *The Company They Keep: C.S. Lewis and J.R.R. Tolkien as Writers in Community*. Kent: The Kent State University Press, 2007.

Gresham, Douglas. Introduction to *Boxen: Childhood Chronicles Before Narnia*, by C.S. Lewis and W.H. Lewis, 7-8. Hammersmith: HarperCollinsPublishers, 2008.

Hooper, Walter. Foreword to *C.S. Lewis's Lost Aeneid: Arms and the Exile*, edited by A.T. Reyes, xi-xv. New Haven: Yale University Press, 2011.

---. "The History of *Boxen*." In *Boxen: Childhood Chronicles Before Narnia*, by C.S. Lewis and W.H. Lewis, 230-240. Hammersmith: HarperCollinsPublishers, 2008.

Lewis, C.S. *An Experiment in Criticism*. Cambridge: Cambridge University Press, 2015.

---. *The Four Loves*. Boston: Houghton Mifflin Harcourt, 1988.

---. *The Great Divorce*. New York: HarperOne, 2002.

---. "On Science Fiction." In *C.S. Lewis Essay Collection: Literature, Philosophy and Short Stories*, edited by Lesley Walmsley, 42-52. Hammersmith: HarperCollins Publishers, 2002.

---. "On Stories." In *Essays Presented to Charles Williams*, edited by C.S. Lewis, 90-105. Grand Rapids: William B. Eerdmans Publishing Company, 1968.

---. "On Three Ways of Writing for Children." In *C.S. Lewis Essay Collection: Literature, Philosophy and Short Stories*, edited by Lesley Walmsley, 97-106. Hammersmith: HarperCollins Publishers, 2002.

---. "Sometimes Fairy Stories May Say Best What's To Be Said." In *C.S. Lewis Essay Collection: Literature,*

Philosophy and Short Stories, edited by Lesley Walmsley, 118-120. Hammersmith: HarperCollins Publishers, 2002.

---. *Spenser's Images of Life*. Edited by Alastair Fowler. Cambridge: Cambridge University Press, 2013.

---. *Surprised by Joy*. Boston: Houghton Mifflin Harcourt, 1955.

---. "Tolkien's *The Lord of the Rings*." In *C.S. Lewis Essay Collection: Literature, Philosophy and Short Stories*, edited by Lesley Walmsley, 111-117. Hammersmith: HarperCollins Publishers, 2002.

Sayer, George. *Jack: A Life of C. S. Lewis*. Wheaton: Crossway, 1994.

C. S. Lewis:
Mere Christian, Evangelist, Author, and Friend
by Mark R. Hall

Mark R. Hall, Ph.D., is Professor of English and Dean of the College of Arts and Cultural Studies at Oral Roberts University. Dr. Hall has written numerous articles and conference papers on C. S. Lewis and the Inklings. He is the editor of two books: *C. S. Lewis and the Inklings: Discovering Hidden Truth* (2012) and *C. S. Lewis and the Inklings: Reflections on Faith, Imagination, and Modern Technology* (2015).

When writing one of his most influential works, *Mere Christianity* (1952)—the title used for the compilation of BBC radio talks he presented from 1941-1944—C. S. Lewis explains what he means by "mere."[1] In this brief apologetic text, he is not appealing to a specific denomination or advocating that one Christian group is superior to another. He observes, "Ever since I became a Christian I have thought that the best, perhaps the only, service I could do for my unbelieving neighbours was to explain and defend the belief that has been common to nearly all Christians at all times" (xv).

In fact, Lewis is self-effacing regarding his expertise in theology and asserts that he is focused on basic Christianity—the foundation of the faith: "Finally, I got the impression that far more, and more talented, authors were already engaged in such controversial matters than in the defence of what Baxter calls "mere" Christianity. That part of the line where I thought I could serve best was also the part that seemed to be thinnest. And to it I naturally went" (xv). The popular Christian author invites all—those who wish to enter into the hall and to participate in the fellowship of faith—to become a "mere" Christian: "I hope no reader will suppose that "mere" Christianity is here put forward as an alternative to the creeds of the existing communions. . . . It is more like a hall out of which doors open into several rooms. If I can bring anyone into that hall I shall have done what I attempted. But it is in the rooms, not in the hall, that there are fires and chairs and meals" (*Mere Christianity* 5).

Lewis references the origin of the term "mere Christianity" from Richard Baxter, an English Puritan clergyman (1615-1691) who "did his best to avoid the disputes between Anglicans, Presbyterians, Congregationalists, and other denominations, even convincing local ministers to cooperate in some pastoral matters. 'In necessary things, unity; in doubtful things, liberty; in all things, charity,' he was fond of saying" ("Richard Baxter"). This belief concerning "mere Christianity" seems to be the *modus operandi* of C. S. Lewis. Since this term reflects the essential Lewis, its application to his life seems appropriate and insightful. He is indeed the "mere" Christian, evangelist, author, and friend.

Not only was Lewis "the most dejected and reluctant convert in all England" (*Surprised* 228-229), he was also reluctant to attend church; even so, he soon discovered not only its importance but its necessity. He writes concerning church attendance: "When I first became a Christian, about fourteen years ago, I thought that I could do it on my own, by retiring to my rooms and reading theology, and I wouldn't go to the churches and Gospel Halls." But he observes, "If there is anything in the teaching of the New Testament which is in the nature of a command, it is that you are obliged to take the Sacrament, and you can't do it without going to Church." Lewis later has a realization:

> I disliked very much their hymns, which I considered to be fifth-rate poems set to sixth-rate music. But as I went on I saw the great merit of it. I came up against different people of quite different outlooks and different education, and then gradually my conceit just began peeling off. I realized that the hymns (which were just sixth-rate music) were, nevertheless, being sung with devotion and benefit by an old saint in elastic-side boots in the opposite pew, and then you realize that you aren't fit to clean those boots. It gets you out of your solitary conceit. ("Answers" 61–62)

Lewis came to understand that for the Christian to mature spiritually and for the "very worship of God to be adequate," he must fellowship with other believers (Martindale). He explains: "God can show Himself as He really is only to real men, and that means not simply to men who are individually good, but to men who are united together in a body, loving one another, helping one another, showing Him to one another. For that is what God meant humanity to be like; like players in one band, or organs in one body" (*Mere Christianity* 90). Lewis continues to describe the importance of the human connection: "If there were no help from Christ, there would be no help from other human beings. He works on us in all sorts of ways: not only through what we think our 'religious life.' He works through nature, through our own bodies, through books, sometimes through experiences which seem (at the time) *anti*-Christian." For example, "when a young man who has been going to church in a routine way honestly realises that he does not believe in Christianity and stops going — provided he does it for honesty's sake and not just to annoy his parents — the spirit of Christ is probably nearer to him then than it ever was before. But above all, He works on us through each other" (102). Lewis definitely sees the significance of the Body of Christ, the Church:

> Men are mirrors, or "carriers" of Christ to other men. Sometimes unconscious carriers. This "good infection" can be carried by those who have not got it themselves. People who were not Christians themselves helped me to Christianity. But usually it is those who know Him that bring Him to others. That is why the Church, the whole body of Christians showing Him to one another, is so important. You might say that when two Christians are following Christ together there is not twice as much Christianity as when they are apart, but sixteen times as much. (*Mere Christianity* 102)

Thus, Lewis realizes that the real Christian must fellowship with mere Christians. Lewis also believed in the importance of sharing his faith. His dramatic conversion had "made him a different person" and from that time forward for the rest of his life, "he devoted himself to developing and strengthening his belief, and almost from the year of his conversion, he wanted to become an evangelist for the Christian faith" (Sayer 231). Owen Barfield, Lewis's lawyer and long-time friend, comments that Lewis "felt it was the duty of every Christian to go out into the world and try to save souls" and was even embarrassed by the author's enthusiasm for Christ (qtd. in Mitchell 20, 23). In his essay "Christianity and Culture," Lewis confirms his view on evangelism: "Yet the glory of God, and, as our only means to glorifying Him, the salvation of human souls, is the real business of life" (14). The apologist shows that he is clearly committed to that endeavor in his essay "Christianity and Literature": "But the Christian knows from the outset that the salvation of a single soul is more important than the production or preservation of all the epics and tragedies in the world" (10).

John Wain, a student Lewis tutored, observes, "Lewis used to quote with approval General Booth's remark to Kipling: 'Young man, if I could win one soul for God by—by playing the tambourine with my toes, I'd do it.' Lewis did plenty of playing the tambourine with his toes, to the distress of some of the refined souls with whom he was surrounded at Oxford" (69).

Lewis established himself as a prolific writer. In fact, he "published almost forty books, nearly seventy poems, 125 essays and pamphlets, three dozen book reviews, and two short stories" (Dorsett, Rev.). He also penned thousands of letters (many now published in the three-volume collection edited by Walter Hooper) and preached several sermons that have been transcribed. His life was dominated by his desire to spread the good news of his conversion and his faith to others. Lewis's evangelism has been described as a four-pronged approach: teaching, writing, praying, and discipling (Ryken 55-78). As Christopher Mitchell notes, "One begins to sense Lewis's enormous drive to save souls." It is therefore no surprise that Lewis has been appropriately labeled a "literary evangelist" (Dorsett, "C. S. Lewis" 8). Lewis admits, "Most of my books are evangelistic," and he sees his role as a translator, "My task was therefore simply that of a translator—one turning Christian doctrine, or what he believed to be such, into the vernacular, into language that unscholarly people would attend to and could understand" ("Rejoinder" 181, 183).

Even in his early fiction Lewis was evangelizing. In a letter to Sister Penelope dated July 9, 1939, he expressed his bemusement at the reviewers of the first book in his Space Trilogy, *Out of the Silent Planet*, noting that "out of about 60 reviews, only 2 showed any knowledge that my idea of a fall of the Bent One was anything but a private invention of my own?" He acknowledges, "But if only there were someone with a richer talent and more leisure, I believe this great ignorance might be a help to the evangelisation of England: any amount of theology can now be smuggled into people's minds under cover of romance without their knowing it" (*CL* 2: 262). Lewis was faithful to this vision. This was confirmed toward the end of his life in an interview with Mr. Sherwood E. Wirt, a member of the Billy Graham Evangelistic Association, on May 7, 1963: "Would you say that the aim of Christian writing, including your own writing, is to bring about an encounter of the reader with Jesus Christ?" To which he replied, "That is not my language, yet it is the purpose I have in view. For example, I have just finished a book on prayer, an imaginary correspondence with someone who raises questions about difficulties in prayer" ("Cross-Examination" 262).

As a result of this commitment to evangelism, Lewis felt compelled to answer every letter that he received. His erudite and penetrating insight into matters theological, his clear and crisp writing style, and his creative and engaging fiction appealed to young and old alike, and because of this multi-faceted writing talent, Lewis continued to grow in popularity—a popularity that demanded he respond to his readers. More and more letters arrived at the Lewis household to the point that even with the assistance of Warnie his brother, C. S. Lewis felt overwhelmed. When his listening audience clamored for more radio talks, Lewis declined because he felt like he could not keep up with the correspondence (Sayer 280). In *Surprised by Joy*, Lewis observes that the "essential of the happy life" is "that a man would have almost no mail and never dread the postman's knock" (143). To a youthful fan who had written him in 1956, Lewis commented that his correspondence was increasing: "[N]ow that I have such a lot to write, I've just got to do them all at once, first thing in the morning" (*Letters to Children* 60). He even answered mail during the year of his death. In a March 26, 1963, letter to Hugh, a young American who was the oldest of eight siblings living in Washington D.C. and had been writing Lewis since 1954, Lewis expresses his frustration at the number of letters he continued to receive: "Don't get any more girls to write to me unless they really need any help I might be able to give. I have too many letters already" (*Letters to Children* 38, 106-107).

Dorothy L. Sayers, a popular apologist in her own right, especially known for her plays and her detective stories, comments on Lewis's evangelism in a letter she wrote to him in May 1943. She, like Lewis, received correspondence from those with religious questions. Sayers complains about her experience with an atheist:

> Meanwhile, I am left with the Atheist on my hands. I do not want him. I have no use for him. I have no missionary zeal at all. God is behaving with His usual outrageous lack of scruple. The man keeps on bothering about Miracles; he thinks Hall Caine's *Life of Christ* is the last word in Biblical criticism, and objects violently to the doctrine of Sin, the idea of a Perfect Man without any sex-life, and the ecclesiastical tyranny of the B.B.C. He is in the Home Guard, can't spell, and has a mind like a junk-shop. If he reads any of the books I have recommended, he will write me long and disorderly letters about them. It will go on for years. I cannot bear it. Two of the books are yours—I only hope they will rouse him to fury. Then I shall hand him over to you. You like souls. I don't. God is simply taking advantage of the fact that I can't stand intellectual chaos, and it isn't fair. (413)

It seems clear that Sayers is being somewhat tongue-in-cheek here, for her editor notes that "the correspondence continued for at least another year and she even permitted him [the Atheist] to call on her twice" (413, n.8).

C. S. Lewis definitely felt that God had called him to share his experience with others albeit not with conventional evangelism but through his fiction and his apologetic works. This wide appeal to varied audiences of children and adults, scholars and students, theologians and laymen shows that Lewis is a mere author in the sense he describes it, for his works are "like a hall out of which doors open into several rooms. [...] [I]t is in the rooms, not in the hall, that there are fires and chairs and meals" (*Mere Christianity* 5). He invites the readers into his "several rooms."

C. S. Lewis was also a gregarious person and tended to be accepting of a variety of fine folk he called friends. One of his closest friends, J. R. R. Tolkien, observes, "But Lewis was a very impressionable man, and this was abetted by his great generosity and capacity for friendship" (362). In his autobiography *Surprised By Joy*, Lewis mentions two of his most important friends: Arthur Greeves and Owen Barfield. He called Greeves his "First Friend," which Lewis describes as "the *alter ego*, the man who first reveals to you that you are not alone in the world by turning out (beyond hope) to share all your most secret delights. There is nothing to be overcome in making him your friend; he and you join like raindrops on a window" (199). Lewis met him in April 1914 (*CL* 1: 51-53) and relates the experience:

> I received a message saying that Arthur was in bed, convalescent, and would welcome a visit. I can't remember what led me to accept this invitation, but for some reason I did.
>
> I found Arthur sitting up in bed. On the table beside him lay a copy of *Myths of the Norsemen*.
>
> "Do *you* like that?" said I.
>
> "Do *you* like that?" said he.
>
> Next moment the book was in our hands, our heads were bent close together, we were pointing, quoting, talking—soon almost shouting—discovering in a torrent of questions that we liked not only the same thing, but the same parts of it and in the same way; that both knew the stab of joy and that, for both, the arrow was shot from the North. Many thousands of people have had the experience of finding the first friend, and it is none the less a wonder; as great a wonder . . . as first love, or even a greater. I had been so far from thinking such a friend possible that I had never even longed for one; no more than I longed to be King of England. . . . Nothing, I suspect, is more astonishing in any man's life than the discovery that there do

exist people very, very like himself. (130-131)

This friendship developed to the point that Lewis writes a letter to Arthur Greeves, dated December 29, 1935, wishing Greeves could live near him in Oxford:

> After all—tho' our novels now ignore it—friendship is the greatest of worldly goods. Certainly to me it is the chief happiness of life. If I had to give a piece of advice to a young man about a place to live, I think I shd. say, "sacrifice almost everything to live where you can be near your friends." I know I am v. fortunate in that respect, and you much less so. But even for me, it wd. make a great difference if you (and one or two others) lived in Oxford. (*CL* 2: 174)

He also writes to Arthur Greeves (July 29, 1930) about meeting two new friends:

> Since writing the last sentence I have come into College to entertain two people to dinner & spend the night.... One of them is a man called Dyson who teaches English at Reading. He is only in Oxford for a few weeks and having met him once I liked him so well that I determined to get to know him better. My feeling was apparently reciprocated and I think we sat up so late with the feeling that heaven knew when we might meet again and the new friendship had to be freed past its youth and into maturity in a single evening.... Such things come rarely and are worth a higher price than this.... The other man was Coghill of Exeter. (*CL* 1: 917)

Both Hugo Dyson and Neville Coghill turned out to be central to the Inklings. C. S. Lewis and Owen Barfield were lifelong friends. In *Surprised By Joy*, Lewis describes him as a "Second Friend":

> But the Second Friend is the man who disagrees with you about everything. He is not so much the *alter ego* as the antiself. Of course he shares your interests; otherwise he would not become your friend at all. But he has approached them all at a different angle. He has read all the right books but has got the wrong thing out of every one. It is as if he spoke your language but mispronounced it.... And then you go at it, hammer and tongs, far into the night, night after night, or walking through fine country that neither gives a glance to, each learning the weight of the other's punches, and often more like mutually respectful enemies than friends. Actually (though it never seems so at the time) you modify one another's thought; out of this perpetual dogfight a community of mind and a deep affection emerge. But I think he changed me a good deal more than I him. (199-200)

In fact, Colin Duriez asserts, "It is no exaggeration to say that his friendship with Barfield was one of the most important in his [Lewis's] life; as important at least, in its different way, as that with Arthur, and with a few others whom Lewis met later" (*C. S. Lewis* 88). The relationship was reciprocated by Barfield. After Lewis's death on November 22, 1963, when Barfield visited Wheaton College on October 16, 1964, he reflected on his friendship with the Cambridge don: "Now, whatever else he was, and as you know, he was a great many things, C. S. Lewis was for me, first and foremost, the absolutely unforgettable friend, the friend with whom I was in close touch for over forty years, the friend you might come to regard hardly as another human being, but almost as a part of the furniture of my existence" (3).

J. R. R. Tolkien, who was instrumental in Lewis's conversion, was a friend of Lewis for almost four decades. Colin Duriez notes, "I have been aware of the friendship between J. R. R. Tolkien and C. S. Lewis for a long time, since first reading the latter's autobiography as a student, but in writing this book I have been surprised to discover how very strong and persistent it was, despite frictions and troughs that, perhaps, one should expect to occur over nearly forty years" (*Tolkien* ix). In a letter to Dick Plotz, "Thain" of the Tolkien Society of America, dated September 12, 1965, written almost two years after Lewis's passing, J. R. R. Tolkien describes his gratitude and his debt to the author: "The unpayable debt that I owe to him was not 'influence' as it is ordinarily understood, but sheer encouragement. He was for long my only audience. Only from him did I ever get the idea that my 'stuff' could be more than a private hobby. But for his interest and unceasing eagerness for more I should never have brought *The L. of the R.* to a conclusion" ("Letter 276," p. 362).

For Lewis, the value of friendship cannot be overemphasized, and his commitment to his friends shows that he was someone who could be trusted—that he stood "side by side," "absorbed in some common interest" with them (*Four Loves* 61). Lewis's attitude toward them is reflected in his very famous sermon, "The Weight of Glory": "There are no *ordinary* people. You have never talked to a mere mortal." His friends are all invited into the rooms Lewis describes—to sit beside him and enjoy "fires and chairs and meals."

To Lewis, "mere" means more, not less, and because of that, his legacy remains and continues to grow. He dedicated himself completely to everything he embraced; thus, he was an exemplary Christian. This "mere Christian" was not a "mere mortal," but he was a "mere" author, evangelist, and friend.

Works Cited

Barfield, Owen. *Owen Barfield on C. S. Lewis*. Ed. G. B. Tennyson. San Rafael, CA: Barfield Press, 1989. Print.

Baxter, Richard. *Cain and Abel Malignity. The Practical Works*. Vol. 10. 473-563. Google Books. Web. 30 July 2016.

---. *The Catechising of Families. The Practical Works*. Vol. 19. 1-292. Google Books. Web. 30 July 2016.

---. *A Christian Directory. Or A Body of Practical Divinity and Cases of Conscience. The Practical Works*. Vol. 2. Google Books. Web. 30 July 2016.

---. *The Practical Works of the Rev. Richard Baxter with A Life of the Author and A Critical Examination of His Writings by the Rev. William Orme*. 23 vols. London: James Duncan, 1830. Google Books. Web. 30 July 2016.

---. *A Treatise of Knowledge and Love Compared. The Practical Works*. Vol. 15. iii-295. Google Books. Web. 30 July 2016.

---. "What History is Credible, and What Not." *Church History of the Government Bishops and Their Councils*. London: Thomas Simmons, 1681. Google Books. Web. 30 July 2016.

Rev. of *C. S. Lewis: A Dramatic Life*. By William Griffin. *Knowing and Doing*. C. S. Lewis Institute. Summer 2006. Web. 1 August 2016.

Dorsett, Lyle, ed. "C. S. Lewis: An Introduction." *The Essential C. S. Lewis*. New York: Simon and Schuster, 1988. 3-17. Print.

Duriez, Colin. *C. S. Lewis: A Biography of Friendship*. Oxford: Lion Books, 2013. Print.

---. *Tolkien and C. S. Lewis: The Gift of Friendship*. Mahwah, NJ: HiddenSpring, 2003. Print.

Lewis, C. S. "Answers to Questions on Christianity." *God in the Dock*. 48-62.

---. *Christian Reflections*. Ed. Walter Hooper. Grand Rapids, MI: Eerdmans, 1967. Print.

---. "Christian Reunion." *C. S. Lewis: Essay Collection & Other Short Pieces*. Ed. Leslie Walmsley. London: HarperCollins, 2000. 395-397. Print.

---. "Christianity and Culture." *Christian Reflections*. 12-36.

---. "Christianity and Literature." *Christian Reflections*. 1-11.

---. *The Collected Letters of C. S. Lewis. Vol. 1. Family Letters 1905-1931*. New York: HarperCollins, 2004. Print.

---. *The Collected Letters of C. S. Lewis. Vol. 2. Books, Broadcasts, and the War 1931-1949*. New York: HarperCollins, 2004. Print.

---. *The Collected Letters of C. S. Lewis. Vol. 3. Narnia, Cambridge, and Joy 1950-1963*. New York: HarperCollins, 2007. Print.

---. "Cross-Examination." *God in the Dock*. 258-267.

---. *God in the Dock: Essays on Theology and Ethics*. Ed. Walter Hooper. Grand Rapids: Eerdmans, 1970. Print.

---. *Mere Christianity* 1952. n.p.: Samizdat, 2014. Web. 30 July 2016.

---. *The Four Loves*. New York: Harcourt, 1960. Print.

---. "Letters." *God in the Dock*. 325-340.

---. *Letters to Children*. Ed. Lyle W. Dorsett and Marjorie Lamp Mead. New York: Simon & Schuster, 1995. Print.

---. "On the Reading of Old Books." *God in the Dock*. 200-207.

---. *A Preface to Paradise Lost*. New York: Oxford UP, 1961. Print.

---. "Rejoinder to Dr. Pittenger." *God in the Dock*. 177-183.

---. *The Screwtape Letters with Screwtape Proposes a Toast*. New York: MacMillan, 1961. Print.

---. *Surprised by Joy*. New York: Harcourt, Brace & World, 1955. Print.

Martindale, Wayne. "C. S. Lewis, Reluctant Churchman." *Touchstone*. Web. 30 July 2016.

McGrath, Alister. *C. S. Lewis—A Life: Eccentric Genius, Reluctant Prophet*. Carol Stream, IL: Tyndale House, 2013. Print.

Mitchell, Christopher. "Bearing the Weight of Glory: The Cost of C. S. Lewis's Witness." *C. S. Lewis: Profile of Faith*. Ed. Joel S. Woodruff and Thomas A. Tarrants. Springfield, VA: C. S. Lewis Institute, 2013. 19-33. Web. 31 July 2016.

"Richard Baxter: Moderate in an Age of Extremes." *Christian History*. Christianity Today 2016. Web. 29 July 2016.

Ryken, Philip. "Winsome Evangelist: The Influence of C.S. Lewis," *Lightbearer in the Shadowlands: The Evangelistic Vision of C. S. Lewis*. Ed. Angus J. L. Menuge. Wheaton, IL: Crossway, 1997. 55-78. Print.

Sayer, George. *Jack: A Life of C. S. Lewis*. Wheaton, IL: Crossway Books, 1994. Print.

Sayers, Dorothy. *The Letters of Dorothy L. Sayers*. Vol. 2. *1937-1943: From Novelist to Playwright*. Ed. Barbara Reynolds. New York: St Martin's, 1997. Print.

Tolkien, J. R. R. *The Letters of J. R. R. Tolkien*. Ed. Humphrey Carpenter. Boston: Houghton Mifflin, 1981. Print.

Wain, John. "A Great Clerke." *C. S. Lewis at the Breakfast Table and Other Reminiscences*. Ed. James T. Como. New York: Harcourt Brace, 1992. 68-76. Print.

Battlefield of the Mind: Examining Screwtape's Preferred Method

by William O'Flaherty

> William O'Flaherty hosts EssentialCSLewis.com which features the *All About Jack* podcast that spotlights authors of books related to Lewis (and recorded several podcasts on site at the 2016 Taylor Colloquium). In 2016 his first book *C.S. Lewis Goes to Hell: A Companion and Study Guide to The Screwtape Letters* was published. ScrewtapeCompanion.com is a website to support the book.

In C.S. Lewis's masterful work *The Screwtape Letters*, the reader is given a peek into the perspective of how the devils work at interfering in a person's life. It is Wormwood's first assignment and he is receiving guidance from his uncle Screwtape on how to make life miserable for his patient. While the book is very short and lighthearted, much can be learned about understanding how the enemy of one's soul might work to hinder our own life. What follows is an examination of what Screwtape calls their most effective method in their toolbox of diabolical techniques. This material is adapted from and an expansion of content from my book *C.S. Lewis Goes to Hell: A Companion and Study Guide to The Screwtape Letters*.

Conventional wisdom is that devils interfere in our life by whispering in our ears. That is, they try to put bad thoughts into our minds. However, when you read the fourth letter from Screwtape, he proclaims their preferred method is "keeping things out"[1] of a person's mind. This comment is found when Wormwood is told that humans fail to recall that "bodily position"[2] in prayers actually make a difference. Thus, Screwtape warns that the patient should not think about this, such truth must be kept out of his thoughts.

This is not an isolated confession about what might be considered an overlooked weapon. Twenty-four of the letters, plus the follow-up essay, "Screwtape Proposes a Toast" makes some reference, or at least suggests this preferred method. However, this does not mean they never try to put thoughts in a person's mind, it's just they focus more on preventing a person from thinking about something that would be spiritually helpful.

---

1   Letter 4, second paragraph.
2   Letter 4, second paragraph.

Previously I gave a talk where the first twelve letters were examined. It was recorded and posted on the All About Jack Podcast.[3] The following material picks up where that address ended and examines the next five letters.

Letter 13

In the twelfth letter Wormwood's "patient" had slowly drifted from his faith and was mostly unaware of what was occurring. However, in the thirteenth the patient experienced "a repentance and renewal"[4] and this upset Screwtape. He tells Wormwood to "prevent his [patient from] doing anything" and to "keep it out of his will."[5] The reference to "will" is a call back to an illustration described in the sixth letter that I elaborate on in the Topical Glossary section of my book *C.S. Lewis Goes to Hell*.[6]

Letter 14

In the fourteenth letter the patient's growing faith is a major concern and Wormwood must do as much as possible to control the damage. Near the end of the letter he is advised to "conceal from the patient the true end of Humility."[7] However, it is revealed that God also uses "keeping things out" as well. Wormwood is told that one of God's aims is to "get the man's mind off the subject of his own value altogether."[8] Screwtape admits a person can keep on improving their abilities and not consider where they might land "in the temple of Fame."[9] But he counters this by telling Wormwood that he must endeavor to "try to exclude this reminder from the patient's consciousness at all costs."[10]

---

3 That program can be heard at http://tinyurl.com/hgg8o3v or http://allaboutjack.podbean.com/e/shining-light-on-screwtape%e2%80%99s-darkest-secret-william-oflaherty.
4 Letter 13, first paragraph.
5 Letter 13, fifth paragraph.
6 This part of *C.S. Lewis Goes to Hell* lists words used in various places in *The Screwtape Letters* and in addition to provide all the letters they are in, also a short summary of what is shared in the various places is included. A free 20 page PDF of the book is available at ScrewtapeCompanion.com.
7 Letter 14, fourth paragraph.
8 Letter 14, fifth paragraph.
9 Letter 14, fifth paragraph.
10 Letter 14, fifth paragraph.

However, the situation is so desperate for Wormwood that Screwtape advises using the "putting in" method to regain the advantage. Because humility is such a problem, Screwtape asks "have you drawn his attention to the fact"[11] that he is being humble? Also in the letter he brings up a mindset the devils have used to lessen the impact of humility, which is by advocating a false notion about it. His example reminds Wormwood that "humans have been brought to think that humility means pretty women trying to believe they are ugly and clever men trying to believe they are fools."[12] Also, in the final paragraph of this letter, Screwtape underscores the fact that while God wants people to not wonder about their own value (and risk being prideful), the devils want us to focus our minds on questions of what our value is.

Letter 15

In the fifteenth letter Wormwood is instructed on the nature of time for humans and how understanding it can help him be a more effective tempter. The "keeping out" is found in the third paragraph where Screwtape proclaims "our business is to get them [humans] away from the eternal, and from the Present."[13] This is in direct opposition to what God stated as wanting people to "attend chiefly to."[14] Thus, Wormwood needs to keep out of his patient's mind anything dealing with eternity or present things. Additionally, to help achieve this objective, the devils can make people ponder the Future. This is an effective method because it "inflames hope and fear" and is "least like eternity."[15] Wormwood is reminded of the usefulness of this because "nearly all vices are rooted in the future."[16] As noted earlier with the word "will," the terms related to time are explained in the Topical Glossary of my book.

Letter 16

In the sixteenth letter Screwtape warns his nephew that it is a concern that his patient is faithfully attending a single church. Then

---

11 Letter 14, second paragraph.
12 Letter 14, fourth paragraph.
13 Letter 15, third paragraph.
14 Letter 15, second paragraph.
15 Letter 15, third paragraph.
16 Letter 15, third paragraph.

after elaborating on a couple of churches Wormwood should get him to visit, Screwtape mentions something other tempters have been successful with regarding their patients. That is, removing "from men's minds what that pestilent fellow Paul used to teach about food and other unessentials."[17]

Letter 17

Finally in the seventeenth letter Wormwood is told about a unique form of gluttony. He learns that Glubose is in charge of his patient's mother and that she is a slave (but doesn't know it) to "gluttony of Delicacy."[18] The initial "keeping out" is in the first paragraph and has to do with hiding this fact from her. Screwtape explains, "She would be astonished…to learn that her whole life is enslaved to this kind of sensuality, which is quite concealed from her."[19] Then a few sentences later he notes that "she never recognises as gluttony her determination to get what she wants"[20] because the amount of what she wants is so small and costs less than the serving already given to her.

Wormwood is given another example of how effective Glubose is at his work. Screwtape points out that when God tries to make his patient's mother aware of her obsession with food, "Glubose counters it by suggesting"[21] something else to get her mind off the point their Enemy (God) is making. It's interesting to note that here God is trying to put something into someone's mind and the demon is putting something else in as a means to keep something out!

Screwtape then informs Wormwood that his patient, because he is a male, is less likely to be tempted to his mother's type of gluttony. Instead, food can be used secondarily as a means for "attacks on chastity."[22] Specific to chastity, Wormwood is told to "never let him notice the medical"[23] benefits of it. Not noticing is the "keeping things out" method.

---

17   Letter 16, fifth paragraph.
18   Letter 17, first paragraph.
19   Letter 17, first paragraph.
20   Letter 17, first paragraph.
21   Letter 17, second paragraph.
22   Letter 17, fourth paragraph.
23   Letter 17, fourth paragraph.

Conclusion

What I've done in this paper is to support my thesis that the preferred method the devils use is not "putting things in" to a person's mind, but "keeping things out." Screwtape clearly states this favored approach in the fourth letter. In fact, nearly all the letters have some direct or indirect mention of this tool in the battlefield for the mind.

Because a previous talk dealt with the occurrences for the first dozen letters, this paper focused on letters thirteen through seventeen. Each had at least one example of "keeping things out." Additionally, it was pointed out that Screwtape isn't against Wormwood whispering into the ear of his patient to suggest or "put in" a thought. In fact, sometimes in order to keep something out another thought might have to be put in, as noted in the last letter explored.

Works Cited

Lewis, C.S. *The Screwtape Letters*. N.Y.: MacMillan, 1961.

O'Flaherty, William. *C.S. Lewis Goes to Hell: A Companion and Study Guide to The Screwtape Letters*. Hamden: Winged Lion Press. 2016

Through the Lens of *The Four Loves*: Love in Perelandra

by Paulette Sauders

> Paulette Sauders has taught at Grace College, Winona Lake, Indiana, for more than fifty years. Her B.A. is from Grace College, her M.A. is from Saint Francis University, and her Ph.D. is from Ball State University, with a doctoral dissertation on C. S. Lewis. She has presented numerous papers at Taylor University and elsewhere.

It is my contention that, when C.S. Lewis wrote his non-fiction treatise, *The Four Loves*, in 1956, he had already been thinking about the various concepts of love for many years. As a matter of fact, he had been including examples of those kinds of love and their perversions in his fiction and other writings since 1936. Each of his novels demonstrates the kinds of loves (and their perversions) that he summarizes in *The Four Loves*, illustrating the various types.

Chad Walsh wrote that, in *Perelandra*, Lewis tries to get his readers "to see the familiar world in a very unfamiliar light" (*Literary Legacy* 109), using "space adventure as the medium for metaphysical, philosophic, religious, and psychological themes" (*Literary Legacy* 83). One of those themes involves the loves that Lewis discusses in *The Four Loves*.

Since *Perelandra* is such a theological and philosophical book, it does not contain nearly as many references to the four loves as Lewis's other books do. Most of *Perelandra* is taken up by a description of the unusual, watery planet and its floating islands, a description of the Un-man's long temptation of Queen Tinidril, and a description of Ransom's attempts to thwart the Un-man and finally destroy it. At the end comes the description of the eldila and the great ceremony honoring Tor and Tinidril for not falling prey to temptation.

However, many of the scenes reveal characters demonstrating the kinds of love Lewis wrote about so consistently in *The Four Loves* and his other novels. For example, in the very beginning of the novel, Ransom's friend, Lewis, the narrator of the story, exhibits true friendship (*Philia*) when he goes to Ransom's home to help him—even though he is strongly tempted by the bad eldila not to go, and he becomes more afraid the further he walks. Lewis, in the course of the narration, says of Ransom, "the man is a friend" (*Perelandra* 10), and as he was nearing Ransom's house, "I was getting nearer at every stride to the one friend" (*Perelandra* 13).

Thomas Howard points out that, even though it goes against the character Lewis's better judgment, Lewis helps Ransom to get packed into the "coffin-like vehicle" for the trip to Perelandra (*The Achievement* 97). This shows true friendship and belief in his friend. Regarding this fantastic trip to an unknown world, there is "mutual respect and understanding" between them. *The Four Loves* considers these to be basic characteristics of friendship (95).

Lewis and Ransom are "kindred souls" (*The Four Loves* 92). They are both philologists, university professors, and single, but more importantly, both are concerned with the spiritual part of life, and both call themselves Christians. They are close enough to confide completely in each other.

As Ransom prepares to leave for Perelandra, Ransom and Lewis converse intimately about taking care of Ransom's affairs while he's gone. "We laid our heads together and for a long time we talked about those matters which one usually discusses with relatives and not with friends" (*Perelandra* 28), showing how close they really are.

While Ransom and Lewis talk, Lewis realizes his friend may be gone for a long time and thus notes, "I found myself noticing and loving all sorts of little mannerisms and expressions in him. . ." (28). Also, Lewis is such a friend that he is willing to be on call to come back and help Ransom when he returns from outer space—even though Ransom has no idea when that will be (27). In the first part of the novel, the great love and friendship between these two men is exhibited and personified in them.

Although Ransom personifies friendship in the beginning of the story, it soon becomes evident that he also personifies Gift-love (*Agape*) in his willingness to go on such a dangerous trip into the unknown in order to be used by God (Maleldil). He does not even know what God expects of him once he arrives, but he puts his complete trust in the hands of the eldila (angels), knowing that they are God's instruments.

Ransom's Gift-love becomes especially evident when he becomes aware of what he has been sent to do—to help keep the newly created man and woman on Perelandra from succumbing to Satan's temptations. He continuously lays aside his own fears and physical comfort in order to help the Green Lady, Tinidril, resist the Evil One's subtle, seductive temptations.

For example, when Ransom sees that Weston, the Un-man, the vehicle for the Evil One, is trying to tempt Queen Tinidril to disobey Maleldil, he resolves to stay by her side to protect her from him and to combat what he has to say to her. But the Un-man does not seem to need to sleep (*Perelandra* 128). Ransom forgoes many hours of sleep–which he truly needs–in order to accomplish this resolution.

"He was dead tired." Yet, "he did not dare to let the enemy out of his sight for a moment, and everyday its society became more unendurable" (128). A few days later, the narrator notes, "But the enemy was never tired, and Ransom grew more weary all the time. . ." (131). He hates being in the presence of the Evil One and tries to stop it as it maims and kills small animals all around him on the floating islands. But he stays with the Un-man out of love—Gift-love. He wants only the best for Tinidril and her husband and their unborn children.

Ultimately, Ransom wants God's best for this new planet, fitting very well the description of Gift-love Lewis gives in *The Four Loves* where he says that God's love is Gift-love (176); it desires only the good of the one loved (197). When a person gives of himself without thought of getting anything in return, that is Gift-love (177). And those characteristics fit Ransom and all he does on Perelandra.

When Ransom physically fights the Un-man, he suffers great pain as the creature's long "nails were ripping great strips off his back" (*Perelandra* 153). He feels "pain as his fist crashed against the jaw-bone—it seemed almost to have broken his knuckles. . ." (152). The Un-man's "nails tore fiercely down his cheek and the pain put an end to the blows" that he was trying to deliver to its chest (154). But throughout the fight, even when the Evil One savagely bites Ransom's heel so that the blood flows and cannot ever after be stopped, "His own pains, where it tore him, somehow failed to matter" (156). He is so intent on doing what is best for Tinidril and Perelandra that the pain does not matter. Since he will not personally gain anything from this battle except injury, Ransom truly manifests Gift-love.

Since Ransom–the lead character–personifies Gift-love, it becomes obvious that this kind of love is one of the main themes of the whole book—especially God's Gift-love.

Toward the end of the novel, when the great ceremony is to begin, honoring the King and Queen of Perelandra for not succumbing to the Evil One's temptations, the Oyarsa (archangel) of the planet Malacandra and the Oyarsa of Perelandra appear to Ransom and then take on somewhat human forms. The expression of their faces reflects "charity. But it was terrifyingly different from the expression of human charity. . ." (199). Instead, "Pure, spiritual, intellectual love shot from their faces like barbed lightning" (199-200).

When King Tor and Queen Tinidril arrive for the ceremony, Tor asks the Oyarsa of Perelandra what she will do now that the King and Queen will be the rulers of the planet. Then he asks the Oyarsa to stay with them on the planet, "both for the love we bear you and also that you may strengthen us with counsel. . ." (207). Next, Queen Tinidril speaks of the "love and trust" existing between Maleldil and herself and Tor (208). King Tor continues the ceremony by speaking eloquently, in response to Ransom, about the gift given him—the rule of his world: "All is gift. . . . Through many different kinds of love and labour, the gift comes to me" (209). In every part of the ceremony, love—Gift-love—is mentioned and extolled.

Then the greatest expression of love for God is presented as all participate in a series of great doxologies, praising God for His love.

> In the plan of the Great Dance . . . all the patterns [are] linked and looped together by the unions of a kneeling with a sceptered love. Blessed be He! (217).

> He has immeasurable use for each thing that is made, that His love and splendor may flow forth like a strong river which has need of a great watercourse and fills alike the deep pools and the little crannies. . . . We also have need beyond measure of all that He has made. Love me, my brothers, for I am infinitely necessary to you, and for your delight I was made. Blessed be He! (217)

> He has no need at all of anything that is made. . . . [W]hat all add to Him is nothing. . . . Love me, my brothers, for I am infinitely superfluous, and your love shall be like His, born neither of your need nor of my deserving, but a plain bounty. Blessed be He! (217)

And Tor's farewell as Ransom prepares to leave them is also a doxology and benediction: "Speak of us always to Maleldil as we speak always of you. The splendor, the love, and the strength be upon you" (222). God's love (Gift-love) is praised in all of these passages.

Gift-love is the major kind of love spoken of and exemplified throughout *Perelandra*, but romantic love (*Eros*), tinged with Gift-love, is also demonstrated through the lives and words of King Tor and Queen Tinidril.

When Tinidril sees Ransom (from a distance) for the first time, she thinks he is Tor, her husband, so her "eyes looked at his full of love and welcome" (54). Then she realizes it is someone else, and her expression changes to surprise. This is Ransom's first indication of the great love between Tinidril and Tor.

During the period when Weston, the Un-Man, is tempting Tinidril to disobey Maleldil, Ransom detects Tinidril's love for her husband many times. For example, the Evil One tells the Green Lady that the new knowledge he is giving her will make her husband the King "love you more" because she is wiser than he is (105). However, she responds, "But how could anyone love anything more? It is like saying a thing could be bigger than itself" (106).

When the Un-man tries to tempt the Queen to disobey Maleldil by telling her she needs to be unselfish and self-sacrificing and daring for her husband's sake, the only times she seems to consider his words are when she responds "out of love for the King . . ." (132-33).

And when Tinidril and Tor come walking to the great ceremony at the end of the novel, they come "walking hand in hand," signifying their love for each other (204).

Of course, Tinidril's love for her husband is more than Eros alone. It also includes Gift-love. Evan Gibson points out that when Tinidril is tempted by the Un-man to sin, the demon-possessed figure describes how the daughters of Eve have surpassed their mother in greatness and abilities. Upon hearing this, however, instead of giving in to disobedience, the Queen praises Maleldil. According to Evan Gibson:

> She rejoices that perhaps her daughters will be greater than she. Her imagination . . . is delighted at the thought of relinquishing her position as Queen and Lady to descendants who will exceed her as much as she does the beasts. And so her selfless love defeats him, and the first temptation fails. (Gibson, *C. S. Lewis: Spinner of Tales* 59).

This "selfless love" is Gift-love, the same kind that Ransom personifies. Like Ransom, Tinidril desires only the good of the ones she loves—her husband and future children. She desires to give of herself without thought of getting anything in return. This is true Gift-love according to *The Four Loves* (176-77).

Just as the novel starts with an emphasis upon friendship (between Ransom and Lewis), *Perelandra* ends with an emphasis on the friendship that has developed between Ransom and Tinidril and Tor. For example, at one point, when Ransom joins Tinidril while the Un-man is talking to her, tempting her, "she was clearly pleased to see him [Ransom]" (133).

Later, when the King and Queen arrive at the great ceremony, "The eyes of the Queen looked upon him [Ransom] with love and recognition . . ." (205), signifying the friendship that has grown out of their many hours of talking together and out of his willingness to help her and to destroy Weston's evil (Hannay, *C. S. Lewis* 96).

Tor, also, speaks of praise and honor for Ransom for keeping the Evil One from him and Tinidril; then he speaks to Ransom and thanks him "and both kissed him, mouth to mouth and heart to heart." They also want him to "sit between them" out of their love for him, but he cannot bring himself to do so (207-208).

After the great ceremony, Tor notices Ransom's bleeding heel (the Evil One had bitten his heel in their battle [cf. Genesis 3.15]), and out of concern for him wants to help him. "'Sit down, friend,' said Tor, 'and let me wash your foot in this pool'" (220). Tor tries to help his wounded friend out of love for him, but he can do no good for the injury.

Tor and Tinidril feel real hesitation and sadness when it is time for Ransom to leave their planet. In the year the three have been together, real friendship has grown. They are "kindred souls" (*Four Loves* 92), having faced the Evil One together and defeated him—having "shared dangers and hardships" as *The Four Loves* puts it (95). A "mutual respect and understanding" (*Four Loves* 95) has developed among them, and each honors the others for what they have done on Perelandra. They fit the description of friendship Lewis gives in *The Four Loves* perfectly.

As Ransom prepares to leave Perelandra, Tor and Tinidril "bent down and kissed him" (*Perelandra* 222), and as he leaves, Tor and Tinidril say together, "Farewell, Friend and Saviour, farewell" (222).

Besides friendship, one other note about love should be added regarding the novel *Perelandra*. Lewis's book *The Weight of Glory* includes much on on the subject of love and on "unselfishness." Here is one excerpt from *The Weight of Glory*:

> If you asked twenty good men today what they thought [was] the highest of the virtues, nineteen of them would reply, Unselfishness. But if you had asked almost any of the great Christians of old, he would have replied, Love. You see what has happened? A negative idea of Unselfishness carries with it the suggestion not primarily of securing good things for others, but of going without them ourselves, as if our abstinence and not their happiness was the main point. I do not think this is the Christian virtue of Love. (*Weight of Glory* 3)

In like fashion, in *Perelandra*, the Evil One keeps telling Tinidril that she needs to exhibit "unselfishness," "self-sacrifice and self-dedication" toward her husband and future children (132). This shows the way Satan distorts the concept of Gift-love for his own purposes.

As Lewis suggests in *The Weight of Glory*, and as Screwtape suggests in *The Screwtape Letters*, Satan tries to substitute "the negative 'unselfishness' for the Enemy's [God's] positive charity" so that he "can, from the very outset, teach a man to surrender benefits, not that others may be happy in having them, but that he may be unselfish in forgoing them" (*Screwtape Letters* 121). This same image is consistently drawn in *Perelandra*. The Evil One harps on Tinidril's need for unselfishness page after page, day after day, hoping to get her to disobey God on that pretext (104-139).

In addition, when Ransom responds to the Evil One's constant plea to Tinidril for "unselfishness," Ransom uses examples just like the ones Lewis uses in *The Four Loves*. Ransom says that "he'd seen this kind of 'unselfishness' in action" in "women making themselves sick with hunger rather than begin the meal before the man of the house returned, though they knew perfectly well that there was nothing he disliked more . . ." (*Perelandra* 132).

This example (as well as others not quoted) sounds like Mrs. Fidget, the woman in *The Four Loves* who "lived for her family," unselfishly working "her fingers to the bone" for them, but in the process showing no Gift-love or concern for what is *best* for the members of the family (75). It is as if people like this are "martyrs" to their families and they want everyone to know about it. They also sound like Pam, the mother in *The Great Divorce*, who cried, "I gave up my whole life" for my son Michael (*Great Divorce* 92). However, her "unselfishness" turns into selfish possessiveness of her son and ruins his life and the lives of the rest of the family members (94).

Lewis is very consistent in all of his books, both fiction and non-fiction, in the way he presents "unselfishness" as perverted, possessive Affection (Storge), opposed to Gift-love, the greatest of loves.

Stella Gibbons summarizes Lewis's presentations of love in his fiction:

> It cannot be denied that Lewis's view of love was both high and severe. Between human beings, in its best form, he seems to have seen it as a form of charity, burningly strong and tempered by a detached intelligence and an unswerving watch upon itself to guard against the smallest hint of the usual heated, half-selfish, satisfyingly sloppy romanticism ever intruding. (96)

Throughout *Perelandra* Lewis demonstrates many of the kinds of love (and their perversions) that he wants his readers to be aware of. These types of love come alive when included in his captivating novels, especially in *Perelandra*. Corbin Scott Carnell, who knew Lewis personally, believes that Lewis had a consistent purpose in his works: "To awaken a desire for love and goodness—this was Lewis's purpose in almost everything he wrote. (*Bright Shadow* 161)

Works Cited

Carnell, Corbin Scott. *Bright Shadow of Reality: C.S. Lewis and the Feeling Intellect.* Grand Rapids, MI: Wm. B. Eerdmans, 1974.

Gibbons, Stella. "Imaginative Writing." *Light on C.S. Lewis.* Ed. Jocelyn Gibb. New York: Harcourt, Brace & World, 1965. 86-101.

Gibson, Evan. *C. S. Lewis: Spinner of Tales.* Grand Rapids, MI: Wm. B. Eerdmans, 1980.

Hannay, Margaret P. *C. S. Lewis.* New York: Frederick Ungar, 1981.

Howard, Thomas. *The Achievement of C. S. Lewis.* Wheaton, IL: Harold Shaw Publishers, 1980.

Lewis, C. S. *The Four Loves.* New York: Harvest Book/Harcourt Brace Jovanovich, 1960.

---. *The Great Divorce.* New York: Macmillan Publishing Co., 1946.

---. *Perelandra.* New York: Macmillan Publishing Co., 1943.

---. *The Screwtape Letters.* New York: Macmillan Publishing Co., 1941.

---. "The Weight of Glory." *The Weight of Glory and Other Addresses.* New York: Macmillan Publishing Co., 1962.

Walsh, Chad. *The Literary Legacy of C. S. Lewis.* New York: Harcourt Brace Jovanovich, 1979.

C.S. Lewis and Christian Postmodernism: Jewish Laughter Reversed

Kyoko Yuasa

Kyoko Yuasa is a lecturer of English Literature at Fuji Women's University, Japan. She is the author of *C. S. Lewis and Christian Postmodernism: Word, Image, and Beyond* (2016), the Japanese translation of Bruce L. Edwards's *A Rhetoric of Reading: C.S. Lewis's Defense of Western Literacy* (2007), and many published essays.

C. S. Lewis's last novel *Till We Have Faces* (*TWHF*) details the tragedy of a queen who fails to find self-fulfillment. It seems to be far from humorous. However, it can be seen as a comedy of Jewish laughter turned into Christian joy. Although G. K. Chesterton's influence on Lewis's comical expression is well-documented, Joy Davidman's Jewish impact on Lewis's humor has not been fully discussed, even though she was deeply involved in the editing of *TWHF*. This paper will compare Lewis's concepts of Jewish and Christian laughter in his *Reflections of the Psalms* (1958), and it will evaluate Davidman's imprint on *TWHF*, finally arguing that Lewis is a Christian postmodernist writer who retells mythologies as is done in postmodernist literature, but reverses them into the completion of the Gospel.

CHRISTIAN POSTMODERNISM

C. S. Lewis challenged the rationalist theology of modernism and expressed his stance through literary approaches similar to those used in postmodern literature, such as metafiction-style multiple stories and blurring the roles of narrator, author, and character. However, although postmodernist literature strives to deconstruct the grand narrative, Lewis ultimately intends to express a greater story that is beyond human understanding by employing mythologies as multiple narrative-subjective perspectives.[1]

HISTORY OF LAUGHTER

Laughing was not satisfactorily discussed in academics until the 20th century, when Henri Bergson began exploring the two sides of laughing, affirmative and negative. In the 21st century, Michael Billig objected to the positive psychology of laughing, arguing for the consideration of the negative

---

[1] For further information on Christian postmodernism, please refer to my book, *C.S. Lewis and Christian Postmodernism: Word, Image, and Beyond.C.S. Lewis and Christian Postmodernism: Word, Image, and Beyond.*

aspects of laughing.

Today, although there are many theoretical approaches to humor, three theories of humor dominate: relief theory, superiority theory, and incongruity theory. John Morreall categorizes the three theories according to different time periods—classical, Renaissance, modern—but Billig finds complementary and simultaneous mechanisms common to the three theories.

In the classical era, Plato focused on laughing about the misfortunes of others; that is, feeling joy and superiority to others. The Christian philosophy of the Middle Ages, therefore, took a negative attitude toward laughing. The Renaissance was open to the incongruity of values, allowing the clown or comedy to be elevated over authority. One of the first examples of incongruity is, as Peter Berger suggests, a Latin work, *The Praise of Folly* by Erasmus in the 16th century.

> Folly ranges across a wide swath of human life and thought in her sermon. Much of the satire continues to bite more than four centuries later, and therefore continues to give pleasure. But for the present considerations, Erasmus's book is important for another reason: Perhaps for the first time here is the presentation of what could be called a full-blown *comic worldview*. (Berger 20)

In the 20th century, the debate on laughing was ignited by Sigmund Freud, Henri Bergson, and Mikhail Bakhtin. Although Freud ascribed laughing to a physical release, Bergson focused on laughing as the incongruity between spirit and body, while Bakhtin considered the world to be inherently comical and foolish, regarding it as an anti-world. Helmuth Plessner harmonized the theories of incongruity and concluded that laughing is produced not only by the physical body, but also from what is beyond the body, or metaphysical, describing "the human position . . . as eccentric" (36).

There appears to be a consensus about laughing among critics like Plessner, Berger, and Billig. They look at both sides of laughing, subjective and objective. When you laugh as a subject, your laugher is an expression not only of joy but also of superiority, incongruity, and release. However, when you are laughed at as an object, you are being mocked. Among the laughs of incongruity, Peter Berger focuses on those of "a fool" who makes us laugh with comical stories and actions. Within the term, *fool*, he includes not only the traditional clown as a producer of laughs, but also the sacred fool who is an object being religiously laughed at.

Laughing in the Bible

The Bible offers no account of Jesus Christ laughing, but there are a number of incidents of Jesus being laughed at by others. Jesus is described as the object of laughter by the Roman soldiers and chief priests (Mark 15:20 and 31). Jesus Christ fell from the highest majesty of God to the lowest level of humanity. In this world, He lived as a sacred fool until He received the highest glory through His resurrection. As the Apostle Paul says, Christ was "a stumbling block to Jews and foolishness to Gentiles" (1 Corinthians 1:23).

Lewis's Idea of Laughing

Terry Lindvall discusses Lewis's idea of laughing, defining it as joy, based on the demon's categories of humor in *The Screwtape Letters* (10). However, Screwtape's analysis of humor is not necessarily trustworthy because Lewis describes the demon as a liar. The demon Screwtape rejects God, instead devouring another demon inferior to him, a hellish act of cannibalism. Although the demon defines the cause of humor as "Joy, Fun, the Joke Proper, and Flippancy" (53), he is not aware that he is being laughed at by readers. He has no understanding of a fool, sacred or otherwise, not only as the subject who makes us laugh, but also as the object of our laughter.

The study of Lewis's use of laughing-related words used in each work, such as "laugh," "mock," and "fool," shows that his fictional books include laughs, both affirmative and negative, but also the laughter of incongruity, which cannot be categorized as either one or the other. Secondly, it is obvious that there are references to fools, especially in Lewis's last novel, *TWHF*.

Lewis ascribes his "light touch" writing style to G. K. Chesterton's humorous tendency:

> I believe this is a matter of temperament. However, I was helped in achieving this attitude by my studies of the literary men of the Middles Ages, and by the writings of G. K. Chesterton. Chesterton, for example, was not afraid to combine serious Christian themes with buffoonery. In the same way the miracles plays of the Middle Ages would deal with a sacred subject such as the nativity of Christ, yet would combine it with a farce. ("Cross-Examination," *God in the Dock* 259)

He was influenced by Chesterton not only as a writer, but also religiously. During his military service in World War I, he read

Chesterton's essays and also his *The Everlasting Man*. Lewis then converted from atheism to Christianity, and thirty years after his conversion, he still remembered Chesterton's skill at humor.

> Liking an author may be as involuntary and improbable as falling in love. . . . His humour was of the kind which I like best—not "jokes" . . . , a general tone of flippancy and jocularity, but the humour which is not in any way separable from the argument but is rather (as Aristotle would say) the "bloom" on dialectic itself. . . . I liked him for his goodness. ("Guns and Good Company," *Surprised by Joy* 220-221)

As Chesterton seeks to use humor as the tool for telling the truth in his literature, Lewis writes a Christian literature in harmony with laughter.

Laughing in *TWHF*

Many of Lewis's novels are written from the perspective of the persona "I," which combines an objective narrator and a subjective character. Unlike earlier works, *TWHF* is nearly monopolized by the different facets of its main character, Queen Orual. The main part of the story consists of two letters by Orual as a fictional author. Although she complains to the gods about their unfair judgement of her sister Psyche, the two letters are written in a form of parallelism that contrasts with the three types of parallelism. Parallelism is a rhetorical form found in the Hebrew Scriptures such as the Psalms, using short sentences made up of two brief clauses.[2]

Orual accuses the gods of using unfair judgement in two different forms of trials or courts of justice: the first letter refers to a civil case and the second to a criminal case. Lewis discusses the two forms of trials in his book *Reflections on the Psalms*, which was published in the same period as *TWHF*.

> The ancient Jews, like ourselves, think of God's judgement in terms of an earthly court of justice. The difference is that the Christian pictures the case to be tried as a criminal case with himself in the dock; the Jew pictures it as a civil case with himself as the plaintiff. The one hopes for acquittal, or rather for pardon; the other hopes for a resounding triumph

---

2   Three parallelisms are synonymous, contrasting, and comparative. This is not only found in the Psalms, but in the wisdom and prophetic literature of the Bible (Job, Proverbs, Song of Songs, Ecclesiastes, and the prophets). https://www.biblegateway.com/resources/asbury-bible-commentary/Major-Characteristics-Hebrew.

with heavy damages. Hence he prays "judge my quarrel," or "avenge my cause." (Lewis, *Reflections on the Psalms* 9)

In the first letter, Orual curses the gods as if she were a Jewish accuser in a civil trial, while in the second letter she speaks first to the gods and later finds herself praying to the Lord for grace as if she were a Christian in the dock in a criminal case. In a metafictional dream, she was dragged into a court just like Christ was delivered to Pontius Pilatus's court. At the end of the second letter, there is another kind of reversal in Orual's spiritual journey. She enters into the picture-scrolls, integrating herself with Psyche in a metafictional medium—a picture-story within a letter-story—transforming herself into a pilgrim wandering to save the world from its sins. In the second letter, she repeatedly reads the first letter, both silently and aloud, until she learns the truth. She realizes that her own accusing voices are the response from the gods or, ultimately, from the Lord:

> Lord, why you utter no answer. You are yourself the answer. Only words, words; to be led out to Battle against other words. Long did I hate you, long did I fear you. I might— (TWHF 308)

The last part, "I might—" looks as if it ends in mid-sentence. Especially for the modernist Priest Arnom, who found Orual dead, this last part may look like a sign with no meaning, but for readers who have experienced everything in the Queen's two letters, it is possible to see a vision of another world beyond the written letters. Lewis deconstructs Orual's words just as postmodernism literature does, but, at the same time, presents an understanding of what transcends human language beyond "I might—" as Christian postmodernism does.

JEWISH CHRISTIAN WRITER JOY DAVIDMAN

C. S. Lewis came to know the mind of a Jewish poet more deeply through his encounter with the Jewish Christian poet Joy Davidman. Davidman was more popularly known at the end of the 20th century through biographical works, such as Brian Sibley's *Through the Shadowlands: The Love Story of C. S. Lewis and Joy Davdman* and the movie *Shadowlands* (1993). However, those works focused on Davidman as Lewis's wife, not as a writer herself. In the 2000s, however, there has been an increasing academic interest in her works.

Davidman was born to Jewish immigrant parents in New York in 1915, converting to Christianity in her thirties. She is introduced as a Jewish Christian writer by Lewis in the foreword to *Smoke on the Mountain*, which she wrote to explain the Ten Commandments of the Old Testament (1954).

> Another point of interest in Joy Davidman's work comes from her race. In a sense the converted Jew is the only normal human being in the world. To him, in the first instance, the promises were made, and he has availed himself of them. He calls Abraham his father by hereditary right as well as by divine courtesy. He has taken the whole syllabus in order, as it was set; eaten the dinner according to the menu. Everyone else is, from one point of view, a special case, dealth with under emergency regulations. To us Chrsitians the unconverted Jew (I mean no offence) must appear as a Christian manqué; someone very carefully prepared for a certain destiny and then missing it. And we ourselves, we christened gentiles, are after all the graft, the wild vine, possessing "joys not promised to our birth"; though perhaps we do not think of this so often as we might. And when the Jew does come in, he brings with him into the fold dispositions different from, and complemenetary of ours; as St. Paul envisages in Ephesians 2. 14-19. (*Smoke on the Mountain* 7-8)

Joy's spiritual contribution to Lewis is described by Lyle W. Dorsett as "something that stimulated—maybe completed—him" (131), and by Abigail Santamaria as "a constancy of contentment" (292). On the other hand, her literary inspiration for Lewis is evaluated by Don King as "a collaborator and shadow editor" (242).

Joy read the drafts that Lewis was writing, giving him incisive comments, and encouraging him as an editor until *TWHF* was completed. She mentions her deep involvement in the writing process of the novel in a letter to William Gresham:

> Jack has started a new fantasy — for grownups. His methods of work amaze me. One night he was lamenting that he couldn't get a good idea for a book. We kicked a few ideas around till one came to life. Then we had another whiskey each and and bounced it back and forth between us. The next day, without further planning, he wrote the first chapter! I read it and made some criticisms (feels quite like old times): he did it over and went on with the next. What I'd give to have his energy! (King 242)

Conclusion

For Lewis, laughing is a religious experience in which an accuser who curses the gods will be changed into a seeker who asks God for grace and salvation. His last novel *Till We Have Faces* is Lewis's divine comedy, in which the main character loses herself, abandoning an accusatory approach, unexpectedly encountering the gods, and ultimately the Lord.

Lewis interprets mythologies as the prophetical tool of conveying the truth, but the analysis of laughing in *Till We Have Faces* reveals that he includes Jewish Scriptures in the mythologies. Joy Davidman's Jewish thought influenced the converted Christian Lewis or, as he called himself, "the graft, the wild vine," contributing to his completion of his last novel. The discussion of laughing and humor thus reveals that Lewis is a writer who deconstructs human language just as postmodernism literature does, but he presents another world beyond the limits of humanity as Christian postmodernist literature does.

WORKS CITED

Berger, Peter L. *Redeeming Laughter: The Comic Dimension of Human Experience.* Berlin: Y.: Walter de Gruyter, 1997. Print.

Billig, Michael. *Laughter and Ridicule: Towards a Social Critique of Humour.* London: Sage, 2005. Print.

Davidman, Joy. *Smoke on the Mountain: An Interpretation of the Ten Commandments.* Forward by C.S. Lewis. Philadelphia: Westminster, 1953. Print.

Dorsett, Lyle W. *And God Came in: the Extraordinary Story of Joy Davidman.* Peabody, MA: Hendrickson Publishers, 2009. Print.

King, Don W. *Out of My Bone: the Letters of Joy Davidman.* Grand Rapids: Eerdmans, 2009.

Lewis, C.S. *The C.S. Lewis Bible.* Edited by Marlene Baer Hekkert et al. New York: Harper, 2010. Print.

---. "Cross-Examination," *God in the Dock.* Edited by Walter Hooper. Grand Rapids: Eerdmans, 1970. Print.

---. *The Screwtape Letters.* London: Bles, 1942. Print.

---. Foreword to *Smoke on the Mountain: An Interpretation of the Ten Commandments*, Joy Davidman, 7–12. Philadelphia: Westminster, 1953. Print.

---. *Surprised by Joy.* London: Bles, 1955. Print.

---. *Till We Have Faces: A Myth Retold.* Orlando: Harcourt, 1956. Print.

Lindval, Terry. *Surprised by Laughter: The Comic World of C.S. Lewis.* Nashville: Nelson, 2012. Print.

Morreall, John. *Taking Laughter Seriously.* N.Y.: State University of New York, 1983. Print.

Plessner, Helmuth. *Laughing and Crying: a Study of the Limits of Human Behavior.* Trans. James Spencer Churchill and Marjorie Grene. Evanton: Northwestern UP, 1970. Print.

Santamaria, Abigail. *Joy: Poet, Seeker, and the Woman Who Captivated C. S. Lewis.* Orlando: Houghton, 2015. Print.

Sibley, Brian. *C.S. Lewis through the Shadowlands: the Story of his Life with Joy Davidman*. Grand Rapids: Fleming, 1999. Print.

Yuasa, Kyoko. *C.S. Lewis and Christian Postmodernism: Word, Image, and Beyond*. Eugene, OR: Pickwick, 2016. Print.

Being *Hnau*:
The Imago Dei in *Gulliver's Travels* and the C.S. Lewis Space Trilogy

by Abby Palmisano

Abby Palmisano is a senior English Literature Major at Taylor University. In the summer of 2016, she received a Faculty Mentored Undergraduate Summer Scholarship grant to do research in the Brown Collection of Taylor University's C.S. Lewis and Friends Center. She also co-authored "A Bibliography of the George MacDonald Victorian Periodical Collection in the Center for the Study of C. S. Lewis and Friends" for *North Wind Journal*.

As a child, one of C.S. Lewis's favorite books was "an unexpurgated and lavishly illustrated edition" (Schakel 191) of *Gulliver's Travels*. As an adult, Lewis wrote that Jonathan Swift's novel fulfills "an imaginative impulse as old as the human race....to visit strange regions in search of such beauty, awe, or terror as the actual world does not supply" (191). The same could be said of Lewis's *Space Trilogy*. In fact, *Out of the Silent Planet* and *That Hideous Strength* bear striking similarities to *Gulliver's Travels*, the third and fourth books in particular. Both authors specifically question what it means to be human, and both conclude that being "human" means two things. On one hand, to be human means to be fallen. On the other, it means to be a reflection of the Divine. Interestingly enough, both Swift's *Gulliver's Travels* and Lewis's *Space Trilogy* probe the issue of what it means to be human through creatures who are distinctly non-human. In both novels, this exploration of "the human" is conducted through the satiric escapades of the human protagonists, Gulliver and Ransom. According to Peter J. Schakel, "As we view and hear Ransom express surprise and confusion over its differences from our world, we grasp an implicit critique of our own world—as one does in *Gulliver's Travels*" ("The Satiric Imagination" 135). Gulliver and Ransom, in conversation with the inhabitants of the worlds to which they travel, begin to recognize and respond to the fallen nature of humanity. What Schakel does not mention, however, are the contrasting ways in which the two men react to this realization. Whereas Gulliver grows in his disgust for humans, and regresses himself into his fallen nature, Ransom turns to the mercy and love of Maleldil, enhancing the reflection of the Divine within himself.

Similarities between the two protagonists can be seen in the introductions of the characters. The initial circumstances which set the stories into motion mirror each other. Both men are travelers waylaid by captors. Transported to a distant land, they encounter a differing species possessing unusual rationality, thus causing each to question his own view of humanity, both in terms of virtue and reason. Both Ransom and Gulliver are well equipped to learn new languages rapidly, allowing them to adapt to the new worlds in which they find themselves with relative ease. However, it is this ability to communicate and relate to the inhabitants of the alien land that becomes the cause of their eventual discomfort. In conversation with these other creatures, Ransom and Gulliver begin to view humankind through new eyes, seeing especially its shortcomings. This transformation of perspective produces a change in the lives of both men.

In Book IV, Gulliver arrives at this disenchantment with humanity after several years spent with the Houyhnhnms, a species of philosophical horses who are the ruling creatures of the island on which they live. This disenchantment arrives slowly, partially through discourse in which he learns that war, lying, and other destructive moral blunders are not a part of the Houyhnhnms' lives. The other source of Gulliver's disenchantment is the constant comparison made between Gulliver's description of humans and the local Yahoos—the irrational and brutal animal in Houyhnhnms Land that not only resemble humans physically but appear to have a similar propensity towards vice. As Gulliver begins to see humans as no more than the animalistic Yahoos, he no longer recognizes the Divine Image in humankind. Ultimately, Gulliver accepts the Houyhnhnm's belief that they are the "perfection of nature," confusing traits of character with physical image, sending him into a misguided attempt to become more like a Houyhnhnm in physicality, rather than virtue. After his return to England, Gulliver's friends tell him that he is obviously trying to think and act like a horse.

Ransom comes to an apparently similar realization through his discourse with the various creatures of Malacandra. In light of this epiphany, and despite his disappointment, Ransom ultimately looks to the mercy of Maleldil, and learns that the word "human" refers to something more than bodily form or even to the rational mind" (*Perelandra* 49). Thus, he grows into the full potential of the reflection of the Divine within himself. As a result of these experiences both Ransom and Gulliver view humankind through the lens of another species and they both witness, for the first time, what fallen man really is. Once they are able to achieve this new view, Ransom and Gulliver arrive at a turning point at which the Divine Image within themselves will either be enhanced, and grow to its full potential, or else take a fatal blow. It is at this crossroads that the protagonists differ. While Ransom views the transgressions of man in context of the ultimate mercy imparted by Maleldil, Gulliver's lack of spiritual understanding renders him incapable of finding any redemption in humanity.

One way in which Gulliver's spiritual understanding falls short is his failure to acknowledge the *Imago Dei*. Gulliver and Ransom initially fail to recognize the equality existing between certain created beings. Equality seems an elusive concept for the fallen order of mankind, as can be witnessed through the human tendency to create royal lineages, as well as the imperialistic pursuit of other lands. Gulliver has a "great...veneration for crowned heads" (236) that contents him with subservient roles that place him near the ruling power of whatever society he currently resides. However, Gulliver eventually is confronted with his own romanticized view of royalty. At the Magician's island, Gulliver meets several resurrected monarchs, all of which possess debased morality and common lineage.

Like Gulliver, Ransom initially accepts that social hierarchy is a part of nature. Ransom attempts to place this human construct onto the creatures of Malacandra. Initially, this is an impediment towards Ransom's recognition of the Divine Image in the Malacandrians. Ransom, along with Weston and Devine, attempts to mentally fabricate a Malacandrian power construct that mirrors human imperialistic structures, placing Sorns (to whom they misattribute superhuman qualities) at the top and the Hrossa towards the bottom. In time, Ransom is confronted with his own contrived view of reality. This occurs primarily in conversation with Augray the Sorn. Augray teaches Ransom that the rational creatures of Malacandra—the seroni, the hrossa, and the pfilltriggi—are all equal because they are all "hnau," meaning they are all equally endowed with the *Imago Dei*. Weston, however, in failing to recognize the equality of all rational creatures, attempts to imperialize Malacandra. These misconstrued hierarchies are typically established based on the perceived degree of reason possessed by an individual or species. Eventually, this confusion flows into the human perception of the higher orders of creation, with the individual envisioning himself "to be a little blind Oyarsa in [their] brain" (*Out of the Silent Planet* 137). It is because of this phenomenon that Weston feels justified in his actions.

The pride displayed in Weston is the same type of pride seen in the Houyhnhnms in Book IV of *Gulliver's Travels*. The Houyhnhnms, although certainly rational, do not seem to possess the moral or spiritual capacities of the *Imago Dei*; instead they are "wholly governed by reason" (*Gulliver's Travels* 318). In fact, all of the virtues of the Houyhnhnms are founded on the single premise of reason. The Houyhnhnms only speak the truth because "the use of speech was to make us understand one another, and to receive information of facts" (285). Therefore, if "one said the thing which was not, these ends would be defeated." However, reason acting of its own accord, without morality or spirituality to guide it, is fallible. In acting on reason alone, the Houyhnhnms are able to rationalize immoral behaviors, such as such as creating a social hierarchy based on physical attributes. The Houyhnhnms are also prideful of their physical form, viewing themselves as the "perfection of nature" (250).

Surprisingly, Lewis's Weston has much in common with Swift's Houyhnhnms. Like the Houyhnhnms, Weston is "wholly governed by reason" (*Gulliver's Travels* 318), and makes use of no other capacities outside of reason. Weston undervalues his moral and spiritual capacities. He sees systems of morality as arbitrary and does not recognize Maleldil. In failing to recognize the value of morality and spirituality, Weston's behavior is rather is rather Houyhnhnm-like. Therefore, he is able to justify his desire to imperialize Malacandra for the preservation of the human race through a rationality that mirrors the Houyhnmhnms view of themselves as the "perfection of nature." Like the Houyhnhnms, Weston views the existence of his own species as the most valuable. This Houyhnhnm-like worldview is further explored through MacPhee in *That Hideous Strength*, who likewise attempts to conduct himself exclusively by reason, undervaluing passions, such as romance, but out of reason has contrived some system of morality.

Just as Weston resembles the Houyhnhnms, Devine, who has no care for the Divine Image within himself or others, shares several traits with the brute species of the Yahoo, who seem to be a characterization of fallen humanity *without* the *Imago Dei*. In *Gulliver's Travels*, "the Yahoos are violently fond" of "shining stones of several colors" (*Gulliver's Travels* 309). They hoard these stones in their kennels, howling if their treasure is stolen away from their keeping. Furthermore, the Yahoos are altogether so irrational that they are looked on by the Houyhnhnms as mere animals, and therefore blamed no more for their barbarous nature than a "*gnnayh* (a bird of prey) for its cruelty" (*Gulliver's Travels* 294). It is for these reasons that the Houyhnhnms see it best to exterminate the Yahoos.

Devine is characterized by the same "natural bent either to profusion or avarice" (*Gulliver's Travels* 298) as the Yahoos. In *Out of the Silent Planet*, this description of fallen nature is shortened to the word "bent" in the language of Deep Heaven. The "shining stones" that attract the Yahoos, referencing precious stones of monetary value such as silver or gold, are likewise prized and sought after by Devine. In fact, Devine's sole enterprise on Malacandra is to gather "Sun's Blood," or gold. Devine's selfish motives that accompany his manipulative and cunning nature are the exact dispositions ascribed to the Yahoos by the Houyhnhnm master. Devine, too, has gone so far into the fallen nature of humanity, and ignored his image-bearing capacities, that the Oyarsa of Malacandra deems him "only a talking animal…and could do no more evil than an animal" who would be unmade on his planet, just as the Houyhnhnms see it profitable to exterminate the Yahoos.

In each of the novels, rationality is recognized by a created being's ability to aptly communicate through language, as well as their tendency towards order. Both authors also employ the concept of communication, and the lack of it, as a signal for a misused capacity for reason. In the third part of *Gulliver's Travels*, the highly "scientific" people of Laputa, who posses a distorted form of reason, can barely hold a normal conversation. Later on, the projectors at the Grand Academy experiment with creating nonsensical academic books and try to do away with language altogether. Their lack of communicative abilities is a reflection of their stunted personhood. For the Houyhnhnms, saying "the thing which is not" (*Gulliver's Travels* 285) hinders the reception of information, and therefore is an impediment to knowledge and reason. Communication, then, proves the presence of reason. It is through the recognition of language that Gulliver first discovers that the people of Lilliput and the Houyhnhnms are rational beings.

In *Out of the Silent Planet* and Book IV of *Gulliver's Travels*, the initial meeting of another intelligent species disorients the main characters, as well as their counterparts. What indicates that they have meet another rational being is the observance of particular patterns and cadences of the vocables being made, which are too specific to not be language. Language, in all its complexities, is similarly identified as a sure sign of reason by Ransom, a philologist. The more reasonable the character, the greater their abilities for communication become and vice versa. Lewis displays the deterioration of communication at the banquet held by the N.I.C.E. As language dissipates into utter nonsense, the room of human beings deteriorates into Yahoos, rioting, fighting, and acting in brutish and irrational manners.

Although some elements from each of the four parts of *Gulliver's Travels* are reflected in *That Hideous Strength*, Lewis primarily echoes the progression of events and ideas explored in the third part of Swifts novels. From the moment Mark Studdock enters the N.I.C.E., the plot lines between the two novels match with great congruity. Both the N.I.C.E. and the people of Laputa place a near veneration on their capacity for reason. However, the types of reasoning used by both groups are distorted; in their devoted striving for logic, their capacities for reason have been damaged. This veneration manifests itself in the Laputans' habit of employing geometrical terms in the description of aesthetic beauty. The Laputans, in their admiration for geometry, misappropriate logic by utilizing complex mathematical formulas and figures in practical matters (such a making clothing or houses) which reason would traditionally determine to require relatively simple equations. These mishaps are "frequent, and little regarded" (*Gulliver's Travels* 190). In the end, Gulliver resolves that the Laputans "are very bad reasoners" (*Gulliver's Travels* 192). Their communication is stunted and a simple answer is a rarity. Gulliver finds the super-intelligent Laputans to be "disagreeable companions" (*Gulliver's Travels* 205). Therefore, he primarily converses with lower-class citizens who are thought to be more disengaged from their thoughts- because they are "the only people from whom [he] could receive a reasonable answer." This misuse of reason is juxtaposed with an example of true rationality. In *Gulliver's Travels*, this juxtaposition is found in the Laputan lord who is considered "the most ignorant person" in the society (*Gulliver's Travels* 205). Despite the lord's poor reputation, he "listened to [Gulliver] with great attention and made very wise observations."

The Institute's near veneration of skewed reason is similar to the Laputans. At the N.I.C.E., reason is likewise twisted into something entirely apart from itself. At the N.I.C.E., Mark, in conversation with Wither, recognizes the meaningless nature of their discourse, wondering "what are we both talking *about?*" (*That Hideous Strength* 53). Wither himself displays the exact behavioral characteristics of the Laputans. Just as the Laputans would "forget what they were about" (*Gulliver's Travels* 187) due to their seemingly "intense speculations" (186), Wither will often not immediately recognize who is speaking to him, stares off "dreamily" (*That Hideous Strength* 101), and is "so far from listening that Mark felt an insane doubt whether he was there at all" (185). This is one of the many occasions where Lewis takes an interpretation of Swift's text and ushers it to the next level of exploration. In this instance, Lewis questions the integrity of the speculations of the Laputans through Wither, examining the possibility of these supposed speculations in reality being the "detachment of the spirit" (248). The character of Hingest, in *That Hideous Strength*, fulfills the role of the Laputan lord; although considered "an embarrassment" (*That Hideous Strength* 55) by the Progressive Element at Bracton, he is seen to be a legitimate scientist who sees through the N.I.C.E.'s scientific facade and recognizes the Institute as a political conspiracy. Not surprisingly, both Gulliver and Mark, upon witnessing all of these things, desire to leave their respective locations.

Once Gulliver leaves Laputa for the mainland of Balnibarbi, he learns of the projectors and visits the Grand Academy, both of which provide further inspiration for the N.I.C.E. The students at the Grand Academy apply backwards reasoning to each experiment conducted, rendering all of their academic endeavors irrational and liable to failure. The landscape of Balnibarbi has been left in ruins by the projectors, who have adopted the twisted logic of Laputa. In the same way, the N.I.C.E. is involved in a backwards scientific experiment of reanimating the dead. Lewis then echoes the irrational destruction of Balnibarbi's landscape in the N.I.C.E.'s destruction of the scenic village of Cure Hardy.

Once Ransom returns from Perelandra, he is a changed man. The *Imago Dei* has been enhanced, thereby ending his similarities with Gulliver. In *That Hideous Strength*, it is Mark, rather than Ransom, who is following in Gulliver's footsteps. Both are out of touch with their spiritual capacities, have misused moral capacities, and in terms of reason, are rendered defenseless due to the same weakness, an overwhelming desire for power and sense of belonging to "the inner circle" of whatever group they are currently involved with. Mark forfeits his true potential in order to become a part of whatever exclusive group holds power within an institution, and Gulliver admits to having "been oft to amuse [himself] with visions of what [he] would do if [he] were a king, a general, or a great lord" (*Gulliver's Travels* 248).

The first capacity of the *Imago Dei* affected for Mark and Gulliver alike is the spiritual. In *Gulliver's Travels*, the possibility for spiritual destruction is seen in the actions of the human race. When asked by the Houyhnhnm master to describe the reasons for which humans go to war, one reason given is religion, specifically in the more arbitrary matters fought over between Catholics and Protestants. Gulliver is a Christian at face value, likely due to the era in which he lives, but spirituality plays little to no role in his life. Despite all this, Gulliver's spiritual capacities remain untouched rather than destroyed. He is unable to trample on a crucifix when asked to in Japan, even though refusal warrants the possibility of death.

For Mark, who is not a Christian, the ability to participate with in a spiritual relationship with the Creator has been left untouched his entire life. In *That Hideous Strength*, Mark is confronted with the possibility of spiritual destruction through Straik, whose personal brand of theology has been distorted to fit the needs of the Institute. He has managed to twist the core doctrines of Christianity into an entirely different religion that places man as the main power of the universe. Furthermore, several aspects of the Christian faith are mimicked by the Institute in its exploitation of spirituality. Filistrato informs Mark that the head would "have every part of" Mark (*That Hideous Strength* 172), as God desires every part of His created beings. The N.I.C.E. even offers a form of eternal life, one that would be absent of the Imago Dei altogether. Fortunately for Mark, his general discomfort for religion turns him away from Straik's heresies. The final test of his religious standing, as a part of his initiation into the N.I.C.E., takes place when he is asked by Frost to trample on crucifix (as happens to Gulliver). Although he is not a Christian, Mark is unable to bring himself to do this, despite the fact that refusal could mean death.

For Mark and Gulliver alike, the potential for immortality proves fascinating and highly desirable. Death, however, is recognized as a natural and ordained part of human life by both authors; the Hrossa and Houyhnhms have set lifespans, and accept death without fear. When Gulliver first learns of the immortal race of the Struldbrugs, he is delighted, and immediately envisions power and eternal youth. The fact that the Struldbrugs are miserable and live eternally powerless comes as a shock to Gulliver. Gulliver's wishful view of immortality is also seen in Ransom. However, Ransom, although highly respected, is powerless, and has no intention of gaining power due to to his obedient relationship with Maleldil. Even so, it is clear that he is not meant to live eternally on the Earth. However, since the members of the N.I.C.E. do not recognize or value the Divine Image, they attempt to create a race of immortals absent of the Image. As MacPhee expresses, the N.I.C.E. looks to this immortal race as "the next step in evolution" (*That Hideous Strength* 194). Members of the Institute, such as Filistrato, look forward to a ruling class of immortals (as did Gulliver) and take it upon themselves to act in anticipation "the next step," the eventual rid of organic life.

The idea of "the next step" in itself is further expanded on in *Mere Christianity*, and delves into the concept of superhuman nature, another prevalent theme of the *Space Trilogy* and *Gulliver's Travels*. In *Mere Christianity*, Lewis states that "imaginative writers try to picture this next step—the 'Superman' as they call him; but they usually only succeed in picturing someone a deal nastier than man as we know him" (*Mere Christianity* 218-219). Gulliver makes this very assumption in Brobdingnag, upon his initial meeting with the giant race of men, as does Ransom when he views the Sorns for the first time. As Ransom learns, there are created beings that are above man, but their physical makeup is antithetical to the popular relation of size and soul. In being more, they seem, to human eyes, to be less, and the Divine Image seen in humankind is magnified in them. Unfortunately for the members of the N.I.C.E., contact with superhuman beings who are "a good deal nastier than man as we know him" has been made. In conversing with the "Macrobes," as Frost calls them, and in rejecting the Divine Image, the members of the N.I.C.E. make themselves vulnerable to the cruel manipulation of the fallen eldils. In the end, it is the cause of their demise.

Although all of the novels possess many satirical moments, a very serious message lies at the heart of the stories. While both authors recognize the fallen nature of humanity, they likewise draw attention to the valuable qualities in human beings that are a reflection of God. The books offer, in conjunction with humorous and exciting adventures, an in-depth exploration of the *Imago Dei*—the capacity for reason in particular, and reveals the danger of undervaluing the Divine Image. In the end, the reader walks away with the realization that the universe, as well as the reflection of the Divine within themselves, is far greater than they ever expected it to be.

Works Cited

Dorman, Ted M. *A Faith For All Seasons; Historic Christian Belief in Its Classical Expression.* Nashville: B&H Academic: 2001. print.

Hanning, Barbara Russano. *Concise History of Western Music, Fifth Edition.* New York: Norton, 2014. ebook

Lewis, C.S. *Out of the Silent Planet.* New York: Scribner, 2003. Print.

- - -. *That Hideous Strength.* New York: Scribner, 2003. Print.

- - -. *Mere Christianity.* New York: HarperOne, 2001. Print.

Schakel, Peter J. "Restoration and Eighteenth Century." *Reading the Classics with C.S. Lewis.* Ed. Thomas L. Martin. Baker Academic, 2000. 187-202. print.

- - - "The Satiric Imagination Of C.S. Lewis." *Studies In The Literary Imagination* 22.2 (1989): 129. MasterFILE Premier. Web. 13 June 2016.

Swift, Jonathan. *Gulliver's Travels, The Tale of a Tub, Battle of the Books, ETC.* London: Oxford University Press. Print.

Two Strategies for Defending Naturalism Against C. S. Lewis's and Victor Reppert's Argument From Reason

by Louis J. Swingrover

Louis J. Swingrover is currently completing his M.A. in philosophy from Gonzaga University in Spokane, Washington, after which he will be pursuing doctoral work. His research interests lie in philosophy of religion and philosophy of science.

Just what positions or actions the Argument From Reason (AFR) justifies one to adopt or perform remains hotly disputed. In this paper I introduce the argument and note some concerns, using the second edition of Lewis's *Miracles* and Victor Reppert's development in *C. S. Lewis's Dangerous Idea*. I then sketch out two strategies by which naturalists might be able to defend their position. In the first strategy Naturalism is assumed for the sake of argument and a dilemma is posed, neither horn of which favors Supernaturalism. In the second strategy proponents of the AFR are accused of committing the genetic fallacy. I consider whether Lewis's argument might dodge this accusation if it is read as a *de jure* challenge to Naturalism. I draw on Plantinga's early account of warrant and put his rebuttal to Freud and Marx in *Warranted Christian Belief* to work against the AFR. After these two strategies are introduced I conclude that while the AFR does not defeat Naturalism *simpliciter*, it calls attention to the deep rift between natural and supernatural worldviews and sheds light on the supernatural assumptions that underlie much of Western thought.

1. INTRODUCTION

The earliest piece of philosophical writing ever published by Elizabeth ("G. E. M.") Anscombe was her critical response to C. S. Lewis's argument that Naturalism is self-contradictory. Lewis's argument was originally published in the third chapter of the first edition of *Miracles*, in 1947. After his scholarly interaction with Anscombe at the Oxford Socratic club on February 2nd, 1948, Lewis invested time into revising his material. He then downgraded his charge against Naturalism from "self-contradictory," indicating that he appreciated the force of Anscombe's concerns.[1] According to the

---

[1] Although he maintains that ."..a strict *materialism* refutes itself. . ." (p. 314, emphasis mine).

post-Anscombe editions of *Miracles*, rather than revealing naturalism as a self-contradiction, reason is responsible for the "cardinal difficulty" facing the naturalist.

Reppert's discussion of the varieties of Materialism and Naturalism is quite helpful; he provides a tidy demarcation of the Naturalism in Lewis's crosshairs: "Any genuinely naturalistic position requires that all instances of explanation in terms of reasons be further explained in terms of a nonpurposive substratum" (51). I will refer to Lewis's and Reppert's alternative metaphysics as "Supernaturalism" which posits the existence of fundamental ("ground floor") explanations that are essentially purposive. The sense of "purposive" here is quite strong. Reppert, with help from Dennet, lays out a naturalistic account of "purpose" according to which the purpose of a heart is to pump blood. The heart is structured in a manner that pumps blood and it acquired that structure in order to pump blood. However such an account of purpose is ultimately grounded in terms of nonpurposive phenomena, namely blind evolutionary mechanisms. "This" explains Reppert "is the exact opposite of what we find in theism, where the apparently nonpurposive order of the physical world is explainable in terms of the intentions and purposes of God" (49).

Specifically what premises the Argument From Reason (AFR) reasons from and just what it attempts to establish require some exposition. I will treat each in turn.

1.1. Lewis's Grounds

Lewis's text touches on several aspects of reason that pose problems for Naturalism. For my part I am able to discern three: the reality of the laws of logic, intentionality, and rational agency.

1.1.1. Logical Laws

According to Lewis, Naturalism has difficulty accounting for the laws of logic, to which acts of reason make recourse. If there is a way "things outside our own minds really 'must' be," that is, if the laws of logic are real, then they cannot belong to nature (313). This is because such laws govern what "must be so always and in any possible world" and not just our own (321). Logic is a part of that *deeper magic* from before the dawn of time, for "from it the orderliness of Nature, which alone enables us to know her, is derived" (320). If the laws of logic are real, according to Lewis, they must be in an important sense prior to, outside, or above nature. At issue here are the nature and reality of logical laws, which Lewis does not address at much depth. It is also far from clear that realism about logical laws could not be at home in a fundamentally nonpurposive (but not strictly materialistic) worldview.[2]

1.1.2. Intentionality

Next, Naturalism faces difficulty in dealing with intentionality, according to Lewis. He says "acts of thinking . . . are 'about' something other than themselves" (316). Yet essentially nonpurposive organizations of material building blocks do not seem able to bear the property of being about anything at all. Natural objects can certainly bear other kinds of properties and stand in other kinds of relations, from 'distance from' and 'later than' to 'more numerous than' and 'greener than.' However intentionality, or *aboutness*, is a kind-defining property that can only be borne by the thought of a rational agent.[3]

1.1.3. Rational Agency

Finally, Naturalism has difficulty making room for rational agency. When an agent reasons, according to Lewis, the agent freely adopts a conclusion on the basis of the apprehension of its logical grounding. However the naturalist must view every event in the universe, including every belief and every behavior, as the inevitable[4] result of non-conscious cause-effect relationships, which seems to exclude any reasoning on the part of a rational agent. He asks "even if grounds do exist, what exactly have they got to do with the actual

---

2   It is possible that the Naturalism Lewis has in mind here does not lend itself to being quite so precisely defined as "nonpurposive." He may have been thinking somewhat *Medievally* here, subconsciously regarding 'Nature' as the concrete, sublunary sphere and what belongs to it or is associated with it.

3   One might wonder about utterances and inscriptions. Are *these very sentences* not about anything? First, if any such strings were to occur as the result of non-mental forces they would not be *about* anything. Second, even if some such strings are the deliberate results of rational agents, they may not really be about anything *in themselves*. They may be regarded as non-intentional instruments by which rational agents signal their thoughts to one another. Third, if these strings are in any way about anything in themselves their intentional states must be entirely dependent on, or derivative of, the intentional states of the rational agents who generate them.

4   or, at best, random

occurrence of the belief as a psychological event?" (315). The majority of Lewis's text is spent on the nature of rational agency and the difficulty it poses for Naturalism.

This aspect of the argument is contingent on two controversial positions that proponents would do well to develop. If cause-effect explanations preclude rational explanations, then *ipso facto* rationality is conditioned by free will. Lewis seems to acknowledge this at times, e.g. when he writes that "the human mind . . . is set free, in the measure required, from the huge nexus of non-rational causation. . ." (*Miracles* 320). However not only is this libertarianism with respect to human freedom controversial in its own right, this account of rationality amounts to a variety of epistemic voluntarism, for it requires agents to freely adopt new beliefs to be rational. The nature and degree of the freedom one has over one's own beliefs is not at all obvious. It should also be noted here that this view creates *prima facie* tension with Reppert's argument from mental causation (discussed in § 1.2.2).

1.2. Reppert's Grounds

Lewis provides Reppert with material for an array of subtly distinct arguments, of which the closest to Lewis's argument from rational agency is an argument from the reliability of our cognitive faculties (discussed in § 1.2.5). Reppert begins by picking up and developing the argument from intentionality (74 ff.), and then lays out five additional arguments.

1.2.1. Truth States

Drawing additionally on Lewis, Reppert lays out an argument from truth (76 ff.). Just as it makes no sense to say of a natural organism that it is *about* something else, it makes no sense to say of any natural organism that it is *true of* something else. According to Reppert the reality of rational inference implies the existence of truth states, which he takes to be inconsistent with Naturalism.

1.2.2. Mental Causation

Next Reppert lays out an argument from the reality of the mental causation operant in rational inference. When a rational inference is made, an agent considers and accepts one premise, and then another, and then adopts a conclusion as a result of the previous mental states. Not only that, but one "mental event must cause another mental event in virtue of the propositional content of those events" (78 ff.). For Reppert to be consistent with Lewis, the sense of causation intended here must not be deterministic; if it were then by Lewis's standards the move from one mental event to the next would not be rational. However if a person achieves insight that permits the deliberate movement from one mental state to the next, then inference can be both Lewis-rational and Naturalism-inconsistent.

Note however that this account of inference limits the usefulness of the AFR. As an example, it would be inconsistent with epiphenomenalism. According to the epiphenomenalist, mental states are sufficiently and exclusively determined by physical states and, more relevantly, never the other way around. This would mean that mental states would not have causal access to one another the way they would on the Lewisian/Reppertian account of inference. Convinced epiphenomenalists will therefore have to look elsewhere for arguments against Naturalism.

1.2.3. Psychological Relevance of Logical Laws

Reppert then lays out an argument from the psychological relevance of the laws of logic (81 ff.). Not only is their existence inconsistent with Naturalism, as discussed above, but the act of rational inference requires that logical laws be psychologically relevant. In order to come to a conclusion from the premises that logically imply it a rational agent must make conscious recourse to the applicable laws. This activity is inconsistent with Naturalism, according to Reppert, because on Naturalism insight into the laws of logic would require the brain to stand in physical relations to the laws of logic, which are not physical.[5]

1.2.4. Unity of Consciousness

After this Reppert lays out an argument from the unity and endurance of consciousness through rational inference (82 ff.). To make an inference one must be aware of each of the premises and their logical relations and then proceed to draw a conclusion from them. This requires that there be some one thing with continuity

---

5 This argument is reminiscent of the mind/body problem consistently raised in objection to Interactionist Dualism. Interactionists propounding this argument must therefore explain why relations between non-physical and physical things are a problem in one case but not the other.

of consciousness, a "metaphysical unit, not merely a functional unit deemed a 'system' by an arbitrary act of the mind," for which Goetz (1999) argues neuroscientists would not seek if it were not for our first-person experience of ourselves.

1.2.5. Reliability of Rational Faculties

Finally, Reppert lays out an argument from the surprising reliability of our rational faculties. Drawing on Plantinga and Nagel, he argues that if Naturalism were true then our rational faculties would not likely be reliable "indicators of the nonapparent character of the world" (pp. 84 ff.). He then argues that our faculties are reliable and therefore Naturalism is false by *modus tollens*.[6] This argument could be symbolized in the following way. Let N = Naturalism and R = Our rational faculties reliably reveal the nonapparent features of the world.

1. $N \to \neg R$
2. R
3. $\neg N$

The plausibility with which one imbues the first premise should depend on how convinced one is that natural-evolutionary mechanisms do not promote the formation of true beliefs[7]. If one establishes Naturalism with a high degree of certainty and one is convinced of the sufficient reliability of our[8] rational faculties one might *modus ponens* one's way to the conclusion that natural mechanisms must in fact promote (or at least result in) as much. This could be accomplished by showing the survival and reproductive advantages of true beliefs; or by showing that the reliability of our cognitive faculties are "accidental" byproducts of the promotion of traits that confer survival and reproductive advantages, e.g. Gould and Lewontin's case for biological "spandrels." Rebutting such objections requires one to shoulder quite a heavy burden: to prove that natural mechanisms cannot or definitely do not in fact result in rational faculties that are reliable in the relevant sense.

A more troubling concern is that attempting to provide direct support for (2) might be futile. Would it be possible to establish that

---

6   In Reppert's explanation, and even in his list of premises, he uses suitably modest terminology, while his conclusion is just that "Naturalism is false."
7   Or true beliefs especially or specifically about the nonapparent character of the world, &c.
8   Or one's own

our "bare metal" cognitive faculties are reliable? Any reasoning one employed would presume the reliability of such reasoning, which begs the question at hand. Reppert seems to take (2) as a presupposition of any putative inference so that any forward movement simply requires its acceptance. However even if (2) is presupposed by any act of inference, it is not obvious that this indicates its truth. What reasons can one give that real inferences are ever truly drawn? Lewis seems aware of this problem: "If . . . a proof that there are no proofs is nonsensical, so is a proof that there are proofs" (319).

(1) also provides the basis for a slightly different argument that Reppert never distinguishes from the one above, although the general idea is discussed. It is also found in passages from *Miracles* and Plantinga's *Where the Conflict Lies*. All three argue that if our rational faculties are not reliable then we cannot assert the truth of anything we infer by them. Thus, if Naturalism is true, its truth may not be rationally asserted (by hypothetical syllogism). One might symbolize this in the following way, where A is a one-place predicate describing a proposition that can be asserted rationally:

4. $N \rightarrow \neg R$

5. $\neg R \rightarrow \neg AN$

6. $N \rightarrow \neg AN$

This will be treated in more detail later. For now it should be noted that the claim that if Naturalism is true then Naturalism cannot be rationally asserted ($N \rightarrow \neg AN$) is significantly weaker than the claim that Naturalism is false ($\neg N$).

1.3. The Aim of the Argument

Throughout Lewis's and Reppert's works there are thus quite a number of grounds from which metaphysical, epistemological, and practical implications are drawn. What is it exactly that these arguments come to when all is said and done? The most ambitious conclusion a proponent of the AFR could hope to establish is that God exists, however Lewis and Reppert both seem aware that their treatment of reason is insufficient to establish theism. Only slightly less ambitious is this: Naturalism is false (a claim consistent with a range of non-theistic worldviews). Less ambitious still is the claim that Naturalism ought not be held (a kind of practical claim not tightly bound to the matter of whether Naturalism is true), followed by the claim that there are no epistemically respectable motivations for holding Naturalism (a claim only weaker than "Naturalism ought not be held" because it is abstract rather than prescriptive and there might be wiggle room for practical reason in between the two). Just down from these are the claims that on Naturalism the truth of Naturalism cannot be rationally asserted (which leaves room for non-rational but somehow broadly epistemically respectable motivations for asserting or at least privately maintaining Naturalism) and that there cannot be rational arguments in support of Naturalism (which says nothing about whether Naturalism can be rationally held or asserted). Finally, the claims that theism can adequately ground the features of the reasoning process under consideration while Naturalism cannot (which leave open questions about the reality of these features) are among the least ambitious claims worth arguing for.

Lewis and Reppert both seem to view discourse on the various aspects of reason as a powerful contributor to a broader case for theism. Lewis, "when he was persuaded by the argument [from reason], accepted not theism (and certainly not Christianity) but rather absolute idealism," which is why "we find Lewis making independent arguments against" non-theist worldviews once he accepts Christ (Reppert, 103). Reppert's own development of the argument is itself aimed at providing motivations for "accepting a theistic understanding of the universe as opposed to a naturalistic one" although he grants that other "worldviews that make reason fundamental to what is real, such as idealism and pantheism" are not defeated by the argument (72). Nevertheless he notes that "for many people today, the live options are some form of traditional theism on the one hand and some form of naturalistic atheism on the other" (103).

2. Defensive Strategies for Naturalism

I will now turn to the task of sketching out two defensive strategies available to the naturalist.

2.1. Strategy #1: Assume Naturalism and Pose a Dilemma

> My propositions serve as elucidations in the following way: anyone who understands me eventually recognizes them as nonsensical, when he has used them—as steps—to climb up beyond them. (He must, so to speak, throw away the ladder after he has climbed up it.)

(Ludwig Wittgenstein, *Tractatus Logico-Philosophicus*)

Can the AFR precipitate a crisis for one who maintains Naturalism? Lewis admits that Naturalism is not *impossible*. Not only did he change the title of chapter 3 and rework the text to avoid making an overbold claim, he includes clear admissions, e.g. "you can if you wish regard all human ideals as illusions . . . without running into self-contradiction and nonsense" (330). In this first strategy by which I attempt to show the theoretical defensibility of Naturalism I argue that Lewis's "Dangerous Idea" does not deliver a motivation to the convinced naturalist to adopt a supernaturalist worldview. I do this by assuming Naturalism for the sake of argument and posing a dilemma of practical reason, neither horn of which favors Supernaturalism.

Giving Lewis and Reppert the benefit of the doubt, bracket any concerns with the AFR such as those raised in the introduction, and grant the Dangerous Idea. Let R' = There is an adequate ground of the laws of logic, intentionality, truth states, mental causation, the psychological relevance of the laws of logic, and the unity and continuity of consciousness. Then let the Dangerous Idea $(D) = N \boxtimes \neg R'$ and the "Extended Idea" (E) be that if R' is false, then nothing can be rationally asserted. One could symbolize this as follows:

7. N p
8. $N \rightarrow \neg R'$ D
9. $\neg R' \rightarrow (\Box x)(\neg Ax)$ E
10. $N \rightarrow (\Box x)(\neg Ax)$ 8, 9, HS
11. $(\Box x)(\neg Ax)$ 7, 10, MP

In (7) Naturalism is adopted as a premise for the sake of argument.

Premise (8) symbolizes the Dangerous Idea, that if Naturalism is right then there cannot be any reason, that is, there are no adequate grounds for the laws of logic, intentionality, truth states, mental causation, the psychological relevance of the laws of logic, and the unity and continuity of consciousness.

Premise (9) symbolizes the Extended Idea, that if there is no reason, then for any proposition x, x cannot be asserted rationally.

(10) says that *if Naturalism is true* then for any proposition x, x cannot be asserted rationally. This follows from (8) and (9) by hypothetical syllogism.

(11) says (*without condition*) that for any proposition x, x cannot be asserted rationally. This follows from (7) and (10) by *modus ponens*.

Lewis and Reppert should agree up to this point and, as discussed earlier, want the naturalist to draw the conclusion that Naturalism cannot be rationally asserted:

    12. ¬AN 11, UI

This does indeed follow—from (11) by universal instantiation. However this formulation of the argument reveals its transcendental nature. One may also conclude:

    13. ¬AD 11, UI

This says that *Lewis's Dangerous Idea* cannot be rationally asserted. But if D cannot be rationally asserted, then nothing premised on it can be rationally asserted either. To proceed down steps (7) through (13) is to descend[9] a Wittgensteinian ladder from Naturalism into Cognitive Nihilism.

This results in a condition in which reason might not have the character that one once thought. How now shall one proceed? Once one abandons the use of pure reason, one faces a dilemma of practical reason: Either one does not trust the deliverances of one's cognitive faculties or one does trust them, fully admitting that reason is an *ignis fatuus*.

If one grasps the first horn of the dilemma and does not trust the deliverances of one's cognitive faculties, then one is just as prohibited from allowing D or ¬N to inform belief and behavior as one is N or any other proposition, resulting in Pyrrhonian Skepticism.

If instead one grasps the second horn of the dilemma and decides to trust the deliverances of one's cognitive faculties as a matter of practice, then one is just as free to assert N as one is ¬N (granting that no assertions are, technically speaking, "rational"). It then becomes a matter of evaluating the evidence for and against each, and no unique motivation is delivered to the naturalist for abandoning Naturalism.

A possible way through the horns of the dilemma may be what Lewis (*Miracles*, 320) describes as a "humbler position," according to which one trusts the deliverances of one's cognitive faculties for practical purposes such as setting bones, building bridges, and launching Sputniks while distrusting them when it comes to speculative philosophy. He says that this position would keep one from affirming Naturalism, as it is "a prime specimen of that towering speculation, discovered from practice and going far beyond experience, which is now being condemned." At best, however, winning this case would mean that both Naturalism and Supernaturalism lie beyond what one

---

9   After all, one can hardly call this *ascending*.

could evaluate. This would result in naught but a Pyrrhic victory for the proponent of the AFR.

2.2. Strategy #2: Accuse Proponents of the Genetic Fallacy

Ceteris paribus any argument for $\neg N$ from the premise that if N then N is believed as a result of cause-effect relationships, is guilty of the genetic fallacy (albeit a subtle one). Anscombe (227) is onto this:

> Whether [one's] conclusions are rational or irrational is settled by considering the chain of reasoning that [one] gives and whether [one's] conclusions follow from it. When we are giving a causal account of this thought, e.g. an account of the physiological processes which issue in the utterance of his reasoning, we are not considering his utterances from the point of view of evidence, reasoning, valid argument, truth, at all; we are considering them merely as events. Just because that is how we are considering them, our description has in itself no bearing on the question of 'valid', 'invalid', 'rational', 'irrational', and so on."

Lewis's and Reppert's work does not engage with any argument in favor of Naturalism: they neither reject a premise nor identify a fallacy. Do they commit the genetic fallacy? Perhaps, as suggested in § 1.3, rather than arguing for $\neg N$, the proponent of the AFR can argue that N ought not be believed. Plantinga (2000) calls this kind of objection a *de jure* challenge, as opposed to a *de facto* challenge. A *de jure* challenge claims that a belief is "is irrational or unreasonable or unjustified or in some other way properly subject to invidious epistemic criticism; it contrasts with the *de facto* challenge, according to which the belief in question is false" (p. 167). A *de jure* challenge goes beyond merely accusing a belief of not being rationally assertable. As discussed above, a belief admitted not to be rationally assertable might nevertheless be held on the basis of some other broadly epistemically or practically permissible grounds, or one might take an agnostic stance toward the proposition if one judges it to be a member a special class that lacks rational assertability. A *de jure* challenge to a position goes so far as to characterize it as having a special quality that commends the withholding or withdrawal of belief.

One can give a plausible reading of Lewis that takes him to be advancing a *de jure* challenge to Naturalism. This is perhaps easiest to do while reading chapter 5 of *Miracles*, where Lewis argues that there is a broad consensus an "individual's views are worthless if they can be fully accounted for by some non-moral and non-rational cause" (p. 331). He takes Freud, Marx, and basically everyone in the world to be at least implicitly committed to this principle, that a naturalistic account of a belief undermines its epistemic and practical credibility.

However Plantinga, while he does not name Lewis as his opponent, opposes this principle. He argues that "giving a naturalistic account of a kind of belief isn't automatically a criticism of that kind of belief" (p. 145). He then provides more nuanced interpretations of Freud and Marx by which Freud (anticipated by Hume) accounts for religious belief by attributing it to a psychological coping mechanism present in human beings called "wish-fulfillment" whose proper function promotes human flourishing but not true belief; in fact it produces delusions. Marx's account (anticipated by Rousseau) attributes it to a perverted social order that causes cognitive dysfunction.

Plantinga characterizes the "F&M" complaint as being concerned with what he calls "warrant," which refers to that which differentiates true belief from knowledge, so that knowledge is warranted true belief. In this text Plantinga develops an account of warrant according to which one is warranted in believing something if it is the result of properly functioning faculties that are designed to produce true beliefs in the relevant context.

Freud characterizes religious belief as lacking warrant on the grounds that it is the result of properly functioning faculties that are not designed to promote true belief while Marx characterizes it as lacking warrant on the grounds that it is the result of improperly functioning faculties. Both criticisms take aim at specific conditions for warrant, and neither criticism springs from a naturalistic account of the beliefs they attack.

Lewis and Reppert, however, fail to show that belief in Naturalism lacks warrant. They do not even attempt to argue that belief in Naturalism is the result of improper function, faculties whose proper operation does not promote true belief, or faculties operating outside the domain within which they were designed to function. Any of those targets would have been fair game for a *de jure* challenge.

Nor would it be any easier of a case to make if they were to argue that belief in Naturalism lacks warrant on the grounds that *if* Naturalism were true then belief in it *would be* unwarranted. The proponent of such a case would be saddled with a similar burden: to establish that if Naturalism were true, then belief in Naturalism would be the result of improper function, faculties whose proper operation does not promote true belief, or faculties operating outside the domain within which they were designed to function.

3. Conclusion

The two defensive strategies sketched above interrelate. For example if a proponent of the AFR were to counter the second strategy by showing that if Naturalism were true then belief in Naturalism would be unwarranted, this would not on its own commend one to withhold or withdraw belief in Naturalism. The first strategy would kick in: So long as Naturalism remains possible (as Lewis himself grants, post-Anscombe), no motivation is delivered to the Naturalist for abandoning Naturalism in favor of Supernaturalism; the Naturalist is simply left with Cognitive Nihilism at the level of pure reason, and a dichotomy of practical reason according to which cognitive faculties are simply either trusted or mistrusted.

Naturalism, however, is revealed by the AFR to come with a very high philosophical price tag. While the proponent of the AFR only needs one variant of the argument to succeed, the naturalist must eliminate or propose dim naturalistic shadows of every aspect of reason discussed by Lewis and Reppert. Furthermore these alternatives must each be held with a very high degree of credence to prevent the probability of Naturalism from dwindling.[10] Perhaps Lewis is right to name reason as the "cardinal difficulty" facing the naturalist. To be sure, many of these individual projects have been undertaken, as Reppert acknowledges, with varying degrees of sophistication and success, in movements including atheistic Existentialism, Naturalized Epistemology, Perdurantism, Neurophilosophy, etc. However while some rare naturalists, such as Rosenberg, are well aware of the full scope of the impact of Naturalism on one's worldview, most, including Dawkins, do not seem to realize it. Dawkins only comes to terms with the bleak implications of Naturalism in specific dialectical contexts where he finally admits, for example, there is "at bottom, no design, no purpose, no evil, no good, nothing but pitiless indifference" (p. 85). He otherwise writes and even quite vigorously argues as if reason is real,

---

10 Even if a naturalist is 90% certain that each of the eight arguments laid out in the introduction fail, the otherwise-unadjusted probability of Naturalism for that person dwindles to 43% ($.9^8$). For the unadjusted probability of Naturalism to exceed that of Supernaturalism, an agent must be, on average, >91.70% certain that each of the variants of the AFR introduced fail ($8\sqrt{.5}$).

life has meaning, and objective moral values and duties really exist. Meanwhile the vast majority of Westerners seem to be (reflective or unreflective) realists at heart when it comes to logic and reason and morality and truth and souls and free will. Western legislation, customs, and languages all carry connotations only intuitively supportable by a supernaturalist foundation. The Argument From Reason is good for bringing this to light.

Works Cited

Anscombe, G.E.M. *The Collected Philosophical Papers of G. E. M. Anscombe, Volume II: Metaphysics and the Philosophy of Mind*. Oxford, 1981.

Dawkins, Richard. "God's Utility Function." *Scientific American*, November 1995.

Dennet, Daniel. "Why the Law of Effect Will Not Go Away." *Journal for the Theory of Social Behavior*, (2), 1976.

Goetz, Stewart. "Review of Whatever Happened to the Soul, by Nancy Murphy et al.." *Philosophia Christi*, 1(2):127, 1999.

Gould, Stephen J. and Richard C. Lewontin. "The Spandrels of San Marco and the Panglossian Paradigm: A Critique of the Adaptationist Programme." *Proceedings of the Royal Society of London, Series B*, 205(1161): 581–598, 1979.

Lewis, C.S. *Christian Reflections*. Grand Rapids, MI: Eerdmans, 1967.

---. *Miracles: A Preliminary Study*. London: HarperCollins, 2000. First published in 1978.

Nagel, Thomas. *The Last Word*. Oxford University Press, 1997.

Plantinga, Alvin. *Warrant and Proper Function*. New York, NY: Oxford University Press, 1993.

---. *Warranted Christian Belief*. New York, NY: Oxford University Press, 2000.

---. *Where the Conflict Really Lies: Science, Religion, and Naturalism*. New York, NY: Oxford University Press, 2011.

Reppert, Victor. *C. S. Lewis's Dangerous Idea: In Defense of the Argument from Reason*. Downers Grove, IL: IVP, 2003.

Rosenberg, Alex. *The Atheist's Guide to Reality*. New York: Norton, 2011.

An Ekphrasis by C. S. Lewis: "On a Picture by Chirico"

by Joe R. Christopher

Joe R. Christopher is a Professor Emeritus of English, Tarleton State University, Stephenville, Texas. His and Joan Ostling's *C. S. Lewis: Writings about Him and His Works* (1974) is one of the earliest and most comprehensive bibliographic studies of secondary materials on Lewis. His *C. S. Lewis* (1978), for the Twayne Authors Series, is a survey of Lewis's prose writings. He has published many essays on Lewis since then.

I. THE EKPHRASTIC POEM

Let me begin at a personal level. While I was still teaching in a university, I began going to one "literary festival" each year, because a friend of mine had started it. Since then I have upped my attendance to three such gatherings each year. One of the things that has struck me about the poetry being read at these festivals has been the occasional appearance of poems written on the topics of friends' paintings or photographs—the appearances of ekphrases, in other words. I have in mind a session that involved a group of enlarged photographs by one person being set up for display and then another person, a friend of the first, reading poems, one poem for each photograph. They were planning to publish a chapbook with the photographs and the poems set on pages opposite each other, and I assume they did.

Next, a different example. Most students (I suspect) will not get through their schooling in the United States without having read John Keats' "Ode on a Grecian Urn." His poem describes and reacts to the pictures on the sides of a large vase. He first describes some young lovers—gods and/or humans, with the males in pursuit of the females—and at least one singer and one player of pipes, and then he describes a religious procession taking a heifer to be sacrificed. In other words, it too is an ekphrasis, although I admit I did not hear the term applied to Keats's poem when I was a student. Scholars have been bothered by the scenes that Keats describes being not a unified group, all lovers or all pious, since Greek vases are decorated thematically—perhaps he was influenced by a late Roman vase,[1] perhaps he simply combined motifs from different vases for his own

---

[1] I have a vague memory of an essay by Gilbert Highet which gave the example of a Roman vase.

purposes. But whatever the sources, Keats is describing scenes such as exist on the vases.

Thus the type of poem I am concerned with is actually well known in educated circles, even if the Greek name of *ekphrasis* is not common outside of the current literary community. All the Greek word means is "description"; the word started out with a broader content than just a description of a work of art. It was then any written description, but *ekphrasis* has become more specialized in modern usage. This is why the current painting-or-photograph-to-poem usage may be called a subgenre. As might be expected, *Wikipedia* has an extended discussion of the term, which will be acceptable for most readers; but I would like to pause briefly on a different authority. Alastair Fowler was C. S. Lewis's final doctoral student at Oxford University, and he later edited Lewis's *Spenser's Images of Life* for publication. Fowler discusses ekphrasis in his *Kinds of Literature: An Introduction to the Theory of Genres and Modes*. He lists a series of historical variations on the descriptive type of writing, but his major emphasis is on the ekphrasis as a modern type: "the modern subgenre has primarily developed from a single influential poem, W. H. Auden's *Musée des Beaux Arts* (1939)." Fowler goes on to enumerate characteristic features of the subgenre, as well as to mention the three paintings by Brueghel in the Belgium museum from which Auden drew his imagery (114-115; the whole discussion continues to 118). More specifically, Pieter Brueghel the Elder painted one of the three; the other two are early copies of other of his paintings made by others. For a consideration of Lewis's poem, all of Fowler's details are not necessary, but perhaps a few characteristic features will be useful, mainly in contrast to "On a Picture by Chirico." Fowler writes, of the subgenre's "casual meditation" and of its "topics [being] suffering, life's pattern, [and] belief." Lewis offers a narrative, rather than a meditation, but in its way his poem presents a suggestion of *past* suffering, of a pattern for a new, post-human life, and of belief, yes, but no longer in a human perspective. *If* Lewis did read Auden's poem soon after its publication, he was not deeply enough influenced by it to write an obvious imitation. Be that as it may, this is a curious instance of Lewis writing in a modern and modernistic poetic subgenre, ten years after Auden's influential revival. As indicated by my "if," I do not argue that Lewis knew Auden's poem; but he did read some of Auden's poetry—in a 1936 letter he refers to him as "one of the few good young poets" (2:197), although his opinion was not always so favorable later (2:424). At any rate, the 1936 letter of praise is only three years before the first publication of "Musée des Beaux Arts"

II. The Painter and What He Meant

As the title of Lewis's poem makes clear, "On a Painting by Chirico," the artist whose work Lewis is describing is De Chirico; more specifically, Giorgio de Chirico, an Italian painter of Greek birth—born 1888, died 1978. So far as I am aware, no one has identified when Lewis saw one of De Chirico's paintings, and certainly the painter's name does not appear in the indices of the three volumes of Lewis's letters. Lewis does not realize—as shown in his title—that De Chirico kept the *De* as part of his family name. I do not suggest any great mystery is involved in Lewis having seen the paintings of a twentieth-century artist. De Chirico was not an artist who produced a limited number of canvases—he was nearly a mass producer, and he also tended to repeat his topics. Perhaps one of the museums in Oxford or one of the Colleges has an example of what may be called the two-horse paintings by De Chirico;[2] certainly some journal may have reprinted one; some individual in Britain or Ireland who knew Lewis may at least have seen one and described it to Lewis. After all, Lewis's best friend, Arthur Greeves, was an artist and studied at one time in Paris (Hooper, "Introduction" to *They Stand Together*, 19). No doubt Lewis knew others who were interested in art.

By De Chirico's "two horse" paintings is meant his series in which two horses—one lighter colored than the other—are on an edge of a lake or the coastline of a sea, with, most often, a section of a classical column in the sand near their feet. At least one such painting has the head of a classical statue in the sand rather than a column section; another substitutes a zebra for one of the horses. In the background on the shore is one or more classical buildings, sometimes in a ruined condition, sometimes not. Often, they are not clear enough for their condition to be certain. I do not know how many paintings De Chirico did in this series, but some brief checking of the internet under his name should turn up six or seven reproductions. The *WikiArt* collection of images related to him contains four of this series (as of 16 May 2016), and they are all given their titles in English, as translations of the original Italian. One of a palomino and a brown horse, facing to the viewer's right, is labelled simply "Two Horses by a Lake." One of a white horse and a black, both with two feathers attached by bands to their heads—two blue feathers for the white horse, two yellow for the black—and with a billowing red cloth attached to the black horse's

---

2   I wrote the Ashmolean Museum and asked about such a painting in its collection, but it does not possess any such (Casley).

back by a yellow strap—both horses facing the viewer's left, is titled "The Divine Horses." The other two titles are "Antique Horses on the Aegean Shore" (horses facing the viewer's right, with two parts of a column, one on the shore, one in the shallow coastal water—the light-colored horse in front, the brown with its head turned to the other) and "The Horses of Apollo" (horses slightly turned to the viewer's left but close to facing forward, with two sections of a column in the sand, the brown horse in front, the lighter in back—both have red ribbons around their bodies, backs and bellies). These four were painted in the period from 1963 through 1974, but at least one such painting is dated to 1928 ("Cavalli in riva al mare"—that is, horses on the seashore). It has a classical head in the sand; the horses, facing the viewer's left, are brown in back, white with blue shadows in front ("Giorgio De Chirico: Image Results," as of 7 June 2016). For reasons that will be apparent later, if De Chirico painted one of these scenes in which the horses were wearing crowns, that must have been the version Lewis saw. But such a version is not necessary for Lewis to have used the imagery he did.[3]

In some ways, De Chirico is an appropriate painter for Lewis to have been conscious of. De Chirico began his professional career as a modernist. In the years 1909 to 1919 (thus including World War I) he was part of an Italian movement called the Metaphysical School. He painted largely empty cityscapes, with shadows, and then gradually turned to "cluttered storerooms, sometimes inhabited by mannequin-like hybrid figures" (Giorgio de Chirico, *Wikipedia*, downloaded 11 February 2015). But next, in 1919 he published an article titled "The Return of Craftsmanship," in which he advocated the return to "traditional methods and iconography." He "adopted a classicizing manner" and "became an outspoken opponent of modern art. "Twenty years later he went further and "adopted a neo-Baroque style." These tidbits from the *Wikipedia* article on him suggest someone who had turned conservative, not religiously, not necessarily morally, but artistically. Lewis, if he knew about De Chirico's progress, would have approved—at least generally, in the leaving of Modernism. The actual result includes a number of thirtyish female nudes in the traditional

---

3   De Chirico also made at least one statuette of the two similar horses in bronze, titled "Cavalli Antichi," in an "edition" of six copies; presented (via the internet) in a show "Homage to de Chirico," curated by Anthony and Gloria Porcella, appearing at the time of this paper (7 June 2016) in the Rome and later to appear in the New York Galleria Da' d'Oro. https://www.artsy.net/show/galleria-ca-doro-homage-da-chirico.

style, so a moralist may have problems.

I have not seen anything that offered De Chirico's comments on this series of his paintings of paired horses, but some points seem obvious. The classical world, the classical culture, is destroyed, as the fallen column suggests. Next, what do the two horses mean? They are impressive horses, so they seem to be a positive statement, in contrast to the broken columns. Their being divine horses and horses of Apollo suggest some sort of spiritual power to them. If one thinks of Apollo as the sun god, then these presumably are the horses which once pulled his chariot across the sky. And what does the lake or sea mean? The Aegean Sea (mentioned in one of the titles) is not between Italy and Greece, of course, but on the far side of Greece, between that country and Turkey. Perhaps it helps that Athens is on that side of the Greek nation. De Chirico may be alluding, in at least *that* one of his titles, to his background in Greece—some sort of survival of the strength of the classical world despite the loss of its physical monuments. He was not only born in Greece but he first studied art there. Admittedly, two horses may be an odd symbol for classical strength *per se*—should one think of the horses pulling the two-man chariots into battles?—but something like this seems to be hinted. However, if "Apollo's horses" (as suggested) are to be identified with the god's daily travel, then the connection is far firmer than a general association of horses with the classics would allow. In some sense, the power of the gods, if not the worship of the gods, survives. And I assume the choice of two horses implies a stallion and a mare, again the symbol of survival—that assumption is made despite the fact that horses pulling a chariot probably would have been two geldings.

In one sense, De Chirico's meaning does not matter, for Lewis's poem tells how he interprets the painting—and he is not concerned with Apollo, or the classical world specifically, so the poem stands on its own. As will be made clear later, Lewis's poem seems to be a reflection on World Wars I and II.

III. Lewis's Stanza Form and His Stanza Sequence

Before considering what Lewis meant by his poem, I would like to discuss the formal aspects of his versification. No certain poetic form goes with the generic content in the modern version of the ekphrasis. W.H. Auden, who wrote in both free verse and traditional forms in his career, used free verse for his famous pictorial description. But, while the rhythm is that of prose, he has rhymed all but one of the lines—and that one, with the end word of "place," off- rhymes with "course" and "horse" later on.[4] The prose rhythm can be shown by the first four clauses of the poem, which cover four lines:

> About suffering they were never wrong,
> The Old Masters: how well they understood
> Its human position; how it takes place
> While someone else is eating or opening a window or just walking dully along[.]

One subject and verb per line: they were (never) wrong, they understood, it takes (place), someone (else) is eating, opening, or walking. But the appositive "The Old Masters" carries over into the second line, the direct object "Its human position" carries over into the third line—and after three lines of (perhaps) five stresses each, suddenly the fourth line runs technically to ten stresses and rhetorically to at least eight.

Obviously this contrasts with what Keats wrote. Keats had developed his monostrophic ode form of a quatrain and a sestet (with some minor experiments)—in effect, a shortened sonnet appearing as a stanza. He used it or some variation of it in five of his six 1819 odes.[5] The iambic pentameter he inherited from the sonnet. The richness of imagery he had learned primarily from Shakespeare's sonnets. "Ode to a Grecian Urn" is well enough known that it does not need quotation.

What then does Lewis do in the form of his poem? Obviously from looking at the poem, one immediately notes it is written in quatrains, the first three lines of each stanza beginning at the same point and the fourth line indented. I would suggest that these first three lines seem to be heptameters: consider the first line:

> Two sóvereign hórses stánding ón the sánd. There áre no mén[.]

Seven stresses. As I have printed it here, it is an iambic heptameter line. Now, I agree that rhetorically a reader who is not delighted by meter may not accent the *on*; a reader who is trained dramatically may add stress to *two* and may shift the accent from *are* to *no*. But the

---

4   Technically, the rhymes of the two stanzas are ABCADEDBFGFGE HHIJKKIJ. The off-rhyme is C and GG. Also, technically Auden ends with an off-rhyme of "shone" (long o) and "on" (short o), set between two other words ending in "n": "green" and "seen."

5   The five odes written in ten-or-eleven-line stanzas are "Ode on a Grecian Urn," "Ode on Indolence," "Ode on Melancholy," "Ode to a Nightingale," and "To Autumn." "Ode to Psyche" is the exception to the monostrophic odes; it fits the pseudo-Pindaric (or Cowleyean) tradition in English.

underlying meter seems to be there.

Likewise I would suggest the fourth line of each stanza seems to be a hexameter: consider the last line of the second stanza:

> The pléasant pástures, résonant wíth their stórmy chárge.

Six stresses. Despite the falling rhythms of four words in the line considered by themselves—*pleasant, pastures, resonant,* and *stormy*—the iambic meter for the line as a whole is basic, with, however, one substitution of an anapest for an iamb: the *-onant* of *resonant* followed by the accented *with*. A rhetorical reading may drop the accent on that *with*.

I have been careful to say that the first three lines of each stanza *seem* to be iambic, but I would now like to modify that, suggesting the impulse in the first line to stress the *no* is correct. Lewis is writing a longer line than is often used in English poetry. He needs to make certain that the lines do not break into smaller units, since English poetry usually consists of four-stress and five-stress lines, tetrameters and pentameters; he needs ways to emphasize his lines as units. In order to do this, he rhymes the second and third lines of each stanza to give emphasis to the lines' ends—*war* and *shore* in the first—but he also does something else to end each of those three lines. He ends each of the unindented lines with a spondee—two accents—usually but not always preceded by a pyrrhic (a contraction of the Latin *pyrrhichius*)—two unaccented syllables. The examples when this is clearest are the third line ("on a báre shóre"), the sixth ("in the greát déarth"), the ninth ("for the fírst tíme"), the tenth ("of the báy, vást"), the fifteenth ("when a dáy shóne"), and the eighteenth ("from the fár síde"). But a reader will find all of the long lines end in spondees. (The only certain example of a line in which there is only one unaccented syllable before the spondee is the second: "thóusand yéars' wár. "On the other hand, the fourteenth line has three unstressed syllables before the spondee: "délicate alárm's góne." The fifteenth line is more uncertain, partly due to it having fifteen syllables, but it also seems—rather awkwardly—to have three unstressed syllables before the spondee "Éden when a dáy shóne.") It would be easy to stress that "when," but I, at least, would then end up with eight stresses in the line. (Only in one case, to be quoted below, do I find Lewis actually having eight accents in a long line.)

It should be noted that the pyrrhic + spondee (together called an ionic foot *a minore*) shows up occasionally in iambic poetry as a substitution for two iambs, but Lewis is doing more than just an occasional substitution.

Let me now complicate the metrics one time more. I picked lines that read as iambics to illustrate the meter, but sometimes Lewis is more irregular than my statement suggests. Here is the example with what seems to be not seven but eight stresses: "Déath-shárp across greát séas, a séminal bréeze from the fár side" (l.18). Perhaps Lewis was just enjoying the writing of three spondees into one line. I have used that one line to suggest the irregularities; but, since I marked the meter of the fourth line of one stanza above, to show the nearly iambic meter, let me add markings to the other fourth lines, to show, more thoroughly, that Lewis is often to a mild degree irregular but mainly iambic:

> Are rólled in a cóld évening when thére is ráin in the áir. (l.4)

An iamb, a pyrrhic + a spondee, a fourth paeon, an iamb, and an anapest. (The accent on "there" is to set up the rhyme with "air." Otherwise, one might well accent "when.")

> They hált smélling the sált in the áir, and whínny with their líps. (l.12)

An iamb, a trochee, an iamb, an anapest, an iamb, a fourth paeon. (Although I call the first four syllables an iamb + a trochee, the effect is a spondee between two unaccented syllables. If one wants classical terminology, the four syllables become an antipast.)

> Fírst upon tóssing mánes and glóssy flánks at pláy. (l.16)

A trochee, an iamb, an iamb, an iamb, an iamb, an iamb.

> The óffer, ís it? The próphecý, of a Hóuyhnhnm's lánd? (l.20)

An iamb, an iamb, an anapest, a light iamb, an anapest, an iamb. (According to the *Oxford English Dictionary*, "Houyhnhnm" is pronounced *hwíhn⌧m*, although it looks to me as if Swift had intended three syllables—a drawn-out whinny. If so, "-hnhmn's land" would be an anapest. A word about that sudden introduction of "light iamb": the English tend to not stress the ends of polysyllabic words such as "prophecy," so I may be giving an American stress upon that ending. If so, perhaps instead the "of" following gets a mild stress, or a theoretic stress, or a rhetorical stress. Then one would call the fourth foot an anapest and the fifth an iamb, reversing the way they are noted here. Or one could call the fourth foot a pyrrhic and the fifth an anapest, making the line short one of the usual six stresses.)

My major point is that Lewis is writing, according to my scansion of the fourth lines—in which I am establishing metrical feet based on the positioning of the stresses—in a six-stress line, most often in an iambic rhythm, but always with one or more different metrical feet in a line. Scansion is something of an art, not a pure science, so another might mark the stresses differently or divide the feet differently. But I think my basic point is solid enough. Lewis, whether or not he was closely analytic about his meter, seems to have planned six stresses per fourth line and wanted enough of an iambic rhythm to fit his ear for the English language. He was not rigid about the number of syllables per line being twelve, as pure iambics would call for (cf. the chart in end-note 6). My analysis of the longer lines—those of seven stresses basically—has not been as thorough, but I believe it would have a similar result: five iambs and a pyrrhic + spondee as the underlying pattern, but with one or more variations in each line.

The third thing Lewis does to strengthen his long lines—both the heptameters and the hexameters—is build internal rhymes whenever he can manage it. They do not appear in any set pattern, but they help keep lines from breaking down into patterns simply because they unify lines without appearing regularly. In what was quoted above, "great *seas*, a seminal *breeze*, " in the eighteenth line, rhymes the stresses in the third and fifth metrical feet. In the first line, one finds "horses *stand*ing on the *sand*," rhyming the stressed syllables of the fourth and fifth feet. In the second line, "the *hou*ses fallen, a *thou*sand years' war" rhymes the stressed syllables of the third and fifth feet, as did the eighteenth. In the third line, "*graves*, and bones, and *waves*" rhymes the stressed syllables of the third and fifth feet again. In the fourth line, "*rolled* in a *cold* evening" rhymes the first and second stressed syllables. Later in that same fourth line, one finds "*there* is rain in the *air*," rhyming the fourth and sixth stressed syllables. (Not all of the subsequent lines have internal rhymes, but most do.)

These comments are intended to touch on the technical aspects which are unusual in this poem, most of them going beyond the standard versification in what is now called "formal poetry," meaning poetry with regular meter, regular stanzas if stanzas are used, and a standard amount of alliteration and assonance. I assume Lewis basically invented the form of "On a Picture by Chirico"; but, since he sometimes used forms invented by his friends, such as in his "March for Strings, Kettledrums, and Sixty-three Dwarfs "which is an adaptation of the verse form invented by J.R.R. Tolkien for his "Errantry," I may just be ignorant of the precise source. However it *does* seem rather like the long lines, reversed, of Lewis's "On the Death of Charles Williams, "which consisted of lines with three spondees in the first part, followed by two iambs and/or anapests. *That* form Lewis adapted from Owen Barfield's "The Merman" (2: 665), except that Barfield had only one foot, iambic or anapestic, after the three spondees. If this conjecture is correct, then Lewis's poem derives its form, in part, in an inverted way, from Barfield.

But one should also note that classical meters had several verse forms ending in spondees (of duration, of course, not stress): the dactylic hexameter, the scazon, and the Sapphic stanza. None of these are identical to Lewis's poem in meaningful ways. If one looks at just the last four syllables of a dactylic hexameter line, one finds two short syllables and then two long syllables, parallel to two unstressed syllables and two stresses syllables in English. But, of course, this ignores the fact that the two short syllables are only the last part of a dactyl. Lewis *could* have been influenced by those four classical syllables, but it certainly is not provable. The dactyls of the dactylic hexameter line are what he would have been taught as a boy. The scazon also has a barely possible influence. It has the same number of metrical feet as the short lines of Lewis's poem, and the scazon is normally iambic before its closing spondee. The length and the iambic aspect are interesting, but Lewis's short lines do not end in spondees—in contrast to the three longer lines in each quatrain. Perhaps Lewis's longer line could be considered as like a scazon with a pyrrhic foot inserted before the closing spondee—but that is the same as saying the longer line is *not exactly* that of a scazon. At best, the classical models of ending lines with spondees may have encourage Lewis to experiment with the accentual equivalent. (Something about the Sapphic stanza will be said below.)

The effect of the poem's artistry is intended, of course, to make the poem memorable. Auden's decision to rhyme his free verse poem "Musée des Beaux Arts" formalizes the comments about the master artists. Keats' invention of the ten-line stanza for "Ode on a Grecian Urn" enabled him to be descriptive with sensuous details, while not using a small sonnet sequence that would not have felt like stanzas in a unified poem. Because of the pentameter lines, Keats has space to ask rhetorical questions, write apostrophes to the figures on the urn, including one to the unseen town of those in the religious procession, and invent a speech by the urn at the end of the poem—in other words, to describe, to emphasize, and to elaborate rhetorically. In short, the ten lines of iambic pentameter, when combined with any needed numbers of stanzas, allowed him to develop his lyric topic in a more leisurely way than, for example, a smaller stanza would have permitted. Lewis's quatrains may hint at a classical lyric form, with three long lines and an indented line, as is done in the Sapphic stanza. But the classical poem has basically three lines of eleven syllables and a final line of five—which is far shorter than Lewis's poem with all of its lines usually running fourteen or fifteen syllables, despite the indented appearance.[6] Lewis's choice of longer lines allows him to develop his content, as will be seen, almost like a piece of fiction.

Thus, I do not come to a certain conclusion about the influences on Lewis's poetic form. The appearance of the poem, with three lines and then one indented, looks as if it is meant to suggest a larger version of the Sapphic stanza, and the use of a spondee at the end of first three lines of each stanza also hint at a classical source. But the playing with regular spondees in poems, if not at the end of lines, had been started by Barfield. (He had also used some internal rhymes, and he indented the fourth lines—a chorus—of his stanzas.) Perhaps there are other elements in the stanza-planning that I have missed.

IV. An Interpretation of Lewis's Poem

The first sentence of Lewis's "On a Picture by Chirico" is this: "Two sovereign horses standing on the sand." Perhaps Lewis was moved by one of De Chirico's paintings that was titled "The Divine Horses," "The Horses of Apollo, "or some such claim for the horses—moved to claim sovereignty for the horses in his poem. Or, possibly, as was said before, De Chirico has a painting in which he gives crowns to the two horses. The painting in which each horse has a headpiece with two large feathers comes close to this, among those located. At any rate, Lewis calls his horses "sovereign," which prepares for how the poem will end by saying the horses are "new-crown'd" (l. 19).

---

6   If one counts the syllables (not the stresses) in the lines of Lewis's poem, one is hard pressed even to say that the fourth lines of the quatrains are shorter than the long lines. By my count, the number of syllables in Lewis's lines are these:

    1—14, 2—14, 3—14, 4—15;
    5—14, 6—14, 7—16, 8—13;
    9—14, 10—15, 11—14, 12—15;
    13—14, 14—16, 15—15, 16—12;
17—15, 18—15, 19—14, 20—14.

Despite the classical appearance of Lewis's stanzas, 3 un-indented + 1 indented, Sappho's 11 + 11 + 11 + 5 is more lyrical than Lewis's longer lines.

The first two quatrains develop into a history of the future, reminding the reader that Lewis was a reader and a writer of science fiction, some of it just barely laid in the future at the time of publication, like *That Hideous Strength*, and some of it still not passed the time of its setting, like "Ministering Angels." In the poem, the first quatrain indicates that mankind is now dead after a thousand years of war, so this is the far distant future, indeed. The second stanza describes the final men as "stunted men" unable to hunt down, and then eat, these two horses. Lewis's reading of H. G. Wells's *The Time Machine* may have suggested a degenerative development—a downward evolution—of mankind. (The upward evolution of the horses is not from Wells, of course.)

The third quatrain says that the two horses "have reached the end of land"—that is, a bay with salt water is before them. And, for the one time in the poem, the month of the action is mentioned—March. Besides rhyming with "arches" later in the tenth line of the poem, the name of the month derives from Mars, the Roman god of war—and the thousand years of war makes this an appropriate month for the temporal setting. Finally, in England, from A.D. 1155 to 1751, March 25 was the start of the year, not January 1—so the name also may suggest the new beginnings, the really fresh New Year, being described in the poem. (Lewis, as a scholar writing a literary history about Britain in the sixteenth century, would have been quite conscious of March 25 as New Year's Day.) Admittedly, the poem says it is in "early March," so the actual new beginning of the year and of the horses' kingdom must await their crossing the bay.

The fourth stanza contrasts the two horses of the poem with the horses ridden today (i.e., 1949). Lewis's freedom to include his reader in a first-person reference ("we," l.13) shows the freedom of the ode form—Keats, for example, in "Ode on a Grecian Urn," in addressing the urn, says that it "tease[s] *us* out of thought" (l.44, stress added).[7] Lewis goes on to compare these two horses to the two in the Garden of Eden. This may seem to distance the poem from the science-fiction, being not a Darwinian acceptance of horses developing rather than being created. But one remembers that Lewis retold an Adam and Eve story in a scientific romance format as *Perelandra*. And, of course,

---

7   Keats also uses "our " (ll. 4) and "ours" (l. 48); the first may be a plural substitution for an authorial "my," but the second, in context, means "mankind's." Auden does not use a first person pronoun, but some of his ode is certainly colloquial: "the torturer's horse / Scratches its innocent behind on a tree" (ll. 12-13).

the comparison to the unfallen "breeding-pair in Eden" prepares for what is to follow.

The final stanza heightens the religious theme. It begins "They are called." Lewis does not say that God calls them, leaving it implicit. "Change overhangs them." Evolution, or God, is developing their ability to speak. Lewis just says, "Now their neighing is half speech." That is, they are becoming rational beings. And all of this is in the first line of the stanza. The predicted leaving of "the places where Man[kind] died" suggests a new beginning for the horses, and Lewis ends with an allusion to the Fourth Voyage of *Gulliver's Travels*. Lewis knew, of course, that those voyages to undiscovered areas of the Earth's globe were the forerunners of modern science fiction, which substitutes far planets for far Earthen lands.

This pair of changed horses, then, are equivalent to Adam and Eve. Readers of Lewis may remember the "Socratic myth" that Lewis offers in the fifth chapter of *The Problem of Pain* about mankind's evolution; it begins:

> For long centuries God perfected the animal form which was to become the vehicle of humanity and the image of Himself. He gave it . . . jaws and teeth and throat capable of articulation, and a brain sufficiently complex to execute all the material motions whereby rational thought is incarnated. The creature may have existed for ages in this state before it became [the equivalent of] man. . . . Then, in the fullness of time, God caused to descend upon this organism, both on its psychology and physiology, a new kind of consciousness which could say "I" and "me," which could look upon itself as an object, which knew God, which could make judgements of truth, beauty, and goodness, and which was so far above time that it could perceive time flowing past. (65)[8]

Likewise, readers of Lewis will remember Aslan's gazing on and breathing on pairs of animals in *The Magician's Nephew*, with a flash of something like fire, making them Talking Animals (113-14). And some of the readers of Lewis may remember his letter of 10 January 1952 to Sister Penelope, a nun in the Community of St. Mary the Virgin, Wantage, Oxfordshire, to whom Lewis wrote that he also "had pictured Adam as being, physically, the son of two anthropoids, on whom, after birth, God worked the miracle which made him Man …" (3: 156). The passage in *The Problem of Pain* suggests the ages of

---

[8] My thanks to Charlie W. Starr who reminded me of Lewis's Socratic myth in *The Problem of Pain*.

development, that in *The Magician's Nephew*, although it speeds up the process, shows that a variety of animals may become the equivalent of Adam and Eve, and the third, again in a speeded-up process, reinforces the prior animality of Adam. None are a new creation from the dust; all are influenced in a general way by Darwinian imagery (not, of course, in a non-religious way). It is in this context that the development of the poem's horses may be understood. The "new kind of consciousness" seems to have not descended on them since "their neighing is [only] half speech," but that development clearly is close.

If Lewis were thoroughly developing his poem as science fiction, he would have had to answer some questions that he does not raise. The major one: how were the two horses to get across the bay, or to another land mass perhaps, when there is no suggestion of their having a boat or the equivalent of hands to build one? Perhaps Lewis simply remembered how Gulliver first saw a Houyhnhnm hold a root "between his hoof and pastern" (Swift, ch. 2; cf. a fuller discussion in ch.9). Obviously, although Lewis is using science-fictional material, his major concern is with it as a parable, not as an end, in and of itself.

Let me return to the form of the poem. Although this discussion so far may have sounded like a typical summary of content, such as is done sometimes by people having problems doing anything but echoing back what a writer has already said, I hope that, beyond such details as the implications of March, this survey has also suggested how carefully Lewis has developed steps in his use of the quatrains. In the first, he introduced the two horses and gave the basic fictional background of the long-lasting war and the dying off of mankind. In the second he discusses the survival of the two horses to this point. In the third he establishes their presence by the bay. In the fourth he contrasts these two horses with horses at present and, in a comparison, refers to horses in Eden. In the fifth, he suggests these horses are to be the replacement of mankind. (Incidentally, this is not the only science-fictional work that has discussed mankind's replacement in this world. One example, if one ignores its final twist, is Alfred Bester's story "Adam and No Eve.") But the point is, Lewis is organizing by quatrains, not doing a simple narrative, for which some type of verse without breaks would be appropriate—blank verse, heroic couplets, or the type of iambic hexameter couplets which Lewis used in his (partial) translation of Vergil's *Aeneid*. This organizational emphasis may not be the most important part of a poem's artistry, but it nevertheless adds to the effectiveness of the poem.

One can also notice Lewis's use of imagery to make his points as a legitimate part of his skill. The thousand years of war concludes, he says, "in charnel, graves, and bones, and waves on a bare shore" (1.3). The bay, with "falling arches"—presumably the bridges of the earlier time—is "vast / And empty in bitter sunset light, where once the ships passed"(10-11).[9] The horses ridden in the present time have an "old look / Of half-indignant melancholy and delicate alarm" (ll.13-14). I leave it to others who have ridden more horses than I to pass judgment on Lewis's summary of equine attitudes, but as a suggestion of a suppressed race it does well. The pair of horses in Eden had "tossing manes and glossy flanks at play" (1.16). (Since the poem refers to the horses as a "breeding pair," this use of "play" may be, but need not be, sexual.) Even if Lewis is often considered didactic, he knew that good poetry is built on images, not on generalizations, perhaps especially not on moral generalizations. Longfellow's "The Psalm of Life" belongs to the Victorian Age, not the second half of the twentieth century with its Imagistic tradition.

However if "On a Picture by Chirico" is only a versified, and nicely written, scientific romance, then it has a certain type of aesthetic appeal and, perhaps, historical interest within the science-fictional community. But I want to approach the question of the importance of the poem through some comparisons and classifications and then a clearer statement of the poem's meaning.

I have said that "On a Picture by Chirico" is an example of an ekphrastic poem. That, by itself, does not guarantee its value, for not all ekphrastic verses are major works. Alastair Fowler names over twenty-five modern poems which contain descriptions of paintings or photographs (115-118). I will not name the poets, but it is unlikely, the more writers one has in a genre, or subgenre, that all of them will be important. Also, I have compared Lewis's poem to "Ode on a Grecian Urn," and Lewis's poem may be considered an ode—in the general sense of an important lyric, in the tradition of Pindar and Horace, if its readers can agree it is important enough. At least, the typical structure of Pindar's surviving odes has a mythic narrative in the middle, so there is nothing unlike an ode in Lewis's poem being narrative; and the scientific-romance content may be considered as a modern "myth"—a narrative presentation of a modern world view. This is the *Weltanschauung* presented in Wells' evolutionary degeneration of mankind into the Eloi and the Morlocks and eventual disappearance of all humans. Species develop and species die off.

---

9   "Falling arches" unfortunately echoes the podiatric "fallen arches."

Further, the writing of "On a Picture by Chirico" in a series of stanzas does not outlaw it from being an ode, any more than Keats's poem is ruled out. Seven of Pindar's odes are monostrophic. So, to some degree by content, by form, by tradition, Lewis's poem is within the possible classification of an ode. I realize that this discussion of whether Lewis's poem can be called an ode is a trivial argument over terminology outside of two points, still to be argued. The second, to be developed starting in the next paragraph, is whether the poem is significant enough in what it says. But the first point is that Lewis was concerned with Pindar at the same time as he wrote his ekphrasis. That is, in the same year, 1949, as Lewis wrote "On a Picture by Chirico," he wrote his long poem titled "Arrangement of Pindar" in eighty-three unrhymed lines. I do not attempt to analyze its meter, but the lines are long—the first line runs sixteen syllables. The poem opens describing the young men dancing Pindar's ode (the word "ode" is not used, and no attempt to shape a strophe, antistrophe, epode pattern is made); the closing lines speak of the audience for the ode; the long middle sections recreate an example of Pindar's content. Lewis is able to present a moral statement in terms of Greek mythology; perhaps the most important passage is when Herakles is seized with "sweet desire" upon looking upon the trees of Hyperborea (ll. 49-55)—although Pindar says madness is the result of longing for that place (l. 58). Lewis's understanding of *Sehnsucht* and Pindar's, as Lewis presents him, are opposed. Nevertheless, "Arrangement of Pindar" shows that Lewis thought in terms of the significance of the classical ode during his time of writing the ekphrasis.[10]

But is "On a Picture by Chirico" important enough? I think there is a way to consider the meaningfulness of the poem. One of the striking things about Don W. King's recent collection of Lewis's poems is that one can now, fairly easily, compare Lewis's poems written and published about the same time. I am interested in the poems published soon after World War II, since "On a Picture by Chirico" appeared in *The Spectator* in 1949. Here are the ones I find most meaningful for my purpose. "On the Atomic Bomb (Metrical

---

10   Lewis thought of Williams's *Taliessin through Logres* as being Pindaric. He mentions the comparison briefly at the end of a 1945 obituary ("Charles Walter Stansby Williams," 148) and in a 1946 review of *Taliessin through Logres* ("Charles Williams," 137); but his clearest statement of the comparison comes in a review of *Taliessin through Logres* before World War II, in 1938 ("A Sacred Poem," 125, 135). These page citations are from the collection of Lewis's reviews, *Image and Imagination*.

Experiment" (pp. 335-36) says that mortals have known they had to die, sooner or later; the Bomb has not brought death in the world for the first time. "On Receiving Bad News" (p. 336) does not define the news but offers a comparison of the receiver to a tired horse not yet close to its stable. "Consolation" (pp. 336-37) ironically celebrates England's appeasement of Communist Russia after the war. "Pan's Purge" (pp. 342-43) tells of the wiping out of the current civilization in which men had taken full control of nature; in it, unlike "On a Picture by Chirico," some small numbers of humans were allowed to survive Pan's destruction of the warped culture—also, the poem is parallel to some elements of *That Hideous Strength* of about the same time (the cleansing carried out by Pan instead of the Oyéresu). "Dangerous Oversight" (pp. 344-45) tells of a "merry-hearted" king who was defeated by his enemies, driven back to "a small river-isle" (l.14), and finally killed by his enemies' cannons ("the grey batteries spoke," l.22). (This example will be returned to.) The first two of these four were written and published in 1945; the third was perhaps written in 1945 and certainly published in 1946; the fourth was perhaps written in 1946 or 1947 and certainly published in 1947; the fifth was written and published in 1947. "On a Picture by Chirico" was written and published slightly later—in 1949.

In short, I believe "On a Picture by Chirico" is a post-World War II poem which reflects, in its thousand-year war, the century of two World Wars and England's losses—both of men in the First and of much of the city of London and other bombed areas in the Second. Rationing and scarcity continued after the Second, which had ended with two atomic explosions. Those Bombs suggested any future war would involve the complete destruction of all large cities and massive numbers of people. Lewis's poem on the Atomic Bomb involves a sort of Stoic acceptance of the weapon—he says it is not up to destroying the whole world—but only predicts a future of more wars. The other poems suggest various disasters or failures. "On a Picture by Chirico," in particular, suggests the sequence of wars will end by wiping out mankind. In short, the years after World War II were not happy times in England, and a number of Lewis's poems of the period reflect this. A somber facing of death, a passing of expectations, a failing of hope that the future will be better—are not these the materials for a great ode?

"Dangerous Oversight" is like "On a Picture by Chirico" in a special way: both of them avoid, in different ways, a complete downbeat ending. "Dangerous Oversight" sets up its merry monarch who is defeated in a series of battles and finally is killed (with his queen, his fool, and his chaplain) on his river island—the island may be meant to suggest Britain, also an island and also bombarded, in one way or another, during World War II. But Lewis has a "tree fair-fruited" growing from their dead, "unpolluted flesh" (ll. 25-26). The last three quatrains (of the nine in the poem) describe this tree growing taller than the "Alps and Andes" (l. 32); its shadow is "poison to the evil-eyed" (1.34). Thus, belatedly, the enemies of the king are killed. Perhaps there is some specific myth or poem that Lewis has in mind, but I do not recognize it. Of course, in some endings of the ballad "Barbara Allen," briars and roses grow from separate graves and eventually intertwine; but that is a relatively small celebration of a human love. That Lewis compares the tree's "smell and taste" to those of Eden (ll. 27-28) suggests this is meant to be a gaining of immortality (through the Tree of Life) despite death in this world—but that tied to the death of the enemies seems unusual. If this is meant to be the Day of Judgment, the tree is a non-Biblical image. The resolution with mankind's complete defeat in this world in "On a Picture by Chirico" likewise has a reference to Eden—for the origin of horses. But it is not so much a Last Judgment poem as a Start Over poem. At any rate, both of these works go beyond the death of a joyous, almost Chestertonian king and the death of the remnants of humankind to a celebration—of a tree, of two horses.

I do not know if an anthology of post-World War II poems has ever been published as a book of residual-war poems. If it were, of course, the publishers would want to collect poems that actually referred to the war, as looking back at it, and "On the Atomic Bomb (Metrical Experiment)" certainly would be appropriate. But if a metaphoric or symbolic way of dealing with the war and post-war were allowed, then Lewis's "On a Picture by Chirico" would be just as appropriate. His ode suggests a complete despair over mankind's tendency to fight one war after another—that is, the despair is complete—unless, like Gulliver, one admires the Houyhnhnms.

Works Cited

Auden, W. H. "Musée des Beaux Arts." *Collected Poems*. Ed. Edward Mendelson. New York: Random House, 1976. 146-47.

Barfield, Owen. "The Merman." *A Barfield Sampler: Poetry and Fiction by Owen Barfield*. Ed. Jeanne Clayton Hunter and Thomas Kranidas. Albany: State University of New York, 1993. 45-46.

Bester, Alfred. "Adam and No Eve. " Originally published in *Astounding Science-Fiction* in 1941. Collected in *Starburst*. New York: Signet Books, 1958.

Casley, Cath, Collections Manager, Department of Western Art, Ashmolean Museum of Art and Archaeology, Oxford. Email to Joe R. Christopher. 10 May 2016.

Fowler, Alastair. *Kinds of Literature: An Introduction to the Theory of Genres and Modes*. Oxford: Clarendon Press, 1982.

Hooper, Walter. "Introduction" to *They Stand Together: The Letters of C. S. Lewis to Arthur Greeves (1914-1963)*. New York: Macmillan, 1979. 9-38.

Keats, John. "Ode on a Grecian Urn." 1819. Widely available.

King, Don W. (ed.). *The Collected Poems of C. S. Lewis: A Critical Edition*. Kent, Ohio: The Kent State University Press, 2015.

Lewis, C. S. "Arrangement of Pindar." King, 363-65.

---. *Collected Letters: Books, Broadcasts and War 1931-1949*. Vol. II. Ed. Walter Hooper. London: Harper Collins, 2004.

---. *Collected Letters: Family Letters 1905-1931*. Vol. I. Ed. Walter Hooper. London: Harper Collins, 2000.

---. *Collected Letters: Narnia, Cambridge and Joy 1950-1963*. Vol. III. Ed. Walter Hooper. London: Harper Collins, 2006.

---. *The Collected Poems of C. S. Lewis: A Critical Edition*. See King.

---. *C. S. Lewis's Lost Aeneid: Arms and the Exile*. Ed. A. T. Reyes. Foreword by Walter Hooper. Preface by D. O. Ross. New Haven and London: Yale University Press, 2011.

---. "Dangerous Oversight." King, pp. 344-345.

---. *English Literature in the Sixteenth Century, Excluding Drama*. The Oxford History of English Literature, Vol. III. Oxford: Clarendon Press, 1954.

---. *Image and Imagination: Essays and Reviews by C. S. Lewis.* Ed. Walter Hooper. Cambridge: Cambridge University Press, 2013.

---. *The Magician's Nephew.* London: The Bodley Head, 1955.

---. "March for Strings, Kettledrums, and Sixty-three Dwarfs." King, 470.

---. "Ministering Angels." *"The Dark Tower" and Other Stories.* Ed. Walter Hooper. London: Collins, 1977. 112-123.

---. "On a Picture by Chirico." King, 362.

---. "On Receiving Bad News." King, 336.

---. "On the Atomic Bomb (Metrical Experiment)." King, 335.

---. "On the Death of Charles Williams." King, 334.

---. "Pan's Purge." King, 342.

---. *The Problem of Pain.* London: Geoffrey Bles, 1940.

---. *Spenser's Images of Life.* Ed. Alastair Fowler. Cambridge: At the University Press, 1967.

---. *That Hideous Strength: A Modern Fairy-Tale for Grown-Ups.* New York: Macmillan, 1946.

E. M. W. Tillyard. *The Personal Heresy: A Controversy.* London: Oxford UP, 1939.

Swift, Jonathan. *Travels into Several Remote Nations of the World. In Four Parts. By Lemuel Gulliver, First a Surgeon, and then a Captain of several Ships.* "Part 4. A Voyage to the Country of the Houyhnhnms." (1726, 1735.) Many editions.

Tolkien, J. R. R. "Errantry" *"The Adventures of Tom Bombadil" and other verses from* The Red Book, *with Illustrations by Pauline Baynes.* London: George Allen and Unwin, 1962. 24-27.

Wells, H[erbert] G[eorge]. *The Time Machine.* (1895.) Many editions.

Strange Bedfellows:
C.S. Lewis and Fred Hoyle

By Kristine Larsen

> Kristine Larsen is Professor of Astronomy at Central Connecticut State University. She is the author of *Stephen Hawking: A Biography* and *Cosmology 101*, and co-editor of *The Mythological Dimensions of Doctor Who* and *The Mythological Dimensions of Neil Gaiman*.

In a May 15, 1952 letter to Genia Goelz, a recent convert to Christianity, C. S. Lewis urges "If Hoyle answers your letter, then let the correspondence drop. He is not a great philosopher (and none of my scientific colleagues think much of him as a scientist)" (*Letters* 3: 192). Lewis goes on to explain that Hoyle "is strong enough to do some harm. You're not David and no one has told you to fight Goliath! You've only just enlisted. Don't go off challenging enemy champions" (Ibid.). Editor Walter Hooper's footnote to the letter explains "Sir Fred Hoyle (1915-2001) was Plumian Professor of Astronomy at Cambridge University, and the founder of the Institute of Theoretical Astronomy" (Ibid.). This hardly sounds like an "enemy champion," which begs the question of who was Fred Hoyle, what did he do to incur Lewis's apparent ire, and did his scientific colleagues really think so little of him? These are the questions I will endeavor to answer in this essay; in addition, I will also posit that, ironically, Lewis turned to Hoyle's astronomy when crafting one of his own famous works of fiction.

It is necessary to begin with an overview of the astronomy in question. Our sun is currently a middle of the road main sequence star, contently generating energy by converting hydrogen into helium in its core, as it has been doing for the past 4.6 billion years. In about 6 billion years the core will be entirely composed of helium, and the sun will begin to die. The outer layers of hydrogen will swell up and engulf the inner planets, possibly including earth. Even if its tenuous gaseous envelope does not reach our orbit, our oceans will boil, the surface of our planet will return to the molten state of its formation, and all life on our planet will be destroyed (Schroder and Smith). The sun will become a so-called red giant because, as the name implies, it will be red in color and titanic in size. Simultaneously, the core of the sun will become hotter, as it shrinks under its own gravity, until the helium eventually reaches a temperature sufficient to begin fusing into carbon and then oxygen. Eventually the core will collapse into a dense corpse the size of the earth, creating a white dwarf, and the outer layers of gas will puff off into space, creating a so-called planetary nebula. If the sun had been born with more mass, it would have the ability to fuse oxygen into heavier elements before dying, perhaps hopscotching down the periodic table as far as iron. But no star can fuse iron, so the heaviest of stars actually explode in a supernova, and in these cosmic conflagrations all the elements heavier than iron are formed. Fred Hoyle played a seminal role in determining many of the details in what has just been explained. Although Hoyle's most famous papers on the subjects of red giants and stellar nucleosynthesis were published in 1955 and 1957, respectively (Hoyle and Schwarzschild; Burbidge et al.), and the popular level book describing the evolution of stars in minute detail, *Frontiers of Astronomy*, appeared in 1955, several years after Lewis's letter, many of the important details were already in place by 1950 (Hoyle and Lyttleton "Structure"; Hoyle "Synthesis"), and, as will be described, had been widely shared with the general public.

This relatively late date for the birth of the modern model of star formation has escaped the notice of many scholars outside of astronomy. For example, in H.G. Wells's *The Time Machine*, the narrator travels millions of years into the future to witness the death of our planet. The sun is described as a "huge, red-hot dome" that "had come to obscure nearly a tenth part of the darkling heavens" (84). This description has erroneously led many a literary critic to assume that this is a description of the sun as a dying red giant. However, it is instead a rather accurate depiction of the sun having cooled to a red *dwarf*, with the earth having spiraled into a much closer orbit, the result being the larger *apparent* size of our star. This is a reflection of the erroneous model of stellar evolution popular in the late 1800s, in which all stars are born as large hot, blue-white main sequence stars, and shrink and cool over their lives, ultimately forming a red dwarf (Eddington 106).

But after the discovery of the existence of red giants in the early 20th century and the resolution of the physics behind the tiny, ultra-dense white dwarfs about a decade afterwards, the model of stellar evolution was modified. Circa 1925 it was thought that stars collapsed from clouds of gas to form swollen red giants, further shrank to become hot main sequence stars, and then continued to shrink and cool over time, ultimately dying as a dim red dwarf before further imploding to become a white dwarf (Eddington 107).

This model is reflected the science fiction of the day, including the novels of Olaf Stapledon. In *Last and First Men* (1930) it is said that the sun would ultimately die by "shrinking to a minute, dense grain with feeble radiation… a typical 'white dwarf'" (240), while in *Star Maker* (1937) it is noted that during its youth, a star "is what human astronomers call a 'red giant'," and afterwards the star shrinks to the smaller "state in which our sun now is" (143). Both works were not only read by Lewis, but were very influential on him. For example, in a 1938 letter to Roger Lancelyn Green, Lewis explains that he was "spurred" to write *Out of the Silent Planet* by Stapledon's *Last and First Men* and geneticist J.B.S. Haldane's *Possible Worlds* (Lewis *Letters* 2: 236). We also see this model of stellar evolution (along with a nod to the ultimate heat death of the universe) in Lewis's 1944 lecture "Is Theology Poetry": "The sun will cool—all suns will cool—the whole universe will run down" (Hooper 149).

But there is another avenue of astrophysical research for which Fred Hoyle was known circa 1950, namely the so-called "Steady State" model of the universe, proposed independently by Hoyle and two fellow Cambridge scientists, Herman Bondi and Thomas Gold in 1948 as an alternative to the Big Bang model (then called the Evolutionary model). As the name implies, the Steady State posits that the universe had no beginning and remains in a permanent unchanging state (although, of course, individual stars are born and die). But the apparent motion of the galaxies away from each other (as discovered through their redshifts by Hubble and others in the 1920s) was compelling evidence, and would make the density of the universe decrease over time—unless, as the Steady State claimed, new atoms of hydrogen are spontaneously created at just the right rate to keep the density of the universe constant. This appears to violate the crucial law of conservation of matter/energy in the universe, unless some new physics is invoked.

Historian of science Helge Kragh reports that at the first public discussion of the Steady State, a December 1948 meeting of the Royal Astronomical Society, the overall response by the scientific community was "reluctant, but not unambiguously hostile" (189). This reaction was due, in part, to the fact that the idea of the spontaneous creation of matter was not original to the Steady State, and had been suggested (albeit briefly) in the unorthodox cosmological models of Oxford astrophysicist Edward Arthur Milne. But Milne voiced clear skepticism at this so-called "New Cosmology," as did many other scientists. Outside of Britain, the Steady State was barely on the scientific radar (Kragh 223). Over the 1950s and 60s, experimental and observational evidence continued to pile up for the Big Bang and against the Steady State, although to his dying day Fred Hoyle rejected the Big Bang and continued to propose alternative explanations for the observed redshift of the galaxies (Mitton 314).

In fact, the Steady State might have died a quiet death long before Lewis's letter if it hadn't been for the BBC, who asked Hoyle (after producing controversial yet engaging talks for the network in previous years [Mitton 125-32]) to deliver a series of five 45-minute long astronomy programs on their *Third Programme* broadcast in January and February 1950. It proved so popular that a book treatment, entitled *The Nature of the Universe*, appeared to strong sales only two months later. The lectures were later rebroadcast over the summer, in a slightly different format, to an estimated audience of 3 million on the popular BBC *Home Service* broadcast (Kraugh 191).

Hoyle used his lectures as a vehicle through which to pitch both his own model of the evolution of stars—including the now correct positioning of red giants as near the end of a star's life rather than the beginning—and the Steady State. Hoyle also used the lectures to espouse his personal beliefs about extraterrestrial life. For example, in the very first lecture, he makes the bold statement (without evidence) that "I would say that rather more than a million stars in the Milky Way possess planets on which you might live without undue discomfort"(*Nature of the Universe* 21). Interestingly, there simultaneously existed three different versions of Hoyle's series. In the printed script, published not long after each initial broadcast in the magazine *The Listener*, Hoyle launches into an attack on religion, which he describes as "a blind attempt to find an escape from the truly dreadful situation in which we find ourselves. Here we are in this wholly fantastic Universe with scarcely a clue as to whether our existence has any real significance" (Mitton 134; Hoyle *Nature of the Universe* 115). Rubbing salt into the wound even further, the atheist Hoyle adds in the book version "I should like to end by discussing in a little more detail the beliefs of the Christians as I see them myself. In their anxiety to avoid the notion that death is the complete end of our existence, they suggest what is to me an equally horrible alternative. . . . [W]hat the Christians offer me is an eternity of frustration" (*Nature of the Universe* 117).

Helge Kragh opines that "Hoyle's attack on Christianity undoubtedly aroused antagonistic feelings in many people and helped to make Hoyle a controversial figure" (192). Lewis's obvious disdain for Hoyle would have put him in excellent company at this juncture, as both scientists and theologians openly attacked Hoyle. For example, Father Daniel O'Connell, Director of the Vatican Observatory, called Hoyle "naïve" and "remarkably foolish" during a three-night-long discussion on Australian Radio (Kragh 195). No less than "honorary Inkling" Dorothy Sayers voiced her own radio critique on the BBC *Home Service*. As an invited speaker, Sayers took the opportunity to attack Hoyle's views on science and religion in general, and the Christian afterlife in particular. She admonishes that "the scientist should beware of too childlike a credulity about data: they may be literally 'data', things given—clues (or red herrings) handed out to him, to look as though he had found them" (497).

But what of Lewis's claim that Hoyle had a dubious scientific reputation overall? A review of *The Nature of the Universe* by Kirtley Mather of the Geology Department of Harvard calls Hoyle "a brilliant young Cambridge University astronomer who displays a commendable flair for presenting intricate data and mind-stretching ideas in a lucid, attractive style" but warns that the book "should be read with great caution," pointing out several topics where Hoyle "writes dogmatically" and "overreaches" (427-28). Hoyle's estimate for the number of habitable planets in the galaxy is described as being built on "a precarious inverted pyramid of speculation piled on speculation after speculation, interlarded with slippery assumptions" (Mather 428). University of Toronto astronomer Ralph Williamson notes in his review that Hoyle is "Brilliant and highly trained in mathematics and astronomy," but warns that "many scientists have severely criticized Dr. Hoyle's current series of lectures," the criticism based on "the deeper issue of the truth or falsity of the material discussed" (185–86). Hoyle's chief crime, according to Williamson, is his failure to be impartial in his "presentation of scientific fact" (186). Williamson actually takes the time to do a statistical analysis of Hoyle's claims, finding them to be "about 20 per cent. pure fact, about 30 per cent. of working hypotheses, and the remaining 50 per cent. was devoted to pure, untested theory. It will not surprise you, at this point, to hear that the theory was, almost without exception, Hoyle's own" (188). Hoyle was therefore recognized as a brilliant, if not controversial, member of the professional astronomical community, a reputation that became even more schizophrenic over the subsequent decades. For example, it is well-known that most of the groundbreaking research on the synthesis of heavier elements inside stars reported in the pioneering 1957 Burbidge et al. paper was done by Hoyle. Yet, it was William

Fowler who received the 1983 Nobel Prize for the research, not Hoyle, a decision that has led more than one author to suggest that the snub was due to Hoyle's troubled relationship with his peers (McKie).

Lewis himself publically took Hoyle to task a number of years after the radio broadcasts, specifically attacking Hoyle's unsubstantiated claims about the likelihood of extraterrestrial life, as well as Hoyle's open hostility towards Christianity. In the 1958 essay, "Will We Lose God in Outer Space" (later named "Religion and Rocketry"), Lewis reflects that when he was a child, the predominant scientific opinion was that extraterrestrial life is highly unlikely:

> Probably life was a purely terrestrial abnormality. We were alone in an infinite desert. Which just showed the absurdity of the Christian idea that there was a Creator who was interested in living creatures. But then came Professor F.B. Hoyle, the Cambridge cosmologist, and in a fortnight or so everyone I met seemed to have decided that the universe was probably quite well provided with inhabitable globes and with livestock to inhabit them. Which just showed (equally well) the absurdity of Christianity with its parochial idea that Man could be important to God. (*World's Last Night* 83)

In "Onward, Christian Spacemen" (1963), also known as "The Seeing Eye," Lewis likewise opines

> When we were boys all astronomers, so far as I know, impressed upon us the antecedent improbabilities of life in any part of the universe whatever. It was not thought unlikely that this earth was the solitary exception to a universal reign of the inorganic. Now Professor Hoyle, and many with him, say that in so vast a universe life must have occurred in times and places without number. The interesting thing is that I have heard both these estimates used as arguments against Christianity (*The Seeing Eye* 235).

Lewis's summary of the scientific establishment's view of extraterrestrial life in the early 20th century is simplistic, but not entirely incorrect. For example, in *The Universe Around Us* (1930), Sir James Jeans (whose popularized works Lewis was not only familiar with, but recommended [*Letters* 2: 1011]) writes "Apart from the certain knowledge that life exists on earth, we have no definite knowledge whatever except that, at the best, life must be limited to a tiny fraction of the universe" (331). This rather pessimistic viewpoint is largely fueled by the then current tidal model of planetary formation, which relies on a passing star to rip material out of a star in order to form planets (Jeans 328). However, Lewis's childhood years were also the time when American amateur astronomer Percival Lowell was publishing a series of popular books claiming that there had been (and perhaps still might be) intelligent life on Mars, as the existence of the so-called Martian canals was not debunked by observational astronomers until the 1909 observing season (Crowe 509).

It is important to note that not all scientists of Lewis's generation were atheists; indeed, to the contrary, there were devout Christians within astrophysical circles, including the aforementioned Oxford astrophysicist Edward Arthur Milne. In a series of lectures written shortly before his death in September 1950 that were never publically delivered but instead published in 1952, Milne criticizes the Steady State model on theological grounds. He argues that it could not be consistent with an Almighty creator, as it relegates creation to merely the "routine production, with penny-in-the-slot regularity and monotony, of hydrogen atoms" (77). Milne also believes that that the concept of Christ having to die on the cross on an infinite number of habitable words is too horrific to contemplate; therefore it happened only once, on our world. Perhaps we were the only world who needed saving, or in the future humanity may spread the gospel to all possible fallen worlds through radio astronomy (153-54). Compare this to Lewis's statement in "Religion and Rocketry": "It may be that Redemption, starting with us, is meant to work from us and through us…. Only if we had some such function would a contact between us and such unknown races be other than a calamity" (*World's Last Night* 88). Milne was ill during the time of the rebroadcast of Hoyle's lectures, and therefore could not join the subsequent condemnation, although Hoyle biographer Simon Mitton describes Milne as "ever a stern critic of Hoyle" (125).

It is unknown to this writer what direct interactions, if any, Lewis had with either Hoyle or Milne. Given the myriad references to Milne's work, not only in scientific but more mundane circles (Kragh 64-65), it would have been nearly impossible for Lewis not to have had at least a passing knowledge of his work. In addition, the three men were in relatively close geographical proximity as academics. It is also interesting to note the timing of Lewis's public attack on Hoyle in "Will we lose God in outer space" (1958), coming in the same year that Hoyle was appointed to the prestigious Plumian Chair at Cambridge, and one year after the publication of Hoyle's commercially successful science fiction novel, *The Black Cloud*, in which a sentient cloud of interstellar gas particles threatens life on earth. At this point, Lewis had been on the faculty of Magdalene College at Cambridge for several years, and most certainly would have had the opportunity to meet Hoyle, if he had chosen to. Similarly there had certainly been opportunities for Lewis and Milne to interact professional or socially, if Lewis had wished it, as Milne had been the Rouse Ball Professor of Mathematics at Oxford, from 1929 until his death in 1950.

Having answered the three questions posed at the start of this essay, we now explore how Lewis ultimately found himself apparently needing Hoyle (or at least his astronomy) in crafting his world of Narnia. Lewis retorted to a complaint by scientist J.B.S. Haldane about the inaccuracy of the science in the Ransom Trilogy that "I needed for my purpose just enough popular astronomy to create in 'the common reader' a 'willing suspension of disbelief'.... There is thus a great deal of scientific falsehood in my stories: some of it known to be false even by me when I wrote the books" (*Of Other Worlds* 76). It is well established that Lewis knew quite a bit of astronomy, not only about the visible night sky, but the history of astronomy (Paxford 126; Lewis *Discarded Image*). His descriptions of the surface of Venus in *Perelandra* are indeed fantastical and original, but do pay homage to scientific presumptions about the Cytherean environment circa 1940 (Dozois xii-xiv).

The astronomical references to Hoyle's work are associated with the deaths of stars in the universe of Narnia, as described in the novels *The Magician's Nephew* (1955) and *The Last Battle* (1956). Despite the fact that Roger Lancelyn Green recalls having been read part of an early draft of *The Magician's Nephew* in 1949, he did not see a completed manuscript until early 1954 (Ward 306). Therefore both novels were essentially written after the infamous radio broadcasts of Hoyle and the publication of *The Nature of the Universe* in 1950. In the first novel, readers visit the dying world of Charn, whose sun is clearly and unequivocally described as an old, dying red giant:

> Low down and near the horizon hung a great, red sun, far bigger than our sun. Digory felt at once that it was also older than ours: a sun near the end of its life, weary if looking down upon that world.... "Was it the Deplorable Word that made the sun like that?" asked Digory.... "So big, so red, so cold."
>
> "It has always been so," said Jadis. "At least, for hundreds of thousands of years. Have you a different sort of sun in your world?"
>
> "Yes, it's smaller and yellower. And it gives a good deal more heat."

The Queen gave a long drawn "A-a-ah!. . ... yours is a younger world" (29-30).

At the end of Narnia, as depicted in *The Last Battle*, that world's sun also becomes a red giant: "Lord Digory and the Lady Polly looked at one another and gave a little nod: those two, in a different world, had once seen a dying star.... It was three times—twenty times—as big as it ought to be, and very dark red" (515).

This bloated behemoth of a sun is then squeezed out of existence into the feeble ember of a white dwarf, leaving the night sky utterly black and cold, not by gravity, but the hand of a giant. The symbolism of a giant forming a white dwarf is simply too perfect to be accidental. Given that the concept of red giants as the end points of stars was largely due to the work of Fred Hoyle in the late 1940s, and would have been all but unknown to the non-scientist save for Hoyle's infamous lectures and the resulting book, Lewis apparently either didn't think so little of Hoyle's science after all, or was pandering to his audience's fascination with and knowledge of Hoyle's lectures. He freely admitted in his response to Haldane's criticism that he didn't feel compelled to use real science, but yet, strangely, in this case, it appears he did.

WORKS CITED

Burbidge, E. Margaret, G.R. Burbidge, William A. Fowler, and F. Hoyle. "Synthesis of the Elements in Stars." *Reviews of Modern Physics* 29.4 (1957): 547-650. *NASA Astrophysics Data System*. Web. 15 Jan. 2016.

Crowe, Michael J., ed. *The Extraterrestrial Life Debate*. Notre Dame: University of Notre Dame Press, 2008. Print.

DeVorkin, David. "The Changing Place of Red Giant Stars in the Evolutionary Process." *Journal for the History of Astronomy* 37 (2006): 429-469. Print.

Dozois, Gardner. "Return to Venusport." *Old Venus*. Ed. George R.R. Martin and Gardner Dozois. New York: Bantam Books, 2015. xi-xvii. Print.

Eddington, A.S. *Stars and Atoms*. 2nd ed. New Haven: Yale University Press, 1927. Print.

Hooper, Walter. "Oxford's Bonny Fighter." *C.S. Lewis at the Breakfast Table and Other Reminiscences*. Ed. James T. Como. San Diego: Harcourt Brace and Company, 1992. 137-185. Print.

Hoyle, Fred. *The Black Cloud*. 1957. New York: Signet Books, 1962. Print.

---. *Frontiers of Astronomy*. London: Harper Collins, 1955. Print.

---. *The Nature of the Universe*. Oxford: Basic Blackwell, 1950. Print.

---. "The Synthesis of the Elements From Hydrogen." *Monthly Notices of the Royal Astronomical Society* 106 (1946): 343-383. *NASA Astrophysics Data System*. Web. 15 Jan. 2016.

Hoyle, Fred, and R.A. Lyttleton. "On the Nature of Red Giant Stars." *Monthly Notices of the Royal Astronomical Society* 102 (1942): 218-225. *NASA Astrophysics Data System*. Web. 15 Jan. 2016.

"The Structure of Stars of Non-uniform Composition." *Monthly Notices of the Royal Astronomical Society* 109 (1949): 614-630. *NASA Astrophysics Data System*. Web. 15 Jan. 2016.

Hoyle, Fred, and Martin Schwarzschild. "On the Evolution of Type II Stars." *Astrophysical Journal Supplement 2* (1955): 1-40. *NASA Astrophysics Data System*. Web. 15 Jan. 2016.

Jeans, Sir James. *The Universe Around Us*. Rev. ed. New York: Macmillan, 1933. Print.

Kragh, Helge. *Cosmology and Controversy*. Princeton: Princeton University Press, 1996. Print.

Lewis, C.S. *The Collected Letters,*. Ed. Walter Hooper. *Vol 2*. San Francisco: Harper Collins, 2004. Print.

---. *The Collected Letters, Vol III*. Ed. Walter Hooper. San Francisco: Harper Collins, 2007. Print.

---. *The Complete Chronicles of Narnia*. New York: Harper Collins, 2000. Print.

---. *The Discarded Image*. Cambridge: Cambridge University Press, 1964. Print.

---. *Of Other Worlds*. Ed. Walter Hooper. San Diego: Harcourt, 2002. Print.

---. *The Seeing Eye*. Ed. Walter Hooper. New York: Ballantine Books, 1967. Print.

---. *The World's Last Night and Other Essays*. San Diego: Harcourt, 2002. Print.

Mather, Kirtley F. "Current Science Reading." *Science* 113 (1951): 427-429. Print.

McKie, Robin. "Fred Hoyle: The Scientist Whose Rudeness Cost Him the Nobel Prize." *The Observer*. Guardian. com, 2 Oct. 2010. Web. 15 June 2016.

Milne, E.A. *Modern Cosmology and the Christian Idea of God*. Oxford: Clarendon Press, 1952. Print.

Mitton, Simon. *Fred Hoyle: A Life in Science*. Cambridge: Cambridge University Press, 2011. Print.

Paxford, Fred W. "He Should Have Been a Parson." *We Remember C.S. Lewis*. Ed. David Graham. Nashville: Broadman and Holman, 2001. 119-128. Print.

Sayers, Dorothy L. "The Theologian and the Scientist." *The Listener* 44 (1950): 496-500. Print.

Schroder, Klaus-Peter, and Robert C. Smith. "Distant Future of the Sun and Earth Revisited." *Monthly Notices of the Royal Astronomical Society* 386 (2008). 155-163. Print.

Stapledon, Olaf. *Last and First Men*. 1930. Oxford: Benediction Classics, 2007. Print.

Star Maker. 1937. Mineola: Dover, 2008. Print.

Ward, Michael. *Planet Narnia*. Oxford: Oxford University Press, 2008. Print.

Well, H.G. *The Time Machine*. Ed. Patrick Parrinder. London: Penguin, 2005. Print.

Williamson, Ralph E. "Fred Hoyle's Universe." *Journal of the Royal Astronomical Society of Canada* 45.5 (1951): 185-189. *NASA Astrophysics Data System*. Web. 15 Jan. 2016.

When Friendship Sours:
A Study of Trumpkin, Trufflehunter, and Nikabrik
by Victoria Holtz Wodzak

Vickie Holtz Wodzak earned her doctorate in medieval and eighteenth century British literature from the University of Missouri-Columbia in 1996. She now teaches writing and literature courses at Viterbo University, a Franciscan liberal arts institution. Her most recent scholarship has considered the influence of World War I on the work of Tolkien. She has presented at a variety of international, national, and regional conferences, and published her work in *Tolkien Studies* and *Mythlore*.

In Lewis's chapter on friendship in *The Four Loves*, he says that when individuals "share their vision—it is then that friendship is born" (92). He continues, quoting Emerson, saying that, to be friends, individuals may disagree, but they must care about the same truth.

The disintegrating relationship among Nikabrik, Trumpkin, and Trufflehunter in *Prince Caspian* can be traced to their inability to continue caring about the same truth. We don't know how the three of them came to share their underground home. I'd like to think that, until Caspian's arrival cast the tensions of their relationship into high relief, that their home looked a lot like the home of Duffle, Rogin, and Bricklethumb, the dwarves who hosted Shasta to his first, and much needed, breakfast and nap in Narnia: they serve him bacon, eggs, and fried mushrooms, draw lots for who must do the dishes, and ultimately make the now-filled, but sleepy, Shasta a bed on their floor. It is a picture of hospitality and mutual understanding (*Horse* 155-56). By contrast, when Caspian wakes up from the blow on the head that separated him from his horse Destrier and landed him on his hosts' doorstep, he finds no such cozy, agreeable hospitality and mutual regard. Instead,

> When he came to himself he was lying in a firelit place with bruised limbs and a bad headache. Low voices were speaking close at hand.
>
> "And now," said one, "before it wakes up we must decide what to do with it."
>
> "Kill it," said another. "We can't let it live. It would betray us."

"We ought to have killed it at once, or else let it alone," said a third voice. "We can't kill it now. Not after we've taken it in and bandaged its head and all. It would be murdering a guest" (*Prince* 60-61)

His hosts' disagreement on what to do with Caspian continues into his recovery:

"And now," said Nikabrik on the first evening when Caspian was well enough to sit up and talk, we still have to decide what to do with this Human. You two think you've done it a great kindness by not letting me kill it. But I suppose the upshot is that we have to keep it a prisoner for life. I'm certainly not going to let it go alive—to go back to its own kind and betray us all." (*Prince* 63)

Trufflehunter and Trumpkin will have none of it. Trufflehunter says that beasts "don't change. We hold on. . . . Great good will come of [sheltering Caspian]. This is the true King of Narnia we've got here; a true King, coming back to true Narnia. And we beasts remember, even if Dwarfs forget, that Narnia was never right except when a son of Adam was King" (*Prince* 64). Trumpkin responds with skepticism. He is, as he had said earlier, morally opposed to "murdering a guest," but he sees little reason to accept Trufflehunter's faith in Aslan and the ways of Old Narnia. He asks "who believes in Aslan nowadays?" (*Prince* 64). The reasonable Trumpkin has some basis for his question. It has, after all, likely been 1300 years or so since the High King Peter and his siblings reigned and Aslan was last seen in Narnia. To Trumpkin, these stories are, at best, fanciful, and at worst deceptive.

Where is the common vision that should cement this friendship? It would seem that, if it existed, it was in a shared fear and hatred of humans in general and Telmarines in particular. Caspian's arrival and predicament show the insufficient vision to hold this friendship together, even though Lewis is careful to point out that, while shared vision is necessary, agreement about that vision is not. Nikabrik speaks repeatedly of hating humans and hating Telmarines. When they go in search of the hidden Narnians, he agrees with his fellow Black Dwarfs' suggestion to recruit ogres and hags to the cause, but he is overruled. When Trufflehunter points out that, were they to recruit hags and ogres, they "should not have Aslan for [their] friend," Trumpkin is skeptical (*Prince* 70-71). And when they discuss their inability to wake the trees and waters, Trumpkin responds "What imaginations you Animals have! . . . But why stop at Trees and Waters? Wouldn't it be even nicer if the stones started throwing themselves at old Miraz?"

(*Prince* 76). Pretty clearly, this is a friendship whose shared vision, if it ever existed, is fraying quickly. Perhaps, rather than a friendship, as Lewis defines the term, it was always what he terms *companionship*, a relationship defined by common needs.

As the relationship sours, it takes its most toxic turn in Nikabrik. His initial hatred of humans becomes a loyalty to his own kind only, and a quick suspicion that, as things get difficult, it is always the dwarfs, and one suspects in his mind the Black Dwarfs like him, who bear the brunt of it. "Who" he asks "is sent on all the dangerous raids? The Dwarfs. Who goes short when the rations fail? The Dwarfs" (*Prince* 149). Finally, he brings new friends—note the choice of word—to council: a werewolf and a hag who offers to conjure up the White Witch. They offer Nikabrik a new vision, one in which Miraz is supplanted by a resurrected White Witch. As for anything bad that might come of her return, Nikabrik is unconcerned. He claims she was always good to dwarfs, and he will support anyone or anything that can rid Narnia of Telmarines. When, in the scuffle that follows this conversation, Nikabrik is killed, Caspian observes

> "I am sorry for Nikabrik . . . though he hated me from the first moment he saw me. He had gone sour inside from long suffering and hating. If we had won quickly he might have become a good Dwarf in the days of peace. I don't know which of us killed him. I'm glad of that." (*Prince* 152)

Nikabrik dies, in part, because he traded hope for hatred, and in doing that, made his vision, as Lewis might call it, incompatible with that of his companions Trufflehunter, Trumpkin, and Caspian. Trufflehunter, because animals do not forget, aligns his vision with Caspian, and when they arrive, with the vision of Peter and Edmund, Aslan's emissaries, who are there, as Peter explains, to put Caspian, the rightful king, on his throne. Trufflehunter embraces Peter in greeting and explains his steadfast lack of doubt: "No credit to me, your Majesty. . . . I'm a beast and we don't change. I'm a badger, what's more, and we hold on" (*Prince* 152). Nikabrik's end, and the ways it contrasts with the story of his companion Trumpkin is instructive in coming to an understanding of Lewis's views on friendship.

The disintegration of the relationship among Trufflehunter, Nikabrik, and Trumpkin is counterbalanced by the eventual friendship Trumpkin shares with Caspian, with the Pevensies, and ultimately with Aslan. While Trumpkin is initially a nonbeliever, and therefore shares little apparent vision with the children, his dedication to justice, as demonstrated in his argument against killing Caspian, and his dedication to his king and Narnia, as demonstrated by his willingness to undertake the trip to Cair Paravel to see if blowing Susan's horn has had any effect, place him in position to align his vision with theirs as his experience brings him new understanding. Trumpkin's emerging shared vision with the children parallels an emerging friendship that carries them through difficulties and will carry Caspian and Trumpkin through to the end of Caspian's life.

Vision and friendship. According to Lewis, they must go together in order for companions to become friends. When Trumpkin sets off on his hike across country to see if help has materialized at the ruins of Cair Paravel, he suspects that "the first result of all this foolery is not to bring us help but to lose us two fighters" (*Prince* 88), but he does it. He does not share the cautious hope of Dr. Cornelius, Caspian and Trufflehunter, but he volunteers because "[he knows] the difference between giving advice and taking orders" (*Prince* 89). He goes, hoping that if anything has happened, it is as Dr. Cornelius suggests, that blowing Susan's horn has called "Peter the High King and his mighty consort down from the high past" (*Prince* 88), but suspecting he will be disappointed.

Trumpkin has a vision problem. He can't see what the others can. He can't see the potential in Susan's horn, suspecting that it is a concoction of superstition and old tales. Even having found the four children, he cannot see that help has come. He says,

> [T]he King and Trufflehunter and Doctor Cornelius were expecting—well if you see what I mean, help. To put it in another way, I think they'd been imagining you as great warriors. As it is—we're awfully fond of children and all that, but just at the moment, in the middle of a war—but I'm sure you understand. (*Prince* 92)

Trumpkin doesn't realize that, when help is needed, Aslan sends children, for whom Trumpkin, as yet, can see no use.

The idea of friendship reenters the story at this point, initially as a kind of throw away, condescending statement from Trumpkin, that he hopes his "dear little friends" (*Prince* 92) will not be offended by his estimation of their abilities, but by the end of the swordsmanship contest with Edmund, the archery contest with Susan, and after a drop of Lucy's healing cordial, Trumpkin declares to Peter that he is "ready to believe in [them]" (*Prince* 98), and ruefully accepts being named their Dear Little Friend, or at least DLF, a name they often used and soon stopped attending to what it stands for. Essentially, he has been given enough evidence to overcome his skepticism. While

Trumpkin's vision is beginning to align with that of the children, and with that of Caspian and Trufflehunter, he is by no means ready yet to concede his objections to the idea of Aslan.

Vision is literally the issue as the companions try to make their way through the forest, navigating with a pocket compass and recollections of geography that are more than a thousand years out of date. When Lucy insists she has seen Aslan, Trumpkin, ever the skeptic, points out that lions, as well as bears, may live in the forest, and at any rate, Aslan, if it was him, would be a "pretty elderly lion by now" (*Prince* 113). Peter tries to explain to him that he must take it on faith that the children know a bit about Aslan (*Prince* 113). Trumpkin is unconvinced, but he is not alone in his blindness. When Aslan commands Lucy to wake the others and make them follow him in the moonlight, Lucy is the only one whose vision does not fail. Lucy's siblings grumble. Edmund "fully intended to back Lucy up, but he was annoyed at losing his night's sleep" (PC 131) and Peter "couldn't help being a little annoyed with [Lucy]" (*Prince* 131) likely because he is tired. Susan bullies and blusters and threatens to remain behind. Trumpkin falls back on loyalty—he will go where Peter goes—and skepticism:

> "But if you ask my private opinion, I'm a plain dwarf who doesn't think there's much chance of finding a road by night where you couldn't find one by day. And I have no use for magic lions which are talking lions and don't talk, and friendly lions thought they don't do us any good, and whopping big lions though nobody can see them. It's all bilge and beanstalks as far as I can see." (*Prince* 131)

It is only gradually, after much scrambling through trees and over rocks, that Aslan allows them the shared ability to see him. As Aslan turns to look at them "they felt as glad as anyone can who feels afraid, and as afraid as anyone can who feels glad" (*Prince* 135). Their contrasting reactions to this opportunity for shared vision is telling. The boys step forward immediately; Susan and Trumpkin "[shrink] back" (*Prince* 135).

Where Trumpkin is concerned, Aslan wants to establish friendship, with himself, and with the children. By revealing himself to them, he offers them shared vision, and therefore friendship. His language in addressing Trumpkin is telling: "[W]here" he roars, "is this little Dwarf, this famous swordsman and archer, who doesn't believe in lions? Come HERE!" (*Prince* 136). The key word is *believe*. Just as it was important for Trumpkin to come to believe in the Pevensie children at Cair Paravel—that they were real children, not ghosts and that they were really of some potential help—here it is important that Trumpkin discard his skepticism and believe in Aslan. After tossing him in the air, and shaking some sense into him, Aslan asks the now-breathless Trumpkin, "Son of Earth, shall we be friends?" (*Prince* 137). In Lewis's terms, this is a loaded question. Aslan has given the skeptical dwarf tangible evidence of his existence. Given that, is the dwarf ready to realign his values?

But then, there is Susan. She tells Lucy that

> "I've been far worse than you know. I really believed it was him—he, I mean—yesterday. When he warned us not to go down to the fir wood. And I really believed it was him tonight, when you woke us up. I mean deep down inside. Or I could have, if I'd let myself. But I just wanted to get out of the woods…" (*Prince* 134-5).

Aslan tells her she has "listened to fears." He breathes on her, and when he asks her if she is brave again, her response is telling: "A little, Aslan." (*Prince* 135). Aslan's breath, and the scent of his mane were enough to make Lucy feel like a lioness (*Prince* 127). Susan can muster only a little bravery. Like Nikabrik's hatred (and likely fear) of Telmarines in particular, and humans in general, Susan's fears will blind her to the vision the others share in friendship.

After this adventure, Susan will never return to Narnia. Aslan tells her that it is so she can come to know him in her own world, but it doesn't seem to happen. She is next mentioned, almost in passing, as the "pretty one" of the Pevensie siblings whom a trip to America will most benefit since she is "no good at school work" (*Dawn Treader* 10). Later, in *The Last Battle*, Peter reports that his sister is "no longer a friend of Narnia" (138). To Susan, Narnia has become "funny games we used to play when we were children" (138) and what seems to be important to her is nylons, lipstick, invitations and being grown up. Her vision has shifted (or clouded), and she is no longer a friend. Perhaps, this loss of friendship is not permanent. Lewis notes in one of his letters that Susan still has time to mend (*Letters to Children* 67), and Rogers argues that the tragic loss of her family in the railway accident that has thrown all of them into Aslan's country might be sufficient to draw her back to friendship with Aslan. But, for the moment, Susan is not one of the nine friends of Narnia.

Friendship, Lewis notes, "is unnecessary, like philosophy, like art.... It has no survival value; rather it is one of those things that give value to survival" (*Four Loves* 93). Aslan intends Narnia to be a kind and gentle country he says, after its creation, not a cruel country like Jadis's Charn. It seems likely that one of the many shortcomings of the later rulers of Charn, whose faces become progressively crueler over time, is a failure of friendship, and arguably, that failure is one of the things Digory's apple is intended to protect Narnia from. When the Pevensies return from their first adventure in Narnia, Professor Kirke warns them not to talk about their experience—share their vision—unless it is with people they learn have had similar experience. In the end, there are nine of them—nine "friends of Narnia" whose shared vision cements their relationship with each other and brings them, together, to Aslan's country.

Friendship, properly understood, runs deep. I'd like to close with a quote from Lewis's friend Tolkien after Lewis's death. In a letter to his daughter Priscilla, he writes

> Dearest, Thank you so much for your letter. . . . So far I have felt the normal feelings of a man of my age—like an old tree that is losing all its leaves one by one: this feels like an axe-blow near the roots. Very sad that we should have been so separated in the last years; but our time of close communion endured in memory for both of us. I had a mass said this morning, and was there, and served; and Havard and Dundas Grant were present. The funeral at Holy Trinity, the Headington Quarry church, which Jack attended, was quiet and attended only by intimates and some Magdalen people including the President. (*Letters* 251)

Theirs was a friendship that carried them far and endured much. Unlike the bitterness that seems to have shredded Nikabrik's friendship with Trumpkin and Trufflehunter, or the fears that have loosened Susan's friendship with Narnia, Lewis's time of "close communion" with Tolkien seems to have left its mark and endures in memory despite the "separation" in their last years.

WORKS CITED

Dorsett, Lyle W. and Marjorie Lamp Mean eds. *C. S. Lewis's Letters to Children*. New York: Scribner, 1996. Print.

Lewis, C.S. *Prince Caspian*. London: Geoffrey Bles, 1964. Print.

---. *The Four Loves*. New York: Harcourt Brace Ivanovich, 1960. Print.

---. *The Horse and His Boy*. London: Geoffrey Bles, 1964. Print.

---. *The Voyage of the Dawn Treader*. London: Geoffrey Bles, 1964. Print.

Rogers, Joshua. "The Overlooked Hope for Narnia's Susan Pevensie." *Christianity Today* (2016): np. Web. <http://www.christianitytoday.com/ct/2016/march-web-only/overlooked-hope-for-narnias-susan-pevensie-.html>.

Tolkien, JRR. *The Letters of JRR Tolkien*. Ed. Humphrey Carpenter. New York: Houghton Mifflin, 1981.

Diana Gyler giving the final banquet talk on Saturday night

II. Essays on Dorothy L. Sayers

Books, Theology, and Hens: The Correspondence and Friendship of C. S. Lewis and Dorothy L. Sayers

by Laura K. Simmons and Gary L. Tandy

Laura K. Simmons teaches at George Fox Evangelical Seminary in Portland, Oregon. She has been studying Dorothy L. Sayers for more than two decades and is the author of *Creed without Chaos: Exploring Theology in the Writings of Dorothy L. Sayers*.

Gary L. Tandy is Professor of English and Chair of the English and Theatre Department at George Fox University in Newberg, Oregon. His book, *The Rhetoric of Certitude: C. S. Lewis's Nonfiction Prose*, was published by Kent State University Press.

In *The Four Loves*, C. S. Lewis suggests that "Friendship arises out of mere Companionship when two or more of the companions discover that they have in common some insight or interest or even taste which the others do not share and which, till that moment, each believed to be his own unique treasure (or burden). The typical expression of opening Friendship would be something like, "What? You too? I thought I was the only one." (96) The reader of the correspondence between Dorothy L. Sayers and C. S. Lewis comes across frequent instances of these "What? You too?" moments. Sayers likely experienced such a moment when she first read Lewis's *That Hideous Strength* and wrote to him mentioning, among many other things she admired, the "marvelous confusion of tongues at the dinner and the painful realism of that college meeting" (Letter, December 3, 1945). Lewis, no doubt, experienced something similar when he read with pleasure Sayers's translation of Dante's *Purgatorio*, writing to her that her translation read like an "exciting story" and noting, "I set out with the idea of attending to your translation, before I've read a page I've forgotten all about you and am thinking only of Dante, and two pages later I've forgotten about Dante and am thinking about Hell" (Letter, November 15, 1949).

That Lewis and Sayers had much in common and that their lives intersected in a number of interesting ways throughout their careers is common knowledge for even the casual follower of either author. What does not seem to have been appreciated or explained sufficiently in the scholarship to date is the nature of the friendship between these two influential Christian authors. Therefore, it is this friendship we wish to shed light on, using as our primary source the correspondence between Lewis and Sayers from 1942-1957. In addition, we look at what the biographers of each author have to say about their relationship.

C. S. Lewis and Dorothy Sayers became friends as a result of their common interests and vocations and, initially, because each admired the other's work. Their correspondence begins with Sayers writing a "fan letter" to Lewis about his *Screwtape Letters* while at the same time Lewis is expressing his admiration for Sayers's *The Mind of the Maker* and *The Man Who Would be King* to other correspondents. Lewis obviously admired her as an author. His letters responding to her books, articles, and her Dante translation are effusive in their praise. While he offers suggestions and a few critiques, the number of these is small compared to the praise. In one letter he jokes that he has included several comments and suggestions, which he knows she will ignore. Sayers writes to praise Lewis's work often, as well, and recommends his books to her friends. Her earliest extant letter to him, sent with a copy of her radio plays, is written in the style of *Screwtape*. She recommends *The Problem of Pain* often to people who contact her seeking reading recommendations. Sayers also passes on praises she hears from others, both for Lewis's *Arthurian Torso* and for *Out of the Silent Planet*.

The two authors are so familiar with each other's work they make frequent suggestions of books or articles the other should attempt. The most notable example is when Sayers complains in one of her letters that there exists no up-to-date treatment of miracles, and in a letter a short time later Lewis tells Sayers that he is beginning a book on miracles. Lewis's suggestions to Sayers are not often as well received, as when he suggests she write a book for a Christian series. Not only does Sayers refuse, but her refusal leads to a lengthy epistolary debate about the motivations and purposes that should drive the Christian writer to create. Likewise, Lewis turns down Sayers's offer to write a preface for a book on existentialism, saying "I know (and care) little about the Existentialist nonsense and wouldn't dream of writing a preface" (Letter, November 1949).

Both were philosophers and theologians who thought deeply about the state of Christianity in the modern world and shared similar, though not identical, worldviews. Both were Anglicans who wrote nonfiction and imaginative literature with apologetic outcomes, causing one contemporary critic to dub them the "Hallelujah Chorus" (Hone 180). Both were students of literature, who loved to read, analyze, and discuss it with other perceptive and appreciative readers. Finally, both were practitioners of the art of letter writing, who took the time to write detailed and interesting letters to their friends and received pleasure from reading the correspondence they received in return, though Lewis denigrated his own letter writing skills while praising Sayers's, calling her "a real letter writer" and suggesting that she would be remembered as "one of the great English letter writers" (Letter, December 14, 1945).

As Lewis notes in *The Four Loves,* friendship often arises between companions who share a common religion, common studies, or a common profession. As he states, "All who share it will be our companions; but one or two or three who share something more will be our Friends." Lewis further qualifies his definition by noting that sharing something more does not necessarily mean agreeing on everything. Quoting Emerson's comment that in friendship saying "Do you love me?" means "Do you see the same truth?—Or at least, "Do you care about the same truth?" Lewis continues, "The man who agrees with us that some question, little regarded by others, is of great importance can be our Friend. He need not agree with us about the answer" (Lewis 97). Lewis's definition adds an important ingredient to the friendship of Lewis and Sayers. While the two authors were of the same mind on many issues, they most certainly did not agree on everything. And both writers relish debating those points of disagreement.

That the two writers share many basic assumptions and preferences is clear. In one letter, Lewis addresses Sayers as "sister dinosaur," referring to his Cambridge inaugural lecture description of himself because of his love for old books and appreciation of the medieval worldview. She, in turn, calls herself "your fellow artefact," and also adopts the dinosaur language. This feeling of shared views comes through often, especially when conspiring to attack a common "enemy," such as F. R. Leavis, Kathleen Nott, or other modernist or secular critics and writers. As Carol and Philip Zaleski note, "Sayers had much in common with Lewis and Tolkien's circle, including a love of orthodox Christianity, traditional verse, popular fiction, and debate" (352). Part of the kinship Lewis felt with Sayers was no doubt because both were part of the "movement" to take seriously orthodox Christianity and write works that would be relevant in the 20th century. Lewis and Sayers shared another key belief: that popular and entertaining literature could achieve excellence while communicating Christian beliefs and values. Examples include Sayers's Lord Peter

Wimsey crime novels and her Canterbury plays and Lewis's children's fantasy novels and science fiction trilogy. Lewis comments on this shared value in his tribute to Sayers, written following her death, where he notes: "She aspired to be, and was, at once a popular entertainer and a conscientious craftsman: like (in her degree) Chaucer, Cervantes, Shakespeare, or Moliere," adding, "I have an idea that, with a very few exceptions, it is only such writers who matter much in the long run" (Lewis, "Panegyric" 92).

A major area of disagreement theologically is the movement toward the ordination of women in the Church of England. Lewis, who opposes the idea, writes to Sayers, assuming she is of the same mind, and asks her to use her influence against it. Sayers declines, noting that she sees no theological reason why women could not be ordained as priests. She tells Lewis, "I fear you would find me rather an uneasy ally" in his objection to the movement (Letter, July 19, 1948).

This last disagreement highlights a fact that to this point we've ignored: that Lewis was a man and Sayers was a woman, yet they became friends. This reality seems important to address for two reasons: (1) Lewis brings up the difficulties of male-female friendships in his own writing, and (2) much discussion has occurred in recent Lewis scholarship around his attitudes toward and relationships with women. In *The Four Loves*, Lewis notes that because friendships arise among companions, in "most societies at most periods Friendship will be between men and men or between women and women" (72); however, he goes on to say that "where men and women work side by side, or in the mission field, or among authors and artists, such Friendship is common" (72). Thus, Lewis would have viewed his friendship with Sayers (along with his friendships with other women like Ruth Pitter and Sister Penelope) as entirely natural. As Alan Jacobs notes, "the tone he uses with female writers such as Dorothy Sayers and female scholars such as Helen Gardner and Joan Bennett is fully as respectful and serious as the tone he uses with their male counterparts, though it is sometimes a bit more courtly" (255). In spite of this, though Sayers maintained friendships with several of the Inklings, she would not have been welcomed in their weekly meetings at the pub or in Lewis's rooms due to basic social proprieties of the day.

To the second point, Lewis's attitude toward women, Sayers's letters shed interesting light on that topic. As we noted earlier, she often recommends Lewis's books to her friends, but these recommendations come with qualifications. Writing to Mrs. Robert Darby, for example, she states, "I do admit that he is apt to write shocking nonsense about women and marriage. (That, however, is not because he is a bad theologian but because he is a rather frightened bachelor.)" (Letter, May 31, 1948). Similarly, she writes to Barbara Reynolds about Lewis: "One just has to accept the fact that there is a complete blank in his mind where women are concerned. Charles Williams and his other married friends used to sit round him at Oxford and tell him so, but there really isn't anything to be done about it. He is not hostile, and he does his best, and actually, for a person with his limitations I think he didn't do too badly with the Lady in *Perelandra*" (December 21, 1955). Finally, we note that the author of a recent study on Lewis and gender argues that Lewis's views on gender slowly changed over time and that the change "owed much to the intellectual and Christian ties he forged with Dorothy L. Sayers, a woman of his own class and educational background" (Van Leeuwen, 12).

While Lewis and Sayers address a variety of theological and literary topics in their letters, the reader of their correspondence comes away with the clear impression their friendship transcended professional and theological interests. They clearly like one another and enjoy each other's company. Lewis frequently invites Sayers to lunch when she is in Oxford or Cambridge and looks for opportunities to meet her when they are attending the same conference. Likewise, in a 1949 letter, Sayers tells Lewis she is coming to Oxford to speak and says, "I do hope you will be there and that we can meet and have a good talk. It is a long time since we set eyes on each other, though we have kept in touch by hand o' write…" (Letter, January 26, 1949).

Reading through the letters chronologically gives a sense of a developing friendship that became warmer and more intimate over time. While the early letters focus more on theological and literary matters, later letters bring in more personal references and revelations. Notably, Lewis's letters to Sayers from 1942 to 1954 all begin with the same greeting: "Dear Miss Sayers" and close with the signature "C. S. Lewis." But, then, in a letter dated September 25, 1954, Lewis for the first time opens with the greeting "Dear Dorothy" and closes with the signature "Jack." Lewis continues this pattern through the remainder of their correspondence. Likewise, Sayers begins addressing him as "Jack" in late 1954. As early as 1947, however, the friendship has developed to the point where Lewis and Sayers feel comfortable sharing, not only grand ideas about theology and literature, but the ordinary details of their lives. Lewis, for example, received great delight from reading this account of Sayers's hens:

> I have purchased two Hens. In their habits they display, respectively Sense and Sensibility, and I have therefore named them Elinor and Marianne. Elinor is a round, comfortable, motherly-looking little body who lays one steady, regular, undistinguished egg per day, and allows nothing to disturb her equanimity. Marianne is leggier, timid, and liable to hysterics. Sometime she lays a shell-less egg, sometimes a double yolk, sometimes no egg at all. On the days when she lays no egg she nevertheless goes and sits in the nest for the usual time, and seems to imagine that nothing more is required. As my gardener says: "She just *thinks* she's laid an egg." Too much imagination—in fact, Sensibility. But when she does lay an egg it is larger than Elinor's. But you cannot wish to listen to this cackle . . . (Letter, June 2, 1947).

Overall, their letters reflect the easy banter of those who are trusted friends and intellectually well matched.

The growing trust over time between Sayers and Lewis is also evident. Several examples will illustrate Lewis's level of trust in Sayers as a friend. In a 1946 letter, in a discussion of apologetic writing, Lewis reveals to Sayers "the fact that apologetic work is so dangerous to one's own faith. A doctrine never seems dimmer to me than when I have just successfully defended it" (Letter, August 2, 1946). George Sayer, in his biography of Lewis, comments on the significance of this revelation: "He [Lewis] valued friends who supported him without fawning over him, who challenged him to improve as a thinker, artist, and Christian. Barfield, Tolkien, Williams, Sayers, and Sister Penelope fit this description. In particular, he worried that apologetics might be bad for his faith. He could not discuss this sensitive question with Tolkien, but to comrade-in-apologetics Dorothy L. Sayers he confessed" it (Sayer 314). Lewis freely shares his personal and family problems with Sayers, for example, the difficult situations with Mrs. Moore's illness and Warnie's alcoholism in 1949. Finally, while Lewis's relationship and eventual marriage to Joy Gresham were kept secret even from most of Lewis's friends, he openly shares what, today, Facebook would call his relationship status with Dorothy Sayers. In a December 1956 letter, he informs Sayers of the marriage though in a very understated way, saying "Certain problems do not arise between a dying woman and an elderly man." However, six months later he discloses to Sayers that his feelings toward Joy have changed, saying "I hope you give us your blessing: I know you'll give us your prayers" (Letter, June 25, 1957). We agree with Alan Jacobs, who calls Lewis's disclosure to Sayers in this letter "uncharacteristically self-revealing" (Jacobs 285).

Given the evidence from the correspondence that reveals Lewis and Sayers to be not only companions but, in Lewis's words, friends who shared something more, it seems fair to say that biographers have tended to underestimate the extent and quality of this friendship. Lewis's biographers typically include only two or three references to Sayers, most commonly focusing on her role as a guest speaker at the Oxford Socratic Club and her contribution to the volume of critical essays in honor of Charles Williams. Sayers's biographers, too, focus less on the friendship than on the content of the correspondence.

Ultimately, when it comes to assessing the friendship of Lewis and Sayers, it seems fitting to let these two masterful Christian writers have the last word: In a 1945 letter to Barbara Reynolds, Sayers says, speaking of Lewis, "I like him very much, and always find him stimulating and amusing" (Letter, December 21, 1955); and, following Sayers's death in 1957, Lewis writes, "For all she did and was—for delight and instruction, for her militant loyalty as a friend, . . .—let us thank the Author who invented her" (Lewis, "A Panegyric" 95).

Works Cited

Hone, Ralph E. *Dorothy L. Sayers: A Literary Biography.* Kent, OH: Kent State University Press, 1979.

Jacobs, Alan. *The Narnian: The Life and Imagination of C. S. Lewis.* San Francisco: HarperCollins, 2005.

Lewis, C. S. *Collected Letters of C. S. Lewis, Volumes 1-3.* Ed. Walter Hooper. SanFrancisco: Harper SanFrancisco, 2004-2007.

Lewis, C. S. *The Four Loves.* New York: Harcourt Brace Jovanovich, 1960.

Lewis, C. S. "A Panegyric for Dorothy L. Sayers." *On Stories and Other Essays on Literature.* Ed. Walter Hooper. San Diego, CA: Harcourt Brace Jovanovich, 1982, 1966.

Sayer, George. *Jack: C. S. Lewis and his Times.* San Francisco: Harper & Row, 1988

Sayers, Dorothy L. *The Letters of Dorothy L. Sayers, Volumes 1-4.* Ed. Barbara Reynolds. Cambridge: Dorothy L. Sayers Society, 1995-2002.

Van Leeuwen, Mary Stewart. *A Sword between the Sexes? C. S. Lewis and the Gender Debates.* Grand Rapids, Michigan: Brazos Press, 2010.

Zaleski, Philip and Zaleski, Carol. *The Fellowship: The Literary Lives of the Inklings: J.R.R. Tolkien, C. S. Lewis, Owen Barfield, Charles Williams.* New York: Farrar, Straus and Giroux, 2015.

Well Met: Common Sense and Humor in the Friendship of G.K. Chesterton and Dorothy L. Sayers

by Barbara M. Prescott

Barbara Mary Prescott, M.A., M.Ed., is a researcher of writing communities and the writing process. She has advanced degrees from the University of Illinois and the University of Wisconsin, including post-graduate research in Language and Literacy at Stanford University. She has published numerous articles on the writing process and is currently researching the poetry of Dorothy L. Sayers.

There was some one thing that was too great for God to show us when He walked upon our earth; and I have sometimes fancied that it was His mirth.
—G.K. Chesterton, *Orthodoxy*

As we consider the myriad facets and profound influence upon twentieth century thought: religious, philosophical, fantastical, of C.S. Lewis and the writers we know as the Inklings, we may also consider the importance of those friendly associations outside of the canonical group which were equally important to this influential society of writers, particularly to C.S. Lewis. I like to refer to those friendly associates and influences as the 'Linklings', and there were many Linklings in the lives of Lewis and his friends. Two of those links with whom C.S. Lewis was acquainted and who were influential to the development of Lewis's own religious thought and profound writing were G.K. Chesterton and Dorothy L. Sayers.

These two writers were Linklings to C.S. Lewis as well as to one another, and they extended those links to us, their readers, through a shared sense of reality, of humanity emanating from the Divine, and a shared gift of humor that allow us, the human, glimpses of insight into the Spirit of God. In our humanity which emanates from the Divine, we have a common sense of one another. As human beings we can understand shared experience and empathize with one another's experience as we can understand the subtle humor that links our common experience. In this paper, I will briefly explore those links of sense and humor shared by Chesterton and Sayers as their own friendship developed through time, realized by similar insights, shared spirit of faith, sense of the absurd, and common sense of experience in early twentieth century Oxford and England.

Chesterton once noted that "the secret of life lies in laughter and humility."[1] Yet he grounded this idea by observing that "the first effect of not believing in God is that you lose your common sense."[2] Chesterton very well understood the use of humor and common sense in reaching out to his readers and audience. Dorothy Sayers possessed, as well, this intrinsic understanding of the power of humor in communication. In point of fact, both Chesterton and Sayers clearly understood how to draw a reader to their message and to keep the reader interested in reading more.

One reason we resonate with the writings of Chesterton and Sayers is that they make us laugh. Chesterton's sympathetically self-deprecating, ironic humor invariably strikes a chord of truth within his reader. We like to read him; we find ourselves in his humor without being made vulnerable. By making *himself* vulnerable, Chesterton saves us the embarrassment yet provides us with a protected mirror of our own foibles and weaknesses. That is, I believe, the beauty of G.K. Chesterton's writings. We like him, we like his words, and we want to read more. We feel safe with him. I believe we feel closest to Sayers, as well, when she leads us to the unexpected irony, to the wit of Wimsey when we are not expecting to find it, to the delightful surprise of her language. Somehow, we instinctively know, along with Chesterton, that, "there is but one step from the ridiculous to the sublime"[3] and, as C.S. Lewis reminds us from the *Screwtape Letters*, "Humour is... the all-consoling and...the all-excusing, grace of life."[4]

G.K. Chesterton excelled in the paradoxical, even in the parody of the paradox. He noted, "Critics were almost entirely complimentary to what they were pleased to call my brilliant paradoxes; until they discovered that I really meant what I said."[5] Sayers' humor often mirrored the paradoxes of Chesterton: "The great advantage about telling the truth is that nobody ever believes it."[6] C. S. Lewis, as well, was the welcome recipient and generator of the profound insights that can best be realized and communicated through humor. These two Linklings shared with Lewis their thoughts, writings, unsparing argument, and language of wit, thus offering an absolutely delightful

---

1   *Heretics*, p. 131.
2   *Penguin Complete Father Brown*, p. 152.
3   *Dickens: A Critical Study*, p. 21.
4   *The Screwtape Letters*, p. 143.
5   *Autobiography*, p. 178.
6   *Gaudy Night*, Ch. 17.

friendship of the mind, a friendship of kindred spirits. Of Dorothy Sayers, Lewis wrote, "I liked her, originally, because she liked me; later, for the extraordinary zest and edge of her conversation—as I like a high wind. She was a friend, not an ally."[7] Of G.K. Chesterton, Lewis noted that Chesterton's *The Everlasting Man* "baptised" his intellect, which, from Lewis, was praise indeed.

As intriguing as it is to consider the effect of two Linklings upon an Inkling, I would like to focus attention now upon the friendship that developed between Sayers and Chesterton until his death in 1936, when Dorothy Sayers acknowledged her debt to G.K. Chesterton with the words, "I think, in some ways, G.K.'s books have become more a part of my mental make-up than those of any writer you could name."[8] In point of fact, Dorothy L. Sayers was influenced by the writing of Chesterton from her adolescent years. Thus, the story of their relationship began far earlier in time than is often thought.

The friendship of G.K. Chesterton and Dorothy L. Sayers was a process in the making, spanning nearly three decades from 1909 through 1936. We can identify at least three stages of the journey from an author-reader relationship, through person-to-person recognition and acquaintance, and finally to a mutually acknowledged collegial friendship. To appreciate the roots of their relation, we must move back to the beginnings, to 1908 and the publication of *Orthodoxy*. The importance of this book upon the minds of young British Christians in the early years of the 1900s should certainly be acknowledged and is, in its own right, a fascinating study yet to be done. Chesterton appealed to young minds, having a relentlessly young mind of his own. One of those young, impressionable, minds was that of Dorothy Sayers at the age of fifteen.

Meeting a Friend of the Mind and Spirit: An Author-Reader Relationship

At this point in her life (1909-1911), Dorothy Sayers attended the Godolphin School, an independent boarding school for girls on Milford Hill in Salisbury and was experiencing the mixed experience of late adolescence. In her own words to Barbara Reynolds, Sayers referred to herself as a "sulky" teenager.[9] Dorothy Sayers appears

---

7   C.S. Lewis, Letter to the Editor, *Encounter Magazine*. January 1963. Also Carolyn Curtis and Mary Pomeroy Key. *Women and C.S. Lewis*, p. 73.
8   Letter DLS to Chesterton's widow, 1936. Also Downing, *Christian History*, 2015.
9   *Dorothy L. Sayers: Child and Woman of Her Time*, p 19. Also Reynolds

to have had a rough time adjusting to the school, difficulty making friends there, and experienced serious health issues. She was also going through the angst of a moral dilemma, distancing herself from her father's religious influence and flirting with the idea of atheism.[10]

Sayers had already become acquainted with Chesterton's fiction through *The Napoleon of Notting Hill* published in 1904.[11] So, she was very aware of G.K. Chesterton and quite liked his writing even before the publication of *Orthodoxy*. In a February 1909 letter, her parents mentioned that they had received a copy of the book. Before reading the book, their daughter responded: "I'm so glad you've got Orthodoxy. I'm not surprised to hear Chesterton is a Christian. I expect, though, that he is a very cheerful one, and rather original in his views, eh?"[12]

Quite soon after this letter, she read *Orthodoxy*. It was this book that changed the direction, in her teenage years, of Sayers' personal philosophy and of her spiritual convictions. That change lasted throughout her Oxford experience, in fact throughout her life, and determined the style and content of many of her apologetic works[40] such as *Strong Meat* (1939), *Creed or Chaos* (1940), *Mind of the Maker (1941)*, and *Why Work?* (1942). Recalling this pivotal point in her life in 1936, while writing the preface to Chesterton's play, *The Surprise*, Dorothy clearly asserted:

> To the young people of my generation, G.K.C. was a kind of Christian liberator. Like a beneficent bomb, he blew out of the Church a quantity of stained glass of a very poor period, and let in the gusts of fresh air in which the dead leaves of doctrine danced with all the energy and indecorum of Our Lady's Tumbler.[13]

Indeed, Chesterton was a sort of jester,[14] a reverently irreverent wise child, firmly committed to the adventure of faith and to the amusing paradoxes of life. "I am the fool in this story, and no rebel shall hurl me from my throne."[15]

Sayers further recalled in 1949 that, upon first reading the book, she had devoured *Orthodoxy*, classing it with St. Augustine's

---

personal interview with DLS. Also Reynolds, Barbara. *Dorothy L. Sayers, Her Life and Soul*, pp.40-43.

10   *Dorothy L. Sayers: Child and Woman of Her Time*, p 19.
11   *The Napoleon of Notting Hill*. London: The Bodley Head, 1904.
12   DLS Letter to Parents. February 1909. DLS Folder 22, Marion E. Wade Center, Wheaton, IL.
13   Dorothy L. Sayers. Preface to *The Surprise*. London, 1952.
14   Gary Willis, *Chesterton*, p. 186.
15   *Orthodoxy*, 1908.

Confessions and Dante's *Divine Comedy*[16]. Even at the age of fifteen, she considered *Orthodoxy* to be thrilling. Dorothy Sayers had found a Christianity that was "beautiful and adventurous and queerly full of humour."[16] This combination was irresistible, struck exactly the right chord with teenage Sayers, presenting her with a fresh perspective to her traditional, somewhat dryly experienced, religious beliefs. Dorothy Sayers explained her unexpectedly joyful reaction to *Orthodoxy*:

> It was stimulating to be told that Christianity was not a dull thing, but a gay thing, an adventurous thing . . . not an unintelligent thing, but a wise thing. . . . Above all, it was refreshing to see Christian polemic conducted with offensive rather than defensive weapons.[17]

Reflecting upon his conversion to Christianity, Chesterton strongly asserted in the chapter of his autobiography titled, "How to be a Lunatic":

> I have grieved my well-wishers, and many of the wise and prudent, by my reckless course in becoming a Christian, an Orthodox Christian, and finally a Catholic in the sense of a Roman Catholic. Now in most of the matters of which they chiefly disapprove, I am not in the least ashamed of myself. As an apologist I am the reverse of apologetic. So far as man may be proud of a religion rooted in humility, I am very proud of my religion. . . . I am very proud of what people call priestcraft; since even that accidental term of abuse preserves the mediaeval truth that a priest, like every other man, ought to be a craftsman.[18]

This remarkable attitude toward Christianity: adventure rooted in faith, common sense rooted in humor, inspiration rooted in work and craftsmanship, gave Dorothy her own direction, and later was the foundation of *The Mind of the Maker* (1941) in which she explored the craftsman-like mind of God reflected in man.

Chesterton's sensible, yet profoundly adventurous, approach to Christianity was highly attractive to this young girl who was captivated by the heroic, the mythic, the splendid adventure of medieval battle. Furthermore, she entirely appreciated the intelligence of wit, wisdom, and sound theology under the amusing adventure. She had opened a door to her own writing future. At this point in her early life, Dorothy Sayers experienced that which she had been seeking through the

---

16   Sayers, Preface to *The Surprise*.
17   Ibid.
18   *Autobiography*, pp.75-76.

anxiety of late adolescence: a meeting of the minds with a kindred soul who possessed an almost recklessly commonsensical intelligence of faith. "There never was anything so perilous or so exciting as orthodoxy. It was sanity: and to be sane is more dramatic than to be mad."[19]

This brings up the question of whether there were the beginnings, in 1909, of a friendship in the new reader-author relationship. Certainly there was influence from Chesterton to Sayers. Certainly there was a meeting of the minds from his writing to her thought. But, as yet, of course, Chesterton was entirely unaware of the existence of Dorothy Sayers, much less of the effect he had made upon a young Sayers. However, to her, Chesterton had opened a door to a new perspective, a new attitude rooted firmly in faith. He was slowly becoming a mentor and friend by virtue of his writings (and her reading).

MEETING THE PERSON: MOVING FROM READING TO RECOGNIZING

In 1912, Dorothy L. Sayers enrolled as an undergraduate student at Somerville College in Oxford. During this time, Sayers usually refers to Chesterton through letters to her parents or to Muriel Jaeger, expecially noting her attendance at Chesterton's evening talks in Oxford. In 1913, she read, *What's Wrong with the World?* (1910). In 1914, Sayers began to attend his lectures in Oxford.

During this period, Sayers most frequently referred to Chesterton as G.K.C.,[20] an unusually familiar referent from one who mentioned her male acquaintances only by their surnames or full names. She seemed to know him as well as to know of him. From 1914 through 1915, she quoted him, worried about his health as one would worry about an acquaintance or friend, heard his lectures in Oxford, met him personally at student attended activities, and possibly invited him to speak at a Mutual Admiration Society meeting.

G.K. Chesterton was seen often in Oxford and became known to Dorothy Sayers as a personality in addition to his reputation as an author. We are given a glimpse of this development of Chesterton into a friendly acquaintance by looking at the letters of Dorothy Sayers at Oxford during the years of 1914-1915. On the 8th of March, 1914, Sayers began to quote Chesterton to her parents:

---

19   *Orthodoxy*, 1908.
20   Letters, DLS to Parents 1912-1914. DLS Folder 22. Marion E. Wade Center, Wheaton, IL.

> Gloom has come upon me. I went to tea with the aunts . . . & Aunt Annie walked back with me & thought it her duty to enquire after my soul's welfare. She will probably send you an account of my spiritual state, so I may as well prepare you. . . . I let her down as gently as possible, but it's difficult to make people see that . . . the only things worth having are the things you find out for yourself. Also, that when so many brands of what Chesterton calls "fancy souls" & theories of life are offered you, there is no scuse in not looking pretty carefully to see what you are going in for. . . .[21]

On April 26, 1914, Dorothy wrote of looking forward to seeing Chesterton speak for the first time:

> On May 16th, G.K. Chesterton is coming to lecture on Romance. I hope he'll be good—at any rate I want to see him, so shall take care to get tickets. We shall have an exciting half term—three Bach Practices a week till the week of the Festival... & G.K.C. on Saturday. Spicy, isn't it?[22]

On Sunday, May 17, 1914, we get a clear account from Dorothy of her first experience hearing Chesterton deliver that lecture about Romance:

> I was very agreeably surprised in him. I had been afraid he would be untidy in his person & aggressive in his manner. He was very huge & ugly, of course, but it is a nice ugliness, & he was well dressed, with plenty of nice white linen, & he looked well-brushed & put together. He had a terrible cold, poor dear, but all the same one liked his voice—it was the voice of a gentleman, & suggested not only culture but breeding. . . . His delivery, perhaps on account of the cold, was not very good—rather hesitating & slow, but he spoke very clearly. We were some distance away, & heard every syllable. His lecture was very Chestertonian, but much sounder than I had expected, & not so fire-worky. He said some really excellent things. I have noted for future use, that his books ought to be read as he speaks—rather slowly, & delivering the paradoxical statements tentatively. His speaking has none of that aggressive & dogmatic quality which his writings are apt to assume when read aloud. Altogether a most pleasant lecture.[23]

---

21 Letter, DLS to Parents, March 8, 1914. Folder 22. Courtesy Marion E. Wade Center, Wheaton, IL.
22 Letter, DLS to Parents, April 26, 1914. Folder 22. Courtesy Marion E. Wade Center, Wheaton, IL.
23 Letter, DLS to Parents, May 17, 1914. Folder 22. Courtesy Marion E.

Sayers was now an observer of Chesterton as a person and personality. She was moving toward a state of interaction rather than being solely a reader of his writing. In the following snippets we may see the "stranger" gap closing, as Dorothy began to accept the person of G.K. Chesterton as part of her Oxford world.

June 1914, To Parents:

> We went to hear G.K.C. at the Newman Society's meeting the other night. His subject was "Capitalism & Culture." I thought he was quite good, but not nearly so good as he was on Romance. Where he was really splendid was when people asked him questions at the end. He was tremendously quick at answering—I don't think I ever heard anyone better & he was very witty. Some people hated him & thought him vulgar... but he certainly had his wits about him on Friday.[24]

By January 1915, Dorothy Sayers was comfortable referring to Chesterton as "poor dear old GK Chesterton."[25] He had moved from author to friendly acquaintance, or at least one to whom Dorothy referred as a known individual. There was affection in her reference to him as she worried about his health.

January 3, 1915, To Muriel Jaeger:

> Dear Jim - have you seen that poor dear old G.K. Chesterton is seriously ill? I saw it in the "Times" on Friday. I'm afraid he's the build of person to take whatever he has pretty badly. It would be dreadful to lose him—[26]

April 15, 1915: To Muriel Jaeger:

> I've just had a note from Miss Walter to say that G.K. Chesterton can find no room for himself at Oriel, so he is to be sent home. It is quite melancholy to think that he will never preside over our revels again.[27]

This last letter was written when the female students of Somerville were asked to transfer from Somerville to Oriel (male college) since Somerville was to be used as a hospital for wounded soldiers.

Wade Center, Wheaton, IL.

24 Letter, DLS to Parents, June 1914. Folder 22. Courtesy Marion E. Wade Center, Wheaton, IL.

25 Letter, DLS to Muriel Jaeger, January 3, 1915. Folder 79. Courtesy Marion E. Wade Center, Wheaton, IL.

26 Letter, DLS to Muriel Jaeger, April 15, 1915. Folder 79. Courtesy Marion E. Wade Center, Wheaton, IL.

27 Ibid.

Apparently, Chesterton had rooms in Oriel and had to leave those due to the transfer. The 'revels' to which Sayers referred may very well have been student activities which Chesterton was asked to chaperone or during which he spoke. It is also possible that Dorothy Sayers had asked Chesterton to speak at a Mutual Admiration Society Meeting.[28]

Toward a Mutual Friendship (1917-1923)

We do not hear about G.K. Chesterton again in Dorothy's correspondence until 1917, when there was rather a dramatic shift in both life situations. Chesterton had become the editor of the *New Witness*. Dorothy Sayers had just written the second of her two books of poetry, *Catholic Tales and Christian Songs*. She again encountered Chesterton, but this time as an author in search of a publisher.

The progression of the road to friendship had entered a new phase. Sayers, as a published author, approached Chesterton within the professional world of publication. She had matured, stepping closer to the beginning stages of professional collegiality. Her language reflected the change. She spoke of "wrangling" with G.K. Chesterton as though she were quite familiar with him at this point and not intimidated by him in the least. To Jim (Muriel Jaeger), she wrote on December 18, 1917:

> I am struggling & wrangling to get G.K.C. to take my "Catholic Tales" for "The New Witness." If he won't, I shall try the "Challenge" & if that fails, Basil shall publish them. They are really rather fun![29]

The *New Witness* did not, finally, publish *Catholic Tales and Christian Songs*, but a review of the book by Mr. Maynard was published in the *New Witness*, a review which rather offended Sayers. She responded by launching a campaign of response with Muriel Jaeger to "The Editor of the New Witness," who was, of course, G.K. Chesterton.[30]

A Friendship of Colleagues (1924-1936)

The third stage of their friendship, that of full collegiality with all

---

28 Ibid.
29 Letter, DLS to Muriel Jaeger, December 18, 1917. Folder 80. Courtesy Marion E. Wade Center, Wheaton, IL.
30 Letters to Muriel Jaeger, Folder 80. Courtesy Marion E. Wade Center, Wheaton, IL.

its attendant humor, argument, critique, and support, occurred during the period of 1923-1936. By this time, Dorothy Sayers had published her detective fiction, achieving a certain fame and credibility in the literary world. Chesterton was now well aware of her as a colleague. He finally remembered her. In this stage, their friendship blossomed into mutual admiration, respect, and equal status. In fact, there existed not only mutual recognition of one another, but Chesterton, in turn, became influenced by Sayers' writings. The humor and communication between them was at its best during this period. They had entered into a relationship of equals, a friendship between authors, and thus a balance of mutual admiration was finally struck within this long standing acquaintance.

A letter sent from Chesterton to Sayers, Christmas 1931, acknowledging the gift of a personal cookbook written by Atherton Fleming, Dorothy's husband, to G.K. Chesterton, illustrated a topic of interest to both as detective fiction colleagues:

Dear Miss Dorothy Sayers

[I]f you will forgive my still starting with the form of address which I have so often hailed on bookstalls with a shout of joy, long before I enjoyed your acquaintance. I do hope you were duly informed before this that I could not acknowledge your very delightful Xmas present as early as I received it: as I was laid flat on my back & not allowed to write a few days before Xmas Day. On that day I had recovered all my normal appetite: but even if I had lost it, I feel sure that the magic book of charms & spells which you sent would have restored it instantly. Will you please thank your husband a thousand times for thinking of trusting so rich and impressive a monograph to me—who who alas cannot cook or do anything useful: but only eat—and drink—and give thanks not only to God but my more creative fellow & creatures: the great Craftsmen of the Guild and Mystery of the Kitchen. I hope he will forgive me if I do not thank him directly—or rather thank you both collectively—but I suppose I must wait a little while before you publish a companion volume, containing all the best ways of poisoning the foods he is so expert in preparing.

Yours very sincerely,
G.K. Chesterton[31]

---

31   Letter. G.K. Chesterton to DLS. DLS Letters, Marion E. Wade Center, Wheaton, IL.

The Detection Club, a society of British mystery authors, including Agatha Christie and Anthony Berkeley, was formed in 1930 with G.K. Chesterton elected as its first president. He served until 1936. Dorothy L. Sayers became the third president from 1949-1957. Along with several others in the club, Chesterton and Sayers collaborated on a mystery entitled, *The Floating Admiral*.[32] She wrote the eighth chapter; he wrote the Prologue. They had become co-authors.

In 1932 Chesterton asked Sayers to write the preface to his play, *The Surprise*. Her preface included the powerful words, "To the young people of my generation, G.K.C. was a kind of Christian liberator," clearly acknowledging the effect of his book, *Orthodoxy*, on her young mind and spirit. The friendship, at this point, was mutually recognized. Even more paradoxically coincidental, according to Dale Ahlquist:

> [T]he plot for *The Surprise* was first suggested in 1908 by Chesterton himself in his book *Orthodoxy*, where he states that when God created the world, he did not write a poem, but a play, "a play he had planned as perfect, but which had necessarily been left to human actors and stage-managers, who had since made a great mess of it."[33]

Therefore, from 1909 when Dorothy first read *Orthodoxy* to 1932 when she wrote the prologue to Chesterton's play, the theme of which had been first suggested in *Orthodoxy*, Sayers' relationship with Chesterton ran the full circle from impressionable reader of his work to active contributor to a work whose roots had been planted in the book that was the first major influence upon her faith. How amusingly subtle were the links in the progression of friendship between these two individuals. Dante would have entirely understood the subtleties of the comedy.

Further, it was not entirely coincidental that Sayers chose the field of mystery fiction as a professional genre choice, starting with *Whose Body?*[34] in 1923 and ending with *Busman's Honeymoon*, 1937.[35] There were many influences pointing her to this route, including that of practicality, the common sense of earning a good living. However, it was providential that Sayers chose a genre that would earn her a

---

32   Agatha Christie, Dorothy L. Sayers, and G.K. Chesterton. *The Floating Admiral*. New York: Doubleday, 1931.
33   Ahlquist, Dale. The American Chesterton Society, Lecture 78. Also *Common Sense 101*, 2006.
34   *Whose Body?*
35   *Busman's Honeymoon.*

living in which Chesterton had already become quite adept and known through his *Father Brown* mysteries.[36] He had, so to speak, blazed the trail again for her. In this, as in so many other of her life choices, although not all, G.K. Chesterton was a continuing influence upon Sayers' professional choices, and certainly had a part, however subtle, in the choice of her writing genres.

Both Sayers and Chesterton possessed an eminently realistic view of the uneven paths of their respective lives. They were very well aware of, and comfortable within, the commonly shared experiences of life. Reflecting upon her reasons for writing popular fiction, Dorothy noted: "I like the common people and I heartily share their love of a lord because I am myself as common as mud in my likes and dislikes."[37]

In the chapter of his autobiography titled "Hearsay Evidence," Chesterton writes:

> The story of my birth might be untrue. I might be the long-lost heir of the Holy Roman Empire or . . . some earnest enquirer [might] come to the conclusion I was never born at all. But I prefer to believe that common sense is something that my readers and I have in common. . . . I was born of respectable but honest parents.[38]

From 1909, when Sayers first read and was profoundly affected by the language and message of *Orthodoxy*, she was very aware of Chesterton as a major social force, revolutionary writer, philosopher, and Christian apologist. To a certain extent, he was always part of her worldview and of her world. Her path of interests and the route of her professional life (i.e., poet, playwright, editor, detective fiction novelist, essayist, critic, among others) often intersected, if not mirrored, that of Chesterton. He was always slightly ahead, somewhat of a guide, in her life path. On the other hand, although G.K. Chesterton was part of Sayers' Oxford world and may have been acquainted with her at that point in time, Chesterton did not formally recognize Sayers until she became part of his published world, that of detective fiction author, essayist, and literary apologist.

At this point, we may come round again to the connection of C.S Lewis to both G.K. Chesterton and Dorothy L. Sayers. As Louis Markos has so elegantly explained, like Chesterton and Sayers, the

---

36   *Penguin Complete Father Brown Mysteries.*
37   Lecture given on February 12, 1936 to the Red Cross. See Brabazon, p. 127.
38   *Autobiography*, p. 178.

key to Lewis was his ability to fuse reason and imagination, logic and intuition, the rational and the emotional:

> Lewis's two-pronged head/heart approach was in great part patterned on the writings of G. K. Chesterton . . . and was seconded in the apologetic works of Dorothy Sayers.... In Chesterton's *Orthodoxy* (1908), *The Everlasting Man* (1925), and Sayers's *The Mind of the Maker* (1941), reason embraces imagination, [at times through humor], in such a way that the latter not only illustrates the former, but provides the primary vehicle for reaching and understanding some of the deepest truths of Christianity. [39]

In summary, we may trace the long process of friendship between Chesterton and Sayers, two writers of very similar character, humor, sense, and insight, which, maturing from influence through acquaintance to a mutual and collegial friendship, led to links with similar forces of intellect such as that of C.S. Lewis. The developing storyline through time of the relationship between G.K. Chesterton and Dorothy L. Sayers may not have been apparent, even to them, during the process of its development. Although, having an historical perspective, we are allowed to recognize the progression, allowed to make the connections, allowed to see the values of common sense and humor repeatedly emerging in each character and writer, then finally coalescing into a full collegial friendship of like mind and spirit. Their links to one another were further extended to form a connected web of authors in the twentieth century who influenced one another and were by virtue of their mutually inspired work, a web of Linklings. By recognition of this linked web, we are also given a glimpse of that which is an infinite web of intellectual threads, links in progression, in movement, in creation, and in common experience, as well as being a manifestation of the divine comedy so profoundly realized by Chesterton:

> That though the jest be old as night
> Still shaketh sun and sphere
> An everlasting laughter
> Too loud for us to hear. [40]

---

39 Louis A. Markos. "Literary Apologetics: The Legacy of G. K. Chesterton and Dorothy Sayers." In *Christian Research Journal*. Article 22, 2011.
40 "A Portrait." *The Wild Knight and Other Poems*. G.K. Chesterton, 1900.

WORKS CITED

Ahlquist, Dale. *Common Sense 101: Lessons from G.K. Chesterton.* San Francisco: Ignatius Press, 2006.

---. *G.K. Chesterton: The Apostle of Common Sense.* San Francisco: Ignatius Press, 2003.

Lecture 78. The American Chesterton Society. http://www.chesterton.org.

Belmonte, Kevin. *The Quotable Chesterton: The Wit and Wisdom of G.K. Chesterton.* Nashville: Thomas Nelson, 2011.

Brabazon, James. *Dorothy L. Sayers.* New York: Charles Scribner's Sons, 1981.

Chesterton, Gilbert Keith. *Autobiography.* London: Hutchison & Co., 1936.

---. *Dickens: A Critical Study.* New York: Dodd, Mead & Co., 1909.

---. *The Everlasting Man.* London: Hodder and Stoughton, 1925.

---. *The Floating Admiral.* Agatha Christie and Dorothy L. Sayers. New York: Doubleday, Doran & Co., 1931.

---. *Heretics.* New York: John Lane Co., 1907.

---. Letter. G.K. Chesterton to Dorothy L. Sayers, December, 1931. DLS Letters, Marion E. Wade Center, Wheaton, IL.

---. *The Napoleon of Notting Hill.* London: The Bodley Head, 1904.

---. *Orthodoxy.* London: The Bodley Head, 1908; New York: John Lane Co., 1909.

---. Penguin Complete Father Brown. New York: Penguin, 1981.

---. *The Surprise.* London: Sheed and Ward, 1952.

---. *What's Wrong with the World?* New York: Dodd, Mead & Co., 1910.

---. *The Wild Knight and Other Poems.* London: Grant Richards, 1900.

Curtis, Carolyn and Mary Pomeroy Key. *Women and C.S. Lewis*. Oxford: Lion Books., 2015.

Dale, Alzina Stone. *The Outline of Sanity: A Life of G.K. Chesterton*. Grand Rapids, MI: William B. Eerdmans Publishing Co., 1982.

Downing, Crystal. "Sayers "Begins Here" with a Vision for Social and Intellectual Change" IN *Christian History*, Issue 113:18, "Seven Literary Sages," 2015.

Lewis, C.S. Letter to the Editor, *Encounter Magazine*, January 1963.

---. *The Screwtape Letters*. UK: Geoffrey Bless, 1942.

Markos, Louis A. "Literary Apologetics: The Legacy of G.K. Chesterton and Dorothy L. Sayers." *Christian Research Journal*. Article 22, 2011. JAF 1342. http://christian1408.rssing.com

Reynolds, Barbara. *Dorothy L. Sayers: Child and Woman of Her Time*. Volume Five, Letters. Great Britain: The Dorothy L. Sayers Society, 2002.

Dorothy L. Sayers: Her Life and Soul. New York: St. Martin's Press, 1993.

Sayers, Dorothy L. *Busman's Honeymoon*. London: Victor Golancz, Ltd., 1937.

---. *Creed or Chaos and Other Essays in Popular Theology*. London: Methuen, 1940.

---. *The Floating Admiral*. Agatha Christie and G.K. Chesterton. New York: Doubleday, Doran & Co., 1931.

---. *Gaudy Night*. London: Victor Golancz Ltd., 1935.

---. *The Just Vengeance*. Lichfield Festival Play for 1946, Gollancz, 1946.

---. Letters, DLS to Muriel Jaeger, 1914-1917. DLS Letters, Folders 79-80, Marion E. Wade Center, Wheaton, IL.

---. Letters, DLS to Parents, 1912-1914. DLS Letters, Folder 22, Marion E. Wade Center, Wheaton, IL.

---. *The Mind of the Maker*. London: Methuen, 1941.

---. Preface to *The Surprise: A Play by G.K. Chesterton*.

London: Sheed and Ward, 1953.

---. *Strong Meat.* London: Hodder & Stoughton, 1939.

---. *Unpopular Opinions.* London: Victor Gollancz, 1946.

---. *Whose Body?* London: T. Fisher Unwin, 1923.

---. *Why Work? An Address Delivered at Eastbourne*, April 23, 1942. London: Methuen, 1942.

Wills, Gary. *Chesterton.* New York: Doubleday, 2001.

Take This Job and Love It: Dorothy Sayers on Work

by Kimberly Moore-Jumonville

Kimberly Moore-Jumonville chairs the English Department at Spring Arbor University. Her teaching interests include Nineteenth Century British Literature and the works of Dorothy Sayers and C.S. Lewis.

Let's face it. In our worst moments of early adulthood, the Zombie Job can lurk in the dark recesses of our imaginations, haunting us with images of hollow men and women creeping through offices, myopically intent on numbers, lists, formulas, equation—the kind of keyboard-crunching, mind-numbing dullness that deadens our spirits. Worse yet, in this nightmare, the hours drag on endlessly for days, months, and years, but we suffer the dread land of this twilight kingdom to pay off debt and accumulate retirement options. The challenging adventure we had hoped for when we trained for this occupation has withered into a pale, red-eyed resolve to survive. And yet, despite our dread, we doggedly pursue our dream of meaningful life-giving work; we slog through job training and internships hoping above hope that training will give way to miraculously satisfying jobs, and hoping above hope that we're not turned into Zombies in the process. The people in this scenario are dying *at* work; we want to be dying *to* work.

What is there to save us from such a soul-deadening life? Dorothy Sayers posits a "gospel of work" grounded in God's nature itself. God is essentially creative; the story through which God reveals himself to us begins with THE creative act. The first verb of scripture is the strongest action verb: "to create"; the first action we see God take is to create: "In the beginning, God created the heavens and the earth" (Genesis 1:1). The Nicene Creed also recounts Jesus as a fundamental presence in God's creative work. Jesus is "God from God, light from light, true God from true God, begotten not made, of one Being with the Father. Through him all things were made."

Made in the image of God, then, made to be like Christ, it is human beings' nature to create. We share in God's creative nature; in fact, creativity is such a critical aspect of humanity that to deny it is to deny part of what it is to be human. Dorothy Sayers's "gospel of work" is that our work "must allow people to fulfill their vocation by being creative, or else it *cheats* them of their essential humanity" (Simmons

112). In other words, we *must* create or become less than human. Sayers's detective Harriet Vane muses in *Gaudy Night* that "to be true to one's calling, whatever follies one might commit in one's emotional life, that was the way to emotional peace" (28). Later Harriet remarks, "When you get the thing dead right and know it's dead right, there's no excitement like it. It makes you feel like God on the Seventh Day—for a bit anyhow" (149). What I like about this is that Harriet is not referring to writing poetry or composing music, typical creative tasks, she is solving a mystery that is haunting a women's college. Her work is detection, and doing it effectively is her creative gift—in other words, *our particular giftedness is our creative work*. (We don't have to dance ballet, play violin, or do graphic design to exercise creativity).

Sayers also describes work in its creative vitality as "the outward and visible sign of a creative reality" (Letter to V.A. Demant April 10, 1941, 247). Such sacramental language should encourage us to regard our work as a sacramental act. In her essay *Vocation in Work* she goes so far as to assign our work a *redemptive* measure, as it is "the creative activity that can redeem the world" (*Creed or Chaos?* 90-91). The upshot of this claim is that fulfilling our unique vocation, doing the thing we are uniquely made to do, serves the creation in such a way that God's work on earth is forwarded. In his biography of Steve Jobs, Walter Isaacson recounts Jobs's response to hearing Yo Yo Ma play Bach: "Your playing is the best argument I've ever heard for the existence of God, because I don't really believe a human being alone can do this" (425). Perceptive observations like Jobs's demonstrate that finding our vocation brings us to full creative vitality. This is what we long for. People of faith can go further to recognize that doing the thing we are made to do gives our soul life. It also fulfills God's intention for our gifts and in some way forwards God's kingdom on earth.

Yet, we have to admit that work does not always give us life; it can drain and frustrate as often as it vitalizes. In fact, we sometimes give our lives to work that actually goes against our value system without realizing it. Even in the church we can work for all the wrong reasons. In her 1947 essay, *Why Work*, Sayers suggests that generally in the West, we are accustomed to value our work in terms of the money it generates. She is quick to remind us that the question "what does it pay?" is the wrong question. If we work only to earn money, then it is an end in itself, a dead end, soul-deadening because comfort and leisure don't make us happy. We work longer hours to secure leisure funds to buy a fancy boat or glitzy vacation package, but wear ourselves out playing hard. We hate Mondays. We exhaust ourselves on a squirrel cage that hopes to secure happiness.

Consider this familiar parable:

> A wise man is happily relaxing in the shade of a tree by a large beautiful lake. He is playing his guitar and beside him lays a fishing rod cast out into the lake. A businessman walks up to him and asks him what he is doing.
>
> He replies that he is waiting for a fish to pass by. The businessman asks whether he has seen anyone else around the lake. The wise man replies that he has not seen anyone else for weeks.
>
> Spotting an opportunity, the businessman advises that he should build himself a boat, cast a net into the lake and sell the surplus fish at the market.
>
> "And what next?"
>
> The businessman replies that he could then use the profits to build himself a bigger boat to catch more fish.
>
> "And then?"
>
> The businessman advises that he could then build a fleet of vessels and hire a crew of people to help him catch even more fish.
>
> "After that?"
>
> The businessman proclaims that he would then be rich and be able to retire early.
>
> The wise man questions, "And then what should I do?"
>
> The businessman replies that he could then sit by the lake, relax and play his guitar!
>
> If leisure and comfort are the goal, then we really can forego the work and take the leisure!

Of course we must work to live, to bring home the bacon as it were; there is some necessity here. But we do well to remember that economic necessity always stands secondary to another claim upon us, given the fact that we are creatures of a creator. The first claim on us follows from God's nature and the creation; thus, Sayers urges us to consider a potential job in terms of the *end* it serves. Rather than "what does it pay," we should begin with the question, "Is it good?" Does this work serve a good? Is it an aspect of creation that warrants cultivation? Does it promote the good of something or someone—an individual, a group or a cause? Does it answer a human need or speak to a human longing? In other words, does it need doing?

And how do we determine whether a job needs doing? Basically, there are two sources of real wealth (and this claim reaches back to thinkers of the Middle Ages like Dante and Aquinas): Nature, the stuff we have to work with; and human labor, the effort we exert upon nature to produce something. Work related to agriculture and ecology obviously draw on the fruits of the earth to serve aspects of Nature. But a plethora of consumer goods not directly related to the earth are also important: the car industry, for example—transportation is a good, after all. The question about car production should go further than profit margin and shareholder gains to issues of employee wages and benefits, working conditions, and also the quality of the product and its relationship to the community and environment. Questions such as "does this product deplete natural resources or put harmful chemicals into the environment?" are important. Asking about a product's efficiency record, about how long it will last is also helpful. Does it perform its function reliably with satisfying results or does it figure in a program of planned obsolescence (not mentioning any names). Would fewer cars or more public transportation in densely populated regions actually offer more humane living conditions? The question, "Is it worth doing?" can be determined by whether it serves a good. That question should be accompanied by another question as well, the question of whether the work is good in itself.

Ultimately, then, the worth of, the value of the job should be assessed not in terms of cost or pay but in terms of what the thing in itself is worth. The question of intrinsic value goes beyond the treadmill of production and consumption to absolute terms of a Christian worldview that begins with absolute values. Because we see ourselves as creatures submitted to a Sovereign Creator, Christians look outside ourselves for the meaning of experience. We see the world in theological terms that take precedence over a secular economic paradigm of work. The absolute value I refer to here is the intrinsic worth of our work well done. Work well done is a life well lived. If the secular paradigm regards the value of the person in terms of what she does, that assumes her meaning lies in earning a paycheck. Therefore, the goal of life becomes money, which assumes the material world is our primary reality; the material world is then the only thing that must be taken into account. However, such a philosophy of materialism denies spiritual reality as ultimate. For us, being created in God's image acknowledges that our soul is the eternal part of us and the source of our uniqueness. Therefore, we are intrinsically valuable and our work with the creation is also intrinsically valuable.

One essential question about our work, then, is "Is it good?" "Have we done it well?" Our reward comes not in dollars but in knowing that we have honored a particular aspect of the creation by exercising our human labor (creativity) upon it as well as we possibly can. The only Christian work, after all, is work well done. No job poorly planned and executed honors the Creator; there is no good Christian music or good Christian book unless it is well-composed or well-performed or well-written. As Sayers admits, "The worst religious films I ever saw were produced by a company which chose its staff exclusively for their piety. Bad photography, bad acting, and bad dialog produced a result so grotesquely irreverent that the pictures could not have been shown in churches without bringing Christianity into contempt" (*Why Work* 80). Furthermore, she insists that ." . . A building must be good architecture before it can be a good church; [a] painting must be well painted before it can be a good sacred picture; work must be good work before it can call itself God's work" (78). Thus, work done as an excellent example of its kind serves the creation and points to the creator.

Sayers's play, *The Zeal of Thy House* (1937), takes up this question of quality (of *work well done*) in the building of the Canterbury Cathedral. Its architect, William of Sens, makes up for his lack of piety with a commitment to the excellence of the product. "At my age, one learns that sometimes one has to damn one's soul for the sake of the work. Trust me, God shall have a choir fit for His service. *Does anything else really matter?*" (emphasis mine) (27). Despite his unorthodox lifestyle, the monks give Sens the job of building the cathedral because they want the church whose grandeur will give God the greatest glory. It doesn't take long for them to question their choice, but the angels in the play, a kind of Greek chorus, validate Sens as one of those "men who work like angels—and whistle while they work. They are much the most cheerful kind" (7). Sayers makes her point clear; the morality of our actions finds its value in relation to the end it serves. The greater sin is to produce a poor product; thus, the quality of the product is what matters most.

If work is good in itself, if it is intrinsically valuable, worth doing because it serves a human need, and honors God when done excellently, we have ample reason to pursue it, a right reason to work. But we also have to ask, does it exercise our faculties, our gifts and abilities to the fullest, because work can make us more fully whole, more fully ourselves. God made us to do the thing that gives us spiritual, mental, and physical satisfaction (Simmons 102). This kind of work could become a prayer, the medium through which we offer ourselves to God. When we are fortunate enough to find work that is our work, it changes the goal from getting paid to working for our fulfillment and reward; it becomes the measure of our life—as long as society gives us enough return to do work properly. It only follows that we need to find the work we are uniquely gifted for. Not the highest paycheck, but the highest level of satisfaction. Bigger is not always better, more is not always advantageous. Numbers in church do not always imply more spiritual success for the community, for instance. The joy of work that fits our giftedness is that in doing it we are becoming what we are created to be; we are becoming what we already are. Right work for the right reason in the right way exercises the strengths God gave us and calls out the particular beauty already latent in us, waiting to be developed. In our beginning, God had a particularly beautiful, breathtaking human being that He hoped we would become; our life is a chance to grow into the fullness of that person and work that exercises our gifts and abilities moves us toward that ideal being we were made to be.

Of course, the culture does not recognize this reality—that being created in God's image predisposes our nature for work, for work that needs to be performed by us for God's glory. We have to admit that social expectations and economic pressures militate against the importance of matching the worker with the work for the good of society. But if we drudge through tasks in order to receive a paycheck at the end of the day, we recognize that frustration, despair, anger, and boredom is a formula for a shoddy, lackluster culture. We know we don't want the Zombie job; we dread living in a Zombie society.

When we do discover the work that suits us, work we were meant for, work that calls out the expression of our full self, work that shapes our selfhood, we realize that it is *sacramental*. In fact, all work, even secular work, can help redeem the world. Therefore, all work is sacred. Christians do not have to think of the so-called Christian vocation or Christian job as the only "sacred work." Any work is potentially sacred, as long as it avoids the soul-denigrating or soul-destroying thing; certainly work as slavery rampant around our world is an outrage. But we can fall into the trap of validating church-related work or ministry as more admirable or more holy than the secular. Specifically church-related work seems more obviously Christian. Sayers urges the church to remember that "every maker and worker is called to serve God *in* his profession or trade—not outside it" (107). The question isn't sacred or secular, the question is, "what am I suited for?" What calls me to it? Because all creation needs to be served. And, as Sayers noted earlier, "the only Christian work is good work well done" (108).

One final reason for work is really the most important for Christians, and that is that we should take on a job in order to serve the work. Frequently, when we describe the goal of work as service, it often gets translated to "serving the community." Sayers warns us, however, that the community can inadvertently become the focus of our work and therefore falsify what we want to offer as a gift. How so? When serving the community, we can take our eyes off the task to see how the community is measuring it. We can end up altering or reshaping what we are doing to get the response we want, which isn't necessarily healthy for the outcome. To ask, 'Do they like me, do they like my sculpture?" isn't helpful because we can end up trying to please the audience rather than striving to create something excellent. Remember, the work needs to be judged by its own standards rather than what people outside the discipline think. And work that is less than quality work serves neither God nor the community. Done for the wrong reasons, it serves only "mammon" (112).

It is also easy for us once we imagine we are serving people to assume they owe us something. We can think it's legitimate to expect a reward, a recognition, or at least some form of gratitude (113) and to resent not getting these. In Sayers's words: "The only true way of serving the community is to be truly in sympathy with the community, to be oneself part of the community, and then to serve the work without giving the community another thought. Then the work will endure, because it will be true to itself" (114). The more difficult thing to do is to serve the work—then our focus is the satisfaction of observing the quality of the thing well done. To serve the work is the thing. It demands our best efforts and gives back what we put into it—labor becomes love. "Take this job and love it," the title for this paper, suggests that to love is to labor at the good thing worth doing, the task that calls out our gifts, that moves us toward being more fully ourselves, nurtures some aspect of the creation and serves the work itself. In the end, the creation is served, the community is served, and love is extended into the universe.

My spiritual mentor describes a vision of heaven in which explosions of creativity resound; people are free to express their gifts fully in the afterlife, and that beauty sets off constant chain reactions that reverberate new waves of inspiration. In a vision like that, Heaven will be so pervaded with joy and love that we will be constantly renewed and energized. The Trinity, the originating force of it all will form its center. I want to spend eternity in such a place. In fact, I believe my work can begin to participate in it now. Such a vision gives continuity to the work I do now; I am participating in the Kingdom of Heaven on earth imagining that it is going to go on for eternity.

Thus, Dorothy Sayers's vision of work helps us see that our task is to find the thing God has created us to do in a way that no one else can because of our unique gifting, and then serve the integrity of that work with all our heart, soul, and mind because it deserves cultivation, because it promotes a good, because it is worth doing well, and because that work calls for the fullest expression of our gifts. We can look to her for ways to avoid the Zombie job and discover we *can* leave home each morning dying *to* work—not dying *from* work!

Works Cited

Edmundson, Mark. *The Ideal English Major.* Chronicle of Higher Education. 2 August, 2013: B14-B15. Web.

Isaacson, Walter. *Steve Jobs.* New York: Simon and Schuster, 2011. Print.

McEntyre, Marilyn Chandler. *Caring for Words in a Culture of Lies.* Grand Rapids, MI: Eerdmans, 2009. Print.

Reynolds, Barbara, Ed. *The Letters of Dorothy Sayers.* Volume 2.

Sayers, Dorothy. *Creed or Chaos?* Manchester, NH: Sophia, 1974. Print.

---. "The Cinema." Letter to the editor. *The Church Times.* Print.

---. "Vocation in Work." A Christian Basis for the Post-War World. Ed. A.E. Baker. London: SCM Press, 1942. 88-103. Print.

---. *The Zeal of Thy House.* Rahway, NJ: Quinn, 1937. Print.

---. "Why Work" In *Creed or Chaos?* Manchester, NH: Sophia, 1974. Print.

Simmons, Laura. *Creed Without Chaos: Exploring Theology in the Writings of Dorothy Sayers.* Grand Rapids, MI: Baker, 2005. Print.

Steiner, George. *Real Presences.* University of Chicago, 1989. Print.

C. S. Lewis and Dorothy L. Sayers: Correspondence

by Marsha Daigle-Williamson

Marsha Daigle-Williamson (Ph.D, University of Michigan) is Professor Emerita at Spring Arbor University where she taught English. She has translated sixteen books from Italian and is an active member of the Dante Society of America. Her book *Reflecting the Eternal: Dante's "Divine Comedy" in the Novels of C. S. Lewis* was published in 2015.

The correspondence between C. S. Lewis and Dorothy L. Sayers began in 1942 and continued until her death in 1957. We have 61 letters from Lewis to her in Walter Hooper's collection, which are either responses to her letters or which call for responses from her. So, although we have only 21 of Sayers's letters to Lewis in Barbara Reynolds's four-volume collection, we know there were more. The letters demonstrate a relationship that evolved over the years from that of being professional colleagues to that of being close friends. There are three main areas of discussion in these letters: requests of each other to write something specific, comments on each other's writings, and discussions mostly on literary topics, especially Dante.

Sayers began the correspondence in the spring of 1942. She was already well-known for her detective novels and plays and was organizing a series of books called *Bridgeheads* that were intended to prepare readers for post-war social and moral reconstruction. The first in the series was her own book *The Mind of the Maker* (1941). She was aware of Lewis's writings up to that point, having already recommended *The Problem of Pain* to two of her correspondents the year before,[1] a book that she continued to recommend as "a brilliant book"[2] and as "excellent."[3]

---

1   See Dorothy L. Sayers, June 5, 1941, and November 26, 1941, *The Letters of Dorothy L. Sayers, Volume 2, 1937-1943: From Novelist to Playwright*, ed. Barbara Reynolds, preface P. D. James (New York: St. Martin's, 1998), p. 265, p. 325. See also Sayers's letter on January 19, 1956, *The Letters of Dorothy L. Sayers, Volume 4, 1951-1957: In the Midst of Life*, ed. Barbara Reynolds, preface P. D. James (Cambridge: Carole Green, 2000), p. 269.
2   Ibid., May 10, 1943, p. 400.
3   Dorothy L. Sayers, May 31, 1948, *The Letters of Dorothy L. Sayers, Volume 3, 1944-1950: A Noble Daring*, ed. Barbara Reynolds, preface P. D. James (Cambridge: Carole Greene 1998), p. 375.

Sayers was reportedly also enormously impressed by *The Screwtape Letters*. Perhaps because Letters XVIII and XIX in particular contained insightful remarks on love and marriage,[4] she wrote Lewis to ask if he would contribute to her *Bridgeheads* series on this topic.

Lewis was likewise already aware of Sayers when he received his first letter from her. Although he did not care for *Gaudy Night* because he did not like detective fiction,[5] he had read and very much enjoyed *The Mind of the Maker*. His response on April 1942 to her request opens in his typical direct manner: "But why not write the book yourself?" The reason he gave was that "every word you wrote showed that you had the book in your own head and just straining at the leash." He suggested she could do it as a novel or a treatise, advising, "I hope you'll do the novel. It wd soften the blow."[6] (Walter Hooper believes that although Lewis did not contribute a book, "much of what Sayers asked him to say probably went into the character of the unhappily married Jane Studdock."[7])

He suggested in his first letter to her that they could perhaps meet sometime. A few days later in his second "refusal letter" to a very persistent Sayers about writing for her series, he took the initiative to invite her to lunch in early June.[8] This would be their first meeting.

Although Lewis turned down her writing invitation this time, it was the first of many back and forth invitations to write something specific. One year later, she wrote Lewis a letter that included a mock memorandum in Screwtape style signed by "Sluckdrib" that she asked him to deliver, presumably to Screwtape, because "you have entrée into the Lowest Official Circles [of Hell]."[9] Sluckdrib revels in "a growing tendency to consider the Bible as Literature"[10] but also complains about the deleterious effect of some religious plays on atheists. At the end of her letter after this memo, Sayers complained to Lewis that

---

4 See Walter Hooper, *Collected Letters of C. S. Lewis*, ed. Walter Hooper, 3 vols. (New York: Harper Collins, 2004-2007), vol. 2, p. 1941.
5 Despite this fact, Lewis must have looked at the novel again because he writes her on September 25, 1954, "Harriet's sonnet in *Gaudy Night* may have come from Milton. Did you know that when you wrote it?" *Collected Letters*, vol. 3, p. 508.
6 C. S. Lewis, April [?], 1942, *Collected Letters*, vol. 2, p. 515.
7 Walter Hooper, *C. S. Lewis: A Companion and Guide* (New York: Harper Collins, 1996), p. 4.
8 Lewis, April 6, 1942, *Collected Letters*, vol. 2, p. 516.
9 Sayers, May 13, 1943, *The Letters*, vol. 2, p. 409.
10 Ibid., p. 410.

"there aren't any up-to-date books about Miracles."[11] He wrote back four days later and included a copy of his sermon "Miracles" that had been published a few months earlier.[12] It was a condensed or miniature version of his eventual 1947 book *Miracles: A Preliminary Study*. Although he says in this letter, "I'm starting a book on Miracles,"[13] Walter Hooper believes, "it is likely that Sayers's observation about the lack of book on miracles was exactly the encouragement Lewis needed to write his own book on the subject."[14] When the book was published, Sayers expressed her appreciation for it to Lewis, saying that "it seems to me to be admirably well argued,"[15] and she also thanked him for his kind mention of one of her books in it (Lewis had written, "How a miracle can be no inconsistency, but the highest consistency, will be clear to those who have read Miss Dorothy Sayers' indispensable book, *The Mind of the Maker*."[16]).

Two days after Charles Williams died, Lewis wrote to ask Sayers to contribute to a volume for Williams that had been meant to celebrate his return to London after the war but that turned into a memorial volume because of his unexpected death. The contributors to this volume, mostly on the art of writing, were all Inklings, with Dorothy being the only "outsider."[17] Lewis's esteem for Sayers's writing[18] plus her friendship with and admiration for Williams after reading his *The Figure of Beatrice* (1943) are probably what opened the door for her to be one of the writers for this volume. Lewis told her she could write "on any subject you like."[19] Responding one week later, she indicated she wanted to write "something arising out of the Dante job I am doing."[20] Six months later, in December, she apologized for her "sprawling 60-page colossus"; since this was the first time she was writing anything on Dante, "all my excitement is apt to come out with

---

11   Ibid., p. 413.
12   C. S. Lewis, "Miracles," *St. Jude Gazette*, October, 1942.
13   Lewis, May [30?], 1943, *Collected Letters*, vol. 2, p. 577.
14   Hooper, *Collected Letters*, vol. 2, p. 573, n. 103.
15   Sayers, June 2, 1947, *The Letters*, vol. 3, p. 304.
16   C. S. Lewis, *Miracles: A Preliminary Study* (New York: Macmillan, 1960), p. 98.
17   T. S. Eliot had also been invited to write an essay for this volume because of his relationship with Charles Williams, but he never did.
18   In his preface to *Essays Presented to Charles Williams* (Oxford: Oxford University Press, 1947), Lewis describes her as a "professional author" (p. vi).
19   Lewis, May 17, 1945, *The Collected Letters*, vol. 2, p. 650.
20   Sayers, May 25, 1945, *The Letters*, vol. 3, p. 148.

a rush, like bottled beer that has stood too long in a warm place."[21] When she received Lewis's editing suggestions for cuts at the end of that month, she wrote, "I am very glad you like the Dante paper—and also that you like the best bits that I was . . . best pleased with."[22] Her revised essay reached Lewis in early January 1946, so we now have *. . . And Telling You a Story: A Note on The Divine Comedy*" included in *Essays Presented to Charles Williams* (1947). Four years later, Lewis, the re-reader par excellence, would write to her that he was reading her Dante essay again "with great enjoyment."[23] (She later asked Lewis permission to reprint the essay in her *Further Papers on Dante*.[24])

It was a different story when Lewis asked her a few months later to contribute to a series of booklets that would constitute a library of Christian knowledge for young people.[25] Although he had told her she could pick her own topic, she declined because she objected to writing things only for edification purposes, what she called "things in which intellect and imagination are not united by the assessment of the will."[26] "Anything I write," she says, "which is not the expression of some apprehended truth which I am bound to communicate, is . . . a sin against truth."[27] Three days later in another letter to buttress her point about the integrity of the artist, she even referred to one of Lewis's own characters in her argument: "The corrupt artist in *The Great Divorce . . .* turned from serving the work and making the work serve him, and no longer paints because he is summoned to express and communicate, but for some other reason."[28] Two years later she also declined a request by Lewis to write a letter or an article about the topic of women's ordination in the Anglican Church because, according to Lewis, "the defense against the innovation must if possible be done by a woman." The job description he gave for that task was "'ANGLICAN (woman): [with] effective dialectical powers: established literary reputation essential.'"[29] Although she agreed with Lewis that such ordination could cause an unnecessary barrier with other churches,[30] she never did write anything on that topic for a journal or newspaper.

21 Sayers, December 3, 1945, *The Letters*, vol. 2, p. 176.
22 Sayers, December 24, 1945, *The Letters*, vol. 2, p. 182.
23 Lewis, November 9, 1949, *Collected Letters*, vol. 2, p. 994.
24 Sayers, April 4, 1955, *The Letters*, vol. 4, p. 221.
25 Lewis, July 23, 1946, *Collected Letters*, vol. 2, pp. 721-22.
26 Sayers, August 5, 1946, *The Letters*, vol. 3, p. 257.
27 Ibid., pp. 255-56.
28 Sayers, August 8, 1946, *The Letters*, vol. 3, p. 258.
29 See Lewis, July 13, 1948, *Collected Letters*, vol. 2, pp. 860-61.
30 See Sayers, July 19, 1948, *The Letters*, vol. 3, 387-88.

Lewis felt free as well to decline her invitations. In the fall of 1949, when she asked him to write a preface for Helmut Kahn's book *Encounter with Nothingness: An Essay on Existentialism*, which was part of her *Bridgeheads* series, Lewis's response was quite clear: "I would'nt [sic] dream of writing a preface" because "I know (and care) little about the Existentialist nonsense."[31]

In tandem with these requests to write something, the letters between Sayers and Lewis often discuss and comment on each other's lectures, articles, or books. In early spring 1943, Lewis wrote to congratulate her on her address to the Public Morality Council.[32] He called it "perfect—i.e., there's nothing one would wish added or removed or deleted."[33] Two months later, he wrote to Sayers about the advance copy she sent him of *The Man Born to Be King*, her series of twelve plays on the life of Christ that had been broadcast at monthly intervals from the end of December 1941 to October 1942, some of which overlapped with Lewis's own broadcast talks that began on August 6, 1941, and would later become *Mere Christianity*. He called her series "a complete success," saying that he read it with tears in spots, and affirmed, "I expect to read it times without number again."[34] This was not a whimsical or hyperbolic statement. Two and half years later, he wrote to her that he was re-reading the book, saying, "It wears excellently."[35] Later he wrote to her in 1955, "I am, as always in Holy Week, re-reading *The Man Born to Be King*. It stands up . . . extremely well."[36] When she sent him a copy of her 1945 lecture "The Faust Legend and the Idea of the Devil,"[37] he responded, "Thanks . . . for

---

31   Lewis, November 9, 1949, *Collected Letters*, vol. 2, p. 995.
32   Sayers's talk, "Six Other Deadly Sins," was delivered on October 23, 1941.
33   Lewis, March 18, 1943, *Collected Letters*, vol. 2, p. 564. Two years later he again remarked on his "delighted enjoyment" of that lecture. See Lewis, May, 17, 1945, *Collected Letters*, vol. 2, p. 650.
34   Lewis, May [30?], 1943, *Collected Letters*, vol. 2, p. 577.
35   Lewis, November 7, 1947, *Collected Letters*, vol. 2, p. 811.
36   Lewis, April 6, 1955, *Collected Letters*, vol. 3, p. 593. See also his remark about this in his eulogy for Dorothy L. Sayers: "For my part, I have re-read it in every Holy Week since it first appeared and never re-read it without being deeply moved." "Panegyric for Dorothy L. Sayers," in *"On Stories" and Other Essays on Literature*, eds. Owen Barfield and Walter Hooper (New York: Harcourt, 1988), p. 93.
37   Dorothy L. Sayers, "The Faust Legend and the Idea of the Devil," Publications of the English Goethe Society, New Series 15 (1946), 1-20. It was delivered on February 22, 1945.

giving me a great deal of pleasure—and knowledge."[38]

Sayers also wrote Lewis in praise of his writings. During the six months between December 1945 and July 1946, perhaps because she was now better acquainted with Lewis because of their work together on the Charles Williams's volume, she sent letters with comments about some of his novels. Sayers admitted to "an unregenerate affection for the 'old furry people'" in *Out of the Silent Planet*.[39] Lewis said he was "exceedingly glad you liked *O. S. Planet*" and thanked her "for the *errata*" that she—ever the careful reader—had also sent along.[40] She also made reference to *Perelandra* as well when she commented that if "all this atomic stuff" might blow up the earth, it "might upset the inhabitants of Malacandra and Perelandra, whose orbits would presumably be displaced, making extra work for the Oyérsu [using the correct plural for 'Oyarsa']."[41] In another letter he thanked her "for the kind things you say about 'Grand Divorce' [*sic*]."[42] In terms of *That Hideous Strength*, her praise did not preclude honesty. Although she said that "the book is tremendously full of good things," she added, "perhaps almost too full." Commenting on the "good things," she felt that "The arrival of the gods [eldils] is grand . . . and the atmosphere of the N.I.C.E. is superb. Wither is a masterpiece. . . . And the death of Filistrato is first-class. . . . Mr. Bultitude of course is adorable." She also highlighted "the marvelous confusion of tongues at the dinner. And the painful realism of that college meeting." On the other hand, she additionally offered, "I'm afraid I don't like Ransom quite so well since he took to being golden-haired and . . . on a sofa."[43]

When she read a copy of the *Arthurian Torso* (1948), which includes Lewis's commentary on Charles Williams's Arthurian poems, she told Lewis, "How thankful I am to have it as a guide to the poems. . . . You have made sense and good order out of it."[44] She

---

38 Lewis, August 19, 1946, *Collected Letters*, vol. 2, p. 737.
39 Sayers, December 3, 1945, *The Letters*, vol. 3, p. 177.
40 Lewis, July 29, 1946, *Collected Letters*, vol. 2, p. 729.
41 Sayers, December 3, 1945, *The Letters*, vol. 3, p. 177.
42 Lewis, January 22, 1946, *Collected Letters*, vol. 2, p. 700.
43 Sayers, December 3, 1945, *The Letters*, vol. 3, p. 177. She also said—but not to Lewis—she was irritated by "the half-hearted attempt made at one point to connect him [Ransom] with the Fisher King on the strength of the wound in his heel." September 9, 1946, *The Letters*, vol. 3, p. 264. A year later, she wrote, "I cannot forgive C. S. Lewis for equating his Ransom with the Fisher King through that very artificial link of the wound in his heel." June 26, 1947, *The Letters*, vol. 3, p. 309.
44 Sayers, October 22, 1948, *The Letters*, vol. 3, pp. 400-401.

proceeded to give it to a friend and met someone else who had found Lewis's commentary very valuable and reported to Lewis, "These are the only two mice I have so far had the opportunity of catching for you, and I lay them at your feet."[45]

In 1956 when he sent her a copy of *Till We Have Faces*, she told Barbara Reynolds that in "The Psyche story . . . [Lewis] has done the woman . . . very well, I think, bearing in mind that it was rather bold of him to attempt it."[46]

Her overall assessment of Lewis's writings in 1948 was "I find most of his books very illuminating and stimulating."[47] In terms of his apologetics, Sayers commented that "Lewis is magnificently ruthless with people who do set out to produce what purports to be a logical argument [and then commit logical errors]. . . . He is down on the thing like a rat; he is God's terrier, and I wouldn't be without him for the world" and "he is a tremendous hammer for heretics."[48]

This assessment did not change over time but she came in the end to prefer his fiction, telling Reynolds, "I think one gets the best of Lewis not in the apologetics . . . but in the three novels and in the Narnia fairy-tales in which Christ appears as a talking Lion, and even the girls are allowed to take active part in the adventures."[49] She later added, "The girls, on the whole, are given as much courage as the boys, and more virtue (all the really naughty and tiresome children are boys)."[50] In general she concluded that "Lewis has a remarkable gift for inventing imaginary worlds which are both beautiful and plausible."[51]

In terms of discussing literary issues and other authors, both Lewis and Sayers pepper their letters with spontaneous allusions to and quotations from English, Latin, French, and Italian authors (as well as the Bible) that were in easy reach. Beginning at the end of 1949,

---

45 Sayers, December 31, 1948, *The Letters*, vol. 3, p. 414.
46 Sayers, September 5, 1956, *The Letters*, vol. 4, p. 328. This is quite high praise given that only nine months earlier she had told Reynolds, "I like him [Lewis] very much, and always find him stimulating and amusing. One just has to accept the fact that there is a complete blank in his mind where women are concerned." Sayers, December 21, 1955, *The Letters*, vol. 4, p. 263. She had much earlier written, "I do admit he [Lewis] is apt to write shocking nonsense about women and marriage." May 31, 1948, *The Letters*, vol. 3, p. 375.
47 Sayers, May 31, 1948, *The Letters*, vol. 3, p. 375.
48 Sayers, July 10, 1947, *The Letters*, vol. 3, p. 314.
49 Ibid.
50 Sayers, February 10, 1956, *The Letters*, vol. 4, p. 271.
51 Sayers, December 21, 1955, *The Letters*, vol. 4, p. 264.

however, their discussions shifted almost entirely to Sayers's writings about and translations of Dante and his *Divine Comedy*. Sayers early on described her problem with Dante: "If one once gets a taste for Dante, one is liable to become a Dante-addict. He acts like a drug—or rather, like an attack of rabies; the people who are bitten rush madly about biting all their friends."[52] This was not a problem for Lewis, who already considered Dante his favorite poet.[53] When her translation of the *Inferno* reached him in November 1949, there was a flurry of letters to her. Lewis responded after reading the first nineteen cantos, "You have got (what you most desired) the quality of an exciting story. . . . Notes & maps excellent." According to him, "the untiring quality and inexhaustible cleverness . . . fill me with astonished admiration. Your version of any passage will always be *one* [italics original] of the things I shall take into account in trying to understand any difficult place: and that . . . [is] saying a lot."[54] This high praise, however, was also accompanied by his gentle assessment that "the metrical audacities are nearly all effective," and as for her colloquialisms, "I approve a great many of them."[55] Four days after finishing his reading of her *Inferno*, he wrote, "There is no doubt. . . . It is a stunning work. . . . *Brava, bravissima*."[56] She responded to this input, saying, "I have had a lot of nice letters about the *Inferno* but I think yours is the very nicest, because you understand so well what the thing's about, and what a translation aims at." Showing her respect for his expertise she added, "Provided people like you" approve it, "I shall feel that I am at any rate on the right lines."[57] Lewis continued the discussion in a letter the following week about the metrics in Dante and in particular about her translation of the "*orazion picciola*" by Ulysses in *Inferno* 26.117 as "little speech." Lewis objected that this translation "conjures up vicars and bazaars!"[58] It was a small point but it rankled Lewis, and he brought it up again in another letter two days later.[59]

As for Sayers's first book of literary criticism on Dante in 1954, Lewis's assessment was enthusiastic: "Your *Introductory Papers* have

---

52 Sayers, July 25, 1946, *The Letters*, vol. 3, p. 249.
53 See C. S. Lewis, "Dante's Similes," in *Studies in Medieval and Renaissance Literature*, coll. Walter Hooper (Cambridge: Cambridge University Press, 1966), p. 76.
54 Lewis, November 11, 1949, *Collected Letters*, vol. 2, p. 996.
55 Ibid.
56 Lewis, November 15, 1949, *Collected Letters*, vol. 2, p. 997.
57 Sayers, November 18, 1949, *The Letters*, vol. 3, p. 465.
58 Lewis, November 21, 1949, *Collected Letters*, vol. 2, pp. 999-1000.
59 Lewis, November 23, 1949, *Collected Letters*, vol. 2, p. 1001.

given me a regular feast. . . . It is a lovely book . . . . Every essay and nearly every page enriched me," [60] he says, and he lists a number of specific examples with their page numbers: "P. 97 is you at your very best. . . . P. 122 at the end of that essay is first-class." But with his typical honesty, he also adds that "On P. 115, I have my only grumble": he objected to her diction in the phrase "evolving in the direction of perfectibility."[61] Although he had earlier raised questions about her interpretation of which things she considered comic in Dante, Lewis wrote to her again a week later, saying, "I'll fight to the death for your lighter and freer view of D. [Dante] against the outer world."[62]

As for her translation of the *Purgatorio*, which did not appear until the summer of 1955, Lewis had said beforehand, "I look forward very much to going up and round the terraces [of the *Purgatorio*] with your guidance,"[63] and again later, "our tongues are all hanging out for the *Purgatorio*."[64] This may have been due to the fact, as Lewis shared with her, that the *Purgatorio* "is perhaps my favourite part of the Comedy." [65] But the long wait was worth it. Lewis's assessment was that "Your *Inferno* was good, but this is even better." As he typically did, Lewis listed out specific things he appreciated, saying that her note on *Purgatorio* 31.60 "is a masterpiece" and he took "especial pleasure to see the metrical licenses." His overall conclusion was that "it makes one hungry for your *Paradiso*."[66] He ended the letter, "With deep congratulations," addressing her with a title in Old French "*grante translateuse*."[67] As Sayers continued working on her translation of the *Paradiso*, she wrote to Lewis, "I shall probably approach you when it comes to launching the *Paradise*, for permission to quote your pregnant words on Dante's style."[68]

When Sayers's second book of Dante criticism, *Further Papers on Dante*, came out in 1957, Lewis wrote her, "I think this book even better than the first." His letter did not include the same kind of list

---

60 Lewis, November 14, 1954, *Collected Letters*, vol. 3, pp. 523-24.
61 Ibid., p. 526.
62 Lewis, November 22, 1954, *Collected Letters*, vol. 3, p. 529.
63 Lewis, December 16, 1953, *Collected Letters*, vol. 3, p. 387.
64 Lewis, April 6, 1955, *Collected Letters*, vol. 3, p. 594.
65 Lewis, December 16, 1953, *Collected Letters*, vol. 3, p. 387.
66 Lewis, July 31, 1955, *Collected Letters*, vol. 3, p. 634.
67 Ibid., p. 635.
68 Sayers, August 8, 1955, *The Letters*, vol. 4, pp. 252-53. Unfortunately, that never occurred because Sayers finished only 20 cantos before her death, leaving Barbara Reynolds to complete the other 13 based on Sayers's notes and to see its publication in 1962.

of specifics this time because he was recovering at home with muscle spasms in his back and the book was back at Cambridge. He had, however, earlier gone through the book thoroughly: "with all the lines in the margins—all prepared for the 'very judicious letter..' . . . There were dozens of good and really illuminating things which I can't remember. I'd like to go through the whole thing with you."[69] Unfortunately that proposed session never happened because of Sayers's unexpected death at the end of that year.

Although they were writers of different kinds, Lewis and Sayers were lumped together during the late 1940s and the 1950s—for good or ill. When Lewis was on the cover of *Time* magazine in 1947, the article describes Lewis as belonging to "a growing band of heretics among modern intellectuals: an intellectual who believes in God," and lists Dorothy Sayers as one of that band.[70] Kathleen Nott's book, *The Emperor's Clothes*, in 1953 was, according to the subtitle on the cover, "An Attack on the Dogmatic Orthodoxy of T. S. Eliot, Graham Greene, Dorothy Sayers, C. S. Lewis, & Others." Nott singles out and couples Lewis and Sayers, often in the same sentence like Bobsey twins, fourteen times in her book, saying that Sayers is "Lewis's fellow-thinker"[71] and "his literary status may be compared to that of Miss Sayers."[72] Lewis wrote Sayers on December 16 of that year, "I see we have been in the pillory together,"[73] which no doubt gave him great pleasure. She responded a week later that she had not read the Nott book: "Why should one pay good money to hear one's self abused?"[74] Even recently the two have been linked as "comrades-in-apologetics" by Philip and Carol Zaleski.[75]

There came a shift in their relationship in 1954. Although their letters generally continued to focus on literary topics and each other's writings, their letters demonstrate a lighter, more playful and personal tone. Up until this point the tone of their letters was that

---

69 Lewis, June 25, 1957, *Collected Letters*, vol. 3, pp. 860-61.
70 "Oxford's C. S. Lewis, His Heresy: Christianity," *Time*, September 8, 1947, p. 65. The article is found on pp. 65- 74. The other two mentioned were T. S. Eliot and Graham Greene.
71 Kathleen Nott, *The Emperor's Clothes* (London: Heinemann, 1953), p. 284.
72 Ibid., p. 256.
73 Lewis, December 16, 1953, *Collected Letters*, vol. 3, p. 387.
74 Sayers, December 21, 1953, *The Letters*, vol. 4, p. 117.
75 Philip Zaleski and Carol Zaleski, *The Fellowship: The Literary Lives of the Inklings* (New York: Farrar, Straus, and Giroux, 2015), p. 314.

of professional colleagues who respected each other and shared the same Christian faith. Sayers had accepted an invitation for lunch in February that year, and Lewis's March letter, which referred to some of her poems and to "your delightful visit," included his poem "Evolutionary Hymn."[76] Sayers, having met Lewis's brother Warnie, was now reading and enjoying his book, *The Splendid Century*.[77]

Up until this time Lewis had addressed his letters to her as "Miss Sayers," and her letters were addressed first to "Mr. Lewis " and then to "Dr. Lewis" after 1946 when Lewis was awarded an Honorary Doctorate in Divinity.[78] Lewis took the initiative in June to ask her, "Call me Jack as others do."[79] By September of 1954, Lewis was addressing his letters to her as "Dear Dorothy" and signing them as "Jack." She responded in kind.

When Sayers felt that Kathleen Nott's book called for a debate, Lewis agreed to her request to join her.[80] The debate was set for October of that year in London. Although Nott in the end decided not to come,[81] it was an opportunity for Lewis to introduce Joy Gresham to her.

After Lewis sent a notice to Sayers in November of his upcoming change of address to Cambridge,[82] she apparently sent him a card with an allegorical image. His request for an explanation of the image on what he called her "cryptic card" took the form of a 16-line poem of rhyming couplets in iambic tetrameter.[83] Two days later, Sayers responded by sending her explanation in a 40-line poem in rhyming couplets in iambic tetrameter.[84]

Sayers was unable to attend Lewis's Inaugural Address at Cambridge,[85] so she insisted that Reynolds go hear it to report on it.[86]

---

76   Lewis, March 4, 1954, *Collected Letters*, vol. 3, pp. 434-37.
77   See Lewis, March 9, 1954, *Collected Letters*, vol. 3, p. 438.
78   Lewis was awarded an Honorary Doctorate in Divinity by the University of St. Andrews on June 28, 1946.
79   Lewis, June 12, 1954, *Collected Letters*, vol. 3, p. 488.
80   Ibid.
81   Nott declined in the end since T. S. Eliot's presence at the debate had been the one condition for her attendance, and he was unable to come at the last minute. The debate did occur with her friend G. S. Frazer in her stead.
82   See Lewis, November 30, 1954, *Collected Letters*, vol. 3, p. 532.
83   Lewis, December 27, 1954, *Collected Letters*, vol. 3, p. 568.
84   Sayers, December 29, 1954, *The Letters*, vol. 4, pp. 197-98.
85   C. S. Lewis's address, "*De descriptione temporum*," was delivered on November 29, 1954.
86   See Sayers, November 24, 1954, *The Letters*, vol. 4, p. 179.

When Sayers received the text of his talk six months later, she was startled to see, and quoted in her letter, Lewis's statement, "I read, as a native, texts you must read as foreigners," because on the evening before she said she had thought and said exactly the same thing with a friend.[87] She signed this letter, "your obliged and appreciative fellow-dinosaur."[88] Lewis's response two day later, referring to Sayers, Warnie, and himself, asked, "Shd. we someday form a Dinosaurs' Club?"[89] A few days later, Sayers, repeated the metaphor when she defined, "Dinosaurs like C. S. Lewis and me" to Reynolds as those who "want to get back to studying the work for its own sake . . . [rather than for] spotlighting the psychology of the authors."[90] In a letter to her two years later, Lewis addressed her as "sister Dinosaur" in the text of the letter.[91]

Although his letters to Sayers are fewer in number after 1954, he does share personally significant and private things with her. By August of the following year, he mentions that Joy Gresham is typing some of his responses.[92] The day before Christmas in 1956, Lewis wrote to inform Sayers of his civil marriage to Joy Gresham on April 23, 1956, and explains, "You will not think that anything wrong is going to happen. Certain problems do not arise between a dying woman and an elderly man."[93] However, as things developed, Lewis did fall in love with Joy and after their Christian marriage on March 21, 1957, when Joy was quite ill, he explained to Sayers, "A rival often turns a friend into a lover. Thanatos [Greek god of death] is a most efficient rival,"[94] and he asks her, "I hope you will give us your blessing: I know you'll give us your prayers."[95] Her quick response must have been positive and understanding because Lewis wrote a few days later, "Joy and I both enjoyed your letter v. much and thought it full of sweetness and light."[96] His last letter to her, on September 29, 1957, thanked her for the copy of her translation of *The Song of Roland*, which he called "a good swinging, readable story," but he found it

---

87 Sayers, April 4, 1955, *The Letters*, vol. 4, p. 222.
88 Ibid., p. 223.
89 Lewis, April 6, 1955, *Collected Letters*, vol. 3, p. 596.
90 Sayers, April 15, 1955, *The Letters*, vol. 4, p. 224.
91 Lewis, July 1, 1957, *Collected Letters*, vol. 3, p. 863.
92 See Lewis, August 9, 1955, *Collected Letters*, vol. 3, pp. 437-38.
93 Lewis, December 24, 1956, *Collected Letters*, vol. 3, p. 819.
94 Lewis, June 25, 1957, *Collected Letters*, vol. 3, pp. 861-62.
95 Ibid., p. 862.
96 Lewis, July 1, 1957, *Collected Letters*, vol. 3, p. 863.

"in places too slangy for my taste."[97] In this last of his letters to her he shares good news about Joy's health and his own. It was his last letter because the next thing he would write to praise her would be his "Panegyric for Dorothy L. Sayers" that he was asked to do for her memorial service.[98]

In assessing these letters in context of their entire correspondence, both wrote letters to a wide variety of correspondents on a daily basis with lively wit and humor that displayed an enormous wealth of knowledge at their fingertips. The biggest difference is that, since Lewis hated writing letters and she loved writing them, his letters tended to be very short and hers very long. Early on Lewis had in fact told her, "You are one of the great English letter writers. . . . But I am not."[99] Her response was to chide him, saying, "It was most rash of you . . . to encourage me to write letters because I am only too ready to do so, at great length, on the slightest provocation,—or none."[100] Lewis later commented to her, "You write such excellent letters that if I were a bad man I should lure you into an epistolary controversy and you wd. find you had written a book . . . without knowing it."[101] On receiving her letter about his commentary on *Arthurian Torso*,[102] he wrote back, "Your letter shines amid the day's mail like a good deed in a naughty world."[103]

P. D. James in the preface to the fourth volume of Sayers's letters, says, "A writer's correspondence, provided it isn't written with an eye to publication, is more revealing of the essential personality than any biography or autobiography."[104] In totality the letters of both Lewis and Sayers are proof of that, and in particular their letters to each other reveal their relationship better than any biography could.

---

97 Lewis, September 29, 1954, *Collected Letters*, vol. 3, 885.
98 See C. S. Lewis, *On Stories and Other Essays on Literature* (New York: Harcourt, 1982), pp. 91-95. Although Lewis was unable to attend the memorial on January 15, 1958, at St. Margaret's Church in London, his eulogy was read by the Bishop of Chichester, George Bell.
99 Lewis, December 14, 1945, *Collected Letters*, vol. 2, pp. 682-83.
100 Sayers, December 24, 1945, *The Letters*, vol. 3, p. 182.
101 Lewis, July 29, 1946, *Collected Letters*, vol. 2, p. 728.
102 See Sayers, December 31, 1948, *The Letters*, vol. 3, pp. 414-15.
103 Lewis, January 1, 1949, *Collected Letters*, vol. 2, p. 902.
104 P. D. James, preface, *The Letters*, vol. 4, p. viii.

Works Cited

Hooper, Walter. *C. S. Lewis: A Companion and Guide*. New York: Harper Collins, 1996.

Lewis, C. S. *The Collected Letters of C. S. Lewis*. Edited by Walter Hooper. 3 vols. New York: Harper Collins, 2004-2007.

"Dante's Similes." In *Studies in Medieval and Renaissance Literature*. Collected by Walter Hooper. Cambridge: Cambridge University Press, 1966.

Miracles: A Preliminary Study. New York: Macmillan, 1960.

"Panegyric for Dorothy L. Sayers." In *"On Stories" and Other Essays on Literature*. Edited by Owen Barfield and Walter Hooper. New York: Harcourt, 1982.

Lewis, C. S., ed. *Essays Presented to Charles Williams*. Oxford: Oxford University Press, 1947.

Nott, Kathleen. *The Emperor's Clothes*. London: Heinemann, 1953.

"Oxford's C. S. Lewis, His Heresy: Christianity." *Time*, September 8, 1947, pp. 65- 74.

Sayers, Dorothy L. *The Letters of Dorothy L. Sayers, Volume 2, 1937-1943: From Novelist to Playwright*. Edited by Barbara Reynolds. Preface by P. D. James. New York: St. Martin's, 1998.

The Letters of Dorothy L. Sayers, Volume 3, 1944-1950: A Noble Daring. Edited by Barbara Reynolds. Preface by P. D. James. Cambridge: Carole Greene 1998.

The Letters of Dorothy L. Sayers, Volume 4, 1951-1957: In the Midst of Life. Edited by Barbara Reynolds. Preface by P. D. James. Cambridge: Carole Green, 2000.

Zaleski, Philip, and Carol Zaleski. *The Fellowship: The Literary Lives of the Inklings*. New York: Farrar, Straus, and Giroux, 2015.

Dorothy L. Sayers and the Mutual Admiration Society: Friendship and Creative Writing in an Oxford Women's Literary Group

by Barbara M. Prescott

Barbara Mary Prescott, M.A., M.Ed., is a researcher of writing communities and the writing process. She has advanced degrees from the University of Illinois and the University of Wisconsin, including post-graduate research in Language and Literacy at Stanford University. She has published numerous articles on the writing process and is currently researching the poetry of Dorothy L. Sayers.

Companions in this airy hermitage.
—Dorothy L. Sayers, *Gaudy Night*

Women students at Oxford University prior to 1920 found themselves in somewhat of a curious situation. They were allowed to attend university, take classes and exams, prove their academic value, but they were not allowed to receive degrees. In point of fact, women attending Oxford University prior to October 7, 1920[1] were not given the rights of matriculation, that is, of full student status. They were there 'on probation', a situation of which these women students were very well aware.[2] However, acceptance to the university was certainly an honor and sought, in fact coveted, by young learned women at the time. Within the Oxford world, Somerville College was noted to be the "school for women" rather than the "school for ladies." From its early days, this college encouraged a strong spirit of individualism among its students.[3] Somerville's proudly held reputation was certainly attractive to the young independent woman scholar of the day. The

---

1 On October 7, 1920, women were officially allowed, by university decree, to matriculate at Oxford (i.e., become a recognized and official part of the Oxford scholarly community) and to graduate with an official Oxford degree and diploma. Therefore, the first class of women to matriculate and receive a degree at Oxford University was that of the 1920 entering class. The first graduation occurred at Oxford also in 1920, officially granting a degree to those women students who had met the requirements previous to 1920. Dorothy L. Sayers was among this graduating class, although she had actually gone down from Oxford in 1915.
2 Frankenburg, 1975, p. 59.
3 Batson, p. 156.

principal of Somerville at the time was Emily Penrose, a strict but forward thinking administrator who made the raising of academic standards one of her chief objectives. She believed that women should take the full degree course even if the degree itself was denied them. Emily Penrose's insistence upon fulfillment of the degree requirements by Somerville students facilitated the later validation, in 1920, of their right to an official Oxford degree.[4]

Into this fairly complex situation, Dorothy L. Sayers, a young and hopeful student recipient of the Gilchrist Scholarship for Modern Languages, arrived in Oxford in October 1912 at the age of nineteen. By November, Dorothy and two other Somerville students, Amphyllis (Amphy) Middlemore and Charis Ursula Barnett, had formed a women's writing community, ostensibly for the purpose of reading and critiquing one another's writing efforts. Dorothy named it the "Mutual Admiration Society,"[5] henceforth referred to as the MAS. Dorothy Sayers chose this name for a variety of reasons, some of which are rather amusing and subtle. First, as she remarked, "if we didn't give ourselves that title, the rest of College would."[6] Secondly, the name was meant to be humorous, meant to soften its closed status, making its existence tolerable, even attractive, among students. Further, one cannot help but think there was additional humor involved (knowing Dorothy's gift for irony), as the MAS, by its very name, threw the ball back to those who looked upon women students at Oxford with hidden disdain or trepidation, aiming, with subtlety, that name toward male dominated Oxford.

For these young students, the opportunity of belonging to a writing circle, a community of like-minded women, within their new, sometimes bewildering, academic environment, was a welcome addition to life at Somerville. Writers gravitate toward one another,

---

4 In 1920, the first class of women graduates, Dorothy Sayers, Muriel Jaeger, and Muriel St. Clare Byrne among them, participated in the university graduation ceremony and had the distinction of receiving an official Oxford BA degree. DLS also received, on that date, an MA in French.

5 This was not the first writing group at Somerville. In the late 1800s, a mysterious society calling itself 'The Mermaids' was also formed by Somerville students to be a writing support community and platform. Somewhat later than 'The Mermaids', an exclusive Somerville writing club was formed called the 'Associated Prigs' who were defined by solemn earnestness in their meetings and writing. The Mutual Admiration Society "shrugged off the excessive earnestness and became a more social network" (Batson, p. 150).

6 Frankenburg, 1975, p. 63.

and writing communities occur frequently in a university environment. The Inklings themselves adopted their name from a former Oxford student writing society. However, roughly twenty-five years earlier than the formation of the Inklings at Oxford came the MAS, another ironically-titled writing circle with very similar intent and raison d'être to that of the Inklings: to share their own poems, stories, and essays; to inspire one another by appreciation, analysis and critique, sometimes severe, of one another's compositions; and to support one another in the friendship of their company. Furthermore, both societies elected into membership only those people with whom they felt comfortable.[7] Both groups were serious about their writing and serious about one another's writing yet discussed their work within an informal yet sometimes argumentative circle, marked by stimulating conversation. They were friends of the spirit and mind.

Despite their similarities, the Inklings and the MAS had two distinct differences: status and gender. The nineteen canonical Inklings, led by C.S. Lewis and J.R.R. Tolkien, were men secure within their professional lives in Oxford and its environs, secure within the closed Inkling circle, sharing mature poetry, prose, fantasy fiction, philosophical and religious essays with their critical yet encouraging writing community. Their sympathy to one another lay in their intent, seriousness of purpose, profound thought, recognized talent, and ties of friendship. In essence, these men shared sympathy of mind and spirit.

The MAS began and remained a student writing community composed entirely of women undergraduates at Somerville College, women who were only just beginning their adult lives and sought a safe haven, a place where "they could relax their guard"[8] and present their burgeoning efforts of poetry, prose, plays, and essays for one another's critical evaluation. In this writing circle, friendship and bonds formed which were to last, for many members, throughout their lives and which would affect both their personal and professional futures. As Charis Barnett noted casually of the MAS: "Dorothy Rowe, Amphilis Middlemore, Dorothy Sayers, Margaret Chubb—we were freshers who enjoyed each other's company, and, with others of our group, have kept in touch over the years."[9]

These women were strong-willed, young, independent thinkers. While clearly respecting the conventions of Oxford and Somerville,

---

7 Brabazon, p. 44.
8 Batson, p. 154.
9 Frankenburg, p. 62.

they "reserved the right to use their own common sense in regulating their behavior and not to get into a state if they unwittingly overturned convention,"[10] often finding humor in the daily situations that were perplexing or confounding to young university women at the time. In fact, it is a testament to the independent spirit of the women of the MAS that they did not ask permission to form the society they just decided among themselves to create the company, acted upon this decision, and continued to keep the writer's circle alive and lively through their student tenure, at least until 1915 when several members, Dorothy Sayers among them, went down from Oxford.

As I continued to find references to the MAS in the pursuit of my interest in the Oxford poetry of Dorothy Sayers,[11] I found myself asking, just who were these women? How many were there? To date, I have found nine securely documented members: Dorothy L. Sayers, Amphilis Middlemore, Charis Ursula Barnett, Muriel Jaeger, Margaret Amy Chubb, Marjorie Maud Barber, Muriel St. Clare Byrne, Dorothy Hanbury Rowe, and Catherine Hope Godfrey.

The MAS was a closed group, an invitation-only writers circle, with entrance criteria. A candidate submitted written poetry or prose, this work was read aloud at a meeting, and the student was voted in, or not. When Muriel St. Clare Byrne applied for membership in her first year, Dorothy Rowe noted that Byrne was "an awfully nice child who writes quite good stuff."[12] Charis Barnett, when speaking of the membership, remarked that they elected only "people we liked"[13] and so the MAS stayed a fairly small community through 1915. Some members were given nicknames, usually informal male names. Muriel Jaeger was "Jim." Catherine Godfrey was "Tony." Amphilis Middlemore was "Amphy." Marjorie Barber was "Bar." Dorothy Rowe was "Tiddler." Dorothy Sayers seems not to have had a verbal nickname, but often signed herself as "John Gaunt" or "J.G.," from her role in *Admiral Guinea* and sometimes as "H.P. Rallantando," or "rAllentando," a not-so-subtle reference to Hugh Percy Allen, the Director of the Bach Choir and her Oxford crush. This tight circle of affectionately nicknamed friends thus grew with the purpose of providing a platform to share their writing and to help one another develop as writers and scholars and persons. "The robust criticism of contemporaries is most salutary, and we undoubtedly had the sense to

---

10   Ibid., p. 156.
11   Prescott, MSb, 2016; forthcoming, 2018.
12   Frankenburg, p. 63.
13   Ibid.

profit from it."[14] Charis Barnett wrote in her autobiography, *Not Old, Madam, Vintage,* the following:

> The items read at our meetings were of all kinds—plays, sonnets, foretastes of future novels, a soliloquy in verse by Nero, a dissertation on Shakespeare's Fairies. My contributions included a criticism of Shaw's plays, the discussion between Dr. Johnson and Boswell on adult suffrage, a short story, and some verse. But my most interesting recollection is that Dorothy Sayers read a conversation between the three Magi— an anticipation of *The Man Born to be King*.[15]

Dorothy Sayers read sonnets, ballads, lais, and other verse at the weekly MAS meetings, as written in her 1912-1914 MAS notebooks, or albums as she preferred to call them. Dorothy Rowe, having an interest in the theatre may very well have read her own plays, later revised and performed by her amateur theatre company. Early drafts of future novels, *The Question Mark* (1926) as well as *The Man with Six Senses* (1927), were read by Muriel Jaeger, as was Nero's soliloquy in verse.[16] A dissertation on Shakespeare's Fairies clearly would have been in the literary world of Muriel St. Clare Byrne or Amphilis Middlemore.

Furthermore, and perhaps as importantly, this community provided its female members a small, safe, friendly literary haven in the midst of a large, sometimes bewildering, male oriented university which was in itself an environment of mixed messages. On the one hand, these women were welcomed to Oxford in recognition of their brilliance. On the other hand, there was a clear, sometimes not so subtle, message that they did not belong, as a group, in Oxford by virtue of their gender. To a certain extent, partly as a result of these mixed messages, the MAS was purposely formed as a closed circle in which to share sensitive thoughts, support one another's writing efforts, and so became for these women student writers, a mutually enhancing writing and reading community. Bonds were formed in the society that lasted throughout the lives of many MAS members. These students became writing comrades-in-arms, and almost all became lifelong friends. Perhaps more significantly, their friendships affected literary and social history.

We do not often think of student writing communities in the light of historical significance, but in the case of the MAS, argument can be

---

14   Ibid.
15   Frankenbug, p. 63.
16   Letter, DLS to MJ, 7-30-13.

made that each of its members became a force within her chosen field and that some contributed appreciably to the professional writing lives of other members. The links that were formed in the MAS grew to be a web of literary, social, professional, and personal support among these gifted women. In essence, the women of the MAS became vibrant and integral parts of what can be titled a Somerville 'school of writers' by virtue of their continuing communication with one another and long term influence upon one another's literary, theatrical, teaching, or social welfare careers and writings. When viewing, in this light, the valuable effect that the women writers of the MAS had upon twentieth century literature and society, one cannot help but wish to know more about these gifted women, their writings, and to bring each from the shadow of anonymity, to rightfully credit them for their valuable lives, for their significant effect upon the history of Somerville, and particularly for their contributions to the professional careers of one another.

Poetry First

The reading, writing, and sharing of poetry were vital to the women of the MAS, and, to a certain extent, the lives of these women were poetic. They were comfortable using the language of literature and used it with the ease of scholarly confidence, sometimes even profoundly so. Most of the MAS women, not unexpectedly at this time of life, wrote verse and read their poetry within the circle. A congenial and supportive environment is almost necessary when sharing sensitive thoughts inherent in youthful poetry. It takes an amount of courage to open one's thoughts to the critique of others, and it is to the credit of this young writing community that members felt at ease so doing. Their confidence in one another was certainly an extension of friendship and mutual regard. This trust of one another, for most, lasted a lifetime.

On Wednesday evening, November 7, 1912, the MAS met for the first time. There were six members present, and those were most probably Dorothy L. Sayers, Charis Barnett, Amphy Middlemore, Muriel Jaeger, Margaret Chubb, and Dorothy Rowe. Dorothy Sayers read two poems, "Peredur"[17] and "Earl Ulfric."[18] Another girl read two

---

17 "Peredur," MAS Notebook, DLS MS-164, 1912-1913. Special thanks to the Marion E. Wade Center for permission to quote.
18 "Earl Ulfric," DLS MS-365, 1910-1911. Special thanks to the Marion E. Wade Center for permission to quote.

pieces, and Amphy served refreshments. It was considered a successful meeting.[19] To give an idea of the work presented, and to give a flavor of this first meeting, the following excerpts from Dorothy's two poems are included:

>Peredur (v.1)
>All day I wander through the meads,
>Or else at random range the wood
>Where the tall pine-trees, rood on rood,
>Stretch o'er the hill-side, dusk & brown
>With heather, that does sloping down
>To meet the river & the reeds.

A second, heroically dramatic, poem read by Dorothy was "Earl Ulfric":

>Earl Ulfric (vs.1-3)
>The winds howl, the waves roar –
>Earl Ulfric stands by the windy shore.
>
>"A boat to sail through the storm & wrack,
>"For the ban of blood is upon my track!"
>
>The winds howl, the waves leap—
>What boat could live on the raging deep?

In the summer of 1913, Dorothy Sayers began to write an epic poem of 700 lines titled "Sir Omez," sending verses throughout the summer to Muriel Jaeger for her opinion and critique. Sayers also sent Jaeger review copies of her poem later published in *Op. I.*, "The Gates of Paradise."[20]

Dorothy Sayers continued to prefer larger-than-life, heroic, and often mythic themes for her ballads, lais, sonnets, and epics, themes which she later applied to her detective fiction, Lord Peter Wimsey himself being a flawed, multi-dimensional, hero figure.[21] Structure was paramount to Sayers; she carefully constructed and adhered to classic rules and rhyme. Muriel (Jim) Jaeger was acknowledged to have a good ear for the language of poetry, and her opinions as well as critiques became valued by Dorothy Sayers, so much so that Sayers continued to send Jaeger copies of her poetry for review throughout her vacations from Oxford and beyond.

An annual venue of publication for the Somerville writers

---

19   Letter, DLS to Parents, 11-10-12.
20   Letter DLS to MJ, Summer, 1913
21   Downing.

was *Oxford Poetry* (*OP*), a yearly book published by Basil Blackwell. Between 1910 and 1913, there were no poems from Somerville students included.[22] However, between 1914 and 1916, there was a distinct blossoming of poetry from Somerville writers included in *Oxford Poetry*, primarily from MAS members.[23] In 1914 Charis Ursula Barnett translated a poem from Theodore De Banville for *Oxford Poetry*, and Dorothy Rowe wrote two poems: "Asleep" and "Morpheus." In 1915, she also wrote "An Old Rhyme Re-Sung" and Dorothy Sayers published a twelve-part "Lay" for the 1915 *OP*. As an interesting aside, along with Dorothy Sayers and Dorothy Rowe, a young student from Exeter College named J.R.R. Tolkien had his poem, "Goblin Feet," published in the 1915 *Oxford Poetry* collection. In 1916, Muriel Byrne published "Devachan." In 1917, Dorothy Sayers published "Fair Erembours, A Song of the Web"; in 1918, "Pygmalion"; and in 1919, "For Phaon," "Sympathy," and "Vials Full of Odours."[22]

The MAS did create at least one unique volume of written work, *The Blue Moon*, containing six pieces, three of which were poems by Sayers.[24] Included, as well, within this published album was a short story by Dorothy Sayers, titled "Who Calls the Tune?"[25] The first issue remained the only issue of *The Blue Moon* by the MAS, with a copy still existing in the Somerville College archives. Elsewhere, Sayers' "Hymn in Contemplation of Sudden Death" appeared in *Oxford Magazine*, 1915,[26] followed by "Icarus" in 1916. The *Fritillary*, a magazine containing news about college activities and debates was also a venue, printing several of Sayers' Oxford poems through 1915.[27]

In 1916, Dorothy Sayers dedicated her first published book of poems, *Op. I.*, in part to her MAS sisters, and particularly to Dorothy Rowe, fellow poet and the director of the Second-Years' December 1913 play, *Admiral Guinea*.[28] The unusual title, *Op. I.* appeared to be a subtle acknowledgement of her experiences with, as well as interest in, music (i.e., Opus I), a nod to the Bach Choir and its director, Hugh Percy Allen, along with a likely nod to the journal, *Oxford Poetry* (*OP*), in which she had already published poems, and to the publisher of

---

22 Oxford Poetry, 1910-1913.
23 Oxford Poetry, 1914-1916.
24 Letters, DLS to Dorothy Rowe (DR), Summer 1913.
25 "Who Calls the Tune?" DLS MS-239; The Blue Moon 1.1.
26 Mead, p. 8.
27 Ibid.
28 Op. I., dedication.

this journal for whom she worked, Basil Blackwell, who, it should be noted, also published *Op. I.* in 1916, and her later volume, *Catholic Tales and Christian Songs* in 1918.

Further in her career, as she began her translation of Dante, Dorothy Sayers often sent translated cantos to both Marjorie Barber, who was skilled in Italian as well as having translated Chaucer into modern English[29], and Muriel St. Clare Byrne, by then a noted Shakespearean scholar, for their expert advice and review. These both, her former MAS co-members, remained an important link of literary support, information, and consultation throughout Sayers' life and various writing careers. As expressly noted by Marjorie Lamp Mead, "Friends were not a luxury in Sayers' life, enjoyed but not essential; rather friends were foundational, as necessary to Sayers as the very air she breathed."[30] Catherine Godfrey Mansfield and Dorothy Hanbury Rowe, as well, retained a personal and professional correspondence with Sayers, Byrne, Barber, and Jaeger, often sharing experiences of daily life with all of these women. The MAS information conduit and support web remained in full effect for decades.

During the Oxford period of her writing life, Dorothy Sayers was primarily a poet. She experimented with a number of poetic structures, such as sonnets, lais, and ballads to complement various themes: medieval stories, epics, religious and classic myths and legends. We do not usually think of Dorothy Sayers in light of her poetry, but she certainly considered herself first and foremost a poet. She began her writing life with poetry and translation and ended her writing life with the translation of poetry.

As I study the poems she wrote during her time at Oxford,[31] I am further persuaded that the skills Dorothy Sayers acquired composing poetry deeply influenced her later prose work. However, in her early Oxford days, Sayers appeared to be somewhat reluctant to write prose:

> "I cannot get any ideas for prose. Prose is a thing (now is it? is it a thing? it's not a person at any rate. Well, thing will have to do)—a thing I only write upon compulsion & then badly" (Letter to Jaeger, July1913). As Sayers continued to experiment with various genres, she also continued to transfer successfully, in very subtle but effective ways, the structure applied to poetry, toward her fiction, essays, and plays. To Dorothy L. Sayers writing poetry and prose became, through

---

29 Letters, Marjorie Barber to DLS, 1935-1949 (423b).
30 Mead, 1994, p. 8.
31 Prescott, MSa, 2015; forthcoming, 2017.

time and experience, a feedback loop, each functioning to support the other, each lending structure to the other. Her command of various genre structures within the writing process, interestingly, can be identified in Sayers' reader friendly, storytelling, approach to the translations of the beautifully dramatic story poems of Dante.

Story Telling and Narrative Fiction

One subtle thread that weaves through the literary lives of several MAS women is the ability to recognize coherent story construction and the skill to write clear narrative that is easily understandable to the reader. Dorothy L. Sayers certainly learned to write a good story. To be a good story teller, one must have a good sense of audience.[32] She noticed everything about people, and in detail.[33] Dorothy Sayers' friend, Amphy Middlemore, was acknowledged as well, at Godolphin and at Somerville, for her own skill in creating narrative, that is, for telling a good story. In fact, Amphy was affectionately described by her friends and, later, by students as "the world's best storyteller."[34] Her gift for story construction, one which she certainly shared during MAS meetings, may have been a factor in Dorothy Sayers' own decision to venture, however reluctantly at the time, into the world of writing narrative prose.

Sayers presented at least one such story at an MAS meeting. The case in point was a puzzle-in-story-form titled, "Who Calls the Tune?,"[35] an intriguing tale written almost as a prototype mystery[36] years before her first detective novel, *Whose Body?* (1923), partly nursed by Muriel Jaeger, was published and almost a decade before her short story, "The [Fascinating] Problem of Uncle Meleager's Will" was published (1925).[37]

The effect of Amphy Middlemore's talent in story construction would not have been lost on Sayers nor the other MAS writers. Dorothy Sayers' sharp observation and appreciation of the writing presented, particularly of those stories she approved, might very well have started a fermentation process in her own mind that encouraged an effort to write clear, interesting, well-structured, narrative, that is,

---

32 Willerton, 2011, p. 47.
33 Brittain, 1933, pp. 105-06.
34 Godolphin News, 1914-1918.
35 "Who Calls the Tune?" DLS MS-239; The Blue Moon 1.1.
36 Prescott, MSc, 2016.
37 Lee, 1994, p. 60.

to create a good story. Furthermore, Sayers developed skill in written dialogue, partly through writing letters. Her engaging letters are written conversations, verbal text. Furthermore, the clear narrative techniques and engaging dialogue which Dorothy Sayers developed in her Wimsey series, in addition to her early ability to structure language in poetry, certainly affected her later style in translation, aiding Sayers' confidence and achievement in tackling the story poems of Dante.

Later in their communication, the reference to enjoyment as a property of good story-telling resurfaces between Marjorie Barber and Dorothy Sayers when Sayers sends her a translated copy of *L'Inferno*. Barber notes that the translation was a joy primarily because Sayers made Dante approachable; he became, "just like somebody sitting there in an armchair and telling you a story."[38] Later Sayers uses this quote of Barber's to title one of her papers about Dante, and she, herself, notes in a letter to Charles Williams, "I knew everybody had got the wrong idea of D., same as I had."[39] Furthermore, Marjorie Barber's own interpretation and modern translation of the works of Chaucer may indeed have partly inspired and encouraged Sayers' decision to attend to her own roots by translating Dante.

Amphy Middlemore, Marjorie Barber, Muriel Jaeger, and certainly Muriel St. Clare Byrne may be seen, in different ways, to have influenced Dorothy Sayers' blossoming interest at Oxford in the writing of fiction as well as to have encouraged later her clear, story-telling, approach to Dante. In addition, Muriel Jaeger took an active part as commentator and encourager while Dorothy Sayers was creating her first novel, *Whose Body?* For that literary support, Sayers dedicated her first detective novel to Muriel Jaeger:

> Dear Jim:
>
> This book is your fault. If it had not been for your brutal insistence, Lord Peter would never have staggered through to the end of this enquiry. Pray consider that he thanks you with his accustomed suavity.
>
> Yours ever,
>
> DLS[40]

Furthermore, the communication channels among the MAS women, remaining open through letters and visits to one another

---

38 Letters Barber to DLS, 1942-1957 (423a).
39 Reynolds, 2006: 122; Folder 423b, Marion E. Wade Center.
40 *Whose Body?* Dedication page.

and spanning decades, recounted the daily doings of their lives and substantially added to the shared narrative of those lives. Sayers' subtly powerful and satisfyingly structured writing, particularly her detective fiction, did not occur spontaneously—it was a long process in the making and influenced by many individuals, however seemingly unexpectedly the venture of detective fiction writing materialized in her career. Sayers was not a solitary writer; she was, however, an experiential writer who gathered from and shared her work with many friends, particularly with members of the MAS.

ACTING, PLAYWRITING, AND THE FUN OF THEATRE

"Amateur theatricals had a permanent place in college."[41] The theatre was always a welcome topic among the students of Somerville, and this writing community was equally enthusiastic for anything dealing with theatre: writing, acting, directing or attending. Playwriting was popular among the writers of the MAS. Charis Barnett and Dorothy Rowe were known for their playwriting efforts. In February 1913, together they wrote, read to the group, and starred together in, a spoof play titled, "Hamlet, the Pragger-Dagger,"[42] brazenly revising the plot of Hamlet and blithely rewriting the play to include a case of measles at Somerville. Cases of measles, apparently, were running rampant through Oxford in early 1913, and this play gave a much needed outlet to the anxiety and inconvenience involved. It was a huge success. Dorothy Rowe played a "wildly hilarious"[43] Hamlet and Charis played Horatio (as well as being stage-manager). According to Charis Barnett, "The show elicited such loud and prolonged explosions of laughter, that we were asked to repeat it to the whole college, dons and students, which we did, with an equally riotous reception."[44]

Dorothy Sayers and Muriel St. Clare Byrne later famously collaborated on the play, *Busman's Honeymoon*. They, however, took this writing very seriously. During the collaboration, both Sayers and Byrne admit to struggling with the structure of the play, with the application of their ideals to the story, ideals of remaining fair to the reader. The authors state that they do not attempt to provide a "perfect dramatic formula for the presentation of the fair-play rule,"

---

41 Frankenburg, 1975, p. 66.
42 Ibid.
43 Ibid., p. 67.
44 Ibid.

but that, "They suggest, however, that the future development of the detective play may lie in this direction, being convinced that neither sensation without thought nor argument without emotion can ever provide the basis for any permanent artistic structure."[45] The fair-play rule was of paramount importance to Dorothy Sayers throughout her detective writing history, and one cannot help but think she was well schooled at Somerville, under the care of Emily Penrose, to adhere unflinchingly to this rule.

Adventuring Writers All

Friendship within a community of women writers takes on additional dimension. Not only are personal lives involved, but professional lives are involved as well. The more deeply I delve into the history of these complex women, the finer and more intricate becomes the web of ties among them: ties of professional association, ties of personal and career influence, ties of affection and support, ties of shared knowledge and continued analysis of one another's writing efforts, continued sharing of ideas, and communication of ties to daily life among them. Some members collaborated with others in authorship, as in the earlier discussion of *Busman's Honeymoon*. Some inspired one another to greater work, notably Marjorie Barber and Muriel St. Clare Byrne in their support and editing efforts toward Sayers' Dante translations, and some inspired one another by their social conscience and practical application of those principles, notably Margaret Chubb Pyke's effect upon the social reform research of Muriel Jaeger.[46] This mission of Margaret Chubb's was reported, by Charis Barnett, to influence other girls at Somerville, as well as the MAS members, toward social welfare work, volunteering, and writing.

During one MAS meeting in the Spring of 1913, Margaret Chubb described to the members a play she had seen, titled *Eugenics*, written by a fifteen-year-old girl.[47] This particular play had a deep effect upon Margaret Chubb who later became Chairman of the UK Family Planning Association.[48] Her son established the Margaret Pyke Memorial Trust[49] for family planning and training. Muriel

---

45   Sayers & Byrne, 1937, Intro.
46   Jaeger, 1956, dedication.
47   Frankenburg, 1975, p. 66.
48   Ibid., pp. 66-67.
49   Ibid., p. 67.

Jaeger consulted Margaret Pyke during her own later historical research on social reform. The drama of all this would not have been lost on Dorothy Sayers who, in turn, later wrote several essays (*Unpopular Opinions*, 1946) on the question of social morality and Christian responsibility toward questions of humanity and welfare.

By these examples, we are given a glimpse into the complexity and richness of the relationships between and among the members of the MAS through their tenure at Oxford, throughout their chosen fields of profession, and throughout their writing and research lives. Despite their divergent paths, the women of the MAS continued to affect, to a great degree, one another's professional and personal lives throughout their post-Oxford days. That which began as a small society of student writers at Oxford grew to be a web of published writers, teachers, and agents of social change.

Concluding Thoughts

My intent through this paper was to bring the Somerville women writers of the MAS out from the shadows, to introduce them as strong, talented, creative student writers who became vibrant women, prolific authors, theatrical figures, social activists, teachers, and scholars in their own right. These women wrote at a pivotal time, each dealing with the dramatic and profound effects of World War I upon their own lives and upon history. Their writings and lives, in turn, had profound effect upon their culture. Furthermore, it is important to recognize how very much this community of women writers and friends deeply affected and continued to affect the life of Dorothy L. Sayers. The Mutual Admiration Society of Somerville became an interrelated web of women writers and activists linked by their mutual interests, shared spirit of independence, their creative collaboration and, most of all, by their enduring friendship. In doing so, they have played a significant, if little-noted role influencing the literary and intellectual culture for women in the twentieth century.

Works Cited

Adams, Pauline. "Somerville and Shrewsbury." The Dorothy L. Sayers Society. *Proceedings of the 200 Convention Christ Church, Oxford, August 12-15, 2005*, 19-36.

---. *Somerville for Women, An Oxford College*. Oxford: Oxford University Press, 1996.

Alighieri, Dante. *The Divine Comedy, Cantica I: Hell (L'Inferno)*. Transl. by Dorothy L. Sayers. Baltimore: Penguin Classics, 1949.

Barber, Marjorie M. *Letters to Dorothy L. Sayers*. DLS Letters 423a (1947-1950; 1953-1954) and 423b (1934-36; 1939-1941). Wheaton, IL: Marion E. Wade Center, Archives. *Selections from Chaucer*. London: Macmillan & Co., 1961.

Barnett, Charis Ursula. "Translated from Theodore de Banville" IN *Oxford Poetry*. London: Basil Blackwell, 1914.

Batson, Judy G. *Her Oxford*. Nashville: Vanderbilt University Press, 2008.

Brabazon, James. *Dorothy L. Sayers*. New York: Charles Scribner's Sons, 1981.

Byrne, Muriel St. Clare. "Devachan" IN *Oxford Poetry*. London: Basil Blackwell, 1916.

Brittain, Vera. *Testament of Youth*. Great Britain: Victor Golancz Press, 1970.

---. *The Women at Oxford*. London: George Harrap & Co. Ltd., 1960.

Byrne, Muriel St. Clare. *Busman's Honeymoon: A Detective Comedy in Three Acts* (final draft). (ca. 1936). DLS/MS-19. 86 pp. cc. TMs. in 86 lvs. with revisions by Muriel St. Clare Byrne. Wheaton, IL: Marion E. Wade Center Archives.

Dorothy L Sayers. *Busman's Honeymoon, a detective comedy*. Anthony Fleming and the executors of Muriel St. Clare Byrne, 1937.

---. *Common or Garden Child*. London: Faber & Faber, Ltd., 1942.

---. *Lisle Letters*. Chicago: Chicago University Press, 1981.

Catherine Hope Mansfield. *Somerville College, 1879-1921*. Oxford: Frederick Hall at The University Press, 1931.

Dale, Alzina Stone. *Maker and Craftsman*. Grand Rapids: William B. Eerdmans Pub. Co, 1978.

---. Ed., *Love All* and *Busman's Honeymoon*. Kent: Kent State University Press, 1984.

---. Ed.543e3432543e34324353, *Dorothy L. Sayers, The Centenary Celebration*. New York: Walker & Co., 1993.

Downing, Crystal. *Writing Performances: The Stages of Dorothy L. Sayers*. New York: Palgrave Macmillan. 2004.

Fletcher, Christine M. *The Artist and the Trinity, Dorothy L. Sayers' Theology of Work*. Eugene, OR: Pickwick Publications, 2013.

Frankenburg, Charis U. *Common Sense about Children*. Bristol: Arco Publications, 1970.

---. *Latin with Laughter*. London: W. Heinemann Ltd., 1931.

---. *More Latin with Laughter*. London: W. Heinemann Ltd., 1934.

---. *Not Old, Madam, Vintage*. Lavenham, Suffolk: The Lavenham Press, 1975.

---. "Further News of Old Girls." Summer 1915. Godolphin School. http://godolphinww1.com (accessed 2 January 2016).

Glyer, Diana Pavlac. *Bandersnatch: C.S. Lewis, J.R.R. Tolkien, and the Creative Collaboration of the Inklings*. Kent, OH: Kent University Press, 2016.

---. *The Company They Keep, C.S. Lewis and J.R.R. Tolkien as Writers in Community*. Kent, OH: Kent State University Press, 2007.

---. and Laura Simmons. "Dorothy L. Sayers and C.S. Lewis: Two Approaches to Creativity and Calling." IN VII, An Anglo American Literary Review. Vol. 21. Wheaton, IL: Marion E. WadeCenter, 2004.

---. *History of Margaret Pyke Centre & Memorial Trust*. http://www.margaretpyke.org (accessed 3March 2016).

Hone, Ralph. *Dorothy L. Sayers, A Literary Biography*. Kent: Kent State University Press, 1979.

---. *Poetry of Dorothy L. Sayers*. Great Britain: The Dorothy L. Sayers Society in Association with The Marion E. Wade Center, 1996.

Jaeger, Muriel. *Before Victoria: Changing Standards & Behavior, 1787-1837*. London: Chatto & Windus, 1956.

---. *The Man with Six Senses*. London: The Hogarth Press, 1927.

---. *The Question Mark*. London: The Hogarth Press, 1926.

Lee, Geoffrey Alan. "The Short Stories of Dorothy L. Sayers: Their Publication History." IN *Studies in Sayers, Essays presented to Dr. Barbara Reynolds on her 80th birthday*. Christopher Dean, Ed., Rose Cottage, West Sussex: Dorothy L. Sayers Society, 1994, 60-63.

Leonardi, Susan J. *Dangerous by Degrees, Women at Oxford and the Somerville College Novelists*. New Brunswick: Rutgers University Press, 1989.

Mead, Marjorie Lamp. "Generosity and Courtesy: Dorothy L. Sayers as a friend." in *Studies in Sayers, Essays presented to Dr. Barbara Reynolds on her 80th birthday*. Christopher Dean, Ed., Rose Cottage, West Sussex: Dorothy L. Sayers Society,1994, 8-12.

"Rejoicing in Truth: Dorothy L. Sayers and the Good of the Intellect." in *Further Studies in Sayers, Essays presented to Dr. Barbara Reynolds on her 90th birthday*. Christopher Dean, Ed., Rose Cottage, West Sussex: Dorothy L. Sayers Society, 2004, 23-30.

"Old Girl News," Christmas 1915. Godolphin School. http://godolphinww1.com. (accessed 4 November 2015).

Parker, C. "*Catalogue of the correspondence of Charis Frankenburg, 1927-1945*." Bodleian Library, Department of Special Collections, University of Oxford, 2002.

Prescott, Barbara M. "The Hero and the Heroic in the Early Poetry of Dorothy L. Sayers." MSb, 2016.

---. *Lyric Muse: The Oxford Poetry of Dorothy L. Sayers.* Forthcoming, 2018.

---. *A Mutual Admiration: Dorothy L. Sayers and the Women Writers of Somerville.* Forthcoming, 2017.

---. "Poems in an Oxford Notebook, 1912-1915: Several Early Unpublished Poems by Dorothy L. Sayers." MSa, 2015.

---. "Who Calls the Tune?": An Early Short Story with Elements of Mystery by Dorothy L. Sayers." MSc, 2016.

Reynolds, Barbara. *Dorothy L. Sayers, Child and Woman of Her Time.* Volume Five, Letters. Great Britain: Dorothy L. Sayers Society, 2002.

---. *Dorothy L. Sayers, Her Life and Soul.* New York: St. Martin's Press, 1993.

---. *The Letters of Dorothy L. Sayers, 1899-1936: The Making of a Detective Novelist.* London: Hodder & Stoughton, 1995.

---. *The Letters of Dorothy L. Sayers, Volume Two, 1937-1943: from Novelist to Playwright.* London: Hodder & Stoughton, 1995.

---. *The Letters of Dorothy L. Sayers, Volume Three, 1944-1950: A Noble Daring.* London: Hodder & Stoughton, 2006.

---. *The Passionate Intellect.* Kent: Kent State University Press, 1989.

Rowe, Dorothy. "An Old Rhyme Re-Sung" IN *Oxford Poetry.* London: Basil Blackwell, 1915.

---. "Asleep" IN *Oxford Poetry.* London: Basil Blackwell, 1914.

---. "Morpheus" IN *Oxford Poetry.* London: Basil Blackwell, 1914.

Sayers, Dorothy L. *Creed or Chaos,* New York: Harcourt Brace, 1949.

---. *Catholic Tales and Christian Songs.* London: Basil Blackwell. 1916.

---. "Earl Ulfric" IN Notebook, DLS/MS-365 POEMS AND BALLADS. (1910-1911) signed. Wheaton, IL:

Marion E. Wade Center, Archives.

---. "Fair Erembours: A Song of the Web" IN *Oxford Poetry*. London: Basil Blackwell, 1917.

---. "The [Fascinating] Problem of Uncle Meleager's Will." *Pearson's Magazine*, Vol. 60, July, 1925.

---. "For Phaon" IN *Oxford Poetry*. London: Basil Blackwell, 1919.

---. "The Gates of Paradise" IN *Op. 1*. London: Basil Blackwell, 1916.

---. *Gaudy Night*. London: Victor Golancz Ltd., 1935.

---. "Hymn in Contemplation of Sudden Death" IN *Oxford Magazine*, 1915.

---. "Icarus" IN *Oxford Magazine*, 1916.

---. "Lay" IN *Oxford Poetry*. London: Basil Blackwell, 1915.

---. *Letters to Charles Williams, 1933-1944 (115a-b)*. Marion E. Wade Center Archives.

---. *Letter to Stanley Unwin, Esq.* 31st October 1947. Messrs. George Allen & Unwin Ltd., The Marion E. Wade Center, Wheaton, IL. DLS Letter Archives (146/21).

---. *Letters to Dorothy Rowe*, 1936-1956, Marion E. Wade Center Archives (427).

---. *Letter to Muriel (Jim) Jaeger.* 22nd July, 1913. Marion E. Wade Center, Wheaton, IL. DLS Letter Archives (22/3).

Letter to Muriel (Jim) Jaeger. 30th July, 1913. Marion E. Wade Center, Wheaton, IL DLS Letter Archives (22/7-10).

---. *Letter to Muriel Jaeger.* 3rd January, 1915. Marion E. Wade Center, Wheaton, IL. DLS Letter (22/15).

---. *Letter to Muriel Jaeger.* Christmas Eve 1916. Marion E. Wade Center, Wheaton, IL. DLS Letter Archives (22/57).

---. *Letter to Parents*. 10th November, 1912. Marion E. Wade Center, Wheaton, IL. DLS Letter Archives (146/21).

---. and Muriel St. Clare Byrne. *Love All and Busman's Honeymoon*, a detective comedy. Anthony Fleming and the executors of Muriel St. Clare Byrne, 1937.

---. *The Mind of the Maker*. New York: Harcourt Brace, 1941.

---. *Op. I*. London: Basil Blackwell. 1916.

---. "Peredur." Notebook. DLS/MS-164 signed; brown notebook with AMs. inscription on recto of front cover. Marion E. Wade Center, Archives.

---. "Pygmalion" IN *Oxford Poetry*. London: Basil Blackwell, 1918.

---. "Sympathy" IN *Oxford Poetry*. London: Basil Blackwell, 1919.

---. *Unpopular Opinions*. Twenty-One Essays. London: Victor Gollancz Ltd., 1947.

---. "Vials Full of Odours" IN *Oxford Poetry*. London: Basil Blackwell, 1919.

---. *"Who calls the tune?"* DLS/MS-239 (n.d.) 10 pp. AMs. in 10 lvs. with revisions. Wheaton, IL: Marion E. Wade Center.

---. *Whose Body?* London: T. Fisher Unwin, 1923.

Somerville College. *"February 1914: Somerville Before the Outbreak of War."* Somerville College, Oxford, Archives. http://www.some.ox.ac.uk/february-1914-somerville-college-before-the-outbreak-of-war/

---. *"June 1914: The Commemoration Dance."* Somerville College, Oxford, Archives. http://www.some.ox.ac.uk/june1914-the-commemoration-dance.

---. *"October 1914: Vera Brittain Arrives for the Academic Year at Oxford."* Somerville College, Oxford, Archives. http://www.some.ox.ac.uk/october-1914-vera-brittain-arrives-for-the-academic-year-at-oxford.

Swarthmore Phoenix. "Middlemore, Amphilis. Obituary." October 7th, 1931.

Tolkien, J.R.R. "Goblin Feet" IN *Oxford Poetry*. London: Basil Blackwell, 1915.

Willerton, Chris. "Dorothy L. Sayers and the Creative Reader," IN VII, An Anglo-American Literary Review, Vol. 28, 2011, 47-60.

III. Essays on George MacDonald

Mutuality in Wonderland: Charles Dodgson, Adopted Member of the MacDonald Family

by Rachel E. Johnson

Until December 2012 Rachel Johnson was the Research Librarian at the University of Worcester, UK. In "retirement" Rachel is currently working part time as a librarian at Tyndale House Library in Cambridge, UK and also volunteering at Homerton College Library, Cambridge, UK where she is working with a special collection of historical children's literature.

As the title indicates, Charles Dodgson had a close and long-standing friendship with the family of George MacDonald. In this paper I aim to explore how their relationship developed to the extent that Dodgson was absorbed into the MacDonald family, with the result that the cross-fertilization of ideas and experiences affected and influenced their writing. I also ask the question—is the mutuality in their writing as great as the critics suggest?

A Bit of Background

Dodgson and MacDonald first met in Hastings between the spring of 1858 and autumn 1859. MacDonald was visiting his homeopathic doctor and Dodgson visiting Dr James Hunt who had a reputation for curing stammering. Dodgson also visited his aunts, the Misses Lutwidge, who lived in Hastings.

The two men were very different in personality. MacDonald was outgoing, a brilliant public speaker, was married with a growing family, had come out of a Scottish Calvinist background and hosted large social gatherings at the family home, whilst Dodgson was shy, avoided public speaking, came from a High Church background and preferred small gatherings if any, since, according to his biographers, he was only completely socially comfortable in the company of children, with whom he lost his stammer.[1] Mark Twain, present at one of the MacDonald gatherings at which Dodgson was also present, described him as "the stillest and shyest full-grown man I have ever met except

---

1   Shaberman, Hudson, Taylor, Cohen

Uncle Remus"[2] (For more on Uncle Remus we may read Joel Chandler Harris, of whom Twain made a similar comment).[3]

Despite these differences in background and temperament, what they had in common was much more important. They were both influenced by the German and English Romantics which led them towards the form of dream-vision in their writing. Both were interested in the positive moral effect of drama. Dodgson was one of the MacDonald family's greatest supporters when they later toured the country with their *Dramatic Presentation of the Second Half of John Bunyan's The Pilgrim's Progress*, although he did once concede that "Lilia (the eldest daughter) was the only one who could act."[4]

Both men were anti-vivisectionists and, key for both of them, they were both committed Christians who had struggled to faith through the rigid religious dogma of their backgrounds. Greville MacDonald, George's eldest son, drawing out their differences, writes:

> How happily could my father laugh over this loving humorist's impromptu drawings, full of absurdities, mock-maxims and erratic logic so dear to the child-heart, young or old! While Dodgson, the shy, learned mathematician who hated inaccuracy, loved to question the very multiplication-table's veracity, my father, the poet, who hated any touch of irreverence, could laugh till tears ran at his friend's ridicule of smug formalism and copy-book maxims.[5]

They already had several mutual friends, and were both influenced by the thinking of F. D. Maurice, whose theology was regarded by the mainstream churches as unorthodox.

THE FRIENDSHIP

During the early 1860s, Dodgson and the MacDonalds were particularly close. It was a time when Dodgson often visited the MacDonalds. Whilst most of MacDonald's fairy tales were written during this period, Carroll was gestating the story that was eventually published in 1865 as *Alice in Wonderland*.

---

2   Shaberman, Raphael. *George MacDonald: A Bibliographical Study.* Winchester: St Paul's Bibliographies, 1990, 117.
3   Wikipedia
4   Raeper, William. *George MacDonald.* Tring: Lion, 1987, p. 346. From Dodgson's Diary entry 26 July 1879.
5   MacDonald, Greville. *George MacDonald and His Wife.* London: George Allen and Unwin, 1923, 342-43.

In 1860, Dodgson first met two of the MacDonald children, Greville and Mary (second daughter), in the studio of Alexander Munro the sculptor. Greville was sitting for Munro's statue of *Boy Riding a Dolphin* which can still be seen in Hyde Park, London. Dodgson immediately began a conversation with Greville, aged five or six, about the benefits of having a marble head. Dodgson writes:

> I claimed their acquaintance and began at once proving to the boy, Greville that he had better take the opportunity of having his head changed for a marble one. The effect was that in about 2 minutes they had entirely forgotten that I was total stranger, and were earnestly arguing the question as if we were old acquaintances.[6]

In his autobiography Greville includes a picture of the event drawn for him by Dodgson and continues to describe the growing friendship with the family in his account of outings which found their way into MacDonald's story *My Uncle Peter*,[7] which I will refer to later in this paper.

Mary was Dodgson's first child-friend to whom he wrote letters, and the longest standing, in that they remained corresponding friends into Mary's adulthood. One of these letters explains that (Derek Hudson's paraphrase)

> the hot weather had made him so sad and sulky that he had thrown a book at the head of a visitor, the Bishop of Oxford ... And then thinking that perhaps he had gone too far he added[8]: '... this isn't quite true—so you needn't believe it—Don't be in such a hurry to believe next time—I'll tell you why—If you set to work to believe everything, you will tire out the muscles of your mind, and then you'll be so weak you won't be able to believe the simplest true things.'[9]

This passage, written before *Alice's Adventures in Wonderland* had been published, although it had been written, is echoed later in *Alice through the Looking-Glass* (1871) when the White Queen states

---

6   Collingwood, Stuart Dodgson. *The Life and Letters of Lewis Carroll*. London: Fisher Unwin, 1898, 83-85.
7   MacDonald, George. *My Uncle Peter* in *The Christmas Stories of George MacDonald*. Tring: Lion, 1982, 7-34.
8   Hudson, Derek. *Lewis Carroll an Illustrated Biography*. London: Constable, 1976 (1954), 102.
9   Quoted in Hudson, Derek. *Lewis Carroll an Illustrated Biography*. London: Constable, 1976 (1954), 102. From *A Selection from the letters of Lewis Carroll to his Child-friends*, edited by Evelyn M. Hatch (1933), 22-25.

that she sometimes "believed as many as six impossible things before breakfast."[10] William Raeper also notes that in "*Through the Looking-Glass* Lilia (MacDonald's eldest daughter) is transformed into Lily, the White Pawn and daughter of the White Queen, while Mary's cat Snowdrop makes an appearance as Alice's white kitten."[11]

The story of Dodgson's creation of *Alice's Adventures Underground* is well-known. After he had begun to write it down, he handed a partially illustrated copy of the manuscript to George's wife, Louisa MacDonald, who read it to the children. As the first child audience to hear the story, they responded enthusiastically, especially Greville, who notes:

> I remember that first reading well, and also my braggart avowal that I wished there were 60,000 volumes of it. Yet I distinctly recall a certain indignant grief that its characters were only a pack of cards; and I still look upon that *Finis* as a blemish upon the sublime fantasy. . . .[12]

George MacDonald not only encouraged Dodgson to publish, which is noted in Dodgson's diary May 9, 1863, but to lengthen the narrative. There are other claimants for this encouragement, but by comparing the dates, it does appear that the MacDonalds were the first to do so. And so the friendship developed to the extent that Dodgson was absorbed further into the MacDonald family, to become known as Uncle Dodgson. I will now move on to briefly examine some parallels between their works.

Influence on Writing

All the major MacDonald and Carroll biographers note the mutual influence, which is described by Hubert Nicholson as "books built with stones from the same ruined chapels and temples,"[13] as well as ideas taken directly from each other's writing.

---

10   Carroll, Lewis. *Alice's Adventures in Wonderland 150th Anniversary Edition with Through the Looking Glass and What Alice Found There*. London: Vintage Books, 2015 (1865,1871).
11   Raeper, William. *George MacDonald*. Tring: Lion, 1987, 172.
12   MacDonald, Greville. *Reminiscences of a Specialist*. London: George Allen and Unwin, 1932, 15.
13   Nicholson, Hubert. *A Voyage to Wonderland and Other Essays*. London: Heinemann, 1947, 13

Nicholson was the first writer to note parallels and mutual influence. Writing in 1947, he commented that "not much ferreting for meanings and origins has been done in the rabbit-hole that Carroll made."[14] Nicholson majors on the parallels between MacDonald's *Phantastes* (1858) and *Lilith* (1890-95) and Carroll's *Alice in Wonderland* (1865) and *Alice Through the Looking Glass* (1871). That *Lilith* was published so much later does not refute his argument since the threads in *Lilith* run through all of MacDonalds work,[15] whilst John Docherty notes what he interprets as "borrowings" from Lewis Carroll's *Alice Through the Looking Glass* (1871).[16] Nicholson also notes the influence of Novalis on both authors, and the parallels found in his work *A Parable* (in *The Disciples at Sais:* Novalis 1772-1801) which MacDonald translated Since then there have been a number of essays, articles, books and one minutely closely read and critiqued study.

I will mention one or two key works in which the parallels are clear but since to drill down into them all would be impossible in the time available, I will then settle on a brief examination of just one of GMD's stories.

I have already mentioned the portrait of Uncle Peter, in GMD's story *My Uncle Peter* (first published in *The Queen* Dec. 21, 1861. Reprinted in *Adela Cathcart* 1864), as a representation of Dodgson. The following quotes demonstrate the reality turned into MacDonald's fiction.

Greville writes:

> Our annual treat was Uncle Dodson taking us to the Polytechnic for the entrancing 'dissolving views' of fairy-tales, or to go down in the diving bell, or watch the mechanical athlete *Leotard*. . . . And there was Cremer's toy-shop in Regent street—not to mention bath-buns and ginger-beer — all associated in my memory with the adorable writer of *Alice*.[17]

And in *My Uncle Peter* MacDonald writes

> The first remembrance that I have of him is his taking me one Christmas Eve to the largest toy shop in London, and telling

---

14 Ibid., 1.
15 See Raeper, William. *George MacDonald*. Tring: Lion, 1987, 346. From Dodgson's Diary entry 26 July 1879, 365.
16 Docherty, John. *The Literary Products of the Lewis Carroll-George MacDonald Friendship*. Revised and Expanded Edition. Lewiston: The Edwin Mellen Press, 1997 (1995), 375
17 MacDonald, Greville. *George MacDonald and His Wife*. London: George Allen and Unwin, 1923.

me to choose any toy whatever that I pleased.[18]

This portrait is apt but the underlying parallel is that Uncle Peter pined away when he lost his child-friend, interpreted by the Carroll and MacDonald critic Docherty as a possible warning to Carroll that his sadness at the loss of Alice Liddell as child-friend must be an accepted rather than become a destructive influence on his life.[19]

PHANTASTES

I cannot move on without a further mention of *Phantastes*, subtitled *A Faerie Romance for Men and Women*, the first of the two adult fantasies which framed MacDonald's output. It was published in 1858, just before the period in which Dodgson and MacDonald first met and five years before *Alice's Adventures Underground* was written down in 1863. Following the German romantics, this bildungsroman in the form of a dream-vision includes a hole and passage down and along which the protagonist journeys, a meeting with a white rabbit and, an image often found in MacDonald's works, a mirror in which is found another country. As MacDonald writes "all mirrors are magic mirrors."[20]

More fundamentally, the structure of both works, or, as some critiques note, the lack of structure, is similar. Both works are structured from the centre outwards, like the spokes of a bicycle wheel. In *Phantastes*, MacDonald's influences include Spenser's *Fairy Queen* whose structure has been likened to:

> the Gothic method of design on gardening—a centre to which all walks have opening but all walks also have their own purpose and destination.[21]

Also, Novalis, whose aim was to create "stories without rational cohesion yet filled with associations,"[22] was a major influence particularly on MacDonald. The cyclical or spiral narrative impetus

---

18 My Uncle Peter in *The Christmas Stories of George MacDonald*. Tring: Lion, 1982, 8.
19 Docherty, 83-84.
20 MacDonald, George. *Phantastes: a Faerie Romance for Men and Women*. London: Paternoster, 2008. Special edition with introduction and notes by Nick Page, 125.
21 Hurd, Richard. *Letters of Chivalry and Romance*. London: Printed by W.B. for A. Millar in the Strand, and W. Thurbourn and J. Woodyer, in Cambridge, MCCCLXIV (1764), 67.
22 Docherty, 109. Novalis—quoted in *Phantastes*

is apparent in *Phantastes* and in the *Alice* books. Many other parallels, in *Phantastes* and *Alice in Wonderland* are examined in detail in the studies available.

MacDonald's final fantasy, *Lilith*, published in 1898 begins the dream-journey through a mirror and also reflects the mutual interest of both writers in psychical research. Dodgson was a founder member of the Society for Psychical Research, a subject which, along with spiritualism, interested many intellectuals of the period. MacDonald initially became interested through his friends the Mount-Temples, although his writing includes many instances of what the Scots term "second sight." The mutual mystical and psychical interest evident in the works of MacDonald and Carroll fed, in the early 1860s, from the meetings held by Dr Hale in Hastings, through subsequent conversations and discussions, into their work. All the biographers record this connection.

CROSS PURPOSES

The story I want to mention particularly is MacDonald's short fairy tale *Cross Purposes*, written during the time of the closest MacDonald/Dodgson friendship, in the early 1860s, and published initially in *Beeton's Christmas Annual* 1862[23]. It was later included in *Dealings with the Fairies* in 1867.

Some critics (notably Docherty) have suggested that the story arose out of a discussion between Dodgson and MacDonald, which led to both writers producing stories about "Alice exploring her subconscious. MacDonald's was *Cross Purposes*; Dodgson's was *Alice's Adventures Underground*."[24]

The beginning of both stories takes Alice into fairyland whilst she is in the dreamlike state between sleeping and waking. On her approach to Fairyland, *Cross Purposes* Alice shrinks twice before the story continues with an emphasis on growth in self-knowledge. MacDonald's concern, as ever, is his protagonist's intellectual and spiritual development. Wolff notes that, even if Carroll had not seen MacDonald's story, which is highly unlikely since they were spending a lot of time together in the early 1860s, he would have "cleared" *his* Alice's experiences of shrinking, journey and dream with MacDonald

---

23 Wolff, Robert Lee. "An 1862 Alice: 'Cross Purposes,' or, Which Dreamed It?" in *Harvard Library Bulletin*. Cambridge (MASS): Harvard University Library, 1975, 199-202.
24 See for example Docherty, 85

before publication. In this scenario the name would have to be purely incidental since Carroll was writing for Alice Liddell.

Cross Purposes exposes the snobbery of social attitudes which dictate that a middle class girl (Alice) should not have anything to do with a working class boy (Richard) but that such attitudes can change when they are thrown together in Fairyland and meet a number of dangerous situations in which initiative and resourcefulness are needed. Docherty discusses the concern of Dodgson that Alice Liddell did not succumb to her mother's lead on such attitudes[25] by challenging the conventions surrounding Alice in his writing, just as MacDonald does in *Cross Purposes*.[26] Although the class divide is shown as insurmountable outside of Fairyland, within Fairyland, or Wonderland, both Alices learn to overcome their prejudice. Amongst many parallels in the stories, are the following situations which fall between entering and coming out of Fairyland (*Cross Purposes*) or Wonderland (*Alice's Adventures in Wonderland*):

> 1) Both Alices enter fairyland between waking and sleeping. *Cross Purposes*, 143; *Alice's Adventures*, 152.
>
> 2) Both Alices encounter a pool, or lake, of water in which they are immersed. *Cross Purposes*, 145 and 152; *Alice's Adventures*, 24-25.
>
> 3) Both Alice (in *Alice's Adventures*) and Alice and Richard (in *Cross Purposes*) are menaced by creatures. *Cross Purposes*, 164, 167, 169; *Alice's Adventures*, 41.
>
> 4) Both Alices encounter and overcome mental illusion. *Cross Purposes*, 164, 167, 169; *Alice's Adventures*, 129.
>
> 5) At the end of the time in Fairyland, Alice and Richard jump from a tree back "down to earth," Alice runs home through a "little gate ... into her father's grounds." *Cross Purposes*, 170; *Alice's Adventures*, 130.
>
> 6) Also, the episodes the two Alices meet happen in the same order.

In *Cross Purposes* MacDonald writes: "many things we never could believe, have only to happen, and then there is nothing strange about them,"[27] and the White Queen expects Alice to believe what at first appear to be impossible things: "I daresay you haven't had much

---

25 Docherty, 111. Mrs Liddell had a reputation for snobbishness.
26 Ibid., 129.
27 MacDonald, George. "Cross Purposes" in *The Light Princess and Other Fairy Tales*. Whitethorn: Johannesen, 1993. 141-171

practice," said the Queen. "When I was your age I always did it for half-an-hour a day."[28]

The letter to Mary MacDonald on believing impossible things has already been noted. Both authors are concerned with the importance not only of the creative imagination but also the importance of not taking any given situation at face-value and assuming that is all there is to it.

Conclusion

When the MacDonald family moved to Bordighera, and visited England less often, Dodgson almost lost touch with them. The last reference to them in his diary of 1882, notes a conversation with George and Louisa after a performance of the play the family toured in the summer months. He also recorded inviting Ronald (2nd son) to dinner at Christchurch College when Ronald became an undergraduate in Oxford, also in 1882. This meeting appears to have been their last.

Finally, is it possible to answer the initial question as to whether the mutuality in their writing is as great as the critics claim? I would suggest the answer is "Yes."

That George MacDonald and Charles Dodgson remained friends and mirrored each other's major themes, consciously or unconsciously, testifies to the depth of their friendship and the acceptance of each other's idiosyncrasies. A major theme of their work, following Novalis, concerned the nature of the dream-vision and the nature of life as a dream. MacDonald quoted Novalis at the end of *Phantastes* "Our life is no dream; but it ought to become one, and perhaps will."[29] Carroll's question "whose dream was it?" the Red King's or Alice's, was further explored in his *Sylvie and Bruno* where dream and what passes for real life are juxtaposed and often inverted whilst MacDonald's *At the Back of the North Wind* (1871) equally poses the same question to the reader. Was Diamond's life with North Wind the reality or was it a dream, or was it delirium?

Dodgson remained an adopted member of the MacDonald family until his death in January 1898. His interest in "the dreamlike quality of this life compared with what was seen as the solid reality of the next"[30] was also a concern that flowed, like Irene's connecting

---

28 Carroll, Lewis. *The Annotated Alice*, edited by Martin Gardner. Rev. Ed. London: Penguin, 2001 (1970).
29 MacDonald, George. *Phantastes*, 269.
30 Raeper, William. *George MacDonald*. Tring: Lion, 1987, 174.

thread in MacDonald's *The Princess and the Goblin* (1872), through all of MacDonald's work and beyond to those he influenced, creating their mutuality in Wonderland and a door into Fairyland for their readers.

WORKS CITED

Carroll, Lewis. *Alice's Adventures in Wonderland 150th Anniversary Edition with Through the Looking Glass and What Alice Found There*. London: Vintage Books, 2015 (1865, 1871).

Cohen Morton. *Lewis Carroll: a Biography*. London: Macmillan, 1995.

Collingwood, Stuart Dodgson. *The Life and Letters of Lewis Carroll*. London: Fisher Unwin, 1898.

Docherty, John. *The Literary Products of the Lewis Carroll-George MacDonald Friendship*. Lewiston.Queenston. Lampeter: The Edwin Mellen Press, Second revised and expanded edition, 1997. (1995).

Gardner, Martin (Editor). *The Annotated Alice*. Revised edition. London: Penguin Books, 2001 (1970).

Hammond, Marie K. "What's in a Name?: Clues to understanding MacDonald's Fairy story 'Cross Purposes.'" In *Inklings Forever*, Volume VI. A Collection of Essays Presented at the Sixth Frances White Ewbank Colloquium on C.S. Lewis & Friends. Taylor University 2008. Upland Indiana.

Hatch, Evelyn (editor). *A Selection from the letters of Lewis Carroll to his Child-friends*, (1933).

Hein, Rolland. *George MacDonald: Victorian Mythmaker*. Nashville: Starsong, 1993.

Hudson, Derek. *Lewis Carroll an Illustrated Biography*. London: Constable, 1976 (1954).

MacDonald, George. *My Uncle Peter* in *The Christmas Stories of George MacDonald*. Tring: Lion, 1982.

MacDonald, George. "*Cross Purposes*" in *The Light Princess and other Fairy Tales*. Whitethorn: Johannesen, 1993.

MacDonald, George. "The Fantastic Imagination" in A *Dish of Orts*. Whitethorn: Johannesen, 1996.

MacDonald, George. *Phantastes: a Faerie Romance for Men and Women*. London: Paternoster. 2008. Special edition with introduction and notes by Nick Page.

MacDonald, George. *The Portent.*

MacDonald, Greville. *George MacDonald and His Wife.* London: George Allen and Unwin, 1923.

MacDonald, Greville. *Reminiscences of a Specialist.* London: George Allen and Unwin, 1932.

MacIntyre, J. *Newsletter of the Victorian Studies Association of Western Canada.* 1977.

Nicholson, Hubert. *A Voyage to Wonderland and other Essays.* London: Heinemann, 1947.

Raeper, William. *George MacDonald.* Tring: Lion, 1987.

Raeper, William. *George MacDonald.* Tring: Lion, 1987. From Dodgson's Diary entry 26 July 1879.

Seper, Charles. http://georgemacdonald.info/carroll.html 2007

Shaberman, Raphael. *George MacDonald: A Bibliographical Study.* Winchester: St Paul's Bibliographies, 1990.

Taylor, Alexander. *The White Knight: a Study of Charles Ludwidge Dodgson.* Edinburgh: Oliver & Boyd, 1952.

Wolff, Robert Lee. "An 1862 Alice: 'Cross Purposes', or, Which Dreamed It?" in *Harvard Library Bulletin.* Cambridge (MASS): Harvard University Library, 1975. Pp. 199-202.

Awaking the Reader to Nature's Aesthetics: A Novel Purpose in *The Seaboard Parish*
by Cynthia DeMarcus Manson

Cynthia DeMarcus Manson is Associate Professor of English at Southern University and A & M College in Baton Rouge, Louisiana. Her previous publications include *The Fairy-Tale Literature of Charles Dickens, Christina Rossetti, and George MacDonald: Antidotes to the Victorian Spiritual Crisis*.

At the 2010 C. S. Lewis and Friends Colloquium, I explored several of George MacDonald's word paintings of natural phenomena, and their interconnections with the art theory and practice of some nineteenth-century Pre-Raphaelite painters. One of the literary landscapes came from the conclusion of MacDonald's 1868 novel *The Seaboard Parish* in which the minister narrator details the physical features of an actual Pre-Raphaelite painting by Arthur Hughes that MacDonald had once seen. Subsequently, the narrator interprets this image—a dying knight in the sunset, just-reaped shocks of corn in the valley nearby, a sky-reflecting lake and slender pines, "which lead the eye and point the heart upward" toward heaven itself (615). *The Seaboard Parish* contains many of MacDonald's radiant word paintings, but my thoughts have returned to the book to consider it more deeply as a whole. Is *The Seaboard Parish* simply a set-piece for MacDonald's artistic, highly pictorial descriptions of nature, or does it strive to meet expectations for its genre—the novel—integrating theme, plot and character development to immerse the reader in a complex representation of reality? I think it does the latter.

First published in book form by Hurst and Blackett of London, *The Seaboard Parish* centers on a long stay in the fictional seaside town of Kilkhaven by Anglican vicar Harry Walton and his family. *The Seaboard Parish* is a sequel to MacDonald's *Annals of a Quiet Neighbourhood* (1867) and a prequel to *The Vicar's Daughter* (1872), though it may easily be read on its own. However, questions about the seriousness of MacDonald's intentions to write a novel arise when reading the first chapter of *Seaboard*, which is entitled "Homiletic," or sermon. Writing in first-person, the minister discursively contemplates old age, writing another book, and the different literary preferences of young and old, before abruptly announcing, "Now, readers in general, I have had time to consider what to tell you about, and how to begin"

(6). The story frame not only delays the action and positions the narrative some years in the narrator's past; it also makes the minister's selection of autobiographical topic seem very casual. One expects a memoir infiltrated with a minister's spiritual insights, rather than the carefully crafted product of a literary professional.

Narrator Walton also undercuts expectations of literary design in the final chapter of *Seaboard*, when he makes various self-deprecating remarks, such as "Now I fancy my readers, looking forward to the end, and seeing what a small amount of print is left, blaming me; some, that I have roused curiosity without satisfying it; others, that I have kept them so long over a dull book and a lame conclusion" (622-23). To answer readers' unanswered questions, the minister quickly states the matrimonial fate of two of his daughters and touches on what has become of some of his other children since the time period of the story. Then, he raises doubts as to whether he will further develop the history of himself and his family in another book, as he suspects that the end of his life is approaching. Walton laments:

> The labour of thinking into sequences, even the bodily labour of writing, grows more and more severe. . . . I must therefore take leave of my patient reader—for surely every one who has followed me through all that I have here written, well deserves the epithet—as if the probability that I shall write no more were a certainty. . . ." (624)

When one contrasts George MacDonald with the persona of the Rev. Walton, one becomes aware of differences in vitality, but most particularly of literary acumen. Part of *The Seaboard Parish* was actually written while MacDonald remained by the seaside in Bude, Cornwall, where he and his family vacationed in summer 1867. As Barbara Amell points out in a *Wingfold* article on "The Bude Holiday," "he spent about two months working on *The Seaboard Parish* in its natural surroundings" (39), even after the opening installment of the novel appeared in the Oct. 1, 1867 issue of *The Sunday Magazine*. MacDonald's proximity to the seaside undoubtedly accounts for the vividness of his description, but the crafting of the novel's purpose and effect indicate that he used his fresh experiences of nature to express and further refine a complex and unified vision that developed long before his visit.

In my opinion, the key interpretive passage in *The Seaboard Parish* is a lengthy declaration that Walton makes to his daughter Connie regarding the aesthetic and spiritual value of the natural world:

> I suspect we shall find some day that the loss of the human paradise consists chiefly in the closing of the human eyes; that at least far more of it than people think remains about us still, only we are so filled with foolish desires and evil cares, that we cannot see or hear, cannot even smell or taste the pleasant things round about us. We have need to pray in regard to the right receiving of the things of the senses even, "Lord, open thou our hearts to understand thy word"; for each of these things is as certainly a word of God as Jesus is The Word of God. (116)

Walton's passage is striking because he claims that the natural world still possesses edenic qualities of beauty and pleasure, and that potentially human beings can enjoy much of the original artistry that the Creator exhibited in the Garden of Eden; Walton's reference to "the pleasant things round about us" highlights sensuous nature as appealing to the human appreciation for and response to the beautiful or to art and culture. In other words, he is talking about the aesthetics or principles underlying the beautiful and artistic. Additionally, Walton asserts that individuals should pray to understand the divine truth or meaning that is being communicated via the aesthetic effects of nature. The concept of creation as speaking of God and his characteristics is emphasized also when Walton contemplates his own continuing ability to enjoy the outdoors. He writes:

> The smell of that field of beans gives me more delight now than ever it could have given me when I was a youth. And if I ask myself why, I find it is simply because I have more faith now than I had then. . . . Now, I believe that God *means* that odour of the beanfield; that when Jesus smelled such a scent about Jerusalem or in Galilee, he thought of his Father. (141)

MacDonald's emphasis on the beauty and meaningfulness of the natural world is not confined to *The Seaboard Parish* or even his realistic novels alone. David L. Neuhouser and Mark R. Hall have written: "An investigation into the writings of George MacDonald shows his love and reverence for nature and reveals how he envisions it as a manifestation of the imagination of God" (144). Neuhouser and Hall also quote from MacDonald's essay on "Wordsworth's Poetry," in which MacDonald writes: "This world is not merely a thing which God hath made, subjecting it to laws; but it is an expression of the thought, the feeling, the heart of God himself" (145).

During the course of *The Seaboard Parish*, the minister guides his two oldest daughters, Connie and Wynnie, as they grow in awareness of and response to the aesthetic and divine communications of nature. The novel's readers vicariously share in Walton's guidance, while observing the different circumstances and processes of change that the daughters undergo. Connie's development begins in the wake of a horseback-riding accident that occurs on her eighteenth birthday. Connie is immobilized for a serious spinal injury, but her confinement indoors strengthens her appreciation of the outdoors. Her father points out that an "interruption" in the enjoyment of gifts from God may be necessary to "make us able to enjoy them as richly as he gives them," and Connie confesses: "[S]ince I have been ill, you would wonder, if you could see into me, how even what you tell me about the world out of doors gives me more pleasure than I think I ever had when I could go about it just as I liked" (36-37).

More enjoyment is ahead for Connie, after a fellow clergyman offers his house to the vicar and his family for the summer, and Walton decides to accept. He shares with Connie an epiphany he had as a young man while viewing the Atlantic on holiday from university. The sky was cloudy, and he was despondent:

> All at once I turned—I don't know why. There lay the gray sea, but not as I had seen it last, not all gray. It was dotted, spotted, and splashed all over with drops, pools, and lakes of light, of all shades of depth, from a light shimmer of tremulous gray, through a half-light that turned the prevailing lead colour into translucent green that seemed to grow out of its depths— through this, I say, to brilliant light, deepening and deepening till my very soul was stung by the triumph of the intensity of molten silver. There was no sun upon me. But there were breaks in the clouds over the sea, through which, the air being filled with vapour, I could see the long lines of the sun-rays descending on the waters like rain—so like a rain of light that the water seemed to plash up in light under their fall. I questioned the past no more; the present seized upon me, and I knew that the past was true, and that nature was more lovely, more awful in her loveliness than I could grasp. It was a lonely place! I fell on my knees, and worshipped the God that made the glory and my soul. (117-18)

Walton tells Connie that he hopes she will see "a vision" by the Atlantic as brilliant as his, and she is taken outdoors for short periods to prepare her for the long journey by railway and then by open carriage to Cornwall.

As the family travels toward its destination, Walton sees "various reflexes of happiness" shining on the faces of his wife and children and reaches for images of nature to convey the nuances of their expressions. Connie's face "was bright with the brightness of a lake in the rosy evening, the sound of the river flowing in and the sound of the river flowing forth just audible, but itself still, and content to be still and mirror the sunset" (142). In other words, Connie's rosy brightness attests to the pleasure she is receiving from the natural world. Alternately, "Wynnie's face was bright with the brightness of the morning star, ever growing pale and faint over the amber ocean that brightens at the sun's approach; for life looked to Wynnie severe in its light, and somewhat sad because severe" (142). Wynnie's face indicates that she is recoiling from nature's beauty. Wynnie suffers from a morbid introspection that prevents her from fully appreciating the aesthetics—and the divine meaning—in the natural world. She has a tendency to feel guilty and blame herself unnecessarily, and though she is a vicar's daughter, she has considerable doubt about God and his purposes.

As the novel progresses, Wynnie remains relatively unmoved by the natural world; that is, until after becoming acquainted with the young, Pre-Raphaelite-like painter Charles Percivale, who is sketching in the vicinity of Kilkhaven. They have several chance encounters, and one day Walton and Wynnie are taking a walk when they come upon the painter. Walton invites him to return with them to the site where the family has been picnicking, when Wynnie suddenly experiences a burst of joy:

"Oh, do look here, papa!" she cried, from some little distance.

We turned and saw her gazing at something on the sand at her feet. Hastening back, we found it to be a little narrow line of foam-bubbles, which the water had left behind it on the sand, slowly breaking and passing out of sight. . . . Such colours! deep rose and grassy green and ultramarine blue; and above all, one dark, yet brilliant and intensely-burnished, metallic gold. All of them were of a solid-looking burnished colour, like opaque body-colour laid on behind translucent crystal. (250)

This feast of color is short-lived, as the bubbles continue to burst, and Wynnie seizes this moment to express her misgivings about the Creator: "I can't think why the unchanging God should have made all the most beautiful things wither and grow ugly, or burst and vanish, or die somehow and be no more" (251). Walton's answer, in short, is that humanity is easily enamored of the physical or visible "bodies" of things to the exclusion of understanding "the spirit that dwells in them" (253). He explains: "But we are always ready to love the body instead of the soul. Therefore, God makes the body die continually that we may learn to love the soul indeed" (252). In response to this explanation, Wynnie tells her father, "I think I understand you a little" (253). It seems that romantic attraction and even blossoming love can begin to open eyes that are closed to natural revelation and its Creator. Eventually in the novel, Wynnie expresses a strong desire to find God, despite her doubts, and it is suggested that both she and Percivale may be helpful to each other in their mutual struggle with doubt.

Meanwhile on a family day-trip, Percivale assists Walton in carrying Connie's litter or pallet over a narrow land bridge that leads to a Cornwall landmark, the ruins of Tintagel, legendary birthplace of King Arthur. Connie is blindfolded lest she become distressed when viewing the abyss below, but finally the two men lay down the pallet near the ruins of a Gothic chapel and leave to help Mrs. Walton. When the company regroups, the narrator reports that Connie "lay in such still expectation, that you would have thought she had just fallen asleep .... But she heard our steps and her face awoke." (361). When Connie's blindfold is removed, she weeps at the glorious view:

> Through the gothic-arched door in the battlemented wall, which stood on the very edge of the precipitous descent, so that nothing of the descent was seen and the door was as a framework to the picture, Connie saw a great gulf at her feet, full to the brim of a splendour of light and colour.
>
> At the foot of the rocks, hundreds of feet below, the blue waters breaking in white upon the dark gray sands; all full of the gladness of the sun overflowing in speechless delight, and reflected in fresh gladness from stone, and water, and flower, like new springs of light rippling forth from the earth itself to swell the universal tide of glory. (363)

Clearly, Connie has attained a brilliant vision of the Atlantic like the one that moved her father in his youth. Moreover, the sharp contrast from darkness to light that is orchestrated for Connie, figuratively links Connie's human experience to divine patterns in the natural world that the Rev. Walton talks about in more than one of his Sunday sermons.

Walton contends that the world is full of types of resurrection: "Every night that folds us up in darkness is a death; and those of you that have been out early and have seen the first of the dawn, will know it—the day rises out of the night like a being that has burst its tomb and escaped into life" (410). Explicitly or implicitly, the text of *The*

Seaboard Parish offers up numerous other patterns of resurrection, ranging from the new plant life of spring appearing following winter, to the transformation of a caterpillar into a butterfly, to a human being waking up from a long night's sleep. Walton stresses that spiritual changes also are resurrections:

> Every blessed moment in which a man bethinks himself that he has been forgetting his high calling, and sends up to the Father a prayer for aid; every time a man resolves that what he has been doing he will do no more; every time that the love of God, or the feeling of the truth, rouses a man to look first up at the light, then down at the skirts of his own garments—that moment a divine resurrection is wrought in the earth. Yea, every time that a man passes from resentment to forgiveness, from cruelty to compassion, from hardness to tenderness, from indifference to carefulness, from selfishness to honesty, from honesty to generosity, from generosity to love—a resurrection, the bursting of a fresh bud of life out of the grave of evil gladdens the eye of the Father watching his children. (421)

In conclusion, *The Seaboard Parish* follows the developing characters of Walton's eldest daughters as they awaken to or move closer to appreciating nature's aesthetic and spiritual bounty. The novel also invites the reader to awaken to the divine artistry and meaning in creation, finding symbolic parallels between humans and the rest of nature. One may conclude that *The Seaboard Parish* is more than a frame allowing MacDonald to insert ecstatic prose paintings and to present his aesthetic philosophy on beauty and art. The novel is unified through its resonant symbolism of resurrection, symbolism that permeates the novel and suggests the degree to which the Creator is reveals new life throughout the creation.

WORKS CITED

Amell, Barbara. "The Bude Holiday." *Wingfold* 91 (2015): 35-45. Print.

MacDonald, George. *The Seaboard Parish*. Whitethorn, Calif: Johannesen, 1995. Print.

Neuhouser, David L., and Mark R. Hall. "Nature as 'God's Imagination': The Environmental Vision of George MacDonald." *Exploring the Eternal Goodness: Selected Writings of David L. Neuhouser with Tributes from Fellow Pilgrims*. Ed. Joe Ricke and Lisa Ritchie. Hamden, Conn.: Winged Lion, 2016. 143-156. Print.

"But What is the Moral?":
A Dramatized Bibliographic Study of the Relationship of George MacDonald's "The Light Princess" to *Adela Cathcart*

by Joe Ricke, Abby Palmisano, Blair Hedges, and Cara Strickland

Thanks to Taylor University's Faculty Mentored Undergraduate Summer Scholarship program, the Center for the Study of C.S. Lewis and Friends Center received a research grant in the summer of 2016 to conduct descriptive bibliographic research on the holdings of Taylor's Brown Collection. Three researchers, Dr. Joe Ricke (Professor of English and Director of the Center) and two Taylor undergraduate English majors, Blair Hedges and Abby Palmisano, began their research in late May.

In the first week of research, as a sample version of what could be done with any book in the collection, the team created a bibliographic history of George MacDonald's fairy tale, "The Light Princess." Our research included exploring the relationship of this, one of MacDonald's most famous fairy tales, to one of his lesser-known novels, *Adela Cathcart*, within which "The Light Princess" was first published in 1864.

For the 10th biennial Frances White Ewbank Colloquium on C.S. Lewis and Friends, the researchers presented their findings in a literally dramatic way. The Lewis and Friends Colloquium has had a long tradition of staged amateur dramatic readings featuring colloquium participants. In fact, "The Light Princess" itself was previously performed in 2010. However, it had never before been performed, here or anywhere, within its original (published) context, the story of Adela Cathcart. To do so, a Reader's Theatre version of "The Light Princess," previously adapted for performance by former Taylor student and now professional writer Cara Strickland, was adapted yet again, this time adding the framework of Adela Cathcart. The script for that dramatic reading follows this brief introductory essay.

In 1862, MacDonald attempted to interest publishers in his manuscript of "The Light Princess," complete with its delightful illustrations by Pre-Raphaelite artist Arthur Hughes, as a children's story. However, according to a leading scholar on Victorian fantasy, U. C. Knoeplmacher, "publishers wondered . . . whether "The Light Princess" might appeal to child readers, let alone be fully understood by them" (ix). MacDonald's good friend, author and art critic John Ruskin, also worried that "the swimming scenes....would be to many children seriously harmful" (Knoeplmacher ix-x). In other words, the story was too improper, especially with its ecstatic mixed bathing scenes (and lots of kissing). So MacDonald was forced to think of a new way to publish his story. Despite the fears voiced by others that "The Light Princess" may be harmful, MacDonald still believed that the tale could provide wisdom and joy for young and old alike. How then to get this story to readers? Rolland Hein writes that "convinced of the value of story as myth, especially parable and fantasy, to minister to the needs of the human spirit, he conceived the plot that became the novel *Adela Cathcart*" (163). Thus, in order to publish his now-famous fairy tale, MacDonald inserted it, along with several other fanciful tales, into the framework of his novel.

Adela Cathcart tells the story of a 21 year-old woman with a sort of "death wish." When she is unable to find any meaning or reason for living from the world around her, her wise and concerned uncle, John Smith, devises a plan to heal her emotionally. His plan involves the recreation of interest in living and feeling for others by telling Adela a number of stories, the first one being "The Light Princess." As Knoeplmacher shrewdly observes, Smith hopes to do for Adela what MacDonald hopes to do for his readers. "Hovering between adolescence and a womanhood she resists, Adela is an ideal audience for MacDonald's purposes" (xiii).

Adela Cathcart was first published in 1864. In the meantime, MacDonald's friend Charles Kingsley had published his surreal children's fantasy, *Water Babies*, in 1863. And MacDonald's very close friend, Charles Dodgson (Lewis Carroll), with the encouragement of the MacDonald family (especially the children), had finished his landmark A*lice's Adventures in Wonderland* (published in 1865). These works opened the door for other fantastic children's tales to be published, until finally the Victorian children's fantasy craze became a highly lucrative market. Thus, in 1867, MacDonald was able to publish "The Light Princess" in the collection, *Dealings with the Fairies*. The *Adela Cathcart* framework, however, provided and still provides an interesting insight into the fairy tale, especially through the reactions of the various characters to whom the story is told. Over the years, readers have voiced various complaints regarding the plot and structure of *Adela Cathcart*. Rolland Hein noted that one "reviewer writing in the *Athenaem* suggested that MacDonald had "ransacked his desk for 'all old bits of writing he had in his possession' and related them by a story-telling club." Hein himself has described the plot as "meager" (164). To us, this criticism misunderstands the purpose of the novel, failing to pay close attention to the links between the "bits of writing" and the larger concerns of the story of the healing of Adela.

In crafting a dramatic version of the *Adela* framework, we chose to highlight the parallels MacDonald established between the characters of *Adela Cathcart* and "The Light Princess" by having the corresponding characters from each story be played by the same actors. For example, Adela is played by the same actress who plays the Light Princess, for, as one scholar suggests, "like Adela herself, the Light Princess resists the relations and responsibilities of adult life" (Knoeplmacher 13). In this way, as the Light Princess transitions from her childhood lack of gravity (in both senses of the word) into the positive, although painful, experiences of adulthood, Adela herself begins to come to life, learning to value her emotions. In performance, the same actor embodies both of these metamorphoses. The young Doctor Armstrong, who has fallen in love with Adela, comments, after hearing the story: "I think the moral is that no girl is worth anything until she has cried a little" (MacDonald, *Adela Cathcart* 104), further displaying the rather countercultural value which MacDonald places on emotional experience.

Just as Adela mirrors the Princess, Adela's father mirrors the King, and was played by the same actor in our version. Dr. Armstrong, who loves Adela, parallels the Prince, and Mrs. Cathcart (Adela's over-bearing and puritanical aunt) becomes the witch. The similarities between Mrs. Cathcart and the witch (the aunt of the princess in the fairy tale) are particularly pointed and satiric. During and after the story-telling, Adela shows a surprising ability to stand up to her domineering aunt. According to Knoepflmacher, "Like the Light Princess herself, [Adela] must continue to challenge the adult limitations embodied in characters such as her literal-minded aunt" (xiii). In fact, the novel seems to suggest that Mrs. Cathcart herself is emotionally stunted, especially evidenced in her general disapproval of fairy tales and "The Light Princess" specifically. Smith, who is the narrator of the entire novel as well as the narrator of "The Light Princess" (but other tales included in *Adela Cathcart* are told by other tellers, as in Chaucer's *Canterbury Tales*) cleverly lampoons Mrs. Cathcart. Throughout his story-telling, she is depicted as knitting. Towards the end of his telling of "The Light Princess," he specifies that the evil witch (the Princess's aunt) sits down and knits after draining the Princess's beloved lake. *Adela Cathcart* likewise satirizes the overly pious and prudish attitudes of Victorian society (and perhaps publishers and critics who found "The Light Princess" too dangerous) through Mrs. Cathcart, who takes offense at the mixed bathing scenes and demands that the story have a clear "mooooowral."

Mrs. Cathcart's demand for a moral (and one of her own liking) sets off one of the most interesting aspects of this framed version of "The Light Princess," in which character after character in *Adela Cathcart* responds with his or her sense of the meaning or moral of the fairy tale. The variety of views, or dialogical interpretive method, provides important insight into MacDonald's views on the imagination, fairy tales, and meaning. Just as Mrs. Cathcart insists that the story must have an obvious moral, publishers who turned down the *The Light Princess* were concerned that children would not "fully understand" the story. MacDonald, however, who ironically is often considered too preachy by some readers, believes that good stories will communicate truth and meaning to the minds and hearts of his readers. In fact, it might communicate different truths and meanings to different minds and hearts. And this is as it should be, according to MacDonald.

In his important 1893 essay, *The Fantastic Imagination*, MacDonald writes that a fairy-tale "cannot help but having some meaning; if it have proportion and vitality, and vitality is truth" (MacDonald, "The Fantastic Imagination" 316). Furthermore, MacDonald insists that "a genuine work of art must mean many things; the truer the art, the more things it will mean" (317). This belief is enacted in *Adela Cathcart* as its characters provide, from their different existential perspectives, different morals for "The Light Princess," several of which MacDonald obviously affirms. MacDonald places a large value on "emotional meaning" and "the feeling intellect," ways of knowing that one may experience through fairy tales (and the imagination more generally). A "meaning," that is, may be as much a feeling as a thought, in traditional terminology. In other words, the "affect" of a work may be the most important part of its effect (its moral energy may be more important than its moral idea). For MacDonald, fairy tales work, when they are allowed to work (contra Mrs. Cathcart) much the way "The Light Princess" works on Adela Cathcart. They speak to the depths of a person's being (mentally but also emotionally and morally), bringing not only "truth" ("meaning") but life ("vitality").

Adela Cathcart numbers among several notable Victorian works (such as *The Secret Garden*) that depict a renewal of life due to a change that takes place in the heart of an emotionally dead character. In fact, MacDonald dedicated *Adela Cathcart* to John Rutherford Russell

M.D. According to Rolland Hein, "John Rutherford Russell was a physician to the Homeopathic Hospital in London" (165). For a number of years, homeopathy, "the practice of medicine that embraces a holistic, natural approach to the treatment of the sick" (American Homeopathic Society) had been gaining popularity in British culture, especially amongst the upper class. "MacDonald was convinced of the soundness of homeopathy, Russell having been a help to him" (Hein 165). Dr. Armstrong of *Adela Cathcart* resembles Russell, especially as he proposes a homeopathic cure for Adela, stating "my conviction is that the best thing that can be done for her is to interest her in something if possible" (MacDonald, *Adela Cathcart* 48). By the end of the novel, the fantastic stories told to Adela (as well as several other factors, including the sermons of Dr. Armstrong's brother) help her return to "vitality." She is then able to become the comforter of her father, who has lost his fortune, and the lover and wife of Armstrong, to whom she becomes betrothed.

For MacDonald, good stories had the power to heal the soul because they communicate spiritual truths. "The laws of the spirit of a man must hold, alike in this world and any world he may invent" (MacDonald, *The Fantastic Imagination* 316). In *Adela Cathcart*, Smith notes of Adela's condition (as he has witnessed in others before), that "without good spiritual food to keep the spiritual sense healthy and true, they cannot see the things about them as they really are" (MacDonald, *Adela Cathcart* 53). But, MacDonald seems to suggest, they might see things truly in fairy-tales. For fairy tales present spiritual truths in a world that is enchanted and strange, and, for those reasons, exciting and "vital." Adela, who has become stuck in a dull vision of supposedly mundane reality, responds to "her" story, refracted by fairy magic and fancy dress. Once these truths are experienced as part of her own reality (as she recognizes, in her "real world," the witch aunt and the healer prince, etc.), the world regains its wonder, her heart begins to beat. Life becomes more than just existence.

WORKS CITED

Chase, Sandra M. "What is Homeopathic Medicine?" *The American Institute of Homeopathy*. Web. 29 June 2016.

Hein, Rolland. *George MacDonald Victorian Mythmaker*. Nashville, Tennessee: StarSong Publishing Group, 1993. Print.

Knoepflmacher, U.C., ed. *George MacDonald: The Complete Fairy Tales*. By George MacDonald. New York: Penguin Classics, 1999. Print

MacDonald, George. *Adela Cathcart*. London, 1864. Reprinted Whitehorn, California: Johannesen, 2000. Print

MacDonald, George. "The Fantastic Imagination." *Dish of Orts*. London, 1893. Reprinted Whitehorn, California: Johannessen, 1996. 313-322. Print.

Morrell, Peter. *A History of Homeopathy in Britain*. Web. 29 June 2016.

The Performance Text of "The Light Princess" with *Adela Cathcart* frame

For this performance and text, the previous adaptation of "The Light Princess" by Cara Strickland was revised and adapted for performance by Dr. Joe Ricke based on research conducted by Abby Palmisano and Blair Hedges. It was performed in the Butz-Carruth Recital Hall of Taylor University on the evening of Friday, June 3rd. The Adela Cathcart "frame" material, with some slight alterations, is in italics. Stage directions and some dialogue are in bold. The characters and actors were as follows:

>John Smith/ Narrator....................Joe Ricke
>Adela/ The Light Princess.............Abby Palsimino
>Doctor Armstrong/ The Prince........Blair Hedges
>Colonel Cathcart/ King.................Donald Williams
>Queen...Laura Schmidt
>Mrs Cathcart(Adela's Aunt)/ Witch...Sørina Higgins
>Minister...................................... Shawn Denny
>Nurse.. Alexis Colón

Narrator: Once upon a time, there was a girl whose life was gradually withdrawing itself—ebbing back as it were to its source. Whether this had a physical or psychological cause, it was impossible to tell. She was 21 years old. Her name was Adela Cathcart. Her father, the colonel, asked the advice of the local doctor.

Colonel: Well, Mr. Armstrong, what do you think of my daughter?

Armstrong: I do not think she is in a very bad way. Has she had any disappointment that you know of?

Col: None whatever.

Arm: Ah—I have seen such a case before. There are a good many of them amongst girls at her age. For the present, my conviction is that the best thing that can be done for her is to interest her in something if possible. Does she take pleasure in anything?

Col: She used to be very fond of music.

Smith: May I be allowed to speak?

Col&Arm: Most certainly.

Smith: With your permission, I will tell you a plan I have been thinking of. Perhaps the interest she cannot find for herself, we might be able to provide for her, by telling stories. If we once got her interested in anything, it seems to me that the tide of life might begin to flow again. She would eat better, and sleep better, and think less about herself. It would be beginning from the inside, would it not?

Arm: A capital plan. And I know my brother, the minister, would want to help. She is in his charge as well as mine, for she in one of his flock. Besides, he can tell a tale better than anyone I know.

Col: There can be no harm in trying it, gentlemen. And thank you for your interest in my poor child.

Arm: You must not let her know that the thing is got up for her.

Col: Certainly not. Come and dine with us, then. This Christmas-tide gives good opportunity for such a scheme.

Smith: Bravo, Colonel. And I am quite willing to open the entertainment with a funny kind of fairy tale which has been growing in my brain for some time.

Col: Very well. And now we will go to church.

......

Smith/Narrator: Finally, the day came, the dinner came, the after-dinner came. Unfortunately, Mrs. Cathcart, Adela's aunt came as well.

Mrs. Cathcart: I trust it is a story suitable to the season, Mr. Smith.

Smith: Yes, very, for it is a child's story, a fairy tale, though I confess I think it fitter for grown children than for young children. If Adela has no objection, I will read it.

Adela: I shall be delighted, uncle.

Mrs. C: So, you approve of fairy-tales for children, Mr. Smith?

Smith: Not for children alone, madam; for everybody who can relish them.

Mrs. C: But surely not at a sacred season like this?

Smith: If I thought that God did not approve of fairy-tales, I would never read nor write one whatever the season. Would you madam?

Mrs. C: I never do.

Smith: I feared not. . . . But I must begin. [clears throat] Title: The Light Princess. Second Title: A Fairy Tale without Fairies.

Mrs. C: I must be very stupid, Mr. Smith, but I can't make head or tail of it.

Smith: Give me leave madam, this is my office. . . . May I?

Narrator: Once upon a time, so long ago that I have quite forgotten the date, there lived a king and queen who had no children.

And the king said to himself:

King: All the queens of my acquaintance have children, some three, some seven, and some as many as twelve; and my queen has not one. I feel ill-used. **[crosses arms over chest]**

Narrator: So he made up his mind to be cross with his wife about it. But she bore it all like a good patient queen as she was. Then the king grew very cross indeed. But the queen pretended to take it all as a joke.

King: Why don't you have any daughters, at least? I don't say sons; that might be too much to expect.

Queen: I am sure, dear king, I am very sorry.

King: So you ought to be.

Queen: You must have patience with a lady, you know, dear king.

Narrator: The king tried, but he succeeded very badly. It was more than he deserved, therefore, when, at last, the queen gave him a daughter—as lovely a little princess as ever cried.

When a princess is born, there must be a christening, and of course, somebody was forgotten. This wouldn't have been so bad, except that the King forgot to invite his own sister.

She was a sour, spiteful creature. The wrinkles of contempt crossed the wrinkles of peevishness, and made her face as full of wrinkles as a pat of butter.

What made it highly imprudent in the king to forget her was that she was awfully clever. In fact, she was a witch.

Therefore, she made up her mind to go without an invitation, and make the whole family miserable. As I said, she was a witch.

So she went to the palace and was kindly received by the happy monarch, who forgot that he had forgotten her.

When the christening water was applied to the princess' face, the witch turned round in her place three times, and muttered the following words, loud enough for those beside her to hear:—

Witch: Light of spirit, by my charms,

Light of body, every part,

Never weary human arms—

Only crush thy parents' heart!

Narrator: They all thought she had lost her wits, and was repeating some foolish nursery rhyme; but a shudder went through them all notwithstanding **[all shudder]**.

The baby, on the contrary, began to laugh and crow; while the nurse gave a start because she could not feel the baby in her arms.

Minister: Bravo, Mr. Smith. An excellent beginning because I have no idea what you are driving at!

Mrs. C: One thing I must object to. That is, introducing church ceremonies into a fairy tale.

Minister: Why, Mrs. Cathcart. Do you suppose the church to be such a cross old lady that she will not allow her children to take a few liberties with their mother? She's able to stand that surely?

Smith: May I continue?

All: Of course . . . by all means . . . carry on my good man . . . please do Mr. Smith, etc.

Narrator: Well, the atrocious aunt had deprived the child of all her gravity. So, the moment the nurse began to bounce the baby, she flew towards the ceiling.

There she remained, kicking and laughing amazingly. The nurse got a ladder, and had to stand upon the very top, before she could catch the baby's dress. Of course, this all caused a terrible commotion in the palace.

The king stood staring up in speechless amazement. At last, turning to the queen, who was just as horror-struck as himself, he said, gasping, staring, and stammering,—

King: She can't be ours, queen!

Narrator: Now the queen was much cleverer than the king, and had begun already to suspect what had happened.

Queen: I am sure she is ours. But we ought to have taken better care of her at the christening. People who were never invited ought not to have been present.

King: Oh, ho! **[tapping his forehead with his forefinger]** Now, I have it. I've found her out. Don't you see, queen? My sister has bewitched her.

Queen: [yawn] That's just what I say.

King: I beg your pardon, my love; I did not hear you.

Narrator: One day, after breakfast, the king went into his counting-house, and counted out his money. The operation, though, gave him no pleasure.

King: To think that every one of these gold sovereigns weighs a quarter of an ounce, and my real, live, flesh-and-blood princess weighs nothing at all!

Narrator: The queen was in the parlour, eating bread and honey. But at the second mouthful she burst out crying, and could not swallow it.

The king heard her sobbing. Glad of anybody to quarrel with, he rushed into the parlour.

King: What is all this about? What are you crying for, queen?

Queen: I can't eat it. **[with mouth full]**

King: No wonder! You've just eaten your breakfast —two turkey eggs, and three anchovies.

Queen: Oh, that's not it! It's my child, my child! **[with mouth still full]**

King: Well, what's the matter with your child? After all, it is a good thing to be light-hearted, I am sure, whether she be ours or not.

Queen: [swallows] It is a bad thing to be light-headed,

King: 'Tis a good thing to be light-handed,

Queen: 'Tis a bad thing to be light-fingered,

King: 'Tis a good thing to be light-footed,

Queen: 'Tis a bad thing—

Proceedings from the Francis White Ewbank Colloquium

King: In fact, in fact, it is a good thing altogether to be light-bodied.

Queen: But it is a bad thing altogether to be light-minded.

Narrator: This last answer quite discomfited his Majesty, who turned on his heel to go. But he was not quite gone when the voice of his queen overtook him.

Queen: And it's a bad thing to be light-haired!

Minister: Oh really, Mr. Smith, you bury us with puns, and not very good ones.

Smith/Narrator: [Stopping him] *Shhh!* The queen's hair was black as night, and his daughter's was, golden. But it was not this reflection on his hair that upset him; it was the double use of the word *light*. For the king hated all witticisms, and punning especially.

King: My dear queen, duplicity of any sort is exceedingly objectionable between married people; and the most objectionable form duplicity can assume is that of punning.

Queen: Oh, I am the most unfortunate woman in the world!

Narrator: She looked so rueful, that the king took her in his arms; and they sat down to consult.

King: Can you bear this?

Queen: No, I can't.

King: Well, what's to be done?

Queen: Perhaps, we can wait till she is older. She may then be able to suggest something herself. She will know at least how she feels, and explain things to us.

King: But what if she should marry?

Queen: Well, what of that?

King: Just think! If she were to have children! In the course of a hundred years the air might be as full of floating children.

Queen: Well, that is no business of ours!

Narrator: Meantime, notwithstanding awkward occurrences, and griefs that she brought upon her parents, the little princess laughed and grew. She reached the age of seventeen, without having fallen into any worse scrape than a chimney.

Nor, thoughtless as she was, had she committed anything worse than laughter at everybody and everything.

For, you see, she never could be brought to see the serious side of anything. When her mother cried, she said,—

Princess: What queer faces mamma makes! And she squeezes water out of her cheeks? Funny mamma!

Narrator: And when her papa stormed at her, she laughed, and danced round and round him, clapping her hands.

Princess: Do it again, papa. Do it again! It's SUCH fun! Dear, funny papa!

Narrator: After a long avoidance of the painful subject, the king and queen resolved to hold a council of three upon it; and so they sent for the princess.

King: My dear child, you must be aware by this time that you are not exactly like other people.

Princess: Oh, you dear funny papa! I have got a nose, and two eyes, and all the rest. So have you. So has mamma.

Queen: Now be serious, my dear, for once.

Princess: No, thank you, mamma; I had rather not.

King: Would you not like to be able to walk like other people?

Princess: No indeed, I should think not. You only crawl.

King: How do you feel, my child? **[after a pause]**

Princess: Quite well, thank you.

King: I mean, what do you feel like?

Princess: I feel like a princess with such a funny papa, and such a dear pet of a queen-mamma!

Queen: Now really!

Princess: [interrupting] Oh Yes, I remember. I have a curious feeling sometimes, as if I were the only person that had any sense in the whole world. **[violent laughter]**

King: But is there nothing you wish for?

Princess: Oh, dear papa!—yes.

King: What is it, my darling?

Princess: Will you promise to let me have it?

Narrator: The king was on the point of saying *Yes*, but the wiser queen checked him with a single motion of her head.

King: Tell me what it is first.

Princess: No no. Promise first.

King: I dare not. What is it?

Princess: Mind, I hold you to your promise.—It is to be tied to the end of a string—a very long string indeed, and be flown like a kite! **[laughter]**

Narrator: A fit of laughing checked her; and she would have been off again over the floor, had not the king started up and caught her just in time. Seeing nothing but talk could be got out of her, he rang the bell, and sent her away.

King: Now, queen, what IS to be done?

Queen: There is but one thing left, Let us consult the college of Metaphysicians.

King: Bravo! We will.

All: No! What? No metaphysics. I thought this was a fairy tale. Really Mr. Smith.

Mr. Smith: Well, if you say so. Let me try this. [clears throat] Perhaps the best thing for the princess would have been . . . to fall in love.

All: Yes. That's more like it. A little more of that. Now you're back on track!

Narrator: May I? As I was saying, perhaps the best thing for the princess would have been to fall in love. But how a princess who had no gravity could fall into anything is a difficulty—perhaps THE difficulty.

Now, the palace was built on the shores of the loveliest lake in the world and the moment the princess got into it, she recovered the natural right of which she had been so wickedly deprived—namely, gravity. **[She makes the sounds one would make if one would fly]**

The passion of her life was to get into the water, and she was always the better behaved and the more beautiful the more she had of it.

Summer and winter it was quite the same; only she could not stay so long in the water when they had to break the ice to let her in.

It must have been about this time that the son of a king set out to look for the daughter of a queen. He travelled far and wide, but as sure as he found a princess, he found some fault in her. Of course he could not marry a mere woman, however beautiful; and there was no princess to be found worthy of him.

Whether the prince was so near perfection that he had a right to demand perfection itself, I cannot pretend to say. All I know is, that he was a fine, handsome, brave, generous, well-bred, and well-behaved youth, as all princes are.

In his wanderings he had come across some reports about our princess; but as everybody said she was bewitched, he never dreamed that she could bewitch him. Besides, what could a prince do with a princess who had lost her gravity? Who could tell what she might not lose next?

She might lose her visibility, or her tangibility; so that he should never be able to tell whether she was dead or alive. Therefore, he made no further inquiries about her.

After traveling for a long while, he found a footpath which led him to the side of a lake. Along this path the prince pursued his way through the gathering darkness. Suddenly he paused, and listened.

Strange sounds came across the water. It was, in fact, the princess laughing. Now there was something odd in her laugh, for a real hearty laugh requires gravity. Perhaps this was how the prince mistook the laughter for screaming.

Looking over the lake, he saw something white in the water; and, in an instant, he had plunged in. He soon reached the white object, and found that it was a woman. There was not light enough to show that she was a princess, but quite enough to show that she was a lady, for it does not want much light to see that.

Now I cannot tell how it came about,—whether she pretended to be drowning, or whether he frightened her, but certainly he brought her to shore in a fashion ignominious to a swimmer, and more nearly drowned than she had ever expected to be.

At the place to which he bore her, the bank was only a foot or two above the water; so he gave her a strong lift out of the water, to lay her on the bank. But, her gravitation ceasing the moment she left the water, away she went up into the air, scolding and screaming.

Princess: You naughty, naughty, NAUGHTY, NAUGHTY man!

Narrator: No one had ever succeeded in putting her into a passion before.

Princess: I'll tell papa.

Prince: Oh no, you won't!

Princess: Yes, I will. What business had you to pull me down out of the water, and throw me to the bottom of the air? I never did you any harm.

Prince: Pardon me. I did not mean to hurt you.

Princess: I don't believe you have any brains; and that is a worse loss than your wretched gravity.

Narrator: The prince now saw that he had come upon the bewitched princess, and had already offended her. But before he could think what to say next, she burst out angrily, giving a stamp with her foot that would have sent her aloft again but for the hold she had of his arm,—

Princess: Put me up directly.

Prince: Put you up where, you beauty?

Narrator: He had fallen in love with her almost, already; for her anger made her more charming than any one else had ever beheld her; and, as far as he could see, which certainly was not far, she had not a single fault about her, except, of course, that she had not any gravity.

Prince: Put you up where, you beauty?

Princess: In the water, you stupid!

Prince: Come, then.

Narrator: The condition of her dress, increasing her usual difficulty in walking, compelled her to cling to him; and he could hardly persuade himself that he was not in a delightful dream, notwithstanding the torrent of musical abuse with which she overwhelmed him. **[abuses him]**

Finally, they came upon the lake at quite another part, where the bank was twenty-five feet high at least; and when they had reached the edge, he turned towards the princess, and said,—

Prince: How am I to put you in?

Princess: That is your business. You took me out—put me in again.

Prince: Very well.

Narrator: And, catching her up in his arms, he sprang with her from the rock. The princess had just time to give one delighted shriek of laughter before the water closed over them.

When they came to the surface, she found that, for a moment or two, she could not even laugh, for she had gone down with such a rush, that it was with difficulty she recovered her breath.

Prince: How do you like falling in?

Princess: Is that what you call FALLING IN? **[panting]**

Prince: Yes. I should think it a very tolerable specimen.

Princess: It seemed to me like going up.

Prince: My feeling is certainly one of elevation too.

Narrator: The princess did not appear to understand him, for she repeated his question:—

Princess: How do YOU like falling in?

Prince: Beyond everything, for I have fallen in with the only perfect creature I ever saw.

Princess: No more of that: I am tired of it.

Minister: Perhaps she shared her father's aversion to punning.

All: Shhhhhh!

Prince: Don't you like falling in then?

Princess: It is the most delightful fun I ever had in my life. I never fell before. I wish I could learn. To think I am the only person in my father's kingdom that can't fall!

Prince: I shall be most happy to fall in with you any time you like.

Princess: Thank you. I don't know. Perhaps it would not be proper. But I don't care. At all events, as we have fallen in, let us have a swim together.

Prince: With all my heart.

Narrator: And away they went, swimming, and diving, and floating, until at last they heard cries along the shore, and saw lights glancing in all directions. It was now quite late, and there was no moon.

Princess: I must go home. I am very sorry, for this is delightful.

Prince: So am I. And I have no other home.

Princess: I wish I hadn't one either!—You see where that green light is burning? That is the window of my room. Now if you would just swim there with me very quietly, and when we are all but under the balcony, give me such a push—up you call it-as you did a little while ago, I should be able to catch hold of the balcony, and get in at the window.

Prince: With more obedience than pleasure. [after delivering her] Will you be in the lake to-morrow night?

Princess: To be sure I will. I don't think so. Perhaps.

Narrator: The prince was intelligent enough not to press her further; and merely whispered, as he gave her the parting lift.

Prince: Don't tell.

Narrator: The only answer the princess returned was a roguish look that seemed to say, "Never fear. It is too good fun to spoil that way."

So perfectly like other people had she been in the water, that even yet the prince could scarcely believe his eyes when he saw her ascend slowly, grasp the balcony, and disappear through the window. All night long he dreamed that he was swimming with the princess.

Mrs. Cathcart: All this is very improper—to my mind!

Adela: But you must remember that this is Fairyland, Auntie. We must not judge the people in fairy tales by precisely the same conventionalities we have. They must be good in their own way.

Mrs. C: Conventionalities! Humbug!

Narrator: Excuse me? When the prince woke up the next morning, he saw the princess already floating about in the lake, attended by the king and queen. It was a very bright day, and soon the prince, burned up with the heat, began to long for the cold water and the cool princess.

But he had to endure till twilight. Then the prince began to sing.

Prince:

Lady fair,
Swan-white,
Lift thine eyes,
Banish night
By the might
Of thine eyes.

Snowy arms,
Oars of snow,
Oar her hither,
Plashing low.
Soft and slow,
Oar her hither.

Cling about her,
Waters blue;
Part not from her,
But renew
Cold and true
Kisses round her.

Lap me round,
Waters sad,
That have left her.
Make me glad,
For ye had
Kissed her ere ye left her.

Narrator: Before he had finished his song, the princess was just under the place where he sat, and looking up to find him.

Prince: Would you like a fall, princess?

Princess: Ah! there you are! Yes, if you please, prince.

Prince: How do you know I am a prince, princess?

Princess: Because you are a very nice young man, prince.

Prince: Come up then, princess.

Princess: Fetch me, prince.

Narrator: The prince reached for her hand, gave a pull and she was beside him. This rock was much higher than the other, and the splash and the dive were tremendous. The princess was in ecstasies of delight.

Mrs. C: *MISTER SMITH!!*

Night after night they met, and swam about in the dark clear lake. The prince often fancied that he was swimming in the sky instead of the lake. But when he talked about being in heaven, the princess laughed at him dreadfully. **[scoffing laugh]**

The prince soon found out that while in the water the princess was very like other people. And besides this, she was not so forward or pert at sea as on shore. Neither did she laugh so much; and when she did laugh, it was more gently. She seemed altogether more modest and maidenly in the water than out of it.

But when the prince, who had really fallen in love when he fell in the lake, began to talk to her about love, she always turned her head towards him and laughed. **[laughter]** After a while she began to look puzzled, as if she were trying to understand what he meant, but could not—As soon as ever she left the lake, she was so altered, that the prince said to himself,

Prince: If I marry her, I see no help for it: we must turn merman and mermaid, and go out to sea at once.

Narrator: The princess's pleasure in the lake had grown to a passion, and she could scarcely bear to be out of it for an hour. Imagine then her consternation, when, diving with the prince one night, a sudden suspicion seized her that the lake was not so deep as it used to be.

Next day she made many observations, which, alas! strengthened her fears. She saw that the banks were too dry; and that the grass on the shore, and the trailing plants on the rocks, were withering away.

The poor princess nearly went out of the little mind she had. It was awful to her to see the lake, which she loved more than any living thing, lie dying before her eyes. It ebbed away, slowly vanishing.

She could not bear to swim in the lake any more, and began to ebb away herself. People said she would not live an hour after the lake was gone. *But she never cried.*

A Proclamation was made to all the kingdom, that whosoever should discover the cause of the lake's decrease, would be rewarded after a princely fashion.

King: Whoever shall discover the cause of the lake's decrease will be rewarded after a princely fashion.

Narrator: The fact was that the old witch was at the root of the mischief. When she heard that her niece found more pleasure in the water than out of it, she went into a rage. [**rage noises**]

Witch: But, I will soon set all right. The king and the people shall die of thirst; their brains shall boil and frizzle in their skulls before I will lose my revenge. [**laughs like a witch**]

Narrator: She went to an old chest in the room, and took out what looked like a piece of dried seaweed. She threw it into a tub of water with some powder, and stirred it with her bare arm, muttering over it words of hideous sound, and yet more hideous import.

Soon, out from the tub came a huge gray snake.

It grew out of the tub, waving itself backwards and forwards with a slow horizontal motion, till it reached the witch. She drew it all out of the tub, and wound it round her body.

Then she went down to her cellar; and as she unlocked the door she said to herself,—

Witch: This is worth living for!

Narrator: Locking the door behind her, she descended and entered a vast cave, the roof of which was supported by huge natural pillars of rock. Now this roof was the under side of the bottom of the lake.

She untwined the snake from her body, and held it by the tail high above her. The hideous creature stretched up its head towards the roof of the cavern, which it was just able to reach. It began to move its head backwards and forwards, as if looking for something.

At last the snake made a sudden dart, and clung to the roof with its mouth.

Witch: That's right, my beauty! Drain it dry.

Narrator: She sat down on a great stone, and she began to knit and mutter awful words. The snake hung like a huge leech, sucking at the stone.

After seven days and nights, the serpent suddenly dropped from the roof and shriveled up again like a piece of dried seaweed.

The witch looked up at the roof. One drop of water was trembling on the spot where the snake had been sucking. As soon as she saw that, she turned and fled, followed by her cat. Shutting the door in a terrible hurry, she locked it, and muttered some frightful words. Then she sat down on the floor listening with malicious delight to the rushing of the water.

Meanwhile, the prince was pining for the princess, as she was pining for her lake. So he disguised himself and went to the palace where he was made shoeblack to the princess. It was rather cunning in the prince to request such an easy post, for the princess, rarely touching the ground, could hardly soil her shoes.

The princess kept to her room, with the curtains drawn to shut out the dying lake. But she could not shut it out of her mind for a moment. She felt as if the lake were her soul, drying up within her, first to mud, then to madness and death.

As for the prince, she had forgotten him. However much she had enjoyed his company in the water, she did not care for him without it.

At length the lake was all but gone.

It happened one day, as it should in such a story, that a party of youngsters found a plate of gold in the lake bed, covered with writing. They carried it to the king. On one side of it stood these words:—

King: "Death alone from death can save.
    Love is death, and so is brave—
    Love can fill the deepest grave.
    Love loves on beneath the wave."

Narrator: Now this was enigmatical enough to the king, but when he turned it over, this is what they saw on the reverse side:—

Queen: If the lake should disappear, you must find the hole through which the water ran. But it is useless to try to stop it by any ordinary means. Only the body of a living man can stanch the flow. AND, the man must give himself of his own will. Besides, if the nation cannot not provide one hero, it is time it should perish anyway.

Narrator: This was a very disheartening revelation to the king—not that he was unwilling to sacrifice a subject, but he was hopeless of finding a man willing to sacrifice himself. Still, the king caused the contents of the wonderful plate of gold to be published throughout the country.

No one came forward.

When the prince heard the announcement, he sat down and thought,—

Prince: She will die if I don't do it, and life would be nothing to me without her; so I shall lose nothing by doing it. And life will be as pleasant to her as ever, for she will soon forget me. And there will be so much more beauty and happiness in the world!—To be sure, I shall not see it. **[Here the poor prince gave a sigh.]** How lovely the lake will be in the moonlight, with that glorious creature sporting in it like a wild goddess!—It is rather hard to be drowned by inches, though. Let me see—that will be seventy inches of me to drown. **[Here he tried to laugh, but could not.]** The longer the better, however, for can I not bargain that the princess shall be beside me all the time? So I shall see her once more, kiss her perhaps,—who knows?—and die looking in her eyes. That will be no death. All right! I am ready.

Narrator: He hurried to the king's apartment, resolving to carry off the whole affair with nonchalance. He knocked at the door of the king's counting-house, where it was all but a capital crime to disturb him.

When the king heard the knock, he opened the door in a rage. Seeing only the shoeblack, he drew his sword. This, I am sorry to say, was his usual mode of asserting his regality.

Prince: Please your Majesty, I'm your butler.

King: My butler! you lying rascal! What do you mean?

Prince: I mean, I will cork your big bottle.

King: Is the fellow mad?

Prince: I will put a stopper—a plug—what you call it, in your leaky lake, grand monarch.

Narrator: Despite his rage, the king thought it would be great waste to kill the only useful man in the present emergency, especially since, in the end, the insolent fellow would be dead either way.

King: Oh! In that case, thank you. Have a glass of wine.

Prince: No, thank you.

King: Then we will go and look for the hole at once.

Prince: Stop, please your Majesty; I have a condition to make.

King: What! A condition! With me! How dare you?

Prince: As you please. Good morning your majesty.

King: You wretch! I will have you put in a sack, and stuck in the hole.

Prince: Very well, your Majesty. But what good will that do you? Please remember that the oracle says the victim must offer himself.

King: Well, you have offered yourself.

Prince: Yes, but upon one condition.

King: Condition again! Well, what is your condition?

Prince: That the princess shall go with me, feed me with her own hands, and comfort me. As soon as the water is up to my eyes, she may go and be happy, and forget her poor shoeblack.

Narrator: Here the prince's voice faltered, and he very nearly grew . . . sentimental.

King: Why didn't you tell me before what your condition was? Such a fuss about nothing!

Prince: Do you grant it?

King: Of course, my boy.

Prince: Very well. I am ready.

Narrator: The prince went to dress for the occasion, for he was resolved to die like a prince.

When the princess heard that a man had offered to die for her, she was so transported that she jumped off the bed, feeble as she was, and danced about the room for joy. She did not care who the man was.

They bore her across to the stone where they had already placed a little boat for her. The water was not deep enough to float it, but they hoped it would be, before long. In a few minutes the prince appeared. The princess recognized him at once, but did not acknowledge him.

Prince: Here I am.

Narrator: He put both his legs into it, sitting on the stone, and, stooping forward, covered the corner that remained open with his two hands. In this uncomfortable position he resolved to abide his fate. Presently a little wave flowed over the stone, and wetted one of the prince's knees. But he did not mind it much.

Princess: This is very kind of you, prince. **[eyes shut]**

Prince: I am sorry I can't return the compliment. **[to himself]** But you are worth dying for, after all.

Narrator: Again a wavelet, and another, and another flowed over the stone, and wetted both the prince's knees; but he did not speak or move. Several hours passed in this way, the princess apparently asleep. But the prince was much disappointed, for he had none of the consolation he had hoped for.

At last he could bear it no longer.

Prince: Princess!

Narrator: But at that very moment up started the princess, crying,—

Princess: I'm afloat! I'm afloat!

Prince: Princess!

Princess: Well?

Prince: Your papa promised that you should comfort me, and you haven't even looked at me once.

Princess: Did he? Then I suppose I must. But I am so sleepy!

Prince: Sleep then, darling, and don't mind me.

Princess: Really, you are very good. I think I will.

Prince: Please, just give me a glass of wine and a biscuit first.

Princess: With all my heart.

Narrator: She got the wine and the biscuit, and leaning over the side of the boat, she finally looked at him.

Princess: Why, prince, you don't look well! Are you sure you don't mind?

Prince: Not a bit. Only I shall die before I can save you unless I have something to eat.

Princess: There, then. **[holds out the wine to him]**

Prince: Ah! you must feed me. I dare not move my hands. The water would run away directly.

Princess: Good gracious!

Narrator: She began at once to feed him with bits of biscuit and sips of wine. As she did, he contrived to kiss the tips of her fingers now and then. She did not seem to mind it. But the prince felt better.

Prince: Now for your own sake, princess. I cannot let you go to sleep. You must sit and look at me, else I shall not be able to keep up.

Princess: Well, I will do anything I can to oblige you. **[with condescension, looks at him]**

Narrator: The sun went down, and the moon rose, and, gush after gush, the waters were rising up the prince's body. They were up to his waist now.

Princess: Why can't we go and have a swim? There seems to be water enough. Just about here.

Prince: I shall never swim more.

Princess: Oh, I forgot.

Narrator: So the water grew and grew, and rose up and up on the prince. The princess sat and looked at him, feeding him now and then.

The night wore on. The waters rose. The moon rose and shone on the face of the dying prince. The water was now up to his neck.

Prince: Will you kiss me, princess?

Narrator: His nonchalance was all gone now.

Princess: Yes, I will. **[kisses him with a long, sweet, cold kiss]**

Prince: Now **[with a sigh of content]**, I die happy.

Narrator: He did not speak again. The princess gave him wine for the last time. Then she sat down again, and looked at him.

The water rose. It touched his chin. It touched his lower lip.

It touched between his lips. He shut them hard to keep it out. The princess began to feel strange. It touched his upper lip. He breathed through his nostrils. The princess looked wild. It covered his nostrils. Her eyes looked scared, and shone strange in the moonlight.

His head fell back; the water closed over it, and the bubbles of his last breath bubbled up through the water. The princess gave a shriek **[shriek]**, and sprang into the lake.

She laid hold of his legs, and pulled, but she could not move them. She struggled to breathe, and then suddenly realized that HE really could not breathe. She was frantic. She got hold of him, and held his head above the water, which was possible now his hands were no longer covering the hole. But it was of no use. He was past breathing.

Love and water brought back all her strength. She got under the water, and pulled and pulled with her whole might, till at last she got one leg out. The other easily followed. How she got him into the boat she never could tell (and I certainly never shall).

Presently, she seized the oars and rowed till she got to the landing. By this time people were on the shore, for they had heard her shriek. She made them carry the prince to her room, lay him in her bed, and send for the doctors.

Somehow, the doctors never came. So the princess and her old nurse were left with the prince.

They tried everything for a long time without success.

At last, when they had all but given it up, just as the sun rose, the prince opened his eyes.

The princess burst into a passion of tears, and fell on the floor. There she lay for an hour, and her tears never ceased. All the pent-up crying of her life poured out from her inside. And a rain came on, such as had never been seen in that country.

But something had happened, for when the princess tried to rise, she found, to her astonishment, that she could not. At length, after many efforts, she succeeded in getting upon her feet. But she tumbled down again directly.

Princess: Ouch!

Hearing her fall, her old nurse uttered a yell of delight, and ran to her, screaming,—

Nurse: My darling child! she's found her gravity!

Princess: Oh, that's it! is it? [**rubbing her shoulder and her knee alternately**] "I consider it very unpleasant. I feel as if I should be crushed to pieces.

Prince: Hurrah! If you've come round, princess, so have I. How's the lake?

Nurse: Brimful.

Prince: Then we're all happy.

Princess: That we are indeed! [**sobbing**]

Narrator: And there was rejoicing all over the country that rainy rainy day.

Of course the prince and princess were betrothed at once. But the princess had to learn to walk, before they could be married with any propriety. And this was not so easy for she could walk no more than a baby. She was always falling down and hurting herself. **[ouch!]**

Princess: Is this the gravity you used to make so much of? **[Prince raises her from the floor]** For my part, I was a great deal more comfortable without it.

Prince: No, no, that's not it. This is it.

Narrator: And with that, the prince took her up in his arms, and carried her about like a baby, kissing her all the time.

Prince: *This* is gravity.

Princess: That's better. I don't mind that so much.

Narrator: I fear she complained of her gravity more than once after this. It was a long time before she was fully reconciled to walking.

The only revenge the princess took upon her aunt was to tread very hard on her gouty toe the next time she saw her. But she was even sorry when she heard that the water had undermined the witch's house, and that it had fallen in the night, burying her in its ruins. There she lies to this day.

All (audience included): Hip Hip! Hooray!! (3)

Narrator: So the prince and princess lived and were happy; and had crowns of gold, and clothes of cloth, and shoes of leather, and children of boys and girls, not one of whom was ever known, on the most critical occasion, to lose the smallest atom of his or her due proportion of gravity.

All: Bravo! Capital! Very good, indeed. Three cheers for Mr. Smith!

Minister: I don't think the princess could have rowed, though, Smith. Without gravity I mean.

Adela: But she DID. And I won't have uncle's story found fault with. It is a very funny and very pretty story.

Mrs. C: But what is the Mooooowral of it?

Adela: That you need not be afraid of ill-natured aunts, though they are witches. [pregnant pause]

Smith: No, my dear, that's not it. It is that you need not worry about forgetting your poor relations. No harm will come of it in the end.

Doctor [thoughtfully]: I think the moral is [pause] that no girl is worth anything until she has cried a little.

Smith: Adela gave him a quick glance, and then cast her eyes down. Whether he had looked at her I don't know. I should think not. It isn't proper, after all. Just before the doctor left, though, he went up to Adela and said.

Doctor: I am sorry to hear that you have not been quite well of late, Miss Cathcart. I am afraid you have may have caught a cold. May I feel your pulse?

Smith: She gave him her wrist directly.

Adela: I feel much better tonight, thank you.

Smith: He stood listening to the pulse for a long while, without consulting his watch, as if he was in immediate communication with the troubled heart itself. Now that his eyes were closed, Adela's eyes glanced up to his face, and rested there for half a minute. He gave her back her hand quite gently.

Doctor: I will send you something as soon as I get home. I presume you will go to bed soon?

Adela: If you think best, doctor.

Smith: And so they parted for the evening. But before we part, dear reader, perhaps you may have one question.

Reader/Armstrong: Pray, Mr. Smith, do you think it was your wonderful prescription of story-telling that wrought Miss Cathcart's cure?

Smith: How can I tell? I hope it had its share along with other things. The doctor's prescriptions, the curate's sermons, or her falling in love with the doctor, or the doctor falling in love with her, or her father's illness and his need for her help, or perhaps the cold weather suited her. In the present case, it is enough to know that Adela recovered. And my own conviction is that the cure was effected mainly from within.

Mrs. C: But really Mr. Smith, I don't understand. What is the Mooooowral?

Proceedings from the Francis White Ewbank Colloquium

Blair Hedges, Abby Palmisano, and Shawn Denny
in "The Light Princess"

Colin Duriez, William O'Flaherty, and Crystal Hurd after Colin's keynote talk on Saturday afternoon

IV. Essays on the Inklings (And Friends)

On the Friendship of Books: F.D. Maurice on the Art of Reading, Writing, and Friendship

by Robert Trexler

Robert Trexler is an independent writer, publisher, and the editor of *CSL: The Bulletin of the New York C.S. Lewis Society* since 2000. Through Winged Lion Press, he has published over 50 books specializing in Inklings related studies including David's Neuhouser's books *A Novel Pulpit: Sermon's from George MacDonald's Fiction* (Winged Lion Press, 2010) and *Exploring the Eternal Goodness: Selected Writings of David L. Neuhouser* (2016).

"On the Friendship of Books" was a talk first given by F.D. Maurice in 1856 and published in a collection of literary lectures a few years after his death in 1872.[1] For students and fans of the Inklings, the primary interest in Maurice (it's pronounced *Morris* not *Maurice*, by the way) is due to his friendship with and influence on George MacDonald. So before discussing the content of his essay, it will be useful to find out more about his life.

Born in 1805 (nearly 20 years before MacDonald), he was the son of a Unitarian minister. At Cambridge University he was influenced by the Platonically derived idealist philosophy then coming from Germany, especially though the works of Samuel Taylor Coleridge—a fact which also forms an intellectual link with C.S. Lewis and Owen Barfield. During the 1820s, he was the editor of various respected magazines and journals.

He entered Oxford University in 1828, was baptized an Anglican in 1831, and ordained an Anglican priest in 1834. A prolific writer, his masterpiece, *The Kingdom of Christ* (1838) was influenced by and dedicated to Coleridge. Among other things, this book makes the claim that politics and religion are inseparable and the church should be involved in addressing social questions. For more on how this idea may have played out in MacDonald's thinking, see David Neuhouser's essay "'The Great Questions of the Day': The Social Conscience of George MacDonald."[2]

---

1 F.D. Maurice. *The Friendship of Books and Other Lectures.* Ed. Thomas Hughes. London: Macmillan and Company, 1874. 1-32
2 David L. Neuhouser. *Exploring the Eternal Goodness: Selected Writings of David L. Neuhouser.* Ed. Joe Ricke and Lisa Ritchie. Hamden: Winged Lion Press, 2016. 131-141.

In 1840, Maurice was appointed Professor of Literature at King's College, so he was not exclusively a theologian and social reformer as people tend to think of him. In the late 1840s and early 1850s, he helped to form what became known as the Christian Socialist Movement. After shocking the principle of King's College with some of his theological views in 1853, he was asked to resign. Soon after, he concentrated on education reform and drew up the scheme for a Working Men's College.

Although MacDonald knew of and probably met Maurice prior to the founding of the Working Men's College, we know that MacDonald attended Maurice's inaugural address there. Maurice was also instrumental in finding a publisher for MacDonald's famous adult fantasy *Phantastes* (1857). Maurice became rector of St. Peter's Church in London in 1860, and when the MacDonald family moved to London in 1865, they started attending his church. MacDonald became an Anglican in 1866.

Much more could be said about Maurice and MacDonald, but it is not a surprise that the theme of the George MacDonald conference being held July 2016 is on his connections with the "Cambridge Apostles," which included F.D. Maurice, Lord Tennyson, John Sterling, and Charles Kingsley. As the conference advertisement says, they will examine "their social activism, diverse writings, and fascination with S.T. Coleridge."

But now it's time to look at the essay "On the Friendship of Books." In the opening paragraph, Maurice sets the stage by saying "an age of reading is not always favorable to the cultivation of this friendship." His first observation on why this might be the case is that "a large part of our reading is given to reviews, magazines, and newspapers." Being the editor of about five different magazines and journals for over a decade, he certainly had occasion to be familiar with this type of literature.

He says that the writer of a newspaper, magazine, or review article "commonly assumes an off-hand, dashing air [. . .] which seems intended to put us at our ease. He speaks in a loud rattling tone, like one who wishes to shake hands the first time you meet him. But then, when you stretch out your hand, what is it you meet? Not that of a man, but of a shadow, of something that calls itself 'We.'"

Maurice uses this principle to determine whether an author can become a friend through his writing: The person you "meet" on those pages can never be a "we." He says, "We can never make any book our friend until we look upon it as the work of an I." By getting acquainted with the writer, you get acquainted with the book, and at that point the book becomes a friend.

Having set up his premise, he continues with case studies from English literature, beginning with the works of Shakespeare. Maurice says that it might be objected that Shakespeare is not to be found in his plays. He is not Othello, Hamlet, Desdemona, or Portia. He states the argument this way: "Shakespeare does not intrude himself into any of their places; he does not want us to know what he thought about this or that matter."

Then, to answer this objection, Maurice steps back and asks a question about friendship, he writes: "Have you found that the man who is in the greatest hurry to tell you all that he thinks about all possible things, is the friend best worth knowing? Do you not become rather exhausted with men of his kind?"

> Have you not met with some men who very rarely spoke about their own impressions and thoughts, who seldom laid down the law, and yet you were sure had a fund of wisdom within, and who made you partakers of it . . . specially by the kindly, humorous, sympathetic way in which they told you about their fellow men, and made you acquainted with them? Instead of being a Reviewer who sits above the universe . . . Shakespeare throws himself with the heartiest and most genial sympathy into the feelings of all, he understands their position and circumstances; he perceives how each must have been affected by them. Instead of being a big, imaginary WE, he is so much a man himself that he can enter into the manhood of people who are the farthest off from him. . . . And so, I believe, his books may become most valuable friends to us—to us especially who ought to be acquainted with what is going on with all kinds of people.

Ah, spoken like a true professor of English literature. It's a great explanation of why Shakespeare's plays can become our friends.

He also briefly mentions George Herbert, the poet/author of "The Temple" which C.S. Lewis listed among the ten books that most influenced his life philosophy and vocation. Maurice says Herbert's poems, "are the utterances of the heart of an affectionate, faithful, and earnest man, they speak directly to whatever is best in ourselves, and give us friendly and kindly admonitions about what is worst."

Next, John Milton is of particular interest to Maurice because Milton wrote in the time of the religious and political controversies of the English Civil War. He says that some may think Milton's political views must exclude him from being a friend, but he has found him a friend "even when I have differed from him most and when he has made me [hurt] most. It does not strike me that on the whole we profit most by the friends that flatter us." Barfield echoed that idea in his book *Poetic Diction* which he dedicated to Lewis with these words from William Blake, "Opposition is True Friendship."

Despite any disagreements Maurice may have had, he says of Milton, "I know of no one who teaches us more habitually that disobedience to the Divine will is the seat of all misery to man."

Of course, Lewis wrote a book called *A Preface to Paradise Lost* in which he wrote:

> The older poetry, by continually insisting on certain Stock themes—as that love is sweet, death bitter, virtue lovely, and children or gardens delightful—was performing a service not only of moral and civil, but even of biological, importance. Once again, the old critics were quite right when they said that poetry "instructed by delighting," for poetry was formerly one of the chief means whereby each new generation learned to make the good Stock responses. Since poetry has abandoned that office the world has not bettered.[3]

Of Spenser's *Fairy Queen*, which was another favorite of C.S. Lewis and MacDonald, Maurice wrote that it "makes us feel [that we are] engaged in a great fight with invisible enemies, and that we have invisible champions on our side." C.S. Lewis wrote his own tribute to this poem in his book *Spenser's Images of Life*.

Regarding Edmund Burke, Maurice greatly admired his moral courage for standing firm in his convictions. He writes:

> "[Burke] told the electors of Bristol that they might reject him if they pleased, but that he would maintain his position as an English statesman and an honest man. They did reject him of course, but his speech remains a model for all true men to follow, as a warning to all who adopt another course, that they make friends for the moment, but that they will not have a friend in their own conscience, and that their books, if they leave any, will be no friends to those who read them in the times to come."

These are just a few of the English authors mentioned in Maurice's essay, indicating books and authors we may want to consider making our friends. Other essays in this collection include: "On Words," "On Books," "Use and Abuse of Newspapers," "Critics," and separate essays on the authors Edmund Spenser, John Milton and Edmund Burke.

---

3   C.S. Lewis. *A Preface to Paradise Lost*. London: Oxford University Press, 1942, 57.

It is somewhat odd and very interesting that after describing these famous English authors and books, he finally mentions one American author of a book that was published in 1856, the same year as Maurice's talk was given. The book's name was *Dred: A Tale of the Great Dismal Swamp*. Has anyone heard of this book, or know the name of the author?

The author is Harriet Beecher Stowe who published *Uncle Tom's Cabin* just three years before. The book used two factual court cases to propel the action of the novel and present Stowe's thesis that slavery corrupted Southern justice and humanity. It was written in response to the violence that broke out between pro-slavery and anti-slavery forces in Kansas following the passage of the Kansas-Nebraska Act of 1854, which permitted white male settlers in those territories to determine through popular vote whether they would allow slavery or not.[4]

One of the characters in the novel is a simple-minded and brave black man who, although he could not read himself, had Bible stories read to him, and knew the characters from those stories as a reality and as friends. Maurice says, "No lesson, I think, is more suited to our purpose. It shows us what injury we do to the Book of Books when we regard it as a book of letters, not as a book of life."

He concludes with these words, "I believe that all books may do that for us, because there is one Book (with a capital "B") that brings before us one Friend (with a capital "F") . . . who is called there the Son of Man."

Now ordinarily, that would be a good place to stop. But I can't resist letting George MacDonald have the last word. In a passage from his novel *The Seaboard Parish*, MacDonald reminds us of how much we treasure our author/friends. Of course, we all realize this at the Lewis and Friends Colloquium as we listen to talks on some of our favorite authors: Lewis, Tolkien, Barfield, Dorothy L. Sayers, and

---

4   MacDonald was sympathetic to the cause of freedom for Blacks in America. During his 1872-3 tour of America he met Harriet Beecher Stowe and John Greenleaf Whittier and was friends with Mark Twain, another abolitionist writer. Furthermore, in 1869, Stowe wrote a book, *Lady Byron Vindicated*, which defended the deceased widow of Lord Byron (the poet) from published accusations that she was a cold, calculating woman. Her book, which raised the issue of Lord Byron's alleged incestuous relationship with a blood relative scandalized the reading public and diminished Stowe's popularity. No doubt, MacDonald would have appreciated Stowe's valiant defense, partly because Lady Byron was a very important benefactress in his own career as well as a personal friend.

MacDonald. But at this year's colloquium, I'm glad that we also have the opportunity to also draw closer to our friend David Neuhouser, because we have each been given a book of his collected writings.[5]

Here is what MacDonald says in his novel,

> I went up to my study. The familiar faces of my books welcomed me. I threw myself into my reading chair and gazed around me with pleasure. It felt so homely here. All my old friends—whom somehow I hoped to see some day—present there in spirit ready to talk with me any moment when I was in the mood, making no claim upon my attention when I was not! I felt as if I should like, when the hour should come, to die in that chair, and pass into the society of witnesses in the presence of the tokens they had left behind them.[6]

---

5   Attendees of the 10th C.S. Lewis and Friends Colloquium were each given a book of David L. Neuhouser's collected writings referred to in endnote 2.

6   George MacDonald. *The Seaboard Parish*. Originally published by Hurst and Blackett: London, 1868. Reprinted Strahan and Company: London, 1869. 620.

The Inklings and Race: Whiteness, Mythology, and Jesus

by Andrew T. Draper

> Andrew T. Draper teaches theology in Taylor's Biblical Studies department and serves as Director of the Honors Guild. Draper earned his Ph.D. in theological ethics from the University of Aberdeen in northern Scotland. His book based on his dissertation, *A Theology of Race and Place*, is forthcoming from Pickwick Publications. Draper is also the founding senior pastor of Urban Light Community Church and Community Development Corporation, a holistic, inner-city ministry committed to reconciliation across ethnic and socioeconomic lines in the urban core of Muncie, Indiana. He lives in Muncie with his wife Leslie, school leader of Inspire Academy, and their two sons, Aidan and Alister.

The Inklings' views on race are not presented systematically. As literary and linguistic scholars, their research interests were not directly related to academic treatments of identity. As men of their times and traditions, they did not consider questions of race and gender in the same manner as more contemporary versions. However, it is possible to construct a reasonable analysis of their perspectives on race by means of their mythical narratives. I will focus my treatment on passages from C. S. Lewis's *The Chronicles of Narnia* and J. R. R. Tolkien's *The Lord of the Rings*. I will attempt to avoid a reductionism that would present either scholar as simply "racist" or "not racist," as the question of race is more complex than such categories.

Having been thoroughly acquainted with both series in my youth, much of my imaginative experiences of good and evil, Christ and cross, Church and world, longing and hope, have been shaped by both authors. As I now share these same series with my own children, I am struck by the subtle yet clear manner in which the Occidental mythologies used by both Lewis and Tolkien encourage us to imagine a battle between good and evil as a contest between lightness and darkness, or more accurately, between whiteness and blackness. As I find myself censoring my reading of their stories by substituting more "palatable" words for their descriptions of the darker skin colors and unfamiliar cultural practices of the "bad" guys, I am increasingly aware of how Christian tradition has been largely enmeshed with Western philosophical and mythological traditions. The resultant mythical appropriations often unwittingly serve to catechize younger generations in a Christian faith that is subtly but powerfully enfolded into myths of white superiority. In other words, I am contending that Eurocentrism and ecclesiocentrism have developed hand in hand. The suggestions I have for disentangling these bedfellows will become apparent throughout this paper.

I am continuously drawn to the works of Lewis and Tolkien because they draw me into an emotive and imaginative experience of the presence of Christ. At the same time, as I am drawn to their Jesus, I find that I have also been drawn into racialized ways of imagining the world, into narratives of non-Western inferiority that reinforce and reestablish my own biases and the ways in which I experience and interpret others. In a globalized world and the pluralistic milieus in which we find ourselves, there is something both comforting and insidious about the ways in which white mythologies allow us to reinforce and reconfirm our own sense of peoplehood and self, our ways of being in the world, and our understandings of flesh and bodies. In an American society in which the lines of racialized being are often policed violently, it is of utmost importance that the manner in which we view bodies (both our own and those of others) is exposed and evaluated according to satisfactory theological criteria.

While Lewis can be considered an apologist and a lay theologian, neither he nor Tolkien were theologians proper. As a theological ethicist, I am interested in the intersection of doctrine and lived commitments, particularly in the realms of Christology and theological anthropology and their concomitant identity issues (especially race and gender). My own scholarly work has centered on the emerging theological race theory of Willie James Jennings and J. Kameron Carter, professors of theology and black church studies at Yale and Duke Divinity schools. While many scholarly accounts of identity have been relegated to the social sciences, what if the problem of race is at heart a theological problem? Jennings and Carter work to fill in the lacunae in theological accounts of race with a more robust account of the origins and maintenance of the racialized imagination. They offer an analysis of race that transcends the narrow contemporary focus on "racism" as primarily a matter of the will or intentions. I will utilize the theological race theory of Jennings and Carter to elucidate what I contend are the racialized imaginations of Lewis and Tolkien.

Unearthing this deeper soil in relation to race is especially needed in Evangelical circles. Evangelicals tend to focus on sin as primarily an individual matter dependent on personal "motivations" (and tend to have an overly optimistic view of their ability to exercise such discernment). They are often reluctant to recognize the systemic nature of the "principalities and powers" and the structural ramifications of the Fall. Many modern Christians seem to believe that if they don't actively harbor animosity in their hearts toward an individual of another ethnicity, then race must not be a factor in the way they view others. This theological naiveté influences the "different languages" spoken by liberals and conservatives in relation to issues of race.

My interest is not in attempting to discern the personal motivations of Lewis or Tolkien but in demonstrating that their mythological imaginations invoke a racialized understanding of the world that harbors racist assumptions and in which racism thereby becomes tenable. From the time of early-modern colonization, this imaginary is the palette from which we as Western Christians have tended to paint the world. Before moving to a summation of Jennings' and Carter's theses, which offer a genealogical account of the missteps to which I am referring, I will first ground my contentions in several passages from Narnia and Middle Earth that demonstrate the manner in which Lewis and Tolkien view "good" and "beautiful" as "white" and "Western" while viewing "evil" and "ugly" as "black" and "non-Western."

Both Narnia and Middle Earth are under attack from forces that threaten all that is true, good, and beautiful. For Tolkien, the gathering menace comes from the East. It is dark and brooding; it threatens the "fair" people of Middle Earth[1] (read "white": an aesthetic description of light-skinned beauty), who are defended by "the captains of the West."[2] Conversely, the peoples who are susceptible to being tricked by the forces of evil and siding with them in battle are the Easterlings and Southrons, described by Tolkien as "black-skinned" and "swarthy"[3] (as opposed to the tall, light-skinned people of Gondor and Rohan whose hair is straight, long, and flowing). Ugliness is likewise embodied in orcs, who are described as "squat, broad, flat-nosed, sallow-skinned, with wide mouths and slant eyes,"[4] while the Uruk-Hai, who refer to the Riders of Rohan as "white skins,"[5] are called "black." Conversely, beauty is embodied in the pale skin and austere countenances of the women of the West. Tolkien presents goodness and beauty as virtues

---

1 Tolkien, *The Two Towers*, 152.
2 Tolkien, *Return of the King*, 200.
3 Tolkien, *Return of the King*, 148.
4 Tolkien, *The Letters of J. R. R. Tolkien*, Letter 210.
5 Tolkien, *The Two Towers*.

inherent to whiteness and unnatural to darker, non-Western peoples. In Tolkien, physical descriptions introduce a sort of naturalized, essentialized racial taxonomy by which the peoples of Middle Earth are distinguished from one another.

Lewis's racialized language is equally explicit. In *The Horse and His Boy*, the Calormenes are thinly veiled references to Arab peoples with their dome-shaped architecture, curved scimitars, and lyrical style of storytelling (think "Arabian nights"), which Lewis derides as flattering and deceitful rather than truthful and brave like the heroic poetry of the West.[6] In *The Last Battle*, Lewis describes the Calormenes as "dark, bearded men" from "that great and cruel country that lies… across the desert to the south," thereby contrasting them with "the fair-haired men of Narnia."[7] The blue-eyed and honest-faced King Tirian[8] is surrounded by these "dark men… in a thick crowd, smelling of garlic and onions, their white eyes flashing dreadfully in their brown faces."[9] According to an evolutionary logic, the antagonistic darker people of a foreign tongue are less developed and more animal-like, serving the ape instead of the Lion and, much to the enjoyment of a Narnian crowd, revert into a donkey at the command of Aslan.[10] While both authors at times present evil as "white" (e. g. the "white witch" or "Saruman the white"), it should be remembered that the characters' whiteness functions literarily as a mask of beauty and truth over the blackness of their hearts.

Many scholars have evaluated the manner in which Lewis and Tolkien present race, with one side maintaining that they are little more than misogynistic racists and the other side softening their offenses by presenting them as men who sought to call stereotypes into question by presenting several females and people of color as exceptions to the aforementioned rule.[11] In my estimation, both of these accounts miss the point. The question at hand is not an evaluation of Lewis's and Tolkien's personal praxis or the aesthetic impact of their mythological works, but the manner in which their Christian identity is maintained by paganizing and marginalizing the

---

6   Lewis, *The Horse and His Boy*, 113.
7   Lewis, *The Last Battle*, 21.
8   Lewis, *The Last Battle*, 12.
9   Lewis, *The Last Battle*, 25.
10 Lewis, *The Horse and His Boy*, 210-211 and *The Last Battle*, 26.
11 Chism, *J. R. R. Tolkien Encyclopedia*, Young, *Race and Popular Fantasy Literature*, Ezard, *The Guardian*, and Brown, *Are the Chronicles of Narnia Sexist and Racist?*.

flesh of non-white bodies. I contend that the Occidental mythologies of Lewis and Tolkien operate according to a supersessionist logic that centralizes white being by pushing Jewish and Muslim bodies to the periphery, thereby recreating them as racialized "others."

This is the point at which the works of Jennings and Carter may shed light on the problematic imaginations of the Inklings by helping us disentangle the convolutions of Christian formation and racial identity. In Jennings' *The Christian Imagination* and in Carter's *Race: A Theological Account*, both scholars contend that the ascendancy of the white male body as constitutive of "Christian" identity is grounded in the marginalization of the Jewish body as religious (and racial) "other."[12] Jennings and Carter use language of "supersessionism," the view that the Church has "replaced" Israel in the plan and purposes of God, to name what they contend is the greatest distortion in Christian theology. Developing out of the Constantinian church's articulation of theological orthodoxy in terms drawn from Hellenistic philosophy (primarily Platonic idealism), and the late medieval church's theological scholasticism (expressed in terms of Aristotelian realism), the Church increasingly imagined her identity at the expense of Jewish (and other near-Eastern) ways of being in the world.

Jennings relates that at the height of the Renaissance, at the dawn of the Age of Exploration, a series of Iberian taxonomies were articulated for the purpose of protecting Christian (read "white") identity by defining Jews and Muslims as "darker" peoples: as racialized "others." In the Spanish *limpieza de sangre* ("blood purity") laws, Jews and Muslims became the "contagion within" the populace, respectively termed *conversos* ("converts") or *cerranos* ("swine"), serving as a buffer to protect "white" identity from the "black" body, which became the "contagion without."[13] "Being" was racialized along a hierarchical scale, a spectrum of skin color. These laws formalized a growing racialized consensus as *blanco* was placed on top and *negro* was assigned space at the bottom with various "blood mixtures," including that of *mulatto*, placed somewhere in between. The most insidious aspect of these laws was that a sufficient dilution of non-white blood made it possible to be counted *blanco*. In other words, Christian conversion was expressed as the possibility of "becoming white." A powerful ecclesiology of assimilation took hold, around which many contemporary theological projects still orbit, including,

---

12 Jennings, *The Christian Imagination*, and Carter, *Race*.
13 Jennings, *The Christian Imagination*, 79.

as I contend, those that represent Christian identity by means of European mythology. As indigenous peoples were displaced and spatially-constituted identities disrupted through colonization, the newly systematized category of "race" was called upon to do what place no longer could: reveal identity. According to Jennings, race became an essentially movable schema capable of binding peoples together in a relentless aesthetic comparison.[14] Therefore, modern race is a distortion of the Christian doctrine of creation. "Whiteness" is not so much a skin color as an *ordo*, an *oikonomia*, a political arrangement organized around the aesthetic and ethical sensibilities of European peoples.[15]

Carter extends Jennings' genealogy of the origins of race into the Enlightenment project. He suggests that Kant's rationalized religion and his use of Jesus Christ as a sort of "ur-human," or a moral ideal for emulation, effectively unhinged the Center of Christian faith from the flesh of the Jewish Jesus and presented it back as a "cultural reflex" Christ, a white male body into which all flesh could be grafted as it ascended out of "crudity" of nature.[16] In this sense, *Aufklarung*, or "the modern project," begins to look like "the racial project," through which certain conceptions of rationality, beauty, morality, and being itself ascend to the "enlightened" heights while others are relegated to the depths of "darkness" and "savagery." I am building the case that many accounts that uphold Western virtue as the antidote to the morass of liberal modernity, including the mythological narratives of the Inklings, centralize the white body in similar ways through appeals to what Hauerwas refers to as the "unity of the transcendentals" ("ontology," "ethics," and "aesthetics").[17] In the Enlightenment and the proto-modern theological rationality that was its genesis, Christian language became the means by which the relative value of non-white bodies was assessed. The non-white body became the soteriological counterweight to the salvific hope extended from a Christian European center. The Jewish center of divine salvation was deposed in favor of a "great white hope" for all the peoples of the earth. Countless historical missiological programs and contemporary soteriological debates could serve as examples.

---

14   Ibid., 40ff.
15   Carter, *Race*, 8.
16   Carter, *Race*, 80.
17   Hauerwas, *The State of the University*, 203. He utilizes MacIntyre's conception of the "transcendentals" to ground his own account of education in the university.

As Lewis and Tolkien conflate Eastern modes of being with evil, they fail to acknowledge the ways in which their own Western mythologies (Dryads, knights, castles, kings, dragons, elves, dwarves, centaurs, fauns, witches, Minotaurs, and Satyrs) are themselves constitutive of the manner in which they envision goodness, truth, and beauty. In his allegorical narratives, Lewis does not hesitate to syncretize pagan British and Greek mythology with the Biblical story of redemption (consider how he represents Creation, Fall, Redemption, and New Creation). At the same time, he is extremely resistant to imagining that Near Eastern cultural and religious imagery could serve a similar iconographic role. This suggests that Lewis has not sufficiently considered the theological relationship between the universality of the Gospel and the scandalous particularity of the Jewish Messiah. He appears to have forgotten that Gentile Christianity is itself a contextualized appropriation of faith in the Jewish God (remember Acts 15) and that Western Christian orthodoxy is itself a syncretism of Greek philosophy and Jewish theology (recall Chalcedon and the fierce debates between *homoousios* and *homoiousios*). I am neither faulting the accommodation of Gentile ways of living into the Jewish faith, nor am I calling into question the veracity of Christian orthodoxy's attempt to safeguard the mystery of faith in Jesus from the comparably systematic heresies that raged in the first few centuries of the Church.[18] Rather, I am simply tagging the fact that the Inklings' racialized imagination is a symptom of the virus of supersessionism coursing through the veins of the Western Christian tradition.

Lewis's admirable (albeit somewhat convoluted) attempts at a nuanced soteriology can be read as at attempt to push against the logical conclusions of the supersessionist vision he had inherited.[19] Even if Lewis's views on the eschaton and the relationship between various "religions" as such are somewhat amorphous, he should be commended for striving toward a more inclusivist theological

---

18 My thinking on this point has been influenced by Justo L. Gonzalez's *A History of Christian Thought*. I am sympathetic with Gonzalez's claim that the development of orthodox Christology was both necessarily and yet problematically reliant upon Hellenistic philosophy. At the same time, I am convinced by Gonzalez's assertion that such rationalization was a faithful buttress against the even more speculative and philosophically systematic heresies against which orthodox doctrine was developed. (See particularly *Volume I*, 394–395 and *Volume II*, 88–89.)

19 See Lewis, *The Great Divorce*.

trajectory. I suggest that his limitations in this regard are due to a problematic conflation of the relationship between Church and world and that of Jew and Gentile. Even when his reflections take on a more universal tone (as we see in regard to the Calormene Emeth's service to Tash that was counted, eschatologically, as service to Aslan[20]), Lewis reads Christian identity as Western *at the expense of* Eastern ways of being in the world. Lewis seems to forget that Christians have been written into another people's story, dine as guests at another people's table, and worship another people's God. The Calormene Emeth calls himself a "dog," invoking the Canaanite woman's posture toward Israel's Messiah,[21] suggesting that Lewis imagines European Christianity as the Israel into which the "races," as Gentiles, can be grafted. Jennings and Carter claim that this way of imagining salvation renders non-white peoples the *ethnos* and the Church "the people of God" while evacuating the Incarnation of its historical particularity.

Like Emeth, Aravis, the Calormene who marries the Archenlandian Shasta, is "grafted in" to the narrative of Occidental qua Christian mythology. Like Rahab, Aravis is effectively brought out of her Gentile identity through inclusion into the people of God by marriage into the genealogy of the great kings and queens of Narnia. The line had been sired (at the dawn of creation) by King Frank I and Queen Helen of Great Britain[22] and would be most fully embodied in four British children fleeing attacks on the United Kingdom by escaping from a castle through a wardrobe.[23] While it is understandable for Lewis's protagonists to be of the same nationality as their author, Lewis demonstrates that he imagines his own tradition as central in the story of redemption in a way that marginalizes the traditions of others (rather than enfolding both those traditions into another story: the story of the Jewish people and their Messiah). The question should not be whether the Calormenes worship the same God as the Narnians, but if either worship a God with a history, and of a people, not their own.

Jennings proposes a Christology of Gentile remembrance as the first step in resisting the racialized imagination. As my family and I have lived for twelve years in a diverse urban community and have worked in relationships of reconciliation across ethnic lines, I have learned that images and myths that resonate with me often do not translate well into the cultural idioms of my non-white neighbors, friends, and colleagues. How can it be that something holding such deep iconographic significance for me is not comparably meaningful to those with whom I share life? The lowest-level answer is that different peoples

---

20 Lewis, *The Last Battle*, 161-166.
21 Matthew 15:21-28
22 Lewis, *The Magician's Nephew*.
23 Lewis, *The Lion, the Witch, and the Wardrobe*.

have different cultural memories and that the images of European mythology are not significant to those whose history is constituted by different cultural stories, which is one explanation for why "classical" approaches to education consistently fail students of color. However, through participation in relationships marked by difference and through submission to scholarly resources from traditions not my own, I have come to recognize that the issue is not simply one of "differing mythologies in need of translation." Rather, because Christian identity was married to imperialism and colonization, the images of conquest and victory throughout the mythologies of Narnia and Middle Earth remind non-white peoples of the marginalization and oppression of their own bodies.

This is not simply an issue of form or medium, nor does it relate to the Idealist quest to embody the supposedly timeless truth of the Gospel in various contingently occurring enculturations. Rather, this is an issue of Christology: Whose Jesus are Christians worshipping? Is it the triumphant Christ of political empires, militaristic campaigns, assaults on the "Black Gate," and battles against the followers of Tash? Or is it the Jesus whom Ted Smith proclaims as beaten, chained, enslaved, lynched, and raped at gunpoint,[24] whom James Cone calls "the Jesus of… the Spirituals" and "Fanny Lou Hamer,"[25] the Moltmannian "crucified God,"[26] the Biblical "Suffering Servant" of Israel?[27] Martin Luther would remind us that the human temptation is always to proclaim a "theology of glory" above a "theology of the cross." As devotees of the Inklings, we would do well to consider in which direction we are being discipled by the mythical images that we so adore.

---

24 Smith, *Weird John Brown*, 153–54.
25 Cone, *God of the Oppressed*, xiii.
26 Moltmann, *The Crucified God*.
27 Isaiah 52:13-53:12

Works Cited

Brown, Devin. "Are the Chronicles of Narnia Sexist and Racist?" Keynote Address: The 12th Annual Conference of The C. S. Lewis and Inklings Society (March 28, 2009).

Carter, J. Kameron. *Race: A Theological Account.* Oxford: University Press, 2008.

Cone, James H. *God of the Oppressed.* 1975. Reprint, Maryknoll: Orbis, 1997.

Chism, Christine. "Racism, Charges of." In *J. R. R. Tolkien Encyclopedia: Scholarship and Critical Assessment*, Edited by Michael D. C. Drout, 558. New York: Routledge, 2007.

Gonzalez, Justo L. *A History of Christian Thought: Volume I.* Nashville: Abingdon, 1970.

---. *A History of Christian Thought: Volume II.* Nashville: Abingdon, 1970.

Hauerwas, Stanley. *The State of the University: Academic Knowledges and the Knowledge of God.* Oxford: Blackwell, 2007.

Jennings, Willie James. *The Christian Imagination: Theology and the Origins of Race.* New Haven: Yale University Press, 2010.

Lewis, C. S. *The Great Divorce.* 1945. Reprint, New York: Macmillan, 1971.

---. *The Horse and His Boy.* 1954. Reprint, New York: Collier Books, 1970.

---. *The Last Battle.* 1956. Reprint, New York: Collier Books, 1970.

---. *The Lion, the Witch, and the Wardrobe.* 1950. Reprint, New York: Collier Books, 1970.

---. *The Magician's Nephew.* 1955. Reprint, New York: Collier Books, 1970.

Moltmann, Jürgen. *The Crucified God: 40th Anniversary Edition.* Minneapolis: Fortress, 2015.

Ezard, John. "Narnia Books Attacked as Racist and Sexist: Philip Pullman Dismisses Work of C.S. Lewis as Blatant Religious Propaganda." *The Guardian* (June 3, 2002). http://www.theguardian.com/uk/2002/jun/03/gender.hayfestival2002

Smith, Ted A. *Weird John Brown: Divine Violence and the Limits of Ethics.* Stanford: University Press, 2015.

Tolkien, J. R. R. *The Letters of J. R. R. Tolkien*, edited by Humphrey Carter and Christopher Tolkien, Letter 210. London: Houghton Mifflin, 1981.

---. *The Return of the King.* 1955. Reprint, New York: Ballantine Books, 1989.

---. *The Two Towers.* 1954. Reprint, New York: Ballantine Books, 1989.

Young, Helen. *Race and Popular Fantasy Literature: Habits of Whiteness.* New York: Routledge, 2016.

Sister Penelope Lawson CSMV: Her Life, Writings and Legacy

by Richard James

> Richard James is a retired pastor who lives in Bowling Green, Kentucky. He is currently serving as an interim pastor at First Christian Church, Albany, Kentucky.

This essay is the nuts and bolts of the oral presentation I made at the 2016 C.S. Lewis and Friends Conference at Taylor University on the life, writings and legacy of Sister Penelope Lawson. I do not discuss in detail two important things that most devotees of Lewis already know: the important twenty-four year correspondence between Sister Penelope and C.S. Lewis found in Volumes Two and Three of his collected letters and his important feedback and help in getting her first translation, *On The Incarnation* by Athanasius, published by Geoffrey Bles, beginning for her an amazing string of translations. Since 1996, two very good essays by Clara Sarrocco (2000) and Will Vaus (2009) have already covered their correspondence, and two additional informative biographical summaries have been written by Walter Hooper (1998, 2004). These letters, these four essays, and Sister Penelope's own spiritual autobiography, *The Meditations of a Caterpillar* (1962) are a basic foundation for anyone who desires to delve further into the contributions that this one Anglican nun has made to the understanding, translation and promotion of the Christian faith. Visual context for a study of Sister Penelope and St. Mary's Convent is provided by Vaus on his blog, *The Lamppost*, where he posted several photographs after he had visited the convent back in 2009. I used some of these with Will's permission in my own presentation.

My purpose in this essay though is to focus more specifically on some of the things about her that have not been shared previously. By doing this, perhaps others will by my example seek to discover even more of the treasures found in her life and work. I start with something that was for me very important yet difficult to find—a contemporary obituary from 1977. Knowing the dates of her birth (20 Mar 1890) and death (15 May 1977) from reading the above mentioned articles and knowing also from Walter Hooper's comments that she had written virtually hundreds of uncollected book reviews for several periodicals, I began to search. I finally did find one obituary of her, but only one, in the Anglo-Catholic weekly, *Church Times*. Titled, "Sister Penelope: A Nun with a Literary Bent," the first column is printed below:

Sister Penelope, a member of the Community of St. Mary the Virgin who achieved a modest fame through her devotional writings, died at Wantage last Sunday, aged eighty-seven. She was born on March 20, 1890, and professed in. the Community on March 25, 1915. Her father was a priest and she was educated at the Alice Ottley School, Worcester, and took her degree at Oxford. She was always considered delicate, and, apart from eleven years of teaching in the Community's schools at the beginning of her professed life, lived mainly at the convent or at St. Michael's House, Wantage, doing librarian or literary work. Her first book, *The Wood*, was published in 1935.

The last two columns contain some personal reflections by Robin Denniston, Chairman of Mowbray's Publishing Company which had published many of her books. He writes of her as "a delightful friend" who "wrote long letters on odd bits of paper about a multitude of matters." Three of his sentences especially impressed me as a helpful summary of Sister Penelope's life and as a way of pointing to her greater purpose:

> In her religion she was a true Tractarian—High but not ridiculously so, self-disciplined, learned and companionable. In her writing she was fluent but not facile. Her books—though quite popular in tone—were all the fruit of great reading and considerable knowledge, particularly of the Early Church.

He ends by connecting and comparing her to her friend C.S. Lewis and saying that "It is sad that there are few like them today!" (20 May 1977, p. 3)

Personally it surprised me that for an author of her accomplishment, no other periodicals or national newspapers, secular or religious, either in the U.K. or the U.S., had even mentioned her death. Also adding to my frustration, and noted also by Denniston and Hooper, is that her religious community's policy until the mid-1960's was not to use either first names or surnames on the works by any of their sisters, but to put on the title page merely the phrases "a member of" or "a religious of CSMV" (Community of St. Mary the Virgin). They did eventually start using the first names only with CSMV, assuming that there was only one person with that name in each community.

I had previously read Lewis's letters to her in both editions of Warren Lewis's compilation of his letters (1966, 1988) and had also seen her mentioned several times in Green and Hooper's biography of

Lewis (1974), in Hooper's pictorial account (1982), and then in others like Sayers (1988, 1994), and Wilson (1990). But these had mentioned little about her life other than that she was an Anglican religious whom Lewis had befriended. The only book of hers that I had at the time was her translation of *On the Incarnation*. But surely there would have been more to her life than what is mentioned in the letters and in one short obituary.

As it turns out, there was; I just did not know where to find it. I found the first indication of this more in 2003 when I read Perry Bramblett's 2000 report of his finding a "dirt cheap prize" in an "old junk bookshop" in Suffolk, Virginia. He had found and bought a used copy of Sister Penelope's book, *The Wood* (1971). With the notes on the dust jacket, there was a flyleaf photograph of her and a brief description of her life and writings (*The Lewis Legacy*, no. 83, p. 3). This same flyleaf photo and history I also found recently on the dust jacket of a copy of this same book while doing research at The University of the South. Incredibly, when the request came to her from the Episcopal Book Club of the United States for a fourth edition, at age eighty-one, she had seen it through with what she called only "sundry obvious updating and minor corrections." Below is part of that flyleaf personal history:

> Sister Penelope was born in 1890 at Clent in Worcestershire, where her father was Vicar. She was educated first at Worcester, under Miss Ottley, at what is now the Alice Ottley School, then at Oxford.
>
> She entered the novitiate of the Anglican Community of St Mary the Virgin at Wantage in Berkshire a few weeks after coming down from Oxford, and was professed there early in 1915.
>
> She worked for six years in the Community's training homes for girls before being put to teach in the schools in Wantage and elsewhere....
>
> In 1939 she took the Lambeth Diploma in Theology by theses, offering the Hebrew text of the Psalms as her special subject; and the following year she received the Archbishop's License to teach Theology
>
> She has written a number of other books ... and she has also published some sixteen translations, including a volume apiece in the Ancient Christian Writers series, Faber's Classics of the Contemplative Life, and the Cistercian Fathers now being published by the Trappists in America.

After reading more about Sister Penelope in *The Collected Letters of C. S. Lewis, Volume II*, I began in June of 2004 to enlarge my library of her books. By July of 2005, I owned twenty-one of her books, mostly bought from used book dealers on the internet, thus expanding my knowledge and appreciation for this gifted woman's ability to write in many different genres. She spoke to me as a biblical theologian, a church historian, a devotional writer, a biographer, a dramatist, a translator of the Greek and Latin Church Fathers, an essayist, and a book reviewer.

Her writings, in all their forms, were a lot to take in, even with my seminary training. As a conservative evangelical, I struggled some with her inclusion of the literary critical approach to the scriptures, especially in the Old Testament that she had learned from her studies of the work of S.R. Driver, a respected British Old Testament scholar. But like him, she was very strong in her orthodox Christian beliefs, often expressing to her readers that her scholarly study of the Bible had not discredited or made her faith untenable. In her opinion "the higher criticism of the Old Testament has rendered untold service to theology," and she had gained from it immensely (*The Wood*, pp. vii-viii, 7).

In the fall of 2007 I traveled to North Carolina to attend a C.S Lewis conference at Wake Forest and while there spent about a week doing research on some of the books from the personal library of C.S. Lewis at the University of North Carolina in Chapel Hill. Also, I had opportunity to view some of the letters related to C.S. Lewis and his friends, including some from Sister Penelope, which Walter Hooper had deposited there.

Then, in the summer of 2011, I began a brief correspondence with Sister Patricia Ann, the Sister Archivist at C.S.M.V. in Wantage. I asked her if she could share with me a bibliography of Sister Penelope's work, possibly a photo of her, and some information on her life and her responsibilities at Wantage. She quickly answered my email, but informed me that it would take some time for her to find the information that I had requested.

It was truly a blessing one month later to receive a very long email from Sister Patricia Ann all about Sister Penelope and a promised photograph and more through the regular mail. Included were the "potted history" shared above from *The Wood* and a list of known books and pamphlets written or translated by Sister Penelope, most of which by now I already knew. But there were two new things sent in addition to the promised photograph. First, she shared with me two poems by

Sister Penelope from two books of poems that had been published by Mowbrays: *Wantage Poems* (1966) and *More Wantage Poems* (1971). When I read Will Vaus's essay in 2014, I noticed that at the end of his paper he had quoted "Behold We Go Up," from the second book, but not "Perseverance in Prayer," her poem in the first book (p. 44). Here is that poem, presented with permission of Sister Patricia Ann.

> "Perseverance in Prayer"
>
> Ask, seek, importune again,
> Though futile seem thy prayer and vain.
> By seeking and by asking, so
> More capable thy soul shall grow
> Those very gifts to take and use
> Which now His wisdom doth refuse.
> God wills not all at once to shed
> His every blessing on thine head:
> But keeps in store, that thou mayest learn
> Greatly for greatest gifts to yearn.

Also, I discovered that it was from this same first book of poems that Sister Patricia Ann had sent me the following further biographical information about Sister Penelope.

> Sister Penelope read German and Theology at Oxford. Shortly after coming down from Oxford, she joined the Community. In 1915 she made her life Profession. She taught in the Community's schools between 1918 and 1931. She began to write and translate as "A Religious of C.S.M.V." in 1932 after she had been invalided home. From 1934 to 1944 she was Community Librarian and during this time she obtained the Lambeth Diploma in Theology. (p. 44)

The remainder of this essay contains what I consider to be the most extensive bibliography available on the published work of Sister Penelope. I have listed these within the following categories in chronological order: essays, book reviews, poems, plays, pocket books and mini books, books and translations. Secondary works cited are listed following her bibliography.

Following the bibliographies is a chart showing six generations of Sister Penelope's family tree. To my knowledge, nothing like this was available when I first started my work on this paper. Even in earlier articles about her, the only other family members mentioned were her mother, Laura Penelope Anstice and her father, Rev. Frederick R. Lawson. In her spiritual biography, *Meditations of a Caterpillar*, Sister

Penelope does mention that her father was of Yorkshire and Lowland Scotland descent, but was born and raised in Worcestershire. But she shared little else about her family (pp. 20, 22)

Looking at this tree, our view of Sister Penelope's family broadens, and we see also all her grandparents, all her great-grandparents, 75% of her great-great-grandparents and 62.5% of her great-great-great-grandparents. From great military and religious leaders on her father's side to the great industrial and literary leaders on her mother's side. They come from Scotland and India, from Somerset and Shropshire, and of course, Worcester. I know who each person listed is and their place in her life, but my space has already been used for other important things shared in the text above. If you have a question about anyone and you cannot find them on the internet yourself, please contact me. The small photo in the upper left corner is a reduced copy of the photograph sent to me by Sister Patricia Ann, Sister Archivist, C.S.M.V. to use in my presentation. Also, if you find an error in this family tree or know a name that should be added in one of the empty slots, please contact me at rvjames@kih.net.

Looking back over the life of Sister Penelope, it is important to note that at the age of forty-two her life took a turn for which Sister Penelope had not planned. As noted above, one source tells us that she was invalided and had to stop doing that for which she had been trained—teaching at the schools in her religious community. Not much is ever said about the specific details. But whatever it was, she and her community took it as an opportunity for her to change her primary vocation from teaching to writing books related to her faith and its history and to translate into English from Greek and Latin, some of the great writings of the early church fathers and the later medieval monastics.

And for that change all who desire to grow in the knowledge of their faith and in their relationship with Christ can be thankful for all the writing that she did over the next 42 years in so many different fields of study and through so many different genres. I marvel at how she was able to communicate so much so clearly in such a short space given to her to review books for both *Church Times* and *View Review*. And, on top of all of that she wrote and published, she was still doing it effectively into her mid-80's. Her work is excellent, but she herself is an even greater testimony to how God can still use us no matter what our age or situation may be, if we will only choose to let him. May there be many more of us like her.

Proceedings from the Francis White Ewbank Colloquium

Bibliography of Sister Ruth Penelope Lawson, C.S.M.V.

Some publisher abbreviations used in Bibliography:
C.L.A. = The Church Literature Association
GFS = The Girls' Friendly Society
SCM = Student Christian Movement
SPCK = Society for Promotion of Christian Knowledge

Essays

"Survey of Books on Christian Doctrine" *Theology*. XLII (Jan 1941): 47-51.
"Survey of Books on Christian Doctrine" *Theology*. XLIII (Dec 1941): 366-368.
"Tribute to Two Tractarians." *Theology*. LI (December 1948): 455-459.
"Believe It or Not? Pre-Advent Thoughts & Hopes." *Church Times* (Nov 17, 1967): 13.
"Lift Up Your Heads: Tales of Flying Saucers May Not Be Pure Fantasy." *Church Times*
(Dec 5, 1969): 13, 15.

Book Reviews

"Book Review: *The Ordination of Women* by P. R. Smythe." *Theology*. XL (May 1940): 388-90.
"Book Review: *The Mystical Theology of St. Bernard* by Etienne Gilson." *Theology*. XLI (July 1940): 59-61.
"Book Review: *Towards a Pattern* by Gwen St Aubyn." *Theology*. XLI (July 1940): 63-64.
"Book Review: *The Church and the World: Church and Society in England from 1800. Vol. III.* By Maurice B. Reckitt." *Theology*. XLII (Apr 1941): 246-247.
"Book Review: *Forgiveness and Reconciliation: A Study in New Testament Theology* by Vincent Taylor. *Theology* XLIV (Mar 1942): 187-188.
"Eight Small Devotional Books." *View Review*. VIII. No. 3 (Jul 1957):31.
"Book Review: *Richard of St. Victor: Selected Writings on Contemplation.* Trans. by Clare Kirchberger. *View Review*. VIII. No. 3 (Jul 1957): 32.

"*Multum In Parvo* (three books)." *View Review*. IX. No. 1 (Feb 1958): 10.

"Five Books on the Love of God." *View Review*. X. No. 3 (Nov 1959): 25-26.

"More Books For Lent (four books)." *View Review*. XI. No. 1 (Feb 1960): 25-26.

"Churches and the Church (three books)." *The Spectator* (Dec 7, 1962): 24-25.

"Prayers and Services (five books)." *View Review*. XIV. No. 3 (Jul 1963): 22.

"Church History (two books)." *View Review*. XV. No. 2 (Apr 1964): 9.

"Spiritual Writings (one book)." *View Review*. XV. No. 2 (Apr 1964): 12.

"Shorter Notices (six books)." *Theology*. LXVIII (March 1965): 162-163.

"Heavenly Architects (four books)." *The Spectator* (Dec 3, 1965): 24-25.

"Worship and Theology (five books)." *View Review*. XVII. No. 4 (Nov 1966): 18.

"The Greatest is Charity (two books)." *The Spectator* (Dec 2, 1966): 25.

"Defending the faith." *Church Times* (Feb 10, 1967): 6.

"Book Review: *Revelation and Tradition* by Karl Rahner and Joseph Ratzinger; *Theological Investigations, Vol. V, Later Writings* by Karl Rahner; and *Authority in the Church* by John L. McKenzie." *Theology*. LXX (May 1967): 233-234.

"Book Review: *Man and Sin: A Theological View* by P. Schoonenberg." *Theology*, LXX (October 1967): 476.

"Presents... for Whom (eight books)." *View Review*. XIX. No. 4 (Nov 1968): 16.

"Conversion." *Church Times* (Jan 1 1969): 7.

"Counsellor." *Church Times* (Feb 7, 1969):7.

"Father & Daughter." *Church Times* (Apr 3, 1969): 6.

"Personal testimony." *Church Times* (Feb13.1970): 6.

"The Religious Life." *View Review*. XXI. No. 2 (Apr 1970): 7.

"Roving life." *Church Times* (Jun 26, 1970): 6.

"Man first?" *Church Times* (Aug 21, 1970): 7.

"Joy in heaven." *Church Times* (Aug 28, 1970): 7

"Final moments." *Church Times* (Oct 2, 1970): 6.
"Biographies (four books)." *View Review*. XXI. No. 4 (Nov 1970): 27.
"Life's memories." *Church Times* (Nov 6, 1970): 7.
"Anthology." *Church Times* (Jan 22, 1971): 7.
"Visitor from beyond." *Church Times* (Feb 26, 1971): 6.
"Mystic poets." *Church Times* (Mar 26, 1971): 7.
"Memoirs?" *Church Times* (Apr 16, 1971): 6.
"Hymns of Ireland." *Church Times* (Apr 30, 1971): 7.
"Up aloft." *Church Times* (May 28, 1971): 6.
"Other-worldly." *Church Times* (Jun 11, 1971): 6.
"Healing Ministry." *Church Times* (Jun 18, 1971): 6.
"Thoughts on hope." *Church Times* (Jul 2, 1971): 6.
"Pioneer Doctor." *Church Times* (Jul 30, 1971): 6.
"Pen-portraits." *Church Times_Supp* (Nov 26, 1971): 5.
"A dedicated evangelist." *Church Times* (Dec 24, 1971): 7.
"Prayer-poems." *Church Times* (Dec 31, 1971): 6.
"N.T. Textbook." *Church Times* (Aug 11, 1972): 6.
"Seeking God." *Church Times* (Aug 18, 1972): 6.
"Friends' Tributes." *Church Times* (Apr 13, 1973): 6.
"Happy memories." *Church Times* (Apr 27, 1973): 6.

POETRY

"Perseverance in Prayer" in *Wantage Poems*, compiled by Sister Sylvia Mary, C.S.M.V.
Preface by John Betjeman. London: Mowbrays, 1966. p. 44.
"Behold We Go Up" in *More Wantage Poems*, compiled by Sister Sylvia Mary, C.S.M.V. London: Mowbrays, 1971. p. 55.

PLAYS

The Dayspring: A Nativity Play. Privately printed. 1922.
Scenes From the Psalms, arranged for use in Schools. [Parish Plays. no. 90.] London: SPCK, 1939.
The House of Mary: A Gospel Play for Passiontide and Easter. London: The Girls' Friendly Society G.F.S., 1947.
They Shall Be My People: The Bible Traversed in A Course of Reading Plays, 2 vols. London: Oxford University Press, 1951.
Handbook to the Plays: They Shall Be My People. London:

Oxford University Press, 1952.
The House of Mary: A Gospel Play for Passiontide and Easter. London: Faith Press. 1960.

POCKET BOOKS AND MINIBOOKS:

In the Beginning. Church Literature Association. 1945.
A Pocket Book for Christians. SCM, 1957.
Light in the Night: A Book for Those in Bed. SCM, 1958.
The Communicant's Pocket Book. Faith Press, 1960.
Concerning Christian Joy. C.L.A. 1960.
Meditating on the Bible. C.L.A. 1960.
Runners after God. The Call to the Religious Life. C.L.A. 1960
A Pocket-Book for Christians. London: SCM, 1957, 1961.
In Face of Fear. 1962.
The Way to Pray. London: Church Union, 1970.
Your Sorrow: a Book for the Bereaved (Wantage minibooks, no. 1). Wantage: St. Mary's Press, 1973.
In Face of Fear (Wantage minibooks, no. 2). Wantage : St. Mary's Press, 1973.
Meditating on the Bible (Wantage minibooks, no. 3). Wantage: St. Mary's Press, 1973.
Runners after God: The Call to the Religious Life (Wantage minibooks, no. 5). London: Church Union, 1970.
Joy (Wantage minibooks, no. 6). Wantage: St. Mary's Press, 1973.
Light in the Night: A Book for Those in Bed (Wantage minibooks no. 7). Wantage: St Mary's Press, Rev ed. 1973.
Saints and How God makes them (Wantage minibooks, no. 8). Wantage: St. Mary's Press, 1973.
The Four Last Things : According to the Creeds (Wantage minibooks, no. 9). Wantage: St. Mary's Press, 1974.

BOOKS

The Wood for the Trees: An Outline of Christianity. Cambridge: W. Heffer & Sons, 1935, 1936.
Leaves From The Trees. Cambridge, England: W. Heffer & Sons, 1937.
God Persists: A Short Survey of World History in the Light of Christian Faith. London: Mowbrays, 1939.
Windows on Jerusalem: A Study in the Mystery of Redemption.

London: The Pax House, 1941.
If Any Man Serve Me: Broadcast Readings for the 6 days in Holy Week. London: Pax House, 1942
Type and Shadows: A Quarry for Teachers. London: The Girls' Friendly Society (G.F.S.),1943.
The Coming of the Lord: a Study in the Creed. London: Mowbrays, 1953.
As In Adam: A Study in the Church. London: Mowbrays, 1954.
Also the Holy Ghost: An Essay on the Bible. London: Mowbrays, 1956.
To See the Lord: a Study in Fulfilment. London: The Church Union, Church Literature Association, 1958.
These Last Days: Time Seen through Christian Eyes. London: The Faith Press, 1959.
The Wood for the Trees: An Outline of Christianity. London: The Faith Press, 1959. (3rd ed., rev)
This Is Life: A Book for the Busy. London: SCM, 1960.
Meditations of a Caterpillar. London: Faith Press, 1962.
The Work of God: A Study of the Divine Office of the Church. London: Faith Press, 1964.
The Wood for the Trees: An Outline of Christianity. London: A.R. Mowbrays, 1971. (4th ed. rev)
The Coming: A Study in the Christian Faith. London: Mowbrays, 1974. (combining *The Coming of the Lord* and *As In Adam*)

TRANSLATIONS BY SISTER PENELOPE, C.S.M.V.:

Athansius. *The Incarnation of the Word of God: Being the treatise of St Athanasius*. Introduction by C.S. Lewis. London: Geoffrey Bles: The Centenary Press. 1944.
Athanasius. *Letter to Marcellinus on the Psalms*. London: A. R. Mowbrays & Co., 1949.
Bernard of Clairvaux. *On the Love of God*. London: Mowbrays, 1950.
A Little Book of the Contemplation of Christ. London: Mowbrays, 1951
Anselm. *Prayers and Meditations*. London: Mowbrays, 1952.
Bernard of Clairvaux. *On the Song of Songs: Sermones in Cantica Canticorum*. London: A. R. Mowbrays & Co., 1952

Athanasius. *The Incarnation of the Word of God: Being the treatise of St Athanasius with Letter to Marcellinus on the Psalms in an appendix*. Introduction by C.S. Lewis. London: A.R. Mowbrays, 1953. 2nd Edition.

Bernard of Clairvaux. *Lent with Saint Bernard. A Devotional Commentary on Psalm 91* . London: Mowbrays, 1953. 2nd imp. 1954. Fleur de lys Series. The Compline Psalm or Psalm of Lent [Fleur de lys series of spiritual classics, no. 1]

William of Thierry. *The Meditations of William of St. Thierry*. New York: Harper & Brothers, 1954.

Bernard of Clairvaux. *On the Christian Year: Selections from his Sermons*. London: A.R. Mowbrays, 1954.

Brother Bernard. *The Threefold Gift of Christ*. London: A.R. Mowbrays, 1954. [Fleur de lys series of spiritual classics, no. 4]

Aelred of Rievalulx. "The Pastoral Prayer" of St. Aelred of Rievaulx. London: Dacre Press, 1955.

St. Thomas Aquinas. *The Golden Chain: Selections from the Catena Aurea*. London: A.R. Mowbrays, 1956.

Hugh of St. Victor. *The Divine Love*. London: A.R. Mowbrays, 1956. ["Fleur de lys" series of spiritual classics, no. 9]

An Augustinian. *Meditations to the Holy Spirit*. London: A.R. Mowbrays, 1957. [Fleur de lys series of spiritual classics, no. 12]

Origen. *The Song of Songs: Commentary and Homilies*. Translated and annotated by R. P. Lawson. *Ancient Christian Writers*, no. 26. Westminster: Newman Press, 1957.

Robert of Bridlington: *The Bridlington Dialogue*, text and translation. London: A.R. Mowbrays, 1960.

Hugh of St. Victor: *Selected Spiritual Writings* . London: Faber and Faber, 1962.

Isaac of Stella. "The Way of Happiness [Sermons 1-4]" *Cistercian Studies Quarterly*. 2.3 (1967): 254-268.

Isaac of Stella. "On the Feast of All Saints, Sermon 6." *Cistercian Studies Quarterly*. 5.1 (1970): 91-94.

Isaac of Stella. "On the Third Sunday after Epiphany, Sermon 12." *Cistercian Studies Quarterly*. 5.1 (1970): 95-96.

Isaac of Stella. "Selections from the Sermons of Isaac of Stella, 4 and 5." *Cistercian Studies Quarterly.* 5.3 (1970): 302-308.

Isaac of Stella. "Selections from the Sermons of Isaac of Stella, 18, 38, 41, 42 [and extracts]."*Cistercian Studies Quarterly.* 5.4 (1970): 388-408.

William of Saint Thierry. *The Works of William of Saint Thierry.* Volume One: *On Contemplating God, Prayer, Meditations.* Translated by Sister Penelope, C.S.M.V. Cistercian Fathers Series, Vol. 1. Spencer, Mass.: Cistercian Publications, 1971.

"The Pastoral Prayer" of St. Aelred of Rievaulx (1955) in *Aelred of Rievaulx: Treatises & Pastoral Prayer.* Spencer, Mass.: Cistercian Publications, 1971.

The Incarnation of the Word of God: Being the treatise of St Athanasius. Introduction by C.S. Lewis. Crestwood, N.Y.: St. Vladimir's Seminary Press, (1978).

SECONDARY WORKS CITED:

Bramblett, Perry. "Sister Penelope, Author" in *The Lewis Legacy,* No. 83 (Winter 2000): 3.

Green, Roger Lancelyn, and Walter Hooper. *C.S. Lewis: A Biography.* New York: Harcourt Brace Jovanovich, 1974.

Hooper, Walter. "Penelope CSMV, Sister" in *C.S. Lewis: Companion and Guide.* San Francisco: HarperSanFrancisco, 1996:718-720.

Hooper, Walter, editor. "PENELOPE, Sister, CSMV" in *C.S. Lewis: Collected Letters, Volume II: Books, Broadcasts and War 1931-1949,* Edited by Walter Hooper. London: HarperCollins*Publishers,* 2004: 1055-1059.

---. *Through Joy and Beyond: A Pictorial Biography of C.S. Lewis.* New York: Macmillan, 1982.

Lewis, Clive Staples. *Letters of C.S. Lewis.* ed. with a memoir by W.H. Lewis. New York: Harcourt, Brace & World, 1966.

---. *Letters of C.S. Lewis.* ed. with a memoir by W.H. Lewis. revised and enlarged. ed. Walter Hooper. New York: Harcourt Brace, 1988.Walter Hooper

---. *C.S. Lewis Collected Letters, Volume II: Books, Broadcasts and War 1931-1949,* Edited by Walter Hooper. London: HarperCollins*Publishers,* 2004

---. *C. S. Lewis Collected Letters, Volume III: Narnia, Cambridge and Joy 1950-1963*, Edited by Walter Hooper. London: HarperCollins*Publishers*, 2006

Sayer, George. *Jack: C. S. Lewis and His Times*. San Francisco: Harper & Row, 1988.

---. *Jack: A Life of C. S. Lewis*. Wheaton, IL: Crossway Books, 1994.

Sarrocco, Clara. "The Kingliness of Friendship: C.S. Lewis and Sister Penelope, CSMV" in *CSL: The Bulletin of The New York C.S. Lewis Society*, 32.6 (June 2000): 1-7, 12-13.

"Sister Penelope: A Nun with a Literary Bent." *Church Times* (20 May 1977): 3.

Vaus, Will. "Some Ladies at Wantage: C. S. Lewis, Sister Penelope & The Community of St Mary the Virgin" in *The Chronicle of the Oxford C.S. Lewis Society*, 6.3 (October 2009): 23-34. [http://inklings-studies.com/wpcontent/uploads/2015/03/csl_chronicle_6-31.pdf, accessed on May 30, 2016]

---. *The Lamppost: C.S. Lewis, Narnia and Mere Christianity* (http://willvaus.blogspot.com/2009/07/sister-penelope.html)

Wilson, A.N. *C.S. Lewis: A Biography*. New York: W.W. Norton, 1990.

Proceedings from the Francis White Ewbank Colloquium

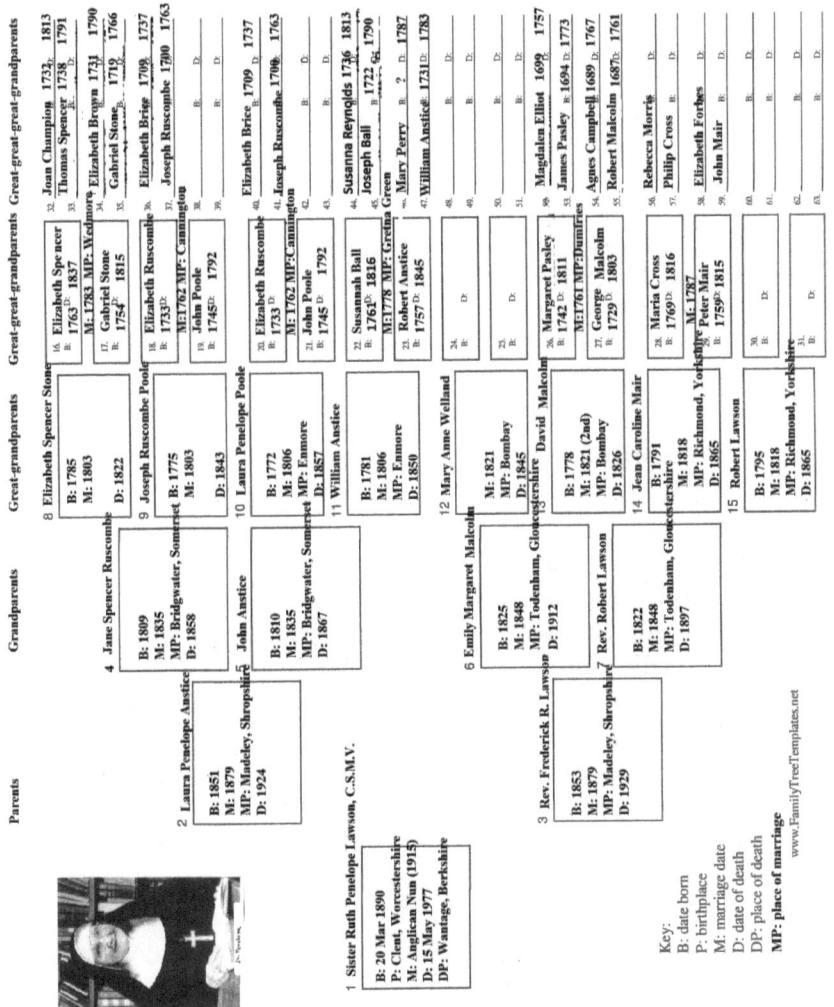

Friendship and Hierarchy in Tolkien and Lewis
by Grace Tiffany

Grace Tiffany is a professor of Shakespeare and Renaissance literature at Western Michigan University, and a near-lifelong aficionada of C. S. Lewis's works. She is the author of "C. S. Lewis: The Antiplatonic Platonist" (*Christianity and Literature* 63:3, Spring 2014). She has edited Shakespeare's *The Tempest* and published two monographs and numerous articles on Shakespeare and Renaissance literature, as well as six novels. She maintains a blog at www.shakespearefiction.blogspot.com.

In many friendships between pairs of fictional characters in the fiction of J. R. R. Tolkien and C. S. Lewis, the authors lay stress on a status difference—on one friend's superiority in some prior way, that is, arising out of and implicit in his formal role as master, king, lord, or husband. Yet in most cases this hierarchical difference becomes blurred for readers, who see the pair of friends functioning in the story as moral and intellectual equals or, in more than one case, the underling surpassing his or her "superior" in either intellect, moral caliber, or both. Is either Tolkien or Lewis, then, critiquing "degree"—the hierarchical friendship model—as inadequate to contain the energies, affections, and purpose of genuine friendship?

Well—not really. In fact, both authors' commitment to a status system ordering human relationships is rooted in the poetic traditions of Anglo-Saxon epic and late-medieval chivalric romance, and those roots remain, challenged but not undercut by the more modern portrayals of friendship that also emerge in the fictions. In *The Lord of the Rings*, Tolkien manages to have it two ways, taking his Shire characters on a medieval adventure where at least two of them exchange the roles of friend-equals for the more hallowed mythic identities of friend-retainers. But the adventure is temporary, bounded by the border between the fairytale domain of elves and dwarves and the more modern land of the hobbits, and left behind upon the "halflings'" return home. By the end of the last book, they are masterless hobbits, back in a Shire that is so latter-day in comparison to the rest of Middle Earth that we almost expect Toad to come rattling past Bag End in a motorcar. Here, friends stand on a more or less equal social footing.

C. S. Lewis undertakes the more difficult task of justifying asymmetrical friendship even outside the medievalesque bounds of his Narnia, in the modern world. He does this even while showing and directly addressing the friends' paradoxical moral and intellectual equality, or even sometimes the superiority of the formal inferior. His prose and his adult fiction provide a rationale for such hierarchical friendship, arguing the importance even among friends of play-acting the roles of superior and inferior. What is most difficult and (to be blunt) annoying for most modern Lewis enthusiasts is his arguments' indebtedness to a classical/medieval view of the sexes, wherein women in those rare male-female friendships are, despite their apparent equality, divinely designated for roles of subservience. Unlike Tolkien, Lewis explicitly argues the validity of such unequal friendships outside the realm of Faerie, where they are less easily accepted by readers. He is brave—though not necessarily successful.

As medievalists, both Tolkien and Lewis were familiar with but departed significantly from the classic Aristotelian teaching that true friendship, or *philia*, is impossible between those of unequal social status. While in his *Ethics* Aristotle defines "complete friendship" as a shared love of the good (Book 8, 159b15), he sees such friendship as possible only between social equals. Thus complete friendship is distinct from the unequal friendship "that corresponds to superiority, e.g. of a father towards his son, and . . . of an older person towards a younger, of a man towards a woman, and of any sort of ruler towards the one he rules" (Book 9, 1158b5). To Aristotle such friendships are unbalanced, in that the inferior friend has more to gain from the friendship than does the superior. "Each does not get the same thing from the other" (1158b5).

As a relation bounded by a pair's social or family connection and mutually focused one on the other, "unequal" friendship in Aristotle differs from asymmetrical friendship in the epic and romance traditions so important to Tolkien and Lewis. For both "unequal" and "equal" friendships in Anglo-Saxon and later medieval literature are not about the friends themselves but about something outside them both: a mutually accepted moral code, a spiritual endeavor, an interest, a quest. The lost lord lamented by the Wanderer in the Anglo-Saxon poem is his "gold-wine," or "gold-friend" (line 23), in a connection valued not just for the rewards given by lord to thane, but for the honorable behavior which elicits the reward, a mode of living which friendship with his "lord of rings" inspires. In Arthurian romance the bond between king and knight involves a commitment on both sides to the Chivalric Code, which orients each "friend" towards Christian virtue, indeed towards Christ himself. The knight's duty is thus not only to serve his lord but—according to an ethic which Sir Philip Sidney would call "*architectonike*" (940), the structuring of all one's actions toward a virtuous goal—to serve truth, justice, charity, and humility. Thus Sir Gawain's shame at having imperfectly fulfilled his obligation to King Arthur when he contended with the Green Knight in the king's stead is that he, Gawain, was "tainted by untruth" during the ordeal, even though Arthur himself finds the knight's duty perfectly discharged (*Sir Gawain and the Green Knight*, l. 2509).

The model for such hierarchical medieval friendship, in which an inferior is bound in love to his superior by the service of both to a greater good, is Christ's bond with his disciples, whom Christ called *filia*, his friends. Christ's followers are friends rather than servants in that they share with Christ the higher spiritual reality—the knowledge of God—that calls forth their service. "Henceforth I call you not servants; for the servant knoweth not what his lord doeth: but I have called you friends; for all things that I have heard of my Father I have made known unto you" (John 16:15).

Lewis's embrace of this notion of friendship is famously articulated in his "Friendship" chapter in *The Four Loves*, where he writes, "the very condition of having friends is that we should want something else. . . . Friendship must be about something" (66-67). While Aristotle used the phrase "fellow voyagers" to describe one species of incomplete friends—those whose connection is bounded by the extent of a physical journey—Lewis *and* Tolkien saw the voyage or journey as the medium and metaphor for profound friendships that cut across social or domestic ranks. Friends who journey together in the service of something more important than their private interests are what Lewis calls "fellow travelers" (*The Four Loves*, 67). It's true that Tolkien finds the journey itself more romantic than does Lewis (who, in *The Great Divorce*, makes fun of the idea that "travel[ing] hopefully" is better than actually reaching one's destination [40]). The hobbit friends in *The Lord of the Rings* begin with a level of friendship that seems to celebrate journeying, and the mere pleasure of road companionship, for its own sake. "*The Road goes ever on and on*," Frodo sings early on in *The Fellowship of the Ring* (with a capital "R" for "Road"). He adds, "Bilbo . . . used often to say there was only one Road; that it was like a great river; its springs were at every doorstep" (*The Fellowship of the Ring*, 110).

But soon enough the Road unites the hobbits and the rest of their fellowship in a purposeful journey toward a destination (Mordor) and a defined heroic action (the unmaking of the ring)—and friendship is sealed in common purpose. In *The Lord of the Rings*, friendship is *about* redeeming Middle Earth from darkness by defeating Sauron. Likewise, in Lewis's Narnia Chronicles, the English children's friendship is *about* reaching Narnia and, finally, knowing Aslan. Among all groups of friends in these works, the assumption of hierarchically distinct roles is necessary to and, in fact, prompted by the larger moral purpose that calls forth the friendship.

In Tolkien, two friendships involving hobbits illustrate this point. The first and most obvious is that of Frodo and Sam. In the Shire, Sam is a hired gardener—he "work[s] for" Mr. Baggins—whose service to Frodo on the ring-quest is directly precipitated by his devotion, not to his employer, but to the elvish world of Faerie in which he discovers Frodo is involved. Caught covertly listening to Gandalf's and Frodo's entrancing discussion of a struggle between good elves and evil orcs well beyond the ordinary Shire, he is chosen by Gandalf to be Frodo's companion. Gandalf chooses Sam because Sam loves elves. "Couldn't you take me to see Elves, sir, when you go?" (*Fellowship*, 98). But on the road, and especially near its end, their friendship— begun by a longing for an otherworld which Frodo, in fact, does *not* exactly share—matures into a shared commitment to fulfill the quest of destroying the ring. That this commitment underlies the friendship rather than the other way around is clear from Sam's assumption of the burden of the quest when he thinks Frodo lies dead in Shelob's lair. Once he's discovered that Frodo is in fact alive, he fights his way back to him, serving him in the manner of a medieval retainer so that they may return to the task as a pair. In this and after this, the pair seem well balanced in terms of virtue.

Frodo surpasses Sam in charity, pitying Sméagol, who follows them, even while Sam treats Sméagol with utter hostility. Yet Sam shows exceeding love and care to Frodo as well as singleness of moral purpose, while Frodo, at the last moment, tries to acquire for himself the ring's power and is saved from doing so only by poor Sméagol's biting teeth. In Mordor, at least as often as Frodo, Sam has been the pair's leader. Yet the ring's destruction, when it is finally complete, is marked not by a gesture suggestive of the pair's equal partnership, like an embrace, but by this: "'Master!' cried Sam, and fell upon his knees" (*The Return of the King*, 276). This reverential action seals them in the roles of master and servant—or perhaps it is more fitting to say, lord and thane.

Sam's assumption of the role of thane to Frodo's lord is a mythic enhancement and deepening of their old relationship of employer and hired help back in the Shire. But *The Lord of the Rings* offers a second instance of the thane-lord friendship which grows entirely from the "heroic adventure" conditions of the hobbits' journey, and which ends, like a dream, with that adventure's completion. That is the feudal bond between Merry and King Théoden.

In *The Return of the King*, Merry adopts heroic language to "lay the sword of Meriadoc of the Shire" on Théoden's lap, and is made by the king "esquire of Rohan of the household of Meduseld" (59). What might be called the adventure-temporary nature of this otherwise lifelong *comitatus* commitment is signaled by Théoden's verbal response to Merry's pledge: their bond will endure "for a little while" (59). During this while, their connection transforms Merry from exotic traveler to sworn subject. At the Pelennor Fields, dazed, wounded, and afraid, he reminds himself that he is "'King's man! King's man!'" Dutifully remaining by his master's side amid the tumult of battle, he discharges his duty by stabbing the monster who slays his gold-friend. He is Wiglaf to Théoden's Beowulf—or, more accurately, an assistant or sub-thane to Éowyn's Wiglaf. Merry has served as something like a squire to "Dernhelm"—who is, of course, Éowyn in disguise—and as Éowyn deals the Chief Ringwraith his chief death-blow, avenging the death of *her* lord and kinsman, Merry assists them both from below. The three friends, separate in status, are united in duty—in the great, compelling task of quelling the monster, an act which is part of the still larger goal of destroying the ring.

Like that of Sam, Merry's service to the goal that united the Fellowship of the Ring has issued directly from his performance of the role of social inferior in a hierarchical bond that joins thane, a higher "thane" (Éowyn), and a king. Yet for both Sam and Merry, the relation smacks of the fantastic, the imaginary, the heroic—the adventure-temporary. After Théoden's death, Merry (of course) seeks out no second lord to serve but goes back to hanging out with Pippin, another masterless hobbit. The two buddies return home, and eventually become the dudes of the Shire. "The two young Travellers cut a great dash . . . with their songs and their tales and their finery, and their wonderful parties" (*The Return of the King*, 377). As for Sam, though he remains subservient to "Mr. Frodo," the heroic quality of the pair's friendship dwindles and dissipates upon their return to their home country of clocks and umbrellas. In the Shire Frodo is not lord or master but deputy mayor, and Sam, with his eventual family, is Frodo's helpful housemate. In Tolkien's *Lord of the Rings*, profoundly hierarchical friendship is the stuff of heroic and temporary adventure.

It arises out of extraordinary conditions that compel characters' dangerous commitment to a virtuous quest, and with the quest it ends.

Unlike Tolkien, C. S. Lewis presents and defends hierarchical friendship in normal everyday life. This is so in both his children's and adult fiction as well as in his prose writings. This isn't to say that in Lewis, hierarchical friendship is the only or even the most important kind. But Lewis's belief in a neo-platonic universe, in which all things are ranked according to their proximity to God, leads him to justify the maintenance of hierarchy in bonds between certain kinds of friends. In the Narnia books, the younger children defer to and are led by Peter, their elder, and by Susan (until Susan goes bad). Even when Lucy proves privy to knowledge and wisdom which the others don't see, their blindness is accounted by the elders a failure of leadership. "I apologize for not believing you," Peter says humbly at once, when the group first finds itself in Narnia. Then Peter proceeds to take charge of their adventure (they'll "go and explore the wood, of course" [*The Lion, the Witch, and the Wardrobe*, 51] . Such unequal roles in friendship between older and younger—between more and less experienced—children are so natural and practical that Lewis nowhere bothers to defend them and (I would venture to say) readers don't especially mark them. And Lewis sidesteps the whole troublesome question of gender and rank among the Pevensey children by making the eldest child male. Yet elsewhere he justifies the hierarchical distinction between males and females purely on the basis of sex difference, specifically when he discusses husbands' lordship over wives. In doing so, he invokes terms drawn not just from Ephesians but from art.

In *The Four Loves*, Lewis defines friendship, we recall, as "fellow voyag[ing]," as well as a bond based on "common interest" (61); in the same chapter he also acknowledges that one can marry one's friend (67), although his subsequent description of most women's ignorance [73] suggests that the odds for doing this aren't good. Still, Lewis's infamous complaint that in his own contemporary society, due to their disparate educations, "The women are to [men] as children are to adults" (73) at least argues no natural intellectual inferiority in women. Hence, in order to explain and uphold the Biblical teaching that wives must "submit [them]selves to [their] husbands, as unto the Lord" (Ephesians 5:22), must, like Tolkien, find justification in fiction or fantasy. Unlike Tolkien, however, Lewis finds the roles afforded by fantasy to be permanently or at least recurrently sustainable, even in our workaday lives, since they require and enable us to participate in the deep metaphysical reality to which fiction gives access.

Hence to Lewis, heterosexual sex is (among other things) a "human participation . . . in the marriage of Sky-Father and Earth-Mother" (*The Four Loves*, 98). He imagines feminine sexual submission in terms drawn from poetry, drama, and opera. Love between marital friends is a "mystery play or ritual" (103), and lovers may "sing like Papageno and Papagena" (99). Erotic behavior contains "sub-plot and antimasque" as well as serious poetry (102). Thus men and women play unequal but complementary roles in erotic relationship. The roles are not ultimately false, as they connect the human partners to a real spirit world which Lewis sees as containing masculine and feminine energies, complementary "natural forces of life and fertility" (98). In his science fiction trilogy, Lewis imagines not just earth but the non-human cosmos as masculine, like Mars (Malacandra), or feminine, like Venus (Perelandra). (That in observable nature the male is frequently dominated by the female seems to have escaped Lewis's notice!)

But what about the other parts of marriage? Are the roles of submission and mastership called forth by filia as well as by eros? Indeed, Lewis's fiction if not his prose suggests this extension. In *That Hideous Strength*, the highly educated Jane Studdock begins to see that the "invasion of her own being in marriage" is in fact "the lowest, the first, and the easiest form of some shocking contact with reality" (312). Her teacher Ransom agrees, telling her the souls of women who choose to live independently, apart from men, must still "meet something far more masculine, higher up, to which they must make a yet deeper surrender" (312). God is masculine. Jane's return (after an estrangement) and her submission to her partner and potential friend, her husband Mark, is an aspect of her Christian conversion, which is a necessary submission to something larger and "so masculine that we are all feminine in relation to it" (313). No equal partner, the feminine is fundamentally, transcendentally, and naturally inferior to the masculine. It follows that in all areas of marital friendship, wifely submission to masculine leadership, though a kind of courtly game, is also a serious spiritual requirement.

The puzzlement Lewis felt regarding the experience of intellectual friendship with women—his difficulty, given his reverence for scripture and for myth, in according the egalitarian status he found in friendships with males to heterogenous or co-ed friend-relationships—is evident in his fiction. In *The Magician's Nephew*, Lewis simply plucks a cabbie and his wife from turn-of-the-century London—a town presumably full of troublesome suffragettes —and deposits the pair in the medievalesque fantasy world of Narnia, where different gender statuses obtain—or are being created. Aslan asks the cabbie, not the wife, if they are willing to be the Adam and Eve of this world, and though the cabbie does ask his spouse for some confirmation of his acquiescence ("I'd do my best, wouldn't we, Nellie?"), her voice in answer is never heard (139). Her agreement is apparently not required, any more than is Eve's in *Paradise Lost*. (Actually, it is considerably less required than is Eve's in *Paradise Lost*.)

The realistic setting of Lewis's adult novel *That Hideous Strength* offers its author no easy recourse to the social or domestic hierarchies of myth or fairytale—despite Lewis's subtitling the book "A Modern Fairytale for Grownups"—and in this story Lewis clearly struggles explicitly to justify the Christian requirement of wifely submission among even intellectually equal marriage partners—that is, between spouses who are or may be friends as well as lovers. Jane Studdock quite reasonably wonders, "Supposing all those people who . . . had infuriatingly found her sweet and fresh when she wanted them to find her also interesting and important, had all along been simply right and perceived the sort of thing she was? . . . For one moment she had a ridiculous and scorching vision of a world in which God Himself would never understand, never take her with full seriousness" (315). Rather than an intellectual resolution to this worried thought, Jane receives, right after she thinks it, a vague "religious experience" which at least temporarily quells her doubts (316).

We readers haven't had the religious experience, so our doubts remain. Lewis allows them to do so. *Lewis* takes Jane seriously. He himself has failed to resolve, in this novel, the question of why men's female intellectual equals should not assume the practical status of equal friends in a marital partnership. Still, he deserves credit for so clearly understanding, articulating, and sympathizing with the obvious feminine objection. Despite his infamous impatience with women who get in the way of masculine friendships, he proves genuinely more interested than Tolkien in literary explorations of friendship *between* the sexes.

It's not my intent here to investigate the complicated connections between Lewis's fictional male-female friendships and those he entertained in his own life. It is worthwhile, however, to note that he found his views on the nearer resemblance to Godhood of masculinity roundly challenged when he finally did marry his friend. George M. Marsden suggests that had Lewis lived longer, his views on the essential differences between men and women would have continued to evolve. I think such evolution would have been the likelier result of Joy Davidman's living longer. It was while he was forming an intimate friendship with her that he created what Andrew Lazo right calls his "most complex character" (142), Orual, the first-person narrator of *Till We Have Faces* (published in 1956). Perhaps Davidman's society provoked Lewis's observation, made to a friend in 1956, that he actually didn't like either the "ultra-feminine" or the "ultra-masculine," but preferred "people" (quoted in Lazo, 142). Unless Lewis was saying he preferred people to God—though this is possible—the comment suggests a somewhat modified view of the deity, as no longer strictly gendered. It is wonderful to consider Lewis's experience of friendship with women—or at least with one woman—expanding his understanding of the fuller nature of the ultimate Person and Friend.

A passage in one of Lewis's letters reveals him in one such possibly transformational moment. In *A Grief Observed*, Lewis records that Joy Davidman disliked his congratulating her on her masculine qualities by asking him how he would like it if she complimented him on his feminine ones. Her reply, which gave him pause, offered a view of gender differences as fundamentally complementary *and* existing on the same plane of value. On the surface Davidman's comment seemed to denigrate "feminine qualities" in comparison to masculine ones—surely Lewis wouldn't want to be called feminine!—and perhaps that is how he took it. But her comment suggests that the word "masculine" is no less insulting when inappropriately applied. In defending her femininity, it isn't likely, given what we know of Joy Davidman, that she was claiming only the attributes Lewis associated, mythically, with women: sweetness and acquiescence as opposed to interestingness and intellectual rigor. She seems rather to have been resisting the artificial gendering of any of these human qualities. Lewis's great friendship with Davidman demonstrated the truth of his earlier observation: in the end, the "ultra-masculine" and "ultra-feminine" are more abstract, less real, than the friend beside you.

Works Cited

Anonymous, "The Wanderer." *The Literature of Medieval England*. Ed. and transl. D. W. Robertson, Jr. NY: McGraw-Hill, 1970. 152. Print.

Aristotle, *Nichomachean Ethics*. Trans. Terence Irwin. Indianapolis, IN: Hackett Publishing Co., 1985. Print.

Holy Bible. King James Version. London: Collins Clear-Type Press, 1959. Print.

Lazo, Andrew. "New Perspectives: *Till We Have Faces, The Four Loves,* and Other Works." *Women and C. S. Lewis: What His Life and Literature Reveal for Today's Culture*. Ed. Carolyn Curtis. NY: Lion Hudson, 2015. 135-143. Print.

Lewis, C. S. *A Grief Observed*. NY: HarperCollins, 2015. Print.

---. *That Hideous Strength*. NY: Scribner, 2003. Print.

---. *The Great Divorce*. NY: HarperCollins, 2001. 40. Print.

---. *The Four Loves: An Exploration of the Nature of Love*. Boston: Houghton Mifflin Harcourt, 2012. Print.

---. *The Lion, the Witch, and the Wardrobe*. NY: Macmillan, 1973. Print.

---. *The Magician's Nephew*. NY: Macmillan, 1973. Print.

Marsden, George M. *C. S. Lewis's 'Mere Christianity': A Biography*. Princeton, NJ: Princeton UP, 2016. Print.

Pearl Poet, The. *Sir Gawain and the Green Knight*. Trans. Simon Armitage. *The Norton Anthology of English Literature, Vol. 1A: The Middle Ages*. Ed. Stephen Greenblatt. 183-238. NY: Norton, 200. Print.

Sidney, Philip. *The Defense of Poesy*. In *The Norton Anthology of English Literature, Vol. IB: The Sixteenth Century, the Early Seventeenth Century*, ed. Stephen Greenblatt. NY: Norton, 2000. 933-53. Print.

Tolkien, J. R. R. *The Fellowship of the Ring*. Volume One of *The Lord of the Rings*. NY: Ballantine Books, 1973. Print.

---. *The Return of the King*. Volume Three of *The Lord of the Rings*. NY: Ballantine, 1973. Print.

Beings of Magic:
A Comparison of Saruman the White in Tolkien's *The Lord of the Rings* and Simon the Clerk in Williams' *All Hallows' Eve*

by Kathryne Hall

> Kathryne Hall is a student at Oral Roberts University, majoring in Writing and Biblical Literature. Kathryne enjoys studying the Inklings and has presented several papers on them at conferences around the country.

Charles Williams and J. R. R. Tolkien were both a part of the popular literary group the Inklings. Williams, an important but lesser known member, penned *All Hallows' Eve* "after he had been among the Inklings for several years" (Carpenter 170), and he often enjoyed the readings of Tolkien's *The Lord of the Rings* during Inklings' meetings (122-123). Despite being a member of this same scholarly circle, their writing styles are very different. Tolkien creates extravagant worlds filled with hobbits, elves, talking trees, and special languages in his *The Lord of the Rings* series, while Williams writes strange thrillers about characters attempting to reach mystical worlds as is the case in *All Hallows' Eve*. However, despite these differences, there are also some significant similarities. In both works, Tolkien and Williams incorporate sorcery as integral parts of the stories and characters. For example, Saruman the White in *The Lord of the Rings* and Simon the Clerk in *All Hallows' Eve* both use magic to do their bidding. Saruman and Simon embody Satanic qualities, and they are both overcome by the spells they practice as a consequence of manipulating others and reaching the supernatural world. Ultimately though, it is their environments that betray them—resulting in their final destruction.

In light of Tolkien's comments on their relationship, it is unclear whether Tolkien and Williams explicitly influenced each other's works; however, their association is undoubted. Tolkien states in his letters that he and Williams were friends, but he also makes "emphatic declarations that he and Williams had nothing in common intellectually" and that their works did not influence each other (Carpenter 122). He writes, "I knew Charles Williams well in his last few years... But I do not think we influenced one another at all! Too 'set', and too different. I think we both found the other's mind (or rather mode of expression, and climate) as impenetrable when cast into 'literature', as we found the other's presence and conversation delightful" (*Letters* 209). Confirming his opinion, Tolkien writes in a later letter, "I doubt if he [Williams] had read anything of mine then available; I had read or heard a good deal of his work, but found it wholly alien, and sometimes very distasteful, occasionally ridiculous" (362). However, before then, Tolkien admits that he "was in fact a sort of assistant mid-wife at the birth of *All Hallows Eve*" (349). It is difficult to discern whether the two intentionally borrowed ideas from each other's characters or not—especially because Tolkien also claims they listened to each other's works in "large and largely unintelligible fragments" (209)—but the likenesses between Saruman the White and Simon the Clerk cannot be overlooked.

The parallels between Saruman and Simon begin with the traditional wizard-like appearance they share; according to the texts of *The Lord of the Rings* series and *All Hallows' Eve*, each character possesses a cloak. Additionally, Tolkien and Williams write specific details about the eyes and facial structures of Saruman and Simon. Saruman is described as "an old man, swathed in a great cloak, the colour of which was not easy to tell, for it changed if he stirred. His face was long, with a high forehead, he had deep darkling eyes, hard to fathom, though the look that they now bore was grave and benevolent, and a little weary. His hair and beard were white, but strands of black still showed about his lips and ears" (Tolkien 601). Simon wore "some kind of cloak" (Williams 51) and "was a tall man, with a smooth mass of gray—almost white—hair; his head was large; his face thin, almost emaciated... The skin was dark and . . . [t]he eyes were . . . deeply set" (52). Additionally, Saruman and Simon have both incorporated magic so heavily in their lives that it has become a part of their very physical beings. Saruman's voice is "low and melodious, its very sound an enchantment. . . . For many the sound of the voice alone was enough to hold them enthralled; but for those whom it conquered the spell endured when they were far away, and ever they heard that soft voice whispering and urging them." Indeed, the tone of his voice mesmerizes his listeners: "none were unmoved; none rejected its pleas and its commands without an effort of mind and will, so long as its master had control of it" (Tolkien 601). In contrast, Simon's voice is "urbane, a little husky, and had the very slightest foreign accent" (Williams 52), but magic clearly affects his smile more, for it is "rather a sudden convulsion . . . a kind of muscular spasm rather than a smile" (65). Simon is arguably not even a human anymore, for he uses magic to clone himself so that he can hold dominant positions in multiple countries simultaneously (Williams 111-113). Magic has taken over Saruman and Simon; evil is eventually personified in them.

Saruman's and Simon's ultimate goal is dominance, though their approach to attain it is slightly different. Captivated by power, Saruman joins forces with Sauron in order to conquer Middle-Earth by possessing The One Ring. He begins to assemble an army to take The Ring by force. Simon's goal is a bit different but still world-dominating and power-seeking. He plans to release the backwards Tetragrammaton into the supernatural world on All Hallows' Eve—the time when Heaven and Hell come closest together. As Thomas Howard writes in his book *The Novels of Charles Williams*, "Simon is more than curious, and we find that his great experiment is to find the word or words that will furnish the man who utters them with *power*" (227). Both magicians have a specific mission in mind and are fueled by greed as well as a yearning for power; additionally, manipulation of others is a key element in both Saruman's and Simon's dominance.

Tolkien explains how the wizards in *The Lord of the Rings* cannot be exempt from free will because "in the view of this tale & mythology, Power—when it dominates or seeks to dominate other wills and minds (except by the assent of their reason)—is evil, these 'wizards' were incarnated in the life-forms of Middle-earth, and so suffered the pains both of mind and body" (*Letters* 237). This humanistic quality—the ability to become fallen—is one of the causes of Saruman's propensity to be in control. Tolkien states that his wizards were "involved in the peril of the incarnate: the possibility of 'fall', of sin. . . . The chief form this would take with them would be impatience, leading to the desire to force others to their own good ends, and so inevitably at last to mere desire to make their own wills effective by any means. To this evil Saruman succumbed" (237). Saruman is clearly forced to this level of impatience when he attempts to control King Théoden through the manipulation of his servant, Grima Wormtongue, in order to have power over the city of Rohan (Tolkien 537-542). Additionally, as stated earlier, Saruman's tone of voice compels his listeners; Tolkien states that "Saruman's voice was not hypnotic but persuasive" (*Letters* 276). This becomes one of Saruman's greatest tools of manipulation, for "[t]hose who listened to him were not in danger of falling into a trance, but of agreeing with his arguments, while fully awake. . . . Saruman corrupted the reasoning powers" (276-277).

Evidenced by his forceful control over Betty, his daughter, Simon also seeks to accomplish his evil deeds through others. Though it is not necessarily the sound of his voice that is enchanting because his reciting of the backwards Tetragrammaton is mostly inaudible (Williams 157), like Saruman, the words Simon say are an integral aspect of his magic. It is through mouthing the letters of the Tetragrammaton in reverse that his plan will work, for when Betty's movement startles him and he is unable to maintain the recitation, the spell cannot continue without his completion of the Name's utterance and without interruption (160-162). Betty is the main vehicle Simon uses to achieve his goal of ruling both the physical and the supernatural world; without forcing her to obey him, his plan of releasing the backwards Tetragrammaton will fail. Every move Simon makes is centered around the need to abuse those around him. Simon's "interest in other selves is simply and solely to have total power over them" (Howard 228), and he also manipulates Richard and Lester to accomplish his goal. He "is interested in Richard because Richard might be the necessary link with Lester, who might supply Father Simon with an answering commodity for Betty, allowing him simultaneously to dismiss Betty from her body and this world and summon Lester into some body here from the world of the dead. He wants an exchange: that will facilitate his black plans" (233). Exploiting those around them becomes one of the primary ways that Saruman and Simon attempt to take control of their worlds.

Both Saruman and Simon function as symbols of Satan. As Lucifer, a fallen angel, was engrossed by his mission to gain power, Saruman also "perverts" his position as a wizard and stains his original purpose to be good. Tolkien explains, "the Wizards . . . first appeared about the year 1000 of the Third Age, when the shadow of Sauron began first to grow again to new shape. . . . They were thought to be Emissaries . . . and their proper function, maintained by Gandalf, and perverted by Saruman, was to encourage and bring out the native powers of the Enemies of Sauron" (*Letters* 180). Though Saruman attempts to achieve power by bending to the will of Sauron, Simon is a representation of the devil himself. As Howard points out, Simon, like Satan, has "contempt for . . . his followers" (225-226). He writes, "The analogy with Satan is unavoidable—the old notion that he hates those whom he dragoons into his camp. Evil is incapable of love that will face death for others" (226). Like Saruman, Simon turns from the choice to be good, and "[i]n his wish for power and control, he is of course guilty of Lucifer's sin: making a grab for what belongs to the Most High alone" (228). Both Saruman and Simon are "satanic" and turn away from good.

Though in different ways, Saruman and Simon each access the supernatural world. Saruman uses a magical *palantír* (while also controlling magic through his staff and ring), and Simon controls his daughter, Betty. Saruman sees what other people are doing through his *palantír* and can also control aspects of the environment (e.g., mountains and snow) through it. He does this in *The Fellowship of the Ring* in an attempt to change the Fellowship's path into one of more peril:

> "I [Aragon] knew the risk of snow, though it seldom falls heavily so far south, save high up in the mountains. But we are not high yet; we are still far down, where the paths are usually open all the winter."
>
> "I wonder if this is a contrivance of the Enemy," said Boromir. "They say in my land that he can govern the storms in the Mountains of Shadow that stand upon the borders of Mordor. He has strange powers and many allies."
>
> "His arm has grown long indeed," said Gimli, "if he can draw snow down from the North to trouble us here three hundred leagues away."
>
> "His arm has grown long," said Gandalf. (Tolkien 306)

As stated before, Simon works through a human being rather than a magical object. He thrusts Betty into the supernatural realm in order to discover the future: "The power which Simon wishes to test out on Betty is his ability to dismiss her spirit from her body and then re-summon it. In other words, he wants the power of life and death over other human beings, Betty being merely the first experiment" (Howard 227-228). Though their modes are different, Saruman, through his *palantír*, and Simon, through his daughter, both reach the celestial dimension to complete their plans for gaining power.

Ironically, Saruman's and Simon's devices that are meant to be evil, the *palantír* and Betty, are both ultimately used for good. Saruman does not choose to get rid of the orb (rather, his servant [Wormtongue] throws it), and Gandalf remarks that the ball "'is not a thing [...] that Saruman would have chosen to cast away'" (Tolkien 607). This action turns out to be a fortunate twist of fate, for now, Sauron thinks the ring-bearing hobbit is in Saruman's capture. Gandalf remarks,

> "There remains a short while of doubt, which we must use. The Enemy, it is clear, thought that the Stone was in Orthanc—why should he not? And that therefore the hobbit was captive there, driven to look in the glass for his torment by Saruman. That dark mind will be filled now with the voice and face of the hobbit and with expectation: it may take some time before he learns his error." (Tolkien 618)

At the end of *All Hallows' Eve*, Betty is able to build a connection with her friend Lester, who recently died and went to the same supernatural world Betty was accessing. Because of this, Betty's life is saved through Lester's substitution when Simon tries to release the backwards Tetragrammaton to kill her. Betty becomes happier than ever and is empowered—no longer afraid of Simon, her mother, or Evelyn (a girl she detests). She even acquires the ability to heal people: "Her immortality was strong in her. . . . She passed, so, round the whole circle, holding, touching, healing—simply and naturally, and with all the gaiety that she could" (Williams 271). The evil that Saruman and Simon try to evoke is eventually thwarted; good still prevails.

In the end, Saruman and Simon finally get their deserved destruction, and interestingly enough, their demises come through their environments. In *The Lord of the Rings*, "[t]he Ents assault and capture Isengard, the stronghold of the traitor Saruman" (Duriez 165). These Ents from Fangorn Forest are so passionate about their march to the south that they made up a chant to sing on their way:

> *To Isengard! Though Isengard be ringed and barred with doors of stone;*
> *Though Isengard be strong and hard, as cold as stone and bare as bone,*
> *We go, we go, we go to war, to hew the stone and break the door;*
> *For bole and bough are burning now, the furnace roars—we go to war!*
> *To land of gloom with tramp of doom, with roll of drum, we come, we come;*
> *To Isengard with doom we come! With doom we come, with doom we come!*

(Tolkien 506-507; italics Tolkien's)

Simon's surroundings also betray him when the City emits a crimson rain, which ultimately, dissolves him: "The rose began to withdraw. He felt himself carried with it and slipping more deeply into it. The smell of blood was in his nostrils; the touch of burning on his flesh; this was what the crimson must be to him. He stared, as he sank and as that in which he was held moved in its own fashion, at the rain of swift-darting points between him and himself" (Williams 266). The Ents of Fangorn Forest and the City turn on Saruman and Simon, helping to destroy the presence of evil.

Saruman and Simon are enchanters of a similar appearance and both represent a fallen Satan. As beings overcome by magic, they evoke evil over other people (primarily through manipulation and through their access of the supernatural world). Additionally, in the end, both characters' actions result in an unfavorable fate as their environments take revenge on them. Tolkien and Williams used these characters to prove that right will always win, for without evil present, one can never know the beauty of goodness. Like a phoenix rising out of the ashes, goodness triumphs out of these fallen characters.

Works Cited

Carpenter, Humphrey. *The Inklings: C. S. Lewis, J. R. R. Tolkien, Charles Williams, and Their Friends.* Boston: Houghton Mifflin, 1979. Print.

Duriez, Colin. *The J. R. R. Tolkien Handbook: A Comprehensive Guide to His Life, Writings, and World of Middle-Earth.* Grand Rapids: Baker Book House, 1992. Print.

Howard, Thomas. *The Novels of Charles Williams.* San Francisco: Ignatius Press, 1991. Print.

Tolkien, J. R. R. *The Letters of J. R. R. Tolkien.* Ed. Humphrey Carpenter. Boston: Houghton Mifflin, 1981. Print.

---. *The Lord of the Rings.* 1954-1955. Boston: Houghton Mifflin, 1993. Print.

Williams, Charles. *All Hallows' Eve.* 1945. Grand Rapids: William B. Eerdmans, 1981. Print.

"Sufficiently Different to Help One Another": The Central Place of Books in the Friendships of the Inklings

by John Stanifer

> John Stanifer holds a B.A. in English from Indiana University Kokomo and a M.A. in English from Morehead State University. His first book, *Virtuous Worlds: The Video Gamer's Guide to Spiritual Truth*, was published by Winged Lion Press in 2011. John says, "I am a hopeless geek who enjoys reading, coffee, and cosplay."

"We read to know we're not alone." These words, spoken by Anthony Hopkins as C.S. Lewis near the conclusion of the 1993 film *Shadowlands*, may not have been spoken by C.S. Lewis himself, but it might as well have been (Attenborough; O'Flaherty). All his life, C.S. Lewis was a bibliophile, reading just about everything he could get his hands on." Yet reading, it turns out, was not just a solitary activity for one's own benefit; for Lewis and his circle of family and friends, it was often a way of forming and cementing friendships that would last for a lifetime. It was never particularly important whether a friend who read the same books got the same things out of them. What mattered was the shared interest, the pursuit of the truth to which books could lead. Using the standard biographies, personal letters, and recollections of Lewis and his friends, readers who are curious about the books that found a central place in the friendships of the Inklings can easily make up a database of titles that helped fuel many a passionate discussion for this group; this essay will focus on a select few titles that are especially significant and are easy to acquire. What makes the exercise so interesting is that it was more often than not the differences in what these friends got out of their favorite books that ensured the passion in that friendship rarely died down.

One of the most natural starting points is Lewis's friendship with his childhood neighbor Arthur Greeves. Lewis and Greeves had attended Campbell College, a grammar school, at the same time without ever meeting. Later, Arthur made some effort to befriend the two Lewis brothers with little initial success. Finally, sometime in the middle of April 1914, Lewis received an invitation—from whom, the record appears unclear—to visit Arthur while the latter was recovering from an illness (Lewis, *Surprised by Joy* 130; Lewis, *The Collected Letters*

1: 53). By this time, Lewis had already delved deep into the world of literature that his parents Flora and Albert had indirectly opened for him by filling their home with books. Lewis describes this wealth vividly in the early pages of *Surprised by Joy*:

> My father bought all the books he read and never got rid of any of them. There were books in the study, books in the drawing room, books in the cloakroom, books (two deep) in the great bookcase on the landing, books in a bedroom, books piled as high as my shoulder in the cistern attic, books of all kinds reflecting every transient stage of my parents' interest, books readable and unreadable, books suitable for a child and books most emphatically not. Nothing was forbidden me. (10)

Within the Lewis household, taste in reading could vary widely. Flora preferred "good novels," such as those of Meredith and Tolstoy, and Albert gravitated to books with a political bent, books that boasted a fine grasp of poetry and rhetoric, and books by "humorous authors," like Dickens and W.W. Jacobs (*Surprised by Joy* 4-5). Neither of Lewis's parents shared his liking for imaginative literature, what Lewis referred to as "the horns of elfland" (5).

Arthur Greeves was apparently the first person, with the possible exception of Lewis's brother Warnie, who shared Lewis's taste in literature. When Lewis arrived at Arthur's sickbed, he spotted a book called *Myths of the Norsemen* on a table beside the bed (*Surprised by Joy* 130). Lewis doesn't identify the author of this book, but several scholars have identified the author as H.A. Guerber (Wilson 37; Hooper 53; Yuasa 51). Beyond naming the book's title and author and the fact that it contains an overview of the major Norse myths, most scholars have given little attention to this specific book—hardly the only book of Norse mythology Lewis would ever read, but well worth exploring if for no other reason than its part in breaking the ice between Lewis and the boy who would become one of his closest companions until his death.

Kirsten Wolf, chair of Scandinavian Studies at the University of Wisconsin-Madison, has been teaching and writing on Norse mythology since the 1980s (Department of Scandinavian Studies). In her introduction to *Myths of the Norsemen*, she describes the author's background. Helene Adeline Guerber, born in Michigan and educated in Paris, "devoted her life to educating her fellow citizens about European literary and cultural history through the publication of about three dozen books on a vast array of topics ranging from famous operas to Jewish history to Shakespeare's plays" (9). The edition of

Guerber's book with the title mentioned in *Surprised by Joy* was first published in May 1908, just three months before Flora Lewis died of cancer (C.S. Lewis Foundation), and would subsequently be reprinted numerous times (Guerber). However, as Wolf points out, the book had originally been published with a different title some 13 years earlier (Wolf 9). The 1895 edition, titled *Myths of Northern Lands*, contains virtually the same text, word-for-word, as the later edition that Lewis found at Arthur's bedside (Guerber, *Myths of Northern Lands*).

What was it about the contents of *Myths of the Norsemen* that so enraptured Lewis and Greeves and led to their immediate and enduring friendship? As soon as the boys realized they were both devotees of Guerber's work, Lewis writes, "we were pointing, quoting, talking—soon almost shouting—discovering in a torrent of questions that we liked not only the same thing, but the same parts of it and in the same way; that both knew the stab of Joy and that, for both, the arrow was shot from the North" (*Surprised by Joy* 130). To Lewis, "North" meant far more than just a direction on a compass; it meant the renewal of the spiritual ache called "Joy" that he had experienced when his brother Warnie had showed him a beautiful toy garden some years before. The ache had faded in the interim, but Lewis claims that his "Joy" returned in full force when he picked up the December 1911 issue of a literary magazine called *The Bookman* and opened it to an article that mentioned, among other things, Arthur Rackham's illustrated edition of *Siegfried and the Twilight of the Gods*. The article's sample illustration featured Siegfried and Mímir, two of the key characters in Norse myth (Lewis, *Surprised by Joy* 73-74; Griffin 34; Tassin 383-385). The effect of simply reading the phrase "twilight of the gods" and experiencing the force of Rackham's artistry, which the article described as worthy of "competition with some of the finest and most adequate stage realisations ever witnessed" (Tassin 385) filled Lewis with awe: "Pure 'Northernness,' engulfed me," he wrote; "A vision of huge, clear spaces hanging above the Atlantic in the endless twilight of Northern summer, remoteness, severity" (*Surprised by Joy* 74). Almost as soon as the longing engulfed him, it was gone, and Lewis claims that he knew having this longing again "was the supreme and only important object of desire" (74).

From the way Lewis describes his first encounter with Arthur, it would seem the two shared more than just an appreciation for Norse mythology in general and for Guerber's work specifically. In *Myths of the Norsemen* and its Northern brethren, the boys found the expression of a cold, hard spiritual longing marked by simultaneous joy and sadness. Given this, Guerber's original title, *Myths of Northern Lands*, may be an even more appropriate summary of what the friends found in the book than its revised title, *Myths of the Norsemen*.

Of course, Lewis's friendship with Arthur did not simply begin and end with Norse mythology, nor did their similarity of taste in this one area mean they never had a disagreement. On the contrary, Lewis says that he and Arthur were "sufficiently different to help one another" (*Surprised by Joy* 150). Elaborating, Lewis mentions several writers whose value he had failed to appreciate until Arthur convinced him to give them another try or a first try in some cases:

> Under Arthur's influence I read at this time all the best Waverleys, all the Brontës, and all the Jane Austens. They provided an admirable complement to my more fantastic reading, and each was more enjoyed for its contrast to the other. The very qualities which had previously deterred me from such books Arthur taught me to see as their charm. What I would have called their "stodginess" or "ordinariness" he called "Homeliness"—a key word in his imagination. (151-52)

Lewis's gratitude to his friend fairly leaps off the page as he confesses that Arthur's taste for the "good, solid, old books" of what he calls "the classic English novelists" was a taste "with which, to my great good, he infected me for life" (151). Lewis's attempts to influence Arthur's literary taste, at least those attempts recorded in *Surprised by Joy*, were not as successful. Lewis claims that Arthur's "great defect was that he cared very little for verse. Something I did to mend this, but less than I wished" (151).

When it comes to verse, there are few literary works that had a wider influence among the Inklings and their circle than the Anglo-Saxon epic poem *Beowulf*. One of Lewis's attempts to sway Arthur to the beauties of poetry came about in a letter dated November 1916. Apparently, Arthur had complained that *Beowulf* was too different from the English novelists he so enjoyed, as Lewis responds to this with, "I know what you mean by that 'crampy' feeling: you mean there are no descriptions in Beowulf as in a modern book, so little is told you & you have to imagine so much for yourself" (Lewis, *The Collected Letters* 1: 244). He goes on to explain to Arthur his belief in the importance of reading literature outside the more contemporary productions of one's own language and culture and making an effort, not just to read the work from the viewpoint of a twentieth-century reader, but to appreciate what the work meant to its original audience

(244). In this early letter, readers of Lewis's book *The Discarded Image* should recognize the argument he makes in that book's preface, almost 50 years after the letter to Arthur, suggesting his views on the topic changed little over the course of his life. In *The Discarded Image*, Lewis is approaching medieval literature in the same way he wanted Arthur to approach *Beowulf*. He says that there are English tourists who carry their Englishness with them all over Europe and "have no wish to realise what those ways of life, those churches, those vineyards, mean to the natives" (x). He does not mean to write for those who are interested mainly in "the impression, however accidental, which an old work makes on a mind that brings to it a purely modern sensibility and modern conceptions" (x). He is writing, he says, for "the other sort" (x).

Lewis would meet and befriend a number of this "other sort" among the students and faculty when he arrived at Oxford. After joining the faculty at Magdalen College, Oxford, he discovered that one of its ex-presidents had outlawed student societies out of a belief that they were "savagely exclusive clubs of rich dipsomaniacs" (qtd. in Poe 49). Lewis quickly found a way to get around this by inviting students to his rooms for literary discussions. For example, Wednesday evenings saw students gathering with Lewis for informal readings of Anglo-Saxon poetry (Poe 50). Walter Hooper writes, "During these sessions [Lewis] introduced his pupils to mnemonic devices he invented for learning Old English, they chanted *Beowulf* aloud, and the beer-jug was passed around" (732). Hence Wednesdays became known as "Beer and Beowulf Evenings" (Poe 50; Hooper 732).

All of these literary and intellectual threads in Lewis's life would converge in his friendship with his fellow faculty member J.R.R. Tolkien. Lewis met Tolkien at a faculty tea party of sorts in May 1926 and would write of Tolkien: "no harm in him: only needs a smack or so" (qtd. in Zaleski 173). But as Philip and Carol Zaleski have so aptly summarized it, "it was Tolkien who would supply the smack, jolting Lewis—with the help of other friends and Lewis's own desperate yearning—into Christian faith" (173).

Though Lewis was by this point an atheist and Tolkien a Catholic, the two found that they had many points of agreement in literary taste and in their attitude to academics. In 1926, Tolkien founded a literary club "devoted to intensive study of Old Norse literature," a club that not only included Lewis but several other members of the more well-known group the Inklings (Zaleski 176). This club and the others that would follow gave Lewis the chance to indulge his love for the ancient characters and stories he had encountered as a youth in books like *Myths of the Norsemen*. Late, late nights with Tolkien and other members of the Kolbítars were common as they discussed their mutual literary obsessions (Zaleski 177).

What happened at these somewhat private clubs would sometimes spill over into their members' professional lives. In the Oxford of the '20s and '30s, debates raged over how much room—if any—should be made in the curriculum for the study of modern English literature. A number of faculty, including Tolkien and C.S. Lewis, feared that this debate would result in a lessening of interest in the study of the classics, including *Beowulf*. Lewis went so far as to argue that it was impossible to understand modern English literature without the close study of *Beowulf* with its "sense of language ... native to us all" (qtd. in Zaleski 175). Together with Tolkien and other like-minded individuals, Lewis formed yet another club called The Cave that would set itself the task of ensuring the classics remained at the forefront of the curriculum (Zaleski 175-76). Tolkien would go on to be one of the most passionate voices in this movement, conducting a now-famous series of lectures on *Beowulf* that convinced many the poem was more than a quaint literary artifact (Zaleski 216); it is, in fact, "a fundamentally Christian myth, revealing the truth that 'a Christian was (and is) still like his forefathers a mortal hemmed in a hostile world" (qtd. in Zaleski 216). In speaking of the literary output produced by Lewis, Tolkien, and other Inklings, Diana Glyer observes that scholars "have found many common sources [in the work of the Inklings], including the Orpheus myth, Norse tales, *Beowulf*, children's books, and fairy stories" (35). On every side, it is clear that these writers took their enjoyment from the level of merely reading and appreciating their favorite books to imitating them and adding their own flourishes to once-familiar fables while trying to persuade the world around them to take note of such books, too.

Yet, as critical as Norse myth, *Beowulf*, and the rest may have been to these friends' professional lives, the impact this literature would come to have on them spiritually was even more significant. Tolkien helped Lewis to see that the longing for something indefinable that Lewis had felt when he encountered Norse myth as a boy was not just a longing for something fictional that had never and would never exist. In September 1931, Lewis took a late stroll with Tolkien and Hugo Dyson, another mutual friend who also happened to be a Christian. Through the persuasions of these two companions, Lewis began to see that all of the books and stories he had most admired, including the Norse myths and *Beowulf*, were really pointing to the "myth" of Christ, the one myth that had actually come true in history. Lewis came to see this conversation as one of the turning points of his spiritual life and would credit these friends as helping him to re-accept the validity of the Christian story for himself (Duriez 53-59; Zaleski 187-89).

It would be all but impossible to catalog more than a fraction of the books that had an influence on the Inklings and their friendships, and here only a handful that cover both ancient myth and modern English literature have been mentioned. Will Vaus, in his introduction to a multi-volume work exploring just ten of C.S. Lewis's favorite books, asserts, "Given a reading life as rich as that of C.S. Lewis, the man probably had a hard time paring down his list to the top ten books that influenced him. An adequate account of all Lewis's literary influences would require numerous thick volumes" (n.p.). The same might be said of Tolkien or any of the other Inklings who would write book after book amidst busy lives, and obviously a short essay is a world away from the "numerous thick volumes" envisioned by Vaus.

Still, whether they were influencing each other in literary taste or in the far deeper matters of faith, several things are clear from even the most superficial survey of the Inklings' reading lists: they loved to read, they loved many of the same books and often in the same way, their tastes—while similar in many points—were different enough so that they could open each other's eyes to new authors and even entirely new genres, their shared tastes overlapped with their academic careers to impact the environment of their university at large, and—arguably the most important point of all—they led each other down new roads of spiritual enrichment. This is a powerful example and a legacy that has been carried on through the work of dedicated Inklings readers, collectors, and scholars around the world, among them the late Dr. Frances Ewbank, Dr. David Neuhouser, Dr. Ed Brown, and Dr. Bruce Edwards—each of whose passion for Lewis and friends has inspired us in multiple ways and will continue to inform the field of Inklings studies for many years to come. May they all rest in peace until we join them "further up and further in" and experience "the Great Story which no one on earth has read: which goes on forever: in which every chapter is better than the one before" (Lewis, *The Last Battle* 228).

Works Cited

Attenborough, Richard, dir. *Shadowlands*. 1993. HBO Home Video, 1999. DVD.

C.S. Lewis Foundation. "The Life of C.S. Lewis Timeline." *Living the Legacy of C. S. Lewis*. C.S. Lewis Foundation, 2016. Web. 25 May 2016. <http://www.cslewis.org/resource/chronocsl/>.

Department of Scandinavian Studies. "Kirsten Wolf." *University of Wisconsin-Madison*. Board of Regents of the U of Wisconsin System, 10 May 2016. Web. 25 May 2016. <http://scandinavian.wisc.edu/80.htm>.

Duriez, Colin. *Tolkien and C. S. Lewis: The Gift of Friendship*. Mahwah: HiddenSpring-Paulist, 2003. Print.

Glyer, Diana Pavlac. *The Company They Keep: C.S. Lewis and J.R.R. Tolkien as Writers in Community*. Kent: Kent State UP, 2007. Print.

Griffin, William. *C. S. Lewis: Spirituality for Mere Christians*. Eugene: Wipf and Stock, 2007. Print. C.S. Lewis Secondary Studies.

Guerber, H. A. *Myths of Northern Lands: Narrated with Special Reference to Literature and Art*. New York: American Book, 1895. *HathiTrust Digital Library*. Web. 25 May 2016. <http://hdl.handle.net/2027/nyp.33433068184989>.

Myths of the Norsemen from the Eddas and Sagas. London: Harrap, 1908. *HathiTrust Digital Library*. Web. 25 May 2016. <http://hdl.handle.net/2027/osu.32435000046136>.

Hooper, Walter, ed. *The Collected Letters of C.S. Lewis*. By C.S. Lewis. Vol. 1. New York: HarperCollins, 2004. Print.

Lewis, C.S. *The Collected Letters of C.S. Lewis*. Ed. Walter Hooper. Vol. 1. New York: HarperCollins, 2004. Print.

The Discarded Image: An Introduction to Medieval and Renaissance Literature. 1964. Cambridge: Canto-Cambridge UP, 1994. Print.

The Last Battle. Norwalk: Easton, 1956. Print. The Chronicles of Narnia 7.

Surprised by Joy: The Shape of My Early Life. San Diego: Harcourt, 1955. Print.

O'Flaherty, William. "We Read to Know." *Essential C.S. Lewis.* N.p., 12 Sept. 2015. Web. 25 May 2016. <http://www.essentialcslewis.com/2015/09/05/we-read-to-know/>.

Poe, Harry Lee. *The Inklings of Oxford: C.S. Lewis, J.R.R. Tolkien, and Their Friends.* Grand Rapids: Zondervan, 2009. Print.

Tassin, Algernon. "Old Spirits and New Seas." *The Bookman: A Magazine of Literature and Life* 34.4 (1911): 379-88. Rpt. in *The Bookman: An Illustrated Magazine of Literature and Life.* Vol. 34. New York: Dodd, 1912. 337-456. *HathiTrust Digital Library.* Web. 25 May 2016. <http://hdl.handle.net/2027/chi.32140075>.

Vaus, Will. *C.S. Lewis's Top Ten: Influential Books and Authors.* Vol. 1. Hamden: Winged Lion, 2014. N. pag. Kindle file.

Wilson, A.N. *C.S. Lewis: A Biography.* New York: Norton, 1990. Print.

Wolf, Kirsten. Introduction. *Myths of the Norsemen.* By H. A. Guerber. New York: Barnes, 2007. 9-15. Barnes & Noble Library of Essential Reading. Nook file.

Yuasa, Kyoko. *C.S. Lewis and Christian Postmodernism: Word, Image, and Beyond.* Eugene: Pickwick-Wipf and Stock, 2016. Print.

Zaleski, Philip, and Carol Zaleski. *The Fellowship: The Literary Lives of the Inklings: J.R.R. Tolkien, C.S. Lewis, wen Barfield, Charles Williams.* New York: Farrar, Straus, and Geroux, 2015. Print.

The Future of Inklings Studies: Keynote Panel Discussion (4 June 2016)

by Diana Glyer, Sorina Higgins, Colin Duriez, and Joe Ricke.
(transcribed and edited by Joe Ricke)

Joe Ricke: What we want to do in this panel is discuss with all of our keynote speakers the future of Inklings Studies.[1] At the end, of course, we will have some question and answer time, so that everyone can take part. You might say, we want to dream and probe the future. But first, let's look back. So I want to ask each of the panelists this question, starting with Diana. Who are the authors and/or what are the works that, looking back, have proven foundational to you? In other words, who or what got you going in the direction you have gone or led you into a direction that has been fruitful? I suppose you could just pay homage, as it were, to the people who have been meaningful to our work—perhaps Inklings scholars, perhaps not. Okay. Is that all right, Diana?

Diana Glyer: Absolutely. It's very exciting to be here today. It is a daunting task to try to think of just a few titles that are significant, especially titles aside from those of the primary texts. One of things that I spend a lot of time talking about, and encouraging young scholars about, is the importance of doing primary research, because it is important for us to talk with one another about our various interpretations. The more we can encourage one another to go back to the original documents and to see what the Inklings really have to say. I think it's incredibly important for us to constantly be checking back and forth. And that's why I'm so grateful for every archivist and librarian in this room. You are our heroes. You make it possible for us to do what we do [applause].

---

1 This essay is a revised transcription of a recording by William O'Flaherty, originally prepared for his podcast series *All about Jack*. The audio version was first published online on 28 June 2016. The edited audio was transcribed by Abby Palmisano and revised for publication by Joe Ricke. The original panel included Carol Zaleski, Professor of Religion at Smith College and co-author of *The Fellowship*, who joined the discussion by Google Hangouts. Although her face was seen and her comments were heard in the room, the audio was not adequate for a clear recording of her contribution. She is referenced, however, several times by other speakers during the discussion.

Let me mention two books that have been very influential to my thinking. When it comes to Lewis studies, one of my favorites, still, and one of the most important books that I've ever read in Lewis studies, is *C.S. Lewis at the Breakfast Table* by James T. Como. That particular collection. What you have there is an assortment of perspectives. One of the reasons that book is so important to me is the very fact that there is so much in it that is contradictory. I think that the differences are helpful and healthy in our field, to have a variety of perspectives, instead of striving for an artificial consistency. What Como has done in that book is allow these individuals to speak clearly from their individual perspectives, and I think that's a model for a healthy intellectual community, modeling the ways in which we can extend intellectual hospitality to a variety of perspectives and voices. I love that book, and I reread it frequently. I think it's still good. I wish he hadn't revised it, because when he revised it, I think he tried to even out the seams a little bit, and I don't think that that was an advantage. I like the original version of that very much. So that was a Lewisian book that has been very important to me.

A book from another field, would be a book by Goran Hermeren called *Influence in Art*. It raises this whole question of what I'll talk about in my address tonight: this idea of what counts as influence. And tonight, I'll be issuing a warning. I think that we view influence much too narrowly. I think that we need to think more capaciously about what we're looking at, and what we're looking for when it comes to the question of influence. So, I will tell you a little more about that tonight. Thanks.

Colin Duriez: What put me on to the Inklings, really, was discovering C.S. Lewis. That is, fairly early on (I must have just finished high school), when I read his *Surprised by Joy*, I came across all of these names, like Tolkien and others. And then shortly afterwards, I was in Istanbul, where I was studying, and an American lent me his copy of *Essays Presented to Charles Williams*. Well, I read the introduction to that. It was written by C.S. Lewis, and it was about the Inklings, which did, in that book, include Dorothy L. Sayers as well. But, I soon realized that she wasn't actually allowed to be an Inkling. And then, a bit after that, I was in North Ireland continuing my studies, and somebody told me that a chap called Humphrey Carpenter was writing a book about the Inklings. So I started to think that was something I wanted to explore, and that really lead me to start writing about the Inklings. But there wasn't really a book to help start writing, until I read Humphrey Carpenter's book when it was finally out, other than doing what I'm sure Diana did as well, and that was to sift away through letters and diaries, manuscripts, and scraps of information, and slowly start to put together a better picture of what the group was. And that really took a long, long time, but that's the only way to do it, really. So it's sort of odd that I went to Turkey and met these Americans who were just discovering Lewis and the Inklings through people like Clyde S. Kilby.[2] By the way, he was one of the great pioneers in Lewis and Tolkien and Inklings studies. He took the time to get to know Lewis and Tolkien and other Inklings and helped to get their materials to Wheaton. He was also a great encourager. Although I never actually met him, he wrote to me and encouraged me. So that's how it all started.

Sørina Higgins: Well, I think I'd like to add on to what they said, and then bring in as well, the power of communities, like this, because, I think the most influential works for me have been works in progress. So one, for instance, is Grevel Lindops' new biography of Charles Williams. Well, you say, wasn't that just published, like last week? Well, actually, it was October of last year, but Grevel's been working on it for over a decade. And he's been extremely generous. I've been in touch with him since pretty early on in the process. And he's shared bits and pieces of it with me all along. And those of you who have seen the *Chapel of the Thorn*, you know that he took his section "Chapel" from the biography, and he and I revised it together and made it into the preface to that book. So I was aware of what he was doing and sort of learning at a distance about how he was doing it. Finding out about archives and manuscript work, even, at a distance was extremely helpful.

And then, four years ago, when I was here, at the Taylor Colloquium, the community was so inspiring that immediately after that, I went to the Wade Center and worked on *The Chapel of the Thorn*. And that's the same time, as many of you have heard, that Brenton made the *Screwtape* discovery. So that was another instance of collaboration and mutual inspiration. And, while I was at the Wade, I also had many wonderful interactions with Chris Mitchell.[3] There was one particular

---

2   The late Clyde S. Kilby was a professor of English at Wheaton College and the Founder and Head Curator/Director of the Marion E. Wade Center at Wheaton College from 1965 to 1981.

3   The late Christopher W. Mitchell was the Director of the Marion E.

conversation that we had, it was just so encouraging, and he sat me down and asked me, "What are your goals? What are your interests?" Then he pretty much told me to stick with Charles Williams, because he knew that there weren't enough people working on that. He put me in touch with several other people who were working on Williams as well.

Another influential book was *Planet Narnia* and, again, that was as a work in progress as far as I was concerned. I heard Michael Ward give a talk on it, way before the word was even out that he had made this discovery. So that was a real blessing and influential on my work.

Joe Ricke: We heard about *Planet Narnia* quite early on too because, as Michael shared at the last colloquium, the very first teaching he ever did, the very first Lewis teaching anyway, was tutoring for the Taylor students I used to take over to Oxford. And so my students would come back and all present papers on the secret planetary influence on Narnia. That was seven or eight years before the book came out, although an earlier essay appeared about that same time in *Christianity Today*, I think.

Now let me just ask a question that I didn't warn anyone about. Is that OK? It's a simple one. Other than your own work, because I know you're all writers, so you're reading your own work a lot through the work of revision, but what are you reading right now that's relevant to your work in Inklings studies. What are you reading right now that you want to recommend to the rest of us, that this is really something we should be looking at ourselves. Why don't we start with Sørina this time, and then we'll come back the other way, all right?

Sørina Higgins: Well, I am just about to finish my chronological read through, and blog through, of Charles Williams. So that's kind of a big priority to me. I want to finish that before I start my work at Baylor in the fall. So I'm just reading or re-reading the last few books that Williams wrote and preparing to blog on those. But, Carol, I'm actually just reading your book right now.[4] I've got the audio version, and I think I'm about a quarter to a third of the way through it. So, that's really great, and we're going to talk about themes to Inklings scholarship soon, and I'll come back to that, but Carol's book has one

---

Wade Center at Wheaton College from 1994-2013.

4   This and other references to "Carol" are to Carol Zaleski. See note 1.

the most important themes that is going on right at this exact moment in Inklings studies. So if you haven't read it yet, do.

Colin Duriez: Just before I left England, I was reading a book which I couldn't bring with me because of the weight of my suitcase, and that's Stephen Thorson's book on Barfield. I am finding it delightfully lucid and helpful in trying to get an overview of his thinking and particularly to understand how best to describe Lewis's philosophical thinking as he developed, because it's really tricky trying to figure out how much he was an idealist and how much he was a realist in philosophical terms.

But also I've been reading tons of books by Dorothy L. Sayers, because I'm currently working on a book about her. I'm trying to put together her many different aspects—a dramatist, a crime writer, a translator of Dante, and a popular theologian. And she is somebody whose prose and conversation are always filled with lots of interesting quotations that leave you wondering where they came from. It would be nice to have somebody annotate all those quotations, but it would be a life-time job, I think. So that's where I am at the moment.

Diana Glyer: I'm afraid that my answer will tell you more about me than Lewis studies. My daughter is fourteen years old, and as she was growing up, it was our habit to read to her constantly. So we read to her half an hour in the morning and half an hour in the evening. Now that she's fourteen, she likes to read to me, and this has been a tremendous privilege, to see the books that she loves best through her perspective. So we've just finished, for the very first time for me, the entire Harry Potter series. And her favorite author right now is an author named Rainbow Rowell. Does anybody know Rainbow Rowell? So she's been reading Rainbow Rowell's *Fangirl* to me. And it's very, very, interesting, the kinds of conversation that are sparked when your children read to you, and you get to ask them questions like, "What do you notice?" "How do you feel about that?" "How do you feel about the choices that these characters are making?" "What would you say if *you* were on the scene and could speak into the situation?" and so on. So we've been doing a lot of that.

My own reading has been related to two projects that I have been working on. One is a book on Dante that I'm very excited about. I've been on sabbatical the last year, working on a book about Dante. I think Dante is incredibly important to all of the Inklings. I think that Dante's influence has been vastly underestimated, particularly on Lewis's thought and worldview. We talk about Lewis's medieval point of view, but we don't talk enough, specifically, on his work on Dante. The specific influence of specific scenes and even phrases in Dante. So I'm very grateful, Marsha, for your book on that.[5]

The other thing that I've been working on, and I'm very excited because I can see the finish line of a project that I've been working on for quite a while, is a book called *The Major and the Missionary: A Love Story*. It's a fascinating project about Warren Lewis and his correspondence with a missionary doctor with whom he became a pen-pal late in life. These letters are fascinating. They start with some inquiries, they become pen friends, and then she gets a little flirty. And it's quite interesting to read their unfolding romance, and to follow the trajectory of their profound relationship that occurred, for both of them. I was late in life but very meaningful to both of them. So I've been reading a lot about missions and about Papua New Guinea, where Blanche was stationed, and I've been trying to understand a little bit about what it meant to be a missionary doctor in that time. She was at the very cutting edge of the ecumenical movement in that country. To watch her efforts, not only to make a difference as a missionary and as a doctor, but also as someone who was trying to promote a kind of "mere christianity" and a kind of collaboration among the various groups that were stationed there, has been fascinating for me.

Joe Ricke: Let's switch, then, to our announced topic—the future of Inklings studies, or new directions in Inklings studies, or however you want to frame that. We can dream, we can complain, we can make a short list. However we want to think about this. So let's start with Colin this time, and then give everybody a chance.

Colin Duriez: I suppose that, up till now, my gripe has been that lots of studies have been on the individual members of the Inklings and usually it's just the four picked out. You know—Tolkien, Lewis, Barfield, and Charles Williams. The reality is much more interesting than that. There are lots and lots of other colorful characters in the group. But I think, now, that it's finally changing. Sometime last year, I think, I said to Diana, "this is the year of the Inklings, isn't it?" Or

---

[5] Glyer refers to Marsha Daigle-Williamson, a conference participant, who had recently authored a book on Dante and C. S. Lewis. See the works cited list.

maybe you said it, Diana, and I picked it up from you. Anyway, it's amazing to see all these books coming out about the Inklings. We've been working for years on things, and suddenly Carol's book came out, and all kinds of others—*Bandersnatch*, and my book on the Oxford Inklings. Grevel Lindop on Charles Williams; he's been working on that for for nine or ten years, I'm sure. So things are changing.

There is one area where I'd like to see more work. I mean, we know the Inklings as a writing group. In its early days, Lewis described its members as being characterized by "a tendency to write and to Christianity." And his brother, Warren, definitely preferred the writing group to the conversational group which formed. But I would like to see more on the other Inklings group, which is the same people, but focusing more upon their conversation and their reading. I think that you can get a hint of the power of their conversation in Humphrey Carpenter's reconstruction of an Inkling meeting, which everybody seems either to like or hate. I know that Barfield really enjoyed the conversations. And everyone knows that Lewis was a famous conversationalist. And a number of people have pointed out that if you knew Lewis very well, you knew that his letters, those wonderful letters in three massive volumes of them, actually echo a lot of this actual conversation.

And I think all of us gathered here care about the part that conversation plays in making culture and are concerned that it isn't playing as much of a part in our culture as it did in the past. But you can notice certain places where you can still get that power of conversation. So, maybe we should ignore Warren a bit and say that the conversation group was also very important. I mean, they kept going to the pub, The Eagle and Child, week after week, to talk. That lasted right into the fifties. Until towards the very end of the fifties, C.S. Lewis was wondering what the group identity was, after Tolkien no longer came and Charles Williams had died. . . . So I would love to see some more on the conversations. It would be hard work, as it was for people who have written on the group, and who have had to do an archaeological dig on the letters, and diaries, and so on. And I think it could also be very worthwhile as to . . . .

Joe Ricke: Go ahead, go ahead. This is our last big thing, and then we're going to open up to questions. So, give it a shot.

Colin Duriez: I would like to see more work on the other Inklings. The group all over the thirty years or so that was made up of twenty or so people. And as far as I know, to come along to a conversation group in the pub, you probably still had to be invited. It wasn't just a matter of barging in. You know, you might find some interesting person in the corner, who turned out to be a right-wing poet. Someone sort of like Strider, who sort of got dragged in, for example. Generally, the Inklings were a noisy lot in the corner of the pub and would probably surprise people by their roughing. There are some people that if you say that they were an Inkling, you'd get in real trouble, you know? Tutt- tutting and all that. One of them is Roger Lancelyn Green, and he actually attended quite a few gatherings of the Inklings in the pub. Obviously, he didn't attend all the time because he wasn't living in Oxford; he was living in Cheshire, in his ancestral home. We know that he played a very important part in Lewis's development of the *The Narnia Chronicles*. And everything he wrote really fits into the ethos of the Inklings. So I suppose I'll just have to develop a thick skin and mention him more. But there's lots of others. People who wrote about Hadrian's Wall, you know, and historical books, and all kinds of other subjects. It was a bit like some of these older groups gathered around Dr. Johnson. There would be people with all different areas of expertise and with very different interests. They were not all Oxford dons from the English Department. There was a wide variety of professional people, and they added to each other's knowledge. I think they were really a remarkable group.

So I'd like to see more work on the other Inklings. And it would be hard work, finding the information, but some people are really good at that, you know? And then, finally, some of what you might call satellites of the Inklings, people who weren't actually members. People like Dorothy L. Sayers had huge affinities with the group, so it's really good to see so much work being done on her now. She's a major writer. And there are many others as well that should be explored. I mean, somebody like Cecil Harwood, one of the anthroposophist friends of Owen Barfield, who became a deep friend of Lewis. In fact, his son, Lawrence, became one of Lewis's godsons, and he's written a very interesting book about Lewis, as his godfather. Lewis would visit and would crawl on the floor with the kids and things, and have a good time. That's not at all, you know, the kind of image that people have of him . These "satellite Inklings" are very interesting. Cecil Harwood, for example, was described by a group of authors in the twentieth century as the "Lord of the Walks," because he used to organize the walks. So it's nice to hear that, isn't it? It might echo something else that took place later on.

Joe Ricke: Thank you. Of course, one of the purposes of the way we conceived the colloquium this year, with the "friendship theme," was to pick up these satellites, and extend the circle of friends so to speak. And I know we couldn't all get to every session, but we had a great paper on C.S. Lewis and the Fred Hoyle, the Astronomer—kind of like the anti-friend—and another wonderful paper on Lewis and Wagner. And of course, that paper brought in Cecil Harwood, because if Lewis was going to hear Wagner, he was almost certainly going with Harwood. And obviously Sayers has been important; we've had two whole sessions on Sayers. And so it's really been encouraging that the way we were conceiving of doing things this year, really worked, at least in terms of recognizing the Inklings' larger circle of influence. Now, back to the future. Sørina, do you want to give this a go?

Sørina Higgins: Sure, thank you. Well, I see three very exciting things happening, and so my dream is that they would continue to happen and gain momentum. And so, first, what I alluded to previously, is the idea of looking at the Inklings as modernists, because I think that at one time, the only places that you could give a paper on the Inklings was either at an Inklings conference or the Tolkien at Kalamazoo sessions.[6] So, you had to look at Tolkien's Medievalism to talk about him. Now, maybe that's just my impression, and sort of overstating the case, but for a long time, all of the books that were coming out, all of the studies, were sort of looking at their sources, were situating them as backwards-looking writers. So even when we were looking at how to put *The Inklings and King Arthur* together, at one stage I was thinking we would have to organize the book according to their sources. So, you know, we would need to move the book through the Welsh sources, then move on to Malory, etc.

But no, that's not really the way that they were looking at Arthur, because they were engaged in this contemporary conversation, right?

---

6   Tolkien at Kalamazoo is a loosely-knit scholarly sponsoring organization for papers given at the International Congress on Medieval Studies, held annually at Western Michigan University. The Center for the Study of C.S. Lewis and Friends at Taylor University also sponsors panels of papers on "Lewis and the Middle Ages" at the Kalamazoo Conference each year. Contact jsricke@taylor.edu for more information.

That's why in my keynote talk, I mentioned the other twentieth century writers who were all working on Arthur. So I think it's very important to look at them in their modernist context. I want to see studies of Williams and James Joyce, and more stuff on Lewis and T. S. Eliot, and I want to see a lot more on their modernist context. And I want to see a lot more on them as war poets, right? I mean, Lewis fought in the war, was wounded, and published a line of poetry in 1919, so why aren't we talking about him in the exact same sentence as Siegfried Sassoon and Wilfred Owen, and so forth. And even Williams, who didn't fight, has so many poems about the war and its effects on the home front and on the people that he lost. So that's a really important topic that we need to do more of. So, I'd like to see that.

The second, is that I really love how the critical conversation is moving forward, and how more and more scholars are picking up on the big critical themes of the latter half of the twentieth century and the critical conversations that are going on right now. There's a lot going on with the Inklings and Genders Studies and Environmental Studies, looking at post-colonial implications of their work, you know, like looking at Williams's "The Vision of the Empire" and so forth. So that's really important, and we need to keep that going, not just to be sort of popular in academia, but because these are really, really, important questions. And we can add those to the more common ones of the theological conversations and the source material, and so forth.

And the last one is finding more of a place for the Inklings in academia, and especially in education. I want to see more to see more courses on them taught at the university level. Obviously, there are whole programs that are developing, and I'm here promoting Signum University as well, so, that's my little edge. But I want to see that these authors are being taken seriously, and we don't have to accept the line between the academic and the popular, right? Over and over and over again, when surveys are done about what are the best books of the twentieth century, *The Lord of the Rings* wins. The surveyors keep trying to ask the questions in different ways so Tolkien doesn't win, right? But it doesn't work; he always wins. And the academy still seems to have this idea that if it's popular, it must not be good literature. Ok, who has had more of an impact on more minds, Joyce or Tolkien? Who has been read more? Now, if I ask you who's been studied more, that would fall down differently, but if I'm walking through the mall, and I'm just asking people, who has read Joyce or who has read Tolkien? The answer is obvious. So I would like to see more undergraduate and graduate study of these authors.

Joe Ricke: I often think this about the way I studied Victorian poetry in grad school. We never studied Elizabeth Barrett Browning, even though she was the most popular poet of the Victorian Age. But she wasn't critically accepted, especially later, in the way that her husband was or in the way that Matthew Arnold was. And how many people read Elizabeth Barrett Browning versus Matthew Arnold? It's a huge gulf between them, and she wins. And so the same thing applies, and it's not just to Inklings. Diana, would you like to take a stab at this?

Diana Glyer: I would love to. I think there's several topics that I'm really excited about in terms of Inklings studies. I am excited to see more on Lewis's family. I think it is great that Don King is working on a biography of Warren Lewis.[7] I hope that my work on Warren Lewis, especially on the later part of his life will perhaps help us to understand and maybe even rehabilitate our understanding of that man. I'm excited about Crystal Hurd's work on Lewis's parents.[8] I think Flora Lewis needs a lot more attention, I think we need to understand her. She was an outstanding individual. Another topic that I think needs more attention is this whole issue of women and C.S. Lewis in its broadest sense. Now there's a collection that came out recently, as many of you know, and many of you contributed to that. I think that it's good, but I think that it's a bit piecemeal. I think that we are really ready, really poised, to have extended, sophisticated, and thoughtful looks at this issue. It's time.

A third topic, that's come up in a lot of conversations here, is that we are ready for some really in depth analysis of Lewis's individual works, and I'm really grateful for that discussion. Honestly, I would point to the setting of the C.S. Lewis stone in Poet's Corner at Westminster Abbey as a kind of watershed moment for the possibility of treating Lewis's work much more seriously than we ever have before. I think that we are there. If there's ever something that gives us an invitation to look at his works more critically, in the very best sense of that word, it was that moment.[9]

---

7   Don King is a professor of English at Montreat College and a prolific Inklings scholar and author. He has written books about and edited the poetry of C. S. Lewis, Joy Davidman, and Ruth Pitter.

8   See her essay in this collection, "Patriarchy and P'daita Bird: The Artistic Influence of Albert Lewis."

9   On 22 November 1963, the fiftieth anniversary of his death, C. S.

So I think those are some of the topics that I would like us to address as a community. I also think that there are some larger issues. So, if I could rabble-rouse a little bit, there are two things that I'm very concerned about relating to how we conduct ourselves as scholars. One thing that I think we have to admit is that the publishing industry is broken. It is very, very difficult, increasingly difficult, for us to do the work that we do, and to get it out, and to make it available without incredible difficulty in working with publishers. I think that we are poised to come up with some more creative ways of making our work available, and I would like to propose that perhaps we can be alert to opportunities to create micro-publishers who would be very happy to publish small numbers of significant works, so that we can create the scholarship that we need to go forward, but without having to meet the demands of the numbers of volumes that are required for these things to become viable from a publisher's point of view. I'm very concerned about how the work that we do here gets out and becomes more widely available, and I want to see us be much more inventive.

The other way I'd like us to be much more inventive is in how we collaborate. Now, it won't surprise you to know that I'm very interested in creative collaboration. I've been coming to academic conferences for a very long time. This is the first one that I've ever attended that had on its first day the opportunity for authors to get together in a round table setting and simply talk about what we're working on, in a large public setting. And even in a session like this, I mean. look who's here! Am I the only one who looks around and says, "Ah! It's my bookshelf come to life!" Can we find new ways of doing a better job, and supporting each other in what we do? Even just simply informing each other—"Oh, did you know that so-and-so has an interest in that?" or "did you hear the paper that was given at Kalamazoo?" "No! I wasn't able to be there." How can we do a better job of encouraging one another, resourcing one another, challenging one another to stay the course, because this work we do is hard and lonely sometimes. How can we do a better job of challenging one another, in the very best sense of bringing out the very best work from one another? Simply by making our papers and our presentations, and even our drafts available before they go to print, and really having each other's back in terms of our creative collaboration.

Joe Ricke: Thanks Diana. We're going to open it up to questions now.

Lewis was honored with a memorial in Westminster Abbey's famous Poets Corner.

But first, just one more thing. I'm going to give a shout out to some people here. Sørina has her *Oddest Inkling* blog, and Brenton blogs at *A Pilgrim in Narnia*. I'm always seeing new things that people are working on, the kind of things that Diana is talking about, in places like that. William O'Flaherty over there hosts the *Essential C.S. Lewis* as well as the *All about Jack* podcasts. This is just a tip of the iceberg, and just from people in this room. So we are seeing some of the work that people are doing in progress, sometimes in very early, even embryonic form. And they're just sharing it, hoping someone is out there reading it. So, that's helpful, and I want to thank those people who are already doing this important work. Now you all need to find their blogs, like them, share them, and so forth. And maybe something more. OK. Questions?

Brenton Dickieson: Yes. My question arises from what you just said and what Diana just said. Sørina, you have an excellent blog on Charles Williams. Recently, you've been featuring guest posts, from a variety of scholars, reading and writing through Williams. I was wondering if you could comment on the blog and other online tools as a forum for the exchange of scholarship and for entry to the marketplace of ideas or community of scholars. Maybe we need a Facebook of Inklings scholars, or something like that?

Sørina Higgins: Thank you for that excellent question. Well, I'll start with the more negative side and move to the more positive. The negative is that the online world is still very fragmented. I'm still really surprised to find out, you know, how many other people are working on Charles Williams who don't know about my blog. And I don't know about their stuff. That's really discouraging, especially when we should all just be able to Google each other and just find it. Right? And maybe that's partly generational or technological; maybe some people aren't as comfortable moving around the internet and finding the different areas. I'm not sure how to unify all of that, because everybody has a favorite platform.. So share your ideas. Let us know your ideas on how we can, not centralize, but network all of these things.

Charlie Starr: Diana, following up about what you said about a new kind of publishing, I just want to give props to Bob Trexler and Winged Lion Press, for the kind of work he is doing.

Joe Ricke: Yes. Bob just published a very good book on David Neuhouser. I don't know if anyone's seen that yet [laughter].[10] Oh! And a book by Charlie

---

10   The Winged Lion Press publication, *Exploring the Eternal Goodness: Selected Writings of David L. Neuhouser*, was distributed to all colloquium participants. Neuhouser founded the Lewis Center at Taylor and started the colloquium in 1997. Winged Lion Press also published Charlie Starr's *Light: C. S. Lewis First and Final*

Starr. Paul Michelson?

Paul Michelson: More a comment than a question. Following on what Sørina said, Diana mentioned that the publishing industry is broken. Well, so is academia. People are coming up for tenure, and they have to fight to even get recognition, especially in the humanities work. Some of it is very substantial, talking about geographical gazetteers, and stuff like that. The difference is, it's volumnized in book form. People have to fight to get any recognition for serious academic work. I don't know any solutions for that, other than just supporting people who are doing these things. But that's another problem we have.

Marsha Daigle-Williamson: I have a question for Diana. When you say that you were working on the Inklings and Dante, are you working on one chapter for each Inkling and Dante, or what? What is the organizational principle?

Diana Glyer: My work on Dante is inspired by the Inklings, but it's really not about the Inklings. It's really about Dante, and really comes out of my life. I fell in love with Dante, in a really, really, big way more than twenty years ago. And it's a book that I study and read at least once every year, and have for those two decades. And when I share my passion for Dante, its often the case that people surprisingly do not share my love for this book. So I want to try to rehabilitate Dante by writing a book that will invite people to enjoy it as much as I do. So that's my goal in writing that. I think that Dante is incredibly relevant and powerful, but I think that it he can also be obscure. So my approach is to take spiritual formation reading of Dante. Sort of Richard Foster meets literary criticism is the kind of the approach that I am taking in that particular book.[11]

Joe Ricke: That's interesting in light of Robert Moore-Jumonville's presentation this morning on C.S. Lewis and the problem of prayer, but from a spiritual formation perspective. And that leads me to saying something about generalism. Some of us heard a great paper

---

Short Story (an edition and interpretation of a Lewis manuscript in the Brown Collection at Taylor) and a number of other books on the Lewis and related authors.

11 Richard Foster is a theologian and spiritual writer in the Quaker tradition whose most well-known book is *Celebration of Discipline: The Path to Spiritual Growth* (1978).

on Thursday, in praise of David Neuhouser, C. S. Lewis, Wendell Berry, and other generalists. It was written by Chris Smith, the editor of *The Englewood Review of Books*, and it was all about the joys and the benefits (and importance for our time) of being a generalist. Of course, "generalist" is kind of difficult to define, but he went into all that. The fact is that Dave Neuhouser was a math professor, but we wouldn't be here without him. And my good friend Chris Armstrong over there is a church historian, who specialized in the nineteenth-century American church. And now he runs a work project at Wheaton College, a vocation think tank of sorts. But he wrote a book addressed to evangelicals, like himself, who maybe need to learn something from the Middle Ages. And his way of doing it—this may seem, a bit cynical, I don't know—his way of doing it, was to approach it through C.S. Lewis. So the book is basically about reading medieval wisdom through the eyes of C.S. Lewis. And I thought, that's the same sort of thing that Diana is talking about. And it's the same sort of thing that Dave Neuhouser did. And it's what Robert was doing this morning. So, that's another area, a broader cultural area, we can kind of be working in. Jennifer?

Jennifer Woodruff-Tait: I was going to pick up on that, actually, I'm the managing editor of *Christian History* magazine, and we did an issue on the seven authors of the Wade Center, using material from the Wade Center, with lists of print and online resources. So that, if you've never read this author before, you could start by looking at websites, all tied together with a time line of connections between the authors. So, if you're interested in something of that kind, that issue pulls this whole world together.

Joe Ricke: Yes. If you haven't seen that issue, it is a great starter. We've given away well over a hundred issues of that this year. The rest of you should consider doing the same. By the way, Jennifer, how many people in this room wrote for that particular issue?

Jennifer: You know, I think that almost everyone who wrote in it or was interviewed for it is in this room. [laughter]

Joe Ricke: So, there you go. I know Colin wrote for it. Edwin wrote for it.[12] Chris wrote for it. Chris Armstrong, here, by the way is the senior

---

12   Edwin Woodruff-Tait, church historian of the early reformation period, a free-lance writer, and a consulting editor for *Christian History*.

editor of *Christian History*, the magazine Jennifer just mentioned.

Chris Armstrong: She does the work.

Jennifer: He has the ideas. And I do the work.

Joe Ricke: Devin?

Devin Brown: I've had the privilege, and many of you have too, of having Colin come into my classroom at the end of each semester through the bonus features of the *Lord of the Rings* and *Narnia* films. And that's another way of getting our scholarship out there. I mean we've talked about the print way and the online way, but what about the video way? I'm just curious, what kind of impact has that had? Because those are great resources. These people had money and were able to pay very well, and were able to feature the very best of scholarship there. And as I said, our students can come into the classroom and see it and hear it. That's another way of bringing Inklings to the world. The bonus material and documentaries that go with it. That's scholarship, just in a different format.

Diana Glyer: Speaking of technology, I want to add in the idea of Skyping into each other's classrooms. And I've had some fantastic opportunities to be present, via technology, talking with students in various settings. So you think about making these connections. What you're seeing right here is an exciting example of the opportunity we have to do better collaboration.[13]

Colin Duriez: Yes, yes. I'm trying to remember how I got into that, because I've done a number of those kinds of interviews, for the BBC for example, and they've often asked me to talk about Lewis or Tolkien. In the case of the *Lord of the Rings* DVDs, they had asked Brian Sibley to do the interviewing. He's a friend of mine, and he knows my work. And so I went to this posh hotel in London and nearly met Christopher Lee, but not quite. He was on a break, so I missed him, unfortunately. I also had to opportunity to be a part of another project; it was the BBC documentary on Freud and C.S. Lewis, *The Question of God*.[14]

---

13   Diana Glyer was referring to the fact that Carol Zaleski was able to be part of the panel discussion from a distance by video and audio technology.
14   The film *Question of God* was actually a PBS production (see works cited).

That was a highly professional film. The people who put that together sent me a whole load of questions to think about so that I could be prepared. When I did the film, we were in the Kilns. And it was the same with the film of *The Lion, the Witch and the Wardrobe*. That was filmed at the Kilns and at C.S. Lewis's home church in Headington. And to me, that was wonderful to do. But, in terms of "paying very well," in none of the cases did I get any payment. Except from the BBC; they paid me. Well, New Lion Cinema did give me a thank you, thanking me for my part in *The Lord of the Rings*. Maybe that's worth something. Anyway, the point is that this is a platform to use. And I think it was well worth doing, because sometimes people looking on a bookshelf will say "I've seen you somewhere!"

Joe Ricke: Unfortunately, we are out of time. I just want to say thank you to everyone, but we have to say goodbye for this session. Please join me in thanking our panelists one more time. [applause]

Roundtable discussion: Joe Ricke (moderator), Diana Gyler, Colin Duriez, and Sorina Higgins

Works Cited

Armstrong, Chris R. *Medieval Wisdom for Modern Christians: Finding Authentic Faith in a Forgotten Age with C.S. Lewis.* Grand Rapids: Brazos Press, 2016. Print.

Carpenter, Humphrey. *The Inklings: C.S. Lewis, J.R.R. Tolkien, Charles Williams and Their Friends.* London: Allen and Unwin, 1978. Print.

Como, James T., ed.. *C.S. Lewis at the Breakfast Table.* New York: Macmillan, 1979. Print.

Curtis, Carolyn and Mary Pomroy Key, eds. *Women and C.S. Lewis.* Oxford: Lion Hudson, 2015. Print.

Daigle-Williamson, Marsha. *Reflecting the Eternal: Dante's Divine Comedy in the Novels of C.S. Lewis.* Peabody: Hendrickson, 2015. Print.

Dickieson, Brenton, ed. *A Pilgrim in Narnia.* Blog. Web. < https://apilgriminnarnia.com/ >

Duriez, Colin. *The Oxford Inklings: Lewis, Tolkien, and Their Circle.* Oxford: Lion Hudson, 2015. Print.

Glyer, Diana. *Bandersnatch: C.S. Lewis, J.R.R. Tolkien, and the Creative Collaboration of the Inklings.* Kent: Kent State UP, 2016. Print.

Harwood, Lawrence. *C.S. Lewis, My Godfather: Letters, Photos, and Recollections.* Downer's Grove: IVP, 2007. Print.

Hermerén, Göran. *Influence in Art.* Princeton: Princeton UP, 1975. Print.

Higgins, Sørina, ed. *The Oddest Inkling.* Blog. Web. < https://theoddestinkling.wordpress.com/ >

Lewis, C.S., ed. *Essays Presented to Charles Williams.* London: Oxford UP, 1947. Print.

---. *Surprised By Joy.* London: Geoffrey Bles, 1955. Print.

Lindop, Grevel. *Charles Williams: The Third Inkling.* Oxford: Oxford UP, 2015. Print.

Neuhouser, David L. *Exploring the Eternal Goodness: Selected Writings of David L. Neuhouser.* Hamden: Winged Lion Press, 2016. Print. C. S. Lewis and Friends Series.

O' Flaherty, William, ed. *All About Jack*. Podcasts.Web. < http://allaboutjack.podbean.com/ >

---.*Essential C.S. Lewis*. Blog. Web. < http://www.essentialcslewis.com/ >

The Question of God. Dir. Catherine Tatge. PBS. 2004. Film.

Rowling, J.K. *Harry Potter* (series). London: Bloomsbury, 1997-2007. Print.

Rowell, Rainbow. *Fangirl*. New York: St. Martin's Griffin, 2013. Print.

Smith, Chris, ed. *The Englewood Review of Books*. Web. < http://englewoodreview.org/>

Starr, Charlie. *Light: C. S. Lewis's First and Final Short Story*. Hamden: Winged Lion, 2012. Print. C. S. Lewis and Friends Series.

Thorson, Stephen. *Joy and the Poetic Imagination: Understanding C.S. Lewis's "Great War" with Owen Barfield and its Significance for Lewis's Conversion and Writings*. Hamden: Winged Lion Press, 2015. Print.

Ward, Michael. *Planet Narnia: The Seven Heavens in the Imagination of C.S. Lewis*. Oxford: Oxford UP, 2008. Print.

Williams, Charles. *The Chapel of the Thorn*. Ed. Sørina Higgins. Berkeley: Apocryphile Press, 2015. Print.

"The Vision of an Empire." *Taliessin Through Logres*. London: Oxford UP, 1933. Print.

Woodruft-Tait, Jennifer, ed. *Seven Literary Sages: Why We Still Need Their Wisdom Today*. Special issue of Christian History. 113 (2015). Print.

Zaleski, Carol and Phil Zaleski. *The Fellowship: The Literary Lives of the Inklings: J.R.R. Tolkien, C.S. Lewis, Owen Barfield, and Charles Williams*. New York: Farrar, Straus, Giroux, 2015. Print.

Eighth Day Books and other vendors featured books written by the plenary speakers and author attendees

V. Essays on Charles Williams

Native Language in a Strange Country: Death and Rebirth in the Friendship of C.S. Lewis and Charles Williams

by Jennifer Raimundo

Jennifer Raimundo has been an Inklings enthusiast for the better part of her life. She is now pursuing an M.A. in Language and Literature at Signum University. She also serves as Institutional Planning Lead at the University.

A book sometimes crosses one's path which is so like the sounds of one's native language in a strange country that it feels almost uncivil not to wave some kind of flag in answer. I have just read your Place of the Lion *and it is to me one of the major literary events of my life—comparable to my first discovery of George MacDonald, G.K. Chesterton, or Wm. Morris.*

—C.S. Lewis, Letter to Charles Williams

That was *The Meeting*. It happened in the Spring of 1936, and it began a most odd but fruitful friendship between two great literary minds: C.S. Lewis and Charles Williams. Although Lewis originally reached out to Williams as to a fellow countryman in foreign lands, their earliest exchange of letters quickly shows at least Lewis that, if Williams and Lewis are from the same country — that place called Romance, they are definitely not from the same province. Williams from the beginning is conceptually lavish where Lewis tends to be most comfortable and homely. But they still remain friends, and very mutually edifying friends. How did this friendship last? Lewis, I believe, answers that question before the friendship even got well on its way. While scrambling for common ground after discovering Williams's very different view of Romantic Theology (whatever that was), Lewis writes: "[W]e touch here: the death and re-birth motive being of the very essence of my kind of romanticism" (*Collected Letters*).

"His kind of romanticism?" What is Lewis talking about? In the letter-writing that flurried over the next few weeks between Lewis and Williams, we find that Lewis was deeply convicted by the heroine of *The Place of the Lion*, Damaris, who, along with her "man," Anthony, undergoes a spiritual transformation through a death by humility to the rebirth of true selfhood and joy. That sounds pretty Lewis, doesn't it? On the other hand, Williams, probably ecstatic after reading certain passages of *The Allegory of Love*, writes Lewis about Romantic Theology—a death and rebirth to be sure, but of a very different kind than the one Lewis loved in *The Place of the Lion*. What we find, then, is that two potential friends have written about the other person's kind of romantic death and rebirth. Basically, their friendship was based on a mistake. But it is a mistake that kept them together, because instead of finding the mirror of themselves like they were expecting, they found in each other iron minds that would sharpen their spiritual and literary lives. Better understanding what romantic death and rebirth was to each friend will help us better understand how it kept the friendship alive. To start, we shall take a quick jaunt through death and rebirth in each of these men's lives just before *The Meeting* happened.

DEATH AND RE-BIRTH BEFORE *THE MEETING*

We begin with Williams and his "Beatrician experience." This experience is fundamental to Williams as a human and to his literature as a theology. It is part of his larger Romantic Theology which he had been developing for some time before meeting Lewis. In essence, it says that the erotic experience of falling in love is a manifestation of divine love, God's love, on earth, within the little "church" of the union. It is based on Dante's vision of Beatrice, which brought his understanding of love closer to God's. Williams's Beatrician experience goes hand in hand with his theology of incarnation and substitutionary love. Christ's incarnation is the defining moment and happening of the Christian life, and so the Christian life is itself an incarnation of Christ. These two ideas do not sound so very unorthodox when stated as such, but put them together and you get Williams's Romantic Theology: the erotic relationship of a man with a woman is an incarnation of God's love and is glorious with all the glory of Christ. In this context, the death and rebirth element is embodied both in the intellectual surrender and recreation of two lovers with each other and in the sexual act itself. Prior to reading *The Allegory of Love*, Williams had begun to write on this subject, both in poetry (his *Poems of Conformity*) and prose (his *Outlines of Romantic Theology*). These are, in fact, the two works that Williams suggested Lewis read in his first letter to Lewis because Romantic Theology is the idea that first got Williams excited about Lewis. Surprised?

But what about Lewis's death and rebirth before *The Meeting*? Unlike Williams, Lewis had developed no formal theology regarding death and rebirth apart from his own experience of conversion and his ongoing, run of the mill, experience of sanctification in daily life. The latter is well-expressed in a letter from Lewis to Dom Bede Griffiths, written just before his first letter to Williams: "[E]very return to ones own situation involves action: or to speak more plainly, obedience. That appears to me more and more the whole business of life, the only road to love and peace—the cross and crown in one" (*Collected Letters*).

There it is—death and rebirth: the only road to love and peace is obedience, the cross and crown in one. The obvious explication of death and rebirth in Lewis's conversion story, though, is *The Pilgrim's Regress*. There we find John undergoing many little deaths—his abandonment of the brown girls, the *Zeitgeist*, less interested companions, fear of killing the dragon, false doctrines—in order, finally, to encounter redemption, real life, in his encounter of Christ and beholding of the real Island. Of course, now that he has found the source of true Joy, the island does not matter so much anymore. Lewis finds the death of himself and his seekings in the life of Christ, and he finds that it brings him back to life. Should we be surprised that *The Pilgrim's Regress* is the work Lewis first suggests to Williams as the expression of his view of romantic death and rebirth? Not at all.

So, here we have Williams, steeped in the development of his Romantic theology, on one hand, and Lewis, a man swept up in the recent discovery of Christ's satisfaction of all his deepest longings, on the other. They have each unconsciously written to the other person's romanticism and have each just stumbled across just the right sample writing to spark a friendship. With this in hand, we are now ready to plunge into *The Meeting* itself.

THE MEETING (PART ONE): DEATH AND REBIRTH AS SURRENDER AND JOY IN *THE PLACE OF THE LION*

I will start with *The Meeting* (Part One), which is Lewis discovering his own peculiar sense of romantic death and rebirth in *The Place of the Lion*. What are the elements of death and rebirth that, considering who Lewis was, attracted him so strongly to *The Place of the Lion*? A few examples drawn from the story of Damaris and Anthony will prove sufficient to answer these questions.

Actually, the entire book is a timeline of the death of Anthony into his new life as the one who exerts his human dominion over the archetypes governing creation and therefore as the Second Adam who names the animals. To come into this new life, he must first undergo self-surrender. The book describes his struggle: "Was he really proposing to govern the principles of creation? . . . It was hopeless, it was insane, and yet the attempt had to be made" (*The Place of the Lion*). Anthony knows he may well die, but it doesn't matter because in a sense he knows he's already begun his death process anyway. The surrendering is even more explicit when he takes on the form of the Eagle for the first time. His life flashes before his eyes like a man about to die—all the good and all the bad he's done—and as he gives himself to this momentary journey of self-knowledge and overpowering, he finds his real identity and new life: "[W]ith an inrush of surpassing happiness he knew that he was himself offering himself to the state he had so long desired" (*The Place of the Lion*).

Anthony then goes on to become the superhero of the book, Damaris, and majestically names the animals, carrying his personal redemption into the redemption of creation in general—just like man ought to have done from the beginning. Here we have a taste of that death and rebirth which had moved Lewis so greatly in his own conversion experience and would continue to move him for the remainder of his life. But Anthony's story is just the beginning. Even more clearly do we see death and rebirth in the character of Damaris, with whom Lewis tells Williams he identifies perfectly. After all, Damaris is a rather stuck-up, self-centered intellectual prig. She has devoted her life to studying the Neo-Platonists and Abelard and angels without ever once thinking that they and their ideas actually had an impact on real life, and especially her own life. Anthony's reprimand of Damaris for her way of thinking is the beginning of her death:

> "O I know such things must be . . . man must use his mind. But you've done more than use it, you've loved it for your own. You've loved it and you've lost it. And pray God you've lost it before it was too late, before it decayed in you and sent up that stink which you smelt, or before the knowledge of life turned to the knowledge of death. Somewhere in you there was something that loved truth, and if ever you studied anything you'd better study that now. For perhaps you won't get another chance." (*The Place of the Lion*)

Can you not see Lewis writhing and sympathizing and cheering as he reads this? The humility, the obedience, the cross that Lewis was just writing to Dom Bede Griffiths about comes alive in this passage. And the crown is soon to follow, for after Damaris sees Quentin's at long-last restful face filled with "beauty of innocence" and realizes that the lamb must take the place of the lion, she undergoes her own inner struggle where all her old selfishness rages against her new spirit of service that wants to discover the "thing" Anthony had already discovered. In pursuit of that thing, she resolves:

> to be savage with herself. . . . A fierce conquest, an innocent obedience—these were to be her signs. . . . The sound of her name still echoed through her spirit when, recovered from her inner struggle, she looked again upon the glade of the garden where the image of Adam named the beasts, and naming ruled them.

After her struggle, after her death, after the surrender of all the rights she once thought hers, and in the midst of the Adamic redemption of creation, Damaris hears her name and is alive again. She joins Anthony in a symbolic rebirth of the world.

This strongly echoes Lewis's recount in *The Pilgrim's Regress*. It also appeals to his natural love of nature and the way its own story reflects the larger redemptive narrative. There is hardly anything in *The Place of the Lion* that Lewis would not like, and it is little surprise that he should jump at the opportunity to write to the book's author. After all, the novel is a romantic expression of death and rebirth.

THE MEETING (PART TWO): ROMANTIC THEOLOGY IN *THE ALLEGORY OF LOVE*

But the enthusiastic letter exchange goes on, and in his reply to Lewis, Williams completely overlooks Lewis's joyous exclamations over Damaris's death of humility and surrender into her new life of joy and selfhood. Instead, Williams plunges into an equally enthusiastic description of his Romantic Theology as he sees it in *The Allegory of Love*. This is Part Two of The Meeting. What is it that Williams saw in *The Allegory of Love* that made him so sure Lewis would agree with his very carnal interpretation of the Incarnation in erotic love? What is the death and rebirth motive in *The Allegory of Love* that made Williams feel like he had found a kindred spirit?

One read of *The Allegory of Love* shows that Williams was justified in his assumption that he and Lewis shared his Romantic Theology. When speaking of Andreas, Lewis writes that the aim of love is fruition inspired by visible beauty, even though true love is not sensuality but rather a "'kind of chastity' in virtue of its severe standard fidelity to a single object" (*The Allegory of Love*). He talks about the "reduplication of experience" and "proportion sum" of divine love to secular love: "*cordis affectio* is to the acts of love as charity is to good works" (*The Allegory of Love*). Can you hear Williams's squeals of delight?

But that is just the beginning. When Lewis moves into Chaucer, he pauses to marvel at "how Chaucer can so triumphantly celebrate the flesh" without becoming delirious or pornographic. Chaucer's secret, says Lewis, lies in his concreteness:

> Lust is more abstract than logic: it seeks . . . for some purely sexual, hence purely imaginary, conjunction of an impossible maleness with an impossible femaleness... But with Chaucer we are rooted in the purifying complexities of the real world. Behind the lovers—who are people, 'rational substances,' as well as lovers—lies the whole history of their love. . . . (*The Allegory of Love*)

Therefore, Lewis claims that Chaucer brought what was once adulterous romance into modern marital romance; that he began to reconcile the conflict between Carbonek and Camelot. That imagery comes straight from Lewis. Thus we have Williams, a grail-seeker, Arthurian fanboy, and founder of Romantic Theology, reading the basics of Romantic Theology in Lewis's Arthurian allusions! Dare we guess that he was excited?

And then Lewis launches into Thomas Usk, saying that Usk uses courtly love as a symbol of divine love, but not in a such a way that courtly love in itself is disregarded. Indeed, one could argue that Lewis's whole thesis in *The Allegory of Love* is that allegory allowed the thing signified (divine love) to at last happily coexist with the signifier (erotic love) in marriage. In Lewis's own words from this passage: "It is a mischievous error to suppose that in an allegory the author is 'really' talking about the thing symbolized, and not at all about the thing that symbolizes; the very essence of art is to talk about both" (*Allegory*). When applied to the realm of romantic love, which is exactly what Lewis does here, this passage could be taken as the banner of Williams's Romantic Theology, the combination of the Beatrician experience and the Incarnation among Christians.

Speaking of the Beatrician experience and the Incarnation, Lewis throughout *The Allegory of Love* obliquely references the fact that of the few medieval poets who attempted to reconcile heavenly and earthy love the only one who succeeded was Dante, the poet who inspired Williams's whole idea of the Beatrician experience in the first place. Beside this touchpoint there is the closing chapter of Lewis's work, the chapter on *The Fairie Queen*. Lewis concentrates on the contrast Spenser makes between the Bower of Bliss and the Garden of Adonis—one being full of pleasure presented through metal and artifice, the other full of pleasure presented through leaves, flowers, fruit, in the flesh. Lewis on Spenser states that pleasure is not bad but that real pleasure is presented in real life on earth: "Like a true Platonist [Spenser] shows us the Form of the virtue he is studying not only in its transcendental unity (which comes at the allegorical core of the book) but also 'becoming Many in the world of phenomena'" (*Allegory*).

In the context of love, this sounds like the Incarnational element of Romantic Theology. And, of course, the death and rebirth of the gods is exactly where Lewis started his *Allegory*. Allegory at all and the allegory of love in particular was made possible through the dying of the ancient gods into symbols, so that the inner life of humans could be examined through the new allegory that was being born. As Lewis says:

> [If the old marvelous is not so stored up but is allowed to perish], then the imagination is impoverished. Such a sleeping-place was provided for the gods by allegory. Allegory may seem, at first, to have killed them; but it killed only as the sower kills, for gods, like other creatures, must die to live. (*Allegory*)

So there we have it, straight from Lewis's pen: Medieval love-lore to modern times has been a history of divine love being reconciled to human love through a series of allegories that involved the death of the gods to be reborn into a new, Christian psychomachia. Of course, this death and rebirth extends beyond erotic love and into the realms of Poesie and Myth themselves. Williams, the developer of Romantic Theology, has just met the consummate romantic, Lewis.

THE MISTAKE

Still, it was a mistake. We have only gotten through the first exchange of letters. After this first meeting, Williams and Lewis, good literary men as they are, send each other supporting material. Williams suggests a specific number of poems from his *Poems of Conformity* to Lewis so that Lewis would better understand Romantic Theology. Lewis reads the whole collection and gives a very honest opinion of the ones containing explicit Romantic Theology. Here is a stanza from Williams's "Orthodoxy," a poem of which Lewis blatantly states he "definitely disliked":

> Now to thy heart the hand hath caught
> The fingers of mine own,
> Thy body's secret doctrines now
> Are felt and proved and known:
> More wisdom on thy breast I learn
> Than else upon my knees:
> O hark, thine honor! orthodox!
> Destroyer of heresies! (47)

And here is a sample from "Churches," a poem that also got a "didn't like" from Lewis:

> What End that is, and what the way,
> What evils upon wanderers prey;
> What Love indeed doth us inspire,
> What doth our shrinking bodies fire
> Till half a sacrifice and half
> A triumph, all a sobbing laugh
> Teaches how sacrifice may be
> Its own exceeding ecstasy... (69)

Again, Lewis didn't like this. At all. So much for death and rebirth in Romantic Theology. As a side note, Lewis did mention a few poems from the collection that he enjoyed. Not surprisingly, they each reflect a different aspect of humility in the soul's quest for true happiness. Lewis was, indeed, a consistent man. In response, Lewis recommends that Williams read Lewis's version of romantic death and rebirth in *The Pilgrim's Regress*. But he leaves no room for error. *The Pilgrim's Regress*, Lewis insists, is not about the death of sexual appetite or even surrender to God-given pleasures but about the death of every desire in light of the satisfaction God offers in Himself, and about how that new life informs and allows the believer to properly enjoy everything else. Lewis brings death and rebirth away from Romantic Theology and back to *The Place of the Lion*.

And there the burst of letters dies out, for our two friends finally meet in person to begin nine years of excellent, ardent friendship.

The Difference

So, here we have Lewis and Williams, natives in a strange country albeit from different provinces. Did these different provinces affect their work, even years into the friendship? Of course. In fact, I would say their different provinces of the Country called Romanticism are as different as *The Four Loves* is from *Taliessin through Logres*. One is analytical, direct, prescriptive, and told. The other is poetic, symbolized, suggestive, and shown. And the differences are more than stylistic. *The Four Loves* and *Taliessin through Logres* are both about Love gone right versus Love gone wrong, but Lewis's version has love submitted to, changed by, filled with, and sometimes stopped by God's love: agape. For Lewis, human love transformed and upheld by divine love is possible, and *The Four Loves* helps readers get to a place where that ideal can become reality. Death and rebirth here covers all categories via a redemptive process. *Taliessin*, on the other hand, frightens us with the terrors of perverted love through dark imagery and failure while inspiring us with the glory of Christ's love incarnate through sea, song, and stars. Williams leaves his readers wincing and reeling, stunned with beauty and perhaps not always quite sure what to do with it. Death and rebirth simply are; some lovers get it, others do not.

But I believe the differences in the death and rebirth motive between Lewis and Williams are their strengths, both as authors and as friends. Like Lewis, readers keep going back to Williams for the shock of expression and therefore conviction. Like Williams, readers keep going back to Lewis for clarity of thought and growth. Thus their friendship was maintained. Lewis never outgrew his ability to upbraid Williams for his at times unintelligible poetry and literary swagger. Williams never outgrew his ability to inspire Lewis with the disinterested sort of love that Lewis always strove to attain. They chiseled at each other in all the right ways, so that, in a sense, their friendship, founded on death and rebirth, was an example of that death and rebirth. They each killed little parts of each other and came out the better for it.

The End

The Meeting happened in 1936. Williams died in 1945. Through the staff work of Omnipotence, Lewis wrote a letter to Dom Bede Griffiths on the day Williams was taken ill. The letter was about the New Creation: "I too have been v. much occupied by the idea of the New Creation. ... In the light of the New Creation all miracles are like *snowdrops*—anticipations of the full spring and high summer wh. is slowly coming over the whole wintry field of space & time" (*Collected Letters*).

Five days later Charles Williams died. But, like New Creation and life following death, Lewis's faith was made strong. Speaking of Williams's death to his friend Owen Barfield, Lewis writes: "It has been a very *odd* experience. This, the first really severe loss I have suffered has given corroboration to my belief in immortality such as I never dreamed of.... 'Local unique sting' alright . . . and yet . . . a sort of brightness and tingling" (*Collected Letters*).

It was an end. But it was also a beginning.

Works Cited

Lewis, Clive Staples. *The Allegory of Love*. 1936. New York: HarperCollins, 2013. iBooks.

C.S. Lewis: Collected Letters. 2004. Ed. Walter Hooper. Vo. 2. New York: HarperCollins 2009. iBooks.

Williams, Charles. *The Place of the Lion*. 1933. gutenberg.net.au. *Project Gutenberg*. BarryHarworth, 2006. Web. 20 May 2016.

Poems of Conformity. London: Oxford University Press, 1917. Print.

Friendship in *The Place of the Lion*

by Dan Hamilton

> Dan Hamilton, an engineer and writer, has edited a dozen George MacDonald novels. His books include *Forgiveness, The Forgotten God trilogy, Should I Home School?* and *Look Both Ways*. He co-authored Dr. Ed Brown's *In Pursuit of C. S. Lewis*. Dan participated in the purchase and preservation of The Kilns, and he co-founded the C. S. Lewis and Friends Society at Taylor University and the Central Indiana C. S. Lewis Society in Indianapolis.

I must warn you that you are in the hands of an engineer, one of those people who like to take things apart and see how they work. That's what I did last year for our Lewis Society in Indianapolis. I took apart *The Place of the Lion* to see what's happening in it and how and why.

I picked *The Lion* because it's one of the Inklings books on which I have fielded the most questions over the years–usually some variation on "I *liked* that book–but I didn't *understand* it. What's it about, anyway?" In this essay, I have three goals: I want to celebrate *Place of the Lion* in the context of friendship; I want to inspire reading or re-reading the book; and I want to give the reader some tools for enjoying it more thoroughly.

This book is *about* friends, but it also *started* a notable friendship when two strangers, C. S. Lewis and Charles Williams, wrote to each other a day apart. This mutual outburst of praise led to the immediate and deep friendship between the two that lasted until Williams' death in 1945, and profoundly affected Lewis, both personally and as a writer.[1]

The best fiction starts with one simple premise: *What if?* In this case, it involves exploring the results IF something like Plato's archetypes or medieval angelic realities suddenly "broke through" from another plane of reality into our world. What would they do? What would they do to us? Would they be dangerous? What would we do in reaction to them?

In the novel, Smetham, a little town in England (just north of London) is suddenly confronted with the true Lion, the true Butterfly,

---

1 These letters are reprinted on pages 183-187 of *The Collected Letters of C. S. Lewis* (Volume II).

the true Serpent, the true Eagle, and other true archetypes. These archetypes are a dire threat to our world not because they are evil, but because by their very nature they attract and absorb everything that is like them, everything that is one of their pale shadows—as the light of a candle is swallowed up by the blaze of the noonday sun. Earth will be a barren, empty, lifeless place roamed by the archetypes unless someone can intervene.

Williams is deliberately vague about details. It is certainly convenient for him that the medieval book from which the ancient information is drawn—the fictional *De Angelis* by Marcellus Victorinus of Bologna—is maddeningly incomplete. Williams hints at several ways to organize the nine archetypes, but does not fill in the charts we would like to have. In one sense, the archetypes are merely the mechanism of crisis by which the humans are exposed for what they are or what they choose to become. In another sense, they are deeply connected to the nature of the humans themselves.

One other barrier to following the narrative is the timeline of events. Many of the later chapters are not sequential, but loop back and actually happen simultaneously. But beyond the timeline, beyond the supernatural dazzle of the events, this book is a story of ordinary people—three friends, against a background of other people with varying motives, levels of perception, and fates. There are three main characters: Anthony Durrant, Quentin Sabot, and Damaris Tighe.

Anthony Durrant

Anthony is a clear-headed man who sees the truth (and the danger) and asks what he must do to see the situation put right. He is a magazine publisher, and he occasionally prints a piece by his cousin Damaris Tighe, whom he loves with a peculiar kind of affection, clarity, perception, and good will. He is patient and adaptable, drawn to truth, whenever, however, and wherever it is revealed to him. He is loyal to his friends; he is patient with Quentin's fears, and is unafraid to serve Damaris while being completely truthful with her and completely undeceived about her flaws. In one passage, he remarks that having an argument with her is like being mauled by a lioness. Only Anthony, by surrendering to the truth and wisdom of the Eagle, is able to control the other archetypes. He can ride the Horse, while the Unicorn will not carry Damaris but will only knock her aside in the road and let her follow. And in the end the Lion and the Lamb come to Anthony and obey his directions as he takes up the archetypal mantle of Adam in controlling an unruly/disordered Creation.

Quentin Sabot

Quentin is a solid friend of Anthony's, and his intellectual equal, but is in some key ways his opposite. The underlying emotion in Quentin's life is fear, the fruit of which is cowardice. He sees dangerous things clearly, but wants to run from any chance of contact with them. He doesn't really mature or learn anything in the course of the whole story. He is saved only because Damaris ultimately agrees that she should find him, because the Unicorn leads her to him, and because she clings to him and keeps them both in the inviolable shelter of the peaceable Lamb that appears in the field.

Damaris Tighe

Damaris is focused on one thing: Damaris, especially her anticipated success as a learned, published, and therefore respected academic with a doctoral degree. She wants only to be left alone to finish "her work," which ironically is all about the very kind of dangerous beings that are about to invade England. The problem is that she thinks these are all *ideas* held by imaginative but lesser-informed people of the distant and ignorant past, and cannot possibly be current *realities*. She is self-centered, though not incurably selfish. If she encounters something that doesn't interest her, she dismisses it as irrelevant and without value; she tolerates her father's quest for butterflies and beauty as a mere "hobby" at best and an unfortunate obsession at worst. Anthony infuriates her, because he is always right; he loves her with an open-eyed love and challenges her on her blind spots. He chooses to serve her, but he refuses to put her on a pedestal.

Damaris is very proud of her learning and her career. She values knowledge especially, but doesn't seem to recognize or care for wisdom. C.S. Lewis noted how the figure of Damaris resonated with him. He recognized himself, and probably more than a few of his colleagues, in her. As a side note, when Lewis wrote *That Hideous Strength* a decade later, he brought forward as a main character Jane Studdock, a young self-absorbed academic who has to be brought rather forcibly to face reality. Both women, at least in the beginning, are intelligent, scholarly, foolish, largely willfully ignorant about reality, and rather silly and shallow in their human and cosmic relationships.

Damaris's goal is getting her doctorate. Everything else that does not contribute to that result is definitely secondary—including her job, her relationships with family and friends, and her neighbors. Even her correspondence with a literary journal is weighed in terms of what influential people it might impress or offend. She uses everyone around her—for her own ends. She is rude and condescending to her father, who presumably is supporting her during her advanced studies. She mainly keeps Anthony around because he occasionally publishes her work and might do so again in the future. She uses Mr. Berringer's little society meeting as (she hopes) a platform to meeting and impressing someone useful to her publishing career. She rejects with disgust Quentin's initial appeal for help; she hardly knows Quentin, barely recognizing him as one of Anthony's friends. The novel suggests that if she truly cared about Anthony as a person, she would be more likely to know and care about his closest friends. She even apparently takes servants for granted; the only time we see an interaction there is when Damaris astonishes the maid by getting herself a sandwich without domestic help.

Of the three main characters, Damaris, knows *all* the relevant information and has the best chance to realize what is happening, but she is blind to it because she sees these archetypes as dead ideas and not actual realities. Her love for mere facts has insulated her from the truth.[2] She is rudely pulled into reality by the intrusion of the Eagle into her awareness. I believe she meets the Eagle as the Pterodactyl, because she is unprepared for Truth (as opposed to facts), unwilling to acknowledge it, and untrained to serve it.

Those who do not love the truth will find truth to be their enemy, and so it has worked out with Damaris. Immediately after Anthony

---

2   There is also irony in her isolation from everything but her thesis. If she had taken some interest in the people and doings in Smetham she might well have encountered Berringer, who was deeply interested in the same topic, though his approach was different—entirely practical and much closer to the truth. Richardson could also have helped her greatly in her studies. In this sense Williams is showing us friendship lost in the midst of a friendship perfected. Williams has also given us a glimpse of the antithesis of friendship. Foster and Miss Wilmot are a duo who form their alliance for purely selfish reasons. They both seek power (of different kinds, and for different reasons), and find the other somewhat useful to those ends. In the end they are separated, alone and lost, devoured and crushed by the archetypes they sought to control. Neither are saved, and perhaps (as Williams shows in his depiction of their beastly final moments) there is not much human left to save at the very end.

rescues her from the Pterodactyl / Eagle, he lectures her about the realities she has willfully ignored. So it could be said that Anthony does not directly save her from the Eagle, but only intervenes and then drives her to acknowledge the truth that sets her free and in proper relation to the Eagle again. It is only because she surrenders to Anthony's protection and leadership (and finally *listens* to his authoritative instruction and wisdom) that she finds herself humbled and ready and willing and enabled to search out and save Quentin (who is in no position to save himself). She had refused to help him at their first encounter, but now she goes meekly to make up for it, though she has no idea how it will turn out. Her "conversion" has been sudden and painful, but complete and lasting. And it is the only one we see in the book. All the other characters become, literally for good or for evil, just what they already were "but even more so."

This idea is also is in harmony with another aspect of Williams' Law of Co-Inherence, which holds that we cannot save ourselves, but can only (and must) save others. On the good side, Damaris is intelligent, and learned, and she displays integrity in her scholarship. She may be proud and arrogant and rude and self-centered, but she is exacting in her research and honest about where it leads her (as far as *facts* are concerned, anyway).

So how does this imperfect three-way friendship ripen, and blossom, and save the world? We have to start with Anthony, the center figure of the trio. He is properly the human hero of the story, but not quite in the usual way. Instead of conquering by his own might and strengths, he conquers by submitting and choosing to serve that which is higher. He is nearly lost in the pit that opens at Berringers, when he first sees and is confronted by the archetypes revealed together. He cannot save himself, but he is rescued by the Eagle. Later, he realizes that the Eagle is the highest of the archetypes that have appeared at that point, and, as Truth, (somehow) controls the others; Anthony then determines to serve the Eagle as the archetype of Truth and take his proper place in the celestial–and now terrestrial–hierarchy. By submitting, he is empowered to do what he wanted to do and must do. He assumes the role of another Adam to restore order to a chaotic universe. The Eagle puts the other archetypes at his service; the Horse comes to him and bears him on its back when he most needs speed to save Damaris. He has been saved, but not for that end alone: now he must turn and save others.

Damaris herself has refused Anthony's initial offer of protection, by stubbornly staying put in Smetham instead of taking refuge in

London. Now she is confronted by the Pterodactyl; on the verge of being destroyed, she turns helplessly to find someone to rescue her. Her father merely looks at her, and says mildly and distractedly, "Well, I was afraid you might get hurt."

Then she encounters the specter of Abelard, a major subject of her studies. But he is dead, and powerless to give her any aid, not even a meaningful word. It is only when she finally calls out to Anthony that she is rescued. At Anthony's feet, with the Eagle on his shoulder, she finally acknowledges the reality that has been surrounding her, and she understands the Eagle in his true guise.

She submits to her place in the hierarchy and realizes that she must now turn and rescue another who is more helpless than she. She chooses to seek for Quentin, not because she has been Quentin's friend in the past, but because he is Anthony's friend and now therefore hers as well.

The archetypes do not serve Damaris as they do Anthony, but they do come to her aid. She has no Horse to ride, but the Unicorn knocks her down to get her attention and then leads the way to Quentin, who is desperately fleeing the brutish Foster with the last shreds of strength in his broken body. She does not directly deliver Quentin herself, but drags him into the safety beside the quietly grazing Lamb while the Lion roars about in the field. And when the danger has passed, she brings Quentin back to her own house and sees to his needs, her former aloofness swallowed by the mercy she has received and must now extend. She is then allowed to watch Anthony from a distance as he approaches the burning fire of the Phoenix and merges, though not forever, with the ninth and final archetype of Man. In his dual being he claims Adam's power over the archetypes and sends them all back where they belong–the Lamb and the Lion appearing at his side for one last moment, a glimpse of Eden as it was and one day shall be again.

There the story in the novel ends, but we can only imagine how deeply enriched will be the friendship among the three. In friendship, the friends have saved one another, and their mutual love and obedience have saved the world. Co-inherence has overcome the incoherent.

WORKS CITED

Lewis, C. S. *The Collected Letters of C. S. Lewis*. Ed. Walter Hooper. Volume II. London: HarperCollins, 2004.

Williams, Charles. *The Place of the Lion*. New York: Pellegrini and Cudahy, 1951

Useful weblinks:

http://www.charleswilliamssociety.org.uk/

https://theoddestinkling.wordpress.com.

*A fuller version of this paper was originally presented to the C. S. Lewis Society of Central Indiana on March 20th, 2015.

The Image of the Library in the Life and Work of Charles Williams

by Michael J. Paulus, Jr.

Michael J. Paulus, Jr., is University Librarian and Assistant Provost at Seattle Pacific University in Seattle, Washington. His administrative, teaching, and scholarly interests focus on the history and future of libraries as well as on technology and ethics.

BEYOND THE BOOK

In her review of Grevel Lindop's biography *Charles Williams: The Third Inkling*, Sørina Higgins commends how well Lindop tells the tale of Williams's life. With Lindop's acute poetic sensibilities and extensive archival research, his book does indeed present a very well told tale. But as Higgins points out, this "is the tale of a life cut short."[1] The premature end of Williams's life and work—with moral failures unresolved, and promising books unwritten—highlights the limits of the traditional biographical form when a life's narrative arc is arrested. When I came to the end of Lindop's book, I was left wanting not just more—such as information about the reception of Williams's works—but something beyond the limits of any single book: something atemporal, or at least nonlinear, beyond the reductive trajectory of time's arrow. To gain a deeper and broader perspective on Williams, in this paper I will explore a concept suggested by Williams's own life and work: the image of the library.

The Church, Williams said, does not look forward: it "looks centrally . . . at that which is not to be defined in terms of place and time."[2] The central "point out of time" that marks the beginning of the Church in Jerusalem also inaugurates its destiny in the New Jerusalem.[3] "We operate, mostly, in sequence," Williams said, "but sequence is not all." Life in the City now and yet to come is a life of

---

1   Sørina Higgins, "Decidedly Odd," *Books & Culture*, March/April, 2016, 30.
2   Charles Williams, "The Church Looks Forward," quoted in *The Image of the City and Other Essays* (Berkeley, Calif.: The Apocryphile Press, 2007), 154.
3   Charles Williams, *The Descent of the Dove: A Short History of the Holy Spirit in the Church* (Vancouver, B.C.: Regent College Publishing, 2002), 1, cf. 15.

interdependence and exchange: "The past and the future are subject to interchange, and the present with both, the dead with the living, the living with the dead."⁴ This is how Williams described the eternal pattern of what he called the co-inherent life.

A book, or even a world full of books, as the fourth gospel concedes, cannot fully represent the reality of the co-inherent life. But when a book is in communication or communion with other books, a deeper center and a larger narrative emerges. What seems fleeting becomes more permanent, and what is fragmentary becomes more unified. The fourth gospel "of John," which Williams said "comes neare[est] to describing the unity of the new thing in the world and soul," is itself extended through intertextual exchange with other books.⁵ Some of these were selected with it for inclusion in the canonical collection that Jerome called a *blibliotheca*—i.e., a library—which inspired a "literary movement" that created a broader library.⁶ Williams actively engaged with and contributed to this broader library, participating in its material reality of divine and human communication.

Books were Williams's vocation. He authored over thirty books— poetry, plays, literary criticism, novels, biographies, theology—and spent most of his professional life working as an editor for Oxford University Press (OUP). As a reader and a writer, he appreciated books with meaningful content. But as a publisher, he understood the importance of books as material containers. Like a human being, a book has a body as well as a soul; and it is through the physical form of a book that one encounters a text incarnate. The book was also a preternatural object for Williams. In his novel *Shadows of Ecstasy*, a character imagines books, nicely shelved in a bookcase, coming to life and releasing something powerful, ecstatic, and transformative.⁷ Williams agreed with Milton, who said: "Books are not absolutely dead things, but do contain a potencie of life in them to be as active as that soule was whose progeny they are."⁸

Yet every book Williams read, discussed, wrote, or published was a compromise—of meaning, form, or craft—reaching the limits of

---

4   Charles Williams, *He Came Down from Heaven*, quoted in *Charles Williams: Essential Writings in Spirituality and Theology*, ed. Charles Hefling (Cambridge, Mass.: Cowley Publications, 1993), 228.
5   Ibid., 43.
6   Williams, *The Descent of the Dove*, 22.
7   Charles Williams, *Shadows of Ecstasy* (Vancouver, B.C.: Regent College Publishing, 2003), 47.
8   John Milton, *Areopagitica*, ed. J. W. Hales (Oxford: Clarendon Press, 1874), 5.

his understanding, expression, and time. When pressed to write for money, he looked for greater depth in his subject. When pressed for time, he hoped for future opportunities for publication. And as he approached his intellectual and physical limits, he sought occult aids that were physically and spiritually destructive. In the end, he left a collection of works incomplete in itself. Beyond work left unfinished, the limits of Williams's extant collection are evident. T. S. Eliot observed that, "what he had to say was beyond his resources, and probably beyond the resources of language." But Williams's collection *is* important for the content and connections within it. All his books," Dorothy Sayers observed, "illuminate one another . . . it is impossible to confine any one theme to a single book."[9] His collection is also important for the connections beyond it, with the works that inspired him and the works he inspired by Eliot, Sayers, C. S. Lewis, W. H. Auden, and many others.

When considering Williams's thoroughly literary life, it is easy to miss the centrality of a literary institution that was significant throughout it: the library. Williams was always in libraries, which mediated access to a cultural, canonical collection that was open to him and his contributions. The importance of the library in Williams's life and work is most evident in his Masques of Amen House, a trilogy of plays set in the library of the OUP London office. Though he would have suppressed any references to these midlife masques in a biography, because of his relationship with the figure of the librarian, the central hopes and struggles of Williams's life are found in these plays. Also found in this hidden center of his life is the image of the library, both real and mythical, which is a mechanism for enabling a book—like a life—to participate in the hope of redemption and reconciliation through its connections, communion, and co-inherence with other books.

THE LIBRARY AND A LIBRARY USER

Before turning to the masques, it is important to define what "a library" is. The library is among civilization's oldest institutions, appearing after the emergence of cities and writing some five millennia ago. Three elements have consistently characterized libraries throughout history and across diverse cultures. First, a library is an intention to configure a culture represented by fixed expressions of

---

9   Quoted in "Introduction: The Pattern of Glory," *Charles Williams: Essential Writings in Spirituality and Theology*, 1f.

knowledge such as books. Second, a library is a collection created through selection, a process that creates a canonical and coherent context for discovery. Third, a library socially and technologically mediates a collection for a community so that its members may actively shape the culture that is shaping them and the library.[10] It is inevitable that mediation includes the creation of writers such as Williams, whose works will be included in libraries when communities favor them.

After his death in 1945, Williams's OUP colleague Gerry Hopkins submitted an entry for the *Dictionary of National Biography*. It is a curious biographical summary, citing "private information" and "personal knowledge," and Hopkins seems skeptical about the canonical value of any of Williams's works. "Many of Williams's contemporaries found him difficult and obscure," Hopkins claimed, and "to be fully equipped for the task of following the thought of any one of his volumes" it is necessary "to have spent many talkative hours in his company." "The art of conversation and the craft of lecturing," Hopkins asserts, "were his two most brilliant, provocative, and fruitful methods of communication."[11]

In spite of the difficulty of Williams's works, and in the absence of further oral encounters with him, many continued to find William's *written* communications of enduring value. Many of William's readers and interpreters would agree with his friend and sometimes publisher T. S. Eliot, who admitted that Williams work "has an importance of a kind not easy to describe."[12] Others may be waiting for the fulfillment of the prophecy of William's employer and sometimes publisher Humphrey Milford, who promised Williams "a reputation in the 21st century."[13] Regardless, Williams's books continue to be read, republished, written about, and collected as his impact on English literature and Christian theology continues to be assessed. For now and the foreseeable future, Williams holds a place in the library. This seems a just end for a library user such as Williams, but also for a

---

10   See Yun Lee Too, *The Idea of the Library in the Ancient World* (New York: Oxford University Press, 2010), 4-5.
11   "Williams, Charles Walter Stansby," *Dictionary of National Biography: 1941-1950*, ed. L. G. Wickham Legg and E. T. Williams (London: Oxford University Press, 1959), 958f.
12   Philip Zaleski and Carol Zaleski, *The Fellowship: The Literary Lives of the Inklings J. R. R. Tolkien, C. S. Lewis, Owen Barfield, Charles Williams* (New York: Farrar, Straus and Group, 2015), 221.
13   Grevel Lindop, *Charles Williams: The Third Inkling* (Oxford: Oxford University Press, 2015), 107.

writer such as Williams—a writer who appreciated how books are always in communication with other books.

The Author and Publisher in the Library

Were Williams's life adapted for a dramatic form, it could be divided into three acts: Act I, early life in St. Albans; Act II, literary life in London; Act III, dislocated wartime life in Oxford. Multiple scenes would be set in libraries: at the St. Albans Grammar School, at University College London, at the British Museum, at the Bodleian Library, and in other public and private libraries. But a simplified dramatization could collapse Williams's whole life into one act, set in one library—the library in Amen House. From this middle point of Williams's life, it would be possible to look back to the past, present through memory, and forward to the future, present through expectation.

Later in life, when Williams prepared an outline of his life for a prospective biographer, he found it centered on a "paradox": his illicit love for his London colleague, OUP librarian Phyllis Jones. This midlife office affair was a source of great inspiration for Williams, but is also created a great amount of pain for him, his wife, and his son. Williams said no mention of or allusion to Phyllis should appear, "and any reference to the Masques should be small."[14] These masques had been initially for and about them, the author and the librarian, and the quest for an impossible union. But as with the *Divine Comedy*, the masques were also about much more. Commenting on Dante's own midlife journey into a dark wood at the beginning of the *Inferno*, Williams acknowledged that "the unifying of our imagination is an arduous business."[15] Williams probably anticipated a period of retirement from employed work, when he could work to understand backwards a life lived forwards, as Kierkegaard put it, but he died within six months of musing about such a time in Hoxton in a letter to Kierkegaard translator Walter Lowrie.[16] If Williams had taken that look backwards, it likely would have included a return to the library at Amen House.

---

14   Ibid., 324.
15   Charles Williams, *The Figure of Beatrice: A Study in Dante* (Berkeley, Calif.: The Apocryphile Press, 2005), 107f.
16   Quoted in Michael J. Paulus, Jr., "From a Publisher's Point of View: Charles Williams's Role in Publishing Kierkegaard in English," in *Charles Williams and His Contemporaries*, ed. Suzanne Bray and Richard Sturch (Newcastle upon Tyne: Cambridge Scholars Publishing, 2009), 38.

Williams joined the London branch of OUP in 1908 "and never left."[17] During his time at the press, Williams was responsible for a number of important acquisitions, editions, anthologies, series, and other projects. In 1924, the London office moved into more spacious quarters in Amen House. The new office included "a long, wide library," beautifully furnished, in which "All the productions of the mighty Oxford University Press from past ages still in print were on the shelves."[18] This dignified reference library was at once showroom, workroom, and common room—a place of inspiration, creativity, and fellowship. This had much to do with the presence of a new "blonde, pretty, lively, and twenty-two[-year] old" librarian Phyllis Jones, who became enamored of Williams, comparing him to "a perfect, heavenly sort of" library.[19]

Inspired by this new central figure in his life and the fellowship that surrounded her, Williams created a dramatization of the work of the press set in the library. A unique blend of Williams's mythic poetry, theological convictions, and esoteric practices, the Masques of Amen House show how the stages of publishing correspond with and manifest the stages of "the re-union of man and God." The first masque, "The Masque of the Manuscript," concerns the "Way of Purgation"; the second, "The Masque of Perusal," concerns the "Way of Illumination"; the third, "The Masque of the Termination of Copyright," concerns the "Way of Union."[20]

"The Masque of the Manuscript," written in 1926 and performed the next year, begins with a song linking the creators of books with the new creation, the "peace and perfect end" "Seen by the seekers of truth." The curtain rises to reveal the Librarian Phillida (i.e., Phyllis) in the library, which is described as an ancient site of revelation where "treasures of words and lives" are preserved against "the dark of future and the void." But the keeper of this accumulated wisdom, caught up in "search on search" with her authors in the movement of time, confesses that her collection is incomplete: "I learn that man only and ever strives; / Nor hath his riddle any answer fair."[21] The library is a work of time, it is also a negation of time, and it points to something

---

17   Alice Mary Hadfield, *Charles Williams: An Exploration of His Life and Work* (Oxford: Oxford University Press, 1983), 13.
18   Ibid., 47.
19   Lindop, *Charles Williams*, 123, 136.
20   Ibid., 153f.
21   Charles Williams, "The Masque of the Manuscript," in *The Masques of Amen House*, ed. David Bratman (Altadena, Calif.: The Mythopoeic Press, 2000), 37f.

beyond time.

A Manuscript, a *Short Treatise on Syrian Nouns*, enters the library and asks:

> Is this the place of achievement, the end of the waiting,
> The portal of freedom, the high city's final ungating?
> Am I come at the last to the house of all holy indwelling . . . ?[22]

Before being admitted to the library, which the Manuscript mistakes for the New Jerusalem, the Manuscript must suffer death and be reborn as the Book: "Nothing at all can live except it die," Phillida announces.[23] Only after the purification of publishing may she be shelved in the place chosen for her and enter the communion of books in the library. The library is not quite Paradise, but the way of purgation that produces the glorious Book marks the beginning of a new creation.

The redemptive work of the first masque continues in the second, "The Masque of Perusal," written in 1928 and performed the following year. Now the Book must "go forth unto its sale," find its way into a "reader's mind," and participate in the creation of another book. As the unread Book observes the publishing staff busy at work, she asks why—after a year on the shelf, untouched—was she ever "brought to be"? Is the library merely a "sepulcher," a "void" of "all that has been," a "great naught"?[24]

The librarian has no words of comfort, but Thyrsis, "an author and a publisher," arrives and desires to share "A wisdom so far hidden." For this he needs knowledge ancient enough to have been found in the library of Ashurbanipal: "a book upon the Syrian noun." He is brought to the librarian with the promise that she "will give such information as is wanted." As Thyrsis is shown the books on the shelves, in what Williams described as "a slow and conventionalized ritual," the actors sing how "The Keeper offers help of every kind" as she "lets her information flow."[25]

Thyrsis leaves with the Book, reads it, and it enters his mind and demands "a newer life."[26] Thyrsis then has a vision of the publishing process *as* and *in* the Procession of the Graal. The Graal, Williams wrote, is "communion with God" and its procession is "the visible

---

22   Ibid., 38.
23   Ibid., 45.
24   Charles Williams, "The Masque of Perusal," in *The Masques of Amen House*, 54, 58, 62.
25   Ibid., 63f.
26   Ibid., 69.

process of reconciliation," promising ultimate union with God.[27] After this vocational vision, of internal love manifested in external labor, Thyrsis is called to feel "the communicating word" and write the book his vision saw.[28] He assents to participate in the pattern of human cooperation with the divine, the pattern of "birth—death—birth."[29] The Manuscript, born to die and become the Book, has generated another book to be added to the library.

"The Masque of the Termination of Copyright," which concerns the full redemption and reconciliation of the Book—reaching its perfect and peaceful end— was written in 1930 but never performed. It begins in heaven, where the Book has been declared immortal. The Book is sought out and found on earth, in a "wretched second-hand bookshop" (an infernal inversion of a library), and the Book is taken to the liminal place of the publishing house so that it may be reissued and return to the library. While the first masque inaugurates a joyful presentation of redemption, the third masque—never completed—ends where the quest began, in the library. We do not see the attainment of the Graal, which Williams said is found in reconciliation, when there is unity of internal love and external labor.[30]

Williams imagined his Canterbury Festival play "Thomas Cranmer of Canterbury," preformed in 1936, as a substitute for the third "ineffective" masque of Amen House.[31] In this play, Cranmer follows the way of union through books. There are the Sacred books and the Book of Common Prayer; the books that bless in early life and the books that weary the eyes in later life; the books "we ever reform ... and not ourselves"; the books whipped "from their shelves" by "the storm in the street"; the books recanted; the books reaffirmed; and the books that survive their authors and become witnesses themselves on the shelves of libraries.[32]

Here the image of the library is more subtle, but the Church's library is shaping Cranmer and the Church, Cranmer and the Church are shaping it, and, beyond their confusions, it is being shaped by

---

27 David Llewellyn Dodds, "General Introduction," *Arthurian Poets: Charles Williams* (Woodbridge, Suffolk: The Boydell Press, 1991), 11; Charles Williams, Arthurian Commonplace Book, 1912-1923, transcribed by David Llewellyn Dodds, 71.
28 "The Masque of Perusal," 73.
29 Williams, Arthurian Commonplace Book, 112.
30 Ibid., 3.
31 Lindop, *Charles Williams*, 246.
32 Charles Williams, "Thomas Cranmer of Canterbury," in *Collected Plays* (Vancouver, B.C.: Regent College Publishing, 2005), 38.

the communicating word of God, "ripe for communion."[33] The way of union passes through the library, which promises greater unity than its contributing authors know. As human and divine communications occur across time and throughout space, the library is an inevitable by-product reflecting the co-inherent nature of God in being and doing: the internal self-communicating love of the triune God manifested in the external self-communicating work of creation and the incarnation.

BEYOND THE MASQUES

In spite of the substitution of "Thomas Cranmer of Canterbury" for "The Masque of the Termination of Copyright," the third masque of Amen House, much like the third act of Williams's life, leaves an incomplete narrative. Although Williams was ambivalent about eschatology, acknowledging that his commentary on the *Paradiso* was the weakest part of his book *The Figure of Beatrice: A Study in Dante*, he believed that in the end all would be known, reconciled, and unified.[34] Dante glimpsed this and attempted to articulate it at the end of the *Paradiso*:

> In [eternal Light's] depth I saw contained,
> by love into a single volume bound,
> the pages scattered through the universe:
> substances, accidents, and the interplay between them,
> as though they were conflated in such ways
> that what I tell is but a simple sight.[35]

Williams life was literally filled with scattered pages that he read, created, shared, edited, and published. And through all the consolations of a central faith, as well as the desolations of a central infidelity, the library was there providing pages to inspire him and collecting pages inspired by him—enabling him and his books to participate in the hope of reconciliation by bringing inchoate and incomplete communications into coherent and co-inherent communion with others and God.

In the Masques of Amen House, Williams presents images of the library along the way of purgation, illumination, and union. The library, reaching deep into and beyond time, has an integral role in the "one work" of "the re-union of man and God" that leads to the place sought by the Manuscript in the first masque: "the place of achievement, the end of the

---

33   Ibid., 20.
34   Lindop, *Charles Williams*, 374.
35   Dante Alighieri, *Paradiso*, trans. Robert and Jean Hollander (New York: Anchor Books, 2008), 915.

waiting, / The portal of freedom, the high city" ungated, "the house of all holy indwelling"—the New Jerusalem.[36] The Apocalypse reveals that the City has no need of a Temple, but one might expect a Library.

---

36   Lindop, *Charles Williams*, 153; "The Masque of the Manuscript," 38.

C. S. Lewis, Charles Williams, and Esemplastic Friendship

by Paul E. Michelson

Paul E. Michelson is Distinguished Professor of History Emeritus at Huntington University. Three times a Fulbright fellow in Romania (1971-1973, 1982-1983, 1989-1990), he was awarded the 2000 Bălcescu Prize for History by the Romanian Academy. From 2004-2014 He served as Secretary of the Conference on Faith and History.

I. Introduction

The sudden death of Charles W. S. Williams on May 15, 1945 (the first member of C. S. Lewis's immediate circle to pass away) had a deep and paradoxical impact on Lewis. On the one hand, he was grief-stricken at the untimely loss of a friend (Williams was only 58) who had become integral to his life and work. On the other, despite the pain, Lewis did not experience depression over the situation or doubts about his Christian faith. As he wrote to Mary Neylan on a few days after Williams' demise:

> I also have become much acquainted with grief now through the death of my great friend Charles Williams, my friend of friends, the comforter of all our little set, the most angelic. The odd thing is that his death has made my faith ten times stronger than it was a week ago. And I find all that talk about 'feeling he is closer to us than before' isn't just talk. It's just what it does feel like—I can't put it into words. One seems at moments to be living in a new world. Lots, lots of pain, but not a particle of depression or resentment.[1]

Lewis—along with Dorothy Sayers, J. R. R. Tolkien, Owen Barfield, Gervase Mathew, and W. H. Lewis—responded to Williams' death by putting together for their friend a commemorative volume of

---

[1] C. S. Lewis to Mary Neylan, 20 May 1945, in C. S. Lewis, *The Collected Letters of C. S. Lewis, Vol. II: Books, Broadcasts, and the War, 1931-1949*, edited by Walter Hooper (San Francisco: HarperSanFrancisco, 2002), pp. 652-653. The "odd thing is" that later Lewis's faith does seem to have been heavily impacted by a death, that in 1960 of Joy Davidman; see C. S. Lewis, *A Grief Observed* (London: Faber and Faber, 1961). Perhaps this reflects a difference between *eros* and *philia*, a subject for another discussion.

*Essays Presented to Charles Williams.*² "We had hoped," Lewis wrote in the preface, "to offer the whole collection to Williams as what the Germans call a Festschrift when peace would recall him from Oxford [where he had spent the war] to London [where he worked at Oxford University Press]. Death forestalled us; we now offer as a memorial what had been devised as a greeting."³

Lewis went on to describe Williams' role in the wartime meetings of their informal literary circle called the Inklings:⁴

> Such society, unless all of its members happen to be of one trade, makes heavy demands on a man's versatility. And we were by no means of one trade. The talk might turn in almost any direction, and certainly skipped 'from grave to gay, from lively to severe'⁵: but wherever it went, Williams was ready for it. He seemed to have no 'pet subject.' Though he talked copiously one never felt that he had dominated the evening. Nor did one easily remember particular 'good things' that he had said: the importance of his presence was, indeed, chiefly made clear by the gap which was left on the rare occasions when he did not turn up. It then became clear that some principle of liveliness and cohesion [coinherence?] had been withdrawn from the whole party: lacking him, we did not completely possess one another. He was (in the Coleridgian [*sic*] language) an 'esemplastic' force. . . .⁶

---

2   C.S. Lewis, ed., *Essays Presented to Charles Williams* (London: Oxford University Press, 1947), reprinted by Eerdmans, Grand Rapids MI, 1966.
3   Lewis, *Essays Presented to Charles Williams*, 1966, p. vi.
4   On the Inklings, see Humphrey Carpenter, *The Inklings. C. S. Lewis, J. R. R. Tolkien, Charles Williams, and their friends* (Boston: Houghton Mifflin, 1979); Walter Hooper, "The Inklings," in Roger White, Judith Wolfe, and Brendan N. Wolfe, eds., *C. S. Lewis and His Circle. Essays and Memoirs from the Oxford C. S. Lewis Society* (New York/Oxford: Oxford University Press, 2015), pp. 197-213; Colin Duriez and David Porter, *The Inklings Handbook* (London: Azure Press, 2001); Diana Pavlac Glyer, *The Company They Keep. C. S. Lewis and J. R. R. Tolkien as Writers in Community* (Kent OH: Kent State University Press, 2007); Colin Duriez, *The Oxford Inklings. Lewis, Tolkien, and Their Circle* (Oxford: Lion Books, 2015); and Philip Zaleski and Carol Zaleski, *The Fellowship. The Literary Lives of the Inklings: J. R. R. Tolkien, C. S. Lewis, Owen Barfield, Charles Williams* (New York: Farrar, Straus, and Giroux, 2015).
5   The allusion is to Pope's *Essay on Man*, Epistle IV.
6   Lewis, *Essays Presented to Charles Williams*, 1966, p. xi. Lewis, ever the optimistic pessimist, had noted in 1939 that "Along with these not very pleasant indirect results of the war, there is one pure gift—the London branch of the University Press has moved to Oxford so that Charles

Lewis's views on friendship are well-known from his widely-read 1960 book *The Four Loves*,[7] which had an entire section dealing with philia or "friendship" (though perhaps this section is less read than the naughty bits on eros). The contention of this paper is that Lewis's more systematic thoughts about friendship published near the end of his life as well as our understanding of his friendship with Charles Williams can be usefully illuminated 1) by looking at how Williams functioned as an esemplastic force, and 2) by examining what Lewis had to say about friendship in his correspondence and other sources prior to the publication of *The Four Loves*. In addition—though it is not a purpose of this paper to systematically survey or to critique Lewis's ideas on friendship in *The Four Loves*[8]—some attention will be given to looking at how Lewis's 1960 exposition squares with the ideas that emerge in this paper.

II. The Esemplastic and Friendship

Esemplastic is a word invented by Samuel Taylor Coleridge in his *Biographia Literaria* (1817) to describe what he called "secondary imagination," the creativity that produces poetry and art.[9] Let's call

---

Williams is living here." C. S. Lewis to Warnie Lewis, 10 September 1939, in Lewis, *Collected Letters*, 2004, Vol. II, p. 272.

7   First published as C. S. Lewis, *The Four Loves* (London: Geoffrey Bles, 1960). References below are to the Collins Fontana paperback edition, London, 1963. The origins of *The Four Loves* was in a series of ten radio lectures that Lewis recorded in August 1958 at the request of the American Episcopal Radio-TV Foundation of Atlanta, Georgia that Lewis had received in January 1958. They were supposed to be broadcast nationally on the weekly Episcopal Hour program from March 29-May 31, 1959, but because Lewis "brought sex" into his talks on *Eros* it was decided to broadcast them only on individual stations. However, the Foundation did make the entire series available on recordings, which are still available today on CD. See Walter Hooper, *C. S. Lewis: A Companion and Guide* (San Francisco: HarperSanFrancisco, 1996), pp. 86-90, 367.

8   Which has been analyzed by others, including Gilbert Meilaender, *The Taste for the Other. The Social and Ethical Thought of C. S. Lewis* (Grand Rapids MI: Eerdmans, 1978); Michael Malanga, "*The Four Loves*: C. S. Lewis's Theology of Love," in Bruce L. Edwards, ed., *C. S. Lewis. Life, Works, and Legacy. Vol. 4: Scholar, Teacher, and Public Intellectual* (Westport CT: Praeger, 2007), pp. 49-80; and William L. Isley, Jr., "C. S. Lewis on Friendship," *Inklings Forever*, Vol. 6 (2008).

9   Samuel Taylor Coleridge, *Biographia Literaria or Biographical Sketches of My Literary Life and Opinions* (London: Rest Fenner, 1817), Vol. 1:

this sense A of Esemplastic. Coleridge's motivation? "I thought that a new term would both aid the recollection of my meaning, and prevent its being confounded with the usual [i. e. prosaic] import of the word, imagination."[10] Coleridge also included in *esemplastic* the sense of shaping as in "moulding my thoughts into verse."[11] It is through the esemplastic power of imagination that the writer/artist transcends mere perception and normality by creating or shaping literature and art.

This was a problem that Lewis had long wrestled with, including a reading—no surprise here—of Coleridge's *Biographia Literaria*. In January of 1927, Lewis wrote in his diary, "Was thinking about imagination and intellect and the unholy muddle I am in about them at present: undigested scraps of anthroposophy and psychoanalysis jostling with orthodox idealism over a background of good old Kirkian rationalism. Lord what a mess!"[12] The following day, he wrote: "Still puzzled about imagination, etc. . . . Decided to work up the whole doctrine of Imagination in Coleridge as soon as I had time. . . . That's the real imagination, no bogies, not Karmas, no gurus, no damned

---

Ch. 10 and Ch. 13. Source: Project Gutenberg, www.gutenberg.org/files/6081/6081-h/6081-h.htm, last accessed 23 May 2016. The title of Ch. 13 is "The imagination or the Esemplastic power." In Ch. 14, Coleridge was the first to use the phrase "willing suspension of disbelief." And in Ch. 15, he describes how the secondary or esemplastic imagination functions as it "dissolves, diffuses, dissipates, in order to recreate," which clearly has affinities with Tolkien's celebrated discussion of "sub-creation" in his "On Fairy-stories," in J. R. R. Tolkien, *On Fairy-stories*, Expanded Edition with Commentary and Notes, edited by Verlyn Flieger and Douglas A. Anderson (London: HarperCollins, 2008), pp. 42, 59 ff, 78. Cf. Paul E. Michelson, "The Development of J. R. R. Tolkien's Ideas on Fairy-stories," *Inklings Forever*, Vol. 8 (2012), pp. 115-127. On Coleridge, esemplasty, and fantasy literature, see Gary K. Wolfe, "Fantasy from Dryden to Dunsany," in Edward James and Farah Mendlesohn, eds., *The Cambridge Companion to Fantasy Literature* (Cambridge: Cambridge University Press, 2012), pp. 7 ff.
10   Coleridge, *Biographia Literaria*, 1817, Vol. 1: Ch. 10. Obviously, Coleridge's term never caught on, except among lexicographers and polymath literature professors such as Lewis.
11   Coleridge, *Biographia Literaria*, 1817, Vol. 1: Ch. 10.
12   Entry for 18 January 1927 in C. S. Lewis, *All My Road Before Me. The Diary of C. S. Lewis 1922-1927*, edited by Walter Hooper, Foreword by Owen Barfield (London: HarperCollins Fount, 1991), pp. 431-432. Similar musings can be found in Lewis's *Surprised by Joy. The Shape of My Early Life* (London: Geoffrey Bles, 1955). References below are to the 1956 Harcourt, Brace edition.

psychism there. I have been astray among second rate ideas too long. . . .[13]

In a letter a few months later to his brother, Warnie Lewis, in April 1927, we find that Lewis was spending mornings reading *Biographia Literaria*, though he often found Coleridge incoherent: "As an attempt at a book (as opposed to mere Coleridgean talk), it is preposterous."[14] Subsequently, in 1933, Lewis wrote to Owen Barfield[15] that a recent article by Barfield on Coleridge was "exciting" but hard to understand, though he now understood why Coleridge frequently appeared incoherent.[16] Barfield had written that Coleridge's "extraordinarily unifying mind was too painfully aware that you cannot really say one thing correctly without saying everything. . . . His incoherence of expression arose from the coherence of what he wanted to express. It was a sort of intellectual stammer."[17] (Since we all fumble with big ideas that seem to escape the bounds of our words and, perhaps, our minds, we can all empathize with Coleridge here.)

Lewis's views on imagination were eventually boiled down in a 1956 letter: "The true exercise of imagination, in my view, is (a) To help us to understand other people (b) To respond to, and some of us, to produce, art."[18] It seems clear that Lewis was intimately familiar

---

13 Entry for 19 January 1927 in Lewis, *Diary*, 1991, p. 432.
14 C. S. Lewis to Warren Lewis, [18 April 1927], in C. S. Lewis, *The Collected Letters of C. S. Lewis, Vol. I: Family Letters, 1905-1931*, edited by Walter Hooper (London: HarperCollins, 2000), pp. 685-686.
15 C. S. Lewis to Owen Barfield, 28 March 1933, in Lewis, *Collected Letters*, 2004, Vol. II, pp. 104-107.
16 Owen Barfield, "The Philosophy of Samuel Taylor Coleridge," first published in 1932 and reprinted in 1944 in Barfield's *Romanticism Comes of Age*, new augmented edition (Middletown CT: Wesleyan University Press, 1967), pp. 144-163.
17 Barfield, *Romanticism Comes of Age*, 1967, p. 146. For more on Lewis and Barfield and imagination, see Stephen Thorson, *Joy and Poetic Imagination. Understanding C. S. Lewis's "Great War" with Owen Barfield and its Significance for Lewis's Conversion and Writings* (Hamden CT: Winged Lion Press, 2015). The interest in Coleridge was keen enough in Lewis's circles that Dom Bede Griffiths proposed to Lewis sometime around 1930 that they subsidize an edition of Coleridge by Owen Barfield. See Walter Hooper's note in the "Supplement," in Lewis, *Collected Letters*, 2002, Vol. II: Note 114, p. 1518; this project did not materialize. Barfield went on to publish an entire book on Coleridge: *What Coleridge Thought* (Middletown CT: Wesleyan University Press, 1971), with two chapters on "Imagination and Fancy," including a discussion of primary and secondary imagination.
18 C. S. Lewis to Keith Masson, 3 June 1956, in Lewis, *Collected Letters*,

with Coleridge, Coleridge's theories, and his view of esemplastic imagination.[19]

In addition to sense A of Esemplastic (as secondary imagination), there are two more senses. In the 20th century, esemplastic also came to be defined as the "forming or moulding into one in the manner of an artist"[20] or, as The Oxford Dictionary has it, "of the process of molding into a unity; unifying."[21] Sense B, then, is the idea of a unifying process or unity in similarity, which many see as the principal basis for friendship. There is also an additional sense C, in which the unifying process brings together opposites. This is another paradox: esemplastic friendship leads to unity in diversity itself.[22]

How do these three senses of esemplastic apply to C. S. Lewis and Charles Williams? It seems clear that Lewis and Williams had nothing in common if not their shared devotion to the esemplastic in sense A (i.e. secondary imagination) and to deep, understanding friendships with others, both similar and dissimilar, that is, the esemplastic in senses B and C. This dated from their first direct contact, a 1936 letter from Lewis to Williams in which Lewis wrote the following:

2004, Vol. II, p. 759. He goes on to recognize that imagination can also be put to bad uses. Compare Lewis's comment that "Friendship (as the ancients saw) can be a school of virtue; but also (as they did not see) a school of vice. . . . It makes good men better and bad men worse." Lewis, *Four Loves*, 1963, p. 75.

19   On fantasy and imagination, see also C. S. Lewis, *The Discarded Image. An Introduction to Medieval and Renaissance Literature* (Cambridge: Cambridge University Press, 1964), pp. 162 ff. On Lewis and Coleridge, see Peter J. Schakel, *Reason and Imagination in C. S. Lewis. A Study of Till We Have Faces* (Grand Rapids MI: Eerdmans, 1984), p. 183; David Jasper, "*The Pilgrim's Regress* and *Surprised by Joy*," in Robert MacSwain and Michael Ward, eds., *The Cambridge Companion to C. S. Lewis* (Cambridge: Cambridge University Press, 2010), pp. 232-233; and J. T. Sellars, *Reasoning beyond Reason. Imagination as a Theological Source in the Work of C. S. Lewis* (Eugene OR: Pickwick Publications, 2011), pp. 48 ff, 194-195.

20   P. L. Carver, "The Evolution of the Term 'Esemplastic'," *Modern Humanities Research Association*, Vol. 24 (1929), p. 330.

21   *Oxford Universal Dictionary on Historical Principles*, third edition with addenda revised and edited by C. T. Onions (Oxford: Clarendon Press, 1955) p. 633. The OUD makes a connection between Schelling's term *Ineinsbildung*, literally "forming into one," which is rejected by Carver, "Esemplastic," 1929, pp. 329-331.

22   For a thorough discussion of the issue of similarities and differences in the Inklings, see Glyer, *The Company They Keep*, 2007, Ch. 1-2.

> A book sometimes crosses ones path which is so like the sound of ones native language in a strange country. . . . I have just read your Place of the Lion and it is to me one of the major literary events of my life—comparable to my first discovery of George Macdonald, G. K. Chesterton, or Wm. Morris. There are layers and layers—first the pleasure any good fantasy gives me: then, what is rarely (tho' not so very rarely) combined with this, the pleasure of a real philosophical and theological stimulus: thirdly, characters: fourthly, what I neither expected nor desired, substantial edification.[23]

Lewis was led to invite Williams to be his guest at Magdalen and join him in "talk... till the small hours" with an "informal club called the Inklings: the qualifications (as they have informally evolved) are a tendency to write, and Christianity."[24] This rapidly evolved into a memorable friendship which ended only with Williams' premature death in 1945.

Both Lewis and his friends were agreed on the Coleridgean esemplastic power of secondary imagination. An illustrative example can be found in a 1955 letter from Lewis to another close friend of Charles Williams, Dorothy L. Sayers. Lewis writes of their shared interest in

> the plastic, inventive, or constructive power, *homo faber*. This wants to make things out of any plastic material, whether within the mind or without; stone, metals, clay, wood, cloth, memory, & imagination. It will take from imagination any of the material I've enumerated. In my own stories it usually takes chiefly 2e: pictures, arising I don't know how, are got hold of by invention which wants to connect them & build a thing.[25]

---

23   C. S. Lewis to Charles Williams, 11 March 1936, in Lewis, *Collected Letters*, 2004, Vol. II, p. 183.
24   C. S. Lewis to Charles Williams, 11 March 1936, in Lewis, *Collected Letters*, 2004, Vol. II, pp. 183-184. For a further elucidation of what Lewis saw in Williams' fiction, see C. S. Lewis, "The Novels of Charles Williams," in C. S. Lewis, *On Stories and Other Essays on Literature*, edited by Walter Hooper (New York: Harcourt Brace Jovanovich, 1982), pp. 21-27, where Lewis also outlines his idea of "supposals." This is the script of a lecture read by Lewis on the BBC, 11 February 1949, which is also available on CD.
25   C. S. Lewis to Dorothy L. Sayers, 14 December 1955, in C. S. Lewis, *The Collected Letters of C. S. Lewis, Vol. III: Books, Broadcasts, and the War, 1931-1949*, edited by Walter Hooper (San Francisco: HarperSanFrancisco, 2002), pp. 683-684.

Lewis's friendship with Charles Williams had a similar source. For example, Lewis was careful to point out to Williams in 1942 "that, far from loving your work because you are my friend, I first sought your friendship because I loved your books."[26] A few years after Williams' death he wrote to I. O. Evans that Williams had the gift of writing books in which "the doctrine is as good on its own merits as the art."[27] And in the preface to *Essays Presented to Charles Williams,* Lewis wrote wistfully that Williams' "face—angel's or monkey's—comes back to me most often seen through clouds of tobacco smoke and above a pint mug, distorted into helpless laughter at some innocently broad buffoonery or eagerly stretched forward in the cut and parry or prolonged, fierce, masculine argument and 'the rigour of the game.'"[28]

An *esemplastic* friendship embodied not only shared artistic vision, but shared agreements as such. Deep friendship was of immense— probably essential—importance to C. S. Lewis. The "friendship as sharing" motif appears repeatedly in Lewis's correspondence. In a letter to Arthur Greeves in 1916, Lewis continues a discussion with Greeves on the difference between books and music in their shared aesthetic. Lewis argues that the difference "is just the same difference between friendship and love. The one is a calm and easy going satisfaction, the other is a sort of madness."[29] In a July 1930 letter to Greeves, Lewis affirmed the importance of shared agreements for their friendship: "our common ground represents what is really (I think) the deepest stratum in my life, the thing in me that, if there should be another personal life, is most likely to survive the dissolution of my brain. Certainly, when I come to die I am more likely to remember certain things that you and I have explored or suffered or enjoyed together than anything else."[30]

---

26 C. S. Lewis, "Dedication. To Charles Williams," 1942, in C. S. Lewis, *A Preface to Paradise Lost* (London: Oxford University Press, 1962), p. v.
27 C. S. Lewis to I. O. Evans, 28 February 1949, in Lewis, *Collected Letters,* 2004, Vol. II, pp. 918-919.
28 Lewis, *Essays Presented to Charles Williams,* 1966, p. x.
29 C. S. Lewis to Arthur Greeves, 14 March 1916, in Lewis, *Collected Letters,* 2000, Vol. I, pp. 685-686. The contrast between friendship and love was frequently mentioned in Lewis's correspondence with Greeves, and need not detain us here. Suffice it to note that this was a 17 year-old Lewis discussing the difference between love and friendship, though, by most accounts, at this stage in life he had had little experience with either.
30 C. S. Lewis to Arthur Greeves, 29 July 1930, in Lewis, *Collected Letters,* 2000, Vol. I, p. 916. It might be observed that in Lewis's early correspondence, the overwhelming number of references to friendship come in his letters to

In a 1930 letter to Arthur Greeves, Lewis wrote about a new friend, H. V. Dyson: "he is a man who really loves truth: a philosopher and a religious man: who makes his critical and literary activities depend on the former—none of your damned dilettante."[31] Dyson also had an "honestly merry laugh," Lewis noted, and asked "Have you observed that it is the most serious conversations which produce in their course the best laughter? How we roared and fooled at times in the silence of the night—but always in a few minutes buckled to again with renewed seriousness."[32]

Lewis further illustrated the bond between himself and Greeves in a 1933 letter: "our correspondence was really like two explorers signalling to one another in a new country... we still thought that we were the only two people in the world who were interested in the right kind of things in the right kind of way."[33]

In a subsequent 1935 letter to Greeves, Lewis wrote "friendship is the greatest of worldly goods. Certainly to me it is the chief happiness of life. If I had to give a piece of advice to a young man about a place to live, I think I shd. say, 'sacrifice everything to live where you can be near your friends.'"[34] And in a 1941 letter, he asked Dom Bede Griffiths, not at all rhetorically, "Is any pleasure on earth as great as a circle of Christian friends by a good fire?"[35]

Greeves. Out of sixteen letters in which it is mentioned in Lewis's letters between 1905 and 1931, fourteen were to Greeves and one each to his father and to Owen Barfield. In his letters between 1931 and 1949, there are ten references, two of which are to Greeves. In the letters between 1950 and 1957, there are twenty references, none in letters to Greeves.

31 C. S. Lewis to Arthur Greeves, 29 July 1930, in Lewis, *Collected Letters*, 2000, Vol. I, pp. 917-918.

32 C. S. Lewis to Arthur Greeves, 29 July 1930, in Lewis, *Collected Letters*, 2000, Vol. I, p. 918. Lewis came to regard Dyson as a friend "of the 2nd class—i.e. not in the same rank as yourself or Barfield, but on a level with Tolkien or Macfarlane." Lewis to Greeves, 22 September 1931, p. 969. Dyson played a key role in Lewis's conversion to Christianity: see Lewis to Greeves, 1 October 1931: "I have just passed on from believing in God to definitely believing in Christ—in Christianity. . .My long night talk with Dyson and Tolkien had a good deal to do with it." p. 974; and Lewis to Greeves, 18 October 1931, pp. 976-977, all in Lewis, *Collected Letters*, 2000, Vol. I.

33 C. S. Lewis to Arthur Greeves, 25 March 1933, in Lewis, *Collected Letters*, 2004, Vol. II, p. 101.

34 C. S. Lewis to Arthur Greeves, 29 December 1935, in Lewis, *Collected Letters*, 2004, Vol. II, p. 174.

35 C. S. Lewis to Dom Bede Griffiths, 21 December 1941, Lewis, *Collected*

Of course, *Surprised by Joy*'s well-known 1955 account of Lewis's first meeting with Arthur Greeves is the locus classicus on Lewis's ideas about friendship and shared ideas:

> I found Arthur sitting up in bed. On the table beside him lay a copy of Myths of the Norsemen. 'Do you like that?' said I. 'Do you like that?' said he. Next moment the book was in our hands, our heads were bent close together, we were pointing, quoting, talking—soon almost shouting—discovering in a torrent of questions that we like not only the same thing, but the same parts of it, and in the same way.... Many thousands of people have had this experience of finding the first friend, and it is none the less a wonder.... Nothing, I suspect is more astonishing in any man's life than the discovery that there do exist people very, very like himself.[36]

Later, in *Surprised by Joy*, Lewis reiterated his description of the First Friend as "the alter ego, the man who first reveals to you that you are not alone in the world by turning out (beyond hope) to share all your most secret delights. There is nothing to be overcome in making him your friend; he and you join like raindrops on a window."[37]

This was the kind of friendship that C. S. Lewis had with Charles Williams. It was a friendship to which Lewis owed a good deal of the inspiration behind his career in the late 1930s and 1940s, including his *A Preface to Paradise Lost* (1942) and *That Hideous Strength* (1946).[38] By 1939, Lewis was writing, only semi-jocularly, to Williams that "I begin to suspect that we are living in the 'age of Williams,' and our friendship with you will be our only passport to fame.[39] And, in 1942, in the dedication to his *A Preface to Paradise Lost*, Lewis thanked Williams for liberating him by showing that "the door of the prison was really unlocked all the time; but it was only you who thought of

---

Letters, 2007, Vol. II, p. 501.

36   Lewis, *Surprised by Joy*, 1956, pp. 130-131.

37   Lewis, *Surprised by Joy*, 1956, p. 131.

38   Grevel Lindop notes that Williams's "feelings about Lewis's enthusiasm for his ideas were mixed. After listening to a reading of *That Hideous Strength* at the Inklings, he told Anne Renwick: 'Lewis is becoming a mere disciple; he is now collecting the doctrine of exchange in the last chapter of the new novel. "That," he says, "is all yours"—I do not deny it, but no-one else will think so; I shall be thought his follower everywhere.'" Charles Williams to Anne Renwick, 13 May 1942, quoted in Grevel Lindop, *Charles Williams. The Third Inkling* (Oxford: Oxford University Press, 2015), p. 360.

39   C. S. Lewis to Charles Williams, 7 June 1938, in Lewis, *Collected Letters*, 2004, Vol. II, p. 228.

trying the handle. Now we can all come out."⁴⁰

In return, Williams benefitted from the generous support that his Inkling friends gave him—including getting for him an influential lecture series at the University on Milton and an honorary Oxford MA.⁴¹ Williams, for all his adoring following and popularity, was a somewhat solitary person. But with Lewis he felt at ease, writing in 1945 to his wife: "somehow, except at home . . . and perhaps at Magdalen [i.e. with Lewis] or with [T. S.] Eliot . . . I am always aware of a gulf. My voice—or my style—goes across it, but my heart doesn't."⁴²

Sense C of esemplastic friendship, unity in diversity, was another aspect that Lewis strongly agreed with. In April of 1920, Lewis wrote to Arthur Greeves, who was considering coming to live in Oxford: "You would find an enormous choice of congenial friends, and you can have no idea how the constant friction with other and different minds improves one."⁴³ This was also true of Lewis's friendship with Dom Bede Griffiths. In a 1934 letter to Griffiths, he wrote: "There was nothing to apologize for. My friendship with you began in disagreement and matured in argument, and is beyond the reach of any dangers of that kind. If I object at all to what you said, I object not as a friend or as a guest, but as a logician."⁴⁴

---

40   Lewis, "To Charles Williams," in Lewis, *Paradise Lost*, 1962, p. vi. The primary reference here was to Williams' 1940 preface to an edition of Milton's poetical works and its influence on Lewis's revolutionary views of Milton.
41   Lewis's lack of snobbery showed in his unconcern for Williams' lack of formal academic credentials: "the vulgarest of my pupils asked me, with an air, if Williams had a degree. The whelp!" C. S. Lewis to Warnie Lewis, 28 January 1940, in Lewis, *Collected Letters*, 2004, Vol. II, p. 335.
42   Charles Williams to his wife, 17 February 1945, in Charles Williams, *To Michal from Serge. Letters from Charles Williams to His Wife, Florence, 1939-1945*, edited by Roma A. King, Jr. (Kent OH: Kent State University Press, 2002), p. 249.
43   C. S. Lewis to Arthur Greeves, 11 April 1920, in Lewis, *Collected Letters*, 2000, Vol. I, p. 481.
44   C. S. Lewis to Dom Bede Griffiths, 26 December 1934, in Lewis, *Collected Letters*, 2004, Vol. II, p. 150. The same was true of Lewis's friendship with another of the Inklings, Dr. R. E. Havard, who wrote "Our differences laid the foundation of a friendship that lasted. . .until his death nearly thirty years later." Robert E. Havard, "*Philia*: Jack at Ease," in James Como, ed., *Remembering C. S. Lewis. Recollections of Those Who Knew Him*, third edition (San Francisco: Ignatius Press, 2005), p. 350. Glyer comments: "The point is clear—Havard does not say similarities formed a foundation

A final Lewisian example of friendship in diversity from his correspondence was Lewis's relationship with Father Don Giovanni Calabria: "It is a wonderful thing and a strengthening of faith that two souls differing from each other in place, nationality, language, obedience and age should have been thus led into a delightful friendship; so far does the order of spiritual beings transcend the material order."[45]

Diversity in friendship was also stressed in a classic passage in *Surprised by Joy*. Lewis introduced Owen Barfield as the second type of Friend, an extreme example of variety or diversity:

> The Second Friend is the man who disagrees with you about everything. He is not so much the alter ego as the antiself. Of course he shares your interests; otherwise he would not become your friend at all. But he has approached them all at a different angle. He has read all the right books but has got the wrong thing out of every one. It is as if he spoke your language but mispronounced it. How can he be so nearly right and yet, invariably, just not right?... And then you go at it, hammer and tongs, far into the night, night after night, or walking through fine country that neither gives a glance to, each learning the weight of the other's punches and often more like mutually respectful enemies than friends. Actually (though it never seems so at the time) you modify one another's thought; out of this perpetual dogfight a community of mind and a deep affection emerge.[46]

Even Lewis's primary academic friend, J. R. R. Tolkien, despite their intellectual agreements and interests, was also quite different from Lewis. As Lewis wrote in *Surprised by Joy*, friendship with Tolkien "marked the breakdown of two old prejudices. At my first coming into the world I had been (implicitly) warned never to trust a Papist, and at my first coming [in 1925] into the English Faculty (explicitly) never to trust a philologist. Tolkien was both."[47] (Tolkien for his part, as a Catholic, doubtless looked somewhat askance at

---

that allowed friendship to thrive in spite of their differences. He says the differences themselves were the foundation." Glyer, *The Company They Keep*, 2007, p. 33.
45   C. S. Lewis to Don Giovanni Calabria, 17 March 1953, in Lewis, *Collected Letters*, 2007, Vol. III, p. 306.
46   Lewis, *Surprised by Joy*, 1956, pp. 199-200.
47   Lewis, *Surprised by Joy*, 1956, p. 216. On p. 190, Lewis remarks that "It would almost seem that Providence. . .quite overrules our previous tastes when it decides to bring two minds together."

Lewis, the Anglican Northern Irishman.)

C. S. Lewis and Charles Williams were opposites who through their friendship and shared imagination were moulded into an esemplastic unity. In a letter to Williams in 1936, Lewis noted that Williams' kind of romanticism was not his "kind at all. . . . Put briefly, there is a romanticism which finds its revelation in love, which is yours, and another which finds it in mythology (and nature mythically apprehended), which is mine."[48] In the same letter, Lewis stressed their unity in disunity, asserting that though he was "a man who is native in a quite distinct, though neighbouring, province of the Romantic country," he "willingly believes well of all her provinces, for love of the country himself, though he dare not affirm except about his own."[49]

Lewis differed from Williams in other significant ways, but this did not affect their friendship. For example, he wrote in 1944 to Griffiths "You're right about C. W. He [Williams] has an undisciplined mind," which Lewis definitely did not, and as a writer Williams "sometimes admits into his theology ideas whose proper place is in his romances," which usually bothered Lewis. But, "What keeps him right is his love of which (and I now have known him long) he radiates more than any man I know."[50] A few years later, on another count, Lewis the master of clarity wrote to Barfield: "Don't imagine that I didn't pitch into C. W. for his obscurity for all I was worth."[51]

Lewis also made the same point, as we have already seen, in his preface to the 1947 Williams festschrift where he stressed that the Inklings were by no means "of one trade." He noted that the collaborators with the volume included "one professional author,

---

48   C. S. Lewis to Charles Williams, 23 March 1936, in Lewis, *Collected Letters*, 2004, Vol. II, pp. 185-186.

49   C. S. Lewis to Charles Williams, 23 March 1936, in Lewis, *Collected Letters*, 2004, Vol. II, p. 185. On romanticism, Coleridge, Williams, and more, see Corbin Scott Carnell, *Bright Shadow of Reality: C. S. Lewis and the Feeling Intellect* (Grand Rapids MI: William B. Eerdmans, 1974); and Wayne Martindale, "Romantics," in Thomas L. Martin, ed., *Reading the Classics with C. S. Lewis* (Grand Rapids MI: Baker Academic, 2000), pp. 203-226, especially pp. 212-213.

50   C. S. Lewis to Dom Bede Griffiths, 25 May 1944, in Lewis, *Collected Letters*, 2004, Vol. II, p. 618. Earlier, he had written to Griffiths, 21 December 1941, that Williams "Both in public and in private he is of nearly all the men I have met the one whose address most overflows with *love*. It is simply irresistible." Lewis, *Collected Letters*, 2004, Vol. II, p. 501.

51   C. S. Lewis to Owen Barfield, 22 December 1947, in Lewis, *Collected Letters*, 2004, Vol. II, p. 817.

two dons, a solicitor, a friar, and a retire army officer." Indeed, "the variety displayed by this little group is far too small to represent the width of Charles Williams's friendships."[52] Here, again, Williams demonstrated an esemplastic influence.

Finally, it does not seem to be too much of a stretch to argue that the esemplastic concepts discussed so far have a good deal in common with one of Charles Williams' pet ideas, "The Way of Exchange," that is, coinherence, substitution, and exchange.[53] Williams defined coinherence as follows: "A certain brother said: 'It is right for a man to take up the burden for them who are near to him, whatever it may be, and, so to speak, put his own soul in the place of that of his neighbor. . . .'"[54] His idea of coinherence was an inherently esemplastic concept, arguing for a commitment to friends that went far beyond a superficial interest in their well-being.

Lewis came to share this view. In 1948, he wrote of coinherence: "We can and should 'bear one another's burdens' in a sense much more nearly literal than is usually dreamed of... one can offer to take another's shame or anxiety or grief and the burden will actually be transferred. This Williams most seriously maintained, and I have reason to believe that he spoke from experimental knowledge."[55] And in 1949, Lewis wrote to Greeves: "it does me good to hear what I believe repeated in your voice—it being a rule of the universe that others can do for us what we cannot do for ourselves and one can paddle every canoe except ones own."[56] Finally, in 1957, Lewis believed

---

52 Lewis, *Essays Presented to Charles Williams*, 1966, p. v.
53 See Charles Williams, "The Practice of Substituted Love," in his *He Came Down From Heaven* (London: William Heinemann, 1938), pp. 114-133; and Alice Mary Hadfield, *Charles Williams. An Exploration of His Life and Work* (New York/Oxford: Oxford University Press, 1983) on Williams' ideas. For a succinct definition of these concepts, see C. S. Lewis, "Williams and the Arthuriad," 1948, in Charles Williams and C. S. Lewis, *Taliessen Through Logres, The Region of the Summer Stars, and Arthurian Torso*, introduction by Mary McDermott Schideler (Grand Rapids MI: William B. Eerdmans, 1974), p. 307.
54 Charles Williams, *The Descent of the Dove: A Short History of the Holy Spirit in the Church* (Grand Rapids MI: William B. Eerdmans, n.d.), 1939, p. 55. See also the Postscript, pp. 234-236; and Williams' novel, *Descent into Hell* (London: Faber and Faber, 1937).
55 Lewis, "Williams and the Arthuriad," in Williams and Lewis, *Taliessen*, 1974, p. 307. See Hooper, *Guide*, 1996, pp. 85-86.
56 C. S. Lewis to Arthur Greeves, 2 July 1949, in Lewis, *Collected Letters*, 2004, Vol. II, p. 953.

he had had a "substitution" experience with Joy Davidman.[57]

This thematically unifying aspect of coinherence was summarized by Helen Tyrrell Wheeler, a student of Lewis's during World War II, who wrote the following:

> Much . . . was owed to a special tang in the air of Oxford at that time and which was specially linked to with the figures of CSL and his entirely enchanting friend, Charles Williams, poet, novelist and critic who had moved to Oxford at the beginning of the war. . . . Was it Williams who revived the Coleridgean word coinherence?[58] Certainly it seemed to be the banner word of the time, and it was to have revealed the coinherence of the most disparate texts, times, dilemmas, and ideas that people crowded out the lectures of both Williams and Lewis . . . at few times can there have been such splendidly exciting lectures . . . coinherence was Charles Williams's label for the quality which they believed in. What it meant to my generation of English Language and Literature undergraduates was that what happened in the great books was of equal significance to what happened in life, indeed that they were the same. . . .[59]

Indeed, C. S. Lewis, Charles Williams, J. R. R. Tolkien, and the rest of the Inklings were living, breathing examples of commitment to the essential unity of texts, ideas, the great books, and life; what we might today call a commitment to a Liberal Arts education and the integration not only of faith and learning, but of faith, learning, imagination, and all aspects of life. In other words, what Lewis called for in *The Abolition of Man*, getting "the trees of knowledge and of life growing together."[60]

---

57 See Hooper, *Guide*, 1996, pp. 85-86; and C. S. Lewis to Sheldon Vanauken, 27 November 1957, Lewis, *Collected Letters*, 2007, Vol. III, pp. 901-902.
58 While the word "coinhere" appears (once in Ch. IX) in Coleridge's *Biographia Literaria*, the word "coinherence" does not. This bears further investigation.
59 Helen Tyrrell Wheeler, "Wartime Tutor," in David Graham, ed., *We Remember C. S. Lewis. Essays and Memories* (Nashville TN: Broadman and Holman Publishers, 2001), pp. 49-52.
60 C. S. Lewis, *The Abolition of Man* (London: Oxford University Press, 1943), Ch. 1.

III. *The Four Loves* on Friendship (Philia)

It is no surprise, then, that when we turn to *The Four Loves*, we find that the importance of shared agreements in friendship (Philia) is a powerful emphasis in Lewis's systematic thinking. This is not to be confused with

> companionship—or "clubbableness" which is only the matrix of friendship.... Friendship arises out of mere companionship when two or more of the companions discover that they have in common some insight or interest or even taste which the others do not share and which, till that moment, each believed to be his own unique treasure (or burden). The typical expression of opening Friendship would be something like, "What? You too? I thought I was the only one."[61]

This, Lewis wrote, is the "common quest or vision which unites Friends."[62]

Secondly, Lewis argued in *The Four Loves* that diversity does not affect Philia since friendship "is uninquisitive. You become a man's Friend[63] without knowing or caring whether he is married or single or how he earns his living. What have all these 'unconcerning things, matters of fact' to do with the real question, Do you see the same truth?"[64] Put another way, "'Do you care about the same truth?' The man who agrees with us that some question, little regarded by others, is of great importance, can be our Friend. He need not agree with us about the answer."[65]

In *The Four Loves*, Lewis also wrote that

> In each of my friends there is something that only some other friends can fully bring out. By myself I am not large enough to call the whole man into activity; I want other lights than my own to show all his facets. Now that Charles is dead, I shall

---

61 Lewis, *Four Loves*, 1963, pp. 61-62.
62 Lewis, *Four Loves*, 1963, p. 67. Compare C. S. Lewis to Charles Moorman, 15 May 1959, Lewis, *Collected Letters*, 2007, Vol. III, p. 1049: "To be sure, we all had a common point of view, but we had it before we met. It was the cause rather than the result of our friendship."
63 Lewis thinks that friendships are usually man and man, woman and woman, but that this isn't inherent in friendship. The reason is that men and women usually don't have "the companionship in common activities which is the matrix of Friendship." However, Lewis also believed that this could be changed. Lewis, *Four Loves*, 1963, p. 68.
64 Lewis, *Four Loves*, 1963, p. 66.
65 Lewis, *Four Loves*, 1963, p. 62.

never again see Ronald's reaction to a specifically Caroline joke. Far from having more of Ronald, having him 'to myself' now that Charles is away, I have less of Ronald. Hence true Friendship is the least jealous of loves. Two friends delight to be joined by a third, and three by a fourth. . . . They can then say, as the blessed souls say in Dante, 'Here comes one who will augment our loves.' For in this love, "to divide is not to take away."[66]

Compare this to what Lewis so movingly and profoundly wrote in 1961 in *An Experiment in Criticism*:

> [W]e seek an enlargement of our being. We want to be more than ourselves. Each of us by nature sees the whole world from one point of view with a perspective and a selectiveness peculiar to himself. . . . to acquiesce in this particularity . . . would be lunacy. . . . The primary impulse of each is to maintain and aggrandize himself. The secondary impulse is to go out of the self. . . . In love, in virtue, in the pursuit of knowledge, and in the reception of the arts, we are doing this. . . . In worship, in love, in moral action, and in knowing, I transcend myself; and am never more myself than when I do.[67]

Interestingly, in *The Four Loves*, Lewis does not see coinherence as a distinctive aspect of Philia: "A Friend will, to be sure, . . . lend or give when we are in need, nurse us in sickness, stand up for us among

---

[66] Lewis, *Four Loves*, 1963, pp. 58-59. "Charles" is, of course, Charles Williams; "Ronald" was what J. R. R. Tolkien was called by his friends. It is not clear that Tolkien agreed with this; he wrote in 1965 that "I was and remain wholly unsympathetic to Williams' mind. . . . We had nothing to say to one another at deeper (or higher) levels" and argued that Williams' influence on Lewis owed mainly to the fact that "Lewis was a very impressionable man, and this was abetted by his great generosity and capacity for friendship." J. R. R. Tolkien to Dick Plotz, 12 September 1965, in J. R. R. Tolkien, *The Letters of J. R. R. Tolkien*, selected and edited by Humphrey Carpenter with the assistance of Christopher Tolkien (Boston: Houghton Mifflin, 1981), pp. 361-361. The question has been raised whether Lewis was aware of some of Williams's more bizarre beliefs and practices. The consensus seems to be that he was not. Cp. Carpenter, *Inklings*, 1979, pp. 120-126; and Zaleski and Zaleski, *The Fellowship*, 2015, pp. 268-269, on Tolkien's reservations about Williams. On the other hand, Grevel Lindop, *Williams*, 2015, pp. 309-301, 410-411, points out that the evidence for Tolkien's negativity concerning Williams dates from later in life, and notes that in 1942, Tolkien even wrote a lengthy and fond poem about Williams (p. 362).

[67] C. S. Lewis, *An Experiment in Criticism* (Cambridge: Cambridge University Press, 1961), pp. 137-141.

our enemies, do what he can for our widows and orphans. But such good offices are not the stuff of Friendship. . . . For Friendship is utterly free from Affection's need to be needed."[68]

Friendship loomed large among the Four Loves. Lewis wrote that friendship is "the happiest and most fully human of all loves: the crown of life and the school of virtue. . . . Life—natural life—has no better gift to give. Who could have deserved it?"[69] On the other hand, "Friendship is unnecessary, like philosophy, like art. . . . It has no survival value; rather it is one of those things which give value to survival."[70]

Finally, Lewis believed that friendship, at least for the Christian, was a divine gift, not a matter of chance or a source of pride:

> A secret Master of Ceremonies has been at work. Christ, who said to the disciples 'Ye have not chosen me, but I have chosen you,' can truly say to every group of Christian friends 'You have not chosen one another but I have chosen you for one another.'... Friendship is not a reward for our discrimination and good taste in finding one another out. It is the instrument by which God reveals to each the beauties of all the others.[71]

IV. Conclusions

So what did C. S. Lewis mean when he described Charles Williams as an esemplastic force in his life and work and that of the Inklings? The Inklings Project had as its unifying objective, in the words of Malcolm Guite: "to heal the widening split between outer and inner, rational and imaginative, microcosm and macrocosm. They aimed to do so by using the power of poetic language, in verse and prose... to heighten and deepen our awareness by re-enchanting the disenchanted, by remythologizing a demythologized world."[72] And they did this through the entirely voluntary community of friends in which they functioned.

To this end, as Diana Pavlac Glyer has effectively argued, the Inklings evolved into "an ongoing, interdependent creative

---

68 Lewis, *Four Loves*, 1963, pp. 65-66.
69 Lewis, *Four Loves*, 1963, pp. 55, 68.
70 Lewis, *Four Loves*, 1963, p. 67.
71 Lewis, *Four Loves*, 1963, p. 83. Compare C. S. Lewis to Genia Goelz, 20 June 1952, Lewis, *Collected Letters*, 2007, Vol. III, p. 204: "the Holy Spirit. . . . speaks through Scriptures, the Church, Christian friends, books. . . ."
72 Malcolm Guite, "Poet," in MacSwain and Ward, *Cambridge Companion*, 2010, p. 306.

community," an idea which:

> has a strong foundation in the Christian faith, a vital link that the Inklings had in common. . . . Each author's work is embedded in the work of others, and each author's life is intertwined with the lives of others. . . . Like filaments joined together in a web, writers work as members of larger communities. As they work, they influence and are influenced by the company they keep.[73]

Lewis saw Charles Williams as an esemplastic force in his Oxford circle of friends because he shared their belief in the power of secondary imagination, real imagination. Secondly, Williams was a unifying force in the development of the Inklings from 1939 to 1945, a key period in the lives and work of Lewis and Tolkien. Thirdly, Williams seems to have won at least some of the Inklings over to the "Way of Exchange," of coinherence, certainly in the case of Lewis. And, lastly, Williams played a role in promoting among undergraduates at Oxford a unified view of the past, of texts, and of ideas, something that Lewis and friends had long had as their intellectual and pedagogical mission.

A week after Charles Williams' death on May 15, Lewis wrote to Williams' widow, Florence (Michal) Williams:

> My friendship is not ended. His death has had the very unexpected effect of making death itself look quite different. I believe in the next life ten times more strongly than I did. At moments it seems almost tangible. Mr. Dyson, on the day of the funeral, summed up what many of us felt, "It is not blasphemous," he said "to believe that what was true of Our Lord is, in its less degree, true of all who are in Him. They go away in order to be with us in a new way, even closer than before." A month ago I wd. have called this silly sentiment. Now I know better. He seems, in some indefinable way, to be all around us now. I do not doubt he is doing and will do for us all sorts of things he could not have done while in the body.[74]

In a subsequent letter, on May 28, 1945, Lewis wrote to Sister Penelope about

---

[73] Glyer, *The Company They Keep*, 2007, pp. 224-226. Lewis was acutely aware of the potential for a positive community of this sort to evolve into a coterie or an inner ring. See C. S. Lewis, "The Inner Ring," in C. S. Lewis, *Transposition and other Addresses* (London: Geoffrey Bles, 1949), pp. 55-64; Lewis, *Surprised by Joy*, 1956, *passim*, and Lewis, *Four Loves*, 1963, pp. 73 ff.
[74] C. S. Lewis to Florence (Michal) Williams, 22 May 1945, in Lewis, *Collected Letters*, 2004, Vol. II, pp. 653-654.

the death of my dearest friend, Charles Williams... it has been, and is, a great loss. But not at all a dejecting one. It has greatly increased my faith. Death has done nothing to my idea of him, but he has done—oh, I can't say what—to my idea of death. It has made the next world much more real and palpable. We all feel the same. How one lives and learns.[75]

And in August 1945, Lewis published a poem, later collected under the title, "To Charles Williams."

> Your Death blows a strange bugle call, friend, and all is hard
> To see plainly or record truly. The new light imposes change,
> Re-adjusts all a life-landscape as it thrusts down its probe from the sky,
> To create shadows, to reveal waters, to erect hills and deepen glens.
> The slant alters. I can't see the old contours. It's a larger world
> Than I once thought it. I wince, caught in the bleak air that blows on the ridge.
> Is it the first sting of the great winter, the world-waning? Or the cold of spring?
> A hard question and worth talking a whole night on. But with whom?
> Of whom now can I ask guidance? With what friend concerning your death
> Is it worth while to exchange thoughts unless—oh unless it were you?[76]

---

75 C. S. Lewis to Sister Penelope, 28 May 1945, in Lewis, *Collected Letters*, 2004, Vol. II, p. 656.
76 See Walter Hooper's note in Lewis, *Collected Letters*, 2004, Vol. II, Note 69, p. 665. The text here is taken from C. S. Lewis, *The Collected Poems of C. S. Lewis*, edited by Walter Hooper (London: Fount Paperbacks/HarperCollins, 1994), p. 119.
Williams, Charles. *He Came Down From Heaven*. London: William Heinemann, 1938.

Works Cited

Barfield, Owen. *Romanticism Comes of Age*, new augmented edition. Middletown CT: Wesleyan University Press, 1967.

Barfield, Owen. *What Coleridge Thought*. Middletown CT: Wesleyan University Press, 1971.

Carnell, Corbin Scott. *Bright Shadow of Reality: C. S. Lewis and the Feeling Intellect*. Grand Rapids MI: William B. Eerdmans, 1974.

Carpenter, Humphrey. *The Inklings. C. S. Lewis, J. R. R. Tolkien, Charles Williams, and their friends*. Boston: Houghton Mifflin, 1979.

Carver, P. L. "The Evolution of the Term 'Esemplastic'," *Modern Humanities Research Association*, Vol. 24. (1929), 329-331.

Coleridge, Samuel Taylor. *Biographia Literaria or Biographical Sketches of My Literary Life and Opinions*. Vol. I. London: Rest Fenner, 1817.

Duriez, Colin. *The Oxford Inklings. Lewis, Tolkien, and Their Circle*. Oxford: Lion Books, 2015.

Duriez, Colin, and David Porter, *The Inklings Handbook*. London: Azure Press, 2001.

Glyer, Diana Pavlac. *The Company They Keep. C. S. Lewis and J. R. R. Tolkien as Writers in Community*. Kent OH: Kent State University Press, 2007.

Guite, Malcolm. "Poet," in Robert MacSwain and Michael Ward, eds., *The Cambridge Companion to C. S. Lewis*. Cambridge: Cambridge University Press, 2010, 294-310.

Hadfield, Alice Mary. *Charles Williams. An Exploration of His Life and Work*. New York/Oxford: Oxford University Press, 1983.

Havard, Robert E. "*Philia*: Jack at Ease," in James Como, ed., *Remembering C. S. Lewis. Recollections of Those Who Knew Him*, third edition. San Francisco: Ignatius Press, 2005, 349-367.

Hooper, Walter. *C. S. Lewis: A Companion and Guide.* San Francisco: HarperSanFrancisco, 1996)

Hooper, Walter. "The Inklings," in Roger White, Judith Wolfe, and Brendan N. Wolfe, eds., *C. S. Lewis and His Circle. Essays and Memoirs from the Oxford C. S. Lewis Society.* New York/Oxford: Oxford University Press, 2015, 197-213.

Isley, Jr., William L. "C. S. Lewis on Friendship," *Inklings Forever,* Vol. 6 (2008).

Jasper, David. "*The Pilgrim's Regress* and *Surprised by Joy,*" in Robert MacSwain and Michael Ward, eds., *The Cambridge Companion to C. S. Lewis.* Cambridge: Cambridge University Press, 2010, 232-233.

Lewis, C. S. *The Abolition of Man.* London: Oxford University Press, 1943.

Lewis, C. S. *All My Road Before Me. The Diary of C. S. Lewis 1922-1927,* edited by Walter Hooper, Foreword by Owen Barfield. London: HarperCollins Fount, 1991.

Lewis, C. S. *The Collected Letters of C. S. Lewis, Three Volumes,* edited by Walter Hooper. San Francisco: HarperSanFrancisco, 2002.

Lewis, C. S. *The Collected Poems of C. S. Lewis,* edited by Walter Hooper. London: Fount Paperbacks/ HarperCollins, 1994.

Lewis, C. S. *The Discarded Image. An Introduction to Medieval and Renaissance Literature.* Cambridge: Cambridge University Press, 1964.

Lewis, C. S. *The Four Loves.* London: Geoffrey Bles, 1960; paperback edition, London: Collins Fontana, 1963.

Lewis, C. S. *A Grief Observed.* London: Faber and Faber, 1961.

Lewis, C. S. *Image and Imagination. Essays and Reviews,* edited by Walter Hooper. Cambridge: Cambridge University Press, 2013.

Lewis, C. S. *On Stories and Other Essays on Literature,* edited by Walter Hooper. New York: Harcourt Brace Jovanovich, 1982.

Lewis, C. S. *A Preface to Paradise Lost*. London: Oxford University Press, 1962.

Lewis, C. S. *Surprised by Joy. The Shape of My Early Life*. London: Geoffrey Bles, 1955); American edition, New York: Harcourt, Brace, 1956.

Lewis, C. S. *Transposition and other Addresses*. London: Geoffrey Bles, 1949.

Lewis, C. S., ed., *Essays Presented to Charles Williams*. London: Oxford University Press, 1947, reprinted by William B. Eerdmans, Grand Rapids MI, 1966.

Lindop, Grevel. *Charles Williams. The Third Inkling*. Oxford: Oxford University Press, 2015.

Malanga, Michael. "*The Four Loves*: C. S. Lewis's Theology of Love," in Bruce L. Edwards, ed., *C. S. Lewis. Life, Works, and Legacy. Vol. 4: Scholar, Teacher, and Public Intellectual*. Westport CT: Praeger, 2007, 49-80.

Martindale, Wayne. "Romantics," in Thomas L. Martin, ed., *Reading the Classics with C. S. Lewis*. Grand Rapids MI: Baker Academic, 2000, 203-226.

Meilaender, Gilbert. *The Taste for the Other. The Social and Ethical Thought of C. S. Lewis*. Grand Rapids MI: William B. Eerdmans, 1978.

Michelson, Paul E. "The Development of J. R. R. Tolkien's Ideas on Fairy-stories," *Inklings Forever*, Vol. 8. (2012), 115-127.

Oxford Universal Dictionary on Historical Principles, third edition with addenda revised and edited by C. T. Onions. Oxford: Clarendon Press, 1955)

Schakel, Peter J. *Reason and Imagination in C. S. Lewis. A Study of Till We Have Faces*. Grand Rapids MI: William B. Eerdmans, 1984.

Sellars, J. T. *Reasoning beyond Reason. Imagination as a Theological Source in the Work of C. S. Lewis*. Eugene OR: Pickwick Publications, 2011.

Thorson, Stephen. *Joy and Poetic Imagination. Understanding C. S. Lewis's "Great War" with Owen Barfield and its Significance for Lewis's Conversion and Writings*. Hamden

CT: Winged Lion Press, 2015.

Tolkien, J. R. R. *The Letters of J. R. R. Tolkien*, selected and edited by Humphrey Carpenter with the assistance of Christopher Tolkien. Boston: Houghton Mifflin, 1981.

Tolkien, J. R. R. *On Fairy-stories*, Expanded Edition with Commentary and Notes, edited by Verlyn Flieger and Douglas A. Anderson. London: HarperCollins, 2008.

Wheeler, Helen Tyrrell. "Wartime Tutor," in David Graham, ed., W*e Remember C. S. Lewis. Essays and Memories.* Nashville TN: Broadman and Holman Publishers, 2001, 48-52.

Williams, Charles. *Descent into Hell.* London: Faber and Faber, 1937.

Williams, Charles. *The Descent of the Dove: A Short History of the Holy Spirit in the Church.* Grand Rapids MI: William B. Eerdmans, n.d.

Breakfast fellowship (L to R) Joe Christopher, John Stanifer, Crystal Hurd, Diana Gyler, William O'Flaherty, Charlie Starr, Brenton Dickieson, and Devin Brown

VI. Essays on Owen Barfield

Owen Barfield and C.S. Lewis: A Critical Friendship[1]

by Colin Duriez

Colin Duriez, one of the keynote speakers for the 2016 Colloquium, is author of a number of books on the Inklings and fantasy literature. They include *Tolkien and C. S. Lewis: The Gift of Friendship*, *J.R.R. Tolkien: The Making of a Legend*, *C. S. Lewis: A Biography of Friendship*, *Bedeviled: Lewis, Tolkien and the Shadow of Evil*, and *The Oxford Inklings: Lewis, Tolkien and Their Circle*. Duriez is in demand internationally as a speaker on these subjects, and has appeared on the BBC, PBS, and the extended box set of Peter Jackson's *The Lord of the Rings*. Currently Colin is writing a study of Dorothy L. Sayers.

The lifelong friendship between C.S. Lewis and Owen Barfield was critical in two senses. First, their conversations were critical in eroding Lewis's atheism and other developing beliefs that were a barrier to his acceptance of a supernatural world and eventually Christianity. Secondly, the friendship was critical in that, unusually, it was founded upon and sustained by mutual opposition, much more particularly in its early days. In fact, the opposition deepened for each of them the very meaning of friendship, where a friend can be truly other, offering a different perspective and take on things. Their friendship helped Lewis find a wholeness that affirmed both reason and imagination, truth and meaning, in harmony. Barfield not only influenced his friend's thinking, but also had a radical impact on Lewis's manner of writing, particularly the increasing importance he gave to imaginative writing. Barfield himself inclined towards esoteric exposition, and Lewis helps us to understand him, though more in the areas in which they agreed than disagreed.

THE HEART OF THE TWO FRIENDS

Though Barfield and Lewis both confessed to having serious differences, Lewis frequently expressed views that Barfield would entirely agree with. Characteristically, he wrote of the universe

---

1   My talk draws upon research for books I've written on the Inklings or authors related to them over the past twenty-five years which are listed in the bibliography. For works cited see the footnotes.

appearing to human beings at the beginning to be full of qualities of life, will, and intelligence. Every planet was a divine lord or lady and all trees were nymphs. Humans were related to the gods. With the development of knowledge the world was gradually emptied even of qualities of smell, taste, colour, and sound, which were shifted from the objective to the subjective in the general account of things. Consequently,

> The Subject becomes gorged, inflated, at the expense of the object. But the matter does not end there. The same method which has emptied the world now proceeds to empty ourselves. ... And thus we arrive at a result uncommonly like zero.[2]

Later, I shall touch upon Barfield's extraordinary second life, where he got increasing recognition in North America. During this later period of his life, the US novelist and Nobel laureate Saul Bellow wrote:

> We are well supplied with interesting writers, but Owen Barfield is not content to be merely interesting. His ambition is to set us free. Free from what? From the prison we have made for ourselves by our ways of knowing, our limited and false habits of thought, our "common sense." These, he convincingly argues, have produced a "world of outsides with no insides to them," a brittle surface world, an object world in which we ourselves are mere objects. It is not only what we perceive but also what we fail to perceive that determines the quality of the world we live in, and what we have collectively chosen not to perceive is the full reality of consciousness, the "inside" of everything that exists.[3]

---

2   C.S. Lewis, "The Empty Universe" in *Present Concerns* (London: Collins Fount, 1986), pp. 81–83. Lewis explores this emptying of qualities in places such as his book, *The Abolition of Man*, and sermon-essay, "Transposition." The reality of qualities are at the centre of both Barfield's and Lewis's views of knowledge. Lewis philosophically was an empiricist, who admired the philosophy of Bishop Berkeley, who like him was both an empiricist and idealist. Barfield was an idealist who believed in the reality of qualities, but had no taste for Lewis's empiricism, which is perhaps why Lewis labelled his friend's views (as an anthroposophist) as "gnostic," and as having "an element of polytheism in it" (see Note 4 below, and letter from C.S. Lewis to Miss M. Montgomery, 10 June 1952, in Walter Hooper (ed.) *Collected Letters, Volume II*, p. 198–199; see also Lewis's letter of 28 March 1958 to W.P. Wylie, Ibid., pp. 928–929).

3   From the cover description of Owen Barfield, *History, Guilt and Habit*, 1979.

Barfield said of Lewis that he was in love with the imagination. It could be said of their mutual friend J.R.R. Tolkien that he was in love with human language. Barfield was also in love with language. Its creation and sustenance was for him a very important function of the imagination. In talking about Lewis and Barfield, and their larger group of friends, the Inklings, the importance of human language is necessarily a prime consideration. This talk however is mainly introductory, and as a result I've found it helpful to partly frame it in Barfield's biography, rather than plunging into what is most esoteric in his thought. However, I shall introduce characteristic themes and some representative books as we go along.[4] Barfield almost made his century, and his long life has much to offer and to challenge a biographer.

Much is made of differences between Barfield and Lewis, not least by the two friends themselves, but in fact Barfield endorsed several writings of Lewis, as did Lewis of Barfield's, which can therefore be taken as indicating some measure of affinity. Lewis's writings can in fact help us to understand some areas of Barfield, whose output at times can be somewhat arcane, whereas Lewis's tend usually to be brilliantly clear. These writings include *The Abolition of Man*, and Lewis's essay-sermon, "Transposition." There are also places where Lewis is clearly trying to explain concepts he owed at least partly to Barfield (which he sometimes acknowledges), such as the chapter "Horrid Red Things" in his book *Miracles*, and his essays "Bluspels and Flalanspheres: A Semantic Nightmare" and "Hamlet: The Prince and the Poem."[5]

---

4   For understanding Barfield, the following are helpful: The biography by Simon Blaxford-de Lange, *Owen Barfield: Romanticism Comes of Age, A Biography*, and, on his thought, Stephen Thorson's recent and lucid, *Joy and the Poetic Imagination*, and Lionel Adey's, *C.S. Lewis's "Great War" with Owen Barfield*.

5   Whole areas can be explored extensively. There is a need to talk of the differences according to Barfield, and according to Lewis. Both for instance give significantly different meanings to consciousness (Lewis sees his friend's account of consciousness as a form of historicism). As a result, Barfield downplays Lewis's *The Discarded Image*, which in fact acknowledges changing human perceptions of the world over time, which are in effect changes of consciousness. Barfield makes the further observation that his point of view on things that didn't change but Lewis's did. He records his shock at Lewis's calling off the "Great War" between them after his conversion, which Barfield wished to continue. An important difference of perception between the two is brought out in Lewis's description of Barfield's views as "a kind of Gnosticism" (see Lewis's letter to a Mr. Fridama of 15

BARFIELD'S LIFE AND SHAPING OF HIS THOUGHT

As well as being a significant friend of C.S. Lewis's (one of the most important in his life), Barfield is also known as an important member of the Oxford literary group, the Inklings, which centered around Lewis, but also Tolkien. The Inklings were friends who met together during the decades of the 1930s, 40s and 50s.[6] Like another significant Inkling, Charles Williams, Barfield was a Londoner. He was born in Muswell Hill, in north London, on 9 November 1898, just weeks before C.S. Lewis. Owen had two sisters and a brother, and was the youngest of the siblings. The household was comfortably secular, and full of books and music. Barfield described himself as an offspring of "more or less agnostic" parents. The natural household air they breathed was of skepticism about religion.

Owen's mother, Lizzy Barfield, was musical, a gifted pianist. His father, Arthur Barfield had been deprived of a proper school education, but achieved the status of a City of London solicitor.[7] Lizzie Barfield, was a suffragette, was active in feminist politics. Owen's school was in Highgate, near when he first lived in Muswell Hill. At school he shone in gymnastics, which correlated with his love of dancing.

In the Spring of 1917, Barfield was called up to the wartime army; he was then eighteen and was anxious to avoid becoming an infantryman (because, he thought, "the average expectancy of life of a young infantry officer by the time we'd got to 1916 or 1917 was about three weeks after he had got out there"). As an alternative, he served with the Royal Engineers. Like Tolkien before him, he served in the signal service. This involved learning about wireless communication, and studying the theory of electricity. Barfield in fact, unlike Lewis and Tolkien, was to have no experience of fighting at the front line. He was posted eventually to Belgium and postwar activity. He found there that, with the war over, there was little to do.

February 1946, in Walter Hooper, ed., *Collected Letters, Volume II,*), which may relate to another sticking point—Barfield's belief in reincarnation. The location of Anthroposophy on Lewis's Mappa Mundi in *The Pilgrim's Regress* (in the lands south of the Main Road) indicate another difference between the two in his perception of Barfield. The latter devotes considerable space to differences from Lewis is his *Owen Barfield on C.S. Lewis*, edited by G.B. Tennyson (1989).

6   For more on the Inklings see my, *The Oxford Inklings: Lewis, Tolkien and Their Circle* (Oxford: Lion Books, 2015).

7   There is an interesting paternal parallel: Like Barfield's, Lewis's father was a solicitor (lawyer).

There was however a chance provided by the army to get involved in education while awaiting demobilization, which helped him to make discoveries in English poetry and encouraged him to write some poetry of his own. As he had already been awarded a scholarship to study at Wadham College, Oxford, all he could do was wait. It was actually October 1919 before he actually got off the train at Oxford railway station.

It was as an undergraduate that Barfield formed his lifelong and enormously influential friendship with C.S. Lewis, being introduced by a mutual friend, Leo Baker. It was this friendship that was to lead to his becoming one of the most important members of the Inklings. Barfield experienced what the *New York Times*, in his obituary nearly eighty years later, insightfully called an "intellectual epiphany."[8] This happened as he was reading through Romantic poets such as William Wordsworth, S.T. Coleridge and John Keats for his university studies. His affinity would be with the Romantic movement for the rest of his life, particularly the poet and thinker Coleridge. Barfield remembered that reading experience:

> What impressed me particularly was the power with which not so much whole poems as particular combinations of words worked on my mind. It seemed like there was some magic in it; and a magic which not only gave me pleasure but also reacted on and expanded the meanings of the individual words concerned.[9]

That moment of illumination seems to have set the course for his entire life. He became fascinated not only with what happens in the mind of a reader of poetry, but with the mystery of human consciousness itself, in play when we recognize faces, see flowers in a meadow, or observe a rainbow. Language, Barfield discovered, had a unique power to transform human consciousness. It also captured changes that took place in this consciousness over time. A sort of archeology could be practised on language, as he undertook when he wrote his book, *History in English Words* (1926). More about this below.

The importance of poetry to the very way that we see the world was a strong element in the friendship of Barfield and Lewis. When the two met, Lewis was far more widely read in poetry. Though, like Lewis, Barfield grew up in a household full of books, Lewis

---

8   *New York Times* obituary, 19 December 1997.
9   Ibid.

was always by far the most bookish of the two. While Lewis thought about everything, Barfield tended throughout his life to stay focused on a number of outstanding insights into the nature of language, particularly poetic language, and upon the historic context of human language. These insights always connected with the changing nature of human beings over the ages—what he purposely called an "evolution" of consciousness. His insights fed into conversations and writings of those who would be associated with the birth of the Inklings, especially Lewis and later Tolkien. It would, in fact, be some years after Barfield's graduation that he would meet Tolkien and stir up the older man's thinking. As with the creator of Middle-earth, Barfield's main intellectual stimulus came from language. Barfield's ideas about how poetry and reading brought about changes in how we see the world were to have an enormous impact upon Lewis and Tolkien.

The friendship with Barfield was undoubtedly one of the most significant Lewis maintained throughout most of the 1920s, especially after Barfield graduated from the English school in 1921 and began working for the distinctive Oxford postgraduate B.Litt.[10] The thesis was to form the foundation of his influential book, *Poetic Diction*. His desire to pursue the relationship between poetry, imagination and knowledge challenged the teaching resources of the English School at the time. Failing to find him a supervisor, the university finally agreed to let him pursue the B.Litt without one! C.S. Lewis however had no difficulty in engaging with his friend on the subject.

THE SILVER TRUMPET

Before finishing *Poetic Diction* however Barfield published two books. In 1925 he brought out an accomplished children's book, *The Silver Trumpet*, published by Faber and Gwyer. Lewis read it in manuscript and, soon after starting, he enthused in his diary (October 20): "I began to read Barfield's faery tale 'The Silver Trumpet' in which with prodigality he squirts out the most suggestive ideas, the loveliest pictures, and the raciest new coined words in wonderful succession. Nothing in its kind can be imagined better."

I've pointed out that Barfield's first love was undoubtedly language (specifically poetry), yet he was in fact the first of the future Inklings

---

[10] The Bachelor of Literature was one of a number of postgraduate Bachelor's degrees awarded by the University. It was eventually renamed the MLitt, one of two research degrees in the Humanities Division (the other being the DPhil).

to publish fiction, and fiction from archives of his work are still appearing. In *The Silver Trumpet* Barfield tells the story of Violetta and Gambetta, twin princesses who have a spell cast over them which makes them love each other even though they constantly disagree about almost everything. A visiting prince, who has a silver trumpet, seeks the hand of a princess, and falls in love with the sweet-tempered Violetta. A servant of the king, a dwarf called (with no awareness of political incorrectness) the Little Fat Podger, has an emphatic presence in the story. The sound of the trumpet affects all that hear it—princess Violetta dreams that she is afloat near the bottom of the sea. In an interview Barfield described *The Silver Trumpet* as a "symbol of the feeling element in life."[11] Some years after publication, Lewis lent his copy of the story to Tolkien, where it was a great hit in his household. Tolkien became the second of the Inklings to publish a children's story, *The Hobbit*.

There are strong affinities of philological interest between Tolkien and Barfield, stronger even than between Barfield and Lewis, especially their archeological digging into sometimes lost meanings of words. In both, there is a kind of linguistic mysticism. Lewis shared this affinity, but not to the same extent. For Tolkien and Barfield there are mythologies or a consciousness revealing a worldview even in individual words.

HISTORY IN ENGLISH WORDS (1926)

This, Barfield's second publication, is a meditation on the etymology of key words—that is, the origins and historical development of meanings of words. Barfield masterfully traced changes in human consciousness, changes he regarded as marking an "evolution of consciousness." This is a fundamental notion in his thought. For Barfield, a history of consciousness must be very different from a history of ideas, as he points out in his book, *History, Guilt and Habit*. Consciousness is intimately related to perception as well as to the products of thinking. Once upon a time, he was convinced, there was a feeling, thinking and a perceiving element unified in a word. The etymology of words often give a glimpse of an ancient unity of consciousness, as Barfield tries to show. Cultural and historical changes might be better explained therefore by shifts in consciousness than by changes in intellectual ideas. He sees Lewis as mainly

---

11 Oral History interview with Owen Barfield, The Marion E. Wade Center, Wheaton College. Il.

focusing on ideas, even in his *The Discarded Image*, which Barfield saw as fragmenting, but actually Lewis had a remarkable ability to bring older and ancient books and beliefs to vivid life, treating them from a perspective that belonged to their time rather than from the distance of a modern view.

Barfield explained the background to the book in an interview with G.B. Tennyson in 1992:

> I . . . found that by tracing the changes of meanings of words, you do get an insight into the kind of consciousness that our ancestors had, which was very different from our own, and by writing a book dealing with individual words in some detail, I could bring that out. . . . What I was anxious to point out, and what I thought was brought out by these etymological observations was that it wasn't just people in the past who think like us but have different ideas, but who didn't think like us altogether at all. They had a different kind of thinking. That impressed itself on me fairly early. . . . Which of course is another way of formulating the concept of the evolution of consciousness.

Poetic Diction (1928)

Owen Barfield in fact believed that an evolution of human consciousness corresponded to steller and biological evolution as a cosmic characteristic. The evolution of consciousness is reflected precisely in changes in language and perception, from a primitive unity of consciousness, now largely lost, to a future achievement of a greater human consciousness. It was this cosmic picture that Lewis consistently rejected as a form of historicism, forcing Barfield to constantly defend it against that charge.

Barfield's concept of changes in perception and consciousness being melded into language inspired Lewis, especially as it was translated into highly original insights into the nature of poetic language. These insights were embodied in *Poetic Diction*, which concerns the nature of poetic language and a theory of an ancient unity in human awareness that was built into speech.

Poetic Diction offers a theory of knowledge as well as a theory of poetry. At its heart is a philosophy of language. Barfield's view is that "the individual imagination is the medium of all knowledge from perception upward" (p. 22). The poetic impulse is linked to individual freedom: "the act of the imagination is the individual mind exercising its sovereign unity" (ibid.). The alternative, argues Barfield, is to see knowledge as power, to "mistake efficiency for meaning," leading to a relish for compulsion.

Knowledge as power is contrasted with knowledge by participation (a key word in Barfield). One kind of knowledge "consists of seeing what happens and getting used to it" and the other involves "consciously participating in what is" (p. 24). The proper activity of the imagination is concrete as opposed to abstract thinking—this is "the perception of resemblance, the demand for unity" (the affinity between Samuel Taylor Coleridge and Barfield can be seen here). There is therefore a poetic element in all meaningful language.

Tolkien read Owen Barfield's *Poetic Diction*; Lewis may have lent him a copy. What particularly struck Tolkien was Barfield's view that in ancient times thinking was not detached from participation in the world. In Barfield's carefully argued view, the way people experienced reality as a seamless whole was embodied at that time in their language. In a way, their thought was completely poetic in the senses of being non-abstract and figurative. In an undated letter to Barfield, possibly written in 1929, Lewis observed:

> You might like to know that when Tolkien dined with me the other night he said à-propos of something quite different that your conception of the ancient semantic unity had modified his whole outlook and that he was almost just going to say something in a lecture when your conception stopped him in time. "It is one of those things," he said, "that when you've once seen it there are all sorts of things you can never say again."[12]

Barfield's complex book was in fact one of the most important single influences on both Tolkien and Lewis, though, for each to some extent, it may have clarified and focused ideas and insights they already had. For instance, Tolkien had already concluded as an undergraduate that mythology could not be separated from language, and vice versa. One of the main observations that Barfield made in *Poetic Diction*, and other books, is how the very way we see the world has changed over time. It is a kind of "chronological snobbery" (to use a phrase of Lewis's) to consider the modern view superior to all past perceptions of reality.

As Barfield has shown in his introduction to the second edition of *Poetic Diction*, the ideal in logical positivism and related types of modern linguistic philosophy is, strictly, absurd; it systematically

---

12 Letter to Barfield, quoted in Humphrey Carpenter, *The Inklings* (London: George Allen and Unwin, 1978), p. 42.

eliminates meanings from the framing of truths, expecting thereby to guarantee their validity. In Barfield's view, the opposite is the case. The richer the meanings involved in the framing of truths, the more guarantee there is of their validity.

Both friends had aspirations as poets, and both were prepared to go as deep as the issues led them. The two had a remarkable facility in philosophical thinking, and had developed an extraordinary knowledge of English and classical poetry. Their discussions were to lay the foundations of their important contributions to understanding literature, the imagination, and the nature of human language. For both, this resulted as much in the writing of poetry and fiction as in works that presented arguments—essays, literary criticism and the history of thought. Some of their prose writing was philosophical or touched on important philosophical issues. Lewis, like Tolkien, was more successful than Barfield is the pursuit of fiction. However, an increasing number of Barfield's stories are now being published by his estate, necessitating a revaluation of his fiction, thanks to the efforts of Barfield's grandson, also named Owen Barfield.

The "Great War": The "New Look," the "Old Look," and Barfield's Anthroposophy

Lewis as an undergraduate had settled comfortably into his intellectual skepticism. To his horror, he found his close friend, Owen Barfield, taking exactly the opposite direction from him. Barfield, the product of a secular home, was now espousing the "Old Look" rather than the trends of what Lewis called the "New Look" that was slowly permeating Oxford. As far back as 1922 a "Great War" began (to give it Lewis's name, taken from the recent conflict) between Barfield and himself. It didn't in any way weaken their friendship; both thought being Other to a friend was part of the proper nature of friendship. Indeed, later Barfield was to dedicate his book, *Poetic Diction*, to Lewis, followed by the aphorism, "Opposition is true friendship." The "war" was carried on by letter and notebook and sometimes in person. It frequently operated on a highly philosophical level, often while the two were walking together. Both drew widely upon their formidable knowledge.

The friendly but at times fierce dispute began soon after Barfield's espousal in the early 1920s of Anthroposophy, a "spiritual science" based on a synthesis of theosophy and Christian thought and pioneered by Rudolf Steiner (1861–1925). Steiner applied "spiritual" research based on his background in mathematics and science to his own experiences which transcended usual perception. Their mutual friend, Cecil Harwood, also was taken by Steiner's views, and soon became an important figure in the anthroposophical movement. According to John Carey, Steiner's "ideas have had a lasting impact on many areas of life, including education, alternative medicine, organic agriculture, art and architecture."[13]

Not long after Barfield abandoned his secular views, he married a professional dancer called Maud Douie, who was some years older. They had met through their mutual interest in dance, in which Barfield was also accomplished. This was soon after his graduation. Barfield was for a large part of the twenties a freelance writer. He and Maud lived for a time in the Buckinghamshire village of Long Crendon, not a great distance from Oxford. Barfield and his wife would also visit Lewis and Mrs. Moore, who was essentially his adoptive mother, whom they liked very much.

Maud was a devout Christian, and became increasingly unhappy with some discordant elements she discovered in Steiner's teaching, such as a belief in reincarnation. In fact, the sceptic Lewis and she became allies against Anthroposophy, which was a foundational element of conflict in the "Great War" between Lewis and Barfield. On one occasion, in the diary he kept at that time, Lewis reported a "heart to hearter" that Maud had with Mrs. Moore during a visit to "Hillsboro" in Western Road, Headington, to the house Lewis shared with "the family." Lewis observed that, according to Janie Moore, Maud Barfield

> "hates, hates, hates" Barfield's Anthroposophy, and says he ought to have told her before they were married: [which] sounds ominous. She once burnt a "blasphemous" anthroposophical pamphlet of his, [which] seems to me an unpardonable thing to do. But I think (and so does [Mrs. Moore]) that they really get on [very] well, better than the majority of married people. Mrs. Barfield is always glad when Barfield comes to see me because I have "none of those views."

In fact, Barfield's anthroposophical beliefs created a good deal of tension in the marriage, much to his sorrow.

---

13   John Carey, *William Golding: The Man Who Wrote Lord of the Flies* (London: Faber and Faber, 2010), p. 48.

"Chronological Snobbery"

Barfield's arguments in their incessant "Great War" began to erode Lewis's espousal of the "New Look." Under his influence, Lewis saw that a dominant myth of his time was that of progress. Change in itself had a supreme value in the modern world. Until meeting Barfield, he had been seduced by this myth, intellectually at least. This is at the heart of why he had adopted the "New Look." He came to see, however, that the "New Look" had the effect of blinding us to the past. One important consequence is that we lose any perspective upon what is good and what is bad in our own time. He explained in *Surprised By Joy*, "Barfield... made short work of what I have called my 'chronological snobbery,' the uncritical acceptance of the intellectual climate common to our age and the assumption that whatever has gone out of date is on that account discredited."[14]

The "war" with Barfield not only refuted his chronological snobbery; it also very gradually helped to convince him that his materialism, if true, in fact made knowledge impossible! It was self-refuting—a view perhaps strengthened by his reading of Arthur Balfour's *Theism and Humanism* and *Theism and Thought* in 1924, though he resisted Balfour's Christian beliefs at the time. Barfield said, after their "war" was over, that Lewis had taught him how to think, but that he had taught Lewis what to think. Lewis, it is clear, passed on to him skills in logical reasoning he had learned. In hindsight, we can see that one of Barfield's biggest contributions to their mutual learning was to help Lewis to become the Christian apologist of the future, lucidly combining imagination and reason. Thinking back over the long years of their "Great War," Barfield said that this was a "slow business." In one central area of his thinking, Barfield failed in his "war" to change the attitude of his materialist friend. Lewis never accepted the idea of an evolution of consciousness, though he would acknowledge historical changes in consciousness, most radically the change from an original unified consciousness.

Barfield's concept of an original unity to human consciousness greatly appealed to Lewis, despite his scepticism about any evolutionary history of language. It also had a great impact upon Tolkien's thinking and fiction.[15] Barfield's genius lay in transforming his remarkable

---

14 C.S. Lewis, *Surprised by Joy*, Chapter 13. Going out of date, Lewis was forced to concede by Barfield's arguments, might well have nothing to do with something's truth or falsity.
15 See Verlyn Fleger's *Splintered Light: Logos and Language in Tolkien's*

insights into the origins of language into an understanding of poetic language itself. So Lewis also grew to accept that there are changes to human consciousness at different times, though, for him, it couldn't be said to be an evolution.

Though C.S. Lewis remained opposed to Rudolf Steiner's Anthroposophy, after the end of the "Great War" between himself and Barfield the influence of his friend is clear in his ideas and writings. Lewis was to make no secret of his debt to his brilliant friend. It was after his conversion to Christianity in 1931 that Lewis brought the "war" to an abrupt end,[16] much to Barfield's sorrow, though their friendship and conversations carried on unabated. Barfield continued to develop his thinking, always imagining how Lewis might counter any step. On one occasion, Barfield was invited to introduce Anthroposophism to a meeting of the Inklings, but he felt he was unsuccessful in conveying his ideas on Steiner.

It is worth mentioning the importance of the two friends' worldviews during the "great war." Essentially, throughout the friendly but hardhitting dispute of many years about the role of imagination in knowledge, Barfield was what Lewis would call a supernaturalist, whereas Lewis was at first a naturalist, moving slowly from atheism via agnosticism to various forms of idealism. After he came first to a belief in theism (around 1929 to 1930) and then to Christian belief, Barfield in effect had won much of the battle, and Lewis, it is evident, was no longer interested in the combat. Both friends were now idealists but, as might be expected, not of the same form.

Their continuing differences, though the two were on the same side of the wall now as regards believing in the reality of the supernatural world, reveal both the complexity of Lewis's thinking and development and the complexity of their friendship. Even his own College, Magdalen,[17] was a stronghold of Idealism.[18] Martin Moynihan, a former pupil and friend of Lewis's, recalls how Magdalen College had been "notably idealist… Besides Bradley there was, for one, [R.G.] Collingwood. He it was who told us how 'idealism' and

---

World (Grand Rapids, MI: Eerdmans, 1983).

16   Barfield in later years remembered where the two were when Lewis declared the war over—they were on a walking trip and had arrived at the historic town of Wallingford, then in Berkshire.

17   See James Patrick, *The Magdalen Metaphysicals* (Macon, GA: Mercer University Press, 1985).

18   The philosopher John Mabbott, a colleague of Lewis's during that period, points out the intellectual isolation of Oxford during this period in his *Oxford Memories* (Oxford: Thornton's of Oxford, 1986), chapter 13.

'realism' were in the Middle Ages one and the same. Ideas and values were *res*, things as much as tables and chairs. And, to quote a later poet, 'good is as visible as green.'"[19] The mature Lewis also seemed to make idealism and realism "one and the same" as he abandoned the Great War with Barfield. This mix can be seen vividly in his book, *Miracles*, where God is the "glad creator" and "Fountain of Facthood" a book which was part of his constant quest to capture the real, the definite, the concrete, the thing in words, expressed vividly in his sermon essay, "Transposition," greatly admired by Barfield.[20]

For all their differences, however, Lewis was greatly shaped in thought and imagination by the influence of his friend. In my view, Lewis's stylistic achievement in writing poetic prose—prose combining reason and vivid imagination—owes much to Barfield's view of the nature of primitive and ideal language. Passages in *Perelandra*, for instance, are so successful as poetic prose that the poet Ruth Pitter was able to turn them poetic stanzas (rather as William Wordsworth turned the prose of his sister Dorothy's journals into poetry, as in her account of the daffodils seen at Ullswater in the English Lakeland).

After the "Great War"; Barfield's Career as a Solicitor

Owen Barfield spent the 1930s, 1940s, and most of the 1950s in the self-imposed tedium of his family's law business in London. He had little time to write, but when he did, the pieces often but not always related to anthroposophical teaching. When he could, he wrote poetry and fiction, including his verse dramas, *Orpheus* (which was staged in Sheffield, at the Little Theatre, in September 1948) and *Medea* (which was read on one of his infrequent visits to the Inklings). Lewis had encouraged him to retell a great myth, and he decided upon Orpheus and Euridice. On one occasion, he used his legal expertise to save his client C.S. Lewis from bankruptcy, when he accrued an enormous tax bill that, in his ignorance, he hadn't expected. Lewis had generously given away all the royalties from his increasingly successful books, such as *The Screwtape Letters*. Barfield wrote a humorous book, fictionalizing his experience as a solicitor, entitled *This Ever Diverse Pair* which recounts the incident.

---

19 Martin Moynihan, unpublished A4 booklet "C.S. Lewis and Oxford," January 1998 (copy in my possession).
20 See my chapter, "Myth, Fact and Incarnation" in E. Segura and T. Honegger (Eds.), *Myth and Magic: Art according to the Inklings* (Zollikofen, Switzerland: Walking Tree Publishers, 2007).

When Lewis was appointed to the Cambridge Chair of Medieval and Renaissance Literature in 1954, he unsuccessfully tried to obtain for Barfield his position as Fellow in English at Magdalen College. He truly understood Barfield's brilliance and insight into language and literature.

It was only in 1959, when he was able to retire from the law firm, that Barfield started an astonishing second life of scholarly and imaginative writing, which included extensive lecturing, much of it in the United States. A prophet overlooked in his own country found acceptance in the USA.

Barfield's Second Life

When Lewis died in late 1963, Owen Barfield was well into his "second life" as writer and speaker, with invitations coming from throughout North America and with a growing readership for his books in literary and intellectual circles. His fiction, though not until then being published outside of specialist or esoteric channels, from this time forward explored contemporary issues such as the environment. He, like Tolkien, knew what he had lost in Lewis's absence. In a talk he gave at Wheaton College, Illinois, less than a year after Lewis's death, he began:

> Now, whatever else he was, and, as you know, he was a great many things, C.S. Lewis was for me, first and foremost, the absolutely unforgettable friend, the friend with whom I was in close touch for over forty years, the friend you might come to regard hardly as another human being, but almost as a part of the furniture of my existence.[21]

The Wheaton talk belongs to the period of Barfield's enthusiastic reception in North America. He never had had a popular appeal, though some of his newly published fiction is more accessible than much of his writing. The year of his talk, 1964, marked a spell as Visiting Professor at Drew University in New Jersey. This was the first of several similar posts at universities in North America right into the 1980s, when he was entering his own eighties. One of his many books of this period, *Speaker's Meaning* (1967), was made up of lectures that he had given at Brandeis University. Over a decade later, his short but seminal book, *History, Guilt and Habit* (1979) came out of lectures he

---

21 A talk given on 16 October, 1964, and published as "C.S. Lewis," in G.B. Tennyson (Ed.), *Owen Barfield on C.S. Lewis* (San Rafael, CA: The Barfield Press), p. 5–16.

gave in Vancouver, British Columbia.

Over the years Owen and Maud Barfield had first adopted two children, Alexander, and Lucy, and then later fostered Geoffrey Corbett (now Jeffrey Barfield) during World War II (to whom Lewis dedicated his *The Voyage of the "Dawn Treader"*). On some occasions, Maud (and Lucy on at least one occasion) accompanied Barfield to the USA on his speaking trips. Lucy Barfield became C.S. Lewis's goddaughter, and his *The Lion, the Witch and the Wardrobe*s dedicated to her.

Barfield thought back at the decade or more of his fruitful visits to the USA. Of the central figures in the Inklings, he was the only one, apart from Warnie Lewis, to have set foot in the new world.

> I first went to America in 1964. . . . Quite a lot was happening, I was writing a lot of articles, I suppose—but then it was rather like starting a new life in America. Although I had no reputation in England, a certain part of the academic world in America, the English departments, quite lot of people... were already interested in my books. It was a strange experience, rather like the "ugly duckling"! . . . "I've read your books, of course"—that sort of thing, you know. And of course it was useful from a financial point of view; they paid you awfully well. I had no responsibilities other than teaching. That went on until 1974–5. . . . The last time was at SUNY [the State University of New York] . . . .It went on for over ten years. I was going fairly regularly to America.[22]

As with paperback publication of Tolkien in the USA and the rise of the Tolkien phenomenon, Barfield's timing couldn't have been better. Thinkers of the counter-culture of the sixties, and others deeply concerned with the direction western culture was taking, were looking for an alternative to what Barfield called the "materialist paradigm" and Lewis had called "the Age of the Machine." Post-modernism was already in the air. Barfield, like Lewis and Tolkien, were in a sense pre-modern (though touching the heart of the culture). They could live imaginatively in the ideas and images of a pre-modern culture such as the medieval period or classical times, and help their contemporaries, through their insights and vision, to have a perspective upon the modern world. It was a way of seeing that, in Barfield's phrase, was not idolatrous. The modern person could be freed from "chronological snobbery." One of the marks of the Inklings was that they unaffectedly

---

22   Oral history interview with Owen Barfield, The Wade Center, Wheaton College, Illinois.

and naturally spoke of older writers and thinkers (from Plato to Dante or Wordsworth) as if they were living. Their attitude was remarkable and attractive to many.

Warren Lewis, a key member of the Inklings, survived his brother by ten years. In his diary, Warnie told of a visit from Owen Barfield on Tuesday 29 July 1969, soon after his visit to Southern California. He had come for dinner with Warnie and to spend the night. Warnie found it pleasant to have "a long chat" with him again. He noticed that Barfield still had his usual mental alertness, but that he grumbled about not remembering names, and forgetting whether or not he had just met someone previously unknown. The two of the surviving Inklings soon got into deeper water, familiar to all who try to fathom Barfield's thought and how it relates to his Christian belief:

> In the course of our talk it emerged that he is that baffling thing, a practising Christian who is a believer in reincarnation; I objected that if there is reincarnation, the essential *me*, WHL dies, and therefore it amounts to the atheist belief that death ends everything. This he would not have, holding that in each life you add something fresh to the basic *you* from which you started. But what about the endless reincarnation of your ancestors, from which you inherit? I doubt if either of us understood the other, but I found it an interesting evening.[23]

C.S. Lewis's Divergence on Meaning and Truth

Lewis particularly owed much to Barfield in thinking through the relation of truth and meaning, despite their differences on this subject. It is on the relationship between concept and meaning, and thought and imagination, that C. S. Lewis makes his most distinctive contribution to our understanding. He argues that good imagining is as vital as good thinking, and either is impoverished without the other. Lewis set out some seminal ideas on this topic in an essay in his book, *Réhabilitations and Other Essays* (1939):

> For me, reason is the natural organ of truth; but imagination is the organ of meaning. Imagination, producing new metaphors or revivifying old, is not the cause of truth, but its condition . . . . The truth we [win] by metaphor [can] not be greater than the truth of the metaphor itself; and . . . all our truth,

---

23 Clyde S. Kilby and Marjorie Mead (Eds.) *Brothers and Friends: The Diaries of Major Warren Hamilton Lewis* (San Francisco: Harper and Row, 1982), entry for Tuesday 29 July, 1969.

or all but a few fragments, is won by metaphor. And thence, I confess, it does follow that if our thinking is ever true, then the metaphors by which we think must have been good metaphors. [24]

This quotation gives the core of the many suggestive ideas in the essay, many of which Lewis developed and refined in later years, leading to his definitive statement about literature, *An Experiment in Criticism* (1961). Some of the basic ideas can be indicated as follows. (1) There is a distinction between reason and imagination as regards roles—reason is to do with theoretical truths, imagination is to do with meanings. (2) There are standards of correctness, or norms, for the imagination, held tacitly and universally by human beings. (3) Meaning is a condition of the framing of truths; poor meanings make for poor thoughts. (4) The framing of truths in propositions necessitates the employment of metaphors supplied by the imagination. Language and thought necessarily relies upon metaphor (and presumably our ability to receive metaphor).

Lewis never agreed with Barfield that imagination is the organ of truth. He did believe however in the ability and importance of myth in making truths tangible and definite. Lewis regarded the historical Gospel narratives as unique in being true myth—myth that had become fact in first century Palestine. But that is another story. Lewis after his conversion did concede that imagination gives knowledge, even though it is not the organ of truth. It is important to distinguish between knowledge and theoretical truths (propositions, abstractions, generalizations). Myths for instance, as Barfield, Lewis and Tolkien believed, can remarkably illuminate truths, which is why Lewis retold the much loved myth of Cupid and Psyche in his novel, *Till We Have Faces*, and Barfield composed his poetic play, *Orpheus*, based on the Greek myth. It is why Tolkien created a plausible legendarium of the early ages of Middle-earth and its divine origin. Though imagination does not, for Lewis, have the function of revelation (contrary to what Barfield believed), it helps us to perceive and receive revelation from objective sources, sources outside of us. It follows that we may imaginatively respond to The Song of Solomon or the Gospel narratives, or to the natural world as God's handiwork, as the early scientists believed in the seventeenth century, and many distinguished scientists today still do.

---

24 In "Bluspels and Flalansferes," republished in C.S. Lewis, *Selected Literary Essays* (Cambridge: Cambridge University Press, 1969), pp. 251–265.

One of Barfield's significant complaints against his friend was that he saw him as following, in effect, the errors of scientism; Lewis was "atomistic" in his empiricism as he divorced imagination and truth. To give a taste of the issues involved, we have Owen Barfield's own brilliant picture of what he saw as limitations in Lewis's makeup:

> He had a pretty sharp line between his intellectual self and imaginative self; he accepted the conventionally scientific basis of knowledge and that all real knowledge depended on scientific evidence drawn from sense experience. Lewis would not admit that the kind of experience that came through imagination had anything to do with knowledge of reality; it just enabled you to have more reality to talk about as experience or subject matter. But when it came to converting that imaginative subject matter into actual knowledge you had to go back to the ordinary scientific method, to put it on the laboratory table, so to speak.[25]

This picture is, I feel, a little over-simplistic. Lewis in fact made it clear in a number of his writings at different periods that there were, in his view, different kinds of truthful knowledge, as when we recognize for example that a beautiful waterfall is sublime—an example given in his philosophical essay, *The Abolition of Man*. He found useful the French distinction between *savoir* and *connaître* as forms of "to know," where *connaître* is employed in being familiar with a person or thing, and *savoir* is knowledge about a person or thing. In Hebrew (retained in English translations of the Bible) "to know" is used for physical sexual intimacy and sensual experience, as well as the usual meaning of knowledge. The Bible typically calls us to "taste and see that the Lord is good" as well as to know its teaching about the maker of heaven and earth.

Like Barfield, Lewis did believe that mankind has moved away from a unitary consciousness into a divorce of subject and object. Theoretical reasoning abstracts from real things, real emotions, real events. In his theory of transposition (set out in his essay-sermon of that name) Lewis revealed his tangible vision of how all things—especially the natural and the supernatural—cohere. He saw this desirable unity, for example, in the Gospel narrative, dominated by incarnation and resurrection, where the quality of myth is not lost in the historical facticity of the events. There is no separation of story and history, myth and fact.

---

25 G. B. Tennyson (Ed.), *Owen Barfield on C. S. Lewis* (Middletown, Connecticut: Wesleyan University Press, 1989) p. 135.

Here is Lewis's big and Barfield-like picture, taken from *Miracles* not "Transposition" (a book Barfield was critical of but which arguably is one of Lewis's best):

> There is ... in the history of thought, as elsewhere, a pattern of death and rebirth. The old, richly imaginative thought which still survives in Plato has to submit to the deathlike, but indispensable, process of logical analysis. ... But from this descent ... if thought itself is to survive, there must be re-ascent and the Christian conception provides for this. Those who attain the glorious resurrection will see the dry bones clothed again with flesh, the fact and the myth remarried, the literal and the metaphorical rushing together.[26]

Lewis sees the incarnation of the divine in the human, and the bodily resurrection of the human being led by Christ, as the complete reconciliation of the abstract-concrete division, rather than Barfield's evolutionary development of consciousness.

To finish: doesn't Lewis sound close to Barfield (or Barfield to Lewis) in this snippet from one of Lewis's most famous passages?

> We do not want merely to see beauty.... We want something else which can hardly be put into words—to be united with the beauty we see, to pass into it, to receive it into ourselves, to bathe in it, to become part of it. That is why we have peopled air and earth and water with gods and goddesses and nymphs and elves.... If we take the imagery of Scripture seriously, if we believe that God will one day give us the Morning Star and cause us to put on the splendour of the sun, then we may surmise that both the ancient myths and the modern poetry, so false as history, may be very near the truth as prophecy.[27]

In an interview, Barfield acknowledged both Lewis's "Transposition" and "The Weight of Glory" as reminding the modern world that there is a spiritual reality.[28]

(c) Colin Duriez, 2016

---

26 From Chapter 16, "Miracles of the New Creation" in Miracles (London: Collins Fontana, 1960), p. 165.
27 "The Weight of Glory," in C.S. Lewis, *Screwtape Proposes a Toast* (London: Fontana Books, 1965), pp. 106-7.
28 Conversation between G.B. Tennyson and Owen Barfield, "Conversations on C.S. Lewis," in *Owen Barfield on C.S. Lewis*, p. 151.

Bibliography

Adey, Lionel. *C.S. Lewis's "Great War" with Owen Barfield.* Cambridge: Ink Books, 2002.

Barfield, Owen. *History, Guilt and Habit.* Middletown, CT: Wesleyan University Press, 1979.

Blaxford-de Lange, Simon. *Owen Barfield: Romanticism Comes of Age, A Biography.*
East Sussex: Temple Lodge Publishing, 2006.

Thorson, Stephen. *Joy and the Poetic Imagination.* Hamden, CT: Winged Lion Press, 2015.

Carey, John. *William Golding: The Man Who Wrote Lord of the Flies.* London: Faber and Faber, 2010.

Carpenter, Humphrey. *The Inklings.* London: George Allen and Unwin, 1978.

Duriez, Colin, and David Porter. *The Inklings Handbook: The Lives, Thought, and Writings of C.S. Lewis, J.R.R. Tolkien, Charles Williams, Owen Barfield and Their Friends.* London: SPCK, 2001.

Duriez, Colin. *The Oxford Inklings: Lewis, Tolkien and Their Circle.* Oxford: Lion Books, 2015.

---. *Tolkien and C. S. Lewis: The Gift of Friendship.* Mahwah, NJ: The Paulist Press, 2003.

Fleger, Verlyn, *Splintered Light: Logos and Language in Tolkien's World.* Grand Rapids, MI: Eerdmans, 1983.

Hooper, Walter, (ed.) C.S. Lewis, *Collected Letters, Volume II.* London: HarperCollins, 2004.

Kilby, Clyde S. and Marjorie Mead (eds.) *Brothers and Friends: The Diaries of Major Warren Hamilton Lewis.* San Francisco: Harper and Row, 1982.

Lewis, C.S. Screwtape Proposes a Toast. London: Fontana Books, 1965.

---. *Selected Literary Essays.* Cambridge: Cambridge University Press, 1969.

---. *Surprised by Joy.* London: Geoffrey Bles, 1955.

---. *Miracles.* London: Collins Fontana, 1960.

---. *Present Concerns.* London: Collins Fount, 1986.

Mabbott, John. *Oxford Memories.* Oxford: Thornton's of Oxford, 1986.

Patrick, James. *The Magdalen Metaphysicals.* Macon, GA: Mercer University Press, 1985.

Tennyson, G. B. (ed.) *Owen Barfield on C. S. Lewis.* Middletown, Connecticut: Wesleyan University Press, 1989 p. 135.

Tennyson, G.B. (ed.) *Owen Barfield on C.S. Lewis.* San Rafael, CA: The Barfield Press, 2006.

Joy and Poetic Imagination: An Introduction to C.S. Lewis's "Incessant Disputation" with Owen Barfield

by Stephen Thorson

> Stephen Thorson earned an MD degree from Pennsylvania State University and an MA in theological studies from Wheaton College. Dr. Thorson contributed most of the topical articles for the award-winning Applied New Testament Commentary as well as those for The Applied Old Testament Commentary He has published many medical research studies, theological articles, and essays on C.S. Lewis. His most recent book is *Joy and Poetic Imagination: Understanding C.S. Lewis's "Great War" with Owen Barfield and its Significance for Lewis's Conversion and Writings.*

> *What an argumentative man Lewis was, in the best sense!*
> —Owen Barfield

Throughout the past three decades, I have remained intensely interested in CS Lewis and Owen Barfield's "Great War" of the 1920s.[1] This "Great War" occurred before Lewis became a Christian, and in *Surprised by Joy,* Lewis lists this "incessant disputation" as "one of the turning points of my life" (207). Yet, major volumes of scholarship on Lewis and Barfield have completely or largely avoided it, at best relegating the topic to a paragraph or two.[2] But the "Great War"

---

1   I am a medical doctor—a pediatrician who has been working in the under-developed country of Nepal for 32 years so far. I also have an MA in Theological Studies, and teach theology in Nepal, as well as working at a hospital that has become a medical school. This article is adapted from my fuller treatment in *Joy and Poetic Imagination: Understanding C.S. Lewis's "Great War" with Owen Barfield and its Significance for Lewis's Conversion and Writings,* published by Winged Lion Press in December 2015.

2   Alister McGrath's recent *C.S. Lewis, A Life: Eccentric Genius, Reluctant Prophet* did not actually use the "Great War" treatises and letters at all. Gareth Knight, in his expanded edition of *The Magical World of the Inklings: J.R.R. Tolkien, C.S. Lewis, Charles Williams, Owen Barfield* mentions the fact of the "Great War" between Lewis and Barfield, but shows no knowledge of the "Great War" materials themselves (246). Philip and Carol Zaleski simply list the names of the treatises in their monumental *The Fellowship, The Literary Lives of the Inklings: J.R.R. Tolkien, C.S. Lewis, Owen Barfield, Charles Williams* (114).

is an essential part of the story of Lewis's conversion to Theism and then to Christianity. Indeed, it should be required reading for anyone interacting with Lewis's later works. I maintain that Lewis never wrote a book, including his Christian books, which did not include arguments first developed during his pre-Christian disputation with Owen Barfield.

Many of the scholars who DO attempt to explain the arguments of Lewis and Barfield during this "incessant disputation" often make two mistakes:

1) They attack Lewis's theory of knowledge without understanding *how his theory changed after his conversion(s)*. That is, they mix up his pre-Christian views during the "Great War" with his Christian views afterward.

2) They argue with Lewis's epistemology without understanding the metaphysics upon which it was based.

Some people are scared off by the words epistemology and metaphysics. All this means is that these scholars argue with Lewis's view of "how we know" without noting Lewis's view of "what we are" as human beings.

Many of these scholars may not have had access to the original documents of the dispute. Even Lewis's "Great War" letters were left out of collections of Lewis letters until the third volume of Lewis's *Collected Letters* edited by Walter Hooper and published in 2007. And the two surviving "Great War" letters by Barfield were only published in 2015, along with the first appearance of the "Great War" treatises that Lewis and Barfield wrote back and forth to each other. This was published as a Supplement to the *Journal of Inklings Studies* in the UK, and only 300 copies were printed.[3]

Surely, all of those reading this essay know about Lewis's particular, recurrent, experience of Joy with a capital "J." This happened to Lewis regularly, or irregularly, throughout his youth and the "Great War"—at first, mainly through "inanimate nature and marvelous literature," he says in *The Pilgrim's Regress* (7). In his *Surprised by Joy*, Lewis points to "the imaginative longing for Joy, or rather the longing that *was* Joy . . ." (175). It was a sudden experience of longing for something ill-defined, that was just as suddenly withdrawn again, leaving only a new longing for the longing that had just passed. In his "Early Prose Joy" Lewis writes, "the longing to recover an old state of longing became

---

3 *The "Great War" of Owen Barfield and C. S. Lewis: Philosophical Writings 1927-1930*, edited by Norbert Feinendegen and Arend Smilde, Inklings Studies Supplement No. 1 (2015), *Journal of Inklings Studies*.

itself longed for in the same way" (18). In his later Introduction to *The Pilgrim's Regress*, Lewis also calls this experience Desire with a capital "D." Many have tried to equate this simply with aesthetic pleasure, but without this second (or third) longing for a longing, we are not truly talking about Lewis's experience of Joy.

Barfield had similar experiences, which only began when he went off to Oxford in 1919, the same year as Lewis. In his *Romanticism Comes of Age*, Barfield writes, *"the intense experience of poetry reacted on my experience of the outer world . . ."* concluding "I found I knew (there was no other word for it) things about them which I had not known before" (10). Barfield believed his experience of Poetic Imagination actually increased his knowledge of the world. He even published two books during the 1920s that argued this. In one of them, *Poetic Diction*, he boldly claimed that his book was "not merely a theory of poetry, but a theory of knowledge" (14).

When Lewis first met Barfield, Lewis called himself a "Realist," a thoroughly modern atheist, who believed that only matter and nature is real—no spirits and certainly no God. This can be summed up as a naturalistic materialism. "Naturalism" can be defined generally as the teaching that only nature exists, and only natural laws (not supernatural or spiritual forces) are operative in the world. "Materialism" in this context refers to the teaching that only matter exists, no spirits of any kind (including God).

A few years later, Barfield became a committed follower of Rudolf Steiner—an esoteric Austrian philosopher who had left the Theosophical Society to found his own Anthroposophical Society. He taught a method of systematic meditation that claimed to lead to visions and knowledge of "supersensible realities" that were "objective" and "reproducible." That is, every trained meditating person should see the same "truths."[4] In practice, the results of Steiner's own meditations produced unorthodox teachings that included many Eastern religious ideas, including interaction with spirit guides, the teaching of reincarnation and karma, two devils, and even two children named Jesus.

When Barfield and another close friend, Cecil Harwood, became Anthroposophists, Lewis was "hideously shocked" (*Surprised by Joy*, 206). There were several reasons for this, including his witnessing a close friend's last two weeks of madness, wallowing on the floor

---

4   For introductions to Steiner's thought, see his *Intuitive Thinking as a Spiritual Path: A Philosophy of Freedom* and his *Occult Science—An Outline*.

and screaming that he was being dragged down into Hell. In spite of this, it may come as a surprise to many that Lewis came very close to accepting Barfield's view of the world. For Lewis credits Barfield with moving him from naturalistic materialism to philosophical Idealism (the teaching that reality is at rock-bottom mental or spiritual, not physical). Barfield had shown Lewis that his view of the validity of logic, his acceptance of moral absolutes, and especially his experience of Joy simply could not be explained by a purely material universe. Lewis came to accept a form of pantheism, close to Barfield and Steiner's view of the universe.

In spite of acknowledging that Barfield's arguments changed his own views in many ways, Lewis never wavered on his rejection of a path to supersensible awareness of higher spiritual worlds through the Imagination. Lewis frequently moved toward Barfield's viewpoint as far as he could go, but only to a point. Then he stopped. It can almost be called Lewis's "signature move." This "signature move" can continue to be seen as late as Lewis's *Letters to Malcolm*, in which Lewis accepts much of Barfield's arguments in *Saving the Appearances*, but quietly corrects Barfield (68-69).

The "Great War" was mostly conducted in person, and sadly, we do not have transcripts of those "dogfights." In *Surprised by Joy*, Lewis says, "...you go at it, hammer and tongs, far into the night...often more like mutually respectful enemies than friends" (200). Lewis and Barfield continued these arguments by notebook and by letter. Lewis's letters can be read in the Supplement to the third volume of his *Collected Letters*. Barfield's two surviving letters have been published in *The "Great War" of Owen Barfield and C.S. Lewis: Philosophical Writings 1927-1930*. This volume was the first full publication of Lewis's 1928 parody of Thomas Aquinas, titled *Clivi Hamiltonis Summae Metaphysices Contra Anthroposophos Librii II*; Barfield replies, *Replicit Anthroposophus Barfieldus* and *Autem*; Lewis's responses, "Note on the Law of Contradiction" and *Replies to Objections in Detail*. Also included are the related treatises, *De Bono et Malo* by Lewis, and the unfinished *De Toto et Parte* by Barfield.[5]

---

5   The manuscripts of Lewis's *Summa, Note on the Law of Contradiction, Replies to Objections*, and *De Bono et Malo* and Barfield's *Replicit* and *Autem* are held as part of the Brown Collection in the Center for the Study of C. S. Lewis and Friends at Taylor University. The manuscripts of the two Barfield letters reside at the Marion E. Wade Center in Wheaton. Barfield's *De Toto et Parte* is held at the Bodleian Library, Oxford.

Lewis's first treatise was called "the *Summa*" for short. Part I of Lewis's *Summa* is titled "Being"—that is, it details Lewis's acceptance of Barfield's idealism, while repudiating any possibility of supersensible awareness. In the first few sections (I.1-3), Lewis agrees with Kant and Berkeley that the world can only be perceived in one's own mind, and Lewis concludes that the world only exists in one's own mind. Second, other minds (or souls) appear in this world, and therefore must be inside our own mind. And third, within this one world, our mind has memories and history (implying time) and even makes mistakes. So Lewis summarizes, "my mind is included in my mind"—a paradox.[6]

Spirit is the mind that includes all, and is "what I really am" and the soul is the mind that is included, he wrote (I.3). Lewis talks about the soul's "emergence" or "separation" from Spirit also (I.12). He sometimes calls this "creation" of the soul, but the word must be understood in the sense of "emergence." He also affirms the need for a "common world" or "neutral system" which is not "malleable to the will of each soul." He ends up with a "real world" (he says) outside each soul, but inside Spirit (I.21). This world is the "creation of what I, at some level, am" (I.3). Further, when Spirit "enjoys" a soul, it creates it; when Spirit ceases to do so, it "annihilates" it (I.12).

So far Barfield agreed. In his *De Toto et Parte*, he writes that he can come to realize "by reflection on the difference between feeling and thought, that 'I', while remaining one of the parts, must also be *in some sense*, the Whole" (section 2). However, shortly before Lewis wrote his *Summa*, he had come across an argument that would help him refute Anthroposophy's (and Barfield's) claim to "supersensible awareness. This was Samuel Alexander's philosophical distinction between enjoyment and contemplation.

It is important to get this correct, as many appear to be confused. In his autobiography, Lewis is, of course, accurate, but I don't think he explains Alexander well enough to prevent confusion. The point to notice is that Alexander was talking about *one* experience of focusing on an object or idea, which can be described in two aspects: *either* as the thinking thought, *or* as contemplation on the object or idea. Lewis found this distinction to be "an indispensible tool of thought" (*Surprised by Joy*, 218), but Lewis applied it to two different mental activities. We cannot *at the same time* both "enjoy" a feeling of love (while "contemplating" our loved one) and "contemplate" our feeling of love (while "enjoying" the new thinking about feelings). The important

---

6 For Lewis's *Summa* and Barfield's *De Toto et Parte*, I will refer to the part and section instead of page numbers.

point is: When we try to turn around and examine our own minds, we no longer are attending to the object!

Lewis included this crucial distinction in part I of his *Summa*:
1) a soul can never turn around and look at Spirit
2) a soul can never turn around and look at intermediaries (spirit guides?)
3) a soul can never explore "higher" spiritual worlds, *as it would cease to remain a soul.*

In Part II of the *Summa* (titled "Value") Lewis discussed how souls experience the higher, Spiritual life. Basically, as souls experience more of the consciousness of Spirit, they became more "Spiritual." This occurs as they get closer to the viewpoint of Spirit. Lewis writes, "the approximation of souls to their *qualitative equality* with the consciousness of Spirit constitutes their spirituality" (*Summa* II.4) Lewis details many "forms" of the Spiritual life—Morality, Science, History, Art, Philosophy, and Charity— but he is most interested in Imagination (with a capital "I"):

> It [Imagination] may . . . appear to us as a rediscovery, as if we came home after long exile; because we are indeed coming to recognize that we are Spirit and are everywhere in our own country and our own home. Or it may appear to us as a longing which is also fruition, and a losing which is also keeping, because we then veritably become aware of our dual nature and our division from our Self, when we are at once the Spirit that possesses all and the soul that is abandoning that possession. . . . [W]e are then pure Spirit so far as we go (for we are still limited, else would not be soul). . . . [Some may] people the hills and trees with vague personality: nor are they wrong, for we share the life of the Spirit which knows itself alive beneath all its vesture. . . . [S]uch moments are our highest life." (II.13)

What a remarkable passage! a good description of Lewis's Joy. Barfield wrote, "Humble congratulations and thanks" in his *Reply* (note on *Summa* II.13). He believed such a description implied his own views.

But Lewis now used his new enjoyment >< contemplation distinction to deny some of the implications Barfield saw in this beautiful description of Imagination with capital "I." Lewis rejected any attempt to apply a "true-false" descriptor to the experience of Joy. He believed that one cannot both "enjoy" the experience of Desire and "contemplate" its "truth-falsehood" *at the same time*. And when one returns to "normal consciousness" for a soul, one is no longer experiencing Imagination. To summarize the *Summa*, Lewis claimed that just as the soul cannot turn around to look at the Spirit and still remain a soul (Part I of the *Summa*), just so the soul cannot turn around and look at Imagination and still remain a soul (Part II of the *Summa*). The previous consciousness is "annihilated."

It is now that the "Great War" letters start to make sense. Although they were written first, they are better understood after reading the *Summa*. Lewis made a clear distinction between "meaning" and "knowledge of truth." He writes, "we can never argue from poetical imagination to the truth of any judgment which springs up in the mind as it returns to normal consciousness" (*Collected Letters* 3, "Great War" letter, Series I/2). Basically, Imagination gives us a "whatness," not a "thatness." It gives us meaning *if* true, but does not give us knowledge that it *is* true.

Barfield disagreed. Lewis seemed to have left out Feeling, which he argued is *between* Thinking and Willing. Feeling allows true self-consciousness, he claimed. He called this in between consciousness "con-enjoyment" (*Replicit*, "1.5.66").[7] Barfield's main objection was based on their shared view of the soul emerging from Spirit. Barfield believed that the imaginative experience of "seeing as Spirit sees" *must* mean seeing truth. He asked Lewis to get rid of his enjoyment >< contemplation distinction.

But Lewis never could reject that distinction. Instead he got out of the pantheistic system he temporarily had shared with Barfield. In reality, Lewis's enjoyment >< contemplation distinction needed a true creation by a God who is "other" than the soul. Subsequently, if Lewis then wanted to overcome this radical separation of the soul from God, he needed a true Incarnation of God. Christianity provided both, but Lewis did not see this second need at first. In the *Summa*, Lewis had flatly rejected the Incarnation; "the Christian doctrine of the Incarnation is an error," he wrote (*Summa* I.15). Even afterward Lewis did not immediately become a Christian. He first became a Theist, with Theism's full doctrine of Creation (but no Incarnation).

Note, however, that in the end game, Lewis did not become a Theist or later, a Christian, through logical argument. His two conversions were experiential, involving surrender to a person. He

---

7   Norbert Feinendegen has pointed out Barfield's misunderstanding of Alexander in his, "Contemplating C.S. Lewis's Epistemology," *SEVEN*, 24 (2007) 29-52. Basically Alexander distinction allows for no "con-enjoyment" at all, but Barfield wanted Lewis to throw out the distinction anyway.

even wrote in a letter to Barfield at the time, "Terrible things are happening to me. The 'Spirit" or 'Real I' is showing an alarming tendency to become much more personal and is taking the offensive, and behaving just like God" (*Collected Letters* 1: 882-883)! We can't go into more detail on this here (read my book). But Lewis did start to think about the Incarnation. I believe that the later annotations to the *Summa* in red pencil were by the Theist Lewis moving gradually toward Christianity. One of these later notes discusses the possibility that a dramatist could put a character in the drama that "in every respect" is himself (*Summa* 1.15 annotation)

So after his conversion what was Lewis's new view of human beings and Imagination? It may have taken 10 years for his mature views to form. But certainly by the early 40's, Lewis was able to describe his views in several essays and books, especially his book on *Miracles* and *The Abolition of Man*. To briefly summarize several chapters in my book, Lewis believed that the created universe was at least two-stories tall—with both a natural world, and a supernatural world. In addition, he believed that the natural world was not just material or physical, but included an immaterial nature as well. When this immaterial nature appeared in human beings (and called a soul), Lewis used the adjective "psychological." And the supernatural component of human beings (the created human spirit of man) can use the adjective "spiritual."

This is indeed a tri-partite view of mankind, although some scholars have flatly denied that this was Lewis's view. Stewart Goetz, in his otherwise excellent book, *A Philosophical Walking Tour with CS Lewis*, claims Lewis believed in two parts to human beings. But Lewis does not leave the question unclear. He writes, "We should be cured at the outset of our inveterate confusion between *psyche* and *pneuma*, nature and supernature" ("Christianity and Culture," 13). Lewis emphatically believed in both a created soul and a created spirit. The created, but supernatural, human spirit includes the logical reason, the moral conscience, and the will. The natural immaterial soul includes personal memories, feelings, and the imagination (small "I").

The absolute Spirit no longer remained "what I really am," but now became a personal God other than the human person. The human spirit (small "s") was a created part of the individual person, although supernatural, or part of Supernature. In *Miracles* and *The Abolition of Man*, Lewis argued that human reason, both logical and moral reason, were at least partially *independent* from the interlocking cause-effect chain we see in nature—therefore he believed that reason is supernatural. We won't go further into those arguments at this time, but I will note that Lewis's tri-partite view is not the usual view espoused by non-theologians in evangelical circles today, but based on the theological distinction between the "rational soul" and "sensitive soul" in older theological anthropologies.

Lewis needed this distinction to counter the tendency among his colleagues to equate cultural taste (of the soul according to Lewis) with spiritual progress. Furthermore, his entire argument that the human Reason and Conscience are derived not from Nature but from Supernature, required the existence of a human spirit that is distinct from the human soul and body.

As for the Imagination: it was now demoted (though still important). His controversy with E.M.W. Tillyard, published as *The Personal Heresy*, provides evidence of this very demotion by Lewis. Lewis himself points this out in an appendix to that book. Lewis wrote that he had "exaggerated" the role of imagination, and that imagination was actually on a "much lower plane" (147). Imagination (small "i") is not evidence of a higher spiritual life, and not evidence that we are in some sense God, but merely evidence that we are human. It is psychological. Lewis wrote in a footnote to *The Problem of Pain*, "We must not fancy we are holy because we are human" (147, footnote). He was referring to the very "immortal longings" his former description of Imagination (capital "I") had claimed were evidence of a higher spiritual life.

Of course, God can use this humbler imagination to lead us to Christ. And Lewis believed that God did do that in his case. Joy did drive him to leave Materialism and accept Idealism. His experience of Desire did drive him to keep looking for the mysterious object of that Desire, and finally to find it in Christ. Although not itself Spiritual, it can be a road *toward* the spiritual, he wrote in *"Christianity and Culture"* (24).

So far, we have seen several crucial distinctions that Lewis made during or at the end of the "Great War." 1) The Holy Spirit and the created human spirit are different in substance. 2) God created both a natural world and a supernatural world. 3) The human soul is part of immaterial nature, while the human spirit is part of created supernature. And 4) imagination can only show us *what* something is like, not *that* it actually exists.

In conclusion, both Lewis and Barfield gave friendly warnings to each other. Lewis's short story, "The Man Born Blind" or "Light," describes the confusion a man, named Robin, feels after getting eyesight for the first time following an operation. He wants to see Light, but is only shown sources of light or objects seen by the light. One day Robin sees a blindingly white fog-filled quarry and plunges into what he thinks is Light, only to fall to his death on the sharp rocks below. This was Lewis's warning to Barfield against seeking "supersensible awareness." In one of the "Great War" letters, Lewis drew pictures to warn Barfield as well, suggesting that an ambulance, an asylum, and even death awaited Barfield's attempt to chip away at the only reality we can ever see, in order to find "supersensible realities."

On his side, Barfield also warned Lewis, most clearly in a long verse drama, "Riders on Pegasus," about "two Lewises" ("Introduction" to *Light on C. S. Lewis*, 23-24). Pegasus, the great winged horse, clearly represents Imagination with a capital "I." Perseus killed Medussa, a gorgon, by using a mirror, and developed a habit of interacting with *reflections* of reality rather than reality itself. Eventually Perseus allowed Pegasus to take him to heaven to interact directly with supersensible reality. Bellerophon killed a different monster, Chimera, with the help of Pegasus and flight, but refused to fly again, "on the ground of impiety" Barfield says. Bellerophon, thrown off by Pegasus, represents the orthodox Christian Lewis who rejected the "supersensible awareness" offered in Anthroposophy. Barfield warned Lewis that Bellerophon remained "earthbound," "grumbling" and "guilt-oppressed."

Both men seem to have intended their warnings to be constructive. That is, they were both trying to bring their friend around to the truth as they saw it.

Works Cited

Alexander, Samuel. *Space, Time and Deity*. N.p.: HardPress Publishing, 2012.

Barfield, Owen. "C.S. Lewis," *Owen Barfield on C.S. Lewis*. Edited by G.B. Tennyson and Jane Hipolito. 1989. 2nd Edition. Oxford, UK: Barfield Press, 2011.

---. "Introduction," *Light on C. S. Lewis*. Edited by Gibb, Jocelyn. 1965. New York: Harcourt, 1976.

---. *Replicit Anthroposophus Barfieldus* In *The "Great War" of Owen Barfield and C.S. Lewis: Philosophical Writings 1927-1930*. Edited by Norbert Feinendegen and Arend Smilde. Inklings Studies Supplement No 1 (2015). *Journal of Inklings Studies*.

---. *Poetic Diction: A Study in Meaning*. 1928. 3rd Edition. Middletown, CT: Wesleyan University Press, 1984.

---. *De Toto et Parte*. In *The "Great War" of Owen Barfield and C.S. Lewis: Philosophical Writings 1927-1930*.

---. *Romanticism Comes of Age*. 1944. 2nd Edition. Middletown, CT: Wesleyan University Press, 1967.

Knight, Gareth. *The Magical World of the Inklings: J.R.R. Tolkien, C.S. Lewis, Charles Williams, Owen Barfield*. Expanded Edition. Cheltenham, UK: Skylight Press, 2010.

Lewis, C.S. *The Abolition of Man*. 1943. New York: Macmillan, 1955.

---. *The Collected Letters of C.S. Lewis, Volume I: Family Letters, 1905-1931*. Edited by Walter Hooper. San Francisco & London: HarperCollins, 2000.

---. *The Collected Letters of C.S. Lewis, Volume III: Narnia, Cambridge, and Joy, 1950-1963*. Edited by Walter Hooper. San Francisco & London: HarperCollins, 2007.

---. "Christianity and Culture," *Christian Reflections*. Edited by Walter Hooper. Grand Rapids, MI: Eerdmans, 1967.

---. *De Bono et Malo*. In *The "Great War" of Owen Barfield and

C.S. Lewis: *Philosophical Writings 1927-1930*. Edited by Norbert Feinendegen and Arend Smilde. Inklings Studies Supplement No 1 (2015). *Journal of Inklings Studies*.

---. "Early Prose Joy": C.S. Lewis's Early Draft of an Autobiographical Manuscript." Edited with an introduction by Andrew Lazo. *SEVEN: An Anglo-American Literary Review*. 30 (2013): 5-49.

---. *Letters to Malcolm: Chiefly on Prayer*. New York: Harcourt, 1964.

---. "Light." Published in Charlie W. Starr. *Light: C.S. Lewis's First and Final Short Story*. Hamden, CT: Winged Lion Press, 2012, 6-9.

---. *Miracles: A Preliminary Study*. 1947. Revised Edition 1960. London: Collins-Fount, 1977.

---. *The Personal Heresy*. With E.M.W. Tillyard. London: Oxford University Press, 1939.

---. *The Pilgrim's Regress: An Allegorical Apology for Christianity, Reason and Romanticism*. 1933. Revised Edition. Grand Rapids, MI: Eerdmans, 1958.

---. *Clivi Hamiltonis Summae Metaphysices Contra Anthroposophos Librii II*. In *The "Great War" of Owen Barfield and C.S. Lewis: Philosophical Writings 1927-1930*.

---. *Surprised by Joy: The Shape of My Early Life*. 1955. New York: Harcourt, 1956.

McGrath, Alister. *C.S. Lewis, A Life: Eccentric Genius, Reluctant Prophet*. Carol Stream, IL: Tyndale House, 2013.

Steiner, Rudolf. *Intuitive Thinking as a Spiritual Path: A Philosophy of Freedom*. N.p.: Anthroposophic Press, 1995.

Occult Science—An Outline. 2nd Edition. Forest Row, UK: Rudolf Steiner Press, 2013.

Zaleski, Philip and Carol. *The Fellowship, The Literary Lives of the Inklings: J.R.R. Tolkien, C.S. Lewis, Owen Barfield, Charles Williams*. New York: Farrar, Straus and Giroux, 2015.

Late night sing-along

VII. Creative Work Inspired by C.S. Lewis and Friends

The Words in the World
by Luke A. Wildman

FIRST PLACE:
STUDENT CREATIVE WRITING CONTEST

Luke A. Wildman was raised in Nigeria, and currently studies professional writing at Taylor. He published a short story with *Havok* magazine and received an Editor's Choice Award for his eventually-to-be-published manuscript *Days to Destruction*. Follow him online at lukelawwildman.blogspot.com. His author page on Facebook may be found at: https://www.facebook.com/luke.a.wildman.writer/

Author's Note: This story is an excerpt from a longer project I'm working on, titled *Song of the Searching*. It's the story of Alp searching across a magical world for his sister, told from the perspectives of those he meets along his journey.

I: The Expected Guest

The magician sat in his marvelously comfortable den, sipping a mulled cider and reading by the helpfulness of the blazing hearth. His favorite reading chair had drawn itself up by the fire.

Outside, the wind howled. It was a night to freeze any little bodies that happened to be caught in it. Yet it didn't dare penetrate the magician's den, which was scooped or carved or molded from the base of a great tree. Some said it was *the* great tree. There was no chimney, but the smoke inside did not pool. The walls were only bark, but the fire did not catch them, except where it had been told to stay. Those walls were crowded with bookshelves that were crowded with many things that were not only books, including no less than three human skulls and a small stuffed crocodile, whose name was Charlie.

The magician set down his leather-bound journal—which was scribbled in runes that bore no resemblance to pentagrams—then checked the time and asked the teakettle to kindly boil itself. A guest would arrive soon. The guest had a little body, which would be half-frozen from his wandering through the woods.

The magician looked at the door. Any time, now. Any time at all.

*

The guest would come stumbling up through the frozen woods, his feet dragging small furrows in the snow. Those furrows would lead back south. His red cheeks would sting with cold, his breath would puff from his lips in staggers and gasps, and his skin would have a crusty, flaked appearance. The guest, whose name had always been Alp, would spot the ruddy glow of firelight through the trees. It would entice him to stray off the path.

So he would come, thorns clutching at his garments, sleep trying to wrap itself around his mind. But finally he would reach the door of the magician's den, and . . .

Ponk, ponk.

*

. . . numb knuckles politely knocked on knotted bark.

"Come in!" the magician called.

The door swung open. Alp stood there, hesitating a moment before the threshold.

"*Ahem.* Fateful prophecies have long foretold this meeting," the magician announced in his gravest of voices. "Come in, young Alp! You'll catch your death of cold."

Alp stepped inside, and the door shut behind him. He didn't appear the least surprised at the magician knowing his name. That was somewhat disappointing, but from everything the magician knew about Alp's character, he was a most *unusual* boy.

"I have just been reading all about your adventures over hills and oceans," the magician said, holding up his journal. "You haven't yet told anyone your full story, but someday you will, and this book contains all the truest stories ever told. It has a full accounting of everything that's happened to you since you left the river valley, searching for your sister. And now, Alp. Let us talk."

Alp tilted his head. He had flaxen colored hair, and the plainest brown eyes.

"I know it's a lovely place, your valley," the magician said. "I've seen it, although that was back when it was still being molded from fire and rock. I hear it has a lot of sheep, now. I cannot abide sheep. Can't stress that enough. More than their stink, it's how they blindly follow anything that cares to lead them, even from clifftops. Only one lamb has ever truly been worthy of being led to the slaughter, and I, for one, am very glad that he did."

"Please, sir," Alp said, "I am only trying to–"

"Yes, yes," the magician said. "After we finish, if you survive,

I will send you on your way. You will continue seeking Ara, the golden-headed sister. But for now you must rest. We have a Perilous Task ahead of us, the sort of task which is fated to happen on any adventure worth having. If you complete it I will offer you wisdom for the road, but you'll need all of your strength to reach that point. Tea and fruitcake, Alp?"

Steam from the teakettle suffused the room with a delicate, mind-swaddled-in-wool sort of smell. It was the smell of confusion and sincerity. Alp shook his head at the offer of tea.

"If you enter through that door," the magician said, "you'll find a cot prepared for you, and fruitcake. Enjoy the fruitcake."

Alp nodded and left the room. The magician turned his eyes back to his journal, where he was currently reading about Alp's future adventure with the giants. That would happen in a few weeks' time, assuming they survived tomorrow's task.

The magician enjoyed his tea and his book very much. He had to, because, as he well knew, the next day was scheduled to be the end of the world.

II: The World's Last Day

On the last day, the magician cooked eggs for breakfast. Sunny side up for the boy, over easy for himself. They ate quickly, the magician mopping up the last salty yoke with a corner of his fruitcake, then chewing it thoughtfully while he smoothed the crumbs from his beard.

"Well, my boy," he said to Alp, "it's time we were off. Button up your coat, please."

Alp turned toward the coat rack, and the magician quickly snapped his fingers. His own nightclothes unfurled into long, purple robes, the silk feeling smooth against his spindly shoulders. His red sleeping cap stiffened into a peaked, conical cap, a foot tall with a silver bell jingling from its tip. Then the magician stretched out a hand and pulled his wand from thin air. He was ready.

"Come, my boy."

The door opened before them. Together, they stepped out into the cool darkness of the pre-dawn hours.

Four wild stags waited outside, harnessed to a rickety sleigh. They snorted and stamped in the snow.

"We must hurry, Alp," the magician said. "We have all the time in the world, but I'm afraid that isn't very much."

Once they'd clambered up, the magician cracked his wand over the antlered heads. Away they whirled.

Snow swished beneath the runners of the sleigh. Branches whipped at them, only just seen before they had to be ducked. This felt like galloping through a void of utter blackness, with even the stars and the moonlight obscured by the trees. Breath trailed from the stags' mouths, like smoke from a locomotive's chimney.

The sky slowly lightened. It changed to the colors of a drink mixed by Apollo. Purple, translucent wisps of cloud became swirled with gold, and beneath them formed a glaze of richer, creamy-pink clouds, which bubbled over the edge of the world. Finally, like a live coal in the bottom of a glass, the sun himself smoldered up, orange and glorious.

The world's last sunrise was spectacular.

"Please, sir," Alp said, huddled on his seat of the sleigh. "What do the words mean?"

The magician raised an eyebrow. "Words, dear boy?"

"The words I see in the sun," Alp said. "And I saw them on the hills where my friend Mr. Gough kept his sheep, and in the ocean with the sea monster. And they were written on the ice where the giants carried their friend who had died. But none of my friends who I traveled with could ever see the words. Only me."

The magician blinked. Surprise was very rare for him. After thousands of years of living in this world, it had given him most of its secrets. But this boy, this child . . . he had seen something that even the wise seldom glimpse.

"You have seen the mortar that sticks our world together," the magician said. "If it ever goes away, or if we every *pretend* that it's gone away, everything we know will fall apart."

"The world is stuck together . . . with words, sir?"

"*All* worlds, Alp. *All* worlds are made through words. The words can be glimpsed in all things, sometimes smudged or twisted till they mean something horrible, but always there, and always more honest in the beautiful, aching places. The lonely cliffs by the sea. The quiet sunsets. The innocent promises of lovers."

Alp shook his head. "But if the words can sometimes be broken, then how can we know when they're true? None of my friends seem to really know. Mr. Gough the shepherd told me that it's always bad to lie, but Hali the highwaywoman said that you sometimes have to lie to protect other people. I travelled with Captain Drakesley over the ocean, and he usually lied, but it always made him less happy."

"Well . . ." the magician began, but Alp wasn't finished.

"And . . . and my sister accidentally lied to me," he said. "I think she meant to tell the truth when she said that she loved me and wouldn't ever leave me. But then she went away with the gypsies, and I am trying to find her again. Does that mean she lied, even without meaning to? And if it does, then how can I know that *any* of my friends aren't accidentally lying when they promise that they love me? How can I know when the words are true?"

The magician shut his eyes. He had the distinct impression that Alp had never spoken so much at once in his life. He tried clearing his mind, but instead heard the sounds of the world: the swish of sleigh runners, the creak of branches, and the sighs of the wind as it fled the coming apocalypse. The apocalypse they were hurtling toward. It smelled like dust and death.

"Even the wisest could never explain why your sister left," the magician said. "Humbly speaking, I *am* the wisest, and all I can say is that most people need help to be shown the words. Most people cannot see them on their own, as you and I are capable of. They also need explanation, because the words you see in this world are only glimpses of the truth in another world, not the whole truth itself. Only beautiful paintings of it."

When he opened his eyes, he saw Alp watching him.

"Sometimes, Alp, people worship the places where truth is found, rather than the truth itself. And sometimes even when they know the truth, they still decide to ignore it. But *you* can see the words because you are the sincerest boy in all the world, and people who are very sincere are always shown the truth. And because you are so sincere, that is exactly why I need your help."

Alp remained quiet, and the sleigh drove on.

A few minutes later, they broke out onto a flat, open country. The dry grass was studded with boulders, and its color had been dusted away by the snow. The sky above them was big and gray and empty, but not so much as the landscape that the magician knew they would soon gaze upon, if 'landscape' was the correct word for it.

The land rose, but not into the gentle slope of a hill. It all rose at once, curving up like the edge of a food platter. Grass gave way to only rock, and then at last they slid to a halt. The magician dismounted to thank the wild stags, and thought about offering them lumps of sugar, but decided against it. Saving their world should be payment enough for their giving him a ride. If he did manage to save the world, perhaps *they* could offer *him* sugar.

At last, Alp and the magician stepped forward and peered over the rim of the world. The gray sky above them darkened, becoming the *lack* of sky. Just an empty, starless void. And far, far beneath them, the world simply ended.

Broken stone stretched away forever. Almost forever.

The stone was pitted. It wasn't brown, red, gray, or any other color; it simply was no color at all, even in the places where the sun's rays died upon it. The magician glanced behind them and saw what he'd expected to see: although it was still dawn, the sun was coming up on the wrong side of them. That made it sun*set*, rather than sun*rise*.

"Sir," Alp said, "what is that?" He pointed a finger toward the void. The magician followed his gaze.

A darkness swelled inside the void, building into a storm. It could only be likened to an enormous sandstorm, although of course there is no sand in that place. There is nothing, and any living thing that enters it should die soon after. A few creatures *have* entered it, over the ages. Monsters, the sorts which devour worlds. But those are long dead, their skeletons strewn thousands of miles away from each other, twisted into ridges of ancient bones. No, this storm wasn't a monster. It was the end of all things.

In the sandstorm, lightning flashed. There wasn't any wind, but the darkness whipped about as if shaken by a gale. And from the heart of the darkness, a face gazed out. The face of a man.

"What is it, sir?" Alp asked. He didn't sound properly afraid.

"Squint your eyes," the magician told him. "Look very carefully, and out beyond the void, you can see the faint rim of another land. There, you see it? It looks like the headland of an island, glimpsed across a foggy sea. That is the place where the world that borders *our* world begins."

Alp gazed with stoic innocence. "I didn't know there were other worlds, sir."

"Oh, yes. And they're all connected, although you and I could never reach them. Not by crossing this void on our own, at least. You see, when the alchemists first built the worlds at the request of the gods, they built all worlds to be accessible from all others. But the evil of the worlds became too great, and so the gods had to separate them. They placed gulfs between the worlds, which are not meant to be crossed. That is the space before us. But sometimes things not physical can seep between the worlds, and in the world next to yours, the world you are looking at, a very wicked man recently did something that his world isn't large enough to contain. It is coming, and it trying to cross the void to reach us. If it does, everything will end. Any attempt to stop it will be too late."

"But sir," Alp said, looking up at the magician, "my sister and all my friends are in this world. Will they be destroyed as well, if the storm reaches us?"

"I'm afraid they will."

Alp and the magician both looked at the storm, and they saw it massing further. Its lightning grew wilder, its darkness blacker.

"Then we have to stop it," Alp said.

"I hoped you would say that. That is why I have brought you here. We have one way of stopping it: with *magic*."

"Mr. Gough doesn't like magic."

"That is because he is shepherd," the magician said, "and most shepherds do not understand what magic *is*—they are only frightened of what it *does*. But magic is just truth that's allowed to fulfill its purpose. To do magic, a person must speak the words which hold the world together. Now, Alp, do you have the flute that your sister gave you?"

Alp didn't look surprised as he withdrew the small reed flute from his coat pocket. He held it loosely, as if it were a delicate friend.

"Good," the magician said. "Now, I want you to play me a song. It must be the sincerest song that any little boy has ever played, played by the sincerest little boy in all the world. Can you do that?"

"I *think* so, sir. At least, I can try."

"We will have to hope it is enough. Now, play. You play, and I will speak the words that may forestall this apocalypse. Than that, we can do no better."

For a long moment, there was only silence. Then Alp blew into the flute, and a note quavered out, high and soft. Beyond the north, the storm began to move, sweeping over infinities of rock in the space of heartbeats. Alp played harder, and the song formed. It was pure and sad. A love song of Absuland, ancient beyond time. The magician listened for a moment, then raised his arms and chanted words of power:

> *Devil, devil, do not trouble,*
> *Skies to burn and land to rubble,*
> *Dead-earth will our green-land make,*
> *Sun will scorch and land will bake.*

The magician's chant didn't fit the tune that the lost boy played. Yet somehow their two songs melded, becoming one as the storm surged toward them:

Eye of World and Soul of God,
Raise your thunders, hear our song.
Blowing winds as reed flute sings,
Halt the death of wicked kings.

Behind them, in the midst of the sunrise that was also the sunset, the colors began to swirl. A new storm formed, forged of pink and gold and flaming orange clouds, boiling together and sluggishly drifting north. The new storm they'd created drifted over the edge of the world.

Put an end to devil's trouble,
Let glory boil and bubble!

At the magician's cries, the new storm picked up speed. It raced over the empty void toward the coming apocalypse. The apocalypse raged toward it.

Devil, devil, do not trouble,
Skies to burn and land to rubble,
Meet the scourge with lightning, God,
Let this end be now forestalled!

The storms met. In the heart of the void, death beat against the sunset. Lighting flashed from the apocalypse, trying to smite the colors of salvation.

It was terrible.

It was beautiful.

Alp stopped playing, his fingers hovering above the flute holes. The magician lowered his arms. This was the end of all things, and they were fighting the apocalypse with a song. How appropriate.

Up until now the battle had been nearly silent, but now, from out of the void, there rolled a single, low, reverberating note. It swept over the world, shivering the pines of the nearby forest. It travelled farther south, rippling the ocean waves, and then, on the hilltops of Aldea, it frightened Mr. Gough's sheep where they grazed. The sound continued until every rock and blade of grass was shaken to its core. Then, after raising dust in the distant desert beyond Ridia, the sound stopped.

The darkness was gone. The world was saved.

Can Love be Blind?

by Bethany Russell

HONORABLE MENTION:
STUDENT CREATIVE WRITING CONTEST

Bethany Russell was a sophomore at Taylor University when she wrote "Can Love Be Blind?" She grew up in the lovely little town of Grabill, Indiana, where she played out countless stories with toys before she could even write. Bethany loves horseback riding, making music, and creating art, which often involves her illustrating her stories. "Can Love Be Blind?" is her first published short story.

If the whole universe has no meaning, we should never have found out that it has no meaning: just as, if there were no light in the universe and therefore no creatures with eyes, we should never know it was dark. Dark would be without meaning.

—C.S. Lewis, *Mere Christianity*

Without warning, the music had dropped into a low yet delicate melody, and the shuffling sounds of shoes filled the courtyard as groups of dancers split into couples. Once realization hit Hannah, she was instantly overwhelmed at the close proximity of him. She'd been so confident before, spinning wildly and bumping into strangers to the bouncy tune, but now somber expectation weighed on both partners. Despite the tension, Blake did not retreat to the side of the dance floor but continued to hold her hands after their spin move at the end of the previous song. As he had first guided the hearing-impaired girl through his world, now he also guided her in slow dance.

His hands were indeed soft as one slipped from her fingers to a considerate spot slightly above her hip. He held her tightly, remaining firm even while she stumbled with her footing.

"I'm so sorry! I can't dance when I can't see."

He let go of her hand and gingerly touched her chin with his thumb, "You don't have to see when you're dancing, silly. Just follow my lead."

As he withdrew his hand from her face, the motion brought to her nose a subtle waft of his natural musk. Such a scent was difficult to describe, but perhaps the closest smell that carried resemblance would be lavender with a sort of masculine aftertaste. This, combined with the mellowness of his voice, drifted her into some kind of surreal trance, entangling her in emotions unlike anything she'd ever experienced.

Halfway through the song, Blake stopped dancing again and they stood silently together for a couple seconds. Hannah could barely hear the chirruping of the insects over the knocking of her own heart in her ears.

"Something wrong?" she asked.

"No, no. I just think," he took and lightly traced the features of her face with his fingers, "you're truly something else."

Her heart soared in ecstasy. As Hannah replayed his words in her head, she smiled broadly; however, it quickly dissolved at a tragic thought. She'd tried dismissing it, but she could not escape the truth that they'd see never each other's smile. How desperately Hannah longed for him to see hers and for her to see his just once. Even so, she swore there were times that she could hear it in his voice. She fantasized what he might look like, imagining a strong complexion being broken by the sudden glow of joy.

Her thoughts were interrupted by the sting of hot breath blowing on her lips. He had edged incredibly near to her, causing her heart to jump at his sigh. The immense magnetism of his proximity drew her in, and she only hesitated before closing the gap between them.

* * *

When Hannah first found herself in this bizarre world, she recognized the absence almost immediately. She was completely captivated by a new "blackness" so deep and penetrating that it extended well beyond the concept of black as a "color." That which she observed was an emptiness, closer resembling a vacuum rather than something tangibly perceived. So thrown by this sudden shift of reality was she that it took her several minutes to notice hands tugging her by the wrists through the waters of an icy, reeking bog. The water soon shallowed, and the hands released her, plopping her face first into the thick muck.

"What's...?" She raised herself up from the slippery mud and clawed at the clomps of ooze on her face, which lodged beneath her fingernails.

"Hey."

The voice was almost inaudible, as were, she'd discover, most of the other voices and sounds. She opened her eyes to see him for she didn't yet realize the absence of light in this world. Initially, she thought mud was still in her eyes, but when she cleared most of it away and still couldn't see, her next reaction was panic in assumption that she had gone blind. Greater was her confusion when the owner of the hands-a boy-did not understand her problem of blindness, as he comprehended all her English with exception to words relating to sight. Since he was a stranger, she doubted it was a joke, and when he seemed to express concern for her she reserved to consider these things in her heart whilst she gathered more information. Hannah quieted herself with the rationale that this was not the oddest thing that she'd encountered for she'd gotten lost before. The best thing to do was let the world carry her through while she sought a way home.

Although she could not exactly pronounce the boy's actual name, it sounded close to Blake, so she ended up calling him such regardless of her likely mispronunciation. This boy, Blake, invited Hannah to his home to get cleaned up and then guided her along the path, for although she tried to feel her way around, she tripped every other step. The swamp was hazardous, ridden with twisted roots, sinkholes, and an autumn chill to top it off. Without him, Hannah knew she would probably have gotten sick-or worse. Even then as she shivered he took her under his arm, covering her messy, smelly body with his windbreaker.

Upon pulling open his door, the lull of soothing fragrances filled her lungs. His parents, whom Blake later informed her worked in the extract industry, were quite hospitable and pleasant despite her intrusion. The mother helped her wash up and brought her to a spare bedroom. As she took a step forward, Hannah thrust her foot into an animal of some kind, which shrieked and scuttled away. This worried the parents, but Blake explained that this girl was significantly disabled in her senses of perception. Next, he seized her wrist and led her hand around the room to feel the furniture. His brusqueness scared her; however, the mere charm of his quiet voice reassured her as he spoke about the room's layout.

Blake steered Hannah around the room in a peculiar sort of dance that was comprised of her being spun in an ovular route while she ran her hand against the many textures surrounding her. At one point, her other hand wandered wayward from their spinning and lighted on his face. She drew back and apologized immediately, but he took her hand and placed it back on his cheek.

"Go ahead."

She still shied away, withdrawing her hand and saying, "I don't understand what you want me to do."

"This is how we introduce ourselves. Here."

She stiffened as the soft tips of his fingers invaded her face and searched her features. Her skin tingled hotly and shivered as they traced the bridge of her nose down to her lips and up again to her eyes where he abruptly stopped.

"What are these things hidden under here?"

Blake poked her eyeball like a button. She reared back, shoved him away, and clutched her eye as she groaned between her teeth.

"Oh, I'm sorry! You can feel that?"

"Yes. That was my eye."

"What's that?"

"An eye. The thing you see with."

"Is this the concept you referred to earlier?"

"Yes. The eye is the organ that captures light so people can see their surroundings. For some reason, mine are not working but that doesn't mean I can't feel them."

"Can I touch them again?"

"No. Go touch your own eyes. You're too rough with mine."

"I can't."

"Why not?"

He took Hannah's hand and raised it to his face, for he was somewhat taller than her. Then Blake proceeded to direct her fingers to feel along his skin as he had done to hers previously. From what she could gather, Blake had a defined jawline, full lips, and a decent nose, but as her fingers approached the place where his eyes would be, there was nothing! All she felt were two valleys in his skull, and she screamed.

"What's the matter?" he asked, nervously.

"Where are … your eyes?"

"I don't have them. No one has those things that you have. I've never heard of such 'organs,' which makes me concerned for you because you might have some kind of tumor or disease that's affecting your brain."

"What? No, they've been here my whole life. Most everyone has eyes."

"Not where I'm from. Hannah, these are anomalies. You should probably see a doctor."

As much as she pleaded with him, Blake and his parents could not be convinced otherwise. Hannah was to be taken to a doctor that lived in town.

The doctor wasn't too far from the country home of Blake and his family. He amiably greeted her and conducted a diagnostic, checking her heart rate, temperature, and reflexes. Following this, he had her take a series of short, specialized tests to determine her senses of hearing, touch, and smell. By the time he finished, he said, "I do believe that I have found the problem."

"Is it an illness?"

"Not exactly. However, I did find the answer as to why she's running into things and speaking exceptionally loud. It seems that Hannah has a rare and serious condition that prevents her from properly perceiving. Specifically, she has two extra organs in her skull that seem to serve no purpose aside from drawing the ability to sense from her ears and nose. To fix her disability, it appears that we will have to surgically cut out the extra organs."

Hannah stood so rapidly she knocked back her chair.

"That's alright, let's just give it time," said the mother.

"I do have a temporary solution." The doctor then explained the procedure before asking, "Hannah, would you please give me your arm?"

The world exploded in a new way. The shot the doctor gave awakened within her a lucidity of perception. She could hear tremendously better, and on the walk back home, she noticed a variety of pleasing scents and enchanting songs of the marketplace.

Blake heard her laugh and squeezed her hand as they strolled along. Although now she could hear everyone coming and sense that which was around her through smell and touch, she hesitated to tell Blake, for she secretly preferred the firm assurance of his grasp.

Delighting in the wonder and life happening around her, Hannah mused to herself aloud, "Blake, I wonder what it's like to live in your world without eyes."

"There is a lot to do here," he said simply.

A thought occurred to her.

"Would you show it to me?"

"Sure. I can take you to some interesting places."

***

A curious child at heart, she reasoned to explore for both pleasure and for clues as to how to escape. With permission, his parents went on home, and the two veered off in a different direction.

"The best way to both experience my culture and talk is at a restaurant, I think," he said, "It could be a trade because I'm interested in this mysterious concept of sight you keep insisting is real."

At the table, they traded answers and questions. Blake told her about how time was formally indicated by the ringing of bells and informally through temperature cycles. In turn, he asked Hannah for more detail about what it's like to see. She told him that it was similar to hearing in that it was perceiving something without direct contact. They talked about this for sometime, but Blake still could not understand it regardless of how Hannah described it. Eventually, there was a break in conversation, which spurred Hannah into asking a default question.

"So…what do you like to do for fun?"

"I like nature and making sculptures."

"Really?"

"Yeah. I can show you when we get back. What do you like?"

"I don't know. Sometimes I like running; other times I like listening to music. It depends on the day. I guess I like doing whatever makes me happy."

"Happiness is nice. I wish I could be happy all the time," Blake sighed.

Hannah sipped her lemony drink. The taste was tart and bittersweet with a tang of something unidentifiable. "Is yours also a rough world to live in?"

"I don't know. Rough compared to what?"

"I mean, is it challenging and difficult to live life here?"

"It's not particularly easy or hard."

"Where I'm from, life is rough. War, for instance, is rough."

"War is natural. People die all the time."

"I don't think so. People die more painful deaths and at faster rates during war."

"So? Everyone is going to die. It's natural."

The food came. They each received a veggie wrap. As she bit into it, Hannah squirmed with glee. A flurry of complementary tastes bombarded her taste buds, and she couldn't help but grin.

"Doesn't that bother you though?" she asked mid-chew, "The fact that you have one life, and you're going to die, too?"

"Hardly. I was already not alive, and right now all I'm doing is living, so why would it be a problem if I wasn't again?"

"Don't you like living?"

"I mean sure, but it's not like I'm going to feel anything when dead."

"So, you don't value your life?"

The ice in Blake's glass clicked against the sides as he took a drink. "I value it. I'm living, so I might as well enjoy it and help others. It'd be a waste if I didn't take care of my life. That's why we have doctors."

She couldn't help but be taken back. Who was this boy that neither feared death nor honestly valued life? How did he stay sane and have the motivation to keep living if life meant nothing?

"Do most people here share your opinion?" she asked.

"Probably."

"So what do you do with murderers?"

"The law takes care of them to help society function. It makes life easier."

Engrossed in conversation and fascinated by the other's polar view of thinking, the two carried on into the cooler hours of the day until Blake suggested they make their way home. This, however, would be far from the last of their times spent together. Thoroughly enthralled by her backward philosophies, Blake found an excuse for Hannah to stay in the guest room as a foreign exchange student and soon began asking Hannah each day to informal events, although he never used the term "date." Little by little, Hannah began to understand his world and his way of thinking. After several months, the two were inseparable and would spend almost every waking moment together. Hannah's feelings quickly began to overshadow her priority to escape, and she started to forget as Blake replaced these thoughts.

When summer vacation was nearing its end, the two were out hiking and had taken a trail past the swamp to a special grove. Here, they listened to the water cascade down a stream between the trees, as it gargled in harmony with the tunes of woodland birds. It was then that Blake finally broke the taboo of their mutual yet unsaid feelings.

"There's something else I'd like to ask you," he began.

"Sure, anything," she replied, impulsively.

"There's a community dance celebrating the end of summer soon. I wasn't going to go initially because those things make me uncomfortable, and my mom was also going to have me run some errands. But, I was thinking she might let me go to the dance if we went together and since you want to experience our world. Would you be interested?"

"Sure, yeah. Why not? It'd be fun."

* * *

This was but a week ago. Now, here they stood, face-to-face, with

Hannah closing the gap between them.

Theirs was a kiss deep yet gallant.

When at last their lips pulled apart, they were at a loss for words, for the bated breath of both dancers had caught them by surprise. Usually, two such as themselves would not find such mutual intimacy until later in time; however, there was uncanniness to the way one complemented the other. Both bloomed in their hearts and were stolen away by the atmosphere. They simply stood, drinking in the sheer presence of the other, and even after the kiss, they held each other tightly, foreheads pressed together.

"I think I really like you," Blake murmured, his voice shaky.

Hannah lightly kneaded his arm. "I don't want to be merely liked," she said. Then, she was still for a moment before asking, "Do you think you could you ever love me, Blake? Even when you find the world this meaningless?"

"I'd care for you deeply." He gave her a peck on the forehead.

Hannah could hardly feel it over the weight of her question. "Yes, but would you love me?"

His honesty was painful. "I don't really know."

She ran her fingers through the downy hair at back of his head. "Let me show you."

Hannah pushed his head to hers and this time, she kissed him with the fullness of her compassion overflowing from within her. Needless to say, he kissed back, ever so flawlessly delivering his benevolence, yet she still could feel something was missing. Though it was wonderful, the kiss felt unbearably empty, not just because she didn't "sense" his love but also since she knew he'd likely never have the capacity. One discovers the profundity of love amidst suffering, struggle, and sacrifice. But even in these trials, neither Blake nor his people would find any value, for they neither found value in life nor anguish. These people merely sought happiness because it feels good and healing because pain is uncomfortable.

She described this to him with much grief.

"I'm afraid I can't understand this different love you talk about, but perhaps it wouldn't be a problem if you perceived the world as I. If you gave up your eyes and recognized the world for what it really is, then we wouldn't have this barrier."

"Yes, but I can't do that. It's not what love is."

"Hannah. . ." he sighed, gently pausing before speaking. "Since I've met you, I've had this fear, and now I've been agonizing it for months. The truth is, I've been so terrified that you'd leave. I was originally scared to fall for you and when I let myself, I dreaded your retreat back to your world. I know it's so selfish! I'm sorry, Hannah. I just want to keep you here and hold you." He took her hands in his. "Forever."

"Oh, Blake. I wish we could be together, too." She took a breath to continue speaking, but he interrupted.

"Really? Oh, I'm so relieved! You have no idea how this has been relentlessly eating away at me every night. It's just been such a burden to think that one day I'd have to ask you."

"Ask me what?"

His hands slipped from hers, and she could hear the sound of rubbing fabric as he dug into his jacket pocket. Before long, he had her hold out her hand as he dropped something cold and metal into her palm. She felt the thing in her fingers and found it to be an elegantly ornamented spoon with a sharp tip.

"What's this?"

"It's a spoon. I'm asking you to make a big sacrifice, and I know it's a lot to ask, but Hannah, the injection and those pills the doctor gave you will soon wear off, and you'll be resistant to them. If we are to be together long term, you have to get ride of these vestigial eyes. They are parasitic, sucking away your capacity to perceive the world around you from your other sensory organs. You would be handicapped and would never be able to do simple things like feel the warmth of my embrace or hear the voices of our children if we have them."

She immediately dropped the spoon, and it rang shrill as it smacked against the stone pavement. "I'm sorry, Blake. I can't!"

"*Why?*"

Hannah cradled herself with her arms. "I'm scared!"

"I know it will hurt, but it won't last long! The spoon has been dipped and coated in painkiller. The doctor himself gave it to me to give to you, so you can stay here with me, and we can be happy."

"Happy? Really?"

"Yes." Blake drew her into an engulfing hug, resting his chin on top of her head. "Just stop for a moment and let me hold you."

Hannah nuzzled against his chest that was adorned in a shirt of a mystically silky yet cozy texture. His body was warm and still smelled of lavender despite the power of his extravagant cologne.

"Wouldn't you miss this?" he whispered rhythmically as if reciting a poem, "Wouldn't you miss how it feels to be cared for? If you do this basic thing, we can enjoy life and be happy forever."

Not wanting him to move, Hannah was silent as she relished his affection, but soon his words caught up to her and she had to respond.

"But what if one dies before the other, Blake? Then, we won't be together forever."

He stroked her hair and tucked it behind her ear. "Forever is what the present time feels like. Forever is as long as you make it. Let us make it a long and happy forever-just me and you."

She leaned back and unwrapped his arms that were around her. "But I don't want that if we can't actually be together forever."

Blake scoffed. "That forever is a fantasy. What I'm referring to is the real forever that's now."

Hannah's voice hardened. "No, your forever is the fantasy because it's not actually forever. Yours is not only temporary but also short. The happiness will end."

"Who cares? Hannah, trust me. I'll give you enough happiness in this life to last all eternity."

She briefly considered doing the deed but quickly shrunk back.

"I can't, Blake. I'm so sorry."

Blake grabbed her hands and entwined his fingers in hers. "Please, Hannah. Please, please hear me out! I desperately need you to stay with me. I don't want to be alone again! You see...I won't love anyone else!"

Hannah wrenched her hands free of his. "Don't tell lies, Blake. You can't love."

"No, Hannah! If you left, I'd be devastated. I beg you!"

"Blake, relax. The answer to the removal of my eyes is no, but I didn't say I'd leave."

"But you *will*! If you don't give up your eyes, this reality will expel you back because you're an unnatural anomaly! However, I talked to the doctor, and he said if you removed your eyes, you'd be safe."

"But I must keep my eyes. I'd need them if I ever returned to my home world, so if it means I have to go back then so be it."

"No! You can't!"

His shoes clunked and metal scraped the floor as he found the spoon. She backed up two steps before he tightly caught her shoulders and forced her against nearby wall.

"I'm so sorry, but I just can't let you go," he grunted, resisting her struggle.

"Blake, please! Don't-!"

"You will thank me one day," he said, amorously as ever, "We will be happy." The cloth of his sleeve rustled as he raised his arm.

"Blake, NO!"

He angled the point of the spoon at the edge of her right eye, and she shrieked. She threw her head back to fight it, when she suddenly saw a star. Amazed at the sight of light, she gasped, as the pinprick exploded into a gigantic mass of white that consumed the totality of the sky.

Blake instantly loosened, and Hannah slipped free in a fall to the ground. She shielded her eyes due to the prolonged lack of exposure. With minor delay, Blake dropped next to her, and the metal spoon harshly chimed, as it struck the ground a second time. The music ceased and was replaced with a chorus of dull, sick thumps as various bodies around her collapsed. Under the radiance of the sky, Hannah could see the forms of all the dancer that now lay ghastly pale and lifeless from the shock of light. She looked to the one next to her and sobbed in both mourning and in horror, for his appearance was so terribly freakish that it closer resembled a soulless corpse than the boy she thought she loved.

Hannah turned away and noticed the luminosity of the sky had focused itself into a single beam. The bright glow of the star was now searched the ground like a wandering spotlight before jerking up and glaring straight into Hannah's eyes with a brilliance so hot it blinded her.

* * *

The beam moved from her face, and the scene sharpened.

Though it was a moonless night, the darkness appeared as day to Hannah, and for a time she just stood there, blankly gazing over the cemetery hills. Rain was billowing down in sheets, pulsing with the gusts that tore at the sparse trees planted between the graves. Hannah shivered, her clothes fastening to her like a second skin. She was surely home, but why in the world was she in Burlough Graveyard? Though it was true she lived just three blocks down, Hannah was still bewildered as to how she woke up here of all locations.

"You there!"

A man sheltered in a dim, yellow raincoat, which obscured all of him from his clerical collar down to his shoes, secured a floppy hat to his head with one hand while shining a flashlight on Hannah with the other.

"Excuse me, miss, but can I help you find someone?"

What was normally a common question now seemed strange to ask in the middle of a typhoon, but still Hannah answered.

"I was looking for someone," she mumbled, "though now I'm not so sure…"

The man nodded, water pouring off his hat. "Then, I can at least take you somewhere dry where you can wait out the storm."

They slogged across the flooding cemetery to a modest building with widows lit amidst the downpour. She glanced behind her, but the man was already gone, so Hannah hurried inside and closed the door.

The place smelt of timeworn wood, and each plank creaked with her footsteps. Rows of battered pews lined both sides of an aisle that led to a single altar, while the magical stained glass windows in the walls showed no trace of chip or fracture. The interior and furnishings were well kept yet visibly historical in age, accruing Hannah's awareness of her dripping, waterlogged state. Meanwhile, someone was playing a cheery hymn, and, despite her self-consciousness, Hannah neared the organ, for the song offered a sense of security in its gladness.

Fully expecting an elderly woman, Hannah was instead bewildered to discover a young man at the bench. Dressed in plain attire, his hair was fair and combed feathery. From what she could tell, he was close to her age, and yet he was incredibly skillful at such an old instrument. She wavered while she fascinated in his hands springing across the keys. Eventually, she conjured up the nerve to sit next to him on the bench for the sake of the music. So absorbed by his work was he that he didn't even notice her beside him for the extent of an entire hymn.

It was only when she began humming along that he glanced over and, upon seeing her, smiled something genuine, crinkling the corners of his kind eyes.

Canto XXXIII
by M. J. Paulus

Michael J. Paulus, Jr., is University Librarian and Assistant Provost at Seattle Pacific University in Seattle, Washington. His administrative, teaching, and scholarly interests focus on the history and future of libraries as well as on technology and ethics.

The only hope, or else despair
Lies in the choice of pyre or pyre—
To be redeemed from fire by fire.

Who then devised the torment? Love.
—T. S. Eliot, "Little Gidding," *Four Quartets*

I.

One of the world's greatest books, Dante's *Divine Comedy*, begins and ends with books. In the beginning, at the edge of Hell, there are Virgil's. At the end, in the highest heaven, there is God's—the book that contains all ideas, forms, and the correspondences between them—the book into which Dante promises God will bind up all scattered leaves.

Unlike Dante, Virgil, or God, I am not the author of a book. I am a keeper of books and of one book in particular. I am also a keeper of particular secrets about the first book of Dante's that appeared in Oxford. The claim that Dante was a student in Oxford was first made by Giovanni da Serravalle, Bishop of Fermo, in the preamble to his 1417 Latin translation of and commentary on the *Divina Commedia*, which was produced under the influence of a former Chancellor of the University at Oxford. The claim is doubted by most, but the record does show that Humfrey, Duke of Gloucester, presented a uniquely illuminated manuscript of Serravalle's book to Oxford in 1444. It was cataloged about a century later, but one bibliographer claims that by 1697 there was no book of Dante's in any of the libraries at Oxford.

I came up to Oxford just before the Second World War to read literature. But I became distracted by the war and, unable to serve in it, accepted a post at the Bodleian. Because of my facility with languages, I was apprenticed to the keeper of rare books. One of my first responsibilities was paging these for readers. This was dreary and dirty work, but it afforded me the opportunity to explore known and unknown volumes that had been housed in the library for centuries. In the third month of my employment, I made a discovery that transformed my job into a vocation. While reshelving quartos among some of the library's earliest accessions, I found Oxford's first Dante.

The book was without markings and bound in tough and dull brown leather. Cradling the tightly bound codex in one hand, with the other I slowly turned over its stiff parchment leaves and followed the vivid illuminations of figures and events running along the lower borders of every page to the last. The penultimate image on the final leaf—a gold, filigreed illustration of the Trinity in diverse but unified figures—was the most beautiful thing I had ever seen. These shimmering figures faced a final image of flashing and blinding light that spread out into colors, a throne, and a door opening up out of the book and pulling me in through it. I quickly shut the book and, with trembling hands, returned it to its secret place on the shelves.

Bibliographic records were minimal, but I became certain that I had found the Dante donated by Sir Humfrey. As I made inquiries, I heard of legends that surrounded the loss of the book—and of other losses that surrounded its loss. Some of the older librarians told me that the book had not been lost but destroyed, to prevent other destructions. Under the cover of reformations and revolutions that spilled into Sir Bodley's library, a succession of readers had suffered strange deaths associated with sudden failures of mental or physical faculties. By the end of the seventeenth century, the book was lost.

Intrigued by the history of the book, I delayed revealing my discovery of it. Initially, I was not clear about my motivations for keeping it hidden. Perhaps it was simply that war and loss were far from abstractions at that point in time, and I had an intuitive sense that the book needed to be protected. As I secretly spent more time with the book, I began to sense a compelling pattern of necessity—of the integration of understanding, redemption, and love. There was something darker, too, which seemed to precede more glorious ends. I began to imagine the book required something of me.

II.

Early during my tenure as the clandestine keeper of the Oxford Dante, I became aware that others knew about the survival of Sir

Humfrey's donation. The first person who approached me about it was the enigmatic editor and author Charles Williams. He first learned of the book through a British Academy tribute to Dante published by his employer, Oxford University Press, in 1921. Nearly twenty years later, war relocated Williams to Oxford and through some esoteric source he found his way to me.

We met in the stone corridor leading to Sir Humfrey's Reading Room. Williams arrived at the library near the end of a workday, visibly weary but intent. He told me he was a poet and that he had written a variety of books, but there remained one book—unwritten and perhaps unwritable—which eluded him. He thought Sir Humfrey's Dante could help him write or not write the great book he was contemplating. He promised he would not reveal the existence of the book, and I sensed he was someone who would not violate his word. If he did, I was prepared to add to the violent history of the book. I led him into the reading room and withdrew to retrieve the book.

When I returned, I found Williams considering, alternatingly, the ancient volumes stacked up around him and the diligent scholars reading beneath them, as if he were looking for manifestations of the discourses between the books that were and the books that were to come. After placing the secret Dante in his eager hands, I surreptitiously watched him during his time with the book. Williams's whole body vibrated as he connected with it, and his vitality seemed to increase as he encountered what had been incarnated in that book centuries ago. He remained with the book for hours, voraciously turning over its pages and scrutinizing its text and images, until it was time for the library to close. He did not flee the final image, which held him for a long time. When I came for the book, he quickly disengaged himself from it, politely thanked me, and said that he had seen what he had needed.

I followed Williams to a pub he frequented with his friends. Near the room where they met, I sat in a dim corner and listened intently as Williams spoke—of the danger and necessity of seeking the psalmist's pure and acceptable words, of what he called the co-inherence of the living and the dead, of the prevailing pattern of love, of Dante—but he said nothing about the book, and I retreated into the night.

A few years later, in 1943, Williams published a book on Dante called *The Figure of Beatrice*. In it he wrote about the image that Dante presents of Beatrice, who points to the way of ascent or affirmation—the way from the awful distinction, the Crucifixion, to the awful likeness, the Resurrection. Williams wrote of the comprehensiveness of the Dantean literary record, which encompasses experience, the environment of that experience, and its expression—the person, the place, and the poem. He wrote nothing explicitly about the secret Oxford Dante, but without his time with it he could not have written what he had.

I was present when Williams died, abruptly and prematurely, two year later. He had written many books, and approached greatness, but he had not written *the* book and I wanted to see what the end of his life would be without it—and if the Oxford Dante would require anything more from me. In his end there was nothing for me to divine, and I was left considering my own fate and the fate of the book I kept.

My encounter with Williams marked the beginning of my own work. Like Dante, I began with the physical dimension of meaning. Unlike Dante, who in innocence glimpsed the glorious Beatrice, my secret copy of Dante was at the base of my ladder of love. In the beginning, it seemed my response to it should be another kind of book. For years I struggled to write a book that was a worthy antecedent to the secret Dante. I will not waste time discussing my futile tour of hell at the peripheries of Oxford and of virtue. I consigned all the books of babble I created during that time to an earthly inferno.

As I approached the middle of my life, and found my duller and determinable passions diminished and my greater and unnamed ones achingly insatiate, I experienced an epiphany. One dark night, in the basement of an old den of iniquity, I saw in the woman slumbering beside me something more than flesh. In the arc and texture of this stranger's shoulder, there was a shock of something more—something spiritual contained in proximate flesh. Something akin to it awoke within me. It was then that I began to see the second sense of Beatrice. I knew, of course, that the literal sense of the *Commedia* was not sufficient to understand it. But I had wrongly read Dante's book as a reverse incarnation. Dante had not sought to return the Word to flesh, through vellum, but to inscriptively reincarnate it to rerelease the spirit through the letter.

I began to think the form of my work should also be spiritual, but that, too, was beyond me. In desperation, I endeavored to move toward Dante's third sense, the moral. I discovered that small and erratic acts of vigilantism, such as sabotaging the work of lazy scholars or helping degenerate students fall, were more productive than anything I could accomplish with words. Dante's splendor increasingly mocked my squalor.

III.

Thirty years after I had shared the book with Williams, I showed the Oxford Dante to the aging Argentine author Jorge Luis Borges. He also, through sources unknown, came directly to me to see the book. I knew that I was nearing the end of my life. Dante, near the end of his, finished the *Paradiso* and in it expressed his hope to return to the octagonal font of his baptism and naming: the Baptistery of St. John, the physical and spiritual core of Florence. Dante had been ready to face that font, dominated by a scene of the Last Judgment, but I was not ready to face my end. I needed to conclude my work, a work that had begun with Williams.

Borges had begun his work on Dante soon after Williams's had abruptly ended. I found Borges's insights on Dante precise and prescient, so for a second time I brought the Oxford Dante into Sir Humfrey's Reading Room. Again, I found an expectant reader pondering his surroundings. Borges was blind, and he seemed to be sniffing out rather than looking for the finite and infinite connections surrounding him. To Borges, who had been given his national library and blindness at the same time, the smells of books and people in time must have been familiar. But as I approached with this book, he seemed to sense something new. He raised his open hands in anticipation. I handed the book to him and withdrew to study him studying it.

Borges's communion with the book was as intense as Williams's, but I could not determine what he could discover through his blind contemplation of it. He looked and touched, taking time with each leaf. And he, too, allowed the final image to hold him for a long time. He was still contemplating it when his time was up. I took the book from him, he thanked me warmly, and he left with the English lecturer who was his guide.

Borges also promised discretion, but I followed him into a pub near the library. I listened from a nearby table as he told his guide and others who joined him how reading Dante was like beholding an immense, serene, labyrinthine painting—one in an exotic library, of course, he added with a smile—a painting that contains everything that was, is, and shall be. Others began to respond to Borges's words while he sat silent, a sad smile settling on his seemingly serene face. Borges eventually rejoined the conversation around him, turning the discussion to the fragmentary books of other great poets. I finished my pint, slipped out into the narrow alley fronting the pub, and hurried home.

Proceedings from the Francis White Ewbank Colloquium

In 1982, Borges published a series of essays on Dante, *Nuere ensayos dantescas*, which showed the influence of the secret Dante. A few years later, after finding love as the antidote to his solipsistic fear of becoming a mere word, he abruptly moved with his lover to Geneva, where early in life he had attended the school established by Jean Calvin. At his end, Borges asked for and received visits from a Roman Catholic priest and a Reformed pastor. I was there, too, for our ends were linked.

At Borges's funeral the pastor, Edouard de Montmollin, read the opening verses of the Gospel of John. He preached about the Word—the true Word Borges had sought, the one Word that was ultimate and complete. Man, de Montmollin warned, cannot on his own discover that

Word; on his own, he becomes lost in a labyrinth. What John's Gospel declares is that the Word comes to man.

As I stood listening in that Genevan graveyard, I closed my eyes and tried to see what Dante saw at the end in the light of eternity:

> In its depth I saw contained,
> by love into a single volume bound,
> the leaves scattered through the universe.

And, beyond that, the circular, tripartite form of the Godhead, which left Dante in a moving state of love. In that vision, Dante's book realizes a unity that comes as close as possible to God's book of creation and reconciliation. This is perhaps most clearly manifested in the copy I have hidden for a lifetime, and the awareness that I have kept this Revelation from others makes me ill.

Inspired by Dante both Williams, the poet and publisher, and Borges, the poet and librarian, had hoped to write the unwritable book, a book that represented a unity analogous to the book of God—a book that would make reality more real and right. But each, before his end, in the end could only write books that pointed to what such a complete book would be: a pattern of transformative reconciliation.

I, too, wanted to write *the* book. I, too, attempted to follow the tripartite path this trinity of poets had taken through education, spiritual enlightenment, and entering a vision of love. I, however, was neither a poet nor an author—in the literal sense. I found myself in a different literary role. This role had been suggested by John Donne, who wrote that when one dies a chapter is translated into a better language. Every chapter must be so translated. God employs many and diverse translators, and by his hand all our scattered leaves, in every translation, will be bound together in his Book. This was the end and Book Dante saw, represented, and joined himself. Williams and Borges saw it, too, in different degrees. In a similar way, each was translated into the Book. And I was there as the keeper of its earthly manifestation and mediator of its severe grace.

After Borges's funeral, I wandered for hours through the streets of Geneva and finally found myself in an ancient garden. Through the garden, thoroughly shaded by trees, ran the purest of rivers. A melody drifted along the river, beckoning, and I followed it. When, after some lost moments, I looked up, I saw on the other side of the river a vision from the Apocalypse. There was, it seemed, a door. And through the door I saw a great throne, from which came a blinding white light that flashed out and broke into the full spectrum of light. All of this I had seen before, and I knew what was coming. The earth beneath me shook; I fell to my knees. Unable to turn away from the terrible light, everything visible was lost to me except what appeared to be leaves of a scroll, unrolling, enveloping me.

I was surprised to wake in the world—still in the park—with a large man standing over me. It was Reverend de Montmollin, holding a small book in one hand and reaching out to me with the other. I took the hand being offered to me and, to the surprise of both of us, I also took the book in the other hand. Recovering more quickly than I, de Montmollin told me in rough English to take and eat it. I knew he wanted to say more, but fearing prophecy, condemnation, and love, I hurried away with his book in my hand and fled—the park, the city, the continent—and retreated to my small cell in Oxford. After my return, I discovered that my work had reached its end.

I, who have spent my whole life with books and the greatest book of man, have never written a book. Instead, I write these leaves to be kept in Oxford's secret archives as a record of what I have done and not done. I hope my translations have served the Book. Now that my own translation nears completion, and the Oxford Dante is destined to become lost again, it seemed necessary to reveal how it bound together these three poets and me for the sake of a justifying, redemptive, and alien love.

DOG CITY AFTER DARK
After reading *The Great Divorce*
by Rick Hill

Everybody has a dog in my neighborhood,
and all the dogs are pacing sad ruts around
their junk-lumber doghouses.

And after dark the dogs bark warnings, inquiries—
bark insults and defiance till morning, bark
short-chain, short-chain, all night long.

Listen, dogs, I understand you can't articulate your more
  complicated longings,
and I realize you're sick of those piles that ring
the end of your lonesome tether.

But we all have to live in this little gray town
Let's try to wag with it, dogs. Let's curb our incessant yipping,
heel our pathetic whine

when the master draws near but then is seemingly
yanked back to his easy chair in the big house.
And let's face it, dogs:

whatever we're trying to get across, all the rest hear is barking,
snarling, irritating, chain rattling, growl bark growl
just dog noise.

So snuffle down now, dogs. Watch the moon sink
and the stars dim. The world is pausing,
steeling itself for morning.

We'll all have our day, brothers, but no one is going
to unhook anyone—not this long tonight,
oh love, not just yet.

(Revised for the conference. Original version published in *Christianity and Literature*, Winter 2000. Also anthologized in *Christianity and Literature*'s Best of Fifty Years issue. 2001 and *Imago Dei*: Poems from *Christianity and Literature*, Abilene Christian University Press 2012)

Chesterton in Heaven
by Jennifer Woodruff Tait

Jennifer Woodruff Tait is an Episcopal priest, the managing editor of *Christian History* magazine, the content editor for The High Calling at the Theology of Work Project, and the author of *The Poisoned Chalice* and the poetry collection *Histories of Us*. She lives in Richmond, KY with her husband Edwin, daughters Catherine Elanor and Elizabeth Beatrice, in-laws, 26 goats, 16 chickens, and a laptop. She invites everyone to check out *Christian History*'s 2015 issue on *The Seven Sages* (MacDonald, Tolkien, Lewis, Williams, Chesterton, Sayers, and Barfield).

> The wine flowed free enough for friends,
> The chairs were large as thrones,
> The walls were white with blazoned saints
> When God's great child came home.
> For him who sang of all the songs
> The wildest and the best
> God's minstrels waited at the gate
> To welcome him to rest;
> And Heaven was a lovely inn,
> The door flung open wide
> The Keeper standing in the door
> With all the world inside.
>
> He threw his faded hat away,
> He cast his cape behind,
> He hurled his staff into the night
> And carelessly he climbed
> Through all the lower clouds of God
> Up to the golden height
> Lit by the windows of the inn
> And burning day and night;
> The crowd was round him at the close—
> Their wingéd mystery beat
> On every shining windowpane
> Along the golden street.
>
> He seized their hands and touched their wings

As each passed into view;
He called them by the names they bore
When earth was all they knew—
Said "Dickens" with a choking sound,
Said "Stevenson" and "Scott,"
And took the wine from open hands
And gazed like one forgot.
His father's eyes, his mother's face,
His brother, tall and proud;
They spoke not, but no other peace
Has ever spoke so loud.

But through the multitude his eyes
Saw keenly who was gone,
Not yet arrived, but laboring still
And waiting to come on.
He missed a City-magnate's hat,
A boyish grin below,
The first and wittiest of all friends
A man might ever know;
He missed a sturdy-shouldered man
With French eyes and English chin
(The gates of Heaven were not yet wide
To let poor Hilary in.)
He missed a hush of blue and green,
He missed an elvish face,
And all the angels round could not
Fill up that empty place.

But all the crowd, they took his hand
And led him to the door,
That inn where all earth's wanderers
Can never wander more.
That Keeper keeps the doors of light
Who guards the gates of pain,
For darkness is as light to Him
Who has death's darkness slain;
And when the pilgrim bent in joy,
In passion like a child,
The Innkeeper looked down on him
And all His glory smiled.

"Don't Believe in Anything That Can't Be Told in Colored Pictures": Notes on a Dramatic Reading of Poems by Lewis, Tolkien, Chesterton, and Williams

by Jennifer Woodruff Tait

This reading was an excerpt of a larger, hour-long presentation that I gave at the New York C. S. Lewis Society in June 2008 and at the Taylor bi-monthly C. S. Lewis meetings in April 2010. Poems read at the 2016 Colloquium are in **bold**.

Opening:

"Commercial Candour" (Chesterton)

Poems of Social Criticism:

"A Confession" (Lewis)
"The Christian Social Union, Nottingham" (Chesterton)
"Wine and Water" (Chesterton)
"The Song of the Strang Ascetic" (Chesterton)
"Evolutionary Hymn" (Lewis)
"A Ballade of an Anti-Puritan" (Chesterton)
"A Ballade of Suicide" (Chesterton)
"A Ballade of the First Rain" (Chesterton)
"The Rolling English Road" (Chesterton)
"The Hoard" (Tolkien)

Poems of Love:

"The Great Minimum" (Chesterton)
"Together" (Chesterton)
"As the Ruin Falls" (Lewis)
"Bors to Elayne: On the King's Coins" (Williams)

Poems of Wonder:

"As One Oldster to Another" (Lewis)
"A Second Childhood" (Chesterton)
"Hermionie in the House of Paulina" (Lewis)
"The Last Ship" (Tolkien)
"Nearly They Stood" (Lewis)
"Fantasia" (Chesterton)

Proceedings from the Francis White Ewbank Colloquium

Poems of Faith:

"Sonnet 3" (Lewis)
"The Wise Men" (Chesterton)
"Love's as Warm as Tears" (Lewis)
"The Convert" (Chesterton)

Coda:

"All that is gold does not glitter" (Tolkien)
"Lines Written in a Picture Book" (Chesterton)

SOURCES:

Chesterton, G. K. *The Collected Poems of G. K. Chesterton.* London: Methuen and Co., 1933.

Chesterton, G. K., ed. Aidan Mackey. *Collected Works*, Volume 10. San Francisco: Ignatius, 1994.

Lewis, C. S., ed. Walter Hooper. *Poems.* San Diego: Harcourt, 1964.

Tolkien, J. R. R. *The Fellowship of the Ring.* Boston: Houghton Mifflin, 1994.

Tolkien, J. R. R. *The Tolkien Reader.* New York: Ballantine Books, 1966.

Williams, Charles, and C. S. Lewis. *Taliessin Through Logres: Region of the Summer Stars: Arthurian Torso.* Grand Rapids: Eerdmans, 1974.

www.brotherthomasfilm.com

The Temptation of Brother Thomas:
A Stop-Motion Animated Short Film

by J. Stephan Leeper

INTRODUCTION

When Joe Ricke asked earlier this spring and if I would present my film-in-progress at the C. S. Lewis and Friends Colloquium, I was at once excited and confused. Excited to present the film I've been developing for over a decade and confused as to the prospects of presenting an unfinished children's film at a scholarly gathering.

The excited part of me wanted to share how much I've been influenced by C. S. Lewis, G. K. Chesterton, Dorothy Sayers, and J. R. R. Tolkien. How as a young artist and storyteller these authors help to shape, inspire and encourage me to reach for stories with lasting qualities. Stories that were grounded in some sense of faith or mystery. The confused part was wondering how these influences would even remotely surface in an unfinished animated film with no dialogue and only a handful of shots completed. To put it bluntly, presenting an unfinished animated film to an audience of non-animator/artists can be tricky business.

I imagined I would begin my presentation with an apologetic as to why and how children's media was a viable art form deserving a level of critical recognition that it seldom receives. From there I would attempt to place my work in context with important children's authors, illustrators and film makers. Fortunately for everyone involved the presentation times were limited so instead I chose to stick with the essentials. In the end I simply told my story accompanied by storyboards, a handful of finished shots and some of the beautiful artwork that's been created in the design stages of the film. What I wasn't prepared for was the response I received from the audience. Clearly I was presenting to an audience ready and willing to be moved by a simple story. I was humbled by their generous response.

Since the story of Br. Thomas is best presented as imagery rather than text I chose not to publish the narrative for this article. Instead I've included a description of the themes, elements (and in some cases) mechanics of the film that will hopefully communicate the heart and scope of the project.

You can also go to www.brotherthomasfilm.com to see how The Temptation of Br. Thomas is progressing or visit our FB page at www.facebook.com/BrotherThomasFilm. For a look at our 2016 teaser you can go to www.vimeo.com/brotherthomas

Abstract

The Temptation of Br. Thomas is a short animated film that celebrates beauty and examines our preconceptions of what we consider sacred. Thomas Aquinas serves both as namesake to the central character and an inspiration to the ideas put forth in the film. The Temptation of Brother Thomas draws from the rich legacy of art within the Western Church while it challenges the modern assumption that true art needs to be cut loose from orthodox faith in order to flourish. True to Aquinas' writings, it also challenges contemporary religious notions that art and beauty are somehow superfluous to a life marked by faith.

The Temptation of Brother Thomas claims the goodness of creation and beauty as an invitation to celebrate the Sacred wherever we may find it.

Project Description

Story Premise: What if a monk found himself so taken with the wonders of the *created* order that he could never fully focus on the duties of his *religious* order? And what if these distractions cast a new and purifying light on his sacred calling?

Theme: *When one sees creation through the eyes of wonder the ordinary is revealed as sacred, and the sacred becomes renewed.*

Plot Synopsis: Brother Thomas is a monk whose day job is to illuminate Scripture and yet his passion is for landscapes. Each morning he makes his way to the abbey and finds the world filled with distractions. His "tempter," in the form of a brilliant blue dragonfly, keeps Thomas' head spinning just long enough to coax him off the beaten path and into a world rich with wonder, subtle mystery, and breathtaking beauty.

Spiritual/Philosophical Inspiration: Thomas Aquinas serves as model and namesake for Br. Thomas, the film's central character. The richness of ancient Church imagery provides both a visual backdrop and thematic baseline for this story to be told. *The Temptation of Brother Thomas* pays homage to the role Western Christianity has played in art history and is a challenge to the kind of religiosity that would separate the created order from its divine author. G. K. Chesterton describes Thomas Aquinas as a theological defender of the arts, the sciences, and the humanities recognizing them as a means to faith and not an obstacle.

> (Aquinas) reconciled religion with reason, (and) expanded it towards experimental science.... (He) insisted that the senses were the windows of the soul and that reason had a divine right to feed upon facts, and that it was the business of Faith to digest the strong meat of the toughest and most practical of pagan philosophies.... St. Thomas was ... taking the lower road when he walked in the steps of Aristotle. So was God, when He worked in the workshop of Joseph.[1]

Formal Issues: The physical world that Br. Thomas inhabits is represented by three dimensional stop-motion sets and fabricated puppets, while the two dimensional stained-glass of the scriptorium serves as an icon, or window allowing us a glimpse into the spiritual world where Mary, the Christ-child and the Apostles reside.

---

1   *Saint Thomas Aquinas; The Dumb Ox* (New York, New York: Doubleday. Reprinted 1956), pp.13, 22

There is a scene in the film where the stained glass Christ-child reaches out with his hand and coos after the stop-motion dragonfly and for a moment these two worlds almost collide. There is a Celtic tradition that refers to *Thin Spaces* where the physical and the spiritual world come close enough to touch.

Aesthetic/Historical Elements: This film pays homage to many of the great aspects of Western Art and acknowledges the church as their rightful steward in the following forms:

1. Illuminated Manuscripts: Br. Thomas by trade illuminates manuscripts magnifying the light of the four Gospels through images created on the very pages that the words are recorded, elevating the letters themselves into fantastic works of beauty.

Inspirational Illuminated Manuscripts

2. Stained Glass: Mary and the Christ child, flanked by the Apostles, are enclosed in their stained glass niches from where they watch closely as events transpire. Ultimately it is the light that cascades through these windows that transforms Brother Thomas' world and the scriptorium where he works.

Inspirational Stained Glass and Gothic Imagery

3. Architecture and Statuary: At first the grandness of design and sheer weight of the Cathedral's beauty make Brother Thomas feel small and inadequate. The statues of the church fathers cast long shadows on Thomas, their history and somber demeanor are more than he can bear. Yet as the film unfolds we find the Cathedral is strangely responsive to Thomas's contributions, which in the end is transformative.

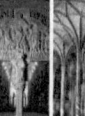

Inspirational Architecture and Sculpture

4. Music: For the score of the film I will use some variation of St. Frances' *Il Cantico delle Creature* and musical patterns from the hymn that it inspired *All Creatures of Our God and King*.

Mixed Media: A combination of animation techniques will be utilized to execute this film stop-motion puppetry, traditionally drawn, 3D computer and the latest in 3D print technology.

 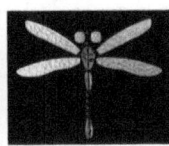   

Br. Thomas Production Images: A Variety of Media

1. Stop-motion Animation will be the main medium of this film. Miniature sets will be constructed for the three-dimensional world while Thomas and the animals will all be physical puppets.

2. 3D Printing aided by 3D animation tools will be used to give Br. Thomas a full range of expression.

3. Digital 2D/Motion Graphics will be used to animate the stained glass world of the Saints.

4. Digital 3D/Computer Graphics will be used to animate the dragonfly.

5. Traditional Drawn Animation will be used to bring life to Br. Thomas' Illuminated Manuscripts.

Intended Audience: *The Temptation of Br. Thomas* is a children's story about a simple-hearted monk remaining faithful and attentive to his circumstances and his calling. While this story grows explicitly out of my own journey and faith tradition I have often found that regardless of spiritual affiliation, this is a story that resonates with all people who value beauty and who gratefully acknowledge creation as a thing to be cherished.

As a short film *The Temptation of Brother Thomas* will be viewed by audiences all over the world through animation festivals and on-line distribution. Eventually we will publish an interactive digital storybook accompanied by targeted curricula. With age-appropriate materials *The Temptation of Br. Thomas* could serve as a guide to the arts for children's ministry or even a catalyst for discussion in adult study groups.

Design and Production Team

There are a number of talented artists and professionals that have joined the Brother Thomas project over the last five years and more to come as we gain funding. Their contribution promises a level of excellence for *The Temptation of Brother Thomas* that previously I could have only imagined. The opportunity to work in such company humbles me daily, challenges me and continues to be a tremendous pleasure.

Media Professionals and Industry Veterans

Steve Leeper: Creator, Director, Production and Story Artist.
"The films that I make draw heavily from my fascination with children's literature and religious faith. As a storyteller the themes that emerge in my work revolve around questions of self-discovery, creativity and belief."

Steve has worked as a Stop-motion animator, model maker, 3D layout artist/supervisor and cameraman. Client list includes Big Idea/Veggie-tales, Cap'n Crunch, Chicago Tribune, Fruit of the Loom, Illinois Lottery and Kroger Market.

Steve helped to build the Digital Media Arts department at Huntington University where he now the Director of Animation teaching classes in storyboarding, stop motion animation and media engagement.

Michael Spooner: Art Direction and Visual Development
Michael has worked in animation for over thirty years from as far back as *"Masters of the Universe,"* to *"Chip'n Dale Adventures,"* right up through Disney's *"Treasure Planet," "The Jonah Movie"* and Sony Picture's new 3D *"Popeye"* film.

Tom Gasek: Director of Animation
Tom is a veteran stop-motion animator excelling in high-level character performance. Tom has worked on *"Wallace and Gromit," "Chicken Run,"* and *"Coraline"* (just to mention a few). He has recently published "Frame by Frame Stop Motion" a definitive guide on the art of stop-frame animation. Tom teaches in the School of Film and Animation at the Rochester Institute of Technology. Tom's most recent film *"Ain't No Fish"* is currently enjoying exposure on the international festival circuit.

Proceedings from the Francis White Ewbank Colloquium

Paul Nethercott: Producer

Paul's films have screened at dozens of festivals internationally and won numerous awards. His film *Jitensha* (*Hidden Beauty*) won the Vision Award for Best Short Film at Heartland Film Festival and was an official selection at the Venice film. Besides acting as Producer on the *Brother Thomas* project, Paul is currently developing *Thin Places*, a documentary/VR experience capturing the power and beauty of Europe's grand cathedral tradition.

Rich Schiller: Sr. Model Maker/Cathedral Builder

Rich's expertise in dimensional model making and his exquisite attention to detail have made him the most sought after Model Maker in Chicago. Rich has created custom models and props for print and video spots for Absolut Vodka, Disney, Quaker Oats, Nestle, McDonald's, Campbell's Soup, Kelloggs . . . to name just a few.

Jeff Jacoby: Sound Designer

Jeff actively practices sound art, sound design, writing, directing and radio production. He has received an Emmy, two Emmy nominations, two Benjamin Franklin's and a host of other awards. His work has been heard on PBS, NPR, and commercial venues, as well as in festivals and art galleries across the country. Jeff is an Associate Professor of Audio & Radio at San Francisco State University.

Kurt Heinecke: *Composer*

Kurt has been the creator of the sound that has defined the world-famous *VeggieTales* and *3-2-1 Penguins* video series. He has composed for over 35 videos and 2 major motion pictures and the recipient of 6 Dove Awards for music production, multiple gold and platinum CDs, and dozens of platinum-selling videos.

Brenda Baumgarter: *Puppet Fabricator*

Brenda is a highly sought after character fabrication artist who has been working in the stop motion industry for well over a decade. Besides being the puppet lead on a television series like *Life's a Zoo* and *Jo Jo's Circus*, Brenda has recently headed up the puppet crew for the soon-to-be released feature film *The Little Prince*. Brenda is currently working as Puppet Fabricator at LAIKA studio in Portland.

J. Stephan Leeper, Copyright 2016 all rights reserved.
www.brotherthomasfilm.com

THE INKLINGS, IN MEMORIAM: A Cycle of Poems
by Donald T. Williams

Donald T. Williams, PhD, is R. A. Forrest Scholar and Professor of English at Toccoa Falls College. He is the author of books of Inklings scholarship such as *Mere Humanity: G. K. Chesterton, C. S. Lewis, and J. R. R. Tolkien on the Human Condition* and (with Jim Prothero) *Gaining a Face: the Romanticism of C. S. Lewis*. His poetry has appeared in *Christianity and Literature, The Windhover, The Rolling Coulter*, and other publications. His latest book is *Deeper Magic: The Theology behind the Writings of C. S. Lewis*.

These poems are excerpted from *Stars through the Clouds: The Collected Poetry of Donald T. Williams* (Lynchburg: Lantern Hollow Press, 2012), and used by permission.

I   THE GRAVE OF C. S. LEWIS

HOLY TRINITY CHURCH, HEADINGTON QUARRY, OXFORDSHIRE

    There was a marble slab, the evidence
        Of burial, with writing on the stone
        Which said, "Men must endure their going hence."
    The mind that had restored my mind to sense
        Was there reduced to elemental bone;
        There was a marble slab, the evidence.
    That well of wisdom and of eloquence
        Was now cut back to just one phrase alone,
        Which said, "Men must endure their going hence."
    No monument of rich magnificence
        Stood fitting one who had so brightly shone;
        There was a marble slab. The evidence
    That plain things have their power to convince
        Was in that simple block with letters strewn
        Which said, "Men must endure their going hence."
    The weight of time was focused there, intense
        With wrecked Creation's universal groan:
        There was a marble slab, the evidence,
    Which said, "Men must endure their going hence."

II SENSUCHT

When the fog obscures the outlines of the trees
>But breaks to show the sharpness of the stars
>And the blood feels sudden chill, although the breeze
>Is warm, and all the old internal scars
From stabbing beauty start to ache anew;
>When mushrooms gather in a fairy ring
>And every twig and grass-blade drips with dew
>And then a whippoorwill begins to sing;
When all the world beside is hushed, awaiting
>The sun as if it were his first arising
>And you discover that, anticipating,
>You've held your breath and find the fact surprising:
>Then all the old internal wounds awake.
>The pain is sweet we bear for beauty's sake.

III SENSUCHT II

God knows no shame in what He will employ
>To win a wandering sinner back again.
>Thus, C. S. Lewis was surprised by joy.
A childish garden made to be a toy
>Of moss and twigs upon a biscuit tin?
>God knows no shame in what He will employ.
The silly garden helped him to enjoy
>The real ones, made him want to enter in.
>Thus, C. S. Lewis was surprised by joy.
Not Athens (first), Jerusalem, or Troy,
>But Squirrel Nutkin's granary and bin?
>God knows no shame in what He will employ.
When Balder the beautiful was dead, destroyed,
>The voice that cried it came into his ken;
>Thus, C. S. Lewis was surprised by joy.
But pagan legend! Could *that* be the ploy?
>Somewhere the path to Heaven must begin.
>God knows no shame in what He will employ;
Thus, C. S. Lewis was surprised by joy.

IV   TO J. R. R. TOLKIEN

On a day when Fall's first leaves were flying
And the wind was howling and geese were crying
And clouds were black and the sun was hiding,
Word first came, on dark wings riding.
        "Tolkien is dead,"
        Was all they said,
        And left us crying.

He heard by light of star and moon
The Elven songs and learned their tunes.
He had long walks with them, and talks,
Beneath the swaying trees in June.

Dwarf-mines deeply delved he saw
Where Mithril glittered on the walls
And mighty kings wrought wondrous things
And reigned in hollow, torch-lit halls.

To forests wild and deep he went
And many lives of men he spent
Where leaves of years fall soft like tears,
Listening to the speech of Ents.

In lofty halls of men he sat
Or rustic rooms of bar-man fat;
In hobbit holes, heard stories told
By an old man in a wizard's hat.

With magic words of dark and light
And days of doom and coming night
And magic rings and hoped for spring,
He wrought the record of his sight. . . .

In Beowulf's bold fleet he sailed,
With Gawain the Green Knight beheld;
By Beortnoth's side he stood and cried
And hordes of pagan Danes he felled,
"Will shall be sterner, heart the bolder,
Spirit the greater as our strength fails!'

On a day when Fall's first leaves were flying
And the wind was howling and geese were crying
And clouds were black and the sun was hiding,
Word first came, on dark wings riding.
       "Tolkien is dead,"
       Was all they said,
       And left us crying.

V   A GLIMMER OF HOPE

When Bilbo Baggins ran off down the road
    Without a hat or pocket handkerchief
    Or even proper time to say, "Good bye,"
Did Smaug, asleep in his usurped abode,
    Dream of Burglars stealing from the Thief?

    Did Sauron shudder without knowing why?
The hobbit, Gandalf later said, was *meant*
    To find the Ring: a thought to bring relief
    To Frodo's mind when it was asking, "Why?"
Iluvatar had left at least that glint
    For them to spy.

VI   ARAGORN, SMELLING THE NIPHREDIL IN PARTH GALEN, THINKETH ON ARWEN

Thou wert not there by trail or stream
Beneath the green, tree-filtered light;
Thou wert not there but as a dream
    Remembered from the night.

Thou wert not there by stream or trail
But as a vision sweet and fair.
I tried to take thy hand, but failed,
    Clasping only air.

And will I ever know thee as my wife,
Or will the future leave us both behind?
How can this valley be so full of life
Yet feel so empty, lacking only thine?

Thou wert not there by glade or glen
Except as memory and desire
That burns as strongly now as when
        It first sprang into fire.

Thou wert not there by glen or glade
Save as desire and memory:
Memory that will never fade
        While life is left to me

And will I ever know thee as my wife,
To tip each other that sweet cup of wine?
How can this valley be so full of life
Yet feel so empty, lacking only thine?

Full soon the long, hard road of grief and strife
Resumes. For now, that destiny is mine.

VII   LOTH LORIEN

From silver trunk the golden leaf
Blows through the old abandoned fief,
For Time, the robber and the thief,
Has brought the hidden realm to grief:
              The wonder is withdrawn.
Now far beyond the Western Sea
The merry folk have gone to be
Naught but a fading memory
              In Caras Galadon.

For untold years Galadriel
Did weave her magic and her spell.
Nor warg nor orc nor dragon fell
Could enter the enchanted veil
        Until it was withdrawn.
Now in the once protected Wood
The Evil mingles with the Good—
Foul things that never could have stood
              In Caras Galadon.

Now through the hushed and chilling air

There rings no voice of minstrel fair,
No melody of sweetness rare,
No magic words beyond compare;
    The music is withdrawn.
The happy sound of harper's glee
    Sounds only far beyond the Sea.
The rasping raven's symphony
    Fills Caras Galadon.

In Cerin Amroth, Arwen's tomb
Lies hidden in the gathering gloom.
The niphredil no longer bloom.
She sleeps within that narrow room,
    All memory withdrawn.
The sons to Aragorn she bore:
They come to mourn her there no more.
They sleep beneath the marble floor
Of cold and deep Rath Dinen, far
    From Caras Galadon.

A lonely wanderer passes by;
He sees there is no shelter nigh.
The stars are twinkling in the sky.
He groans, and on the ground doth lie
    Within his cloak withdrawn.
The leaves are rustling on high.
It seems to him they softly sigh
A sad lament—he know not why—
    In Caras Galadon.

VIII   THE QUEST MOTIF

What Lewis and Tolkien Knew, but Peter Jackson Does Not

Snaking out across the vast expanse
    Of History and Legend lies a trail,
    The footing treacherous, the markings pale,
And peril lies in wait for those who chance
    To travel it. But if they can advance,
    And if their luck and courage do not fail,

They may emerge into a mystic vale
And find the magic realm of fair Romance.

The landscape's always changing. There is no
      Map that can be trusted once you swerve
      Aside; you only compass is your quest.
If, true to friend, implacable to foe,
      You're faithful to the Vision that you serve,
      You'll find that country which the Muse has blessed.

IX   TO CLYDE S. KILBY

A

I wandered through the silent trees
      Of fair Loth Lorien,
At Cerin-Amroth saw the leaves
      Blow o'er the tomb of Arwen.

I wandered North to Rivendell,
      To Elrond's homely halls,
And watched as evening shadows fell
      On long deserted walls.

Then West I turned, past hill and tree,
      Til I stood by the shore.
But Cirdan was gone, and elves to the sea
      Down Anduin sail no more.

B

And I have stood as tall as a king
      On a hill top windy and bare
And drunk the air of a Narnian spring
      When no one else was there.

And I have seen Cair Paravel
      And stood by Aslan's Howe,
But where the king was none could tell
      For no one goes there now.

C

And homeward I my feet have turned
        But there I never came,
For in my soul a fire burned
        And "home" was not the same.

And human eyes I seldom find
        Who seem to comprehend
The longing of a pilgrim mind
        For distant Fairie lands.

But when I find such eyes, I call
        The man who owns them "friend."
And together we wander through leafy halls
        In fair Loth Lorien.

Stephen Thorson and Nina Mullins reading a letter by
C. S. Lewis from the Brown Collection

Afterword: About the Center for the Study of C. S. Lewis and Friends at Taylor University

The Center for the Study of C. S. Lewis and Friends is housed in the Zondervan Library of Taylor University in Upland, Indiana. With a mission to promote the integration of faith, scholarship, and the imagination, the center serves the Taylor University campus, the local community, as well as a worldwide academic and lay audience. We offer several programs to reach these various groups. For our students, we hold classes on the works of C. S. Lewis and several related authors—primarily, but not exclusively, George MacDonald, Dorothy L. Sayers, Charles Williams, and Owen Barfield. For our local community, we offer invitations to learn from visiting Lewis & Inklings scholars, as well as other events both educational and inspirational. For both of these audiences, as well as our more distant friends, we organize the biennial Frances White Ewbank Colloquium on C. S. Lewis and Friends, which gathers scholars and readers from across the United States and around the world. Over the years we have hosted hundreds of scholars and *aficionados* alike for this most friendly of conferences.

For all of these groups, we maintain a fine rare book and manuscript collection, named after its original collector, the late Dr. Edwin W. Brown of Indianapolis, Indiana. The Edwin W. Brown Collection includes first English and American editions of books authored, edited, or with prefaces by C. S. Lewis, published essays and lectures of Lewis, over a hundred Lewis letters, and two very special Lewis manuscripts ("Light"—a previously unpublished short story and "*Clivi Hamiltonis Summae Metaphysics Contra Anthroposophos Libri II*"—a notebook containing the majority of what has come to be called "The Great War," a philosophical debate between C. S. Lewis and his great friend, Owen Barfield).[1] The collection also contains significant books about C. S. Lewis, as well as first and reprint editions of Lewis's brother and his friends, Charles Williams, Dorothy L. Sayers, and Owen Barfield. Since its relocation to Taylor University in 1997, the collection has more than tripled in size.

---

1 · Both of these manuscripts have been recently published: Charlie W. Starr, ed., "*Light*": *C. S. Lewis's First and Final Short Story* (Hamden, CT: Winged Lion Press, 2012); Norbert Feindendegen and Arend Smilde, ed., *The "Great War" of Owen Barfield and C. S. Lewis: Philosophical Writings, 1927–1930* (Oxford: *Inklings Studies* Supplements, no. 1, 2015).

After C. S. Lewis, however, the author most prominently featured in the collection is the Scottish writer George MacDonald. The George MacDonald portion of the collection contains more than five hundred volumes, including first edition books, biographies, critical works, and books with inscriptions and/or annotations by MacDonald. Among these, visitors to the collection will find one hundred early or first editions of MacDonald's work, a forty-six volume set of his complete works in a very fine series of reprints, fifty bound copies of nineteenth-century periodicals containing the first state versions of many of MacDonald's works, including serialized novels, poems, and essays. The periodicals also contain early versions of works by other significant Victorian writers. The MacDonald holdings also include twenty books by MacDonald's wife, sons, and grandson, forty-two PhD dissertations, several Master's theses, and a wide variety of manuscripts, letters, and articles on microfilm.

Some of the many highlights of the collection include the following:

- MacDonald's personal copy of Shakespeare's *Hamlet*, which contains MacDonald's extensive handwritten notes for lectures that he gave on the same, and comprising a sort of rough draft for his book on *Hamlet*.

- Two George MacDonald novels with handwritten notes by C. S. Lewis, one from Lewis's personal library and one from the library of his friend Arthur Greeves;

- Eight books from MacDonald's personal library, five of which include notes in MacDonald's hand;

- Joy Davidman's copy of *Mere Christianity*;

- *Prince Caspian* inscribed by Lewis to its seven-year old owner;

- Mary Neylan's copy of *George MacDonald: An Anthology*, inscribed by Lewis, who dedicated the book to her;

- The Lewis letters to Jill Flewett-Freud, who, as a school girl, live with the Lewis household at the Kilns during World War II.

- Signed copies of books by Barfield, Dorothy Sayers, and Charles Williams

Proceedings from the Francis White Ewbank Colloquium

Individuals or groups interested in visiting the collection are welcome during the academic year, when we hold regular hours; special arrangements can also be made for other times. We are always eager to share our collection with new friends.

To facilitate our outreach work, the center has recently added the Lewis Room to complement the Brown Collection. The hundreds of books, journals, DVDs, and other materials in this room feature recent publications as well as reader's copies of books written by the authors and a comprehensive collection of Inklings scholarship. It is our goal to collect and provide ongoing support to new scholarship in the field of Inklings Studies. On-campus students find this a pleasant study room, and the occasional game of Narnia Monopoly brings out the Eustace Scrubb in visitors of all ages. Small seminar classes on the Inklings meet here regularly. Best of all, the books in the Lewis Room are available for circulation, both locally and through interlibrary loan, thus enriching the research opportunities for students, faculty and scholars alike.

In a nearby lounge, a "Lewis Tea" is held most Friday afternoons during the school year, featuring tea, biscuits (and sometimes Turkish Delight), and a presentation or reading in the spirit of the Inklings.

*Lisa Ritchie, Program Coordinator for the Lewis Center revised, expanded, and updated this from an earlier document by Thom Satterlee, former Director of the Center for the Study of C. S. Lewis and Friends.

OTHER BOOKS OF INTEREST

C. S. LEWIS

C. S. Lewis: Views From Wake Forest - Essays on C. S. Lewis
Michael Travers, editor

Contains sixteen scholarly presentations from the international C. S. Lewis convention in Wake Forest, NC. Walter Hooper shares his important essay "Editing C. S. Lewis," a chronicle of publishing decisions after Lewis' death in 1963.

"Scholars from a variety of disciplines address a wide range of issues. The happy result is a fresh and expansive view of an author who well deserves this kind of thoughtful attention."
— Diana Pavlac Glyer, author of *The Company They Keep*

The Hidden Story of Narnia:
A Book-By-Book Guide to Lewis' Spiritual Themes
Will Vaus

A book of insightful commentary equally suited for teens or adults – Will Vaus points out connections between the *Narnia* books and spiritual/biblical themes, as well as between ideas in the *Narnia* books and C. S. Lewis' other books. Learn what Lewis himself said about the overarching and unifying thematic structure of the Narnia books. That is what this book explores; what C. S. Lewis called "the hidden story" of Narnia. Each chapter includes questions for individual use or small group discussion.

Why I Believe in Narnia:
33 Reviews and Essays on the Life and Work of C. S. Lewis
James Como

Chapters range from reviews of critical books , documentaries and movies to evaluations of Lewis' books to biographical analysis.
"A valuable , wide-ranging collection of essays by one of the best informed and most accute commentators on Lewis' work and ideas."
— Peter Schakel, author of *Imagination & the Arts in C. S. Lewis*

C. S. Lewis: His Literary Achievement
Colin Manlove

"This is a positively brilliant book, written with splendor, elegance, profundity and evidencing an enormous amount of learning. This is probably not a book to give a first-time reader of Lewis. But for those who are more broadly read in the Lewis corpus this book is an absolute gold mine of information. The author gives us a magnificent overview of Lewis' many writings, tracing for us thoughts and ideas which recur throughout, and at the same time telling us how each book differs from the others. I think it is not extravagant to call C. S. Lewis: His Literary Achievement a tour de force."
— Robert Merchant, *St. Austin Review*, Book Review Editor

WWW.WINGEDLIONPRESS.COM

In the Footsteps of C. S. Lewis: A Photographic Pilgrimage to the British Isles
Will Vaus

Over the course of thirty years, Will Vaus has journeyed to the British Isles many times to walk in the footsteps of C. S. Lewis. His private photographs of the significant places in Lewis' life have captured the imagination of audiences in the US and UK to whom he has lectured on the Oxford don and his work. This, in turn, prompted the idea of this collection of 78 full-color photographs, interwoven with details about Lewis' life and work. The combination of words and pictures make this a wonderful addition to the library of all Lewis scholars and readers.

Exploring the Eternal Goodness:
Selected Writings of David L. Neuhouser
Joe Ricke and Lisa Ritchie, Editors

In 1997, due to David's perseverance, the Brown Collection of books by and about C. S. Lewis and related authors came to Taylor University and the Lewis and Friends Colloquium began. This book of selected writings reflects his scholarship in math and literature, as well as his musings on beauty and the imagination. The twenty-one tributes are an indication of the many lives he has influenced. This book is meant to acknowledge David L. Neuhouser for his contributions to scholarship and to honor his life of friendship, encouragement, and genuine goodness.

Speaking of Jack: A C. S. Lewis Discussion Guide
Will Vaus

C. S. Lewis Societies have been forming around the world since the first one started in New York City in 1969. Will Vaus has started and led three groups himself. *Speaking of Jack* is the result of Vaus' experience in leading those Lewis Societies. Included here are introductions to most of Lewis' books as well as questions designed to stimulate discussion about Lewis' life and work. These materials have been "road-tested" with real groups made up of young and old, some very familiar with Lewis and some newcomers. *Speaking of Jack* may be used in an existing book discussion group, to start a C. S. Lewis Society, or as a guide to your own exploration of Lewis' books.

Light: C. S. Lewis's First and Final Short Story
Charlie W. Starr
Foreword by Walter Hooper

Charlie Starr explores the questions surrounding the "Light" manuscript, a later version of story titled "A Man Born Blind." The insights into this story provide a na ew key to understanding some of Lewis's most profound ideas.

"*As literary journalism, both investigative and critical, it is top shelf*"
James Como, author of *Remembering C. S. Lewis*

"*Starr shines a new and illuninating light on one of Lewis's most intriguing stories*"
Michael Ward, author of *Planet Narnia*

C. S. Lewis' Top Ten: Influential Books and Authors, Volume One
Will Vaus

Based on his books, marginal notes, and personal letters, Will Vaus explores Lewis' reading of the ten books he said shaped his vocational attitude and philosophy of life. Volume One covers the first three authors/books: George MacDonald, G.K. Chesterton, and Virgil. Vaus offers a brief biography of each author with a helpful summary of their books.

"Thorough, comprehensive, and illuminating"
  Rolland Hein, Author of *George MacDonald: Victorian Mythmaker*

C. S. Lewis & Philosophy as a Way of Life: His Philosophical Thoughts
Adam Barkman

C. S. Lewis is rarely thought of as a "philosopher" per se despite having both studied and taught philosophy for several years at Oxford. Lewis's long journey to Christianity was essentially philosophical – passing through seven different stages. This 624 page book is an invaluable reference for C. S. Lewis scholars and fans alike

C. S. Lewis Goes to Heaven:
A Reader's Guide to The Great Divorce
David G. Clark

This is the first book devoted solely to this often neglected book and the first to reveal several important secrets Lewis concealed within the story. Lewis felt his imaginary trip to Hell and Heaven was far better than his book *The Screwtape Letters*, which has become a classic. Readers will discover the many literary and biblical influences Lewis utilized in writing his brilliant novel.

C. S. Lewis Goes to Hell
A Companion and Study Guide to The Screwtape Letters
William O'Flarety

The creator and host of "All About Jack" (a podcast feature of EssentialCSLewis.com) has written a guide to *The Screwtape Letters* suitable for groups or individuals. Features include a topic index of major and minor themes, summaries of each letter, questions for reflection, and over a half-dozen appendices of useful information.

Joy and Poetic Imagination: Understanding C. S. Lewis's "Great War" with Owen Barfield and its Significance for Lewis's Conversion and Writings
Stephen Thorson

Author Stephen Thorson began writing this book over 30 years ago and published parts of it in articles during Barfield's lifetime. Barfield wrote to Thorson in 1983 saying, ""...*you have surveyed the divergence between Lewis and myself very fairly, and truly 'in depth...*'". This book explains the "Great War" between these two friends.

CHRISTIAN LIVING

Keys to Growth: Meditations on the Acts of the Apostles
Will Vaus

Every living thing or person requires certain ingredients in order to grow, and if a thing or person is not growing, it is dying. *The Acts of the Apostles* is a book that is all about growth. Will Vaus has been meditating and preaching on *Acts* for the past 30 years. In this volume, he offers the reader forty-one keys from the entire book of Acts to unlock spiritual growth in everyday life.

Open Before Christmas: Devotional Thoughts For The Holiday Season
Will Vaus

Author Will Vaus seeks to deepen the reader's knowledge of Advent and Christmas leading up to Epiphany. Readers are provided with devotional thoughts for each day that help them to experience this part of the Church Year perhaps in a more spiritually enriching way than ever before.

"Seasoned with inspiring, touching, and sometimes humorous illustrations .... I found his writing immediately engaging and, the more I read, the more I liked it. God has touched my heart by reading Open Before Christmas, and I believe he will touch your heart too."
    The Rev. David Beckmann, The C.S. Lewis Society of Chattanooga

God's Love Letter: Reflections on I John
Will Vaus

Various words for "love" appear thirty-five times in the five brief chapters of I John. This book invites you on a journey of reading and reflection: reading this book in the New Testament and reflecting on God's love for us, our love for God, and our love for one another.

Jogging with G.K. Chsterton: 65 Earthshaking Expeditions
Robert Moore-Jumonville

Jogging with G.K. Chesterton is a showcase for the merry mind of Chesterton. But Chesterton's lighthearted wit always runs side-by-side with his weighty wisdom. These 65 "earthshaking expeditions" will keep you smiling and thinking from start to finish. You'll be entertained, challenged, and spiritually uplifted as you take time to breath in the fresh morning air and contemplate the wonders of the world.

"*This is a delightfully improbable book in which Chesterton puts us through our spiritual and intellectual exercises.*"
    Joseph Pearce, author of *Wisdom and Innocence: A Life of G.K. Chesterton*

GEORGE MACDONALD

Diary of an Old Soul & The White Page Poems
George MacDonald and Betty Aberlin

The first edition of George MacDonald's book of daily poems included a blank page opposite each page of poems. Readers were invited to write their own reflections on the "white page." MacDonald wrote: "Let your white page be ground, my print be seed, growing to golden ears, that faith and hope may feed." Betty Aberlin responded to MacDonald's invitation with daily poems of her own.

Betty Aberlin's close readings of George MacDonald's verses and her thoughtful responses to them speak clearly of her poetic gifts and spiritual intelligence.
   Luci Shaw, poet

George MacDonald: Literary Heritage and Heirs
Roderick McGillis, editor

This latest collection of 14 essays sets a new standard that will influence MacDonald studies for many more years. George MacDonald experts are increasingly evaluating his entire corpus within the nineteenth century context.

This comprehensive collection represents the best of contemporary scholarship on George MacDonald.
   Rolland Hein, author of *George MacDonald: Victorian Mythmaker*

In the Near Loss of Everything: George MacDonald's Son in America
Dale Wayne Slusser

In the summer of 1887, George MacDonald's son Ronald, newly engaged to artist Louise Blandy, sailed from England to America to teach school. The next summer he returned to England to marry Louise and bring her back to America. On August 27, 1890, Louise died leaving him with an infant daughter. Ronald once described losing a beloved spouse as "the near loss of everything". Dale Wayne Slusser unfolds this poignant story with unpublished letters and photos that give readers a glimpse into the close-knit MacDonald family. Also included is Ronald's essay about his father, *George MacDonald: A Personal Note*, plus a selection from Ronald's 1922 fable, *The Laughing Elf*, about the necessity of both sorrow and joy in life.

A Novel Pulpit: Sermons From George MacDonald's Fiction
David L. Neuhouser

Each of the sermons has an introduction giving some explanation of the setting of the sermon or of the plot, if that is necessary for understanding the sermon. "MacDonald's novels are both stimulating and thought-provoking. This collection of sermons from ten novels serve to bring out the 'freshness and brilliance' of MacDonald's message." *from the author's introduction*

Behind the Back of the North Wind: Essays on George MacDonald's Classic Book
Edited and with Introduction by John Pennington and Roderick McGillis

The unique blend of fairy tale atmosphere and social realism in this novel laid the groundwork for modern fantasy literature. Sixteen essays by various authors are accompanied by an instructive introduction, extensive index, and beautiful illustrations.

Through the Year with George MacDonald: 366 Daily Readings
Rolland Hein, editor

These page-length excerpts from sermons, novels and letters are given an appropriate theme/heading and a complementary Scripture passage for daily reading. An inspiring introduction to the artistic soul and Christian vision of George MacDonald.

Shadows and Chivalry:
C. S. Lewis and George MacDonald on Suffering, Evil, and Death
Jeff McInnis

Shadows and Chivalry studies the influence of George MacDonald, a nineteenth-century Scottish novelist and fantasy writer, upon one of the most influential writers of modern times, C. S. Lewis—the creator of Narnia, literary critic, and best-selling apologist. This study attempts to trace the overall affect of MacDonald's work on Lewis's thought and imagination. Without ever ceasing to be a story of one man's influence upon another, the study also serves as an exploration of each writer's thought on, and literary visions of, good and evil.

POETS AND POETRY

In the Eye of the Beholder: How to See the World Like a Romantic Poet
Louis Markos

Born out of the French Revolution and its radical faith that a nation could be shaped and altered by the dreams and visions of its people, British Romantic Poetry was founded on a belief that the objects and realities of our world, whether natural or human, are not fixed in stone but can be molded and transformed by the visionary eye of the poet. A separate bibliographical essay is provided for readers listing accessible biographies of each poet and critical studies of their work.

The Cat on the Catamaran: A Christmas Tale
John Martin

Here is a modern-day parable of a modern-day cat with modern-day attitudes. Riverboat Dan is a "cool" cat on a perpetual vacation from responsibility. He's *The Cat on the Catamaran* – sailing down the river of life. Dan keeps his guilty conscience from interfering with his fun until he runs into trouble. But will he have the courage to believe that it's never too late to change course? (For ages 10 to adult)

Pop Culture

To Love Another Person: A Spiritual Journey Through Les Miserables
John Morrison

The powerful story of Jean Valjean's redemption is beloved by readers and theater goers everywhere. In this companion and guide to Victor Hugo's masterpiece, author John Morrison unfolds the spiritual depth and breadth of this classic novel and broadway musical.

Through Common Things: Philosophical Reflections on Popular Culture
Adam Barkman

"Barkman presents us with an amazingly wide-ranging collection of philosophical reflections grounded in the everyday things of popular culture – past and present, eastern and western, factual and fictional. Throughout his encounters with often surprising subject-matter (the value of darkness?), he writes clearly and concisely, moving seamlessly between Aristotle and anime, Lord Buddha and Lord Voldemort.... . This is an informative and entertaining book to read!"
     Doug Bloomberg, Professor of Philosophy, Institute for Christian Studies

Spotlight:
A Close-up Look at the Artistry and Meaning of Stephenie Meyer's Twilight Novels
John Granger

Stephenie Meyer's *Twilight* saga has taken the world by storm. But is there more to *Twilight* than a love story for teen girls crossed with a cheesy vampire-werewolf drama? *Spotlight* reveals the literary backdrop, themes, artistry, and meaning of the four Bella Swan adventures. *Spotlight* is the perfect gift for serious *Twilight* readers.

The Many Faces of Katniss Everdeen: Exploring the Heroine of The Hunger Games
Valerie Estelle Frankel

Katniss is the heroine who's changed the world. Like Harry Potter, she explodes across genres: She is a dystopian heroine, a warrior woman, a reality TV star, a rebellious adolescent. She's surrounded by the figures of Roman history, from Caesar and Cato to Cinna and Coriolanus Snow. She's also traveling the classic heroine's journey. As a child soldier, she faces trauma; as a growing teen, she battles through love triangles and the struggle to be good in a harsh world. This book explores all this and more, while taking a look at the series' symbolism, from food to storytelling, to show how Katniss becomes the greatest power of Panem, the girl on fire.

Myths and Motifs of The Mortal Instruments
Valerie Estelle Frankel

With vampires, fairies, angels, romance, steampunk, and modern New York all in one series of books, Cassandra Clare is exploding onto the scene. This book explores the deeper world of the Shadowhunters. There's something for everyone, as this book reveals unseen lore within the bestselling series.

Virtuous Worlds: The Video Gamer's Guide to Spiritual Truth
John Stanifer

Popular titles like *Halo 3* and *The Legend of Zelda: Twilight Princess* fly off shelves at a mind-blowing rate. John Stanifer, an avid gamer, shows readers specific parallels between Christian faith and the content of their favorite games. Written with wry humor (including a heckler who frequently pokes fun at the author) this book will appeal to gamers and non-gamers alike. Those unfamiliar with video games may be pleasantly surprised to find that many elements in those "virtual worlds" also qualify them as "virtuous worlds."

BIOGRAPHY

Sheldon Vanauken: The Man Who Received "A Severe Mercy"
Will Vaus

In this biography we discover: Vanauken the struggling student, the bon-vivant lover, the sailor who witnessed the bombing of Pearl Harbor, the seeker who returned to faith through C. S. Lewis, the beloved professor of English literature and history, the feminist and anti-war activist who participated in the March on the Pentagon, the bestselling author, and Vanauken the convert to Catholicism. What emerges is the portrait of a man relentlessly in search of beauty, love, and truth, a man who believed that, in the end, he found all three.

"This is a charming biography about a doubly charming man who wrote a triply charming book. It is a great way to meet the man behind A Severe Mercy."
    Peter Kreeft, author of *Jacob's Ladder: 10 Steps to Truth*

Remembering Roy Campbell: The Memoirs of his Daughters, Anna and Tess
Introduction by Judith Lütge Coullie, Editor
Preface by Joseph Pearce

Anna and Teresa Campbell were the daughters of the handsome young South African poet and writer, Roy Campbell (1901-1957), and his beautiful English wife, Mary Garman. In their frank and moving memoirs, Anna and Tess recall the extraordinary, and often very difficult, lives they shared with their exceptional parents. Over 50 photos, 344 footnotes, timeline of Campbell's life, and complete index.

HARRY POTTER

The Order of Harry Potter: The Literary Skill of the Hogwarts Epic
Colin Manlove

Colin Manlove, a popular conference speaker and author of over a dozen books, has earned an international reputation as an expert on fantasy and children's literature. His book, *From Alice to Harry Potter*, is a survey of 400 English fantasy books. In *The Order of Harry Potter*, he compares and contrasts *Harry Potter* with works by "Inklings" writers J.R.R. Tolkien, C. S. Lewis and Charles Williams; he also examines Rowling's treatment of the topic of imagination; her skill in organization and the use of language; and the book's underlying motifs and themes.

Harry Potter & Imagination: The Way Between Two Worlds
Travis Prinzi

Imaginative literature places a reader between two worlds: the story world and the world of daily life, and challenges the reader to imagine and to act for a better world. Starting with discussion of Harry Potter's more important themes, *Harry Potter & Imagination* takes readers on a journey through the transformative power of those themes for both the individual and for culture by placing Rowling's series in its literary, historical, and cultural contexts.

Hog's Head Conversations: Essays on Harry Potter
Travis Prinzi, Editor

Ten fascinating essays on Harry Potter by popular Potter writers and speakers including John Granger, James W. Thomas, Colin Manlove, and Travis Prinzi.

Repotting Harry Potter: A Professor's Guide for the Serious Re-Reader
Rowling Revisited: Return Trips to Harry, Fantastic Beasts, Quidditch, & Beedle the Bard
Dr. James W. Thomas

In *Repotting Harry Potter* and his sequel book *Rowling Revisited*, Dr. James W. Thomas points out the humor, puns, foreshadowing and literary parallels in the Potter books. In *Rowling Revisited*, readers will especially find useful three extensive appendixes – "Fantastic Beasts and the Pages Where You'll Find Them," "Quidditch Through the Pages," and "The Books in the Potter Books." Dr. Thomas makes re-reading the Potter books even more rewarding and enjoyable.

Deathly Hallows Lectures:
The Hogwarts Professor Explains Harry's Final Adventure
John Granger

In *The Deathly Hallows Lectures,* John Granger reveals the finale's brilliant details, themes, and meanings. *Harry Potter* fans will be surprised by and delighted with Granger's explanations of the three dimensions of meaning in *Deathly Hallows.* Ms. Rowling has said that alchemy sets the "parameters of magic" in the series; after reading the chapter-length explanation of *Deathly Hallows* as the final stage of the alchemical Great Work, the serious reader will understand how important literary alchemy is in understanding Rowling's artistry and accomplishment.

Unlocking Harry Potter: Five Keys for the Serious Reader
John Granger

"I got so hooked I had to stop everything else I was doing and just read, read, read. I carried it around the house, read it while using the excercycle, I hid in rooms away from the daily life so I could take it all in. A spectacular read for all serious fans of Rowling's works. Compelling, well-argued, fun, and funny. Engaging. Thought provoking. Erudite."

> Tom Morris
> author of *If Harry Potter Ran General Electric*
> Chairman of the Morris Institute for Human Values

Sociology and Harry Potter: 22 Enchanting Essays on the Wizarding World
Jenn Simms, editor

Modeled on an Introduction to Sociology textbook, this book is not simply about the series, but also uses the series to facilitate the reader's understanding of the discipline of sociology and a develops a sociological approach to viewing social reality. It is a case of high quality academic scholarship written in a form and on a topic accessible to non-academics. As such, it is written to appeal to Harry Potter fans and the general reading public. Contributors include professional sociologists from eight countries.

Harry Potter, Still Recruiting: An Inner Look at Harry Potter Fandom
Valerie Frankel

The Harry Potter phenomenon has created a new world: one of Quidditch in the park, lightning earrings, endless parodies, a new genre of music, and fan conferences of epic proportions. This book attempts to document everything - exploring costuming, crafting, gaming, and more, with essays and interviews straight from the multitude of creators. From children to adults, fans are delighting the world with an explosion of captivating activities and experiences, all based on Rowling's delightful series.

www.ingramcontent.com/pod-product-compliance
Lightning Source LLC
Chambersburg PA
CBHW052042280426
43661CB00084B/35